MANAGING

NEW

ENTERPRISES

MANAGING

NEW

ENTERPRISES

RICHARD H. BUSKIRK
The Herman W. Lay Professor
of Business Management
Southern Methodist University

PERCY J. VAUGHN JR.
Alabama State University

WEST PUBLISHING CO.
St. Paul • New York • Boston
Los Angeles • San Francisco

COPYRIGHT © 1976 By WEST PUBLISHING CO.
All Rights Reserved
Printed in the United States of America
Library of Congress Cataloging in Publication Data

Buskirk, Richard H.
MANAGING NEW ENTERPRISES

Includes index
1. Small business — management
I. Vaughn, Percy J., joint author   II. Title

HD69.S6B87   658.022   75-3799
ISBN   0-8299-0071-3

PREFACE

There is a standing need in the field of business management for a more comprehensive and practical book assimilating, clarifying, and interrelating various concepts of the small business. The authors are interested in the problems of the entrepreneur and are distressed at the over-emphasis on the problems of the large corporation in many business courses. Indeed, for a number of years it has seemed as if the small businessman was to be lost in the forest of corporate giants. Thus, it is with relish that the authors detect among students today an interest in going into business for themselves. They hope the reader will share their enthusiasm for this revitalized treatment of small business management.

First, the authors will not include some material normally taught in the other functional business courses. There is little sense in repeating things usually covered in accounting, marketing, management, and finance texts. Because this book will not cover those traditional core areas, the reader is expected to have knowledge of such materials already or to acquire it by examining books on those subjects.

Second, this book will not be generalized advocacy of the virtues of free enterprise and the American system. The authors assume the reader is already interested in going into business for himself.

Third, this book is neither a readings book nor a textbook. Rather, it is a hybrid creature consisting of part *cookbook* — how to do it; part *policy book* — what are the key policy decisions confronting the entrepreneur; part *case book* — see how other people have done it and the problems they encountered; and some *readings* on pertinent topics.

In the book, the reader is given a definite and detailed idea of what he must do to start a business. In this way, the book can be used as a handbook. Most of the classic pitfalls awaiting the new enterpriser are noted and some advice is given on how these problems may be avoided. Much material on the various aspects of operating a small business is provided so that the reader can better understand these operations.

In teaching the subject, the greatest success has been achieved by the authors when the course was built around a term project in which each person developed a venture capital proposal for some ideas he wanted to examine, complete with all the plans the individual would have to formulate before going into such a venture. Such a term project gives the teacher a marvelous vehicle for seeing many of the practical problems encountered in beginning a new business. Moreover, the students find a project most helpful, particularly when they have an actual business in mind that they want to start. This book is best used in conjunction with such a project because various illustrations in the book are directly applicable to them, for example, the material on incorporating, the formulation of a venture capital proposal, cash flow planning. Also, a book of this nature can be an invaluable aid to persons involved in giving technical and counseling assistance to small businessmen. Readers involved in the Small Business Institute (SBI) program of the Office of Management Assistance, U.S. Small Business Administration, will find this book a significant aid in giving more valuable assistance and counseling to each individual business owner and manager. This aid will come alive in the area of communicating with clients in simple direct language that both the reader and his clients can understand.

The authors are greatly indebted to a number of people in connection with this work. Sincere thanks are extended to the various authors and publishers who permitted us to reprint their material, and to Ms. Nita Parks and Ms. Sheri Behne, secretaries in the authors' departments at Texas Tech University and at Southern Methodist University who efficiently provided typing and clerical assistance.

Dr. Buskirk particularly wants to acknowledge his gratitude to Professor Jack Wichert who first stimulated his interest in the area at the University of Kansas in the late 1940's; to the College Department at West Publishing Company for their help in making this

book possible, and to Dean Jack Grayson of Southern Methodist University for his vigorous support of Dr. Buskirk's programs in entrepreneurship.

Mr. Vaughn extends his thanks to West Publishing for bringing the authors together; to Jack Steele, Dean of the College of Business Administration, Texas Tech University, who provided valuable insights on small business management; to J. W. Terry, Southern University at Baton Rouge, a long-time consultant partner; to Vincent and Louise Luchsinger and John A. Ryan; and to Bob Justis of Texas Tech University whose encouragement has contributed to whatever success these efforts may attain.

The authors extend their thanks to their wives and families who have put up with them during the struggle to put together a manuscript. Finally, the authors thank Mrs. Sylvia Arnot, of Boulder, Colorado, without whom they would be lost.

Richard H. Buskirk
Percy J. Vaughn, Jr.

✳✳✳

Test your entrepreneural quotient — EQ

1. Does a million dollars sound like a reasonable amount of money to raise for starting your new company?
2. Do you want to start your company in some pleasant place to live?

3.   Do you prefer to enter a highly competitive industry?

4.   Are your savings too small to be of help to your firm?

5.   A really good idea sells itself.

6.   Do you plan to attract good people to your firm by giving them good individual offices with secretaries?

7.   Do you plan to build up your firm then sell it quickly for a profit?

8.   Would you refuse to bend your normal ethics if by doing so it would help your company get off the ground?

9.   Do you think that you should be paid more as the founder of the enterprise than you were getting in your old job?

10.   Is it important to you to reserve some time for your family?

11.   If you were faced with failure, would you stick to your guns rather than try to shift quickly to something else?

12.   Do you feel that your subordinates would best be selected from close friends whom you could trust completely?

13.   Do you think that management of a new enterprise should be free from interference from outside investors?

14.   Do you feel it is wrong to use the savings of relatives to start a business with?

Each of the previous questions to which you answered — yes — *would make an experienced venture capitalist flee for the hills!*

*

CONTENTS

Preface   *v*

I: CREATING THE ENTERPRISE   1

1 THE CONCEPT OR IDEA   3

2 FEASIBILITY STUDIES   7
   Assessing retail opportunities in low-income areas   8

3 BUSINESS MORTALITY   22
   *The uncertain future of small business: can
   this picture by changed?*   22

4 A CASE HISTORY OF BUSINESS FOR SALE   34
   Robo car wash   34

5 TO OWN OR TO FRANCHISE   38
   Controversy: Franchise vs company operations   38
   Some things to look for in franchise agreements   43

6 THE ENTREPRENEUR — YOU?   54

7 JOE KARBO   57
   Joe's awfully rich – for a 'lazy man'   57

8 WHEELING AND DEALING   60
   *The acquisitor – how an Iowa farm boy came
   to own a casino and much, much more*   60

9 NEW DIRECTION FOR MINORITY
   ENTERPRISE   65
   Minority enterprise lures more activities   65

10   THE "7-ELEVEN" STORY   70
     Family affair   70

11   LEGAL ASPECTS OF STARTING A
     NEW BUSINESS   78

12   CHOOSING A FORM   87
     Choosing organization form for engaging in
     business   87

13   AND THEN THERE IS BIG BROTHER   96
     OSHA, big government and small business   96

14   LEASES   105
     Selected problems in store leasing   105
     Clauses in a shopping center lease   118

II: FINANCING THE ENTERPRISE   131

15   DETERMINING FINANCIAL NEEDS   133
     How much working capital for the new
     project?   136

16   SOURCES OF FUNDS   139

17   THE JARGON   160
     Financial terminology in business
     agreements   160

18   GOVERNMENTAL PROGRAMS FOR AIDING
     SMALL BUSINESS   173
     A new day at the SBA   173
     Urgently required: A reordering of SBA
     priorities to save small business   177
     A perspective on the MESBIC program   194

III: CREATING THE VALUE   203

19   ACQUIRING PRODUCTIVE CAPABILITIES   205
     Three approaches to inventory control   210

20   PRODUCT PLANNING   217
     *A primer on patent, trademark, and
     know-how licensing*   220

IV: MANAGEMENT   235

21   PEOPLE AND ORGANIZATION   237

22   CONTRACTOR OR EMPLOYEE   246
     *Current factors that distinguish between
     "employee" and "independent contractor"*   246

24   THE ADVANTAGES OF MANAGING A
     SMALL ENTERPRISE   263
     *Peter Drucker attacks: Our top heavy
     corporations*   263

V: MARKETING   271

25   BUILDING DISTRIBUTION   273
     *How to sell the mass merchandiser
     (Interviews with two experts on selling)*   276

26   SELLING TO SMALLER CUSTOMERS   284

27   LOGISTICS   288
     Transportation report   288

28   GOVERNMENTS AS CUSTOMERS   301
     *The risks inherent for a small business
     taking a contract as a prime – or as a
     sub-contractor*   303

29   PRICING   315
     What is the best selling price?   322

30   PROMOTION   342
     A helluva way to learn salesmanship   346
     Sales promotion pointers for small retailers   348
     Advertising for profit and prestige   353

VI: CONTROL   361

    31 CONTROLLING THE ENTERPRISE   363

        *Using the computer for distribution of
        fashion goods*   367

        *Cost reduction: "Panic from
        the word Go"*   371

        *Designing a bookkeeping system
        for a new enterprise*   376

    32 INCOME TAX   400

        *A practitioner's guide to avoidance v.
        evasion: Basic concepts change*   400

VII: GROWTH   411

    33 THE MANAGEMENT OF GROWTH   413

        Jet propulsion in drug discounting   417

        *Homey hustlers – down-East look helps
        Maine outdoors store build national business* 425

VIII: TERMINATING THE ENTERPRISE   429

    34 SELLING A GOING ENTERPRISE   431

        How to play "You Bet Your Company"   440

        The expert's role in a company valuation   442

        *Representing the seller of a closely-held
        business*   460

Epilogue: Some Basic Business Philosphy   471

Index   479

†

I

CREATING THE ENTERPRISE

. . . and on the seventh day the entrepreneur was still at work, for there is rest neither for the wicked nor the industrious.

Anyone can look around and see that the vast bulk of enterprises in our nation are small businesses. Moreover, all one has to do is keep his eyes and ears open and he can see all sorts of people going into business and going out of it all the time. So there is little point in starting out this book with the usual trivia about how many small businesses there are, how important they are, and why free enterprise will be the salvation of our souls. So let us get on with it and into this matter of starting your own business.

THE CONCEPT OR IDEA

1

Many people harbor the impression that in order to go into business they must have some unique idea, a great invention, an inspiring thought. Perish the thought, for it is simply not so. In fact, some of the most successful businesses are "me-too" operations in which the entrepreneur has copied some successful enterprise almost down to the last detail.

Harry is an entrepreneur in every sense of the word. He started with a small lumber operation in Los Angeles and from there went into the real estate development business and then into building apartment houses which, over the past decade, he has managed to erect at a rate of at least 500 units a year — the whole operation starting from practically nothing. But, more to the point, Harry and a couple of his cohorts decided to go into the restaurant business. (Don't ask why; such decisions are those from which bankruptcies are spawned!) Since they knew little about the restaurant business, they copied the operations of a successful chain in Southern California called "Coco's." Harry and his pals now have six restaurants and have done exceptionally

well with all of them. As Harry said, "If Coco's doesn't do it, we don't do it!"

Here is a well-established product, food, and a new operation which came in as a copy of another. Harry has no claim of originality whatsoever but was able to get six locations, put them together with a management team, and make some money. One does not have to be a pioneer or inventor to go into business. In fact, it may help **not** to be one.

Indeed, a strong case can be made that the risks are much greater for the pioneer than for the Harrys of the world. Consider the advantages of Harry's strategy: he knew there was a tremendous demand for coffee shop food operations and he could count the dollars spent in them in his area each year. Contrast Harry's situation to that of the entrepreneur who has developed a unique, new product: he does not know how many he will sell, and the over-all market risks are much larger for him than for the person going into an established line of business.

Harry copied a proven operational system and the importance of this cannot be minimized. In any new operation there are a great many things that must be learned from experience. It is impossible to plan ahead how everything should be done and how everything will work. On paper it may appear as if a certain operation should be done one way, but actual practice might prove it should be done a different way. Thus the start-up costs of a new enterprise are always increased because of such unpredictable factors. Contrast that pioneering venture with that of the new McDonald's franchisee who is given in one package exactly how everything should be done, how all the food should be cooked, and how the business should be run. The franchise holder benefits from the results of many years of experience in more than a thousand operations — Rest assured that McDonald's headquarters knows how to run a hamburger stand. Too many entrepreneurs fail to recognize the time and money it takes to perfect an operating system.

There are companies that follow a policy of pirating the proven products of others, all quite legally. A small chemical company began operations by copying a product (it had no legal protection) that was selling quite well to the floral industry. In time it did improve on the product somewhat, but it was still no new idea. Subsequently, management would spot some chemical product that was selling well, have it analyzed, then bring it out for a lower price.

GO INTO SOMETHING YOU LIKE

Experience proves that the person who does something he likes is far more likely to be successful than one who does something for which he has little taste. If you are uncertain about what you want to do, follow your instincts toward the activity you like most. Never go into a business you dislike just because it looks profitable. If you do not know what you like, go work for others until you find something that interests you.

BASIC SOUNDNESS OF THE CONCEPT

Many new enterprises fail because the concept upon which they were based was faulty. For example, a woman opened a small dress shop called "The Villager" which featured fashions from the manufacturer of the same name. Sales were fine as long as that manufacturer's styles stayed in fashion, but fashions changed and the line did not. Basing a business on one manufacturer is dangerous, for one may have difficulty changing with the fashions.

The classic failure, of course, is the new manufacturer whose "great new product that everybody will buy" fails to find market acceptance. There is no point in belaboring this obvious failure.

It is usually a mistake to begin a business based on fad. The people who started trampoline jumping pits, model auto raceways, miniature golf courses, and such had little chance for success. Few fad businesses last for long. The recreational dollar is fickle and competition for it is keen.

One should study the history of businesses similar to the one in which he is interested, for it will disclose interesting economic facts about their success and longevity. For example, large hotels have a high rate of initial failure. The party who picks them up out of bankruptcy, after the initial equity has been wiped out and the debt has modified its terms, may have a chance at success. When the financial risk is reduced this way, business is apt to prosper.

The economic soundness of the business concept is critical; no one should go into a venture that does not make good economic sense. Investors have been bilked of billions by schemes that were economic nonsense — remote recreational real estate, and other sorts of get-rich-quick schemes. With good, hardheaded economic analysis many such schemes are exposed — chinchilla ranching, vending machine routes, pyramid sales schemes, or similar ventures.

First, keep in mind at all times that no one else has the slightest interest in making you rich. Those who promise you quick riches are lying to you. The riches they have in mind are destined for their own pockets. Flee from those who would have you believe that they bring instant wealth.

Second, few ventures are immediate successes; most take a good deal of time and much effort to develop into valuable properties. Easy routes to fortune are rare; most ventures require much hard work.

Third, if entry into an industry is easy and it is being strongly promoted, then rest assured that the industry will be quickly over-expanded, which will place great downward pressure on prices. The programs of Ralston Purina to expand the primary demand for its products by helping farmers go into egg or broiler production caused over-production in many regions. Bear in mind that attractive profits will be short

---

TABLE 1-1: Economic analysis check list

	Yes	No
Does the firm have a differential advantage that cannot be easily copied?		
Is the risk/reward ratio reasonable?		
What investments are needed?		
Upon what basis do firms in the industry compete:		
Price		
Promotion		
Service		
Product		
Location		
People		
Are you capable of competing on the same basis?		
If not, is there a market niche in which you can profitably exist using whatever capabilities you have?		
Is the primary demand for the product favorable?		
What does it take to be successful in the industry?		
Are there problems with needed resources, i.e., raw materials, labor, technology?		
What are the cost characteristics of production?		
How large need you be to compete?		
What are the product's substitutes?		

lived in an industry into which entry is easy. Moreover, the industry over-swings in its expansion and creates more supply than the market demands, complicating the situation.

The firms entering an industry late in its product life-cycle usually encounter difficulty. Table 1-1 presents an economic analysis check list to assist in evaluating an industry.

FEASIBILITY STUDIES

2

Once the concept has been settled upon and refined to a reasonable degree, a feasibility study is called for, particularly if outside capital will be needed. This step usually causes problems because the entrepreneur may not have the skills or knowledge needed to conduct the study. The consultant enters the picture when the would-be businessman seeks outside help from someone familiar with feasibility studies.

Naturally, such studies vary depending on the kind of enterprise. However, a general outline can be used as a guideline for the topics that should be covered.

OUTLINE FOR NEW ENTERPRISE FEASIBILITY STUDY

   I. The concept

  II. Evaluation of market opportunity

 III. Production plans

 IV. Marketing plans

  V. Financial plans

 VI. Profiles of management team

Early in the planning for a new venture, some fairly good studies should be done on the market for the concept and its competition. The following article focuses upon a retailing operation, but the same type of approach can be used for a wide range of other types of businesses.

Retailing is a large segment of small business, and for many good reasons: ease of entry, capital requirements, and the economics of optimum size. While the following article seems to dwell on low income areas, actually everything that is covered is equally applicable to other areas. Bear in mind that in most instances the key to successful retail operations is the location of the store. It is difficult to make money in a poor location.

Assessing retail opportunities in low-income areas

William Rudelius
Robert F. Hoel
Roger A. Kerin†

> *"Fires Set, Rocks Thrown in*
> *City Mob Outbreaks"*
>
> *"600 Guards Mobilized to*
> *Keep City in Order"*

The actions of concerned businessmen can be crucial factors in preventing such headlines. They must recognize the spiral of events that are both causes and effects of urban violence: the fleeing of many middle-income black and white families, the deterioration of housing, an increase in vandalism, the exit of larger retail stores, a decline in local employment opportunities, the closing of "Ma and Pa" stores, and increasing numbers of boarded and razed buildings. The final result: a general frustration and anger felt by the remaining residents.

One of the critical needs for such an area is to rejuvenate its inadequate or possibly nonexistent retail structure. Because few men with the power and funds needed to repair the decay live in the area, assistance from business leaders throughout the metropolitan

†William Rudelius, Robert F. Hoel, and Roger A. Kerin, *Journal of Retailing*, Vol. 48, No. 3, Fall 1972, pp. 96-114.

area is required. An impediment to action by these leaders is often the lack of information that could be available through systematic study incorporating the desires of local residents in an objective evaluation of retail opportunities in these low-income areas. This article, which is based upon a study undertaken on the north side of Minneapolis, attempts to provide a systematic framework for this evaluation.

Objectives

A basic problem in north Minneapolis — the locale of the headlines cited above — is how to provide satisfactory retail services to residents. This same problem is encountered in hundreds of retail centers in cities across the country. Using Minneapolis as a background, our specific objectives are: (1) to identify the principal steps involved in determining the kinds of stores that should be included in a proposed neighborhood shopping center in a low-income area; (2) to discuss some results of a study using these steps that may be useful in similar studies. In developing these objectives, we shall stress the importance of working with local groups and of adapting the research to the conditions present in the trading area. Where possible, we shall cite references that may aid businessmen involved in similar feasibility studies.

In the last five years several important publications have described the problems faced by low-income households, the role of businessmen in solving urban problems and the need to stimulate minority businesses. However, very little work has described the specific steps necessary to involve the community in planning for the development of future retail stores or to undertake the actual feasibility studies. As will be seen, analyzing consumption behavior in low-income areas presents severe problems in obtaining accurate estimates. Ultimately, obtaining adequate financing and insurance depends on a favorable feasibility study — which, in turn, depends on data that must demonstrate that the shopping center will serve the residents satisfactorily and will be economically profitable.

Figure 2-1 illustrates the steps involved in opening a shopping center in a low-income area. These steps may be divided into three main groups: (1) the preliminary work in obtaining ideas from groups of local citizens and businessmen, (2) the feasibility study, and (3) the effort required to translate the feasibility study into bricks and mortar. The direct assistance that can most often be given by businessmen or business school students and faculty is in undertaking the feasibility study. Consequently, this step receives the major emphasis here. For simplicity in this discussion, we shall use the word "stores" to refer to all retail establishments that might be included in a shopping center; this includes service establishments like barber shops and restaurants, as well as traditional stores like supermarkets and drugstores.

Preliminary work

Step 1 in Figure 2-1 — obtaining ideas on retail store needs from local citizens and businessmen — is essential to the ultimate success of the shopping center for two reasons. First, these people live and work in the area and have a thorough understanding of what the present retail situation is and how it got that way. They have insights that outsiders can never obtain. For example, one supermarket chain store in the area studied changed the store name twice, accompanying the name change with a reduction in the merchandise quality, according to area residents. They felt — with some justification — that they were receiving poorer quality merchandise than suburban stores in the chain. This resulted in comments in interviews such as "we're tired of overpricing and junk for merchandise just because the other parts of town think we're too dumb to know the difference" and "my money spends as good as anybody else's, even if I don't have quite as much."

The second reason is that without local people's involvement in the planning for the shopping center, reports and feasibility studies gather dust. Community involvement stimulates interest and a sense of urgency that will result in implementation. Furthermore, low-income residents are particularly suspicious of studies by outsiders that promise too much. This involvement has a price: as with any group in a democracy, there will almost never be complete agreement on a simple issue — much less something as complex as the characteristics of stores in a new shopping center. Nevertheless, if community groups believe an honest attempt was made to listen — to attempt to understand their needs — the project has a solid start. In the case of north Minneapolis, although there were many divergent views on details, there was unanimity in believing that a shopping center is essential. This desire for "something better" provides the impetus for subsequent help and cooperation. In summary, the support of neigh-

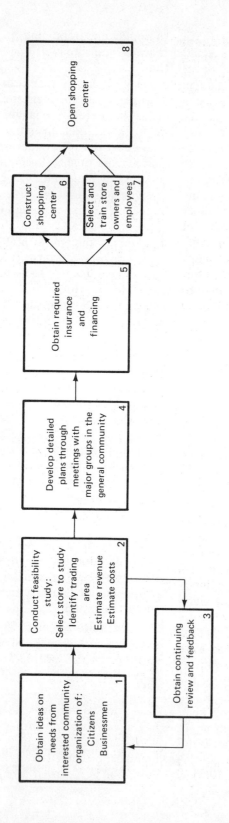

FIGURE 2-1:   Principal steps in developing a new shopping center from generation of the idea of opening of the center

borhood organizations will speed acceptance of change; their veto could create disaster. In our study north Minneapolis organizations and the outside researchers met frequently, with a prominent businessman in the area providing liaison.

Feasibility study

The method used in Step 2 to assess both the desirability and feasibility of possible stores to be located in the north Minneapolis low-income area is relatively simple and not original. However, obtaining the information necessary to use this method proved to be a formidable task.

Obtaining adequate information

The information required for any feasibility study includes (1) the revenue data provided by the market analysis and (2) the cost data. In the preliminary analysis, we assumed that data on the number of households and median income per household would be readily available; as will be seen, this was a poor assumption. Thus, our first concern was obtaining data on attitudes and behavior of consumers. Nonresponse problems precluded using mail questionnaires. The possibility of interviewing door-to-door was finally eliminated for three reasons. First, some detailed information was required that extended the interview beyond the 15 to 20 minutes that we felt to be an upper limit on a door-to-door survey in the area. Second, black and white households in the area are about evenly split; because we felt black households might be reluctant to describe their attitudes honestly to white interviewers and vice versa, we wanted blacks to interview

blacks and whites, whites. However, we were unable to develop a simple procedure that would ensure this interviewer-respondent match. Third, the area has been oversurveyed by both private and governmental groups, making it doubtful whether real consumer cooperation could be obtained. A comment heard in one of the meetings we had with local businessmen summarizes this problem: "Every sociology Ph.D. that's graduated from the University during the last ten years has been up here doing door-to-door interviews." Although the statement is exaggerated, residents' suspicion of interviewers is not.

Finally, we chose to have group interviews with six to eight adult women per session. These groups were stratified on two bases, race and census tract, because we felt the likelihood of a woman's shopping at the proposed shopping center might depend heavily on both factors. The advance recruiting of the women made it possible for the black and white female interviewers to interview a group of their color. The interviews, which took about an hour and one-half and for which the women received payment, fell into seven main parts:

1. Introduction — Described the survey objectives and identified the proposed location of the shopping center on a map.

2. Attitudes toward the proposed shopping center — Established group rapport, while obtaining attitudes (tape-recorded).

3. Card rating of potential stores — Each woman received 22 cards, each having the name of a different store on it; she then sorted cards, with names of four most preferred stores in one group, next four in a second group, etc. This

enabled each woman to assign each store to one of five groups based on how important she felt the store was for her family needs.

4. Other stores wanted in the center — Each woman estimated the amount of various goods that she might buy in stores in the center as (a) none, (b) about half, or (c) almost all (self-administered).

5. Attitudes on favorite stores, as well as services, quality, and prices desired — Open discussion (tape-recorded).

6. Estimate of dollars spent per week or month on various items — Twelve different items were estimated, ranging from groceries purchased per week to shoes purchased per months (self-administered).

7. Demographic data — Family size, income, availability of a car for shopping (self-administered).

The format of the group interview was intended to establish rapport among the interviewer and all the group members, to break up the monotony of the interview with useful group discussions, and to enable the interviewer to lend assistance to respondents on the self-administered questions when necessary. This format proved very successful.

The data from the group interviews were supplemented with information from a variety of business, government, and community organizations. In the market analysis these organizations provided both quantitative data on the number of households and annual household income in the area and also subjective judgments about a variety of political and economic factors. On the cost side of the feasibility study, these organizations gave detailed data on costs of retail operations, lease and fix-turing expenses, insurance problems, and financing costs and opportunities.

Developing a list of stores to analyze

The initial list of possible stores considered for the shopping center was subsequently modified and expanded by area residents through the group interviews described above and through meetings with neighborhood organizations. Unfortunately, the realities of the marketplace restrict the number and kinds of stores having a chance of survival. The need to offer a wide variety of products and services to low-income area residents, coupled with a limited trading area, sometimes necessitates the merging of several specialized lines into single stores. The limited market precludes large department or discount stores from locating in these neighborhood shopping centers. Service operations such as bowling alleys and theaters often are not feasible because they produce almost insurmountable insurance problems. Legal or political restrictions may prohibit construction of facilities such as a liquor store or a post office branch.

Consumer rankings for various kinds of stores were estimated through the card piles from the group interview sessions with area residents. Later, during general discussion, participants were given an opportunity to discuss why they ranked the stores the way they did. Of great concern at the outset of the research was whether both black and white housewives would agree on the stores that should be considered for the shopping center. Figure 2 shows that both groups had a remarkable consistency in their rankings and that the concern was unwarranted. The

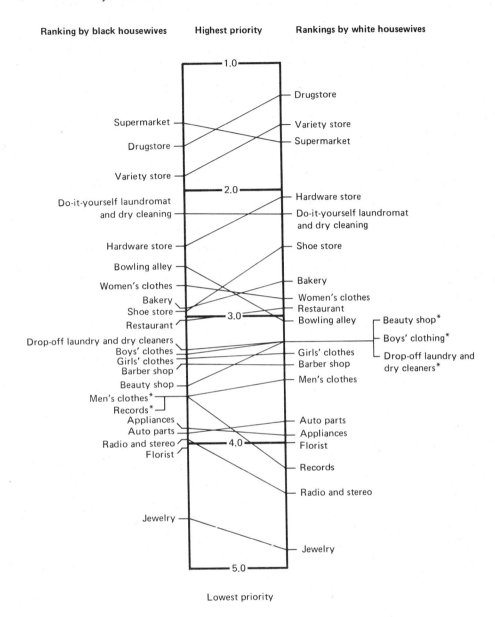

Ranking by black housewives   **Highest priority**   **Rankings by white housewives**

Drugstore

Supermarket
Variety store
Drugstore
Supermarket

Variety store

Do-it-yourself laundromat
and dry cleaning

Hardware store

Do-it-yourself laundromat
and dry cleaning

Hardware store

Shoe store

Bowling alley

Women's clothes

Bakery

Bakery

Women's clothes

Shoe store

Restaurant

Restaurant

Bowling alley

Beauty shop*

Boys' clothing*

Drop-off laundry and dry cleaners

Drop-off laundry and
dry cleaners*

Boys' clothes

Girls' clothes

Girls' clothes

Barber shop

Barber shop

Beauty shop

Men's clothes

Men's clothes*

Records*

Appliances

Auto parts

Auto parts

Appliances

Radio and stereo

Florist

Florist

Records

Radio and stereo

Jewelry

Jewelry

Lowest priority

*Indicates a tie in the rankings.

FIGURE 2-2: **Rankings of black and white housewives of stores they would like to see in the proposed shopping center from highest priority (1.0) to lowest priority (5.0)**

scale varies from 1.0 (if all women put a store in the most important group) to 5.0 (if all women put a store in the least important group). Figure 2-2 shows that both groups of women ranked a supermarket, drugstore, and variety store in the top three and a jewelry store as the least important.

Identifying the retail trading area

Five general factors have a profound effect on the boundaries of the retail trading area of shopping center stores located in low-income areas: (1) the number of stores in the shopping center; (2) the natural or man-made boundaries such as parks, rivers, or limited-access throughways; (3) competing stores or shopping centers that adequately service the needs of consumers; (4) family ownership of a car and the availability of public transportation facilities; and (5) the level of racial or ethnic harmony. Often the trading area of a store in the shopping center varies appreciably according to the type of goods or services offered. These factors point out the need to survey the physical area, competition, and residents' attitudes carefully, as well as to determine future highway and housing developments. For example, 31 percent of the families in the survey had no car to use in shopping. This factor, coupled with a sizeable number of housing units for the elderly in the area, suggests the need for improved public transportation or a retail delivery service. The analysis suggested that at least 90 percent of the sales by stores in the shopping center would come from eight census tracts, which were assumed to be the trading area for the center.

Estimating revenue

As a general rule, the most serious estimation problems in retail feasibility studies lie on the revenue side, not the cost side, of the problem. In estimating potential revenue, it is helpful to utilize available subdivisions of the total retail trading area such as census tracts; each store's retail sales can then be estimated for each of the census tracts. The sum of the store's sales for each census tract in its trading area is then taken as the basis for an estimate of total revenue for the store. This estimate is based mainly on the households living in the trading area; the estimate may be augmented if individuals living outside the area may contribute to the store's sales through (1) being employed in the store's neighborhood or (2) being "intercepted" on the way to or from work. Figure 2-3 illustrates a systematic method of converting population, income, expenditure patterns, and shopping inclination information into retail sales projections for census tracts or other small geographical areas. The estimate of the store's sales to a census tract is simply the product of the four factors. To illustrate the method of obtaining estimates of these four factors, including the problems, each factor is discussed separately.

Number of households

One surprisingly difficult task is estimating the number of households located in low-income census tracts, the first factor shown in Figure 2-3. These areas are characterized frequently by high mobility, changes in the number of households per dwelling unit, and changes in the number of dwelling units through recent demolitions and urban

FIGURE 2-3:   Example of the method used to estimate the annual revenue obtained by a supermarket from a specific census tract located in the store's retail trading area

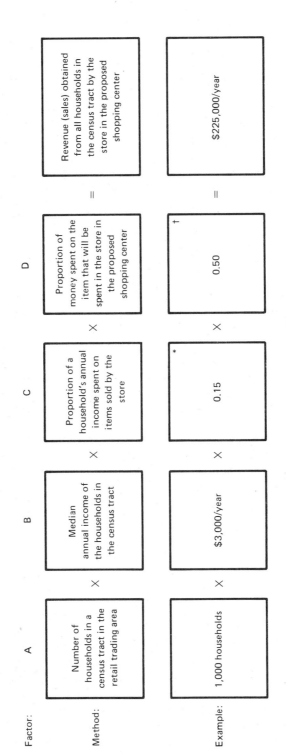

Notes: *The proportion of 0.15 means that 15 percent of the typical household's annual income of $3,000 per year is spent on groceries and meats.

†The proportion of 0.50 means that 50 percent of the groceries and meats purchased by all the households living in this census tract will be from the supermarket located in the proposed shopping center.

redevelopment construction projects. The 1960 Census data are clearly not current, and there is the added problem that these data might have been incorrect when originally compiled because of the failure of many low-income residents to report information to the Bureau of the Census.

Median annual household income

The problems inherent in estimating the number of households continue when attempting to estimate the median annual income of households living in each census tract in the trading area, the second factor in Figure 2-3. The limited sample of area residents included in our group interviews provided some information about the income of the households they represented. The women were informed that in order to determine whether stores could serve the area effectively we required the most honest answers they were able to provide. We believe that a sincere attempt was made to give good estimates.

An example illustrates the magnitude of the problem of estimating the annual income of all households in a census tract in a low-income area. The 1970 Census data were not available. A search of other sources such as a 1967 real estate study of the area and a 1969 probability sample of all housing units in Minneapolis gave purportedly current estimates of the number of households and median annual household incomes for census tracts within the trading area. In total there were three available estimates for each of these two factors. These values are plotted in the two left-hand graphs of Figure 2-4 for one of the census tracts in the area. Multiplying the two factors together gives the total annual income of all households in

the census tract, the right-hand graph in Figure 2-4. The result is that the high estimate ($8,280,000) is about 2.7 times the low estimate ($3,090,000) of total annual household income. The middle estimate ($3,888,000) is the product of the middle estimates of the two initial factors.

A check of local agencies did not resolve these discrepancies. Because we believed it necessary to develop a single "best estimate," the research group constituted itself into a "panel of experts." Each expert scrutinized all objective and subjective information available and made an independent estimate of what he considered to be the most likely value of the factor. The median of these individual estimates was chosen as the collective best estimate of the panel.

Proportion of annual income spent by kind of store

A 1968 study of a low-income area in Cleveland and Bureau of Labor Statistics data on the total United States identify the proportion of a family's annual income spent in various kinds of stores. In the group interviews, we attempted to determine some key items for which the housewife might be able to remember approximate expenditures, such as dollars spent for groceries and meats per week. We concluded that recall of exact expenditures was very difficult and possibly misleading in some cases. Nonetheless, these values were given to our self-proclaimed panel of experts. The best estimate by our panel largely reflected a compromise between Cleveland and national expenditure data, modified in some cases by the local group interview data. This estimate represented the third factor shown in Figure 2-3.

FIGURE 2-4:   **Variation in estimates of total annual income of all households in a census tract resulting from variation in underlying factors of number of households and median annual household income**

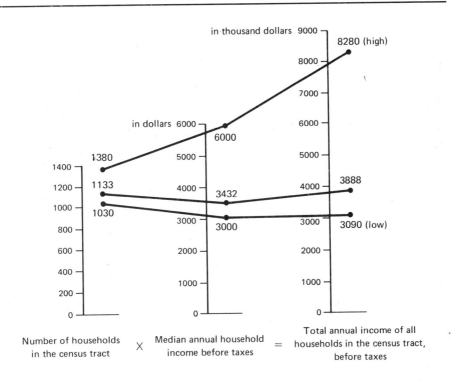

Number of households in the census tract × Median annual household income before taxes = Total annual income of all households in the census tract, before taxes

Proportion of trade captured by proposed store

The proportion-of-capture value, the fourth factor in Figure 2-3, is the estimated proportion of the *total* funds spent annually on the category that will be spent in the proposed store in the shopping center; it is not the proportion of people who merely buy something during the year at a given store. Any estimate of this proportion depends upon key assumptions about the quality of operation of both the individual stores and the entire shopping center. We assumed that the stores in the proposed shopping center would be well run, adapt to the needs of the locality, and offer products at competitive prices. Each resident participating in the group sessions was told this, given a list of product categories, and asked, "Assuming that the stores have the quality and price that you want, think about how much of the things you and your family would buy at the store in the shopping center." They were instructed to check one of three categories: None at All, About Half, Almost All. These responses and information about competitors were analyzed carefully.

In an attempt to be conservative, the estimates of the women made in the group interviews were deflated by the panel of experts. This was because the panel felt the women's enthusiasm for the shopping center may have caused them to overestimate the proportion of their purchases in the center. The panel may have been naive on this count; in the eight census tracts in the primary trading area of the proposed drugstore in the shopping center, the proportions varied from a low of 0.44 to a high of 0.98. This variability lends credence to these estimates. Yet the 0.98 means that 98 percent of the expected annual drugstore purchases made by women in one census tract would be in the shopping center — an astounding response until one understands that there are now only two drugstores in all eight census tracts; that for some families the nearest drugstore is over a mile away; and that almost one-third of the families have no car to use in shopping. Still, we attempted to be conservative and deflated the estimate.

Estimating costs and profitability

After summing the potential sales from all census tracts for each kind of store to estimate total revenue, both fixed and variable costs must be estimated. Community business leaders provided estimates of store rents and common-area costs (such as mail and parking costs) for the proposed shopping center. The Small Business Administration (SBA) assisted in outlining costs of store financing. Experienced small businessmen and franchisers, as well as SBA publications, guided estimation of operating costs. Data on operating ratios were obtained from National

Cash Register publications and trade publications such as the Lilly Digest that gives operating ratios for drugstores.

Sales revenue less fixed and variable costs, of course, provide an estimate of the annual profitability of individual stores. Final recommendations of stores to include in the shopping center are based on estimated profitability, modified by judgments about the degree to which an establishment assists the total shopping center in offering a sufficiently diverse mix of products and services to be successful. Thus, a store that standing alone would be marginal, might be a successful unit in a shopping center if it can both contribute to the "one-stop shopping" concept and benefit from the greater traffic generated by the shopping center. Clearly, the whole of a successful shopping center is greater than the sum of its individual parts.

Final steps:
future conditions for survival

In terms of Figure 2-1, we have discussed the development of the shopping center only through the feasibility study. Many low-income area residents bitterly charge that this is "about as far as any 'do gooder' project ever goes." Continuing guidance and assistance from businessmen and firms must go beyond this point to ensure improved retail facilities.

In the case of north Minneapolis, preliminary work has been done to meet with community groups on the detailed plans, to evaluate the availability of insurance and financing, and to select and train store owners and employees, which appear as steps 4, 5, and 7 in Figure 2-1.

Meetings with community groups

Local businessmen have held both formal and informal meetings with community residents to discuss detailed plans for the shopping center (Step 4, Figure 2-1). As an example of the difficult decisions that must be made, there are two opposing views of what the final configuration of the shopping center should be. One group argues for a "strip center" along the main street in the area in the belief that it is "in keeping with other developments along the street." The opposing view is that a mall configuration with a central landscaped courtyard would be preferable because it would "give a nicer atmosphere for shopping." Whichever configuration is eventually selected, there is great concern that the shopping center not be oversold. It will be a neighborhood shopping center of about ten to twenty stores. When many residents hear the terms "shopping mall," they immediately conjure up images of enclosed regional centers with 50 to 100 stores. Unless this image is corrected, the final result will be a terrible disappointment for neighborhood residents.

Obtaining insurance and financing

Insurance coverage for the shopping center can be obtained through the FAIR Plan (Fair Access to Insurance Requirements). The FAIR plan denies insurance companies the right to reject an application for insurance because of the neighborhood or any environmental hazard beyond the control of the property owner. Consequently, the retailers will not be penalized for locating in a low-income area. However, the insured retailer must maintain his facility if coverage is to continue in the future. It is crucial that plans for the shopping center be developed with the assistance of knowledgeable insurance men who may make suggestions on construction and layout that significantly reduce the insurance cost.

In a period of tight money, financing a new operation is a problem for any firm, particularly for a small retailer in a low-income area. However, his opportunities for financing are brighter because of the support provided by the detailed feasibility study described earlier. Financial assistance from the governmental sector may come from the Small Business Administration and through the Economic Opportunity Loan program. In addition, some private institutions now have loan programs designed for the financial requirements of small retailers.

Selecting and training store owners and employees

To assist in developing management skills, business school faculty of the University of Minnesota teach courses in small business management to present the prospective owners of retail establishments in low-income areas. Developing a supply of skilled store owners is crucial to the success of the shopping center, but three related problems must also be resolved: (1) selecting stores for the shopping center from among the existing retailers in the area, (2) determining the mix of white-owned and minority-group-owned stores for the center, and (3) determining the degree to which chain stores should be present in the center.

On the first point, there are some retailers presently operating in the trading area of the prospective shopping center. A successful shopping center will adversely affect some of these existing stores. Consequently, some of these retailers desire tenancy in the planned center. The problem that local groups are just starting to face is how to select the beauty shop for the center (assuming it can only support one) from among three or four prospects.

If about half the residents of the trading area are white and the other half are black or Indian, should an attempt be made to obtain a balance of store owners and employees from among these groups? Militant blacks in the area answer, "No, the stores should all be black-owned!" However, the general reaction of the black women in the group interviews was that all the stores in the center should *not* be black-owned. They responded with such comments as "I don't care who owns the store," or "get all black-owned businesses and the whole thing will go down the drain." White residents emphasized that, "I don't give a damn what color they are as long as they're pleasant and act like they want to help you." Both black and white residents repeatedly stressed the need to utilize owners and employees from the immediate neighborhood, whenever feasible, and to have the center "integrated or it won't get rolling." They implied what the feasibility study made explicit. The shopping center would fail unless it could attract both black and white shoppers; attracting just one of the racial segments is insufficient to generate the necessary retail volume.

In general, major emphasis was not placed on the racial issue, but on store merchandise, prices, service, and public safety. In reference to the store characteristics noted above, both black and white residents maintain that the facility should be "like shopping centers

in other parts of town." Merchandise should be "honest merchandise, not a bunch of 'off' brands" and "be the same as you'd buy anywhere else." Prices on identical merchandise should not be conflicting ("I mean the same prices on different boxes of the same thing,") or too high for low-quality merchandise because "we're supposed to be poor or black or too dumb to know we're getting the shaft." And finally, in-store help should "give service to everybody no matter what color they are or how much or how little money they spend." One shopper responded with the classic plea of the times: "I want to be treated like a human being." Because of the history of vandalism and unrest, public safety is definitely considered a threat to the success of the shopping center with white residents perceiving the problem to be slightly more serious than black residents. Both groups generally wanted the shopping center protected to ensure a pleasant place to shop.

There are also mixed reactions with respect to the third problem, whether to exclude all chain stores. Some residents — both black and white — feel that under no circumstances should chain stores or outlets of large downtown stores be allowed in the proposed shopping center. Their reasoning is that these stores are largely owned or managed by suburban residents who effectively pump profits out of the low-income urban areas. Urban residents believe this is exploitation and resent it. At odds with this position is the more prevalent feeling that "we don't deserve something drab and second-rate just because we live on the north side;" residents with this opinion often equated "Ma and Pa" stores with second-rate treatment and welcomed the idea of a Wards or Sears outlet — although sales volume might limit it to a catalog operation — or other retail chains.

Both the prospective retailer and shopper find themselves in an ambivalent position on the question of chain outlets in the center. The unfortunate fact is that franchised chains, such as a possible restaurant for the shopping center, pose the greatest initial opportunity for comparatively inexperienced entrepreneurs because detailed procedures have been established for them based on the experience with previous outlets. Similarly, the housewife in the neighborhood is caught between opposing forces. As a champion of better local employment opportunities, the housewife wants the stores owned by her neighbors. However, as the principal buyer for her family, the housewife wears a different hat and wants to shop in pleasant stores having reasonable prices and good quality "like they do in the suburbs." She is astute enough to understand that running these successful stores takes experience that her neighbors may not have; she is practical enough to recognize that the shopping center needs some "name" chain outlets to generate traffic to make it a success. The best solution probably lies in a compromise that will allow some stores in the center to be part of national or regional chains, while retaining local ownership of the remaining stores.

Conclusion

Whether the proposed shopping center will be successful depends on a myriad of variables — economic, racial, political, and entrepreneurial. Perhaps the most important variable is the degree to which the entire community plans, supports, and maintains the shopping center. With all of the potential problems, the success of such a center is certainly not assured. Yet this chance for success deserves to be exploited for it has been observed that "the greatest opportunity to assist and to revolutionize the daily lives of the poor rests in the retailing communities serving the poverty area." As one local businessman commented, "What the area needs most is the confidence that comes from success — not promises." The attempt to understand the shopping needs of area residents and to include these in a feasibility study that is provided to local businessmen should increase the opportunities for the proposed retail stores to taste this success. Talents of concerned businessmen and firms — both inside and outside similar low-income areas throughout the United States — are needed to assist in designing, conducting, and implementing the findings of such studies.

BUSINESS MORTALITY

3

Most people assume that small businesses fail largely because of inept management. Here is a closer look at that problem.

The uncertain future of small business: can this picture be changed?

Harold K. Charlesworth†

What is the role of small business in American society today: Is its role the same as it was before the advent of the

†Harold K. Charlesworth, pp. 13-20, *MSU Business Topics*, **Spring 1970.**

Reprinted by permission of the publisher, Division of Research, Graduate School of Business Administration, Michigan State University.

corporate giants? Will rapidly changing technology force small business to the wall because of its inability to compete with large, well-managed, and adequately financed firms? Does the urban society, with its growing interdependence, rapid transportation and communication, and increasing social services, provide an environment in which small business can take root and grow? Would the demise of small business endanger the maintenance of basic American political freedoms? The Committee for Economic Development implied answers to these questions when it stated:

Whatever its type or stage of growth, the small business is a manifestation of one of the basic freedoms of American life. This is the freedom to enter or leave business at will, to start and grow big, to expand, contract — or even to fail. This freedom to be enterprising is an aspect of the economic democracy without which our political democracy cannot exist.

In many lines and in many markets — notably in home communities and for customers desiring individual service or products made to particular specifications — small business is able to do a better job than big business. Furthermore, the ingenious small enterpriser often is a source of new materials, new processes, new services, that older, better established firms cannot or will not offer. The whole pattern of any commercial system is enlivened and enriched by the independent businessman.[1]

The above quotation draws three important conclusions: that political democracy cannot exist without "freedom to be enterprising," that small business is more efficient than big business in certain markets and business activities, and that small business is a principal source of innovation of both materials and ideas. If all three conclusions are true, the future for small business is indeed very bright and encouraging. But if one or more of these conclusions becomes false or problematical, the prospects for small business become questionable; in fact, as the editors of the *Harvard Business Review* have stated, "in some industries the small business seems to be heading inexorably toward extinction."[2]

The future for small business can be measured in part by the study of its past growth and by estimates of future growth, by analysis of past economic conditions and by forecasts of future conditions, and by the number of old business discontinuances and of new business starts.

Past and future growth

In 1940 there were about 3.2 million small businesses in the country.[3] By 1961 this number had grown to 4.5 million,[4] and by 1968 to 5.2 million.[5] Between 1961 and 1968 the number of small businesses grew at an annual rate of 2.1 percent, as compared to a slower rate of 1.3 percent during the period 1940-60. The total number of business firms estimated by the Small Business Administration (SBA) for fiscal year 1969 is about 5.4 million; and about 6.0 million are forecast for 1975, as shown in Table 1. Assuming that 95 percent of all business firms may be classified as small business,[6] and recognizing that Table 3-1 is based on fiscal not calendar years, the number of small businesses at the end of calendar year 1975 would be about 5.7 million.[7]

National economic climate

The probability of success of new small business firms and the survival chances of existing firms depend heavily upon sustained and rapid

[1]*Meeting the Special Problems of Small Business*, a statement on national policy by the Research and Policy Committee of the Committee for Economic Development, New York, 1947, pp. 13-14; and cited by Small Business and Venture Capital Associates, *Encouraging Venture Capital for Small Business*, p. 6.

[2]The Editors commenting on "Meeting the Competition of Giants," *Harvard Business Review*, May-June 1967, p. 172.

[3]Edward D. Hollander et al., *The Future of Small Business*, prepared by Robert R. Nathan Associates, Inc. (New York: Frederick A. Praeger, 1967), p. 219.

[4]Small Business Administration, *17th Semi-Annual Report*, July 1-December 31, 1961, Washington, D. C., p. 1.

[5]Small Business Administration, 1968 *Annual Report*, Washington, D. C., 1969.

[6]Bank of America Small Business Advisory Service, *Small Business Reporter* 8, no. 1 (San Francisco: Bank of America, 1967): 3.

[7]It is interesting to note that the business population is estimated to be 5,655,800 in 1976. See Hollander et al., *Future of Small Business*, p. 220.

TABLE 3-1: Number of business firms, fiscal years
1969 and 1975 (thousands)

Industry	1969 (estimated)	1975 (forecast)
All industries	5,420	5,990
Contract construction	540	640
Manufacturing	340	350
Services	1,090	1,230
Retail trade	2,240	2,360
Wholesale trade	380	430
All other	830	980

SOURCE: Office of Planning, Research, and Analysis, Small
Business Administration, *Quarterly Economic Digest*, Winter
1969, p. 18.

national economic growth.[8] Since 1950 the United States has witnessed strong economic expansion which has fostered small business growth. Population increased from 151.3 million in 1950 to 199.9 million in 1968, an increase of 32.1 percent. Total personal income grew from $226.2 billion in 1950 to $683.7 billion in 1968, or by 202.3 percent; and per capita income rose from $1,496 to $3,421, an advance of 128.7 percent. Not all of the increased annual growth rate of small business (2.1 percent) between 1961 and 1968 can be attributed to the general affluence of the sixties. Part of the lower growth rate (1.3 percent during 1940-60) is a result of a longer measurement period during which World War II, the Korean War, and several recessions occurred. Yet, the difference is great enough to suggest that part of the growth was due to the more favorable economic climate of the sixties, compared to that of the forties and fifties.

Business starts and discontinuances

Vitality and continuity are important characteristics of small business growth. This is seen in the cycle of births and deaths which accompanies expansion of the business population. It is estimated that in recent years between 450,000-500,000 business concerns have been started annually and that between 350,000 and 400,000 have been discontinued annually.[9] Unfortunately, current data on business births and discontinuances are no longer available since the U. S. Department of Commerce stopped estimating these data in 1963. In the

[8]Office of Planning, Research and Analysis, Small Business Administration, *Quarterly Economic Digest*, Winter 1969, p. 13.

[9]Dun & Bradstreet, Inc., *The Failure Record Through 1967*, New York, 1968, p. 2. Dun & Bradstreet estimate business starts somewhat lower at over 400,000. Recent evidences, however, place the starts at well over 400,000.

ten-year period between 1953 and 1963 business births averaged about 9.2 percent of the business population and business discontinuances about 7.8 percent. If it is assumed that these same percentages would apply in 1969 and that 95 percent of the business population represented small business, the number of new business starts would be estimated at about 474,000 and the number of discontinuances at about 402,000 with a net of 72,000 businesses remaining in 1969. Based on the same assumptions, the forecasted number of new business starts in 1975 would be about 524,000 and the number of business discontinuances about 445,000.

One would conclude from the above discussion that the future growth of small business is all but assured. But nothing is further from the truth, for at least two reasons: first, the variance among relative and absolute growth rates of the eight geographic regions of the United States; second, the despondency, frustration, and bitterness — due to high rates of unemployment, underemployment, and low per capita incomes — which govern the future of small business in rural America and in the central cities of our large metropolitan areas.[10]

In large metropolitan areas and in rural regions of the nation, geographic location, poor transportation, lack of communication, discrimination, and segregation have created a tariff-type wall which has protected small business from competition in the same way that a tariff protects an infant industry. However, such protection is rapidly fading and with it many small businesses.

Recent studies by the SBA of major metropolitan areas suggest that "the urbanization process appears not to be conducive to the establishment or survival of the smallest concerns."[11] Economic deterioration in the inner city, witnessed mainly during this decade, "has taken a heavy toll of business concerns, particularly small concerns without paid employees."[12]

The same report points out that rural areas are the stronghold of small business:

Their survival and growth potential depend principally upon the course of economic development of rural America. Unless persistent outmigration of the youngest and best trained elements of the population can be halted through the development of diversified job opportunities, prospects for this major segment of the small business population are far from bright.[13]

The future for small business

The future for small business depends upon two forces working closely together: the federal government, which must expand its efforts to promote small business ownership, and management, which must be by those who live in the poverty areas. By its own efforts, small business stands no chance of stemming the economic decay existing in our central cities or reversing the tide of rural poverty

[10]Stanley Foster Reed, "Entrepreneurship and the Depressed Area," *Yale Review*, Autumn 1964, p. 39.

[11]Office of Planning, Research, and Analysis, Small Business Administration, *Quarterly Economic Digest*, Winter 1969, p. 16.

[12]Ibid., p. 17.

[13]Ibid.

flowing from "declining employment in agriculture, mining, and other primary industries."[14]

Unfortunately, it is often believed that federal funding alone can save small business. But federal programs cannot do the job by themselves. This conculsion was underlined by Lawrence R. Laughlin, head of the SBA's Boston office, in his comments to the *Wall Street Journal* on ailing entrepreneurs: "Money isn't the main problem any more; it's management assistance that is needed."[15]

Thousands of small business failures and discontinuances may be attributed to costs associated with inadequate business management. Historically, management has suffered from:[16]

1. lack of qualifications to run a business,

2. lack of training as a manager,

3. improper pricing of products and not buying at the best price,

4. poor selling programs, and

5. inadequate records.

Without basic skills, small business often has operated only marginally, and frustration and despondency have developed with disastrous results.

The operating conditions of small businesses in the depressed areas and the ghettos were described in the final report of the Small Business opportunities Corporation to the Economic Development Administration:

Many of the existing small businessmen are operating marginally and out of ignorance rather than through understanding of the proper techniques for running business. Little thought was given to such features as choosing a location, layout, controls (inventory and cash notably) merchandising, maintaining suitable records, cash reserves for contingency purposes, etc. Planning in any real sense is conspicuously absent, and forecasting is simply one of the unknowns. Success is associated with hard work and long hours, so that "mule power" is substituted for good business sense, and the financial returns are proportionate to the former in far too many instances to justify the business. Frustration, despondency, and defeatism "spill over" to affect the entire family, which "pitches in" in the effort to maintain an already inadequate income and virtually hopeless situation. Unjustifiably long hours are maintained which do not produce even the statutory minimum wages available through normal employment opportunities, so that the family, individually and collectively, ends up subsidizing a business which did not start out as a nonprofit organization, even though that may well be the net result.[17]

Evidence of the prime importance which management plays in small business growth and survival is emphasized in enumerating the reasons for business failure given by Dun and Bradstreet. If it is true, as assumed, that the causes of business discontinuance are similar to those of business failure, then poor management is the root cause of most business problems. If the four items in Table 3-2 (lack of experience in the line, lack of managerial experience, unbalanced experience, and incompetence) are combined, over 90 percent of the business failures shown may be attributed to poor management.

[14]Ibid., p. 29.

[15]*The Wall Street Journal*, 23 September 1969, p. 1.

[16]Clyde Bothmer, "Management Counseling for Small Business," *Defense Industry Bulletin*, September 1968, p. 27.

[17]Small Business Opportunities Corporation, *Final Report July 1, 1969 – December 31, 1967*, Philadelphia, 1968, pp. 27-28.

TABLE 3-2: Causes of business failures (in percent)

Cause	1964	1965	1966	1967
Neglect	2.8	3.8	3.1	2.7
Fraud	1.9	1.8	1.4	1.4
Lack of experience in the line	8.8	9.9	11.3	8.7
Lack of managerial experience	20.9	18.8	17.4	15.1
Unbalanced experience	19.7	21.4	18.4	20.2
Incompetence	42.5	41.3	46.3	48.5
Disaster	0.9	1.2	1.0	1.3
Reasons unknown	2.5	1.8	1.1	2.1

SOURCE: Dun & Bradstreet, Inc., *The Failure Record Through 1964; 1965; 1966; and 1967.*

Behavioral attitude of small business managers

If the basic problem of small business failures has been poor management, then why have effective programs not been designed to correct this deficiency?

The answer lies in the failure on the part of previous assistance programs offered by universities, federal and state agencies, and private institutions to recognize that "those who would shape any program designed to supply managerial assistance to the small businesses which need it most must find securing its acceptance more difficult than solving operating problems."[18]

The failure to concentrate on securing acceptance of past educational programs by many small business managers comes about because such programs do not view problems of small business management from the standpoint of "the habit patterns and attitudes of individuals or social groups."[19] What is needed to secure the acceptance of management assistance by small businesses is a "behavioral approach" which focuses its attention on the kinds of business behavior that have become so routine that they pass almost unnoticed.

Programs concentrating on the behavior pattern and psychology of small business management consider entrepreneurship a function of the socioeconomic environment or climate of the country or region concerned, not simply a function of the profit or money motive.[20]

What small business management needs then is a program which will change its present attitude of reticence

[18]Karl Morrison, *Small Business and Management Counseling* (University, Miss.: The University of Mississippi, Department of Economics, 1965), p. 12.

[19]Frank A. Heller, "Management's Contribution to Economic Development," *MSU Business Topics* 17, no. 1 (Winter 1969): 39.

[20]David C. McClelland, *The Achieving Society* (Princeton, N. J.: D. Van Nostrand Company, Inc., 1961), p. 376.

and suspicion of modern management practices to one of acceptance. The psychological resistance to change and to the acceptance of new ideas must be replaced by an "achievement motivation" or "need for achievement" on the part of small business managers.[21]

Role of the change agent

Given the suspicion and distrust held by small business today toward change, how can this conversion be made? The best known method of changing outmoded and outworn behavior patterns is to inject a *change agent* into the environment. The agent's objective is to introduce and establish new and permanent behavior patterns which will allow the people of a given culture to deal more effectively with their own environment.

The change process is sociocultural in form rather than economic, scientific, or technical. Person-to-person encounter is currently one of the most effective methods for accomplishing change. Most small businessmen are not book oriented and learn much better in a face-to-face meeting. This is particularly true for small, nontechnical firms which must have their problems translated into terms they understand, and must have help in adapting available information to fit their specific needs.

Essentially, the change agent provides the link between the world of small business (where managerial, technical, and financial problems exist) to the world of professional expertise (where the solution to the problem is found). To transfer knowledge and understanding of how to use that knowledge successfully, an agent must be able to play any or all of a variety of roles.[22]

Analyst. In this, the agent's main role, he interprets the business problem in the context of the firm's environment in an effort to arrive at an understanding of the firm's needs, to judge priority among those needs, and to assess the availability of resources to satisfy the needs.

Adviser. Here the agent presents to the small business alternatives applicable to the problem.

Advocator. As the advocator, the agent recommends alternative solutions, or ranks different alternatives in their order of applicability to the problem.

Innovator. In this capacity, the objective of the agent is to initiate a change or an innovation that will satisfy the needs of his client — the small businessman. In this role, the agent must apply his own expertise and knowledge of a technical subject such as management technology, engineering, or finance to initiate a program which is responsive to the needs of the business and is supported by his analysis.

The agent is expected to play these roles either singly or in combination. The challenge to the change agent is to selectively mix the necessary knowledge, skills, and attitudes to accomplish the desired results of transferring knowledge and understanding to his

[21]*Business Leadership Training Project, 1967-68* (Boston: Behavioral Science Center, Sterling Institute, 1968), p. 17.

[22]By role is meant the behavior expected of a person involved in a given situation as a change agent. Art Gallaher, Jr. and F. A. Santopolo, "Perspectives on Agent Roles," *Journal of Cooperative Extension*, Winter 1967.

client. It is ridiculous to bombard clients with potential solutions to problems they may not have. Rather, the change agent must first help them to define and understand their own needs if assistance is to be successful.

The concept of change agent is not new. Probably its most notable example of success in the United States has been the agricultural extension agent. The American farmer, responding to the suggestions of his county agent, has changed many of his older and less productive farming techniques. The result has been a revolution in American agricultural production over the past fifty years.

The hypothesis

The hypothesis posed in this article is that through the medium of a change agent it is possible as in the case of the American farmer, to bring about changes in the attitude of small business management toward modern management practices which will significantly affect the future of small business, particularly in the urban ghettos and the disadvantaged rural areas.

The evidence which exists to date to test this hypothesis points encouragingly to its acceptance. The Economic Development Administration of the U. S. Department of Commerce has funded twelve university centers in the distressed regions of the United States to offer technical assistance and counseling to small businesses. After two or three years of operation, evaluations of these centers suggest that a change agent can introduce new management concepts among small businesses which will be respected and maintained over time. Based upon the observations of

university centers in Kentucky, Georgia, Oklahoma, Wisconsin, Washington, D. C., and elsewhere, several preliminary observations may be drawn.

Because the small businessman is a product of his sociocultural environment, he is apprehensive of the consequences of making the necessary decisions required to achieve greater profits. He recognizes the risks facing small business where the odds of achieving success are "about one chance in 10" and the odds of dismal failure "about one chance in two."[23] His performance record in the ghettos and disadvantaged regions of the United States, therefore, should not be surprising.

Unlike the American farmer, whose status was enhanced among other farmers by improved agricultural production, the small businessman is wary of competition and hesitates to show how well he is doing. He does not wish to call attention to his business because he believes competition may increase.

Business clinics and management training programs offered by universities and federal and state agencies have not been strikingly successful in promoting better small business management, particularly in the urban ghettos and disadvantaged rural regions of the United States. The small businessman is hesitant about entering into formal class discussions or seminars that will reveal confidential knowledge about his business or show his lack of knowledge about business matters.

Most important in achieving attitudinal change toward business management is the establishment of

---

[23]Lawrence L. Steinmetz et al., *Managing the Small Business* (Homeword, Ill.: Richard D. Irwin, Inc., 1968), p. 29.

TABLE 3-3:   Small business clients — assessment of attitudes

	Initial attitude		2nd visit	3rd visit	4th visit
	Number	Percentage	Number	Number	Number
Hostile	36	15	2	0	0
Indifferent or passive	140	58	88	41	30
Receptive	66	27	70	42	11
Declined assistance	0	0	16	7	0
Total	242	100	176	90	41

SOURCE: Office of Development Services and Business Research, University of Kentucky.

rapport between two individuals, one offering assistance (the change agent) and the other receiving it (the client). The offer has to be made in such a way that it will not downgrade the client's self-respect whether he accepts it or not. The agent must have the necessary technical competence and business background plus the unique capacity to establish a relationship between himself and his client, if rapport is to be established. Only then can he be useful to his client. Unfortunately, such individuals are hard to find. Retired business executives often do not have such unique abilities, as the SBA has recognized.[24]

Many small businessmen living in rural areas are by nature, reticent and suspicious of "do-gooders." They are unwilling to accept any offer of advice from an outsider. For example, many businessmen living in eastern Kentucky are respectors of their own "kith and kin" and seemingly uninterested in the opinions of the outside world, because their emotional boundaries and ties keep their interests localized in their own small community.

To overcome this reticence, it is necessary to develop a methodology and technique for providing assistance which would be acceptable to the client. Since many small businesses are not cognizant of the value of management assistance or of a consulting service, a large part of the initial effort must be devoted to the recognition of the need for such assistance on the part of small business.

In quantitative terms some measures of the success or failure of the hypothesis that change agents can induce positive change among businessmen were found in studies of individual trip reports made by change agents of the University of Kentucky. In 242 cases studied — covering more than a two-year period — a marked difference was noted in attitude between the initial and final visit of the change agent, as shown in Table 3-3. Comparisons were made in terms of (1) the initial attitudes of clients toward the agent as compared with later attitudes, (2) the number of repeat requests

[24]*Wall Street Journal*, 23 September 1969, p. 1.

TABLE 3-3 (Continued):

Total visits		Final attitude	
Number	Percentage	Number	Percentage
38	7	0	0
299	55	30	12
189	34	189	78
23	4	23	10
549	100	242	100

coming from the same client, (3) the number of requests from unsolicited or new clients, (4) the growth in demand upon an agent's time by the same client, and (5) the types of questions asked — elementary or sophisticated.

The initial reaction to an offer of management assistance indicated that the attitudes of 140 businessmen were indifferent to the idea, 36 were hostile but did not reject the concept outright, and 66 were receptive. A second visit made within two to three weeks to only those who were hostile or indifferent on the first visit (176 in all) produced a significant change in attitude: an additional 70 were convinced of the value of the offer of management assistance, 88 remained indifferent, sixteen rejected the offer of assistance, and 2, who although still hostile, asked the change agent to call again. The third visit made to the 90 who still remained hostile or indifferent at the end of the second visit changed the attitudes of 42 businessmen from indifference to receptivity. A fourth and final visit increased the number of receptive businessmen by 11. Out of the original 242 business contracts, by final count, 78 percent expressed a sincere interest in working with the program, 10

TABLE 3-4:   Resolution of small business cases: Visits required and time spent

Visit	Time between visits	Cases resolved	Cumula- tive percentage	Average hours per visit*	Total hours
First	—	16	10	2.0	32
Second	2-4 weeks	31	29	4.5	139
Third	3-4 weeks	52	61	6.0	312
Fourth	4-6 weeks	34	82	6.5	221
Fifth	6-8 weeks	17	92	3.0	51
Six or more	7-9 weeks	13	100	2.0	26
		163			781

SOURCE: Office of Development Services and Business Research, University of Kentucky.

*Hours per visit include research and special consultant's time, if any.

percent declined, and 12 percent remained indifferent.

To develop these 189 active small business cases, 549 visits were required — an average of 3 visits per case. Of particular importance were the 299 visits made to businesses which had initially indicated indifference to management assistance. Out of the original 140 expressing indifference, only 30 maintained this attitude.

Within six to seven months, 163 business problems present in the 189 active cases had been resolved. Eighty-two percent of the 163 problems were answered within two or three months, as shown in Table 3-4. The remainder (30) required an additional three to four months before implementing an effective final solution. Twenty-six problems related to the original 189 cases, remained unsolved at the end of the study.

In most cases the solution of the original problem did not terminate the relationship with the program. For example, of the 189 original businesses, 119 requested further assistance in solving a second problem, and 78 found a third problem requiring outside assistance. In total, 298 additional requests for assistance were generated from the original 189 cases. Likewise, as the management assistance program became better known, new but unsolicited clients appeared. In the first six months 4 unsolicited clients applied for assistance. During the next six months, 13 additional unsolicited clients were obtained, and 8 more the following six months. At the end of three years, a total of 101 unsolicited entrepreneurs had applied for assistance.

The growth in demand upon an agent's time and the sophistication of the questions asked depended on the client's ability to change his attitude and to implement new business methods. In general, the more primitive the business, the more visits required and the less time spent per visit. Also, the time required per visit reflects the learning potential of the businessman and his willingness to take the initiative in solving his own problems and implementing new techniques. In the earlier periods more time was required than in later periods. These are direct correlates with the concept that many small businessmen by virtue of their sociocultural environment and past experience are prone to low self-confidence. This negative self-image has a retarding effect on performance and motivation. The use of a change agent as a technique to enhance self-confidence on the part of small businessmen results in better task performance, improved profit potential, and often leads to business expansion.

The small businessman who refuses to either seek or accept professional assistance in identifying problems and developing appropriate and realistic solutions, given his unique sociocultural environment, will face growing business risks and dim prospects for business success. Most likely his business will fail. But, by convincing him that he does not have to fear change, a favorable climate for small business growth can be created. It is this aspect of change which provides hope for the small businessman in his struggle for existence.

QUESTIONS

1. Why don't entrepreneurs seek help more frequently?

2. What might be done to attack this problem?

3. What is this inept management that causes so many failures? Specifically, what does "inept" really mean?

4. It was stated in the article, "Money isn't the main problem any more; it's management assistance that is needed." Is it?

A CASE
HISTORY OF A
BUSINESS FOR SALE

4

At any one time, if the entrepreneur cared to investigate the number of businesses that were for sale, the number would be rather frightening. Look in the want ads under Business Opportunities some day! Suppose you happened to come across some business for sale that seemed to appeal to you. What would you do to evaluate it? Here is one such business that was being considered by a young college graduate.

Robo car wash

Richard H. Buskirk

Evaluation of a prospective business acquisition

Mr. Thomas Charles had just left a meeting with Mr. Wright, who was trying to sell him a Robo Car Wash. Mr.

Charles had recently sold a tavern for a good profit and was actively seeking some other business activity in which to engage. He had learned of the availability of Mr. Wright's car wash and wanted to learn the details of the deal.

Mr. Charles was particularly interested in learning the reason Mr. Wright desired to sell the property. Mr. Wright claimed he wished to free his money from this car wash to facilitate development of a large number of them throughout the state. He had been granted a franchise for Robo Car Washes in the state of Colorado, and terms of the franchise required that a number of new washes be installed each year, but he was behind the quota because too much money was tied up in the ownership of individual locations. Mr. Wright was more interested in the overrides obtained by setting up and selling a large number of Robo Wash units in the state.

Boulder, Colorado, was a rapidly growing city of about 70,000 population. The particular car wash unit under consideration was advantageously located on the main thoroughfare through the town. It would be difficult to procure a better location. Mr. Wright had prepared a four-page resume concerning the business, which is presented in Tables 4-1 and 4-2.

At the close of their meeting, Mr. Charles promised Mr. Wright that he would investigate the matter carefully and let him have an answer in three days.

At the time there were two other car washes in town. One was a full-service drive-through for $1.75 in which the car was cleaned inside and dried off, and the other was a nonservice 50-cent drive-through. The service stations in town charged $2.50 per wash and preferred to turn away the business.

QUESTIONS

1. What & where should Mr. Charles investigate in evaluating this project?
2. Is $77,000 a fair price for this business? If so, why?
3. If not a fair price, what would you offer? Explain why.

TABLE 4-1:   Robo Car Wash sales information

Location: 1965 28th STREET, BOULDER, COLORADO

Price: $77,000

Sales price includes
1. Robo Wash equipment and building.
2. Franchise protection.
3. Robo Wash sign.
4. Land lease for 10 years with two 5-year options for renewal.
5. Gasoline equipment and outside lights are owned by Texaco.

Location information
1. Traffic count 30,000 per day.
2. Residential supporting area good.
3. Car agencies in area.
4. Large site — stacking area excellent.

Robo Car Wash franchise
1. Franchise fee of 2 cents per car wash.
2. Franchise fee of 8 cents per car wax (no charge for wax).
3. National and local advertising.
4. Franchise patent protection on equipment.
5. One-mile radius protection on location.
6. Maintenance advantages.
7. Robo Car Wash company status and growth.

TABLE 4-1 (Continued):

Texaco sales agreement
1. Agreement for three-year period, giving operator a 2 cents per gallon reduction on tank wagon price.
2. Profit margin of 9.6 cents per gallon regular gasoline and 9.9 cents per gallon on premium gasoline.

Monthly operating expenses

Wages	$ 880
Payroll taxes	83
Uniforms	3
Soap	100
Franchise	120
Supplies	40
Salt	10
Telephone	12
Maintenance (approx.)	100
TOTAL	$1,348

Overhead

Heat, light, water	370
Insurance	40
Rent	400
Taxes (estimated)	
Property	60
Personal Property	40
Advertising	100
TOTAL	$1,100
TOTAL MONTHLY EXPENSES	$2,448

Robo car wash franchise

TABLE 4-2:   Robo Car Wash — Boulder: Sales data, 11-month period

| | Gasoline (gals.) | | | |
Month	Reg.	Prem.	Free wash	Free wax
Jan.	11,955.4	7,244.8	1,844	270
Feb.	12,750.3	8,845.7	2,201	422
Mar.	14,866.5	10,374.4	2,560	474
Apr.	11,302.3	7,434.7	2,065	352
May	8,344.9	6,180.7	1,521	308
June	8,951.1	7,223.1	1,598	251
July	11,846.8	9,048.3	2,115	203
Aug.	13,631.0	11,110.2	2,299	55
Sep.	16,344.6	13,094.1	2,778	763
Oct.	16,496.0	12,300.1	2,693	561
Nov.	18,176.1	14,334.3	3,092	690
TOTAL	144,665.0	107,390.4	24,766	4,349

	Total no. wash	Wash-wax receipts	Vacuum	Chamois
Jan.	5,014	$ 1,808.75	.20	10.10
Feb.	5,713	2,008.00	40.35	
Mar.	6,045	1,949.50	51.10	18.30
Apr.	4,409	1,416.70	42.25	15.80
May	3,344	989.75	16.00	6.60
June	3,380	1,046.75	52.40	8.00
July	4,095	1,193.80	45.65	14.10
Aug.	4,203	1,069.00	49.55	19.80
Sep.	4,200	1,011.40	52.25	13.85
Oct.	4,170	871.75	22.80	6.60
Nov.	5,421	1,436.00	21.60	9.30
TOTAL	43,211	$14,801.40	395.15	137.35

Projected income

30,000 gallons gasoline sales @ 10¢/gal.	$ 3,000
5,000 cars	$ 1,500
	$ 4,500
Less average monthly expenses	$ 2,400
Projected net profit	$ 2,100
Average monthly net profit	$ 2,100
	×12
PROJECTED NET INCOME PER YEAR:	$25,200

TO OWN OR
TO FRANCHISE?

5

Some concepts are conducive to franchise operations. Indeed, there is more than one good entrepreneur who maintains that franchising is the fastest way one has of gaining a national base for his concept. The franchise method of business organization is something that most people give at least some thought to. Perhaps the following article will help better explain franchising.

Granted that the days when franchising was the hottest trend in business are over, still it remains an important form of organization for small businessmen.

Controversy: Franchise vs company operations

Leon Gottlieb & Associates†

†**Leon Gottlieb & Associates,** *Franchise Journal,* **March 1973, pp. 10-12.**
Reprinted with permission of: Leon Gottlieb,

Lucky you . . .

For the purposes of this article, you have a marvelously successful operation and you are trying to decide how to expand without culturing a new ulcer.

You can pump your own money, time and know how into a new location and own it all yourself.

Or, you can let someone else pump their money, their time, and your know how — note the words *your know how* — into the new spot and still come up a winner.

How do you make that kind of decision?

Both marketing methods of distribution can be excellent. Franchise oriented organizations and company operated have been in existence for decades. Tens of thousands of franchisees exist, purveying a multitude of products or services. There are also those who practice the straight-line method of expansion commonly referred to as a "company operation." Does there exist one method — one answer?

Leon Gottlieb & Associates, Franchise Management Consultants, Tarzana, California.

Let's take the position that you wish to expand; to grow; to add more outlets for your products or services. You may not have all the monies or financing you would like to have. Possibly, you're not satisfied with your management team at every level.

You are in a position to alter your methods of operation if you had solid reasons — something with which to compare.

What are basic criteria that will aid you to differentiate between franchising and company owned operations, their advantages and disadvantages?

The use of your franchisee's investment as leverage to increase the monies available to you is one of the great advantages in franchising. The theory, if not the practice, is that the franchise fee should make ready and open the franchise unit utilizing the fresh, incoming monies as working capital without the input of extra capital.

In company operations you depend upon your own resources. There is no influx of new monies at any time, save those that you are paying for in interest or equity. If you do not have the capital; if it is too expensive or unavailable; then the franchise method might be your answer and supply you with needed leverage.

A key element in your decision regards management. What are we talking about when we compare franchise management with company operation management?

Your franchise agreement is much like an employment agreement that allows your franchisee to have a place in which to work. A place to conduct his business without any guarantee as to his net profits and income. Your contract obligates him to perform certain managerial functions; to follow your systems and procedures and provide the motivation and enthusiasm of an owner to earn a better-than-average return on his time and investment.

An employee, on the other hand, whom you have promoted to manager of one of your units is not an independent agent whose income is based on the units profit or loss picture. He is dependent upon you. He knows that he must try to work within certain parameters of volume, costs and percentages. He will try to maintain a reasonable orderly operation, try to minimize losses and achieve some level of net profits.

A franchisee may be more proficient in people-to-people skills, whereas your employee-manager may be more technically proficient.

In either case, attitude is an important element. A franchisee is usually motivated and involved. He lives the business, literally night and day, and is proud of his investment. His dream has come true.

An employee, unless motivated and encouraged by his superiors, will perform adequately, earn a specified income, and generally expect advancement. His staying power is apt to be more tempermental and psychological, than financial.

In choosing which way to go, the issue of reliability is of importance.

A franchise owner will, to a greater degree, "be on the job" through good and bad times, in all kinds of weather and business conditions. It's his business, his investment. And he intends to protect it.

Employees are prone to "be sick," absent from their work, and allow others to fulfill their obligations, especially when under severe pressure. They are more apt to quit than work out their business problems.

The construction of your unit is completed. You're ready to open the doors to the first customers. Your man, be he franchisee or employee, is on the line. How will he meet the demands placed on him?

A franchisee generally will not at first be as proficient in your business. He probably has changed his profession to enter yours, through the purchase of a franchise. He will, in substantial form, become what you will teach him to be. Your training and supervisory activities are of vital importance to his well being. Firm controls, methods of communication, inspection and supervision are absolute necessities. Later on the franchisee will be more apt to resist authority for he knows he will not "be fired."

Company personnel generally assume a different posture. They are more proficient at work, having been at it longer; will accept changes in work orders and conditions more readily, and know from experience the latitude they have to achieve profit goals. Those with tenure could develop poor work habits that might offset good ones. Re-training and supervision are as important with employees as with franchisees.

After their initial period, franchisees often become suspicious of company intentions, and are less apt to accept changes in merchandise, procedures or services. Your first and best method in handling this problem is to show them how they can improve their net profits.

Company personnel do not relish changes either, but they will accept them more quickly and require less subtle tactics.

In getting down to business, the franchisee has chosen you and your concept because he can afford it, grasps the idea and relates to it. He knows he needs considerable support. He must be taught everything. Therefore, you can't take anything for granted. Strong support and inputs from you will make the difference when you add up those final figures in your financial column.

The employee, by comparison, is usually more experienced in his work, technically speaking. He may lack the ability to handle people well, and too, he may not be aware of the more sophisticated skills of business management. Therefore, you must give him the same strong support you would your franchisee.

In the area of profit orientation lies the strength of your program. Your franchisee, if he does not already know it, must be taught to earn a profit from his operation. This sounds like a simple concept, but most franchisees have never before in their business careers had the responsibility of producing profits. They must learn what items are fixed and those that are variable. They learn to control to produce net profits.

Nothing so awakens a franchisee as when he learns he will no longer receive a weekly paycheck and that his expenses will continue each day, and that only through close control will he maintain a proper balance of volume, overhead and profits. You must be very aware of this new psychological impact and help him handle it.

Managers, too, may not know how to make money; to earn profits! People are not good managers by accident. Those of your employees who have been properly and thoroughly trained will become professionals and operate within the limits you require. If you are to keep them happy, you will need to devise methods of compensation that are equitable. A "piece of the action" may be the answer.

Let's discuss further an average "profile" of a franchisee vs. an employee-manager.

Generally speaking, franchisees prove to be more stable and dedicated to the amassing of monies for their future investment, your franchise. As such, they are usually responsible, family-type individuals. Once granted their license they tend to remain for longer periods than an employee holding a comparable position. Franchise owners often become an active part of their community. Active in local affairs, communicating with fellow businessmen. An employee may not be as active, knowing he may be promoted or moved to another location in the future. Turnover can be greater with employees.

Franchisees require sensitive handling. Persuasion rather than fear of termination is necessary and desirable to encourage compliance in following directives to maintain standards of quality, image, trademarks, etc.

Owner-operators will tend to make more decisions; thus, greater decision-making supervision is generally required during the first year with some reduction afterwards. Franchisees seek support and recognition no matter how independently they speak or act.

Employee-managers depend more completely on their supervisors for important decisions and support. They use this contact for short-term consideration, favorable reports and recognition to achieve greater income and promotion. If denied supervision, they may try to operate by their own rules with the end justifying the means, if necessary, to achieve goals they "believe" you want.

Your franchisee wants respect and will object to being treated as an employee. He is more apt to question and resist company direction if he cannot see immediate net profit potential.

Conversely, a manager accepts his subordinate role and management's overall interest in quality of service, image and standards of product excellence, and will attempt to satisfy his employer to maintain job security.

The critical difference between your franchise owner "partner," and your "employee," is the manner in which he views his security and income.

The franchisee has a long-term contract assuring him of not being "fired" without several and just cause. He knows he can be terminated for serious transgressions and will on occasion test and bully you and your personnel to extreme limits if he feels wronged, put upon or when he is in financial trouble. A franchisee realizes his stake and investment, his equity and potential capital gain should he sell his business in the future. He will do all he can to protect this advantage.

Your employee-manager, on the other hand, has no such stake in his business. He can feel insecure due to the fact that his performance at all times is subject to review, and for any number of reasons, logical or illogical; for any number of circumstances within or beyond his control, he can be terminated and find himself without a job. Your manager views his cost of operation as being your cost, your money, and your investment . . . not his! An extremely conscientious manager will take his position seriously but when hard-pressed will generally admit that "the company can afford it," meaning, of course, his losses or errors.

Managers and franchisees alike, have a distorted opinion of company extravagance, executive salaries and expenses and frequently feel their particular overages are excusable.

When we speak of support and guidance, it begins during the training and pre-opening period through the grand opening and post opening weeks and months. During this time your franchisee will lean heavily on you, his Parent Company. The shock of being on his own, of being his own boss with others depending upon him is a new situation and one that calls for your assistance.

He paid for your services and he must receive them. Your patience and understanding are vital to his psychological success. The tricky part comes when your franchisee knows as much about his daily operation as you and your supervisors. When this occurs you had best listen to him. He can become more vocal as time goes by and needs to be heard. Give him the opportunity. How you handle this maturation process will become a major factor in the respect you command from your franchisee.

On the other hand, your manager employee has no doubt served his apprenticeship and grown into his position of responsibility and authority. You assume he knows his role and will maintain control over his comments and actions that could be considered upsetting to management or be prepared to suffer the consequences.

Franchise oriented companies value the need to convince their franchisees to cooperate and will often conduct seminars and communicate with greater care suggestions, ideas and promotional campaigns designed to persuade and obtain their cooperation.

This compares with company personnel who follow orders that, in most organizations, are issued from one direction, namely, the top down with little regard for dialogue upward from subordinates.

Franchising has prompted those who have selected this method of distribution to develop complete manuals of operation, training and supervisory techniques, bookkeeping and other technical knowledge to not only mark the progress of their franchisees but to establish parameters and controls over them. The need for controls is dictated by the fact that most continuing income and fees, as stipulated in the license agreements, are earned by the Parent Company for services rendered and based upon a percentage of gross volume. So, you, of necessity, should develop weekly or monthly profit and loss statements and other forms of measurement and record keeping to obtain all the monies due you.

In turn these standard operating procedures will enable each of your units to become a profit-center with full responsibility for all direct costs of operation placed in the hands of your franchisees.

There are other good reasons for you to want to know how well your franchise owners are doing; are they financially stable and able to repay balances and obligations due you and others; are they spending their monies faster than their income?

You want to know these things and you will use their gross volume figures, cost of sales, variable items, gross and net profits as a sales tool to sell more franchises as you expand. Their success becomes an integral part of your company's reputation and sales presentation.

These, then, are some of the differences between a franchise oriented organization and a company that owns and operates its own units.

Both have merit.

Evaluate each method. Do not assume that one is necessarily all bad or all good. In fact, a combination and balance between the two may well be your best solution.

Depending upon your particular business . . . you may wish to establish company owned and operated units in major population areas while franchising the satellite units around it. Your company units can become your training centers, warehouses or executive management training grounds. The satellite franchised outlets could supply fresh operating capital, involved and motivated management, and you could obtain the leverage from the initial fees as an off-set to the out-of-pocket expenses you will need to establish each new franchise unit. Again, this is one of the primary reasons for franchising.

If you have all the funds you need; if you have a wealth of executive talent both in-line and waiting for their promotion; if you already have the systems and controls, volume operations and net profits, you need not share your equity or profits with a franchisee.

You have what you need and don't require the advantages of franchising.

It is your question.

Do you franchise or not?

It is your decision.

QUESTIONS

1. What other reasons might an entrepreneur have for not wanting to become a franchisor?

2. For what reasons might one *not* want to became a franchisee?

3. Describe the situation in which the franchisor-franchisee relationship is most apt to work.

Franchising has been a hot topic and a most controversial one. Here is a legal view of it.

Some things to look for in franchise agreements

Harry Kemker†

Franchising has expanded so rapidly as a means of distributing goods and services that almost every lawyer finds himself involved in franchising. Either his franchisor client requests that he draw a franchise agreement or his franchisee client is requesting advice as to whether he should sign a proposed franchise agreement.

The purpose of this article is to point up some of the significant problems in drafting or advising a client concerning franchise agreements. The emphasis will be on the practical rather than the legalistic. Because of the wide variance of what is designated as "franchise agreement," the observations will necessarily be general.

From the franchisee's point of view, modern franchising permits little, if any, negotiation. It is a contract of

†**Harry Kemker,** *The Practical Lawyer,* **December 1970, pp. 55-67.**

adhesion, which he signs on a "take it or leave it" basis, as the franchisor insists on uniformity of franchise language.

Despite the usual absence of negotiation, the franchisee's attorney plays a vital role in interpreting and explaining the franchise agreement to his client. The franchise agreement can be a deceptive document, and all too frequently the franchisee client's enthusiasm to become a franchisee causes him to ignore the hard realities.

The franchise agreement may consist of more than a single document. Frequently the franchisor requires an application for a franchise agreement that incorporates by reference a manual or separate book containing franchise operating instructions, building specifications for the franchise facility, product and service standards, and the like. While the three documents make up what is properly called the franchise agreement, the focus of this article will be on the basic agreement.

The recitals.

Like any other contract, a franchise agreement traditionally begins with recitals or "whereas" clauses. The recitals of most franchise agreements describe the business of the franchisor generally and define the franchise "system" with particularity.

The "system"

The word "System" is usually stated to include the franchisor's:

- Trade name;
- Trademarks;
- Service marks;
- Copyrighted materials;
- Trade secrets and know-how;
- Building design and layout;
- Operating procedures;
- Operating manuals;
- Business systems, and the like.

The System is what the franchisee will exploit in carrying out the franchise agreement.

The scope of the franchisor's business defines the commercial area in which the franchised System will be practiced. Accordingly, the makeup of System and the definition of the franchisor's business are important to both the franchisee and the franchisor.

From the franchisor's point of view, the System should embrace everything of significance that the franchisor imparts to the franchisee. The wise franchisor particularizes every item in the System, as he wishes to commit the franchisee to the recognition of the proprietary and exclusive right of the franchisor not only in the franchisor's trade name and trademarks, but in all things that the franchisor has developed that cannot readily be protected by registration — such as operating procedures, product standards, and the like.

The franchisee should look carefully at the definition of the System to see if he is willing to accept that all of the System belongs to franchisor and to concede that, except for the purposes of the franchise agreement, he may not use any part of the System during or after the term of the franchise agreement.

Scope of business

Another aspect of the recital clause is the careful analysis of the business to which the franchisor's system relates. From the franchisor's point of view, he wishes to be sure that he chooses language that permits expansion of the franchised System (from the sale to the lease of franchisor's products, or from hamburgers to fried chicken). Accordingly, the franchisor will frequently draft the franchise so as to require the franchisee to agree that the System may be expanded to apply to business areas in which the franchisor is not presently active.

A franchisee, on the other hand, may be active in one of the potential expansion areas and may not wish to agree that the System may thereafter apply to a business in which the franchisee is already engaged.

Modification of the system

A similar problem is that of modification of the System. A well-drafted franchise agreement will usually provide that the makeup of the System is as presently defined or "as it may be changed from time to time by franchisor" during the term of the franchise agreement. In other words, the franchisor has an interest in keeping the System current to meet changing market conditions and consumer preferences.

To this end the franchise agreement may permit the franchisor unilaterally to change what constitutes the System. The effect of this provision may require the franchisee during the term of the franchise agreement to make additional expenditures in implementing such changes in the System.

Creating the franchise relationship

A franchise agreement has historically been a license to use a trade name or trademark coupled with some incidental agreements. Over the years

it has now evolved to the license of the entire System described above.

The basic questions the franchisee asks are, Where may he use the System and For how long? The granting clause answers these questions.

The franchisee desires to know that he will enjoy the protection from competition from additional franchisees and wants the security of an extended term within which to carry on the franchise operation. The franchisor's interest is to achieve the greatest distribution of its product and services.

Antitrust laws

Here the antitrust laws of the United States affect the agreement that the franchisor and franchisee may validly make. Relatively recent case law has made illegal franchise agreements that prevent franchisees from competing with each other or that prevent franchisees from dealing with certain prospective customers.

The appointment of the franchisee at a specific address surrounded by a "protected area" is a different thing from granting a "primary area of sales responsibility" and then limiting the location of the franchise facility within that area. Accordingly, the franchisee's focus will be on the clarity of language with which he is protected or insulated from the franchisor's appointment of additional franchisees in his "protected area" or within his "area of primary sales responsibility."

How certain is the franchisee that additional franchisees will not be appointed? Close scrutiny of the language is imperative.

Exclusivity

When the System is granted to a franchisee in a given area, he should be careful to examine whether the right to use the System within the protected area is exclusive or nonexclusive. The franchisor may designate it as nonexclusive because it wishes to engage in what an antitrust parlance is referred to as "dual distribution" — that is, the franchisor may wish to sell products or render services within the "primary area of sales responsibility" in direct competition with his franchisee.

Frequently the franchisor can serve a given class of customers more effectively because of its size and financial strength and thus compete with his franchisee within the "area of primary sales responsibility." By so doing, the franchisor does not violate the agreement because the franchisor is not appointing an additional franchisee. He is competing directly.

Many franchisors grant a nonexclusive use of the System because this is consistent with the franchisor's appointment of other franchisees for different franchise system in the same primary area of sales responsibility.

Modern franchise agreements usually appoint a franchisee in a specific "primary area of sales responsibility." To protect the franchisee from competition, the franchisor agrees that additional franchisees will not be appointed within the assigned "primary area of sales responsibility."

As a matter of law, however, the franchise agreement may not legally prohibit franchisee *B*, appointed by the franchisor in a "primary area of sales responsibility" adjacent to *A*, from competing in the area assigned to franchisee *A*, so long as franchisee *B* does not open a franchise facility within the area assigned to franchisee *A*. Similarly, provisions of preempting a franchisee from dealing with certain customers are illegal. *United States v. Sealy, Inc.*, 388 U.S. 350 (1967).

Many franchisors solve the problem by appointing a franchisee a specific street address or location, and providing in lieu of a "primary area of sales responsibility" a so-called "protected area" that surrounds a franchisee's facility. Some franchisors provide that the "protected area" protects the franchisee until the population therein expands to a certain number, whereupon an additional franchisee may be appointed.

The use of the "protected area" phraseology is derived from the antitrust problems created by the so-called "one location" clause, a franchise provision that limits the location of the franchise facility to a particular place with a "primary area of sales responsibility."

If franchisee *A* succeeds in Washington County with "Blue Plate" Burgers, how well will he do when franchisee *B* opens "Blue Plate" Fried Chicken in Washington County? This will depend on the definition of the System and the business to which it relates, but it may be controlled by whether the grant to franchisee *A* of the right to use "Blue Plate" in Washington County is exclusive or nonexclusive.

Lastly, a nonexclusive grant is consistent with the practice of a franchisor appointing additional franchisees when the "protected area" or "area of primary sales responsibility" expands.

Cost of changes

Franchising is relatively new, but it is clear to most that all franchise systems will not be outstanding successes. Many franchise systems will hereinafter need modification and change to improve their commercial prospects. As mentioned before, the astute franchisor builds into the franchise agreement the capacity to modify and change its System as market situations and competition dictate.

The franchisee, on the other hand, must be mindful of the potential of this modification. It may cost him a great deal of money to adopt or achieve the changes that the franchisor requires.

Usually the granting clause will provide that the franchisee license its system "as it presently exists or as it may be modified hereafter." The franchise agreement may provide that the franchisee will "erect and maintain" a franchise facility that will permit him to meet a particular sales goal or other performance standards set by the franchisor.

The word "maintain" can be interpreted as requiring the franchisee to upgrade or even relocate the franchise facility in order to meet franchise performance requirements. This, of course, is an extreme example but is a very real problem for automobile dealers.

In counseling the franchisee, the potential of additional expense occasioned by acts of the franchisor should be seriously considered.

Specific term

The granting clause also provides for a specific term. The range of provisions is almost limitless. Some franchise agreements are from year to year, whereas others are for 20 years with automatic right of renewal. The length of the term is usually co-extensive with the investment of the franchisee.

The shortness of term is, of course, an effective means of eliminating poor franchisees by simply not renewing them. It is also a good occasion to require a modification in the franchise agreement. Many franchisors who do

not provide for modification in the initial agreement impose considerably different agreements on their franchisees at renewal time.

Operation of the franchise

A good portion of most franchise agreements is taken up with provisions concerning the operation of the franchise facility. Not infrequently, franchisors shorten their basic franchise agreements by incorporating by reference a separate manual containing many of the operating provisions. The operating criteria particularized in various franchise agreements vary so greatly that it would serve little purpose to comment thereon except as to a few of the really troublesome provisions.

Best efforts

One of the most deceptive but important provisions is that which requires that the franchisee use his "best efforts" in operating the franchise facility. When the franchise agreement is between a franchisor and an individual franchisee, this provision, in effect, requires a franchisee to commit the major portion of his personal business efforts to the operation of the franchise.

Moreover, the use of additional words such as the "best personal and continuing efforts" impose additional requirements. The word "personal" requires the franchisee to operate the franchise facility. The word "continuing" emphasizes that the franchise agreement runs only to this particular franchisee.

The franchisor's justification for this language is that he has carefully selected a given individual he regards as competent, financially sound, and reliable to operate the franchise and he wants this particular individual to be personally involved in the day-to-day management of the franchise facility. He does not want the franchisee's efforts diluted by other work that does not further franchise purposes.

The franchisee must be reminded of this personal obligation, which may be non-delegable. The franchisee finds himself faced with the prospect of breach of contract if he attempts to pursue other business endeavors.

Equipment and supplies

Also classified as operating criteria are the requirements setting standards as to the equipment used in the franchise facility, the products or ingredients of products sold by the franchise facility, or the equipment or products with which the franchise facility renders a service. The basic problems here are again those involving antitrust laws.

It may be a violation of section 1 of the Sherman Act [15 U.S.C. § 1] or section 3 of the Clayton Act [15 U.S.C. § 14] if the franchisor conditions the grant of the franchise on a requirement that the franchisee purchase such equipment, products, or supplies from the franchisor.

Such standards may be appropriate and not a violation of the antitrust laws if they are reasonable and designed to maintain the quality standards of the products or services of the franchisor.

Competitor's products

An analogous provision is one that prevents a franchisee from dealing in the products of a competitor. Such a provision that requires the franchisee to deal exclusively in the products of the franchisor may likewise constitute a violation of section 1 of the Sherman Act or section 3 of the Clayton Act if competitors of the franchisor encounter problems in marketing their products because the franchisee is foreclosed from dealing with them by the exclusive dealing arrangements.

Similarly, sales performance requirements or inventory and stocking requirements that are set so high as to require exclusive dealing may also run afoul of the antitrust laws.

These provisions are important to the franchisor, not only to protect the integrity of the franchise system and its trademarks and other symbols, but also important as a device for marketing his products. The restriction may be a sincere effort to maintain quality standards, or they may simply be an attempt to control his franchisee as a market.

From the franchisee's point of view, he will want to consider carefully such provision in the franchise as it may limit his profit potential. The franchisor's products may be too expensive to permit a profitable operation, or perhaps the franchisee can acquire products from sources other than the franchisor and still maintain the quality standards.

The lesson to the franchisee is to analyze the franchise closely to measure its impact on his potential operation. How well will he do if he must deal only with his franchisor as a supplier?

Fees

Traditionally, a franchise agreement provides for an initial fee that is earned when the franchise agreement is signed or when the facility is opened and thereafter for continuing fees in terms of percentage of gross sales, unit sales, or the like.

A number of successful franchise systems have found that their franchise fees based on a percentage of revenue are unusually low and that a much greater return could have been achieved had a higher rate been adopted. This experience has resulted in many new franchisors setting fees of five to as much as 10 per cent of gross sales. The problem is an economic one of business judgment in setting franchise fees at the outset.

From the franchisee's point of view, care should be taken in reviewing the franchise agreement to measure the full impact of the franchise fee requirements on the franchisee. It is usual for a franchise not only to require continuing percentage of gross revenue, but to require additional fees in terms of percentage of gross revenue earmarked for the purposes of advertising, promotion, and the like.

It is not always clear that a particular franchisee will enjoy the benefits of the advertising and promotional effort, as a national franchisor may not always expend an aliquot portion of the advertising fees in the franchisee's service area or on a basis that will benefit all franchisees equally. Clarification in order to require franchisors to expend this money equitable should be pursued.

Restrictions placed on the franchisee

The usual franchise agreement places rather harsh restrictions on the franchisee's use of the System, including the trademarks, service marks, copyrights, and the like named therein. To be sure, these trade symbols are properly the property of the franchisor and are licensed to the franchisee only for the use of franchise purposes. Thus, it is usual to require the franchisee to admit:

• That the System is the exclusive property of the franchisor;

• That the elements of the System will be displayed and used only as particularized by the franchisor; and

• That the franchisor controls the matters relating to infringement of the trademarks and trade names.

Transfer of franchise

There are additional restrictions, however — the full impact of which are not frequently appreciated by franchisees. Many franchises flatly prohibit the transfer or alienation of the franchise facility and prohibit the franchisee from selling or assigning the franchise agreement or any right that exists under the franchise agreement.

What the franchise should require is a provision that will permit a franchisee to transfer the franchise to a corporation so long as the franchisee remains substantially liable personally for the obligations of the franchise agreement. While some limitations may be proper to protect the franchisor, certainly the franchisee wants the ability to change to a corporate or other business form if this proves advantageous for him for tax or business reasons.

Further, the franchisee wants to be able to sell his franchise facility to a third party if he so desires. Now the reference to "personal, best, and continuing efforts" takes on an additional meaning.

If the franchise agreement is expressly a personal franchise, the franchisor will argue it simply will not exist in the absence of the franchisee's personal involvement. Even if the purchaser hires the original franchisee as the franchise operator, this may not meet the requirements of "best personal and continuing efforts" of the original franchisee, as this language implies the efforts of such person as an owner.

Moreover, if the franchisee desires to sell the business, he probably wants to be out of it altogether. Accordingly, no great solace is found if the franchise agreement provides that the approval of sale of the franchise will not be "unreasonably withheld" by the franchisor.

The franchise is personal. The language of the franchise agreement emphasizes the reliance by the franchisor on the personal ability, confidence, and integrity of the franchisee. It is difficult reasonably to argue that one franchisee should be replaced with another. The short of it is that the franchisee must recognize that the right to operate as a franchisee may not be an asset he can sell at will.

The language of the franchise agreement that restricts alienation of the franchise agreement or any right thereunder may also prevent the franchisee from sharing his profits with other investors. These limitations of the franchise agreement may restrict a wide range of commercial conduct by the franchisee — from preventing the franchisee from being involved in a public offering of stock to simply prohibiting the use of the franchise agreements as security for a loan.

Engagement in similar business

Most franchise agreements provide that franchisee will not be engaged in any business similar to that of the franchisee (or franchisor) during the term of the franchise agreement. Frequenty, franchise agreements further prevent the franchisee from being a member of trade associations or organizations whose members compete with other franchisees. Thus, a franchisee of one motel system may be prevented from owning a motel of a competing system even though the respective motels do not compete.

These provisions should be carefully reviewed with the franchisee, as some franchise agreements tend carefully to prevent even the remotest form of competition. In the rush to obtain franchise agreements, many franchisees are in breach at the moment of signing because they have not carefully reviewed their holdings in light of franchise restrictions.

Competition after termination

Perhaps the most significant restrictions on competition are those that apply after the termination of the franchise agreement. Many franchise agreements contain the usual covenant not to compete, presumably setting reasonable limitations in both area and time. In some states such restrictions are invalid, and alternative provisions are used in the franchise agreement.

Thus, after the term of the franchise agreement, the former franchisee may be prohibited by the so-called "diversion of trade" clause from approaching former customers of the franchise facility. Some franchise agreements provide an option on the part of the franchisor to employ the former franchisee as a consultant, thus preventing the former franchisee from accepting employment from competitors of the franchise facility.

The franchisee must, of course, consider the impact of this language, but it is the franchisor who has the major problem. He must select language that will furnish post-term protection from franchisee competition but be effective in numerous jurisdictions. Perhaps the most useful provision is one that provides a combination of restrictions coupled with the usual clause providing that partial invalidity will not affect the balance of the agreement.

Protection of the franchisor from the franchisee's acts

Most franchise agreements provide that the franchisor is not liable for acts or debts of the franchisee and require that the franchisee indemnify the franchisor from loss arising from operation of the franchise facility. Further, the franchise agreement may require the franchisee to maintain insurance that protects the franchisor as well as the franchisee with reference to the operation of the franchise facility.

Thus, the franchisor assumes he is free from liability for the debts or acts of his franchisees. Here there are considerations for attorneys' fees for both the franchisee and the franchisor.

Ostensible agency

First, there is the possibility that the franchisee will be held to be the ostensible agent of the franchisor, resulting in the franchisor's liability to third persons for acts of his franchisee. This liability is in part predicated upon the control of the franchise operations by the franchisor. The franchisor protects the integrity of the franchised system by control of operations of the franchise facility, the display of trademarks and the like, but this very control may impose liability to third parties. The franchisor's compromise is invariably insurance protection.

Product liability

If the franchisee sells a defective product that injures a third party, may he sue his franchisor-supplier? Presumably he can, for the transaction in which a franchisee purchases products from his franchisor is like any other sale and involves the usual warranties of the *Uniform Commercial Code §§ 2-312 to 318.*

The franchisor should perhaps control this question to his advantage in the franchise agreement by limiting his responsibility. However, few seem to have done so.

Termination

Other than operating standards, no topic takes up more space in the usual franchise agreement than provisions relating to termination. It is traditional to provide that a franchise may be terminated for violation of the terms of the franchise agreement, bankruptcy or other insolvency, violation of law, and a host of other reasons.

The franchisee should ask a number of questions. Is the language calculated to allow the franchisor to terminate for any picayune reason? Are there fair and reasonable provisions affording the right to cure violations of the franchise agreement?

If not, the franchisee is in constant jeopardy that any breach, no matter how slight, will subject him to termination. The franchisor may be able to coerce the franchisee by threats of termination if the termination provisions are too stringent.

The proposed Franchise Competitive Practices Act, the so-called "Hart Bill" [S. 1967, 91st Cong.], seeks to make effective only those franchise provisions that are "essential" to the franchise relationship and "reasonable."

Destruction of premises

What happens if the franchise facility is destroyed by fire, windstorm, or some other casualty, or the facility is closed because the property is taken by eminent domain proceedings? Under most franchise agreements, failure to operate for a short period of time is a basis for termination.

It seems reasonable to require the franchisor to provide that, in the event of the destruction or loss of the franchise facility by casualty or eminent domain, the franchisee will not lose the balance of his term, but have a reasonable chance to rebuild or relocate and continue operations for the balance of the term of the franchise agreement.

Value to franchisee's estate

Perhaps the most important aspect of termination of the franchise is the potential value of the franchise to the franchisee's estate. Most franchise agreements provide that the franchise terminates on the death or incapacity of the franchisee. This is consistent with the franchise being granted to an individual based on his personal performance.

If possible, however, the franchise agreement should permit the franchise to remain an asset of the franchisee's estate, and that, if qualified, the widow or nominee could be approved to continue as the franchisee for the balance of the term. The total goodwill pertaining to the franchise facility does not arise only from the trademark of the franchisor, but may well have a great deal to do with the manner in which a competent franchisee operates the facility.

Franchising contemplates that the franchisor's trademark be the sole trade symbol used. Thus, the franchisee's goodwill arising from years of effort may be largely lost if the franchisor prevents continued use of that trademark after the death or incapacity of the franchisee. It would seem appropriate, therefore, to provide in any franchise agreement the right to continue the operation of the facility after the death or incapacity of the franchisee.

Rights of the franchisor on termination

Perhaps the most extensive and sometimes arbitrary provisions of the franchise agreement are those rights that are accorded the franchisor on termination. It is not unusual to find a franchise agreement that not only permits the franchisor to recover all sums due it from the franchisee, but also to enjoy the right of setoff against the franchisee.

Franchise agreements frequently provide for attorneys' fees to the franchisor's attorney and a specific measure of damages if termination is based on nonperformance or breach of the franchise agreement by the franchisee. They may go so far as to provide that any amount due to franchisor automatically becomes a lien on the fixtures of the franchise facility that are owned by the franchisee. The franchisee's attorney must point out these problems and be clear that his client understands their impact.

One of the franchisor's problems concerning termination is that the franchisor needs continuing representation in the distribution of its products or services and thus needs immediate control of the franchise facility on termination. Many franchise agreements provide for an automatic right of re-entry at the expense of the franchisee in continuing the operation of the franchise facility.

Other franchise agreements have employed the technique of requiring that the lease of the property on which the franchise facility is located be assigned to the franchisor upon notice to the landlord of the franchisee's breach. Of course, the landlord must consent to the assignment when the lease is executed.

Each of these provisions may run afoul of the rule of law existing in some states prohibiting the contract forfeiture of interest in real property and providing that the only remedy to remove a tenant is ejectment or some specific statutory remedy.

Conclusion

Space limitations prevent the discussion of other provisions in the franchise agreement. The foregoing discussion attempts merely to point up some of the more important provisions and the considerations that underlie them.

It is hoped this article will assist attorneys for both franchisors and franchisees to be mindful of the need for careful consideration of the terms of such agreements.

QUESTIONS

1. Why should one be concerned with such legal details when considering a franchise?

THE ENTREPRENEUR — YOU?

6

Experience indicates that the biggest risk in new enterprises is the enterpriser himself. Immediately the question of his talents arises. Has he the technical know-how to operate the business? Has he the necessary business knowledge? Has he the requisite administrative skills? Has he the energy? Has he the desire?

There is a great deal to know about any business. It is all too easy for one to jump to the conclusion that he can open a filling station, restaurant, or operate a trash collection service with little or no knowledge, but such is simply not the case. Naturally, some businesses are more complicated than others, thus requiring a higher level of expertise for their operation, but nevertheless there are things that must be known if one is to succeed in any business. Many people fail solely because they lack such knowledge. The person without experience in the business in which he intends to begin is an exceedingly high risk. Even a few months of actual working experience in that line of endeavor would greatly increase his chances for success. Most successful entrepreneurs serve an apprenticeship

until they are confident that they know the business — know the customers, know the suppliers, know the industry, know the competition, and know what it takes to be successful in that business. One successful haberdasher worked for two years as an assistant buyer for men's wear in a large department store before he felt that he had sufficient knowledge to open his own store. During that time he worked diligently at planning his own store. He contacted suppliers and talked to them about obtaining their lines for his operation. When the time arrived for him to open his shop he had everything ready to go. In another instance of careful preparation, the average fast food franchisee is given more than ten days' training before he opens up and is carefully supervised thereafter. McDonald's operates Hamburger University at which its franchisees are thoroughly trained.

After picking the business one wants to enter, then it is a good idea to get a job working for someone who is known to be particularly adept in that calling. Study under the best! You will not learn much from those who don't know much.

Just as important as technical proficiency are intangible factors such as the entrepreneur's philosophies, work habits, attitudes, and personality. Studies have shown that the entrepreneur is a different animal. He is not like his bureaucratic, big-business brother. He is different in many ways, some of which have been measured and others which can only be surmised. The list of his differences could be rather lengthy, but some of the more salient points need to be brought out against which the reader may measure himself.

First, the entrepreneurial personality tends to rebel against authority. He wants to be boss. He does not like taking orders from other people. He tends not to work well in groups or with other people. He tends to be a lone wolf. Moreover, he is strongly oriented toward achievement; he wants to accomplish things, make things happen. He wants action and becomes impatient when frustrated by red tape and the inertia of other people.

Surprisingly, the background from which entrepreneurs come is not what one might expect — the modestly wealthy upper classes. Rather, they seem to evolve from the lower middle classes where a strong sense of the Puritan values of materialism, hard work, and achievement have been inculcated in them. But let us get down to some of the personal factors that seem to cause the failure of new enterprisers.

FAMILY DEMANDS ON ENTREPRENEUR'S TIME AND RESOURCES

There are some families that simply will not allow an individual to be successful. They will not leave him alone long enough to allow him to do the things that must be done if he is to be successful. Many times his family demands that he act as their chauffeur, buying agent, companion, or whatever, when he should be tending to business affairs. Make no mistake, the time demands on the entrepreneur are great. The man seeking the forty-hour week need not look into his own business, for it's not to be found there. It is not unusual for a man to have to work weekends and nights, particularly in the early stages of the business in which he must do a great many things himself to conserve cash. The family that does not understand this and will not help him will cause his failure. Have you control over your time? Does your family understand what you must do? Does your family agree with your going into business? If you get the wrong answers to such questions, forget being your own boss — you aren't!

MENTAL TOUGHNESS

Adversity is the lot of the entrepreneur. Harrassment is its handmaiden. As one new enterpriser put it, "It's just one damn thing after another!" Things go wrong daily, problems must be solved, and authorities dealt with constantly. Some people do not have the mental tenacity, determination, or patience to deal with the unending stream of problems confronting them. It wears them down. It takes a particular type of individual who has a very high tolerance point to handle the situation. People with low boiling points carry a large liability. Many people quit simply because they tire of the fight. Make no mistake about it, harrassment, and that is the word for it, from all sorts of sources, particularly governmental authorities, is very real. The fire inspector orders the back room cleaned up due to such-and-such; the building inspector tells you that you must make some changes; the food and drug people seize some merchandise; the tax people walk in for an audit; the safety people serve you with a notice to do something or other. It is an amazing monument to man's desire to have his own business that one is established at all under today's governmental regulations. It is impossible to exaggerate the difficulties that the entrepreneur must endure.

JOE KARBO

7

Yes, there still are people who are making large profits from small enterprises. Here is a brief story of one such man. Perhaps you've seen his ads.

Joe's awfully rich — for a 'lazy man'

Steve Mitchell†

Joe Karbo got together with creditors 12 years ago and said, "Listen. I owe you guys about $50,000. Now you can make me file a petition for bankruptcy, but I'd rather just pay you off.

"If you'll agree to a repayment program I can live with — that means no harassment or attaching my bank

---

†**Steve Mitchell,** *The Daily Pilot,* **Newport Beach, Ca., November 7, 1973, p. 36.**

account every time I make a couple of bucks, I can pay you back."

Today, sitting in his plush Sunset Beach office overlooking the Pacific, Karbo recalls, "I placed about $1 million worth of advertising that year and paid off the creditors in three years."

Dressed in a casual shirt and shorts, and with his stocking feet propped up on his cluttered desk, Joe Karbo is the prototype for his book "The Lazy Man's Way to Riches" which he published this year. The book has sold 139,000 copies at $10 per — a price Karbo terms "ridiculous." The publishing company? F.P. Publishers of Huntington Beach, a firm which is owned, naturally enough, by Joe Karbo.

"Lazy" isn't his first venture in the writing field. An earlier book entitled "How to Get Out of Debt" was written while he was in debt.

"It helped pay some of the bills," he noted.

Karbo and his wife Betty used to host an all-night talk show on television.

"Instead of having to depend on sponsors for the show, we decided to become our own sponsors by forming a mail order business."

When they lost the television show in 1962, Karbo recalls, "Mail order was the only game in town."

That was when he had the chat with the creditors.

"I had a crummy car that I was still making payments on and eight kids to feed when KTTV dropped our program."

Joe's secret for success?

"There's really only two ways to make a buck — as a commercial salesman or by working for yourself. You'll never make a fortune working for someone else," Karbo claims.

He ought to know. The 48-year-old Huntington Beach man expects to make $500,000 in 1973 alone, according to a recent article in the business section of Time magazine.

His book describes the way to millions in two steps. The first is positive thinking. He describes a system of what he calls "dynamic psychology" or "the programmed study and practice of achieving success by the planned application of important but little understood natural laws."

Karbo claims "Dyna-Psych" is what got him out of debt 12 years ago and says it can be applied to anyone's life. He advises readers to see themselves as winners and to set up a list of long-term goals in a spiel that would entice the laziest of men.

His second suggestion is for readers to get into the mail order business, "not by selling someone else's product, mind you."

His secret is to "come up with your own product ideas — develop a product and sell it by mail — find a need and fill it," Karbo harps. "What I usually do when I come up with an idea is, take it to

a manufacturer and say, 'here's a good product. You make it and I'll sell it.'"

In this manner, Karbo reasons he only has to come up with one good idea a year.

"I usually try out two or three products a year in case something goes wrong with a couple of them — which frequently happens."

One of the first products Karbo sold successfully was a Christmas ornament that lights up without electricity.

"We were testing some invisible powders that we thought would help trap thieves," Karbo explained. "That didn't work out the way we hoped, but then somebody said, 'Hey, that would make a neat Christmas ornament.' With a little switching and changing we developed a product that was shatterproof, glowed in the dark and sold it for a little more than five cents apiece. We sold millions of those gadgets and are selling more every year."

A Huntington Beach dermatologist came up with a new skin care product. Karbo heard about it, went to see the doctor and is now selling the product nationwide in magazines and newspapers.

He once commissioned a physician to write a book about sex that would be easy to understand and "in good taste." The book was a success.

He says he was once the largest dealer of door viewers in the nation and his wife's diet plan is still a hot item after more than a decade on the market.

"The nice thing about this business is you can test your ads for very little capital by trying them out in a small area. If the test works out you can build into a national business overnight because it's self-financing. Besides, you use the same street address for orders," Karbo explains.

Things aren't that easy anymore for Joe Karbo, a man who only works six months a year. He now has processing offices in Los Angeles and Huntington Beach but does the "thinking portion" of his job at the Sunset Beach office.

Karbo gets about 50 letters a day from people who have purchased his book and want to air their ideas with the author.

"I'm really snowed under with correspondence, which bothers me because it's just not my lifestyle to have to work this hard," Karbo complains. He does give most of them personal attention, however.

What does he do during his six months off each year?

"Betty and I spend about three months at our cabin in Washington with some of the kids." he said.

The Karbos travel a lot, flying to Europe in the spring, "partly on business, but mostly for fun."

Karbo says he could make twice as much if he worked all year but "that would be defeating my purpose. After all, I'm basically a lazy man."

QUESTIONS

1. Why do you suppose Joe preferred to stay out of bankruptcy?
2. What are the characteristics of a good mail order product?

WHEELING AND DEALING

8

The so-called "wheeler-dealer" has his unique place in our system. Naturally, some are more adept at it than others. It takes time to evaluate such promoters, for many of them owe what fleeting success they enjoy more to luck than to skill. Unfortunately, luck is usually short lived; skill usually wins in the long run. Here's the story of one wheeler-dealer. Note his apparent ability to see values where others do not. This sense of values is a most critical trait to develop.

The acquisitor — how an Iowa farm boy came to own a casino and much, much more†

Frederick C. Klein†

LAS VEGAS — Deil O. Gustafson thinks that cash is overrated. "Anyone who says you have to have it to make it doesn't know what he's talking about," he says. "If that were true, I'd still be back teaching school."

As it is, a look at Mr. Gustafson's current surroundings suffices to confirm that the dapper, 43-year-old former Iowa farm boy has come a long way since he stopped teaching business courses at the University of Minnesota 12 years ago. His expensively shod feet are propped atop a handsome mahogany desk in the board room of the Tropicana Hotel and Casino on this city's gaudy "Strip." He owns the Tropicana.

He also owns the Carousel casino in downtown Las Vegas, banks, apartments, office buildings and large chunks of real estate in Minneapolis, a hotel in Phoenix, a cattle ranch in northern Nevada and 20 or so companies engaged in selling insurance, leasing equipment, making movies and other things. Assets under his control

†**Frederick C. Klein,** *The Wall Street Journal,* **January 3, 1974, p. 1.**

are estimated to exceed $150 million. His net worth, which stood at close to zero in his teaching days, has been placed at $20 million to $30 million.

And that, he says, is just the beginning. "If my plans here pan out — and I have no reason to think they won't — I'll have the biggest resort operation in Las Vegas in a half-dozen years," he declares with characteristic confidence. "Some of my ideas are so good I have to shake myself to make sure I'm not dreaming."

Those who have followed Mr. Gustafson's career believe he has an excellent chance of bringing this off, and more. "He's the most unusual businessman I've ever come across," says B. John Barry, senior vice president of American National Bank & Trust Co. in St. Paul, which has financed several of his ventures. "He has an uncanny knack of taking the most unpromising-looking properties and making them tremendously valuable in a short time."

A Minneapolis real-estate man puts it somewhat differently. "When he makes a deal, you wonder what made him do it. A year later, you wonder why you didn't make it yourself."

A different song

Mr. Gustafson is something of a loner in business, often buying out the partners he takes into deals and demanding control of anything he enters. His flamboyant ways haven't set well with some here and in Minneapolis, so his rise hasn't been unanimously applauded. There are whispers that his enterprises stand on shaky ground.

He has no patience with the latter assertion. He says, and Minneapolis banking sources confirm, that he has avoided the sort of borrowing and collateralizing practices that have sent other real-estate empires tumbling under a load of debt when income from a project or two fails to come up to expectations. The recent Chapter 11 bankruptcy petition filed by Florida builder Walter Kassuba is the latest example of this.

Further, "I've never bought anything that I wasn't sure I could sell at a profit the next day," Mr. Gustafson claims. "When you buy properties at a fraction of their value, as I have, you build up equity very fast. If I ever have to go to the well, the money is there."

He will admit to the possibility of failure ("I suppose I'd have trouble starting new things if I had a really big flop"), but the subject doesn't particularly engage his interest. "The last time I worried about anything I was seven years old," he says. "I had to sing a song in a school play, and I wasn't a very good singer."

As the above indicates, the story of Mr. Gustafson's path to riches is one of the more unusual in modern business. He was born in Chicago and spent his youth on a Casey, Iowa, farm run by his Swedish-born parents. His unusual first name resulted from his mother's lack of facility with English. "She wanted to name me 'Dale' but it came out sounding like 'Deel,' and the nurse spelled it the way she wanted to," he says.

"Economics of a multiple-purpose cow"

Except for a two-year stint as an Army enlisted man and a year as a $150-a-week federal bank examiner, he spent the time between his 18th and 30th birthdays — the late '40s to the early '60s — pursuing a variety of academic degrees. He holds a bachelor's degree in business, economics and psychology from the University of Minnesota, a master's degree in economics from North Dakota State University (where he peddled his master's thesis on "The Economics of a Multiple-Purpose Cow" to the state government for $4,800), and a law degree from William Mitchell College of Law in Minneapolis. He completed his course work for a doctorate while teaching at Minnesota, but never got around to writing his thesis. Besides earning his law degree at night, he also took time out from his scholarly chores to serve as an advance man and deputy director of Sen. Hubert Humphrey's 1960 bid for the Democratic presidential nomination.

Accounts of his lengthy sojourn in academia vary. "I got into it, and I liked it," he says simply. A one-time faculty colleague at Minnesota tells it differently: "I always got the impression that he was there mainly to mark time and make business contacts. He was not your typical graduate student."

Whatever the case, when the opportunity to strike out on his own finally arrived, he grabbed it. "A banker that I'd met told me about a small bank in Somerset, Wis., that was for sale," he recalls. "I had no money, but he liked my qualifications, and he lent me the $55,000 purchase price plus $5,000 more. I used the extra $5,000 to live on. I went down there, cleaned the place up, collected some overdue loans, and sold out a year later at a profit of $6,000."

His next move was to form a syndicate to obtain a national bank charter for Minneapolis. The fact that no new bank charters had been issued for the region in more than 30 years didn't deter him. "I knew the banking laws, and I knew that if you had the

backing and the qualifications they couldn't turn you down frivolously," he says.

His previous association with Sen. Humphrey didn't hurt, either. "He never got involved in the thing, but because I'd worked for him the people in Washington knew they weren't dealing with some glump off the street," he says.

He got the charter, which entitled him to a free, one-seventh interest in the resulting bank. Shortly thereafter, he sold his interest to his six partners for $24,000. "That was when my net worth climbed to above zero," he says with a smile.

He later obtained another federal bank charter and either started or purchased three state banks around Minneapolis. He's chairman of all four, and their combined assets total about $50 million. He's currently dickering to buy a fifth bank in that city.

"A great way to do it"

His first venture into real estate also was accomplished without the benefit of cash. In 1963, he and a partner, whom he has since bought out, learned that Nicolette Village, a development of 160 townhouse-type apartments in the Minneapolis suburb of Richfield, was available at a bargain price. He went to a bank in search of the financing.

"They asked me what I was paying for the property. I told them to go out and appraise it and tell me how much they'd put up," he says. "They did and said they'd give me $1.3 million, which I guess was 80% of what they thought it was worth. I said fine. The actual purchase price was $1.1 million. I used the $200,000 that was left to start some other things. It wasn't income, so I didn't have to pay taxes on it. When you're young and need funds, that's a great way to get it." He says that the development has been profitable almost from the outset and that it's currently worth "at least twice" his purchase price.

Next, he ventured into downtown Minneapolis, buying a half-interest (again for no money down) in the 12-story Flour Exchange Building, an elderly edifice that was sparsely occupied and losing money. "It was dirty, but it was built like a fortress," he says. He painted the building's exterior white from top to bottom ("so that people would notice it"), remodeled its interior and installed air-conditioning. It quickly filled up and moved into the black. "We are close to retiring the mortgage on it," he says.

An old elephant

Mr. Gustafson's biggest Minneapolis real-estate coup was his 1966 acquisition, with partners he later bought out, of the 562-acre Earle Brown Farm from the University of Minnesota. The property was smack in the middle of a growing industrial and residential area just north of Minneapolis, but it involved no little risk. It had only limited access to highways, no utilities and a potentially large tax burden. Its purchase price at auction was about $1.8 million.

Within three years, highway access and utilities were obtained, and the tenants were standing in line. The tract now is about one-third filled with offices, warehouses, apartments, stores and restaurants, most of which Mr. Gustafson owns and leases to such tenants as General Electric Co. and Northwestern Bell Telephone Co. Minneapolis sources place the development's current value at around

$25 million. "It'll be worth several times that when it's finished," a Twin Cities banker says.

Mr. Gustafson's 1972 move into Las Vegas also had a Twin Cities base; the 550-room Tropicana was run by Texas International Airways, which was partly owned by MEI Corp. of Minneapolis. It, too, had liabilities. Situated at the south end of the Strip, it is a good distance from other major hotel-casinos. It was somewhat run-down and had barely broken even in the previous two years. It was he says, "an old elephant that needed a stab in the rear."

In a complex transaction that still isn't complete, he bought the operating rights to the hotel for about $10 million, this time putting up cash and properties worth about $1.5 million as a down payment. He's still negotiating for the land on which the hotel sits but expects to have it in a few months.

Some high-rollers

"What brings people to Las Vegas is the excitement — the action," he says, and he has set out to provide it. He signed Sammy Davis Jr. to a long-term performing contract that gives the entertainer an 8% share of the hotel's profits. He added a 1,400-seat showroom to the existing hotel; it opened Oct. 5 amidst appropriate hoopla. He spent $1.5 million on an indoor tennis facility that gives guests something to do when they aren't bellied-up to the tables.

His proprietorship of the hotel hasn't been without incident. John and James Sheehan, who held a small piece of the hotel deal and who had been associated with him in Minneapolis real-estate ventures, were blackballed by the Nevada Gaming Control Board for giving "false and misleading" financial information on their license application. They have since bowed out. Last summer, eight reputed members of the Kansas City Mafia turned up at the hotel with a high-rollers' junket, causing a local flap (hotel personnel said they didn't know who the men were). Mr. Gustafson relaxed credit policies to attract more high-rollers, and bad debts edged up.

The hotel, however, has moved back into the black, showing a $1.2 million profit for 1972. "If you count receivables the way most operations here do, the profit was twice that," he says.

But the glamor of running a Las Vegas hotel wasn't what brought him here: it was land. The sprawling Tropicana sits on a 40-acre tract that was only partially developed. In addition, it owns a 110-acre golf course across the road. After buying the casino, Mr. Gustafson added a 48-acre piece of land next to the golf course, giving him a total holding of almost 200 acres.

Having and eating cake

Mr. Gustafson has big plans for the property. He recently announced his intention to spend $46 million to build a 1,000-room hotel tower and a convention facility and casino on the site. The hotel's rooms and suites will be sold as condominiums at prices ranging from $38,000 to $150,000. Condominium owners will be permitted to occupy their rooms only three weeks a year; the rest of the time the rooms will be rented out with the owners sharing in the proceeds.

"The condominium idea is new here, but it has been successful elsewhere," he says. "It's a beautiful concept. By

selling the suites, I'll get my money out right away, and at a profit. We'll rent the suites we don't sell. Either way, the people will be playing at my casino. I'll be able to eat my cake and have it."

If the first hotel tower fills up the way he expects, he says he'll build three more. This would give him some 4,500 hotel rooms on the Strip, more than twice as many as the largest facility provides at present.

Mr. Gustafson's working habits are as unconventional as his methods. Despite his far-flung holdings, his personal staff of lawyers and accountants numbers just six. He is peripatetic, hopping from one project to another and rarely lighting for more than a week. When he started dealing in Minneapolis real estate, he turned the back seat of a chauffered limousine into his office.

He wears no watch and keeps no appointments calendar; if you want to talk business with him, you phone, and if he's free he'll see you right away, day or night. His round-the-clock working habits ended his first and only marriage in divorce several years ago.

He rejects the idea of taking his businesses into the public realm. "I never want to have to answer to any shareholders," he asserts. "I learned a bit of business history in all those years I spent in college, and I know darned well that wheeler-dealers like me and public ownership don't mix.

QUESTIONS

1. Why do the wheeler-dealers seem to have an affinity for banks and real estate deals?

NEW DIRECTION FOR
MINORITY ENTERPRISE

9

Certainly one clear cut trend in small business management is the vastly increased interest in it by members of various minority groups. Many members of minority groups, having been fairly well rejected by big business as potential top management material, have opted to seek their passport out of the ghetto and and poverty by starting their own businesses. As could well be expected, the road has been rough for them. It is normally quite difficult under the best of circumstances, but add to the normal situation the additional burden of the almost total unawareness and orientation of minority people toward business management and the problems become even more difficult. In the past few of them were reared in environments in which they were exposed to business thinking.

In contrast, in a business simulation at the University of Southern California during which the students could assume top management positions in their own companies if they so wished, in each case the president of the simulated company was the son of someone who was the president of a leading corporation. The same experience was observed at the University of Colorado. Offspring seem to learn how to be leaders or entrepreneurs from their parents.

Thus the new direction for entrepreneurship entails nurturing minority enterprises until their managers gain the experience they need to survive on their own. Here is a news article on the subject.

Minority enterprise lures more activists

Francis Ward†

†**Francis Ward**, *Los Angeles Times*, **October 8, 1973, p. III-12.**

CHICAGO — A few days ago a West Side Chicago organization run by a onetime "street militant" signed an agreement to operate 30 new fast food outlets here.

It was the most significant business venture yet undertaken by the Industrial & Commercial Assn., subsidiary of the Garfield Organization, a federation of West Side community groups formed in 1967 by an aggressive black activist named Frederick Douglas Andrews.

The agreement also symbolizes a kind of philosophical turnaround for activists like Doug Andrews from "street militancy" to economic activity as the way to carry on the black struggle.

Ironically, many of the new Burger King outlets will be constructed in the same riot-ravaged area that Andrews and five Garfield Organization companions were accused of conspiring to burn down in April, 1968, following the assassination of the Rev. Martin Luther King Jr. They were subsequently acquitted.

In the past four years, many former militants like Andrews, and most national civil rights organizations, have shifted from demonstrations to some kind of economic activity.

The Rev. Jesse L. Jackson, president of Operation PUSH (People United to Save Humanity), primarily an economic rights group, has characterized the shift as a change "from civil rights to civil economics."

Mr. Jackson and others strongly advocate strengthening black entrepreneurship as the key to full black empowerment and equality.

Perhaps sensing the shift among blacks and other minorities toward wanting "a piece of the action," the Nixon Administration has stressed minority enterprise over the social welfare programs emphasized under Presidents Johnson and Kennedy.

But after five years, the record of black enterprise, or black capitalism, as some call it, is so lacking in achievement that many authorities now question whether it will lead to economic power for blacks or simply the enrichment of a relatively few businessmen and hustlers.

Berkeley G. Burrell, president of the 73-year-old National Business League, the oldest, most established black trade association in the country, said he believes black business "is in a pretty precarious position, partly because it has to operate in high crime areas and also because there is no real commitment to it by the corporate structure."

The major weakness of black businesses, he said, is the lack of equity capital, which he says has forced many black businessmen to borrow money to set up shop. Repaying the loans with interest eats up so much of the earnings, Burrell said, that too little is left for reinvestment in the business, thus hobbling growth.

"It also suffers from rhetoric and fantasy more than any other segment of our economy," Burrell said. "There seems to be developing an antiblack businessman syndrome that is based on some ill-conceived notion that profit going into the pockets of merchants, be they white or black, is not in the best interest of inner city residents."

Burrell scoffs at the suggestion that investment capital will come from programs appealing to white corporate responsibility to aid minority businesses.

"This kind of money lasts only until there is a downturn in the economy and then minority businesses are the first ones cut," he said. "It's like the corporations thinking they're investing in the NAACP."

Government responses, primarily through formation of MESBIC (Minority Enterprise Small Business Investment Corp.) "have been very meager," Burrell said, because they're too small — capitalized at $150,000 each.

(In a MESBIC, an investment company is formed with private funds which are matched on a 2-for-1 basis by federal money through the Small Business Administration.)

The ultimate answer, he said, is "educating blacks to save, then invest, thereby creating a large enough pool of equity capital. It can be done."

Burrell was interviewed at the National Business League's annual convention in Chicago, where executives of the nation's 100 top black businesses, as cited by Black Enterprise magazine, were honored.

The companies are ranked according to gross sales in 1972. The largest is the Motown Industries music company of Los Angeles, run by Berry Gordy, who developed the "Motown sound" in popular music in Detroit.

Motown's sales were $40 million last year, according to Black Enterprise figures, followed by Johnson Publishing Co. of Chicago, the world's largest black publishing complex, with sales of $23.1 million. Fedco Foods Corp. of New York, operator of a 14-store chain of supermarkets, ranked third with $20.6 million in sales.

Among the top 100 were 15 automobile dealerships, eight publishing companies, four liquor and beer distributorships, and 25 manufacturing companies. Two Los Angeles firms, Watts Manufacturing Corp. and Shindana Toys, were ranked 29th and 91st.

The 100 companies employed 9,267 persons and had total revenues of $473.4 million last year, according to the magazine. The gross sales figure would place 268th in the Fortune magazine ranking of the 500 top corporations.

But, then minority enterprise is, by definition, small business.

A survey by the federal Office of Minority Business Enterprise (OMBE) for 1969 — the last year for which complete statistics are available — lists 322,000 minority-owned businesses with total receipts of $10.6 billion. A little over half — 163,000 — were owned by blacks with total income of $4.5 billion. Businesses owned by Spanish-speaking persons total 100,000 with gross revenues of $3.3 billion, according to OMBE.

At the time, California had the highest number of minority-owned businesses of any state — 64,200 with gross receipts of $2.4 billion.

The study added "that 322,000 minority-owned businesses represented 4% of the total number of enterprises . . . (and) accounted for 0.7% of the 1967 receipts of $1.498 billion reported by all firms."

Supporters of black entrepreneurships, while not contesting its relatively infinitesimal size, point out that many new businesses have started since the survey, and that 58 of the Black Enterprise 100 have started since 1967.

Since it takes the average small business at least three years to become stable and profit-making, argue these supporters, black business has not had a chance to prove its real potential for black self-sufficiency, pride of ownership, community improvement and empowerment.

Perhaps the biggest advocate of black economic power is Mr. Jackson. PUSH began in 1966 as the economic arm of the

Southern Christian Leadership Conference, but became independent in December 1971.

As Operation Breadbasket, under Mr. Jackson's leadership, it has negotiated — under threat of boycott — agreements with a number of Chicago food chains, soft drink and milk companies for jobs for blacks and for shelf space in chain store for products manufactured by blacks.

More recently, PUSH has signed "covenants" with corporate giants like General Foods, Schlitz and Miller breweries and Avon Products for jobs, and for a host of ancillary benefits like a portion of their insurance business to black companies, more advertising in black-owned media and deposits in black banks.

The Rev. Mr. Jackson says these agreements have been worth $165 million to black communities nationally (though he hasn't provided any specific data on their implementation) and that through organized economic activity in major cities, blacks can control their communities and substantially affect the national economy.

One of the most persistent critics of the black economic power theory is Andrew F. Brimmer, the only black ever appointed to the Federal Reserve Board, who has called black-owned financial institutions "mere ornaments" with no substantial impact on the total economy.

Unless they merge into perhaps a half dozen or so larger institutions black-owned banks, insurance companies, real estate companies and savings and loan associations will never become strong enough to significantly lift black communities out of their present economic weakness, Brimmer argues.

He also says that small businesses which employ only a few people don't have much of a future in the American economy, and counsels blacks to seek middle and upper management jobs in major industries, creating a residue of skills and increasing the purchasing power of the black middle class.

But the advocates of black enterpreneurship don't seem deterred by these criticisms.

New ventures, like the one by Doug Andrews, continue to flower. And government programs to foster minority business are being stepped up.

Federal loans and guarantees, including those from the Small Business Administration, have gone to $400 million from $105 million in the past three years. The Administration claims its assistance to minority business will be $1 billion for fiscal 1974, the current period — a huge jump since 1970.

OMBE's budget went from $3 million in 1969, when it started, to $91.3 million for fiscal '73-74, OMBE does not fund businesses, but offers technical and management assistance to minority businessmen "for as long as they want our help," said its new director, Alex M. Armendaris, a 43-year-old Mexican-American who replaced John L. Jenkins, a black, earlier this year.

Armendaris said OMBE has helped about 20,000 minority businesses, less than 5% of which have failed. He, like others, sees the need for substantially more capital to assist minority businesses, but believes it will come "once we can provide more profitable business situations."

"This Administration wants to get more minority businesses out of the Ma and Pa situation," Armendaris said.

So, while black entrepreneurship may not be bursting with energy and strength, it's holding on with enough dogged determination to maintain a high degree of public confidence — and to keep the optimists within the Administration optimistic.

QUESTIONS

1. And what ails Mr. Brimmer? How many small enterprises (or even large ones, for that matter) have a "substantial impact on the total economy"? What are some of the other justifications for small business?

2. Is it wise, or necessary, to isolate minority enterprises for special treatment rather than help all small businesses?

THE "7-ELEVEN" STORY

10

Here is how one franchise system operates.

![Family affair]

Family affair†

Franchise Journal†

Back when franchising was in its infancy, franchises were very much family affairs. Whether it was an ice cream stand, a hamburger carry-out, a dry cleaning shop or what have you, one spouse would open the store in the morning and the other would close it at night, their shifts overlapping during the peak business hours. The kids, depending upon their ages and abilities, also pitched in. Other employees were a luxury the profit and loss sheet usually

†*Franchise Journal*, **August 1972, pp. 10-16.**

could not accommodate. These operations were, as they are referred to somewhat disparagingly today, "Mom and Pops."

But with the passing of the smaller, lower-investment franchises came a new breed of franchisee, better educated, better trained, more career-oriented. The wife and kids stayed home and the franchisee hired the help he needed. Some franchises became so large and costly that two or more professionals would form a corporation and hire others to run it for them. Absentee ownership became an attractive selling point for many franchises.

Despite this trend, however, the "Mom and Pop" concept is far from passe. It too has changed, for the present-day "Moms and Pops" are also better educated, better trained and they are definitely more career-oriented. As a case in point, take the parents of Karen Mah, the new *Franchise Journal's* first cover girl. John and Stella Mah are the franchised owners of a 7-Eleven convenience food store in Alameda, California, one of almost 1,800 franchised outlets in the its final decision on whether to grant the franchise and that decision hinges in large part on how the prospective franchisee's family feels about its new life style.

One of the first things 7-Eleven impresses upon a prospective franchisee and his family is that their new store is not a "get rich quick" gold mine, but that profits in the grocery business result from a delicate balance of sales, costs and expenses. To help its franchisees strike this delicate balance and maintain it, the company provides close and continuous assistance in marketing and merchandising.

Critics of the 7-Eleven franchising program are quick to point out that the company takes unfair advantage of its franchisees by charging them 55 percent of their gross income to operate under the 7-Eleven name. When he starts up, the franchisee puts up an investment for inventory, an initial cash register fund, initial licenses and fees and a security deposit, all of which 7-Eleven will finance at the legal rate of interest in the state in which the franchisee operates, if he desires the financing. The loan is secured by the inventory in the store and can be repaid by leaving a portion of the profits in the business.

The franchisee also pays a training and service fee, which includes the cost of the training school and follow-up training. The franchisee, however, is reimbursed for his travel (up to $300), meals and lodging while attending school. As for the service fee, the franchisee pays for the cost of site selection, development fees, legal fees, a bookkeeping setup and owner recruiting.

A typical franchisee's cash payment could amount to $15,200 — $13,100 for inventory, $150 for his cash register fund, $350 for initial license and permits, and $1,600 for a security deposit. For this investment he turns the key on a $150,000 to $170,000 investment in land, a building, equipment and signs, all of which he leases from 7-Eleven. Under this arrangement, the franchisee is freed from investing in a building, purchase of equipment and long-term contingent liability. The company pays the taxes on the property, the building and the equipment, leaving only the business tax, inventory tax and employer taxes to be paid by the franchisee.

The 7-Eleven financing plan might well be described as a revolving charge account on which the franchisee pays according to how much he makes in the operation of his store. This continuing arrangement insures the franchisee a profit by providing the money necessary for his day-to-day operation and eliminating the concern for cash flow to pay for purchases, expenses, payroll, business taxes and licenses.

While the charge of 55 percent of the gross profit is relatively uniform throughout the 7-Eleven franchise system, the contract provides for a reduction of that charge if it is necessary to protect the owner's gross income. The owner is assured a gross income of from $16,000 to $22,000 annually.

Thus, if a franchisee's sales slump and reduce his gross income before costs have been figured in, the company will in turn reduce its charge so that the franchisee has an assured gross income before subtracting the expenses from that gross income. Net income may be taken from the business weekly as a draw on anticipated profits, or quarterly as a draw on net worth increase.

For its 55 percent charge, 7-Eleven provides a complete bookkeeping service for its franchisees. It pays all company's 4,729-store coast-to-coast system. The Mahs, who operate the store with John's brother, Edward, are typical of the men and women who last year pushed franchised 7-Eleven stores gross sales to $328,600,000 and helped the parent company, The Southland Corporation, reach its first billion dollar year in 1971.

While it is probably best known for its franchised 7-Eleven operation, Dallas-based Southland is a diversified giant which also owns Barricini and Lofts Candy Stores, Gristede's and Charles & Co. Food Stores, Bradshaws Super Markets, Pak a Sak Food Stores, 30 dairy processing plants, a truck rental company, a chemical plant and, as it did when it began, an ice company, now called Reddy-Ice. Internationally, Southland has joined with Cavenham Ltd. and its specialty shops in England and Scotland, and with Wright's Biscuits Ltd. and Moore Stores Ltd. retail grocers in Britain. 7-Elevens are also operating in Western Canada and in Monterrey, Mexico.

The birth of 7-Eleven (the only division of Southland which offers franchises) was humble enough to satisfy the most demanding admirers of Horatio Alger-type stores. In 1927, John Jefferson "Uncle Johnny" Greene came up with a suggestion for his boss, the Southland Ice Company. Because business at his retail ice dock in the Oak Cliff section of Dallas fell off during the winter months, why not stock a few convenience items to keep customers coming in year-around?

A young Southland Ice executive, Joe C. Thompson, liked the idea and soon "Uncle Johnny" and other ice retailers around the city were stocking and selling bread, milk, eggs and a few other grocery staples to the Model T set. As the idea caught on with Dallas residents the ice docks were christened "Tote'm

Stores" and they soon spread to Fort Worth and other Texas cities.

Throughout the depression in the 1930's and World War II in the 1940's, ice continued to be the mainstay of Southland. The sale of milk and other dairy products, however, grew to the point that Southland bought its first milk processing plant — Oak Farms Dairies in Dallas — in 1936 and has added 10 others to date.

Southland did not begin franchising its 7-Eleven stores — the name was changed from "Tote'm Stores" in 1945 to reflect the stores' hours of operation — until 1964 when it bought "Speedee Mart," a California-based chain of franchised convenience food stores. Along with the acquisition came Palmer J. Waslien, vice president of "Speedee Mart" and a strong exponent of franchising.

As director of franchising for 7-Eleven for the past eight years, Waslien has developed a successful family franchise system around a common goal: profit. He believes — and the system's growth has borne him out — that a man and his wife who have an investment in their own business will work harder to improve their store's profitability than would a salaried employee whose only stake in the store is his job.

The 7-Eleven franchise philosophy puts strong emphasis on the man and wife team. As with most franchises, convenience store management requires long hours and concentrated effort on the part of the owner. If his wife and family are not completely sold on what he is doing, the store is in trouble before it opens. To eliminate this potential problem, 7-Eleven interviews both the husband and wife and, if they desire, sends them both to one of its four training centers. It is at the training school that 7-Eleven makes approved bills, prepares payroll checks and maintains payroll records, inventories the store and audits its money, issues periodic financial statements and business tax reports and returns, provides merchandise movement information and any additional reports on the status of the store.

The 7-Eleven assured franchisee gross income program is not based upon a gamble, but upon thorough planning before a new owner puts the key in his door. Franchisee selection and training are, of course, important to the success of a 7-Eleven store. Equally important, however, is where the company builds that store.

With several new franchised and company-owned 7-Elevens opening weekly throughout the nation, the company keeps 47 site selection men combing the countryside for new locations. When a potential site is found and is available, the field men evaluate it according to specific criteria, such as traffic flow, population density, land costs and other factors. This data is sent to Dallas where a computer analyzes the criteria against the performance of presently operating 7-Elevens and prints out a go or no-go decision.

With all deference to modern technology, however, the success of the 7-Eleven franchise system is due in large part to a well-known but often neglected human factor: communication. One of the most common problems in all franchise systems is that as the parent company grows and often diversifies, it loses contact with its franchisees. This rupture results in alienation and discontent and, in some cases, has led to lengthy and debilitating litigation.

It was noted at the outset that Southland is a diversified international giant, yet this giant maintains daily face-to-face contact with every one of its franchisees through an organization that would cause envy in the Pentagon.

The Stores Division of Southland is headed by J. W. Thompson, executive vice president and son of the founder, Joe C. Thompson. Under him is a staff which handles franchise operations and training as well as merchandising and advertising. Each of these staff members has his own staff which provides assistance in the field. The Stores Division is divided into two regions — Eastern and Central — each containing three divisions. Four other separate divisions bring the total number to 10. Each of the 10 divisions also has its own vice president in charge and necessary staff.

The divisions are further broken down to zones and each zone is divided into districts. It is on the district level that 7-Eleven maintains continuous contact with its franchisees through field representatives, each of whom daily calls on eight stores. On these visits the field representative finds out what problems the franchisee might be having, answers any questions he might have, and makes suggestions on the store's operation. If the representative encounters a situation he cannot handle on the local level, it "goes upstairs" and keeps going up until it is resolved. This constant interchange of information allows 7-Eleven to anticipate and act rather than react to problems which may arise and provides the franchisee the means to make his feelings known to the company.

When all is said and done, however, it is not the capitalization of the parent company, nor the contract, nor the training, nor the organization that builds a viable franchise system, although all are important contributions. What really counts are the John and Stella and Edward Mahs and the thousands of men and women like them who make all companies in the nation's $134 billion-a-year franchise system work. Those franchisors who keep this firmly in mind have a long leg up on turning a profit year after year.

And, as they say at The Southland Corporation, that's the name of the game.

7-Eleven franchise agreement

The Southland Corporation entered franchising in 1964 with the purchase of Speedee Mart, a chain of 126 franchised stores in southern California. Since that time, Southland has expanded franchising to 1,740 7-Eleven Food Stores in 20 states and the District of Columbia, and there have been five major modifications of the 7-Eleven franchise contract, each resulting from suggestions of operating franchise owners and designed to clarify the terms of their agreement with 7-Eleven.

Since profit margins in the grocery business are very small, operators must carefully control costs if they are to make a profit. The 7-Eleven franchise contract is designed to offer the franchise owners a proven system of operating procedures which will assure them maximum profit.

In its franchise program for individual 7-Eleven stores, Southland selects qualified applicants and trains them in the operation of convenience stores. Southland provides marketing, administrative and financial services to its franchisees, leases or subleases the store premises and equipment to them, and licenses them to use Southland's trademarks.

Generally, each franchisee pays Southland a fee for training, makes an initial cash investment of a minimum of $3,000 and pays a continuing fee computed on the basis of the store's gross profit. The franchisee's initial cash investment includes $1,600 as a security deposit, $500 to cover the costs of necessary licenses and permits, an initial cash register fund, and $900 which is applied to the purchase of inventory.

The franchisee may elect to increase his investment to an amount equal to his store's inventory (approximately $13,000) plus the $2,100 for the security deposit and the costs of necessary licenses and permits with the initial cash register fund to be determined. A portion of the full investment will be financed by 7-Eleven at an interest rate not to exceed the legal rate specified by the state in which the particular store is located. If he prefers, the franchisee may secure his capital from any other source. Aside from these costs, franchisees need no additional operating capital to go into business.

7-Eleven provides its franchise owners with an opening inventory for the store which varies depending upon the size and type of the location and upon its potential volume. The inventory serves as the only collateral for his loan from 7-Eleven. Under the terms of the agreement, 7-Eleven maintains the leased building, provides insurance for fire and extended coverage on the building and equipment, provides the franchise owner a complete bookkeeping service including processing of payroll checks authorized by the franchise owner, periodic inventory reports, net worth condition reports, and profit and loss statements, and provides continuing merchandising assistance.

7-Eleven franchisees may procure any additional insurance or substitute comparable coverage for the insurance provided by 7-Eleven if they wish. If they elect to provide their own coverage, the franchisees are given credit for the saving to 7-Eleven.

Franchise owners hire and discharge their own employees, establish their work schedules, wages and any taxes related to employees. They also determine and execute grocery and other merchandise orders. Periodically, 7-Eleven provides lists of suggested vendors, merchandise, and retail prices. However, since the franchisees are independent contractors and are expected to control their businesses as independent retailers, they are not required to use the services of the vendors, buy the merchandise, or sell at the prices suggested by 7-Eleven. According to the terms of the agreement, "Owners are not required to purchase from vendors recommended by or affiliated with 7-Eleven, to purchase only that merchandise which is recommended by 7-Eleven, or to sell merchandise at retail prices suggested by 7-Eleven."

7-Eleven owners deposit the cash receipts from their operations into a bank account established by 7-Eleven, or account to 7-Eleven for receipts expended by them in the operation. The 7-Eleven bookkeeping service processes payment to vendors for merchandise ordered by the franchisee and for all additional costs approved by the franchisee and related to the operations. These receipts and disbursements are handled through an open account which assures the franchisee of adequate operating capital at all times.

The agreement also assures the franchise owners a regular income through a weekly draw against their anticipated profits, in an amount which, when added to the payroll for the week, will not exceed eight to eight and one half percent of the previous week's sales

or $200-275, depending on geographic location, whichever is greater. This amount is intended to cover the owners' payroll and personal expenses. In addition, at the end of each calendar quarter, the franchise owner may withdraw from the business 70 percent of their net worth increase for the quarter. (Net Income less weekly draw equals net worth increase.)

The provision for weekly and quarterly draws are among the unique features of the 7-Eleven agreement as is the fact that owners are not required to make specific monthly or quarterly payments on their indebtedness to 7-Eleven. Instead, the balance of any net worth increase reduces the amount borrowed on open account from 7-Eleven. If there has been no increase in the net worth balance during the period, no payment is made on the indebtedness to 7-Eleven. Of course, as with any indebtedness, the greater the amount applied to the obligation, the less amount of interest is paid.

7-Eleven operates under the philosophy that franchised businesses are most successful when the franchisor and franchisee are working toward a mutual goal. For this reason, the 7-Eleven fee for the rights, privileges and services provided to franchise owners is a percentage of gross profits, rather than a fixed amount or percentage of sales.

In most areas, the 7-Eleven fee is 55 per cent of the owner's gross profit. Although this may at first appear to be an excessive part of the income from the business, closer examination indicates that 7-Eleven pays from this amount a large part of what would otherwise be the franchise owner's operating expenses: buying, occupancy (principally building and equipment rentals, utilities and property taxes) and general selling and administrative expenses. Normally, franchisees in businesses similar to a 7-Eleven operation pay monthly rent on the lease, are required to finance and purchase their equipment, to maintain the building, to pay all utilities, pay taxes, insurance and maintain enough capital to assure an adequate inventory — as well as to pay a royalty on gross sales.

Under the 7-Eleven system, these costs are absorbed in the 55 percent 7-Eleven charge. The franchisee bears all payroll and other in-store controllable expenses including losses. Moreover, under the terms of the agreement franchise owners are assured a gross income, depending upon geographical location, of from $16,000 to $22,000 a year, from which all expenses borne by the franchisee are deducted.

The term of the 7-Eleven agreement is for fifteen years unless the master lease on the store location is for a lesser period, in which case the franchise term is for the term of the master lease. However, provisions are made for the franchisee, if he wishes, to terminate the contract after giving only 72 hours' written notice. 7-Eleven, on the other hand, may terminate the contract only after thirty to sixty days' written notice, depending on local statutory requirements.

The only exceptions are that, if the owner's net worth drops to less than $3,000, which would happen only if there were a breakdown in operating procedures, or if the owner fails to deposit or account for merchandise sales receipts, file a voluntary petition in bankruptcy, or vacate and desert the premises, then 7-Eleven may terminate the agreement by giving 72 hours' written notice, provided the default is not corrected within that period.

Upon termination, 7-Eleven credits the owner's open account with any portion of the security deposit that has not been used, conducts an inventory and credits the account with the purchase price of the inventory, and within sixty days after termination delivers to the owners a final statement and any credit balance owed to them. The franchisees are charged $200 for closing and auditing the account, and any money that may be owed to 7-Eleven becomes due and payable at the time of final statement.

A franchise owner may sell his inventory to someone other than 7-Eleven if the purchase price is at least equal to that offered by 7-Eleven and the proceeds are applied through the open account. In addition, franchise owners may sell their business if the new owner meets 7-Eleven's then current franchise qualifications and the proceeds are applied through the open account. All disputes between franchise owners and 7-Eleven, except the effectiveness of a termination, are submitted to arbitration by the American Arbitration Association.

Because merchandising and procedures may vary, depending upon local conditions and owner's wishes, there are several standard amendments to the 7-Eleven agreement which provide for situations that are unique to a particular store. These relate to the sale of liquor and gasoline, extended hour operations and the use of credit cards.

In addition, Southland has granted six exclusive area franchises covering certain areas of Michigan; Pennsylvania and West Virginia; Texas; Oklahoma, Kansas, Arkansas and Missouri; Nebraska and Iowa; and West Virginia and Kentucky under which the area franchisees presently operate or franchise a total of 40 7-Eleven stores.

QUESTIONS

1. Would a 7-Eleven franchise be of interest to you? Why?

LEGAL ASPECTS OF STARTING A NEW BUSINESS

11

There was a time when all a businessman had to do to begin operations was to unlock the door, but such has long since ceased to be the case. Any romantic ideas that the businessman is operating in a free enterprise society are quickly dispelled when he comes up against the procedures demanded of him by the various government authorities under whose jurisdiction he intends to operate. Indeed, there are situations in which aspiring enterprisers have been prevented from beginning business because of legal blockages.

A young man with some experience in running fine restaurants initially wanted to open such an establishment in Boulder, Colorado. He had developed rather magnificent plans but soon gave up the enterprise after talking with various city fathers who refused to give him the utilities he needed. He had planned to serve liquor and the city fathers were not in favor of such enterprises. He transferred his activities to Denver, Colorado, and established a chain of excellent restaurants there — The Hungry Farmer and The Hungry Dutchman.

A young man who wanted to locate a clothing store in Columbia, Missouri, found an excellent location on Ninth Street close to campus, but was prevented from building a fine store there by the zoning ordinances which demanded that one parking place had to be provided on the premises for every 100 sq. ft. of floor space. While this might make some sense in certain locales, in a downtown area it was nonsense. A 4,000 sq. ft. store had to have 40 parking places. Experience indicates that no more than ten are really neeeded. But the city fathers found it a convenient way to keep out competition. Guess who was on the city council and zoning board — the town's leading men's apparel merchant. It is rather difficult and quite expensive to fight city hall. The young man went elsewhere with his clothing store.

Such illustrations could go on for some time, for the bitter truth is that a prospective businessman must first make certain it is legally possible to do what it is he wants to do where he wants to do it considering the zoning laws and other such regulations. But there are more mundane legal aspects which must be attended to by the enterpriser.

Table 11-1 is a checklist of the various legal steps the new enterpriser must attend to in the process of beginning a business in the state of California. This procedure would hold for most states except those not requiring sales tax licenses.

LOCAL LICENSES

In the majority of cases, the city or county in which the business is located requires a business license. A firm intending to do business in several cities may have to get licenses in each of them. At times the license fees are nominal, $5 or $10, and other times they can be rather substantial — $50 to $100. Sometimes they apply to all businesses and other times only to retail establishments.

Many times cities levy a number of licenses that must be procured for the sale of various things, such as cigarettes, alcoholic beverages, use of vending machines, or any other item the city fathers can isolate and conjure up justification for taxing under the disguise of licensing. The states vary tremendously in what they allow the various municipalities to do in the way of taxing local businesses, so each situation is different. It is necessary to do a lot of checking.

STATE SALES TAX LICENSES

In states that have sales taxes, businesses must register, and frequently post bond, if they must collect and remit sales taxes. Nonretailers must usually get a sales tax number in order to be exempt from paying sales taxes on things they buy to

---

TABLE 11-1: Legal steps for beginning a new business in the state of California

---

Obtain Employer's Identification Number from the Internal Revenue Service
Obtain sales tax license from the State Board of Equalization
Obtain business license from city if required
If incorporating:
  1. File Articles of Incorporation with the Secretary of State
  2. File a certified copy of Articles of Incorporation with the clerk of the county in which office is located
  3. Clear stock issue with Corporation Commission
If not incorporating, file Certificate for Transaction of Business under Fictitious Name
File with the Department of Human Resources for Workmen's Compensation and Unemployment Compensation
Get special licenses for selling:
  Alcohol
  Cigarettes
  Vending machines
  Drugs
  Firearms

sell at wholesale. A close check should be made with the state authorities on the matter.

Moreover, in some states the cities can levy a sales tax. Thus the businessman must also obtain a sales tax license from such municipal authorities.

EMPLOYER'S IDENTIFICATION NUMBER

Every business must apply to the Internal Revenue Service for an Employer's Identification Number which must be shown on practically everything thereafter filled out for governmental authorities. Fortunately, it is one of the few things that is free. The card can be obtained at the local Internal Revenue Service office. An example is shown in Figure 11-1.

REGISTERING WITH THE LABOR AUTHORITIES

Each state has an agency in charge of administering its unemployment compensation and workmen's compensation programs. Workmen's compensation is not what it sounds like. It is insurance to cover the medical expenses of employees who are injured while on the job. Coverage may be taken with the state or with a private insurance company. The rates vary depending upon the dangers connected with the work your people do. Every business with employees must comply with the provisions of these laws. In California it is called the Department of Human Resources. Other states have varying euphemisms for labor, but whatever the department is called, it must be contacted.

Having employees is rather expensive. The wages paid are only the beginning of their cost. Add to their wages Social Security costs, unemployment compensation, workmen's compensation insurance, plus whatever fringe benefits are provided. These are not minor costs; they can run anywhere from ten to fifteen percent of payroll, depending upon the type of business. This is mentioned here, for many businessmen fail to take into account these substantial costs in their cash flow planning for beginning a business.

INCORPORATION

Those entrepreneurs who want to incorporate will follow the procedure shown in Figure 11-2 which shows a sample Articles of Incorporation.

While this procedure varies slightly from state to state, it is essentially the same for all. Details are explained in a copy of the Corporation Code at either the Secretary of State's office or a local library. One common misconception is that a lawyer must incorporate the enterprise. True, it is best if one can afford to have a lawyer, but it is not necessary under the laws of most states. A person can do it himself with a bit of study and possibly some guidance from some knowledgeable people. There are several books on the subject.[1] It may cost from $300 to $3,000 to have a lawyer do the incorporating, depending upon the lawyer's inclinations. Sometimes a game attorney will speculate and take stock for his work, but this practice is not recommended.

In some states a proprietor who intends to do business under a name

[1]See Ted Nicholas, *How to Form Your Own Corporation Without a Lawyer for Under $50.00,* (1000 Oakfield Lane, Wilmington, Del.: Enterprise Publishing Co., Inc., 1972) or go to a business law library.

☆ U. S. GOVERNMENT PRINTING OFFICE: 1974 — 532-237

FORM SS-4 (3-69)
PART 1   U.S. TREASURY DEPARTMENT—INTERNAL REVENUE SERVICE
APPLICATION FOR EMPLOYER IDENTIFICATION NUMBER

1. NAME *(TRUE name as distinguished from TRADE name.)*

2. TRADE NAME, IF ANY *(Enter name under which business is operated, if different from item 1.)*

3. ADDRESS OF PRINCIPAL PLACE OF BUSINESS *(No. and Street, City, State, Zip Code)* | 4. COUNTY OF BUSINESS LOCATION

5. ORGANIZATION
Check Type
☐ Individual   ☐ Partnership   ☐ Corporation   ☐ Other *(specify e.g. estate, trust, etc.)*
☐ Governmental   ☐ Nonprofit Organization
(See Instr. 5)   (See Instr. 5)
6. Ending Month of Accounting year

7. REASON FOR APPLYING *(If "other" specify such as "Corporate structure change," "Acquired by gift or trust," etc.)*
☐ Started new business   ☐ Purchased going business   ☐ Other
8. Date you acquired or started business *(Mo., day, year)*
9. First date you paid or will pay wages *(Mo., day, year)*

10. NATURE OF BUSINESS *(See Instructions)* | 11. NUMBER OF EMPLOYEES→ IF "NONE" ENTER "0" | Non-agricultural | Agricultural

12. If nature of business is MANUFACTURING, list in order of their importance the principal products manufactured and the estimated percentage of the total value of all products which each represents.
A   %
PLEASE LEAVE BLANK
R | DO | TA
B   % | C   %
FR | FRC

13. Do you operate more than one place of business?   ☐ Yes   ☐ No
If "Yes," attach a list showing for each separate establishment:
a. Name and address.   b. Nature of business   c. Number of employees.

14. To whom do you sell most of your products or services?
☐ Business establishments   ☐ General public   ☐ Other (Specify)

PLEASE LEAVE BLANK→ | Geo. | Ind. | Class | Size | Reas. for Appl. | Bus. Bir. Date

FORM SS-4 (3-69)
PART 2
DO NOT DETACH ANY PART OF THIS FORM. SEND ALL COPIES TO
INTERNAL REVENUE SERVICE
PLEASE LEAVE BLANK

NAME AND COMPLETE ADDRESS

1. NAME *(TRUE name as distinguished from TRADE name.)*

2. TRADE NAME, IF ANY *(Enter name under which business is operated, if different from item 1.)*

3. ADDRESS OF PRINCIPAL PLACE OF BUSINESS *(No. and Street)*

(City, State, Zip Code) | 4. COUNTY OF BUSINESS LOCATION

5. ORGANIZATION
Check Type
☐ Individual   ☐ Partnership   ☐ Corporation   ☐ Other *(specify e.g. estate, trust, etc.)*
☐ Governmental   ☐ Nonprofit Organization
(See Instr. 5)   (See Instr. 5)
6. Ending Month of Accounting year

7. REASON FOR APPLYING *(If "other" specify such as "Corporate structure change," "Acquired by gift or trust," etc.)*
☐ Started new business   ☐ Purchased going business   ☐ Other
8. Date you acquired or started business *(Mo., day, year)*
9. First date you paid or will pay wages *(Mo., day, year)*

10. NATURE OF BUSINESS *(See Instructions)* | 11. NUMBER OF EMPLOYEES→ IF "NONE" ENTER "0" | Non-agricultural | Agricultural

12. Have you ever applied for an identification number for this or any other business?   ☐ No   ☐ Yes
If "Yes," enter name and trade name (if any). Also enter the approximate date, city, and state where you first applied and previous number if known. →

DATE | SIGNATURE | TITLE

FIGURE 11-1:   Application for employer's ID number

FIGURE 11-2: Sample Articles of Incorporation

Filed with County Clerk

_____ County

Filed with Secretary of State

_____, 19___

ARTICLES OF INCORPORATION
OF
THE CALIFORNIA ELECTRIC CAR CORPORATION

ARTICLE I

The name of the corporation is ___The California Electric Car Corporation___

ARTICLE II

The corporation's purposes are:

(a) Primarily to engage in the specific business of __manufacturing and distributing an electric car.__

(b) Generally to engage in the buiness of __manufacturing__

(c) To engage in any business or transaction, whether related or unrelated to those described in Paragraphs (a) and (b) above, which may from time to time be authorized or approved by the Board of Directors of this corporation.

(d) To act as principal, agent, partner, joint venturer, or in any other legal capacity in any transaction.

(e) To transact business anywhere in the world.

(f) To have and exercise all rights and powers which are now and which may in the future be granted to a corporation by law.

The above statement of purposes shall be construed as a statement of both purposes and powers, and the provisions of each paragraph shall not be limited by reference to or inference from one another, but each shall be considered as separate statements conferring independent purposes and powers upon the corporation.

ARTICLE III

The County in the State of California where the principal office for the transaction of the business of the corporation is located is the County of __Orange__

ARTICLE IV

(a) The number of directors of the corporation is ___3___, provided that the number of such directors may from time to time be changed by amendment of the By-Laws of this corporation.

(b) The names and addresses of the persons who are appointed to act as first directors of the corporation are:

NAMES	ADDRESSES
John Doe	123 First St. San Diego, Ca.
Richard Roe	456 Second St. Newport Beach, Ca.
Harry Moe	789 Third St. Irvine, Ca.

(c) The Board of Directors of the corporation shall be permitted to take any action authorized by Division 1 of the California Corporations Code without a meeting, provided all members of the Board consent in writing to such action and such consent or consents are filed with the minutes of the proceedings of the Board.

ARTICLE V

The corporation is authorized to issue only one class of shares having a total number of 1,000,000 shares. The aggregate par value of such shares is $100,000,000 ___, and the par value of each share is $ 100.00 ___. (If no-par shares are to be authorized and issued, omit the foregoing sentence and in its place insert: "Each share shall be without par value.")

FIGURE 11-2: (Continued)

ARTICLE VI

No distinction shall exist between the shares of the corporation or the holders of such shares.

ARTICLE VII

(a) All shares issued by the corporation shall be fully paid and nonassessable and shall not be subject to assessment for the debts or liabilities of the corporation.

(b) Each shareholder of this corporation shall be entitled to full pre-emptive or preferential rights, as such rights are defined by law, to subscribe for or purchase his proportional part of any shares which may be issued at any time by this corporation.

(c) Before there can be a valid sale or transfer of any of the shares of this corporation by any shareholder, he shall first offer such shares to the corporation and then to the other shareholders in the following manner:

(1) Such offering shareholder shall deliver a notice in writing by mail or otherwise to the Secretary of the corporation stating the price, terms, and conditions of such proposed sale or transfer, the number of shares to be sold or transferred, and his intention so to sell or transfer such shares. Within fourteen (14) days thereafter, the corporation shall have the prior right to purchase all or any full number of such shares so offered at the price and upon the terms and conditions stated in such notice. Should the corporation fail to purchase all of said shares, at the expiration of said fourteen-day period, or prior thereto upon the determination of the corporation to purchase none or only a portion of such shares so offered, the Secretary of the corporation shall, within five (5) days thereafter, mail or deliver to each of the other shareholders a notice setting forth the particulars concerning said shares not so purchased by the corporation described in the notice received from the offering shareholder. The other shareholders shall have the right to purchase all of the shares specified in said Secretary's notice by delivering to the Secretary by mail or otherwise a written offer or offers to purchase all or any specified number of such shares upon the terms so described in the Secretary's notice if such offer or offers are so delivered to the Secretary within ten (10) days after mailing or delivering such Secretary's notice to such other shareholders. If the total number of shares specified in such offers so received within such period by the Secretary exceeds the number of shares referred to in such Secretary's notice, each offering share-holder shall be entitled to purchase such proportion of the shares referred to in said notice to the Secretary, as the number of shares of this corporation, which he holds, bears to the total number of shares held by all such shareholders desiring to purchase the shares referred to in said notice to the Secretary.

(2) If all of the other shares referred to in said notice to the Secretary are not disposed of under such apportionment, each share-holder desiring to purchase shares in a number in excess of his proportionate share, as provided above, shall be entitled to purchase such proportion of those shares which remain thus undisposed of, as the total number of shares which he holds bears to the total number of shares held by all of the shareholders desiring to purchase shares in excess of those to which they are entitled under such apportionment.

(3) If none or only a part of the shares referred to in said notice to the Secretary is purchased, as aforesaid, by the corporation or in accordance with offers made by other shareholders within said ten (10) day period, the shareholder desiring to sell or transfer may dispose of all shares of stock referred to in said notice to the Secretary not so purchased by the corporation or by the other shareholders, to any person or persons he may so desire; provided, however, that he shall not sell or transfer such shares at a lower price or on terms more favorable to the purchaser or transferee than those specified in said notice to the Secretary.

(4) Within the limitations herein provided, this corporation may purchase the shares of this corporation from any offering shareholder, provided, however, that at no time shall this corporation be permitted to purchase all of its outstanding voting shares. Any sale or transfer or purported sale or transfer of the shares of the corporation shall be null and void unless the terms, conditions, and provisions of sub-part (c) of this article SEVENTH are strictly observed and followed.

IN WITNESS WHEREOF, the undersigned and above-named incorporators and first directors of this corporation have executed these Articles of Incorporation on ___December   7____, 19__73__.

John Doe

Richard Roe

Harry Moe

STATE OF CALIFORNIA } ss.
COUNTY OF _____ }

On_____, 19____, before me, the Undersigned, a Notary Public in and for said State appeared

known to me to be the persons whose names are subscribed to the foregoing Articles of Incorporation, and acknowledged to me that they executed the same.

WITNESS my hand and official seal.

_____
Notary Public in and for said State

other than his own must file a certificate of doing business under a fictitious name, such as shown in Figure 11-3, with the appropriate authorities.

An attorney can give guidance in these matters. If the cost of an attorney is out of the question, the Small Business Administration may be of assistance.

Note that throughout this book there is no discussion of partnerships. They are not a viable form of business organization in today's world in most instances. It is so easy to incorporate and the tax advantages for doing so are so substantial, since the traditional tax disadvantages have been removed with Subchapter S, that it is simply not advisable to go into partnership. If going into business with other people, one should incorporate for self-protection. In a partnership a person's entire fortune is risked if things should go bad in the enterprise. No matter how attractive the business may look, the risk of things going wrong is substantial. Thus it is folly not to limit the extent of one's personal liability in the venture. Partnerships are now used mainly in the investment field for income tax reasons. If an enterprise is exposed to any significant liability, doing business either as a proprietor or partnership is not wise.

One note of warning: it is extremely important to understand the philosophy of the corporation laws and the importance *to oneself* of carefully abiding by all of the legal procedures specified by the state corporation code. Remember that the corporation is a separate legal entity. The individual is not the corporation. If a person acts as if he and the corporation are one and the same thing, the courts will strip him of the limited liability the corporation provides. In legal terminology it is called "piercing the corporate shield," in which a creditor's lawyer proves to a judge that by various actions it is clear a person has considered the corporation to be one and the same as himself. Thus a person must take great care not to pay corporate debts with his personal money nor cover personal debts with corporate funds. The individual's money and the corporation's money must be kept totally separate. In short, a person should treat his corporation as he would one in which he held no stock. At arm's length!

Just as importantly, the legal details of holding stockholders' and directors' meetings and putting all important decisions in the corporation's minutes must not be overlooked. Minutes can prove to be extremely important in later legal dealings with the IRS and other such government authorities. It is in this area that a good lawyer can be helpful.

Do not overlook the possibility of putting the corporation under Section 1244 of the Internal Revenue Code, for it is a free ride, so to speak. A word of explanation here: one of the problems in attracting equity money into new enterprises has been that while the profits are fully taxable, losses can only be deducted to the extent of gains or a maximum of $1,000. If the investor does not have other capital gains during the year in which he liquidates a bad investment in a new enterprise, he is limited to a $1,000 loss which is a pittance compared to his investment of $25,000 to $50,000. Thus, from a tax point of view, he stands a distinct likelihood of not being able to take his losses off his income, a most disadvantageous position and one that has stifled investment in new enterprises. However, if the corporation from the beginning has elected to qualify under Section 1244, the investor in a new enterprise can

FIGURE 11-3:   Certificate for transaction of business under fictitious name

CERTIFICATE FOR TRANSACTION OF BUSINESS UNDER FICTITIOUS NAME

• • •

THE UNDERSIGNED___does___ hereby certifies that ___he is_____ conducting a
             do - does   they - he - she   are - is

___men's apparel_____ business located at
                                   description of type of business

___765___   ___4th Street___ ___Anaheim___, ___Orange_____County, California,
   number   street   city

under the fictitious firm name of_____ ___The Wardrobe_____
                                                        exact name of business only

and that said firm is composed of the following persons, whose names in full and places of residence are as follows, to-wit:

___Paul Poe , 9578 35th Street, Villa Park, Ca._____

_____

_____

_____

_____

_____

_____

_____

_____

_____

_____

WITNESS_____ hand____this_____day of _____, 19_____
        our - my

                                        SIGNATURES: *Paul Poe*_____

_____

_____

_____

STATE OF CALIFORNIA.
                         } SS.
County of_____

ON_____, 19_____, before me, the undersigned, a Notary Public in and for said

State, residing therein, duly commissioned and sworn, personally appeared_____

_____

known to me to be the person_____ whose name_____subscribed to the within instrument, and acknowledged to me

that_____ executed the same.

WITNESS my hand and official seal.   _____

                                               _____
                                             NAME (TYPED OR PRINTED)

NOTE:—Each member must sign and acknowledge before qualified officer.   Notary Public in and for said State.

treat any loss within the first two years as an ordinary operating loss (fully deductible), thus availing himself of sizable potential tax benefits. This removes some of the sting for a person in a high tax bracket. If a man in the fifty percent tax bracket invested $20,000 in a venture and lost it in the first two years, his tax savings of $10,000 makes his net loss on the venture only $10,000 which helps somewhat. There are no drawbacks to Section 1244 stock. All that is required is a simple statement in the minutes saying that the corporation's directors have so elected to qualify under Section 1244. The exact wording of the minutes is important and can be obtained from a tax service.

CHOOSING A FORM

12

Here is an article presenting a traditional treatment of the advantages and disadvantages of each form of business organization. One person may place great value on limited liability while another is most concerned with income tax considerations.

Choosing an organization form for engaging in business

William K. Daugherty
Douglas J. Wall†

†William K. Daugherty and Douglas J. Wall, *Arizona Business Bulletin*, pp. 22-28.

Reprinted by permission of the publisher, Bureau of Business and Economic Research, College of Business Administration, Arizona State University.

In the modern economic world of today the undertaking of a business venture frequently requires a capital investment that exceeds the amount that an individual is willing or able to dedicate to the venture. A person confronted with this situation must either forgo the opportunity or secure the cooperation of others who are willing to provide capital to the undertaking. In the event of the latter and assuming that such participants are available, the problem becomes one of choosing the form of organization that will best fit the needs of those who are willing to participate in the business venture. The choice of the appropriate vehicle for bringing the participants together will hinge upon a number of factors, the most important of which are likely to be related to the liability of participants for debts incurred in connection with the venture and to the tax implications inherent in the choice of organizational form.

The ideal organizational form will generally be one in which:

1. the liability of a participant for debts of the organization is limited, at

organizational form for specific situations.

The corporate form

The corporate organization form is widely used in a variety of business situations. A corporation is a legal entity brought into being by the compliance of a group of incorporators with the appropriate statutes that govern the formation of corporations. Compliance with the requirements for forming a corporation generally involves the filing with a designated officer of the state an application in which the name of the corporation, the nature of the business it will conduct, the amount of authorized capital stock and the numbers of shares into which it is to be divided, and the names and addresses of the original subscribers to the stock are set out. There may be other requirements that must be met before the corporation is authorized to do business, such as the publishing of the application, the meeting of the stockholders and the election of directors, and the issuance of stock in exchange for assets that are paid into the corporation. When all requirements have been met the corporation will receive a charter, authorizing it to do business as a corporation, from the state.

The corporate form of organization embraces four of the seven characteristics previously described. Owners (stockholders) are not generally liable for the debts of the corporation. There is no income tax imposed upon the owner until he receives a distribution of earnings in the form of cash or other property. The legal existence of the corporation is not affected by the death or bankruptcy of a stockholder nor is it affected by a stockholder becoming mentally or legally incompetent. A stockholder may freely dispose of all or part of his interest by any legal means at any time he chooses.

On the undesirable side, the corporate form fails with regard to three important characteristics. It is a taxable entity for state and federal income tax purposes. At the federal level it must pay income tax at the rate of 22 percent on the first $25,000 of its annual earnings, and at the rate of 48 percent on all ordinary income earned in excess of $25,000 annually. Earnings distributed to stockholders are taxed again as income to the stockholders. This double taxation characteristic of the corporation, coupled with the prohibition against a corporation retaining earnings in excessive amounts, constitutes the greatest disadvantage of doing business as a corporation. The third characteristic on which the corporate form fails is that not every kind of business can be legally operated in general corporate form. The restriction generally applies to business activities of a professional nature such as the practice of medicine, law, or accounting.[1] In most instances the failure of the corporate form to meet this desirable characteristic is of no significance since most types of business activities can be accommodated in the corporate form.

The corporate form of organization, because of its characteristics, is particularly appropriate where the risk of substantial loss is very high, and in

---

[1] Recent legislation at both the state and national level has modified previous prohibitions against the practice of a profession in corporate form. Since the profession corporations that are now allowed under certain conditions are a rather specialized form of organization with limited applicability they are not considered in this paper.

the most, to the amount of the investment provided by him;

2. the organization is not a taxable entity for income tax purposes thereby avoiding the imposition of a double tax, first on the earnings of the organization and again on the owners when earnings are distributed;

3. the organization is able to retain, without restriction or penalty, all or part of its earnings for reinvestment on behalf of its owners;

4. there is no income tax imposed upon a participant until he receives his share of earnings in the form of cash or valuable property;

5. the legal existence of the organization is unaffected by the changes in the financial fortunes of the participants with regard to either their personal affairs or other financial interests, by changes in the legal competency of participants, or by their withdrawal from participation whether such withdrawal is voluntary or involuntary;

6. a participant may freely transfer all or part of his interest in the organization by whatever legal means that he chooses;

7. the type of business transactions which may be undertaken are not restricted by the form of organization chosen.

An organizational form in which these seven characteristics are found without qualification would be ideal from an individual investor's point of view and from the point of view of the investors as a whole. Consider an individual investor. His potential loss in the event the venture encountered an adverse situation would be limited to the amount of the investment; his personal fortune, however large or small, would be beyond the reach of creditors of the organization who might be seeking satisfaction of their claims. The organization would pay no income tax on earnings, and he would pay tax only on his share of the earnings when they were received by him in cash or other property. He could dispose of his interest by sale, gift, or by any other legal means at any time he should be so inclined.

Conversely, from the point of view of the investors as a whole, the organizational form would permit the undertaking of a business venture that, individually, they could not or would not undertake. The assets provided by their investments would be immune from attachment in satisfaction of debts owed by individual participants. The legal existence of their organization would not be threatened by the bankruptcy, mental or legal incompetence, or death of any one or more participants.

Unfortunately there is no organizational form in which all of the above characteristics are found. Therefore, the choice of an organization form under which to shelter a business venture must be made in the context of a specific situation after careful consideration of all factors. Consideration must be given to a determination of the most desirable characteristics that are needed in the situation and to the tradeoffs between characteristics. In the absence of a specific situation, it is impossible to ascertain the form of organization that would be best. However, it is possible to analyze some basic alternative organizational forms that are generally suitable for carrying on business activities and to evaluate them against the seven criteria of a hypothetical "ideal" organization. From this analysis some general statements can be derived as to the appropriateness of a specific other situations where large amounts of capital must be raised and where it is desirable to appeal to relatively small investors for at least part of the capital. In these types of situations the undesirable characteristics are likely to be secondary to other considerations.

The general partnership form

A partnership as defined by the Uniform Partnership Act "is an association of two or more persons to carry on, as co-owners, a business for profit." The requirements for the formation of a partnership are considerably less rigorous and less formal than the requirements for forming a corporation. A partnership is created by a contract between two or more parties. Although it is preferable to have the partnership agreement reduced to writing to avoid misunderstandings between the partners, a written contract is not a requirement. The partnership may be brought into existence by an oral agreement or it may be implied from the actions of the participants themselves even through they have made no oral or written agreement. By whatever means they are created, partnerships embody only three of the desirable attributes of our hypothetical ideal organizational form. The partnership itself is not a taxable entity and therefore is not subject to the imposition of state and federal income taxes at the partnership level. Profits and losses of partnership are passed on to the partners, each of whom must pick up his share of the partnership profits or losses on his personal income tax return along with his other taxable earnings. Since a partner must pay tax on his share of the earnings whether they are actually distributed or not, taxing

authorities are indifferent to the retention of earnings in the partnership for reinvestment or any other purposes. Generally, any kind of business that can be carried on by an individual may be carried on in partnership form. While the partnership form of organization meets the criteria of avoiding double taxation on earnings, of allowing retention of earnings without restriction or penalty, and of no restriction on the type of business activity, it fails on all other counts. Each general partner is liable to the limit of his wealth for the debts of the partnership. He is taxed on his share of the earnings whether he receives them or not. The partnership is terminated upon the death or bankruptcy of any partner, or if a partner becomes mentally or legally incompetent. This may force the discontinuance of a business and the forced liquidation of partnership assets at an inopportune time. This undesirable characteristic of partnerships may be at least partially overcome by agreements entered into by the partners themselves prior to the occurrence of such an event. A participant may generally transfer only his interest in partnership profits without the approval of all other partners, but he may not transfer his rights to participate in the management of the business to anyone else without permission of all of the other partners.

Partnerships are most appropriate in situations requiring no more capital than can be provided by only a few partners and in which the risk of loss is relatively insignificant in relationship to the wealth of the partners. The partnership form is usually found among relatively small businesses although it is sometimes used in other situations such as large public accounting firms, law practices, and other businesses in which personal responsibility is a significant factor in the owner-client relationship.

Corporations and general partnerships are two basic types of organizations. The favorable characteristics of one are generally lacking in the other (and vice versa). All other organizational forms are generally hybrid forms that embody some of the favorable characteristics of corporations and partnerships. Two hybrid forms — Subchapter S Corporations and Limited Partnerships, are briefly examined and evaluated in terms of the seven characteristics of our ideal organization in the remainder of this paper.

Subchapter S Corporation

Subchapter S corporations derive their name from the subsection (S) of the chapter of the Internal Revenue Code which provides for special treatment, in some circumstances, of certain corporations for federal income tax purposes. In substance, Subchapter S permits corporations that meet specific criteria to be treated for tax purposes as if they were in fact partnerships rather than corporations. Subchapter S corporations do not meet all the characteristics of our hypothetical "ideal" organization. However, since it combines the legal liability characteristics of the corporation with the income tax characteristics of a partnership, it does meet several important criteria.

Since this type of organization is, in fact, a corporation, stockholders are not liable for its debts and their potential loss is limited to their investment in the corporation. A Subchapter S corporation is not a taxable entity. Each shareholder must pick up his pro rata share of the corporation's net income or loss, whether distributed or not, on his personal income tax return. Since the tax is collected whether the earnings are distributed or not, there is no restriction or penalty on the amount of earnings retained by the corporation. The legal existence of the Subchapter S is not affected by changes in the fortunes of the participants, by changes in their legal competency, or their death. A participant may freely transfer all or part of his interest in the organization. The Subchapter S corporation fails on two desirable characteristics. First, the shareholder pays tax on his pro rata shares of earnings whether they are actually distributed to him or not. Second, there are some restrictions on the kind of business activity that may be engaged in by the corporation. In addition, there are requirements that must be met to become and remain a Subchapter S corporation; these, to some extent, restrict the favorable attributes possessed by this type of organization.

First, the corporation must be a domestic corporation and must not be a member of an affiliated group. Therefore, foreign corporations and subsidiaries of other corporations do not qualify for the special treatment afforded under Subchapter S.

Second, there must be not more than ten shareholders. How husbands and wives are counted for determining the number of shareholders depends upon the legal form in which they hold stock.

Third, shareholders must be individuals or decedent's estates. Partnerships, other corporations, and estates of bankrupts do not qualify. Thus, although the legal existence of the corporation would not be affected by the bankruptcy of a shareholder, its special tax treatment as a partnership could be terminated if a shareholder should become bankrupt.

Fourth, a nonresident alien may not be a shareholder.

Fifth, the corporation may have no more than one class of stock.

Sixth, the corporation may not get more than 80 percent of its gross revenues from outside the United States.

Seventh, the corporation may not get more than 20 percent of its gross revenues from rents, royalties, dividends, interest, annuities, and gains from sales or exchanges of securities.

Eighth, all shareholders must consent to the election to be taxed as a partnership at the time the election is made. Further, all additional shareholders must also consent at the time they become shareholders. Otherwise the election will be terminated and the organization will revert to the tax status of a corporation. This provision, to some extent, adds a qualification to the desirable criteria of our ideal organization that participants should be free to transfer all or part of their interests without restriction or reservation.

The Subchapter S corporation is particularly appropriate when it is desirable to restrict the liability of participants for corporate debts; when only a small number of participants are needed and they are all U.S. citizens; when 80 percent or more of the business activities as measured by gross revenues is to be within the United States; and when 80 percent or more of the business revenues will be provided by the active operation of a merchandising, manufacturing, or service type of business as opposed to "passive" types of investments such as investments in securities, and rental property. When these conditions are met, the Chapter S corporation provides an organization form that closely approximates our hypothetical "ideal" organization.

Limited partnerships

The limited partnership, like the Subchapter S corporation, is a hybrid type of organization in which may be found some of the favorable characteristics of both general partnerships and corporations. Further, some of the limitations of the Subchapter S corporation may be overcome by using the limited partnership form of organization. This form of organization has been receiving increased attention in recent years particularly in the real estate development sector of the business community.

A limited partnership is a partnership formed by two or more persons, having as members one or more general partners and one or more limited partners. Like a general partnership, the rights and obligations of the partners are established by contractual agreement, but unlike a general partnership a limited partnership can be formed only under statutory authority. Generally, this requires the filing, with a designated official, of a certificate showing such information as the name, character, and location of the business, names and addresses of the partners, the contributions to be made by limited partners, the term for which the partnership is to exist, and how profits are to be shared among the partners.

Properly formed and operated, a limited partnership meets in some measure most of the criteria of our hypothetical "ideal" organization. Furthermore, it overcomes some of the limitations of the Subchapter S corporation with regard to the number that can participate, the kind of business activities that can be carried on, the nationality of the participants, and the geographical area in which revenues may be generated.

With regard to the liability of participants, limited partners are not liable for the debts of the partnership except to the extent of the investment that they agreed to make in the partnership as stated in the certificate required by the statutes. General partners are, like all partners in a general partnership, liable, individually and collectively for all debts of the partnership. Thus, the limited partnership meets the first criteria with regard to limited partners but not as to general partners.

A limited partnership is generally not a taxable entity for income tax purposes, therefore there is no double taxation of partnership earnings.[2] Earnings of the partnership are taxable to the partners on their personal income tax return whether the earnings are actually distributed or not. Each partner must report and pay income tax on his pro rata share of the partnership earnings. Thus the limited partnership, like the general partnership and the Subchapter S corporation fails on the criterion that only earnings received by the owner in cash or other property should be taxed to him. Each of these

types of organizations may, however, retain earnings without restriction or penalty for reinvestment on behalf of their owners.

Limited partnerships, like general partnerships, fail to meet the fourth criterion of being unaffected by changes in the financial fortunes or changes in legal or mental competency of participants. In both forms, the death or bankruptcy of a general partner will cause a dissolution of the partnership. Further, on application by or for a partner a court will decree a dissolution of the partnership under certain conditions such as mental or physical incapacity of the partner to perform his part of the partnership contract; generally this is not true, however, in the case of a limited partner. It is possible to overcome the deficiency to some extent with regard to general partners by providing in the certificate of the limited partnership that the remaining general partners may continue the business. When legal to do so, the deficiency can be overcome by having one or more corporations as the general partner or partners.

With regard to the sixth criterion, the free transferability of interests, a limited partner may assign all or a portion of his interest in the partnership, and the assignee of this interest may become a substituted partner if given that right by the certificate or if his status as a limited partner is consented to by all other partners. Further the interest of one or more limited partners may be divided into units and sold as limited partnership interests, which are much the same as stock in a corporation. Free transferability may or may not be allowed depending upon the provisions of the Certificate of Limited Partnership.

[2]A word of warning is in order with regard to taxation of both limited and general partnerships. The Internal Revenue Service will look to the substance of the agreements and if the organizations have more of the characteristics of corporations than of partnerships, the organization will be treated as a corporation for tax purposes, regardless of what it is called by its owners. Agreements should be drafted with the advice of competent counsel to avoid this problem. Generally, there will be no difficulty with limited partnerships formed in compliance with the Uniform Limited Partnership Act that has been adopted by many states including Arizona.

With regard to the seventh criterion, no restrictions on the type of business activities that can be undertaken, any business activity that can be carried out by a general partnership may be carried out by a limited partnership (except banking and insurance in Arizona).

A comparison of the limited partnership with the Subchapter S corporation reveals that they share many of the same characteristics. However, the restrictions associated with limited partnerships are considerably less than with the Subchapter S corporation. For example, there may be no more than ten shareholders in a Subchapter S corporation but there is no restriction on the number of partners that a limited partnership may have. The amount of revenue that a Subchapter S corporation may have from passive investments such as rents and royalties is limited to 20 percent, but there is no such restriction on limited partnerships.

In general, limited partnerships may provide the most appropriate form of organization in situations where a large quantity of investment capital must be raised from a relatively large number of investors and where it is desirable to protect most of those investors from the liability for debts of the organization. Properly formed and operated, a limited partnership may come very close to our "ideal" organization without the limitations imposed upon Subchapter S corporations.[3]

Other organizational forms

Other organizational forms such as joint ventures, trusts, joint stock companies (in some states), and partnership associations (in some states) may be appropriate in certain circumstances. In general, trusts are taxed on the same basis as individual taxpayers, and other forms of organizations are treated either as partnerships or corporations depending upon the characteristics of the entity itself. Detailed analysis of these types of organization is beyond the scope of this paper.

Summary

An analysis of four types of organizational forms — corporations, general partnerships, Subchapter S corporations, and limited partnerships that are generally suitable for sheltering business enterprises that require the participation of two or more individuals reveals that, to some extent, each meets some of the criteria of a hypothetical "ideal" organization, Two "hybrid" organizations. Subchapter S corporations and Limited Partnerships, may be used to overcome some of the undesirable characteristics of the traditional corporation and the traditional general partnership forms. The limited partnership is slightly better than the Subchapter S corporation where restrictions upon ownership and business operations are concerned.

We have discussed each of four organization forms in terms of their general characteristics and have attempted to provide businessmen or potential businessmen with some insight into the nature of each type. Of course, there are many technical and detailed considerations that must be taken into account when choosing an organizational form. Only through the joint effort of the businessman, his attorney, and his certified public accountant and after due consideration

[3]Attention is again directed to the warning issued in the previous footnote with regard to the tax status of partnerships.

of all relevant factors of the situation
can the appropriate choice be made.

QUESTIONS

1. Under what conditions would a
   Subchapter S corporation be more
   advisable than trying to take the
   profits of the enterprise out through
   salary and expenses?

2. By what means could a sole
   proprietor protect his estate from
   the liabilities of his business?

AND THEN THERE IS BIG BROTHER

13

Some small businessmen complain of governmental restrictions. Here is some documentation on the subject.

OSHA, big government, and small business

Jack R. Nicholas, Jr. †

Until the late 1960s most small businessmen didn't have too much contact with the federal government other than to pay taxes of various types.

†Jack R. Nicholas, Jr., of the American University, pp. 57-64, *MSU Business Topics,* Winter 1973.

Reprinted by permission of the publisher, Division of Research, Graduate School of Business Administration, Michigan State University.

Then came the Equal Employment Opportunity Act, the Environmental Protection Agency legislation, and other laws and executive actions such as wage and price controls. These increased regulation of business operations and the cost of doing business. In 1970 the Occupational Safety and Health Act was signed into law. This act is perhaps the least understood, most technical, most complex, most comprehensive, and therefore most exposed of the recent regulatory efforts of big government. It covers virtually every employer and employee in the United States.

The law is designed to protect the American worker at his work place. Provisions for safety and health standard setting and enforcement, intergovernmental cooperation, research, and the compilation of statistics represent a radical change in the approach to occupational safety and health. The most important section of the act places responsibility upon the employer to ensure a place of employment free of recognized hazards. Developing, modifying and enforcing safety standards is the responsibility of the Secretary of Labor, acting through the Occupational Health and Safety Administration (OSHA). Non compliance with standards, or failure to maintain adequate records or satisfy posting requirements results (in all but a small number of cases) in written citations from the Department of Labor describing the violation and fixing a time limit for correction. The law requires that employers post citations prominently at or near the site of the alleged violation. Civil and criminal penalties of up to $10,000 and six months confinement are provided. Failure to correct violations for which citations have been issued and all administrative review is complete can result in additional penalties of up to $1,000 per day. Appeals are handled by a three member, quasi-judicial Occupational Safety and Health Review Commission which is independent of any government department. Commission rulings may be appealed to the U. S. Court of Appeals. The National Institute for Occupational Safety and Health (NIOSH) was established by the act to develop and establish occupational safety and health standards; it functions under the Secretary of Health, Education, and Welfare in the field of technical and medical research needed to support OSHA.

There were compelling reasons for passage of the act. The National Safety Council, based on voluntary reports of its own members (including 95 percent of America's largest companies), estimated that in 1971 there were 14,200 deaths from accidents on the job; 2,200,000 disabling injuries (out of 7,000,000 total injuries); and $9.3 billion lost in wages, insurance, property damage, and medical expenses.

Bureau of Labor statistics show the injury frequency rate increasing alarmingly between 1961 and 1970: from 11.8 disabling injuries per million man hours worked to 15.2 — an increase of 29 percent. In 1970, the U. S. Public Health Service estimated that 390,000 persons contract occupational diseases each year.

It was President Lyndon B. Johnson in 1968 who proposed the first nationwide occupational and safety bill. Extensive hearings were held, but the bill never got out of committee. In 1969, upon recommendation of the Labor Department and after consultation with representatives of business, labor, and safety organizations, President Richard M. Nixon proposed his administration's version of an Occupational Health and Safety bill. Hearings were held all through 1969 and 1970. The AFL-CIO changed its position of opposition in 1968 to one of strong support for an effective health and safety law. The AFL-CIO made this subject their number one legislative priority for the Ninety-first Congress. As public awareness of the issue grew, representatives from business also decided to give support for passage and began to make constructive recommendations to give Congress the benefit of their experience in enforcement of then existing safety standards. Those with substantial safety programs wanted a law which was compatible with their efforts so that revamping and reorientation would be minimized. Testimony was given by members of the Chamber of Commerce of the United States, the National Association of Manufacturers and various trade associations. The result was a compromise bill which did not completely reflect the views of any one group.

A little more than a year later it became obvious that the impact of the act upon the small businessman had not been seriously considered during the hearings. The only reference in the whole legislative history of the act is the provision for financial aid from the Small Business Administration to help businessmen make safer work places.

This oversight created tremendous problems. These problems were compounded by lack of effective communications concerning the law from big government to the small businessman.

Early in 1972 senators and congressmen indicated in committee and in debate that they were receiving a considerable number of complaints concerning OSHA. At the completion of the first year of inspection (in mid-1972) constituents really started bringing pressure to bear. Inspectors were finding many violations. Figures released by OSHA showed that 32,701 inspections were conducted in fiscal 1971 and that 23,231 citations were issued alleging 120,861 violations of the standards. Penalties amounting to $2.3 million were proposed. Fear of being fined without prior warning, inability to easily determine how to comply with the law, and the burden of additional federal record keeping requirements were frequently recurring objections raised by representatives of small business before congressional committees.

Why burden small business with OSHA?

When the small businessman began to petition Congress for relief from OSHA there were attempts to change the law. There were more than 100 related amendments proposed during the Ninety-second Congress. Many were intended to gut the law through a cut in appropriations. Other amendments would have exempted

whole industries (such as agriculture) from having to comply. In the latter days of that Congress it became apparent that no long lasting constructive change could be achieved. In order to provide some indication to the small businessman that Congress recognized his plight, a unique but temporary device was used to try to relieve small businesses from the threat of inspection. OSHA is funded with the appropriations for Health, Education, Welfare, and Labor. In the specific section allocating money to OSHA the following provision was included:

None of the funds appropriated by this act shall be expended to pay the salaries of any employees of the Federal Government who inspect firms employing three persons or less for compliance with the Occupational Safety and Health Act of 1970.

This would have exempted 47 percent of all employers and 10 percent of all employees in the nation. The intent of the amendment was to gain time so that proper attention could be paid to the basic law. This appropriations bill was one of those vetoed by President Nixon in late October 1972. Thus the act remains in effect even for employers with only one employee.

The reason the small businessman was not simply exempted is that small business worksites are no less dangerous than places of employment having larger numbers of workers. Recent research on violation of safety codes, work related fatalities, and injuries requiring rehabilitation was conducted by the Department of Industry, Labor, and Human Relations of the State of Wisconsin. The frequency of fatalities for all of 1971 and up to July of 1972 is shown in Table 13-1 (based on a statistical sample of cases on file) for businesses having different sizes of work forces. The table shows

TABLE 13-1:   Percentage distribution of fatalities by employment size in Wisconsin, 1971 and 1972

Employment size class	Number of employees	Number of fatalities	Percentage of total cases	Deaths per 100,000 employees
0-19	312,139	68	42	21.78
20-49	177,337	28	17	15.79
50-99	131,430	22	13	16.74
100-249	156,559	19	12	12.14
250-499	131,912	11	7	8.34
500 and more	329,834	14	9	4.24
		Total 162	100	

that the working conditions at the places of business of smaller employers are more dangerous in terms of number of fatalities occurring during a given time period than are the working conditions at the worksites of larger firms.

Table 13-2 relates frequency of injuries requiring rehabilitation to businesses of different sizes. The critical part of Table 13-2 is reflected by the ratio displayed in the last column. In spite of the large number of cases reported for the 0-19 size group, the frequency of cases per employee is not significantly different from the next two larger size groups. This indicates that the number of accidents causing a need for rehabilitation is just as high for small size employers as for larger size employers. No reason can be given for the higher frequency per employee ratios of the largest employee groups are much lower, a result consistent with the data on fatalities.

Approximately 10 percent of all compensation cases of Wisconsin workers are investigated to see if added compensation is due because of a safety violation resulted in an injury. Cases

closed in 1971 were used as a sample to determine if differences in the number of violations and related injuries existed for groups of workers of varying sizes. The results are illustrated in Figure 13-1. When examining injuries and violations per employee by size of the employee group, it is apparent that the safety record deteriorates as the size of the business employee group decreases.

Objections to OSHA by small businessmen

Fear of citation and fines without warning.   An inspector who enters a premises on official business for OSHA is required by the law to issue a citation for all but the most minor (**de minimus**) violation of the standards. The principle being followed is "citation in the first instance." The employer may not be warned; he must be cited when violations (other than well-defined **de minimus** violations) are detected. First instance citation was included in the law to help ensure voluntary compliance by employers in advance of any OSHA inspection. It was found during studies

TABLE 13-2: **Percentage distribution of rehabilitation cases by employment size in Wisconsin, 1972**

Employment size class	Number of employees	Number of rehabilitation cases	Percentage of total cases	Cases per 10,000 employees
0-19	312,139	159	28	5.09
20-49	177,337	88	16	4.96
50-99	131,430	65	12	4.95
100-249	156,559	90	16	5.75
250-499	131,912	53	09	4.02
500 and more	329,834	105	19	3.18
		Total 560	100	

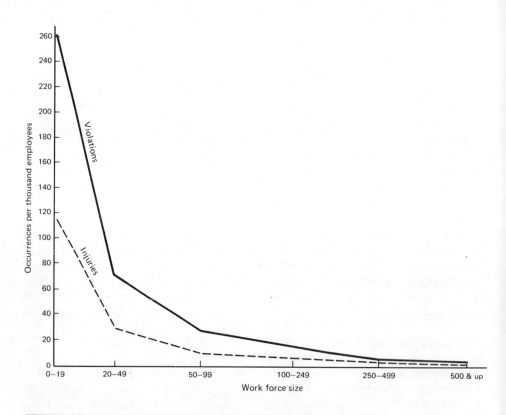

Figure 13-1: **Investigated accident cases settled in Wisconsin in 1971 by size of work force**

of state-run safety and health programs that only programs which were truly effective as determined by lower death and accident frequency rates were those having first instance citation provisions. Under this principle there is no question about whether a citation will be issued. The employer can expect to be cited if a violation is detected; the OSHA inspector can expect to be without a job if he doesn't issue a citation and is caught at it. One need only do some simple arithmetic to recognize why voluntary compliance is necessary. With the 500 inspectors presently in OSHA, assuming each can conduct 200 inspections per year, it would take forty-one years to inspect all businesses one time.

Lack of information on the safety and health standards. The Occupational Safety and Health Act directed the Secretary of Labor to adopt national consensus and pre-existing federal job safety and health standards issued under other acts "as soon as practicable." OSHA employees managed to get the general industry standards published in just five months but without an index to the 248 pages of fine print, tables, and graphs. There were many standards which were in need of more specific interpretation. One small paragraph in the middle of the standards under Article 1910.151, Medical Services and First Aid, reads as follows:

In the absence of an infirmary, clinic, or hospital in the near proximity to the work place which is used for the treatment of all injured employees, a person or persons shall be adequately trained to render first aid. First aid supplies approved by a consulting physician shall be readily available.

Matters for interpretation include the phrases "near proximity," "a person or persons," and "adequately trained." Obviously, considerable effort has to be expended in ensuring that proper interpretation is rendered and that the information is widely disseminated. Only when this is done could penalties be fairly assessed for non-compliance. The list of more complex safety standards which are considered necessary at any one time is constantly changing. The act contains no specific standards. It merely establishes machinery to promulgate and update appropriate standards for each industry and delegates responsibility for this to the Secretary of Labor. It is the machinery for promulgation which has not served the small businessman very well to date. The problem manifests itself in two ways. **First,** he must locate sources of information on the standards applicable to his business; and **second,** when he locates a source, the information begins coming in such a deluge and is so arranged that direct application is difficult, if not impossible for reasons of cost, feasibility, and exact interpretation. Thus, even when he can establish a source of information the businessman may not be able to comply. He can't even request an OSHA inspector to visit his premises without being subject to the requirement of citation for violations. At the present time he may phone or visit any nearby office of OSHA and request guidance, but he must know what questions to ask in order to get proper answers with uniform interpretation.

Excessive record keeping and reporting requirements. The act authorizes the Secretary of Labor, in cooperation with the Secretary of Health, Education, and Welfare, to prescribe record keeping requirements necessary or appropriate for developing information regarding the causes and prevention of occupational accidents and illnesses. Regulations were promulgated which require the recording of every work-related injury or illness which involves loss of consciousness, requires medical treatment, or prevents an employee from carrying out all of his regularly assigned duties. Only simple first aid treatment need not be recorded. To the businessman this means having to prepare and maintain the following OSHA documents: a log of occupational injuries and illnesses, a supplementary record of occupational injuries and illnesses, and a summary of occupational injuries and illnesses. The result is a statistical analyst's dream but a burden to the small businessman. None of these documents is very simple, although the number of entries from any small business may be quite small. In terms of time spent trying to understand the record keeping requirements, the cost to the small businessman apparently seemed unacceptable. Along with the other complaints mentioned in this article, excessive record keeping and reporting requirements were frequently listed as most objectionable.

Big government's response to small business

Legislative action: One of the more than 100 amendments proposed in the Ninety-second Congress to change the Occupational Safety and Health Act was submitted to the House of Representatives by Congressman William Steiger of Wisconsin. The amendment was specifically designed to assist the small businessman by providing, at the request of the employer, on-site consultation visits which do not trigger the entire enforcement procedure. Without being subject to a first instance citation and penalty, the employer could, on his premises, openly consult with OSHA inspectors on interpretation or applicability of safety and health standards or on possible alternative ways of complying with applicable standards. The proposed amendment limits matters for consultation and advice to those specified in the employer's request affecting conditions, structures, machines, apparatus, devices, equipment or materials in the workplace. The fact that consultation is held would not preclude issuance of a citation in a subsequent inspection whether or not the particular matter resulting in citation was discussed. The bill anticipates that on some visits a hazard posing an imminent danger to the lives of employees might be discovered. In this case the consultant would be required to bring the condition to the attention of the OSHA area director as well as to the employer. The employer would be expected to abate the danger immediately. The area director in this case would be required to ensure that this is done, even if he must use enforcement procedures to protect the lives of the employees. In addition, any serious violation of a rule or standard or regulation which is noted during the consultation would be subject to a written notice to the employer describing the violation and the action which must be taken (within reasonable time) to abate the violation. An employer failing to abate the violation within the specified time, or who fails to report abatement, would be subject to an inspection under the normal rules of first instance citation. In testimony before the House Select Subcommittee on Labor, Assistant Secretary of Labor George C. Guenther enthusiastically supported a similar proposal to aid small businesses.

Passage of Congressman Steiger's amendment or a similar one should abate the worst of the hostility to OSHA exemplified by testimony of representatives of small businessmen in House of Representative committee hearings on this bill. At the same time responsibility for voluntarily complying with the act can not be avoided by the businessman. The employer must still become knowledgeable about those safety and health standards which are established to protect his employees. The proposed amendment is aimed specifically at helping the small business with twenty-five or fewer employees. It clearly distinguishes between consultation visit and inspection. It would not be possible that one could be substituted for the other for the convenience of either the businessman or OSHA. Thus the law could continue to be a strong one which can be complied with more effectively.

Administrative action: OSHA has been engaged in a massive information program using many different means of communication. The information program started with a series of speeches and seminars held across country, with more than 10,000 speeches made by members of the OSHA staff in fiscal 1972. A variety of courses and free seminars for employers and employees has been offered throughout the country and an OSHA school has been established at O'Hare Airport, Chicago, offering forty-hour courses to interpret established standards for the construction industry and general industry.

In addition, the Education and Training Department of OSHA has other types of instructional materials under development to cover subjects such as record keeping requirements and a voluntary compliance program. The latter is a "programmed instruction" course for self teaching. OSHA and NIOSH are nearing completion of a jointly developed college level correspondence course on occupational safety and health, with the hope that the course will be qualified by universities for credit through college extension services.

Information is available

OSHA has made available through the U. S. Government Printing Office a series of self inspection guides for applying safety and health standards — a comprehensive locator to applicable sections on safety in the law and regulations which are published in the Federal Register.

A direct source of information now available is the monthly publication of the Occupational Health and Safety Administration, *Job Safety and Health.* The *National Safety Council Self-Evaluation Checklists* offer an elaborate set of guides to the standards. These checklists transform the regulations promulgated by OSHA into question and answer lists designed for fact finding about the status of occupational health and safety at a workplace. They are recommended for use by safety professionals in large companies, or in consulting firms, as well as for use by owners and foremen responsible for safety in smaller firms.

Development of the checklists is merely one example of OSHA participation with non-government groups to disseminate information. OSHA also has assisted interested trade associations, employee groups, insurance companies, and even individuals in finding out more about OSHA and its methods of operation.

The *Compliance Operations Manual*, which is used by OSHA field personnel in proposing penalties, is available to the public through the U.S. Government Printing Office. This manual and the guide which prescribes the procedure for appealing penalties to the new independent Occupational Safety and Health Review Commission are essential documents which should be referred to in the event of a citation which an employer wishes to challenge.

Conclusion

Initial difficulties are bound to occur with any new program as complex and comprehensive as one for nationwide occupational safety and health. Even though the deficiencies of the act are causing the worst problems for the small businessman, the best solution would not be to exempt small businesses from compliance. The statistics in this article indicate that employees of smaller businesses in one state are experiencing far higher frequencies of fatalities in occupational accidents than are employees of larger companies. Small business employees work in establishments where, on a per capita basis, safety violations resulting in disabling injuries are most frequent. The frequency rates of disabling injuries in various sizes of employee groups do not exhibit as wide a range of values, but the smallest size group does have a higher frequency of disabling accidents than the two employee groups with the largest membership.

Help is on the way to abate the major objections to OSHA voiced by small businessmen. More effective information services and reduced record keeping requirements are beginning to ease the burden. OSHA relaxed the record keeping requirements for employers who have no more than seven employees at any one time within any year. Effective 1 January 1973, most of the employers in this category are not required to maintain any of the records listed earlier in this article. The only requirement is that fatalities or multiple hospitalization accidents be reported within forty-eight hours. In order to continue receipt of statistical data for injury and illness analysis as required by the law, a representative sample of the affected employers are to be notified annually that they must maintain the log, one of the three records maintained by larger employers. They will also be required to make an annual report.

The machinery of big government, although slow, is being geared for response to small business needs. Congressional action will be needed to obtain the most direct and effective assistance. Improved occupational safety and health will increase the cost of doing business — but the anticipated rewards of fewer fatalities and injuries justify the cost. In the long term, the diminished financial drain of these tragedies may partially offset the cost of making a work place safer.

QUESTIONS

1. Are there any other factors that might exist to explain the apparently more dangerous environment in small business?

2. What other evidence might one want?

3. How might the government accommodate the small businessman in this matter?

LEASES

14

Leases are important. Very much so! We must delve into them for you cannot always rely on others for protection.

Selected problems in store leasing

Milton R. Friedman†

Modern store leases present a wide range of solid problems — the resolution of which is often determined by the relative desirability of the store operator as a prospective tenant.

†**Milton R. Friedman,** *The Practical Lawyer,* **December 1969, Volume 15, No. 8, pp. 41-57.**

Reprinted with the permission of *The Practical Lawyer,* 4025 Chestnut Street, Philadelphia, Pa 19104. Subscription rates: $12 a year; $2 a single issue.

This article will consider the issues in a number of these areas — including contracts to build, percentage leases, fire and casualty insurance, repairs, rent escalation, competition among tenants, and shopping-center leases. It will also offer some sample clauses that would be desirable from the tenant's standpoint — assuming that he has sufficient bargaining power to have them included in the lease.

Contracts to build

You represent a store operator who has found a piece of undeveloped land that appears to be a desirable store site. The owner may be a builder or, if not, is willing anyway to enter into a contract to build a store to your client's specifications and lease it to him.

It is reasonably clear that if he is highly responsible and a desirable tenant, and remains so; if the deal promises to be profitable to the landlord, and continues so; if the costs of construction do not rise substantially; and if a competitor of your client does not come around in the interim with a better offer — he has a reasonably good chance of moving into the new building.

But if some of these conditions change for the worse, what can your client do? If he is thinking of recovering damages, measured by the loss of future profits at a presently unimproved site — with no history whatever of past profits — you have an uphill struggle that the writer does not envy. Furthermore, the likelihood of the corporation (or other entity with which you will probably be compelled to deal) being able to respond to such a judgment is not overpowering.

Specific performance

What of the right to compel actual performance? Traditionally, courts have refused to decree specific performance of a contract to build, on the ground that it would not be feasible for them to superintend the construction of a building, just as they would never order an opera star to sing.

The modern tendency is to enforce specific performance unless difficulties of supervision outweigh the importance of specific performance to the plaintiff.

Percentage leases

The author's experience with percentage leases dates back to the 1930's. The first two percentage leases the author saw involved a motion picture theater and a stadium.

Both leases contained the same defect from the landlord's point of view, because they merely gave him a percentage of the "box office receipts." The sale of pink lemonade and popcorn supplied a major source of income for the theater at that time, but under this clause the landlord picked up nothing

from their sale. At the stadium, slick paper programs were sold for 50 cents each. The result was the same.

Over the years, it seemed that landlords' lawyers had become sufficiently sophisticated to avoid this sort of thing. But only a few years ago, the landlord of a theater in New Haven, Connecticut, learned from the state's highest court that his percentage clause deprived him of rent based on program advertising, checkroom facilities, the value of complimentary tickets, and the sale of sheet music, candy, and soft drinks.

Problems for tenants

By and large, however, landlords have learned how to take care of themselves in this situation. Usually it is the tenant who has the problems.

The author once prepared a percentage lease to a florist-tenant, on behalf of a landlord. Some time later the question arose of how the percentage clause applied to the delivery of flowers by telegraph.

If, for example, a customer placed an order with the tenant, in New York, for $10 worth of flowers to be delivered in San Francisco, the tenant might keep about $2 and send the rest to the corresponding florist at the place of delivery. The lease made no provision for this, and required the tenant to pay the landlord a percentage of the full $10.

If, by chance, the customer belonged to the Diner's Club or a similar credit plan, the latter might take, perhaps, one dollar of the 10. Percentage rent for the florist may run as high as 10 or 20 per cent. Theoretically, the florist could make a $10 sale and lose 20 cents on transaction — without regard to overhead.

Other problem areas come to mind. If the tenant is an automobile dealer and sells a car for $2,500 — $1,000 in cash and $1,500 by way of a trade-in — should the landlord be credited with $2,500 and then another $1,500 when the trade-in is resold? And how about the trade-in on the trade-in?

Should the percentage rent include employees' discounts and the employees' cafeteria where food is sold — perhaps at cost? How about the tenant's sales of money orders and postage stamps as an accommodation to customers? Or a bulk sale of merchandise at the end of the season or in connection with a sale of the business? Are these part of the tenant's gross sales?

Percentage clause for tenant

One national chain has developed an excellent sales clause from the tenant's point of view, which is set out in full in Form 1. It permits the tenant to deduct from gross sales, for purpose of percentage rent:

• Returns and allowances (as such terms are used in the tenant's profit-and-loss statement);

• Delivery service and installation charges not included in the sales price of merchandise;

• Sales of merchandise ordered through tenant's mail-order catalogs;

• Amounts in excess of tenant's cash sales price charged on sales made on credit or under a time payment plan;

• Taxes, such as sales, use, excise, and occupation taxes;

• Sales of departments or divisions not located on the leased premises;

• Premiums collected on life-insurance policies sold from the leased premises.

FORM 1 — TENANT'S CLAUSE FOR PERCENTAGE LEASE

Net sales means gross sales made upon the leased premises by Tenant and Tenant's concessionaires, deducting or excluding, as the case may be: returns and allowances as such terms are known and used by Tenant in the preparation of Tenant's profit-and-loss statement; delivery, service, and installation charges not included in the sale price of merchandise; sales of merchandise ordered through Tenant's mail-order catalogs and filled through Tenant's catalog channels, regardless of the place of order, payment, or delivery; amounts in excess of Tenant's cash sales price charged on sales made on credit or under a time payment plan; the amount of all sales, use, excise, retailer's occupation, or other similar taxes imposed on a specific amount or percentage upon, or determined by, the amount of retail sales made on the leased premises; sales of departments or divisions not located on the leased premises; premiums collected on policies of insurance sold from the leased premises; all receipts from weighing machines, vending machines, snack bars, amusement devices and public telephones; and all receipts from vending machines and snack bars operated for the use of Tenant's employees only.

Within 15 days after the end of each calendar month (except July and January, and within 25 days after the end of July and January), Tenant will furnish to Landlord a statement of Tenant's net sales (as herein defined) for such month. Landlord shall be deemed to have accepted each statement as correct, unless within 30 days after Landlord's receipt of any such statement, Landlord gives Tenant written notice of Landlord's dissatisfaction therewith, in which event, Landlord shall have the right, at Landlord's expense, within 60 days notice after the giving of such notice, to cause any impartial, reputable firm of certified public accountants, nationally known and doing business on a nationwide basis, mutually satisfactory and approved in writing for that purpose by Landlord and Tenant, to audit Tenant's net sales (as herein defined) for the period covered by said statement; *provided*, that if said firm does not submit a detailed report to Landlord and Tenant in support of its findings within 45 days after its selection and approval by the parties, Tenant's statement of net sales shall be deemed correct and conclusive.

Tenant makes no representation of warranty as to the sales that it expects to make in the leased premises, and Landlord agrees to hold in confidence all sales figures and other information obtained from Tenant or upon the inspection and audit of Tenant's books and records.

• Receipts from weighing machines, snack bars, and amusement devices; and

• Receipts from vending machines and snack bars operated for the use of tenant's employees only.

This clause also provides that the tenant's statements will be deemed accepted as correct unless objected to within 30 days. In other words, if the tenant is not caught within 30 days, he is safe.

Although the clause requires the landlord to hold this information in confidence, this is unrealistic. If the landlord wants to borrow money or to sell the property (or some interest in it), he will be asked for these figures, and they will not be kept confidential.

A tenant would have to be extraordinarily desirable to induce a well-represented landlord to accept this clause as is. Nevertheless, the clause obviously represents the distillation of much experience and thought and is worth considering for that reason, whether or not it can be used in toto.

Fire and casualty insurance

Many store tenants regularly get a clause in their leases requiring the landlord to maintain fire and casualty insurance on the property. A practical reason is to assure the tenant that the landlord will have the funds to restore the premises.

To accomplish this purpose, the amount of the insurance must be adequate. A level frequently required is 80 per cent of "insurable value."

This term is not clear, however, and often landlords and tenants could use insurance counsel in this respect. Many landlords cut the insurance too low and, as a result, do not have sufficient funds to restore without new financing. The effect of this may be to kill the landlord's income from the property — something that does neither the landlord nor the tenant any good.

Subrogation

Sometimes a requirement that the landlord maintain fire insurance is invoked in an entirely different connection. The circumstances of this are substantially as follows:

A fire occurs due to the negligence of the tenant or his employees; the landlord collects from his insurance company; and the insurance company then claims a right of reimbursement against the tenant. The fire gave the landlord a claim against his tenant for negligent damages. The insurer, on payment to the landlord, acquires this claim by subrogation — stepping into the landlord's shoes.

Insurance companies have always had this right of subrogation but rarely exercised it against tenants until about 20 years ago. *General Mills, Inc. v. Goldman* [184 F.2d 359 (8th Cir. 1950)] was the case that opened the box.

In that case, the insurance company recovered a judgment in the trial court against the tenant for the value of an entire building. On appeal, this was reversed by a divided court.

The reversal was based on a clause in the lease that provided that, on expiration of the term, the tenant would surrender the premises in good condition, "loss by fire . . . excepted." The majority of the Court felt that this was intended to excuse the tenant from liability for fire.

However, the very fact that the Court needed to rely on this clause was a recognition of the rule that the tenant would otherwise be liable for negligent fire damage. This was the startling part of the *General Mills* case.

Negligence of parties

Another startling thing is that many states do not construe this surrender clause as a release from negligence and hold, partly for historical reasons, that the clause merely relieves a tenant from the consequences of non-negligent fire. Inasmuch as most fires are due to the negligence of a party in occupation, the *General Mills* case raised some serious problems.

Since the *General Mills* case, there has been a string of cases in which landlords' insurers have recovered against tenants. The converse is also true: a landlord whose negligence has resulted in damage to his tenants' property is liable, under the same theory, to his tenants' insurer.

Immunity against subrogation

Subrogation is not inevitable in the life of a tenant, and there are ways to avoid its impact. An insurance company can have no claim of subrogation against its insured.

That is a reason for buying insurance. If a tenant is insured, he is immune to subrogation. If a tenant is included in the landlord's policy, this is enough — he thereby becomes an insured.

But suppose the tenant is not insured. In some actions by insurance companies against a tenant, the tenant has pointed to a lease clause requiring the landlord to insure, claiming that this clause required the landlord to insure not only for himself but for the tenant as well, and that, as a consequence, no right of subrogation arose.

Some courts have upheld this argument — on the ground that, since the landlord could always insure for his own benefit, the inclusion of an obligation to this effect could only mean that the landlord was to insure for both.

Windfall The rationale of the latter decisions, apparently, is that the sole purpose of this clause is to make sure the landlord will have funds for restoration. The effect, however, is to give insurance companies a windfall. The desirability of this is questionable on two grounds:

• An insurer will generally waive the right if requested in advance; and

• Subrogation plays little or no part in fixing insurance premiums.

Risk to landlord Fire policies covering both landlord and tenant will, as mentioned above, protect a tenant against subrogation. But this poses some risk for the landlord unless the policy provides that it will not be invalidated as to the landlord by reason of some act or omission by the tenant (for example, the tenant's violation of a condition of the policy by maintaining benzine on the premises).

Even this provision may not sufficiently protect the landlord if the policy had no proper inception — for example, if the tenant made a misrepresentation in the application. Furthermore, in the case of a multi-tenant building, it is not practical to write the names of all the tenants into the landlord's fire policy, particularly when the tenancies frequently change.

Tenants have, therefore, sought other ways to bar the right of subrogation. One method has been to have the landlord agree, in the lease, to make no claim against the tenant for fire damage. Because the insurer's right of subrogation is derivative, if the landlord has no claim, the insurer can have none.

There has been some question, however, whether a landlord could cut off a right of his insurer without prejudicing the enforceability of his policy. This is now academic, because in all states insurance companies will now agree to waive the right of subrogation.

Waiver of rights in tort However, waiver by the insurer is not a full solution to the problem. Waiver merely means that the landlord's right to recover for a negligent fire remains with the landlord instead of passing to the insurance company.

It is also necessary to get the landlord to release in advance his rights in *tort*. The converse of this is also true.

Accordingly, the landlord and tenant should mutually release each other from liability for fire and other damage included in extended-coverage fire and casualty insurance, to the extent that such damage is insured, by policies that release each other from subrogation. The releases and waiver of subrogation should include not only landlord and tenant but the respective officers, directors, and employees of both of them.

Indemnities

In most fire clauses found in leases, the tenant's liability is based on his fault or the fault of somebody for whom he is responsible. In some leases, the tenant agrees to indemnify the landlord against loss from various causes, including fire. When an indemnity is involved, the tenant is liable whenever such a loss occurs — even if he has been entirely free of fault.

The liability is not only to the landlord, but also to an insurer who pays the landlord.

This kind of subrogation applies to all indemnities. Indemnities, therefore, are dangerous things. It is preferable to supply insurance rather than indemnities.

When giving an indemnity is unavoidable, you should add the qualification that it will not extend to any matter against which the landlord shall be effectively protected by insurance.

Repairs

The repair clause inevitably produces a struggle in which each party tries to assume a minimum obligation to repair and to impose a maximum obligation on the other. In this reverse tug-of-war, the battle is to the strong, the experienced, and those who are sophisticated in this field.

A well-prepared repair clause, from the tenant's point of view, should contain the provisions set forth in Form 2.

FORM 2 —
TENANT'S REPAIR CLAUSE

Lessor agrees:

1. That the leased premises are properly constructed and will be delivered to tenant in good condition, including initial decorating.

2. That during the term of the lease it will make all necessary repairs:

    (a) To the sidewalks, driveways, service areas, curbs, and parking areas;

    (b) To the exterior and to the structure of the building;

    (c) To the exterior water, sewerage, gas, and electrical services up to the point of entry to the building;

    (d) To the interior walls, ceilings, floors, and floor coverings, when such repairs are made necessary because of faulty construction or lessor's failure to keep the structure in proper repair;

    (e) To the heating and air-conditioning systems, except ordinary maintenance;

    (f) All repairs or restoration made necessary by fire or other peril covered by the standard extended coverage endorsement on fire insurance policies or by reason of war, windstorm, or acts of God.

Lessee agrees:

1. To do its own redecorating;

2. To make all repairs necessitated by the negligence of its agents and employees, except where covered by the standard fire and extended coverage insurance policy;

3. To provide ordinary maintenance for the heating and air-conditioning systems;

4. To make all other repairs not required to be made by the Lessor.

Landlord's
continuing obligation

A landlord who agrees to turn a building over to a tenant is likely to say: "Here is a brand new building. Look it over thoroughly before you accept possession. I will have a certificate of occupancy, a certificate of electrical inspection, of plumbing inspection, and so forth. I will assign to you all the builder's guaranties that I receive. Furthermore, I will make all repairs that may be necessary for the first full year of your term, whether these repairs be structural repairs or otherwise, excepting only repairs necessitated by your own acts or omissions. But from then on it is your baby."

The tenant may not see eye to eye with the landlord on this. The lapse of a year is no assurance of the structural soundness of a building.

The writer is familiar with a store that was abandoned by reason of a condition that first became noticeable after 18 months. The builder's failure to discover an underground stream on the site resulted in a gradual and uneven sinking of the structure. At another store, a center beam collapsed after seven years, without warning.

A tenant who rents air-conditioned space will pay more than for non-air-conditioned space. If the motors and blowers are run for 12 hours a day, these will probably wear out before expiration of the term. When this happens, the tenant will still be paying for air-conditioned space, but not getting it — unless the landlord makes the replacement.

If the floor is of terrazzo, it will probably last for many terms. If it is vinyl, as most are today, it will not. By the same logic, the landlord should replace the vinyl.

However, at this point the landlord may say: "Your rent was negotiated on my costs — land, construction, service of mortgage — and an income to me. If you expect me to make structural replacements, the rent must be revised upward."

And so it goes. The landlord might also argue: "I live 50 miles from your store. You are not going to call me every time a toilet is stopped."

Sometimes the solution is on the practical side. The tenant may pay for all repairs costing no more than $75, for example. There are no easy answers.

The clause set out in Form 2 was prepared for a high-credit tenant with substantial bargaining power. Although a smaller tenant may not succeed in getting all the provisions in this clause, he can at least get ideas from it.

Rent escalation

Taxes and assessments

Tax escalation clauses are thrown at tenants with frequency these days. These require the tenant to pay any increase in taxes above those that existed during a base period.

The clause may raise some questions: Does it include special assessments as well as taxes? What is the base year for the taxes — or better, the base amount?

Suppose, for example, a lease is made this year and requires the tenant to pay any increase over the year's tax. The tenant signs the lease, knowing the exact amount of tax that had been assessed for this year. However, the landlord later succeeds in getting this assessment reduced, with the result that this year's tax — that is, the base amount — is less than the tenant had in mind. Thus, there will be a larger spread between the first and second year's taxes, and, to make things worse, the landlord will have less inducement to try to reduce taxes after the major burden has been passed on to the tenant.

The landlord is apparently under no legal duty to seek a reduction in this situation. He may sell out to a purchaser who in good faith believes that the tax base is the amount of the first year's taxes, as finally determined.

Tax base   There would be no such problem if the tax base were specified in a dollar amount — for example, if the tenant were to pay any increase above $1,000 per year. This is not feasible, however, in the case of new construction, when neither party knows the amount of a future tax assessment.

The tax base should be so defined as to allow for its adjustment in the case of additional construction by the landlord. If the landlord builds additional stores in a shopping center, a tax increase will follow. This is not the sort of increase a tenant should pay. The same is true when a landlord adds stories to an urban structure.

There is a possibility — or so chain tenants fear — that local bias may result in comparatively low taxes during the first, or base year, when the owner pays them, with substantial increases thereafter when the tenants pay. For this reason, some tenants prefer to make the tax base the average of, for example, the first three years' taxes.

Operating expenses

In city buildings, escalation clauses are apt to be based not only on increased taxes, but on increased costs of building operation — for example, increased wages of the cleaning and elevator employees. A store tenant that does not receive these services may well take the position that it should not be asked to pay for any of these increases.

An escalation clause used in this situation should be sufficiently flexible to allow for changes in building operation.

When a landlord converts elevators from manual to automatic operation, the wages of elevator operators will be eliminated. If these wages are, inflexibly, one of the items constituting the escalation base, their elimination will ruin the landlord's right to escalate, despite the fact that the conversion entailed a substantial investment.

This has been handled by adding to the annual cost of operation a sum equal to four per cent of the cost of installing some labor-saving device, but not in excess of the annual saving in cost of labor thereby effected.

Occupancy as factor   If there is less than full occupancy during the base year, the operating expenses of that year will not constitute a fair base. Incomplete occupancy thereafter will fail to evidence full escalation.

These can be corrected by adding a sum appropriate to reflect full occupancy. These and other problems are worked out well in the clause set forth in Form 3.

FORM 3 —
RENT ESCALATION CLAUSE

(a) The Tenant shall pay to the Landlord as rent, in legal tender, at the Landlord's office in the Building or as directed from time to time by the Landlord's notice, the annual sum or sums (hereinafter called "the Rent") of $ _____ , payable in equal monthly payments of $ _____ each, in advance promptly on the first day of each calendar month of the term. (b) It is understood that the Rent specified in Paragraph (a) does not anticipate any increase or decrease in the amount of taxes on the Property or in the cost of operations and maintenance thereof. Therefore, in order that the rental payable throughout the term of the lease shall reflect any such increase or decrease, the parties agree as hereinafter in this section set forth. Certain terms are defined as follows:

Building rentable area: The total number of square feet of rentable floor area of office and store space in the Building.

Tenant's share: The amount of the tenant's pro rata share of the increase or decrease, as the case may be, in Taxes and Operating Expenses over the Base Year for Taxes and Base Year for Operating Expenses, all as hereinafter defined. The Tenant's Share is agreed to be _____ per cent of such increase or decrease.

Base year for taxes: The first full calendar year of the term of this lease in which at least 50 per cent of the Building Rentable Area is occupied by tenants and real estate taxes have been payable to the City of _____ based on an assessment of the Building as complete.

Base year for operating expenses: The first full calendar year of the term of this lease during which at least 50 per cent of the Building Rentable Area is occupied by tenants.

Taxes: (i) All real estate taxes, payable (adjusted after protest or litigation, if any) for any part of the term of this lease, exclusive of penalties or discounts, on the Property; (ii) any taxes that shall be levied in lieu of any such taxes; (iii) any special assessments for benefits on the Property (except any payable in whole or in part during the Base Year for Taxes), which, for purposes of this lease, shall be deemed payable in 10 equal annual installments, whether or not actually so payable; and (iv) the expense of contesting the amount or validity of any such taxes, charges, or assessments, such expense to be applicable to the period of the item contested. If during any calendar year, including the Base Year for Taxes, the assessed value of the Property shall be lower than otherwise due to the fact that any part of the Building is not occupied or because finishing work in rentable areas has not been completed, said real estate taxes payable or paid, as used in clause (i) of this paragraph and in Paragraph (c) of this section, shall be deemed to be the amount calculated as though such assessed value had not been so lower.

Operating expenses: Those expenses (including the premiums for all kinds of insurance carried by the Landlord, except insurance against the loss of rents) incurred or paid on behalf of the Landlord in respect of the operation and maintenance of the Property, which, in accordance with accepted principles of sound accounting practice used by the Landlord, as applied to the operation and maintenance of first class office buildings, are properly chargeable to the operation and maintenance of the Property, and the cost, as reasonably amortized by the Landlord, with interest at the rate of four per cent per annum on the unamortized amount, of any capital improvement made after the Base Year for Operating Expenses which reduces other Operating Expenses, but in an amount not to exceed such reduction for the relevant year. Operating Expenses shall not include: (i) franchise or income taxes imposed on the Landlord; (ii) interior painting in tenant spaces; and (iii) the cost of any work or service performed in any instance for any tenant (including the Tenant) at the cost of such tenant.

In determining the amount of Operating Expenses for the purpose of this section, either for the Base Year for Operating Expenses or for any subsequent year, (1) if less than 100 per cent of the Building Rentable Area shall have been occupied by tenants and fully used by them, at any time during the year, Operating Expenses shall be deemed for the purposes of this section to be increased to an amount equal to the like operating expense which would normally be expected to be incurred had such occupancy been 100 per cent and had such full utilization been made during the entire period, or (2) if the Landlord is not furnishing any particular work or service (the cost of which if performed by the Landlord would constitute an Operating Expense) to a tenant who has undertaken to perform such work or service in lieu of the performance thereof by the Landlord, Operating Expenses shall be deemed for the purposes of this section to be increased by an amount equal to the additional Operating Expense that would reasonably have been incurred during such period by the Landlord if it had at its own expense furnished such work or service to such tenant.

(c) Not later than the 31st day of March (or within a reasonable time thereafter) in the first year following the Base Year for Taxes and the Base Year for Operating Expenses, in each year thereafter during the term of this lease, and in the year following the year in which the lease terminates, the Landlord shall deliver to the Tenant a statement setting forth the amount of Taxes payable or paid by the Landlord and Operating Expenses paid or incurred by the Landlord during the immediately preceding calendar year and, except in the case of the statement for the Base Years, comparable figures for the Base Years. Within 30 days after the delivery of such statement, other than the one for the Base Years, the Tenant shall pay to the Landlord as Additional Rent (if the statement indicates an increase in Taxes and Operating Expenses) or the Landlord shall pay to the Tenant (if the statement indicates a decrease) the Tenant's Share. If the Base Year for Taxes and the Base Year for Operating Expenses shall be different, the foregoing provisions of this paragraph shall apply only to the earlier, until the later occurs. If the term of this lease ends on other than the last day of a year, the Tenant's Share shown on the statement delivered after the end of the term shall be reduced proportionately and paid as aforesaid or, at the Landlord's option and upon 30 days notice by the Landlord, at the end of the term the Tenant shall pay as Additional Rent, or receive from the Landlord, an appropriate proportion of the Tenant's Share for the immediately preceding year.

(d) If tenants of 55 per cent of the Building Rentable Area shall request the Landlord in writing to protest any real estate assessment imposed on the Property during the term of this Lease and execute and file a petition with the Court having jurisdiction for a review thereof, Landlord, at such tenants' expense (to be deducted from any saving in taxes, otherwise to be reimbursed to the Landlord as Additional Rent), shall duly institute such proceeding, and shall diligently prosecute such proceeding to final determination, accept a settlement, or discontinue such proceeding, as directed by a majority (in terms of rental area) of such requesting tenants.

[Taken from lease prepared for an office building in Chicago of the Equitable Life Assurance Society of the United States, and made available through the courtesy of Howard E. Thomas, Vice President and Associate General Solicitor.]

Competing neighbors

It is not easy to discuss restrictions of tenants' competing uses and to try to decide, for instance, whether a restriction against a restaurant is violated by a luncheonette or if "separates" are the same as two-piece dresses.

Some useful articles on the subject include the following: Sturtevant, *Restrictive Covenants in Shopping Center Leases*, 34 N.Y.U.L.Rev. 940 (1959); *Lessor's Covenants Restricting Competition: Drafting Problems*, 63 Harv.L.Rev. 1400 (1950); Annot., 97 A.L.R.2d 4-135 (1964).

It is clear that about every large tenant wants to branch out for himself and to restrict somebody else. Supermarkets want to sell nonfoods and junior department stores want to sell foods. Supermarkets and drug stores are tending to become discount houses, and many tenants want to bar discount houses.

A provision barring discount houses is enforceable.

Compromises among tenants

The struggle is not so much with the landlords as between the tenants themselves. Each generally has to give a little.

The supermarket may agree that the junior department store can use up to 10 per cent of its space for the less profitable foods — canned meats, beans, and the like, but nothing fresh. The supermarkets may waive as to a delicatessen, a fish market, or a candy store selling for off-premises consumption.

The junior department store may agree to the supermarket's use of a specified percentage of its space for the sale of nonfoods, but may try to limit this to a few items and to bar an entire department.

It is generally agreed that supermarkets may sell the nonfood items they customarily sell — such as soap and soap products, detergents, paper napkins, facial and toilet tissues, floor wax, wax paper, matches, and tobacco products. In fact, these items have occasionally been referred to by grocery chains as "food".

Shopping-center leases

Common areas

A tenant going into a shopping center will probably be asked to pay a share of the cost of maintaining the common areas. He may be adamant against this.

He is not renting a free-standing store but a part of a shopping center, which includes common areas. That is what his rent is for. Why pay for it twice?

Nevertheless, he usually pays the charges. Sometimes he succeeds in placing a ceiling on what he pays — such as five cents for each foot of his floor space per year. Sometimes the amount he pays is credited against the percentage rent he earns.

In small shopping centers, the landlord's claimed charges for common areas may not be well substantiated. There is rarely an accountant permanently connected with the center. Trying to audit these charges may be a frustrating experience.

As a practical matter, it may be adequate to see that no charges for supervisors or executives are included and that the items charged — which might include such things as flowers and shrubbery — bear some reasonable relation to the legitimate purposes involved.

Combined attraction of customers

The distinguishing feature of a shopping center is that it is not a free-standing store or a cluster of free-standing stores, and that if one takes a free-standing store and merely adds a parking area and other facilities, it is still not a shopping center. A shopping center is, in essence, an ensemble of many stores, with their combined pulling power.

A prospective shopping-center tenant should not want to be bound to any shopping-center lease without assurance that this ensemble is in existence or, if not, that it will come into existence. It is equally important that it continue as such.

The ordinary lease of a free-standing store generally makes some provision with respect to fire or other damage and with respect to possible condemnation. These provisions relate to the leased store only.

In a shopping center, you should contemplate the possibility of fire or condemnation that has no effect on your client's store alone, but which may remove some of the other stores and to this extent destroy the ensemble. It is conceivable, though not likely, that condemnation will pass all the stores by and take only the parking area.

Withdrawal of major tenant Suppose your client is a little fellow who takes a lease in a shopping center — for which he must invest his all, plus borrowings from others. In the center there is a large department store, which is expected to draw customers for your client.

What if the department store decides to discontinue its operation? The little fellow may think of this possibility, but he may have some difficulty in getting the landlord to put something in the lease about it.

A clause of this nature was construed in *Lilac Variety, Inc. v. Dallas Texas Co.* [383 S.W.2d 193 (Tex.Civ.App. 1964)], in which a landlord had agreed that certain major tenants "shall remain as tenants and located as per proposed location on Exhibit C," for breach of which the named tenant was empowered to cancel.

A major tenant discontinued its business, but left its fixtures and continued paying rent. The named tenant was held justified in canceling, on the ground that, although the major tenant had "remained," the condition

could be satisfied by nothing short of active business.

Description of premises

The description of the premises in a shopping-center lease should include more than the demised store, because the tenant's rights extend beyond the store. These rights include the use in common of access roads and parking areas. If the tenant has a right to an exclusive use, this right affects the entire shopping center, and all other tenants should be put on notice of this right.

A tenant who is without notice of a restriction in favor of another tenant is not bound thereby.

Some shopping centers have been sold in parcels to different purchasers. In this situation, recordation of a lease against the demised premises alone may be ineffective to give notice to purchasers and other tenants, in those jurisdictions where recordation is constructive notice only of instruments recorded in the direct chain of title.

Accordingly, it is advisable for a tenant to place an instrument on record that by metes and bounds or plot plan, or both, shows the demised store, the common areas, and the entire shopping center.

QUESTIONS

1. How can the tenant protect himself against the landlord's nonperformance?

2. When should the prospective tenant reject a proposed lease?

Now for a less legal look at shopping center leases.

Clauses in a shopping center lease

Benjamin Pollack†

The shopping center space lease of today is quite different from the lease of even 10 years ago. There have been changes in the attitudes and philosophy of the developer and in the techniques and practices of development, operation, and financing — and some added income tax considerations that have come into play.

The landlord-tenant relationship

Negotiating a shopping center space lease is in some respects like, and in many respects unlike, the negotiation of a commercial space lease in a multitenant project. The shopping center is a very different animal from the office building, and the goal and problems of the owner are entirely different. The tenants in a shopping center are all retail merchants banded together with a common purpose.

†Benjamin Pollack, *The Practical Lawyer*, May 1970, Volume 16, No. 5, pp. 31-44.

Reprinted with permission of *The Practical Lawyer*, 4025 Chestnut Street, Philadelphia, Pa. 19104. Subscription rates: $12 a year; $2 a single issue.

Complicating the whole structure is the position of the implacable mortgage lender, who must perforce fix the framework within which the parties must negotiate. Further complications arise if there is a ground lease and a "subordination" of the fee to the leasehold mortgage. The space tenant seeks to be assured that his lease will survive a foreclosure sale or a termination of the ground lease.

Bargaining position

The bargaining position of the department store tenant, the well-rated tenant who occupies a small unit, and the satellite tenant depends on the desirability of the tenant for the purposes of the shopping center — that is, its public image and "pulling power" (its ability to generate sales, its net worth for mortgage borrowing purposes, and, to a lesser extent, its place in the "tenant mix"). Another factor is the stage of the developer's progress at the time of negotiating.

Major tenants The leases of the department stores and other major tenants present a picture quite different from those of the smaller shops (sometimes called "line tenants" or "satellite tenants"). In making a lease, the major tenant is in the dominant position and the developer is usually in the position of anguish.

The major tenants dictate the essential planning of the center, often pass on the esthetics, reserve the right to pass on some tenancies, and lay down the requirements and limitations for its development, the conditions to the commencement of the term and the liability for rent. Their rents are low — sometimes nominal — and not infrequently the developer loses money on their space just to get them into the center, impart the necessary prestige, and attract the satellite tenants who pay high rents and provide the developer with his profits.

The lease of a major tenant affords him certain protections that reduce his risks to a minimum. He is in a position, which the smaller tenants are not, to cut his losses if the center turns out badly. He can usually close up shop and let the premises remain idle, though he is obligated to pay the minimum guaranteed rent for the balance of the term. He is also permitted to sublease the premises.

Satellite tenants The middle-sized and satellite tenants are, of course, in a much less comfortable position. They pay a high price for the venturesomeness of the developer who furnishes the marketplace they need to carry on their businesses.

They have no say in the planning or development of the center. They can lay down no enforcible conditions to the commencement of the terms or their liability for rent.

The developer's lease forms usually offer them few protective provisions. They take the risk that the center will turn out well and are in no position to cut their losses if things go bad; they cannot assign their leases or sublet the premises.

They are obligated to remain in occupancy throughout the term and "continuously operate" the store, come hell or high water, and fully staff and stock the store and attempt to do a "maximum volume of business."

An outline of lease clauses

This article will present a brief outline of some of the clauses that are commonly found in shopping center leases of satellite tenants. It will also indicate, in passing, a few of the issues and problems that may arise during the negotiation or administration of these clauses.

Use of lease form in general

The developer should have a printed form suitable to the center and should try to keep his store leases as uniform as is practicable. The developer invariably presents a landlord-oriented form. Some tenants of smaller space have their own forms, and their success in getting acceptance depends on their desirability as tenants and on the landlord's need.

Courts have recently shown a tendency to give the tenant a break if he signed a tough lease form, especially if it was done without consulting a lawyer. Therefore, landlords should encourage tenants to see lawyers; it will help if the lease ever gets into court.

Variations Variations from the printed form in many cases are inevitable. These must be worked out individually in the framework of the tenant mix, the financing requirements, and the leasing program. Landlord should keep an accurate chart of individual variations from the standard form.

Major tenants have their own lease form requirements. These are onerous and hard for the developer to accept; the lender does not usually accept them without change or without side agreements. Early leases must be worked out carefully to avoid freezing developer's planning for the future.

The developer's form and special forms of chains should be submitted to the lender before signing.

The lease often provides for changes required by lender after execution. In providing safeguards for tenant in this clause, keep it all "reasonable" — say that it will not cut down his rights or increase his burdens or the risk of losing his leasehold estate.

Description of store premises

If the shopping center is yet to be built, refer to the "store to be erected" at the location shown on an attached site plan. Attach the legal description of shopping center shown on the site plan as separate exhibit. This is useful when the lease provides for restriction of competition and in connection with a radius clause.

The dimensions and area of each store should be "approximate" — "to centers of side walls" and "to outside of front and rear walls." If a basement, describe the dimensions and location as approximate and refer to a sketch, if possible.

Right to use common areas

The tenant will naturally object to having only a "revocable license" to use common areas; he wants the right to use common areas as an appurtenance to the lease.

There is no reason why he should not have this. The limitation found in some leases goes further than necessary in order to preserve landlord's right to change the site plan.

Reservation of landlord's rights

The landlord prefers not to include the land under the store in the demise.

The landlord seeks to reserve right to use land under the store (for tunnels, conduits, sewers, and so forth). The landlord wants to exclude roof and outer walls from the demise and to reserve right to build upwards (that is, the use of "air rights").

The site plan

The site plan should be based on an engineer's survey and show the entire intended layout of roads, buildings, parking and other facilities. If the center has two levels, it should show both. However, it need not show the location of other tenants unless necessary to carry out lease provisions.

The landlord's lease form will provide that the site plan and location of the tenant and other stores are subject to change — that additional buildings may be erected, additional stories or basements added, and the location of access roads and common areas shifted. This will be resisted by the tenant.

Limitations on changes Compromise, if feasible. State that changes:

- Will not be substantial;
- Will not reduce parking space below a given ratio or minimum number;
- Will not interfere with the visibility of the store or access to it;
- Will not permit any store front to project beyond others; and
- Will not result in more than a small lateral shift of tenant's store or change the tenant's location relative to certain major tenants or to the entrance to the mall.

Construction of center and store premises

The landlord usually does not affirmatively covenant to build the shopping center or even to erect the building that will contain the store. The tenant, however, may ask for such a covenant. Most developers will only say that, if the shopping center is not complete by an outside date, the tenant may cancel the lease.

Turnkey; shell and allowance

Landlord will covenant to build the store premises, either on a "turnkey" or "shell and allowance" basis. Under the turnkey arrangement, the landlord erects the whole store, the tenant furnishes drawings for the layout and fixture plan (subject to landlord's approval), and the landlord does everything to enable the store to receive trade fixtures.

Under a shell-and-allowance arrangement, the landlord builds a "shell" and the tenant does the rest of the construction and finishing work.

An "allowance" is made by the landlord to the tenant for the doing of the work, usually a fixed amount calculated at so much per square foot (varying from about $2 to about $10 or more, depending upon the circumstances), which is payable when the lease starts. Payment is conditioned on satisfying landlord that tenant's work complies with the requirements of the lease, particularly the work letter (see below). The allowance is usually less than the actual cost to the tenant.

Under a shell-and-allowance arrangement, the lease contains "work letters," describing in prose the work to be done separately by each of the parties. The landlord usually furnishes only the roof, the studs for side walls, a partial back wall, and in some cases the floor slab.

The landlord furnishes to the tenant the basic building plan; the tenant draws plans for "finishing work" and submits them to landlord for approval. The tenant's work would include floor slab, walls, ceiling, store front, air-conditioning, electrical, plumbing, hung ceiling, distribution of utilities, and so forth.

Work letters

Lawyers too often ignore the work letters in drafting or reading the lease. Architects who draw the work letter often insert substantive provisions that bind the parties (often without their realizing it) — such as allocating expenses of certain work, providing for consents, indemnifications, insurance, and so forth.

Tenant's lawyer should become familiar with the contents of the work letter. He must learn to detect those items that may involve greater expense than was contemplated.

Other matters that may be covered are: insurance and indemnification during tenant's work; performance bond; endorsement to tenant's liability insurance; waivers and releases from contractors and subcontractors; "compatible" labor clause; and delivery of the certificate of occupancy.

Tenant's counsel should be sure that the construction contract calls for the delivery of waivers and other matters required in the work letter. He should know in advance how to fulfill all the conditions to payment of the allowance. He should familiarize himself with the practices of waiving and releasing mechanic's liens in the jurisdiction. (For example, can the general contractor waive or release the mechanic's lien of a subcontractor without an express provision in the subcontract?)

In practice, "shell and allowance" often results in delays in completion —

sometimes making impossible a simultaneous grand opening — that are often hard to control. Delays often occur in agreeing on plans.

Notices to begin work are sometimes too early. There may be many separate contractors at work, usually with no coordination.

Commencement of lease

When the shopping center is in existence and the lease will commence upon expiration of an existing lease to another tenant, a specific commencement date should be inserted. The landlord usually disclaims liability for the refusal of existing tenant to remove in time to give possession to new tenant. In some jurisdictions, the burden may be on the landlord to remove the old tenant, and the landlord may try to put the obligation on the new tenant.

When the center is not complete, some leases start their term immediately on signing and have an ascertainable date for the beginning of rent. This creates a leasehold estate immediately on signing, sometimes even before the developer has acquired his own title. It is preferable to have lease term and the rent obligation start together.

The commencement date should be keyed to the earlier of:

• Date of opening by tenant; or

• X days (30 to 90, depending on whether it is a turnkey or a shell-and-allowance arrangement) after notice from the owner that the store is ready for tenant's work. This gives tenant time to build or fixture if the landlord's work will not slow him up.

Conditions

The tenant should be bound by all the terms of the lease, except rent, from the time it starts its work. The tenant may ask to be relieved of "indemnification" and "insurance" clauses until it enters to do any work.

The tenant should agree to defer opening, at landlord's request, to permit one or more joint openings.

The tenant may ask for conditions to the obligation to open and to the commencement of the lease term, some of which are contained in the leases of major tenants — for example:

• That one or more major tenants have noncancellable leases for 10 or more years and will be open or will open simultaneously with tenant;

• That stores with x percent of gross leaseable area also open;

• That shopping center be substantially complete;

• That parking meets a given standard; that storm drainage and parking lot lighting are adequate; and

• That a certificate of occupancy has been issued for the building.

Some tenants also want assurance that one or more major tenants' leases require them to remain open for at least 10 years.

Reluctance of landlord Although these conditions may be fair enough, landlords shy away from them and will not or cannot make the representations. Some landlords, without making any representations, will allow tenant to appraise the risk by showing him the other leases or an operating agreement, though most will refuse to do that.

From the landlord's standpoint, any representations of existence of length of leases of major tenants must be carefully drawn to avoid the implication that major tenants are obligated to conduct business in the center throughout tenant's term. If the lease does not disclaim such implication, there is danger in making the representation.

The landlord will ask for the right to cancel if he cannot get satisfactory financing or is prevented from building the center for causes beyond his reasonable control.

Tenant's opening

The tenant should be given enough time to fixture. A 30-days' notice is enough for smaller stores. In a shell-and-allowance deal the tenant is given 90 days or more to build his part of the store; the fixturing time is added to that.

Some tenants with seasonal business may ask to defer necessity of opening in slack season or if new merchandise cannot be bought until later. Some landlords go along, depending on the facts of each case. Some tenants will not open until another named tenant opens.

Construction deadlines

Often the landlord's only covenant is to build the "leased premises," the access roads, and so forth, "as shown on Exhibit A" (the site plan). Beyond this, there might be no covenants to build the center or the buildings.

The tenant may ask for some deadlines:

• Completion of foundations;

• Completion of the shopping center;

• Completion of the demised premises; or

• Opening of the shopping center.

The tenant will want the right to cancel if any deadlines are not met. The deadlines are liberal and are not usually refused.

Additional charges

Common area expenses

Common areas should be defined, and each tenant should pay a proportionate share of the cost of their operation and maintenance. Sometimes this will be a fixed square-foot charge; sometimes it will have an escalation provision based on the consumers' price index.

The proportion is usually the relation of tenant's square-foot area to gross leasable area in the shopping center, but sometimes is based on the ratio of tenant's square-foot area to square-foot area of all *occupied* space. Under the latter, the landlord does not absorb the shares of the vacant stores. Other formulas are also used for apportioning tenant's fair share.

It is better to specify items of expense that go into common area costs — for example, heating, air-conditioning, lighting and maintaining closed malls, cleaning, fire protection, snow removal, rubbish removal, landscape maintenance and supplies, cost of utilities, liability insurance premiums, wages of those employed in maintenance, and workmen's compensation. Capital expenditures should be excluded. A question may arise about including landlord's office expense.

Some landlords include depreciation on equipment, personal property taxes, and real estate taxes on parking areas. There should be a separate tax bill for the parking area. Avoid conflict with the general real estate tax escalation clause, to avoid payment of same tax twice. Some leases have maximums.

Annual statements are sometimes given showing the aggregate costs and each tenant's share. Each tenant should be given the right to examine records. The landlord will want to avoid the necessity of accounting for receipts and expenditures.

Tax escalation

Mortgagees insist on a tax escalation clause. Thus, leases seek to require all tenants to share in increases in taxes on the center.

The tenant's arguments are that taxes are normally the landlord's burden; that the tenant should not have an "open-end" rent expense; and that the percentage rent takes care of inflation. Most tenants must nevertheless pay it, and major tenants deduct payments from percentage rent.

Some also require tenants to share assessments for public improvements. Are these paid by tenants apart from real estate taxes? Are they added to amount of taxes? Are they spread over years in installments? Will an assessment in the first year add to the base year tax, thus helping the tenants?

Usual tax increase provisions require tenant to pay a "proportionate share" (as defined) of the *increase* in real estate taxes on the mall building and the land on which it stands, over the taxes in a "base year" (as defined). The entire tax (not just an increase) on the parking area is paid by the tenants in proportionate shares as an expense of the operation of the common areas.

Proportionate Share Who bears the burden of the tax increase otherwise to be borne by the tenants who would occupy vacant mall space?

The problem is the same as in the common area expense sharing. Other "fair share" formulas refer to the ratio of the value of the store to the value of all buildings or the ratio of tenant's rent payments to the aggregate rents paid in the center.

Problems of apportionment also arise out of the failure to obtain separate tax bills for the parking area, mall buildings, and space rented to a major tenant who has a net lease and pays the entire tax on his store and the land it stands on. Sometimes the tax assessor will show his work sheets with the breakdowns. Otherwise there is no feasible way to make the breakdown.

Base year Usually the "base year" is the first year in which the shopping center is assessed as completed. Some centers are not completed for years. Some tenants ask that the base year be the average of the first three or five full years.

Other problems include the situation where there is an unreasonably low base year (resulting from a negotiated assessment for the first year) and the need for weighting basement, mezzanine, and second-floor space in calculating leasable area.

Tenant's payment In some leases, the tenant's percentage rent payments reduce the tax increase payable by him. The lease should say whether the percentage rent must be earned in the period for which tax accrues—with no spillover into other years. Problems of drafting an accurate clause arise if the lease year and the tax year are not identical.

When the increase in tax on the center is because of tenant improvements, the tenant should pay. Personal property taxes of tenants are sometimes found in the real estate tax bill.

This formula for sharing tax increases recently came into use: tenant pays any tax over x cents per square foot. It has good and bad features. This and most other formulas ignore tax increases for later additions to the center.

Operation of stores

Use clause

In the "use" clause it is advisable to say: "Tenant *may* use the premises *only* for the sale of ..." Try to be specific and narrow in describing business. Where possible, spell out items of merchandise. Add: "and for no other purpose."

Avoid generalities like "TV store," "men's shop," "shoe store," "restaurant," "supermarket," "drug store," and so forth. If possible, use expressions like: "sale of misses' and ladies' sport dresses, evening dresses, coats (excluding fur coats), lingerie, hosiery, handbags, in the popular price range"; and "self-service sale of foods for off-premises consumption, not cooked or otherwise prepared at the premises."

Limit the size of space used in a food market for nonfood items. Do not use "restaurant" when counter service or self-service is intended. Exclude "children's wear" from ready-to-wear, unless the intention is otherwise.

Restrictions against competition

Parties are slowly getting away from "exclusives" or "restrictions," though they are still a large problem. The landlord seeks to avoid expressions like, "Landlord covenants not to permit any other tenant to sell ...," but wants to draw the clause in terms of landlord's agreement not to "lease any space in shopping center to a tenant whose main business ..."

These clauses must allow for overlapping of merchandise. For example, a supermarket should agree to the sale by others of baked goods, kosher foods, seafood specialties, baby foods, dietetic foods, and so forth; a candy store should permit the sale of loose candies and candy bars, but may limit the sale of based candies to a maximum size rack or counter; and a drug store should permit others to sell aspirin and other drugs not requiring prescriptions.

The courts look at actual competition rather than words to determine the extent of enforceable restriction on merchandise carried. Try not to cut out competition altogether, but limit the size and number of competing stores.

The tenant may be satisfied with eliminating a specified chain from the center, but it is better to avoid this technique — since there is no certainty that the courts will not hold that it violates antitrust laws. In a small center, try for later elimination of exclusives if the center is enlarged.

Radius clause

The tenant's opening another store within three or five miles of the outer boundaries of the shopping center is usually prohibited. The tenant, however, will ask for an exception as to any existing store. In response, the landlord may require that tenant not enlarge the existing store or renew the existing lease.

The tenant may ask for exclusion of a store in a downtown shopping area within the radius or a store within the radius under another name.

Should the landlord forbid advertising that mentions the locations of other stores of the tenant and shifting of personnel to other stores? How about advertising other stores of tenant by signs in the interior or on sales checks, packages, shopping bags, and delivery trucks? Some landlords insert a clause forbidding referral of customers by sales personnel to other locations of tenant.

Signs

The landlord should retain control over the design and appearance of store-front signs. Tenant will want an individual style of lettering. Usually they can agree on drawings and specifications at the time of signing of the lease, making elaborate lease provisions unnecessary. Limited rights, if any, might be granted for such items as roof signs, pylons, and paper strips on windows.

Continuous operation

One of the most important clauses in the lease is the requirement of continuous operation. The tenant may not cease the conduct of his business. Store hours may be designated as per the tenants' Merchants' Association or equal to the hours of a given department store.

The lease usually requires six days' operation a week, with no closing except for certain national and religious holidays (perhaps stating a maximum number every 12 months). Tenants will object to a covenant to do the "maximum possible gross sales" and will want to be excused for causes beyond their control.

The landlord usually asks for a "complete" stock of merchandise; a full staff of employees at all times; minimum advertising; inventory taking at overtime expense; or diligent prosecution of business.

Major tenants ask for and usually get the right to discontinue and pay minimum rent (or average of total annual rent theretofore paid) at any time, or, in some cases, after five years. Is there an implied obligation to remain in business and in good faith to try to build up sales? "Good faith" is often the test in permitting tenant to discontinue or to compete with itself.

Parking areas

Should landlord give guaranties of minimum parking? Such a clause may specify a given number of cars regardless of gross leasable area, a ratio of number of cars (usually 5.5 as a minimum) to each 1,000 square feet of gross leasable area, or a number of square feet in the parking lot to the number of rentable square feet in the center (often expressed as three to one, 2½ to one, and so forth).

The clause might contain ratios for office building and nonretail space needing parking. Restrictions on tenant and employee parking might be enforced by fine — x per day — per car. Other items may include rules and regulations governing parking; the right to charge, by meter or otherwise, and give tenant right to validate free parking tickets; and the right to close off the parking lot to prevent easement by the public.

The tenant may ask for landlord's express obligation to maintain parking areas—which is not always included in lease form. The language in the lease sometimes carefully skirts the positive expression of the obligation by saying that the tenant may have the use of such facilities as the landlord may furnish from time to time, and giving the landlord the *right*, for example, to install lighting in the common areas.

Merchant's association

Require each tenant to join a Merchant's Association. If this organization must be newly created, such questions must be decided as the form of entity (corporation or association), the voting rights formula, the assessment formula, and the tenants' maximum liability.

The landlord should be able to tell the tenant what form it will take. Some leases have organization papers attached. Be sure that the association makes no profit. Some developers contribute up to one third of the annual budget or a percentage of what the tenants contribute.

There are other questions. Who receives dues — the landlord or the association? Is this a contract for the benefit of a third party? Is failure to pay a breach of the lease? This is generally held "yes," depending on the wording. Some tenants want a maximum on the annual dues and on the assessment for the grand opening.

Destruction of premises

Damage and destruction by fire

Landlord should restore after damage or destruction if the loss is an insurable one or a minor one; otherwise, he should have the option not to restore, in which event the lease should terminate, ipso facto, on the giving of landlord's notice of election, as of the date of damage, and prepaid rent returned to tenant. If there is extensive damage in the last two or three years of the term (or of last extended term) either party should have the right to cancel.

Extent of damage can be measured by ability of tenant to conduct its business. There should be an equitable reduction in rent during the work of repair, depending on the duration and extent of the inability to conduct business in the normal manner. A dispute on this should go to arbitration.

Where the original construction was under a shell-and-allowance arrangement, should landlord and tenant each rebuild its part? This depends on who carries the insurance. Should landlord, or tenant, or both have option to cancel the lease if a substantial part of shopping center is destroyed without being rebuilt? A clause covering that matter should be submitted to the lender, who abhors cancellations.

Parties should bear in mind statutes that may give tenant the right to surrender in case of severe damage, unless the lease provides otherwise.

Condemnation

The lease should say that upon a total (or almost total) taking it will terminate on the date of title vesting.

Should either party have the right to terminate if there is a partial taking of tenant's store, or if there is a taking of a substantial part of the shopping center? This depends on the extent to which the tenant's store premises are or are not reasonably useable for tenant's business and the extent to which the center has been reduced.

The lender is important at this point because he abhors cancellation. Most lenders will permit cancellation if 20 per cent or more of the parking area is taken, or if enough of the store is taken to render the premises not reasonably useable for the tenant's business.

If the lease is not canceled, landlord should at its expense restore the premises to an architectural unit adapted to tenant's business, and the tenant should have a reduction in rent from the time of the taking, either on a proportionate bases (ratio of floor area taken to original floor area) or on the new appraised rental value of the premises.

Tenant gets no award except the unamortized value of leasehold improvements to the extent landlord has not paid for them, and except statutory awards for loss of fixtures, moving expenses, and other awards that do not cut into landlord's award.

Clauses of interest to mortgage lender

The mortgagee's requirements must be kept in mind during negotiations with tenants. The mortgagee contemplates the problems arising out of a foreclosure sale and envisions itself a possible future owner or ground lessee of the center.

It therefore is watchful for landlord's covenants for breach of which tenant may be excused from paying rent or may rescind the lease, and for remedies given tenants that may impair the steady flow of rental income or the strength of the security.

Troublesome clauses

Here are some of the clauses the mortgagee worries about:

• Self-help clauses that give tenant the right to cure landlord's default and recoup the cost out of minimum rent (but this is permissible if taken out of percentage rent).

• Any clause giving tenant the right to cancel the lease, surrender premises, or suspend payment of rent. (Exceptions: destruction or eminent domain in certain circumstances where

insurance proceeds and condemnation awards reduce the lender's risk.)

• Clauses that give tenants "exclusives" or which limit competition. (If breached, they may in some circumstances give rise to the right to cancel.)

• Clauses restricting competition on land owned by the landlord outside the shopping center. (This limits possible future activity of mortgagee as to such other property.)

• Clauses requiring or giving tenant right to make improvements for which he is to be reimbursed by landlord, or requiring landlord to do the work (such as future expansion of the store).

• Security deposit clauses that give tenant protection against failure to return deposit. This may in some cases constitute a lien on the center superior to the mortgage. Tenant in some leases gets an extended term with free rent to use up the unpaid security deposit. There is a possible obligation of mortgagee or purchaser at foreclosure sale to pay back the security deposit.)

• Option to purchase the center. Lessee's purchase of the fee may merge lease with fee and destroy lease considered valuable to mortgagee. In some states an option is an "encumbrance" preventing a regulated lender from making a first mortgage loan.

• Clauses committing landlord to use insurance proceeds to restore building, regardless of their adequacy.

• Condemnation provisions giving tenant the right to cancel lease or failing to deprive tenant of right to share in the condemnation award.

• Clauses committing landlord to restore after partial condemnation, regardless of adequacy of award.

• Subordination clauses. In some states, the mortgagee is better off being subordinate to the lease rather than having the lease surbordinate to it. Reason: a foreclosure in some states will have the effect of cutting off the lease, whether or not the mortgagee wants it to, unless lease is superior. But attornment and an agreement to accept the attornment may cure the problem in most cases.

✻

QUESTIONS

1. What are the pros and cons of a turn-key lease versus a shell-and-allowance one?

II

FINANCING THE
ENTERPRISE

Many people maintain that financing the enterprise is unquestionably the most important part of the undertaking, for unless the money is available nothing will happen. This may be an overstatement. In one recent book about new enterprises entitled *Fun and Guts*[1] the author makes his observations with the assumption that the entrepreneur is starting out with

[1]Joseph Mancuso, *Fun & Guts – The Entrepreneur's Philosophy* (Reading, Mass., Addison-Wesley, 1973).

about $250,000 capital and is manufacturing some new product. The model that he has in mind perhaps fits one new enterprise in 10,000. It is a rare item in the scheme of things. Few new enterprises will have available to them a quarter of a million dollars — nor should they, for they usually don't need that much money. Indeed, Bob Teller, an entrepreneur whose feats will be described later, stoutly maintains that the shrewd enterpriser only goes into ventures that require little or no capital. There is great truth to what he says. There are many enterprises that don't require much money. It is strongly suggested that such avenues be sought, for risks are thereby minimized. One can do many things when he doesn't stand to lose much money doing them. One might be tempted to add, "Yes, but aren't the profits also limited in such enterprises?" Not necessarily. Teller has an investment of about $6,000 in each of his ice cream stores, certainly a minimal amount that normally can be raised without tapping the professional money market. But he got into business on much less than that. True, operating on such a shoe string may limit one's growth rate and scope of activities, but such enterprises can still be surprisingly rewarding and furnish the entrepreneur with a good living.

The advantages of using one's own money are tremendous. When a person uses his own funds he escapes the problems that plague those who use other people's money. Much time is spent on investor relationships, to the detriment of operating the business. Many times control of enterprises is lost when investors become dissatisfied with the way things are being managed. Moreover, as long as a person is using his own money, charges of fraud, misrepresentation, embezzlement, and all of the other nasty aspects of using other people's money are avoided. Stockholder relationships in small, closed corporations are extremely volatile, to say the least. Conflict of interest arises because the investor wants to take money from the business while management wants the funds on which to operate and grow.

DETERMINING
FINANCIAL NEEDS

15

Quite early in the enterprise the operator must formulate some estimates of how much money will be needed to do what it is he wants to do. A cash flow analysis is the major tool used in this planning. A sample cash flow analysis of a new enterprise is shown in Table 15-1. It is developed through many contacts with suppliers and by forecasting income. The problem in cash flow management is that the enterprise must spend a lot of money before it starts receiving any in return. Thus the difference in time between expenditures and income must be financed from some source. There are only a few sources of funds: money received from cash sales, money received on account, loan proceeds, money obtained from sale of equity, credit extended by suppliers, and the sale of assets.

One of the mistakes made in cash planning is that the entrepreneur assumes that sales are cash and in many cases they are not. He may sell $10,000 worth of goods in June but not actually receive the cash until August and then he may not receive all of it because of some bad debts. Thus in cash flow analysis one must account very severely for money flowing through the doorway — money going out and money coming in. The firm may buy something and receive extended terms of sixty to ninety days, in which case the money flows out two to three months after the purchase. Fortunately, many of the estimates of operating costs can be made routinely by people of some experience. They can accurately estimate how much will have to be spent for office supplies, telephones, travel expense, utilities, and all of the overhead factors entailed in operating a business. However, the individual who has not previously been through this process will have to check out such things for himself.

Note some of the comments made on the items shown in Table 15-1. Note at the bottom the difference between outgo and income; this is the amount of money that will be needed to finance operations. This analysis becomes a most important document in procuring funds. Financiers want to see this cash budget to learn when the loan can be repaid. An excellent cash flow analysis impresses other people that a person

TABLE 15-1:   Cash flow format for retail men's store (store to open doors March 15th),

	January	February	March	April	May
Income:					
Planned sales			8,000	10,000	10,000
Cash sales[1]			3,200	4,000	4,000
Charge sales[2]			4,800	6,000	6,000
Received on account[3]				3,360	5,160
Other income[4]	30,000				
Total income	30,000		3,200	7,360	9,160
Cumulative income	30,000	30,000	33,200	40,560	49,720
Outgo:					
Planned purchases[5]	20,000	15,000	4,000	2,000	2,000
Payments for goods[6]		19,600	14,700	3,920	1,960
Wages			2,500	2,500	2,100
Occupancy costs[7]	700	700	700	700	700
Promotional costs			4,000	2,000	200
Administrative overhead[8]	400	400	800	600	400
Interest					
Automotive	50	150	150	30	30
Travel[9]	800				
Entertainment			500		
Freight/Postage		50	100	100	50
Loan payments					
Equipment purchases		20,000			
Other outgo					
Total outgo	1,950	40,900	23,450	9,850	5,440
Cumulative outgo	1,950	42,850	66,300	76,150	81,590
Difference between income and outgo[10]	28,050	12,850	−33,100	−35,590	−31,870

[1] 40 percent of sales in cash.
[2] Cash not received on these sales.
[3] 70 percent of accounts received paid in month following sale; 20 percent in second month; 9 percent in third month; 1 percent bad debt.
[4] Equity and loans.
[5] Cost of goods received in stock.
[6] Payment of 98 percent of previous month's purchases — take 2 percent cash discounts.
[7] All costs of store premises.
[8] All costs of office.
[9] Two trips to market.
[10] Indicates financial needs each month.

TABLE 15-1: (Continued)

June	July	August	September	October	November	December
6,000	7,000	15,000	18,000	15,000	20,000	25,000
2,400	2,800	6,000	7,200	6,000	8,000	10,000
3,600	4,200	9,000	10,800	9,000	12,000	15,000
5,832	4,260	4,200	7,464	9,738	9,270	11,172
8,232	7,060	10,200	14,664	15,738	17,270	21,172
57,932	65,012	75,212	89,876	105,614	122,884	144,056
5,000	20,000	12,000	4,000	2,000	2,000	2,000
1,960	4,900	19,600	11,760	3,920	1,960	1,960
2,100	2,100	2,800	2,800	2,500	3,000	3,000
700	700	700	700	700	700	700
200	200	1,000	1,000	200	1,000	1,000
400	400	400	400	400	500	500
50	50	50	50	50	60	60
		800				
		500				500
50	50	100	100	100	200	200
5,460	8,400	25,950	16,810	7,870	7,420	7,920
87,050	95,450	121,400	138,210	146,080	135,500	161,420
−29,118	−30,438	−46,188	−48,334	−40,466	−30,616	17,364

knows what he is doing. Without doubt it is one of the most important planning documents that a new businessman can prepare.

One word of caution in all affairs: Inevitably things cost more than anticipated, so put "fudge" factors in everything. Never go into business on the basis of being able to do so on all of the minimum cost figures obtained. There are always unseen costs, price increases, waste, and inefficiency. Calculate all expenditures on the basis of maximum expectations and all income on the basis of minimum expectations. Then if actual experience is otherwise, so much the better.

However, if a person enters business on the basis of high income expectations and low expense budgets and these plans fail to materialize, he may face bankruptcy if he cannot finance the difference.

How much money is needed? Always a key question!

How much working capital for the new project?

Thomas B. Lyda†

Failure to provide adequate working capital — the money required for the day-to-day operation of a business over and above the fixed investment for land, buildings, and equipment — has been a classic cause of bankruptcy among companies whose expansion policies ran too far ahead of their cash flow.

Some managers may think of working capital for a new venture as money in the bank that can be easily recovered and reassigned should the project fail. But a substantial part of the working capital may be tied up in inventories that can only be liquidated at a substantial loss.

†**Thomas B. Lyda**, *Management Review*, December 1972, pp. 54-56.

Condensed by special permission from CHEMICAL ENGINEERING (September 18, 1972). Copyright (c) 1972, by McGraw-Hill, Inc., New York, N.Y. 10020.

For these reasons, a realistic estimate of working-capital requirements is very important in venture analysis.

One obvious form of working capital is money that must be supplied by a company to buy inventories for raw materials and finished products and to provide credit to customers. Any funds coming into the treasury that can be retained or any payments that can be delayed until further funds are received reduce the working-capital requirement. An example would be an account payable — an unpaid bill — for a raw material. The goods for which the bill is payable are used and thus provide revenue that can be retained until the bill is due.

An accruing liability also reduces working-capital requirements. A good example is the company payroll. Halfway through a pay period the firm owes half the payroll to its employees. Because the efforts of its employees presumably produce continuous income, the cash reserved in the treasury for paying them temporarily reduces the amount of outside money required to operate the business.

Averaging the requirements

Because working-capital requirements are not constant, they pose a difficulty in venture analysis where it is desirable to have a single, time-independent quantity that can readily be used in return-on-investment or discounted-cash-flow calculations. For this purpose, however, an average working-capital requirement will prove useful.

A detailed study of the day-to-day cash requirements of a particular venture will show that the working capital required at any moment of the venture's life is the algebraic sum of five items: the cost of raw-material and supplies inventories, plus the cost of the product inventory (excluding non-cash depreciation costs) plus accounts receivable at selling price, less the accounts payable, less the sum of all accrued liabilities.

There are two methods of averaging these components. The first four are best considered as being set by operating and sales policy. For example, sales considerations may dictate that 60 days of production be maintained in inventory so that prospective customers can be reassured of a dependable supply. Similarly, shipping and distribution considerations may fix the average inventories of products and raw materials.

The last of the five items, made up of all accruing liabilities, best lends itself to a different type of averaging. These liabilities vary between two predictable values: a minimum (usually zero) and a maximum reached after some fixed period. Wages, again, are a good example: Immediately after pay day, no wages are owed. But just before the next pay day (say, a month later) the full payroll has accrued. Because preliminary economics are usually tabulated on an annual basis, it is convenient to take as average a fraction of the estimated annual amount determined by the duration of the accrual. Since, in the wage example, the accrual period was a month or 1/12 year, the average is reached in half that time or 1/24 year. Therefore, the average of the amount of accrued wages is 1/24 of the annual wages.

Liabilities from profit

The liabilities created by a profit deserve special mention. Part of the profit must be paid to the government as income tax, part to the stockholders as dividends, and the remainder is retained for business expansion. Since the first two are normally paid quarterly, funds to pay them are reserved as profits are made. These cash balances held in the company treasury decrease a profit-making venture's working-capital requirements.

Since the tax rate is set by law, determining an average liability for taxes is simple. The division of the remainder of the profit, however, is a matter of management's discretion. Although the division may vary from year to year as profits or management policies change, a particular company will usually maintain the same approximate ratio of dividends to retained earnings over the years. The manager will have to establish the ratio for his company before making estimates of working capital.

Corporate expansion in its various forms (including normal growth of existing businesses as well as new ventures) creates an ever-present demand for cash, and it can be assumed that these profit-derived expansion funds are not allowed to accrue for later payment but are paid immediately. This portion of the profit, therefore, does not make a negative contribution to working-capital requirements.

The effect of taxes and dividends create two paradoxes.

1. A venture's profits do not in themselves reduce its working-capital requirements, but a profit-making venture nevertheless requires less working capital than a break-even venture. Assuming that the revenues are the same, this paradox can be explained by considering the taxes payable. A break-even venture creates

no net revenue nor does it create a tax liability, while a profit-making venture produces cash income that may be retained in the treasury until the taxes are due. The part of profit that is dedicated to future tax payments temporarily reduces the treasury's need to borrow working funds and thus incrementally reduces the firm's working-capital requirements.

2. The average working capital required by a venture undertaken by a company that pays its stockholders a dividend is lower than that required by the same venture if undertaken by a company that pays no dividends. This is again explained by the venture's incremental effect on the firm's total working capital. The reserve built up by a dividend-paying firm for its stockholders can constitute a major part of its total working capital.

A company that pays its stockholders no dividends need not accumulate this reserve and may well have a lower total company working-capital requirement. However, in evaluating a single venture, the absolute value of the company's total working capital is immaterial. Only the incremental increases or decreases caused by the venture are pertinent.

SOURCES OF FUNDS

16

Traditionally, the person's funds and whatever the family might contribute have been the first places the entrepreneur looks for capital. Some people maintain that the entrepreneur should not take money from his family to finance the operation, but this all depends upon the nature of the family relationships. In some cases there is nothing wrong with accepting help from your family and there are a great many advantages in doing so. One problem is the matter of pride. There are many people who do not want to go to their parents for financial help and that can be a valid factor to consider. Another problem arises should the enterprise fail. Remember that new businesses are risky affairs. Money can easily be lost. If it is, family relationships may be strained. It may not be wise to risk Aunt Sally's savings in an enterprise, no matter how good the venture looks. There can be no generalizing upon one's use of family resources. Suffice it to say that if they are available, they are the most convenient funds to use.

LENDING INSTITUTIONS

Typically, the new businessman first looks to his bank to see if he can borrow some money for his venture. Up to a certain limited amount he may be able to do so. If all the individual needs is a few thousand dollars, he may be able to borrow it from his bank if he has good credit and a reasonable relationship with the bank. He could borrow the money for his business much like he could borrow it for buying a new car or a housefull of furniture — on his signature alone.

After a certain level, depending upon the credit of the individual, the bank wants security for its loan — stocks, bonds, mortgages, whatever. There are many instances in which it is wise to borrow money on assets rather than selling those assets to raise the money. In other instances, the entrepreneur is only raising his costs of operation by the interest he is paying by hanging onto his assets. It all depends upon the nature of the assets and it is not possible to generalize here on that decision.

If the money is to be used for tangible assets of recognized market value, banks may make loans taking those assets as security. Thus if one wants to build a store, he can borrow up to about 70 percent of the value of that property, using it as security just as he does his home. If the money is to be used for inventory that has a hard market value, banks have been known to make inventory loans. One merchant of men's wear who was building a new store in Denver, Colorado, managed to do so without investing a nickel of his own money. The store fixtures and improvements to the concrete shell that was turned over by the shopping center builder were financed by the $35,000 allowance provided by the shopping center. Plans called for putting $75,000 worth of inventory in the store. The company was able to borrow that amount by signing a note pledging the assets not only of that store but also the inventory of its other store. Thus the entire operation was financed by other people.

Accounts receivable also can be financed in many instances. If a company's customers are good credit risks (so-called "hard" accounts receivable) banks may lend up to 90 percent of their value upon receipt of the invoice. Indeed, it is not at all unknown for some entrepreneurs to be able to borrow money on the basis of a firm order from a large, well-known customer. One manufacturer of canvas bags was able to borrow money needed to buy canvas and zippers on the basis of a large order from Sears. The banker recognized that Sears was good for the order; it was a firm contract. He had faith that the businessman would be able to produce and meet that contract, thus he made the loan based upon such

knowledge. One's ability to get a bank loan depends to a great extent upon his relationships with his banker. Make no mistake about it, banks do vary considerably. Most banks simply refuse to make any loans whatsoever to new enterprises, as demonstrated by the following examples.

A manufacturer of overnight bags approached a banker in Norman, Oklahoma, requesting an accounts receivable loan on an amount due from various Post Exchanges throughout the world. It so happens that Post Exchanges are rather slow paying; it takes them about 90 days to go through all the red tape to get the checks to the suppliers. The checks are forthcoming and bad debts are not a problem. However, this small manufacturer did not have enough money to finance his customers for 90 days. He clearly needed an accounts receivable loan, but the banker refused to even discuss the matter — "It is too risky!" Clearly this Neanderthal financier did not want to make business loans.

Banks are like that — some want to deal with manufacturers, others deal with merchants, and some prefer consumer paper. It is all a matter of bank policy. Thus the enterpriser needs to find out which banks cater to his type of action. Before making banking connections ask around to find out which bank looks most favorably upon lending to your type of enterprise.

Bear in mind that banks vary in their ability to make loans, which is a function of the characteristics of their depositors. Typically, banks with a lot of "retail" business (wage earner or consumer accounts) will have more money to lend than banks that deal largely with business concerns. Non-business customers do not require the loans that commercial and industrial accounts generally demand.

It has been said many times over that banks only lend to those who do not need it. There is truth in that adage. Banks will shun the advances of persons without assets or some solid income flow. Banks are not in the business of taking risks and lending to new enterprises is risky.

But there are other lending institutions with more liberal loan policies. Commercial loan companies such as CIT are more prone to make loans to small businesses, particularly inventory or accounts receivable loans. However, their costs are significantly higher than banks. These commercial loan companies are of little use in starting up most new businesses.

One merchant had maintained his account at one bank for five years with excellent relationships. When he began building a new store in Boulder, Colorado, his banker continually assured him, "Don't worry, we'll take care of you!" When the merchant walked in "to be taken care of," the banker threw him to a mortgage broker. On such last-minute notice he was forced to pay a relatively high interest rate and a large brokerage commission to get the money he needed. It was assumed that the bank was going to make the modest mortgage loan being requested. No one needs a banker like that. The merchant realized it and changed his account to another bank who handled the expansion of the next store in magnificent fashion.

Another example which shows the extent to which a banker can go when he really wants your business: A bank was aggressively seeking to expand the industrial base of its trading area. A moderately sized electronics firm located in Chicago was thinking of moving its research laboratory to town. It had purchased 20 acres on which to build a 10,000 sq. ft. plant. The rest of the land was held for speculation. The bank financed the entire cost of the land and the building — $140,000 — a 100 percent loan. Critics will immediately say, "But that's against banking regulations!" Yes, it is, but they found a way to do it legally, for it was a matter of the valuation of the land. If the valuation on the property is high enough, the 70 percent loan limitation will cover 100 percent of the actual cost or even more.

The point is that when a banker really wants to be cooperative, when he wants business, he will go out of his way to meet a customer's demands. When he does not want business, he will have all sorts of good excuses for why he cannot loan money. Try to find a banker who wants business, who wants to be accommodating, because, unquestionably, bank money is most convenient to use. One can get it rather quickly and it is usually the cheapest source of borrowed money.

One word of warning about banks: If the capital needs will be large, be careful of dealing with small banks, for their attitude toward a loan depends somewhat upon whether they can handle it in-house or whether they must get participation from a correspondent bank. This situation is created by the legal limitation that no bank can lend more than 10 percent of its capitalization to any one party. Thus, if a bank has a capitalization of a quarter of a million dollars, it can only make a $25,000 loan to any one customer. For a $100,000 loan, the small bank must put together a syndicate of other banks to participate in the loan. In such circumstances, the banker makes certain that the proposition is on the up-and-up in every respect. However, if the entire loan is in-house he can bend some rules, take some risks, that he might not otherwise take. Thus, if one will be needing

$100,000 he had better be dealing with a bank that has a capitalization in excess of $1-million. This is one reason large banks get larger. It is also one of the advantages of branch banking systems. The disadvantage of the branch banking system is that the entrepreneur usually gets to know the branch manager rather well, but seldom can make good contacts with the people who decide on large business loans. In the small bank the businessman can gain rapport with the people who actually make the loan decisions. Branch banks are rather difficult to deal with in making loans on new enterprises, despite all the publicity that Bank of America puts on TV.

Your chances of walking into a bank off the street cold and getting a loan are next to nil. You must get to know the banker and impress him with your ability to make money, for that is the key to getting a loan, convincing the lender that he will be repaid. He knows the real basis for a successful loan is profits from which to repay it.

BORROWING FROM OTHER SOURCES

There are other institutions that will lend money, but usually their costs are so high that they are economically prohibitive. Remember that interest costs mount rapidly. It is not unknown for some institutions to demand 20 or 30 percent interest per year on their money. This is rough and should scare off prudent businessmen.

Incidentally, the bag manufacturer who was turned down by the bank on his Post Exchange accounts receivable was thrown into the arms of a local loan shark from whom he borrowed the money at 30 percent a year. Outrageous, but it was profitable for the businessman under those

circumstances. Stay away from the loan sharks.

SMALL BUSINESS ADMINISTRATION (SBA) LOANS

Once a businessman has been turned down for a loan by two banks he can apply for a so-called SBA loan, which is really only a guarantee. It is a bank loan of which 90 percent is guaranteed by the SBA.

From a practical standpoint, the SBA loan is not of much use. First, the number granted is quite limited. Second, the paperwork and governmental supervision is troublesome. Third, most such loans are now made to minority businessmen and therefore not useful to a person who does not belong to a minority group. Fourth, SBA loans are seldom made for start-up costs. Finally, they take a great amount of time and effort to negotiate — perhaps six months. Do not base financing plans on the SBA.

LEASING COMPANIES

Physical assets can be financed by leasing them from organizations that specialize in this, but the costs of such funds are high — often 20 to 30 percent per year. Moreover, the lease payments are an immediate cash drain.

SMALL BUSINESS INVESTMENT CORPORATIONS (SBIC)

Congress, in its feeble and misguided attempts to help the small businessman, set up provisions in the tax laws for the so-called SBICs in which companies are allowed to form for the sole purpose of financing small businesses and are granted certain tax advantages for doing so. Moreover, for every dollar of equity invested in an SBIC the government will loan three dollars at an attractive rate of interest. The record of these SBICs has been spotty, but they can be a source of funds for some firms in certain circumstances. However, there are some problems involved.

Typically, they demand a claim on equity along with a strong creditor position. Thus, if the businessman is not careful he may end up not owning his company. Banks have created SBICs to take care of the new enterpriser's requests for funds. For example, one SBIC was created by The Central Bank and Trust Company of Denver, Colorado. An entrepreneur coming to The Central Bank for financial assistance was referred to their SBIC, who carried the ball from that point on.

Three major problems arise from using this source of money. First, it takes a great deal of time and effort to solicit funds from them, for they demand a rather complete venture capital proposal. No small amount of management time must be devoted to such negotiations. Second, their acceptance rate is something less than one in ten; thus the chances of getting money after going to all the trouble of preparing the venture capital proposal makes the effort a bad gamble. Third, if a businessman is successful in getting participation from them he has usually acquired a partner, for they will demand to play a role in management and will keep close tabs on the business. Unless these conditions are palatable, SBICs should be avoided.

EQUITY

The cheapest source of money is usually equity. The entrepreneur may never have to pay anything for it. He only has to pay to equity what he wants to pay it if he controls the company. Thus minority stockholders in small, closely held corporations, if they have their wits about them at all, demand protection from potential greed, for they are well aware of the propensity of the entrepreneur to hang onto all the money he can. Consequently, they may demand preferred stock in which the entrepreneur must pay some dividends or eventually lose control of the enterprise. There is no end to the arrangements minority stockholders may request in their quest for protection; however, all have serious drawbacks. There is a serious conflict of interest between the entrepreneur and his financiers which can only be settled by negotiation. On the entrepreneur's side he must take care that in his eagerness to get funds he does not give away too much or agree to arrangements that will prove to be difficult to live with later. In particular, care should be taken in agreeing to a date when the investor will receive money from the enterprise. Timing of payouts is most difficult to predict.

Get rid of the idea that you can sell your stock in a new venture publicly. It rarely happens. Granted, there are some situations in which stock can be sold to the general public, thus raising funds for the enterprise. One example comes to mind. In the mid-1950's a group of chemistry professors at the University of Colorado decided they would form Arapahoe Chemicals Company to manufacture rare organic chemicals. They advertised·its stock for sale in the local newspapers. The reputation of these men plus the basic concept of the enterprise was such that they were able to raise the money by such methods. With a good story to tell and the appearance of being able to execute the plans, money may be raised this way. In the case of Arapahoe Chemicals, the venture was very successful and later sold out to Syntex at a handsome profit — a beautiful case history of success in new enterprises.

There are stock brokerage companies that specialize in new issues. Talking with a few of them will indicate whether or not a proposition is of interest to them. Basically they are looking for a good story to tell.

Shortly after World War II a man named Tucker was able to raise several million dollars by proclaiming that he was going to start manufacturing automobiles — the infamous Tucker escapade. It so happened that the psychology of the American market at that time was such that it was hungry for automobiles. Tucker caught its fancy and sold his stock. He never produced an automobile and was later prosecuted unsuccessfully for fraud.

If a story is right and the timing is right, an entrepreneur can raise money publicly. However, it is hazardous. In the first place, when going public the businessman must conduct himself with careful regard to the law so he will not be prosecuted and jailed for some violation of the securities laws. Irate stockholders are continually bringing suit and will seize upon the slightest opportunity to do so if a venture has not made them happy — or even if it has.

In point of fact, many of these public stock flotations border on being swindles. Here is a true tale proposed by a gentleman located in New Jersey, right across the river from New York City. He is in the printing business. While talking about getting some sales promotional literature printed, one of the authors of this book noticed that the printer turned out a large volume of prospectuses for various Wall Street underwriters. Upon learning that the

author's business was new, the printer related another business activity in which he was involved. He had taken five companies public, including his own, the previous year. Here are the details of his own public offering.

He sold 40-million shares (25% of those issued) in his printing corporation for one cent a share, a price that represented 400 times earnings, from which he obtained $400,000. The firm did not need the money. Rather the president invested it in high grade bonds from which $24,000 interest a year was earned. He smiled and said, "Of course, we'll never pay any dividends, for after all we are a growth company." And he had a good laugh. It was a rip off, pure and simple. He knew the propensity of some people to invest in penny stocks so he sold them a minute share of his company for which he will never have to pay them a mill. He availed his company of $400,000 capital and $24,000 profit as a free ride. Interestingly, he said the attorney general of New Jersey was investigating such situations and was trying to make a company sell at least 40 percent of its stock in such offerings.

If you want to play such games, fine, but make certain you walk hand-in-hand with a very good lawyer who is skilled in meeting all of the requirements of the Securities and Exchange Commission and the various state corporation commissions. You'll need him!

Traditionally, legitimate stock brokers do not care to take a company public until it has at least three years of good operating results plus a story that promises a good future. At the time of this writing it is doubtful if much of anything could be taken public, for the stock market is sour. Unquestionably it is much easier to raise equity money in times of a bull market than a bear one. Thus timing has a great deal to do with whether or not one taps this source of funds.

While in theory one has absolute control of a firm if he owns 51 percent of its common stock, he can own much less and still have working control if the other stock is held in the hands of many small stockholders widely dispersed geographically. As long as he is selling stock to widely dispersed small investors, his control of the company is secure; it is unlikely that they will be able to get together to vote him from power.

Let's examine the game another entrepreneur played in the electronics business. He had a marginally profitable little firm making a consumer electronics device. In the early 1960s, when the electronics stocks were hot, he went public, selling his own stock holdings for a handsome profit. His cost was $1 a share; he sold for $60 a share, knowing full well that the valuation the market was placing on his company was grossly high, but such was the psychology of the times.

When electronics stocks fell out of bed with a big bang in 1962, the price of his stock dropped to $3 at which point he bought back his controlling interest, for he knew that he could show some substantial profits in the next two to three years, which he subsequently did. As the price of his stock climbed again into the twenties he sold out once more, taking a large profit (which was a capital gain taxed at that time at a maximum of 25 percent). Then by the endeavors of his creative accountant he managed to have his company show a loss the next year. They charged off all R&D and everything else in sight against revenues. The price of his stock once again dropped below $3, at which point he started rebuying only to repeat the cycle over again. As he said, "I'm not in the electronics business. That's a

sideline. My main business is buying and selling my own stock. That's where I make the money."

Simply put, he runs the price of his stock up and down like a yo-yo, selling out when it is high and buying back when it's low. All of this trading was reported and abided by the laws regulating trading by insiders.

What is suggested here, in what seems to be an aside, is that when the enterpriser gets into the financial arena he is really getting into a completely different business. It is one that is not only hazardous but can also take up a great deal of time and may tarnish one's reputation if things go badly.

THE VENTURE CAPITALIST

In the annals of business folklore, the venture capitalist holds an honored place, for he captures the imagination of people and assumes most of the virtues of an angel, which he is frequently called.

He is usually a man of considerable wealth who is in love with new business. That is important. The man enjoys building an enterprise from scratch. He is a creator. Many times he has soured on traditional investments or has become bored with them. It is rather difficult for a man of any business acumen to accept the low rate of return that is to be had from stocks on the organized exchanges. At best, the dividend return is six percent; overall, authorities cite a ten percent return on such investments, taking capital gains into consideration. Such is nonsense to the economic man for he realizes he can get a better deal than that from other investments such as real estate or municipal bonds. Such an investor feels that the stocks on the exchanges are grossly overpriced and one of the basic principles of business is that no one makes much money when he pays too much for the things he buys. Moreover, case histories show that an investment in a good new enterprise can pay extremely handsome rewards.

As a general rule, venture capitalists are looking for a rate of return in excess of 25 percent a year on their money, and at times far more (see Table 16-1). In 1972 an investor joined a partnership in which he invested $3000 to finance the purchase of an industrial plant. They sold the plant a year later and each received $9000, a 300 percent return on their money. That seems to be a reasonable rate of return. They went into the deal because they spotted an opportunity, a good plant that the owner wanted to sell rather badly. The investors felt they could sell it for a lot more if they waited for business conditions to improve in that area. This proved correct and they were duly rewarded. It is such cases that make venture capitalists.

In a manner of speaking, the venture capitalist is much like a horse player. The challenge of trying to pick horses that are going to pay off seems to be the lure that attracts millions to the tracks every year. Similarly, the challenge of trying to ferret out the business opportunity that will pay off seems to be one of the lures of the venture capitalist. Moreover, the situation is usually such that the venture capitalist may participate to some extent in management and this can be attractive to him. In some enterprises he can play a helpful role, either from his expertise, experience, or his contacts. Sometimes such investors have a wide range of contacts and can open doors for the enterprise that would be otherwise closed.

TABLE 16-1: Rates of return expected by venture capitalists for investments in enterprises in various stages of development (rates compounded)

Start Up and First Stage	48-58% per year or 7 times their investment in 5 years
Second Stage	35-40% a year
Third Stage	25-30% a year

Definitions of stages of an enterprise:

Start Up: Sometimes referred to as seed money or seed deals.

    Companies that are being organized or have been in business less than a year but have not yet completed a prototype or have taken orders for a product.

First Stage: Company has expended its money on prototype, has evidence of commercial interest in its product, has some type of organization, perhaps has a small pilot production line, and may even have a limited line of credit at the bank.

Second Stage: Company is producing and shipping product. It has accounts receivable and inventories are building up. Firm needs working capital. Probably is still operating at a loss.

Third Stage: Company is breaking even or making a profit. Needs money for expansion and working capital.

Several things should be noted before going further. First, the venture capitalist expects a high rate of return on his money. Second, he may expect to participate in management. Third, he usually knows his way around in business better than the entrepreneur, thus he is in a position to drive a rather hard bargain.

If the venture capitalist is such an attractive source of funds, then why isn't he more widely used by entrepreneurs? First, he is a rather rare animal. You do not find one on every street corner[1]. One authority estimated that perhaps there were only one hundred in the city of Boston. It is unknown how many venture capitalists are in Los Angeles, but there are at least 100 in Newport Beach, California.

To illustrate, a real estate agent approached a friend to see if he were interested in buying a golf course in Fresno. The situation was rather fascinating in that it appeared that one could get into the venture without much money. It was a $4-million deal, most of which consisted of taking over existing loans. It would take about $400,000 hard cash for the deal. However, the operation had assets (some building lots ready to be sold) which would bring in more than that amount; thus, if one wanted to own a golf course, he might be able to do so without a permanent investment.

The friend was not interested in the proposition himself, but mentioned it to two golfing buddies, both of whom immediately responded that they were interested in looking it over. Nothing ever came of it, but largely due to reasons of inertia. The real estate man did not push it. His friend did not push it because he was not really interested in owning a golf course in Fresno. One of the other men had a heart attack and lost his interest, and the remaining man could not handle the action by himself.

The point to this story is that these two gentlemen were interested in making an investment in such a venture if it proved attractive. All it would have taken was some entrepreneur to put the deal together; that was the missing element. There was no entrepreneur who wanted to take over and push the thing through. On this last point, the availability of someone to actually ramrod the operation is critical.

As a further example, a wealthy investor said that someone was trying to sell him a big hotel in San Francisco and it looked attractive, but he was not able to spend the time to supervise the deal. It takes many meetings and much time to complete a deal and oversee it aside from the actual management of the operation. Such are the complexities of going into business and actually pulling off a deal that it takes a tremendous amount of time and someone on the scene to make sure that everything goes according to plan. The investor offered an acquaintance half of the action for no investment if he would oversee the action and push the deal through. The acquaintance had neither the time nor the inclination to accept it, but the story shows some of the problems entailed in putting together deals. This investor recognized that it would take an entrepreneur to tie the deal together. If that party was not in the picture, it would not happen.

Now, how does someone find a venture capitalist? First, ask around; it is not at all unusual for bankers to know

[1] One excellent book, *Guide to Venture Capital Sources* (1974), Capital Publishing Corporation, 10 South LaSalle Street, Chicago, Ill. 60603, estimated that there are 400 to 500 professional venture capital companies who invest a total of from $500 to $600 million a year. This excludes private individuals for whom there is no way of counting.

such men. Sometimes an advertisement in the newspapers under "Investors Wanted" will attract his attention.[2]

One financier responded to an "Investors Wanted" advertisement. The enterpriser wanted a modest amount of money to go into manufacturing men's trousers from double knit fabrics. The financier responded to the telephone number given in the advertisement and made an appointment to see the man. He was taken through an embryonic "plant" and saw all of the patterns, etc. It took about three minutes to resolve this proposition. The man did not know what he was talking about and his motives were all wrong. The man had no idea of how he was going to sell the trousers. His reason for going into business was that he had been fired as a cutter from a local firm making such trousers and he knew the amount of business they were doing. His motive was to put them out of business. Run ... not walk ... away from such maniacs!

The venture capitalist will look at more than a hundred such deals for every one he invests in. Most of the time either the deal is wrong or the entrepreneur is weak or the concept is wrong. All three elements must mesh together before anything can happen. The entrepreneur must be capable, his plans must be sound, and the proposition he offers must be satisfactory.

A man started a record store. The first year's volume was good, but $40,000 was lost through inept management. He contacted a venture capitalist to see if he would finance the operation. His proposition was that he would give the investor ten percent of the company for $40,000. The financier

politely left the meeting with the firm conviction that the gentleman would never make it because he did not seem to have the slightest grasp of basic business. If someone wanted to be in the record business, it would take a lot less than $40,000 to own the whole store, so why should the investor put up all of that money for only ten percent of it?

Now this is a very important point you must understand. *You must be able to look at your proposition from the viewpoint of the venture capitalist.* The deal must appeal to him. Do not think for one moment that you are going to be able to entice money from him for a small share of the business. Indeed, some venture capitalists will not invest unless they have control. They will retain the entrepreneur as president to operate the business, but he does not control it. Sometimes the businessman can obtain "buy-back" privileges so that, if things go well, he can buy the investor out from earnings. He insists on control so that he can get rid of the entrepreneur if he does not work out. The reason for the investor's insistence on control is that he has learned that the biggest risk in new enterprises is the entrepreneur himself. In most cases there comes a time when, if things are going sour, the entrepreneur must be thrown out and someone brought in who can salvage the business. Moreover, the venture capitalist has learned that unless he has control of the operation, he may be frozen out of the picture if it proves successful. He is not at all interested in having to go to court to enforce whatever contractual arrangements were made to protect him. He simply takes the direct route by keeping control of the enterprise. His insistence on this usually ends conversations rather quickly, for most entrepreneurs want to keep control for themselves.

[2]Ibid. The book gives a detailed list of most significant venture capital companies.

On the other hand, there are many times when one should shun the investor's deal. For example, a young man wanted to go into the business of making and selling smoked meats. A man in the food business offered him $5000 for two-thirds of the business. The deal was refused. "I can get the money elsewhere for less," the young man said, and he was right.

You might ask how the venture capitalist finds any action. The answer is that there are people who want to go into business sufficiently bad, who are sufficiently confident of their plans, and who have enough trust in the venture capitalist that they are willing to take his money under his terms rather than not go into business at all. The entrepreneur usually has no other alternative so he accepts the proposition. It is better to own 49 percent of something than 51 percent of nothing, he may think.

A young man wanted to get into the high quality restaurant business. He met a successful restaurant owner who was willing to finance a new operation in the southern part of Denver, Colorado. Through the help of this benefactor, the would-be restaurateur developed and opened a highly profitable restaurant called the Northwoods Inn. He claimed that he was making $6000 a month when, in his own words, "One day a board meeting was called. I walked in and the chairman of the board said, 'First item on the agenda: the replacement of Mr. X as general manager of the Northwoods Inn.' All of a sudden I was out. He was the majority stockholder and I'd had it!"

He had learned his lesson, however. In his next venture he protected himself by obtaining capital from people with the agreement that he could buy out their interests after giving them a good return.

Buskirk & Vaughn—Man. New Ent.—11

Thus the entrepreneur should bear in mind that in dealing with venture capitalists he should try to put an escape hatch in through which he can get rid of them at some point in the future, even though the price might seem to be high.

Then there are instances in which the entrepreneur takes the investor's money, giving him whatever he asks, knowing that he can convert the deal to whatever he wants when it suits his purpose. Several questionable tactics have been used to effect such maneuvers. Sometimes the entrepreneur is so important to the success of the firm that his threat to take his talent elsewhere, usually to a new firm in which he will have the deal he wants, forces the outside investor who cannot run the business to grant the entrepreneur his demands.

One inventor-entrepreneur retained ownership of patents which he licensed to the firm for ten years. When the license expired, he bought out the other investors quite reasonably when he threatened to not renew the license but instead start a new firm to sell the invention, which was most profitable.

In other instances outside investors have had their property stolen from them by devious entrepreneurs; valuable corporate assets sold for a fraction of their true worth to firms owned by management; competing enterprises have been started and nurtured *sub rosa* by using corporate assets; other times the entrepreneur manages to take from the company what he wants so he has no reason to bother with trying to oust the outside investors.

Now that we have presented the bad aspects of venture capitalists, let us look on the other side, the bright one. We just did not want you to begin by thinking that the venture capitalist was the pat answer to your financial problems. He probably won't be. However, there are experienced venture capitalists who do not want control of an enterprise, who do not want to participate in managing it (If you so much as hint that you would like their help, they will flee in fear.), and who *do* want to invest in legitimate new enterprises.

Do not assume that you must beg money from the investor. True, you have a problem finding money, but he also has a problem finding a good investment. Investors have more money than they have good investing opportunities. So he wants to hear your story; you're there to make him money, so keep it strictly business.

One factor you must be aware of. You cannot rush a venture capitalist. If you come at him with a "I must have the dough next week!" pitch, he will run for the exit. He wants time to investigate and think about it. He knows it takes time to pound out deals. He wants time to size you up for he knows that you are the key to the whole affair. Negotiations can easily take several months.

Few investors are interested in furnishing you start up costs. They want in on the first or second stages of development. Moreover, they want you to commit all of your resources and your time to the enterprise.

WAYS TO
SCARE OFF INVESTORS

1. Be concerned about your expenses, salary, office furnishings, and other luxuries. They do not like those who want to play big business on their money.

2. Give him reason to believe you are a chiseler; if you cheat other people, he knows he will in turn be cheated.

3. Do not provide a way for him to bail out of the investment when the time comes. Most professional investors want to sell out for capital gains in about five years.

4. Emphasize your need for management counseling.

5. Rush him!

6. Fight him on protection clauses.

7. Have a third party do all the negotiating. He wants to get to know you.

8. Be greedy and appear unwilling to pay capital its reward.

9. Tell him, "There is nothing like this product on the market today." Maybe there is no market for it either. Or perhaps you haven't done your homework.

10. Tell him, "We've got to rush this product to market to beat the competition." That is expensive and usually nonsense.

11. Show him a dozen products and tell him of the other ideas you are going to produce. He wants just one good product on the market making money.

FINANCING OPERATIONS
ON SUPPLIERS' MONEY

Some entrepreneurs are able to finance much of their operation on the credit of other firms. Here's how.

A young man had an idea for a certain printed product to be sold to the health food trade. He ordered 10,000 units which would cost $6000. They were to be delivered at the end of August. He negotiated terms so that he would pay half at the time of delivery and the other half at the end of sixty days; thus he was able to finance half his action on his supplier's money. If he could manage to sell that amount ($3000) between the time of delivery and the end of sixty days he would finance half of his business on the supplier's money.

The turnover of the proposition has to be quick; if an entrepreneur can convert the product into cash within a month or so, then he may be able to operate on suppliers' credit. Why would a supplier agree to such an arrangement, knowing full well what is going on? The supplier wants business and unless he is willing to make such accommodations, the entrepreneur may take it elsewhere. Such liberal credit by the supplier is used as a means of locking the business to him.

Another example of such an arrangement is provided by the men's apparel store which was referred to previously. It financed a portion of its shirt inventory by a $5000 "credit freeze" given by one shirt supplier. The merchant paid only the amount owed in excess of $5000; thus the supplier was financing $5000 worth of inventory. He did this because it allowed him to hold that merchant's business. The merchant loses his freedom to throw out the line, because if he does so he will have to pay off the supplier. Unquestionably, liberal credit is a tremendous competitive weapon in the hands of suppliers.

In one restaurant, the soda fountain was financed by the local dairy that put in everything connected with dairy products. The coffee machine was financed by the supplier, as was the orange juice dispenser, the hot chocolate dispenser, and the various soft drink dispensers.

Certain of these practices were illegal under state laws. When a supplier says that he cannot legally do something, usually what he is really saying is that he does not *want* to do it. If he wants to do it, he will usually find a way that is legal. In the case of the soda fountain, it was illegal for dairies to do this in the state where the restaurant was located. However, the dairy salesman just happened to know where a soda fountain could be picked up free of charge from an unmarked warehouse in another city. Nothing goes on anyone's books and there is no way to prove a thing.

This same restaurant owner was told by the Coca-Cola salesman that their policy prohibited putting in Coke dispensers free of charge, to which the owner replied, "Okay, that's fine. Pepsi Cola will, so we'll sell Pepsi." The Coke salesman responded, "Now don't get in a hurry! I may know a wholesaler who has some that we can get for you." Somehow the Coke dispensers got into the restaurant, free.

Bear in mind that suppliers do not want to give away anything. That costs them money. The only way to pierce their first protests is to make it clear that unless they do these things they are not going to get the business at all. Remember, threats do not have to be carried out. They can be phrased to include an escape hatch.

In the dairy situation above, the salesman was made most cooperative when the owner replied to his initial refusal to cooperate by saying, "Well, if I'm going to have to put all that money into one of those fancy soda fountains, I think it would be best for me to bring in a Swensen franchise in which they furnish an ice cream machine. Then I can make all of my ice cream, which will be a lot cheaper than buying it from you." The salesman turned perceptibly paler upon hearing those words. There was $3,000 a month ice cream volume at stake.

As a buyer one does have a certain amount of power over suppliers, no matter how much they want to pretend otherwise. Smart suppliers go to great lengths to keep businessmen from thinking that they have any power over them, continually citing shortages and such. A wire rack supplier was going on about how difficult it was for him to get wire and that he probably could not do this and could not do that and they had so much demand that they probably would not be able to deliver the racks for some time. He was told, "Well, I'm glad to hear business is so good. I'll tell you what, it would probably be best for me to find someone who has some available capacity." Suddenly the supplier started back-pedaling. It seemed that they would be able to work the order in and give preferential delivery. No one likes to see business walking out the door, but many times until a businessman threatens to do so he is not going to get the service he wants. It does not always work, but little is lost by trying.

If these power tactics seem offensive, bear in mind that customers use them too.

DEALING WITH THE MONEY MARKET

Here are a few suggestions on dealing with the money market, no matter which institution is involved. First, all financiers strongly prefer to deal with people who have proven experience in doing what it is they are proposing to do. Inexperience scares them, and rightly so. Thus, the burden of proof is upon the entrepreneur to show them that he knows what he is talking about and that he is able to do what must be done. This situation exists because many new entrepreneurs do not know what they are talking about and do not know how to do what needs to be done, thus their ventures fail. It is critical, therefore, that an entrepreneur be able

to show some experience in the proposed activity. Without the experience, he is a very bad risk indeed.

Second, financial men love numbers, the more numbers they see, the more they are reassured. They want to see *pro forma* balance sheets, profit and loss statements, cash flow analyses, budgets, and financial controls. They want to know how the entrepreneur is going to use their money and when they are going to get it back. The entrepreneur who demonstrates an ignorance of accounting and financial controls will be treated rather roughly by the financier.

To create a venture capital proposal is an art in itself. The basic elements in a venture capital proposal are:

I. *The idea*
II. *The market*
III. *Production plans*
IV. *Marketing plans*
V. *Financial plans*
VI. *Management*
VII. *The deal*

While essentially it is a rather simple document, in actual practice the actual proposal can be complicated because considerable data is necessary. First, the financier wants to know exactly what the business is that he is being asked to finance. This may seem to be a simple request, but it isn't. One must carefully delineate exactly what it is that he intends to do. Second, the financier wants to know what the market is for the proposal. A careful market analysis must be presented. Then he wants to learn the plans for making and selling the product, production and marketing. Next he wants to know about financial plans; he wants financial projections, what's going to be spent on what, how much is going to be needed, and when it can be returned. He would like to know about the operating plan of the enterprise. What's the timetable? He wants to know something about management. Who is going to be connected with the venture and their qualifications? Finally, a proposition needs to be made in which the entrepreneur says, "You do such-and-such for me and this is what I will do for you."

CLASSIC PITFALLS

Probably the biggest pitfall awaiting the entrepreneur is in grossly underestimating the amount of money he will need. He begins operations with too little money, gets his neck stuck out too far, and then does not have anywhere to go to get the money he needs to save the enterprise. It is most important that the entrepreneur obtain enough money from the start that he is able to carry his project through to success. If he has to negotiate for additional funds at some point in midstream, at which he usually has a loss to show, he will find one or a number of things to be true, all of which are to his distinct disadvantage. First, he has little to show for his efforts, thus placing him in a weak bargaining position. Second, because he is on weak bargaining ground, he will pay far more for the money than he did originally. Third, many investors believe that it is unwise to send good money after bad; thus, they may write off their original investment rather than plunge deeper. The taste in their mouths may be rather bitter already. Fourth, he has already proven an inability to forecast his financial needs, so there is little confidence that his new projections will prove to be any better. It is usually easier to get money initially than it is after a period of time in which there is

only failure to show. On the other hand, if the firm needs more money to finance expansion, it is an easier task.

UNWISE USE OF DEBT

Many entrepreneurs, in their unbridled optimism, are so firmly convinced that they will make large sums of money quickly in their ventures that they hasten to borrow substantial sums of money, many times at unreasonably high interest rates, thoroughly convinced that repaying the debt will be no problem. It is tragic to see a family forced to move from its home because the entrepreneur has mortgaged it to the hilt to finance some venture, only to discover his forecasts were overly optimistic. Debt must be repaid. If it isn't the creditor is in the driver's seat.

Three young men started a chemical compounding company which lost $50,000 the first year. The company was about to fold when one of the founders offered to loan the money for one year at a reasonable interest rate. The other two men accepted his offer. They each owned one-third of the enterprise. At the end of the year he presented his note for payment. Although the firm had turned the corner and was now making a small profit, it still did not have $50,000 with which to pay the note, nor did it have any source from which it could raise that money. The other two owners were at the mercy of the lender. He proposed to settle the note by taking stock at a very low price, which resulted in his owning 60 percent of the enterprise. He moved them out of the business as the venture prospered.

Creditors secured with notes are able to cause the entrepreneur much inconvenience. The minute they sue for collection on the note the company's credit is ruined. Suppliers panic and the run is on. The entrepreneur will find himself harrassed hourly by creditors wanting their money. Debt is not to be taken lightly. It is extremely unwise to promise to repay money unless one is certain he will have the funds with which to repay, which brings up another matter: predicting the future.

Some lenders, particularly banks, refuse to loan money for periods longer than one year. While a bank may go three to five years, it will do so on one-year notes. They say that they will renew the note routinely when it comes due. This is done because bank auditors dislike notes maturing beyond a year in the bank's portfolio. While it is true that such notes may be renewed, it is most assuredly not a matter of routine. They will examine the advisability of extending it at that time. Moreover, the terms may change unfavorably. If there is a shortage of funds and the banks are shrinking their portfolios, they may demand that the note be liquidated. This presents some interesting situations for both the bank and the entrepreneur, for the bank is also posed with some problems in liquidating a note.

A bank loaned a nonprofit swimming pool association $70,000 on a one-year note under the assumption that all memberships would be sold and the note paid off within the year. Sales did not go as expected, although the note had been reduced to $18,000 by the time it was due. The banker wanted his money. The treasurer of the corporation asked the president of the bank, "Do you know anything about running a swimming pool?" The president said he did not, to which the treasurer replied, "Well, you better start learning, because you're going to own one!" The treasurer had made his point. The last thing in the world the bank president wanted to do was to take over that nonprofit swimming pool and try to liquidate it with all of the attendant bad publicity. It was something he could do without, particularly when it appeared quite likely that the $18,000 would easily be paid off with the coming year's membership drive. Moreover, in that situation the banker was being rather difficult, for the dues structure of the operation was sufficient that the debt could be adequately serviced. He really had nothing to worry about.

There's an old saying that it's rather difficult to call a dog if he isn't around. Bankers have the same problem when they try to call notes when the company cannot pay off. The Banker's Hall of Shame is lined with gullible loan officers who extended loans to companies that subsequently got into difficulty and came back for more and more money in an attempt to salvage the original loan. Bankers do not like to write off large loans, for it makes them look bad. They will go to great lengths to avoid court suits and other activities that are public confessions of their lending ineptitude.

However as that may be, the moral of the story is still clear, debt poses dangers if plans fail to go as anticipated. There has yet to be a company go into bankruptcy that did not owe money. Debt can put a person into bankruptcy; equity, never.

SPENDING SPREES

One of the most pitiful experiences one can witness is an entrepreneur who, upon obtaining a substantial sum of money on which to operate his enterprise, proceeds to squander it stupidly on nonessentials to the point where he does not have sufficient working capital on which to operate. You think it does not happen? Let's look at an actual case.

A noted chemist decided there was an opportunity for an aerosol packaging concern and his reputation was such that he was able to sell $500,000 worth of stock to the citizens of a small, midwest town who thought they knew him well. He proceeded to build a monument to his ego which he called "the plant." It was a fine structure of brick and mortar, costing about $300,000, which he paid for in cash. Then he hired a lot of people, bought lots of furniture, and began to play Big Businessman. Unfortunately, when the time came to market his products he did not have enough money for inventory and accounts receivable. In what is known as a "working capital crisis," he had to sell his plant to get money on which to keep his enterprise alive. Within a year he was "belly-up," all $500,000 squandered.

Marshal your resources carefully. Do not let a fat bank account lure you into a feeling of false prosperity. Careful, iron-clad budgeting must be maintained. Every one of those dollars originally obtained must be ticketed for some end use. Do not rob Peter to pay Paul. If it's going to take $25,000 to finance inventory, make certain there is $25,000 with which to do it when the time comes.

As intimated, there are two culprits that help dig this pit into which the neophyte businessman frequently plunges. First is his ego. Too many businessmen want to play big business executive. They feel they must surround themselves with posh offices, fine furniture, and fancy secretaries. This is usually a lot of nonsense. Initially many businesses are started in basements using orange crates for furniture and wives for secretaries.

And there is not a thing wrong with it! Pride costs money!

Another story: An enterprise selling a supply item to the floral trade had lost a great deal of money in its first year of operation. A consultant was summoned to analyze the situation for the owner. It did not take long for the consultant to pinpoint the trouble. The owner was ensconced in a nice office served by two secretaries. He had three men working for him in the office, an accountant, a sales manager, and a production manager. There were three men in the plant. He had a solid $15,000 a month in revenues flowing into his enterprise. It did not take an hour to see that the owner was playing big businessman. He was not doing one lick of work, but rather was hiring it done. He did not relish being told that his only problem was that he was not working. All he needed was one secretary, one man to handle the office, and one man out in the plant. If he got off his chair and did some work, he would have a profitable business. He did not even need the accountant, for he could hire the same work much cheaper by an outside accounting firm. Overhead was eating him up.

On the other hand, numerous examples could be cited of ventures that have spent some time in basements, garages, or old warehouses, gaining financial strength before committing themselves to normal overhead costs. Indeed, some of the things that entrepreneurs do to cut costs are incredible.

Admittedly, there is another side to this matter. There are some situations in which it is important that the new firm appear to be a substantial profitable concern, for its customers will not do business with it otherwise. It all depends upon the nature of the business as to what other people expect of the concern. Not many people care to patronize firms that appear to be managed by amateurs. In particular, certain new retail businesses should usually avoid appearing to be rag-tag operations.

Initial capital, as much as possible, should be used for working capital, the financing of inventories and receivables. Use money where it is critical, where it is really earning money. Sometimes it is advisable to let other people invest in the fixed assets such as plant and equipment, even though in the short run costs may increase. It may be cheaper to own a plant than rent it in the long run. It may be cheaper to manufacture something oneself rather than subcontract it in the long run. However, in the short run the pressures on working capital may be such that it would be folly to tie money up in such fixed assets, particularly when their capacity may not be used sufficiently or the product proves unmarketable. Pay the higher costs and stay liquid.

This squandering also refers to personal living. Observers of the entrepreneurial scene quiver when they see the new businessman start paying himself a handsome salary and start living it up with large expense accounts on founding money. It is almost certain that failure is not far behind. They know that the true entrepreneur behaves otherwise. Most investors shy away from ventures in which the entrepreneur is unwilling to make considerable personal sacrifice. They want a situation in which the man must make the business successful to be rewarded.

One example is Charley, the founder of a top-selling line of guitar amplifiers. Charley walked up to the house of a financier with his idea. Charley was a "good old country boy" from the Ozarks whose experience in country music and his selling talents looked to be a winning combination. The financier found venture capital for him in Chanute, Kansas, from a local industrial development concern. He started operations in an old garage; he and his wife lived under most austere conditions in the attic. They hardly spent a dime until they had it to spend.

The adage the good businessman adheres to is, "Don't spend money until you've earned it and after taxes have been paid on it." Unless the entrepreneur is willing to sacrifice, his chances for success are slim.

A VENTURE CAPITAL COMPANY

Few new enterprises rely on venture capital for financing; however, they are of such interest and do serve such a vital function in our system, that careful note should be made of them. The advice seems sound, but what protects the venture capitalist if he does not have control or some other protective clauses in the agreement?

The following letter and brochure provides an example of what some venture capitalists are currently seeking.[3]

[3]"Messrs. Alexander L. M. Dingee, Brian Haslett and Leonard E. Smollen who founded the Institute are now structuring a privately-financed venture capital fund that would focus on the creation of ventures using some of the methods described in the Institute's pamphlet."

INSTITUTE FOR NEW ENTERPRISE DEVELOPMENT

375 CONCORD AVENUE

BELMONT, MASSACHUSETTS 02178

———————

(617) 489-3950

28 September 1973

Professor Richard H. Buskirk
Graduate School of Business Administration
University of Southern California
University Park
Los Angeles, California 90007

Dear Professor Buskirk:

Thank you for responding to our recent advertisement "Entrepreneurs Wanted".

The Institute for New Enterprise Development is working with six economic development agency partners that have $2 million to invest as equity in starting and expanding new companies. Because our partners are willing to invest in startups as well as very early stage expansions, they represent a rare source of equity capital for entrepreneurs. The enclosed brochure has more detail in our operation.

We would like to hear of any start-up ventures that you might come across. The kind of ventures we are interested in should fit the following general criteria:

-The venture's product or service should have regional or national market

-Venture has potential of surpassing $100,000 net after taxes in 3-5 years

-Maximum equity investment from our investment partners should not exceed $300,000

-Investment should purchase at least 30% of business

-Venture requires moderate level of technology

-Ventures should be capable of being located in one of the six areas mentioned in the brochure.

If you see or hear of any situations that you feel might interest us or want more information about what we do, please give me a call.

Sincerely yours,

Leonard E. Smollen
Associate Director

LES/rrl
Encl.

INSTITUTE

FOR

NEW ENTERPRISE

DEVELOPMENT

How it Helps People
Start and Build
Their Own Businesses

GETTING STARTED

Early errors cripple many new ventures. If, however, an entrepreneurial team takes a systematic approach and gets advice from those experienced in business start-ups - their chances of securing financing and launching a successful business can be improved.

INED has developed a wide range of venture-creation aids for people wanting to start a business. Because of its grant support, INED can only offer these aids to people willing to locate in areas where we are operating.

INSTITUTE FOR NEW ENTERPRISE DEVELOPMENT (INED)

INED works with enterprising men and women to help them create and build substantial businesses of their own. Founded by a successful entrepreneur, the Institute operates with an annual budget of $400,000. These funds come from a major private foundation and a federal agency: both seek to promote economic development in various parts of the country.

To illustrate what we do: In the Summer of 1972, INED worked with two men and a community economic development corporation in Appalachia to create a company manufacturing canvas products for the leisure time market. This company was started late in 1972 with initial financing of $650,000. After seven months of operations, it had profitable sales of $500,000 and was employing 54 people.

CURRENT PROGRAMS IN 6 STATES

During 1973, INED is working in partnership with six community economic development corporations across the nation. Our objective is to do in six areas what was accomplished last year in Appalachia; — i.e. to build substantial businesses that prosper, thereby increasing employment and cash flow in our investing partners' communities. Each community economic development corporation has between $200,000 and $500,000 to invest this year, *as equity,* in businesses that can be started, expanded or moved into communities near:

* *Salt Lake City ... north central Utah*
* *San Antonio ... southwest Texas*
* *Eau Claire ... northwest Wisconsin*
* *Greenville ... Mississippi Delta*
* *London ... Appalachian Kentucky*
* *Sanford ... central Florida*

INED is playing a lead role in identifying business opportunities *and* enterprising people attracted by the idea of starting or expanding their own business, or acquiring and reviving someone else's, in one of these six areas.

We will work with these people to build a strong management team and develop a comprehensive business plan. Selected entrepreneurs will be financed by the community economic development corporation in that area.

HOW INED HELPS

INED assists entrepreneurs put ventures together and get them started. We do this by offering:

Participation in entrepreneurial development weekends:

INED works with groups of would-be entrepreneurs over two weekends. We help them develop a thorough understanding of their own skills, motivation and commitment and compare these with those of successful entrepreneurs.

Access to available product/service ideas and the sources of such ideas:

INED has developed a network of corporate, government and university sources from which we obtain data on products/processes and services that may be purchased or licensed for business starts or expansions. INED is also collecting data on unsatisfied needs in various growing markets.

Venture screening and business planning guidelines:

Business plans acceptable to experienced venture capitalists require many man-weeks to prepare *and* must be well presented. Several leading venture capitalists collaborated with INED to produce guidelines the entrepreneur can use to screen, analyze and plan a venture - using the venture capitalist's criteria. We critique these analyses and plans, and advise when and how to present plans to our partners with venture capital funds.

Access to investment capital from the community economic development corporations with whom we are working:

In return for some equity in the entrepreneurs' businesses, these corporations are ready to invest in ventures with acceptable plans that will operate in their areas.

INED'S STAFF

INED's eight-man professional staff has considerable experience in starting, managing and counselling new business ventures.

Three of us have been founders/managers of independent businesses. Three more have started new ventures for established corporations. The others have trained managers and entrepreneurs for several years.

We bring to the program our experience in

* Market Research
* Business Analysis and Planning
* Management Team Development
* Raising and Investing Venture Capital
* Direction of New Business Ventures
* Entrepreneurial Management
* Acquisitions and Turn-Arounds

Together with a small group of accountants, attorneys, business teachers and consultants, we offer a full range of skills needed to organize and launch a business.

INED'S NEEDS

We want to hear from enterprising people who are interested in working with us to start, expand or move a business into any of our areas.

We also want to hear from individuals or companies with products for sale, or license, businesses for sale, or ideas about unsatisfied market needs.

INED
375B Concord Avenue
Belmont, Massachusetts 02178
(617) 489-3950

THE JARGON

17

Business agreements are loaded with all sorts of technical terms which have been given specific meaning through usage. A person signing such an agreement must understand all its terms. When some critical aspect of an agreement hinges on a term, then define the meaning of that term in writing within the body of the agreement. The following reading describes some of the definitions of more commonly used terms.

Financial terminology in business agreements

Irving Kellogg†

The attorney who drafts an agreement undertakes to exercise due care so as

†Irving Kellogg, CPA,
The Practical Lawyer, **December 1969, pp. 15-30.**

not to injure his client. The attorney who represents the opposing party undertakes a responsibility to his client when he reviews that agreement. If the agreement contains financial terminology, both attorneys encounter unique risks.

In drafting financial agreements, the attorney blindly using agreement forms in form books that are not current or not financially oriented is not unlike a nonattorney preparing wills and trusts. Unless the attorney understands the meaning and ramifications of the terminology or, failing that, gets an expert to review the agreement, he may be charged with failure to exercise due care.

Approach to terminology

Financial terminology is technical and is not always well understood. To avoid the pitfalls of vagueness, ambiguity, or misapplication, you can use either or both of these methods:

• Define the terms, if you understand the application of the definitions, or

- Familiarize yourself with the facts of the situation before using the terminology.

Definitions should be used only when necessary and should be as full as necessary. The draftsman should avoid creating his special meaning or a special meaning applicable only to this specific situation, even though his special definition is a paragon of clarity.

The cost in communication failure is too high for you to undertake this procedure of establishing your own special definition. You would be wiser to use standard definitions.

Knowing the meaning of the terms qualifies the attorney to raise substantive problems relating to the transaction. Knowledge of all the facts in the transaction enables you to recognize the application of the terminology in the same sense that knowing all the facts in a legal problem enables you to recognize the legal issues hidden in the facts and to apply legal rules and reasoning.

Kinds of documents

These are some of the kinds of documents containing financial terms:

- Merger and acquisition agreements;
- Profit-sharing agreements;
- Property settlement agreements;
- Loan agreements;
- Partnership agreements;
- Stockholder buy-sell agreements;
- SEC prospectuses; and
- Leases.

Recurring terms

These terms are most likely to occur in these agreements:

- "Audit";
- "Unaudited";
- "Book value";
- "Gross receipts";
- "Accounts receivable";
- "Inventories";
- "Current assets";
- "Current liabilities";
- "Current ratio";
- "Depreciation";
- "Net worth" ("capital," "equity");
- "Gross profits";
- "Net profits" ("net income," "net loss"); and
- "Generally accepted accounting principles."

Most ambiguous terms   The terms most loaded with ambiguity potential are listed in approximate descending importance:

1. "Book value"
2. "Net profits" ("net income," "net loss")
3. "Generally accepted accounting principles"
4. "Audit"

Book value

All deficiencies in financial statements merge into the term "book value." Its appearance in an agreement should warn the attorney that one of the parties to the agreement may receive less than his bargain because the term is a fiction in value.

You should shun "book value" unless no other words can express the concept of value in the specific agreement.

Official definition

"Book Value is the amount shown on accounting records or related financial statements at or as of the date when the determination is made, after adjustments necessary to reflect (1) correction of errors, and (2) the application of accounting practices which have been consistently followed." Accounting Terminology Bulletin No. 3 (AICPA 1956).

The obvious inadequacy of this definition destroys its utility. The amount shown on the books must be checked as to whether the amount is *both* correct and has consistently followed prior accounting practices.

The attorney using "book value" states in effect, therefore:

"This value is the basis for the agreement of the parties, but the value should be checked as to whether any errors were made in computing or recording the value, and whether the 'practices applied to this particular amount were consistently followed.'"

A counselor must reject this concept. A scrivener accepts it from ignorance.

Recognizing the controversy-laden potential of the term "book value," the Committee that attempted to define it concluded its report:

In view of the fact that the intent of the parties to arrangements involving sale or transfer of business interests should govern, and the foregoing definition may not reflect such intent, the Committee recommends that the term "book value" be avoided. Instead of this term it is recommended that any agreement involving the general concept of book value should contain a clearly defined understanding in specific and detailed terms.

Court decisions

On the other hand, some courts have simplified the definition. By their nature in resolving controversies, court decisions are retrospective. Courts are not under pressure to be prospective; they have the security of hindsight and the power of decision.

A court may find that, since it cannot remake the contract, it can clarify the term "book value" contained in the contract. One court used this definition: "As applied to finance, the value of anything as shown in the books of account." *Davis v. Coshnear*, 129 Me. 334, 151 A. 725, 727 (1930).

The definition, albeit simple and deceptively practical, illustrates to the knowledgeable practitioner the uselessness of the term for the draftsman.

Reasons for ambiguity

Why is "book value" so unreliable? Because it does not reflect the intention of both parties. Because it inherently ignores: the variations from "generally accepted accounting principles" (about which more is said below); deliberate distortions and window dressing; and variations from the values that would result in fair and equitable treatment to one or all the parties to the agreement.

For example:

• All assets are recorded at historical cost. In this era of inflation, cost bears only a coincidental relationship to market value, utility value, or replacement value.

• Valuation of "accounts receivable — customers" depends upon the judgmental factor of deductions or allowances for uncollectable accounts.

• Valuation of merchandise inventory can be computed using at least six methods:

⟶ Cost — first in, first out (FIFO);

⟶ Cost — average cost;

⟶ Cost — last in, first out (LIFO); Market;

⟶ Cost or market, whichever is lower (market being related to quoted prices); or

⟶ Cost or market, whichever is lower (market arbitrarily determined by management "cushion"method).

• Property, plant, building, equipment, furniture, vehicles, and leasehold improvements, in the category generally referred to as fixed assets, are subject to as great a margin for inequity as any. The policy of the management in either increasing these assets by additions from certain repairs or factory supplies, or not increasing the assets by charging to expense these certain repairs or factory supplies, can cause swings in book value of hundreds of thousands of dollars, depending upon the size of the fixed assets category. When to this variable policy is added the variable policy of depreciation — whether to use accelerated method or nonaccelerated, straight-line method, or whether to use a five-year life or a 15-year life — the attorney grasps the extent of the unreliability of the amounts in the accounting records proposed to be used for the agreement with whose legal effect he is charged.

• Research and development may not appear on the accounting records or balance sheet, but the asset in fact may exist. Or, it may appear in the records and balance sheet, but its value is not truly determinable. It is placed there to report greater earnings by deferring research and development in accord with an alternative procedure of "generally accepted accounting principles." The same uncertainty would apply to patents and other intangibles like trademarks.

Occurrence of term

"Book value" as a term is used mainly in these agreements:

• Partnership agreements;

• Merger and acquisition agreements;

• Property settlement agreements;

• Buy-sell agreements, among shareholders of a closed corporation, or among partners; and

• Stock-option agreements.

Form book criticized   In the light of the foregoing explanation of the difficulties with the "book value," the attorney can criticize the uncertainties in the following clauses taken from a popular form book:

"The purchase price shall be the book value of the stock, as of the date of death, as determined by the certified public accountant then servicing the books of the Company. His determination as to book value shall be made according to accepted accounting practices, and shall be binding upon the parties. No adjustment shall be made in the book value of such shares of stock for operations of the Company from the end of its last preceding fiscal year to the date of death."

This is an analysis of the inadequacies contained in the foregoing paragraph:

• The book value could not accurately be determined as of the date of death, because the company could not properly take, price, and extend the physical inventory, and close its sales, purchase, and cash books at that date.

• The CPA is given a complete license to determine what accepted accounting practices should be applied in this set of facts. He is not generally privy to hidden assets or contingent liabilities. Alternative methods of treating accounts raise questions of judgment.

• If the seller dies one week before the end of the fiscal year, he is penalized because he does not share in the profits from the end of the previous fiscal year, and he benefits in not being charged with the loss that might have occurred.

Net profits, net income, and net loss

To the nonaccountant, net income is the "bottom line" of the income statement and should be easy to determine. Nothing could be further from the truth! Just as "book value" is a snare and a delusion, the "net profits," "net income," or "net loss" terminology must be used by the attorney with great care.

Consequences of misuse

This clause (from an actual agreement between two shareholders owning 100 per cent of a corporation) will illustrate the results likely to occur as the result of the draftsman's failure to consider the consequences of his wording:

Purchase price: For purposes of this agreement, the value of all the issued and outstanding stock of the corporation shall be an amount equal to 2½ times the excess of the aggregate of the net profits over the aggregate of the net losses of the corporation for the three fiscal years next preceding the fiscal year in which the death of a stockholder occurs. The net profits or net loss for any fiscal year of the corporation shall be the net income or net loss as disclosed on the federal income tax return of the corporation for that year.

Important questions The possible inequities of the above formula were not recognized until the two stockholders were asked the following questions:

• Would each of you sell your stock of the corporation for the amount that the formula would dictate, based on the past three years? [In this instance, the amount was $78,750, computed as follows:

1st year	$ 33,000
2nd year	18,000
3rd year	12,000
Total "net income"	63,000
Multiplier	× 2½
Total price	157,500
Each stockholder's share (50 per cent)	$ 78,750

However, the stockholders total tangible equity was actually $260,000, of which each stockholder's share was $130,000.]

• Were you conservative when you counted and priced your inventories at the end of each year? Did your conservatism result in a greater markdown of inventories at the end of the third year than the markdown at the beginning of the first year?

• Did you charge off much of the improvements (electrical wiring and equipment) when you moved into your new factory?

• Did you charge off to expense all your design expense and patterns of the past three years?

• How much in dollars did your personal fringe benefits [including but not limited to entertainment, promotion, country club, entertainment facilities (such as boats or cabins), travel, Internal Revenue section 105(b) medical plan] total during the past three years?

• Were there any large nonrecurring items of income or loss during the past three years?

• Did you understand the "net profit or net loss" to be the amounts *before* deduction of federal income tax or *after* deduction of federal income tax?

• Did you use accelerated methods of depreciation on the corporation's plant and equipment rather than the straight-line method? Were the lives used shorter than true useful lives? Was salvage value recognized in determining amounts to be written off?

• Were all catalog expenses charged to expense in each year?

• What was the value of the sales distribution organization?

After answering the questions, both stockholders realized that the agreement as drafted might result in the decedent's estate receiving about $50,000 less than it should receive under a reasonable valuation of the corporation.

Lawyer's responsibility

Is the attorney-draftsman responsible for such an inequity should it occur? An analysis should be made of two apparently different but basically similar fact situations:

1. The attorney does not meet with the certified public accountant for the corporation, and

2. The attorney meets with the certified public accountant for the corporation.

In the first instance, the attorney is faced with two burdens:

• He has undertaken the total responsibility and might be held to a standard of care of a specialist in financial matters; or

• He might be charged with failure to seek specialized advice if in fact he was not qualified in financial matters. The failure to seek advice might be construed to be the failure to act as a reasonable counselor who should have known of his lack of expertise and therefore, to service his client better, should have sought advice.

This article does not purport to explore further the concept of the lawyer's responsibility for financial statements. The questions are merely raised for the reader to think about.

Protecting against inequities How can the lawyer protect himself and his client in this context of net income or net loss? The obvious but not complete answer is to enlist the aid of the certified public accountant for the company; but the CPA cannot supplant the attorney as draftsman.

The CPA supplies historical facts, definitions, and information. In contrast, the attorney must use this grist for his mill, looking into the future within his and his client's power of foreseeability for every contingency and every consequence of his financial language.

Applying foreseeability to the purchase-price clause above, the lawyer may project hypothetical results by inserting various figures to represent the net income or net loss before federal income taxes for each of the three years. By this exercise, the absurdity of the above formula becomes evident.

For example, the purchase price would not reflect whether the business of the company was increasing or decreasing. The first year could have shown a substantial loss, followed by a steady rise in profits during the next two years, yet the three-year total would be the same as if the profits and the loss had occurred in the reverse order.

A business with increasing annual net income should be worth considerably more than a business with decreasing net income. Any attorney who has invested in the stock market knows this elementary rule of valuation from bitter personal experience.

The actual purchase-price formula that should be used in such cases is beyond the scope of this article. The prevention of inequitable results challenges the creativity of the attorney and may well make the difference between the fee due a scrivener and the fee due a counselor.

Precise terminology

The uncertainty surrounding the determination of net income or net loss can be minimized by adherence to precision of definition, and by knowledge of the factors influencing the arithmetic used to compute "the bottom line."

The attorney should not use the terms "net income," "net profits," or "net losses," as such in agreements. The terms, depending upon the intent of the parties, should be:

- Earnings from operations;
- Earnings before income taxes and nonrecurring items;
- Earnings after nonrecurring items and after income taxes; and
- Earnings after income taxes.

There could be other specific terms used depending upon the situation.

Earnings or losses When losses are contemplated, the word "losses" should be substituted for the word "earnings." In addition, if certain items of income or expense are to be added or subtracted or other adjustments are to be made, you could include the following statement in the definition section of the agreement:

Earnings or losses. The terms "earnings" or "losses" mean the earnings or losses before deduction for federal income and state income taxes, increased or reduced by these amounts in accord with the principles of accounting and record keeping:

a. Entertainment expense in excess of $15,000 per year;

b. Internal Revenue Code section 105(b) benefits for the benefit of the President-shareholder and the Treasurer-shareholder;

c. Donations of company merchandise from company inventories to charitable organizations, which donations were included as expenses of operation;

d. Salaries and bonuses in excess of $40,000 per year for the benefit of the persons listed in item b.

Other adjustments More increases or decreases could be listed:

- Allowances covering uncollectable accounts;
- Allowances or reserves for discounts, warranties, or returns;
- Inventory valuations;
- Depreciation adjustments;
- Research and development;
- Expenditures for intangibles; and
- Plant improvements, equipment, furniture and fixtures, and leasehold improvements charged to expense, and vise versa.

The attorney now perceives that between the two terms "book value" (which relates to the equity section of the balance sheet), and "net income" (which relates to the income statement), there exists an interrelationship that he must keep constantly before him. The term touching the balance sheet also touches the income statement.

Sample definition clause The following clause, contained in a merger agreement, illustrates the care one draftsman gave to the definition of "net income" in order to represent accurately the intent of the parties. Acquirer X Co. is a public company; acquiree Y Co. was a closed corporation.

Net Income. For the purpose of this paragraph 6, the term "Net Income" shall mean the *net profits of X Co. after provision for federal, state, or other taxes relating to income.* Notwithstanding any changes of rates, however, in determining Net Income, provision for such *taxes shall be calculated on the basis of rates applicable to the fiscal year ended November 30, 1966. Such computation of Net Income shall be made by the independent certified public accountant of X Co. in accordance with generally accepted accounting principles applied on a basis consistent with that employed by Y Co. in the prior year.* The determination by such certified public accountants shall be binding on the parties hereto. *The net gain on the sale of property assets disposed of shall be excluded in computing Net Income.* If Y Co. requires funds for its operations and X Co. lends the same to Y Co., then for the purpose of determining Net Income of Y Co. for the purpose of this paragraph 6, its *operating results shall be charged with interest thereon at the same rate which is paid by X Co. for its short term borrowings,* but no interest shall be charged with respect to funds replacing cash previously withdrawn by X Co. from Y Co. on account

of borrowings by X Co. or on account of payment of dividends. For the purposes hereof, Y Co. *operations shall not be charged for services rendered by officers of X Co. but will be charged for other services furnished by X Co. at X Co.'s cost, provided,* however, that until December 1, 1967, *no such services shll be furnished by X Co. without the consent of the Sellers.* (Italics supplied.)

Audit

The term "audit" means an *examination* of financial statements pursuant to generally accepted auditing standards, the result being a report in which the independent public accountant gives an opinion on whether the financial statements present fairly the financial position of the company, and the results of its operations for the period under review.

In all other senses, the auditing services performed by the accountant should be referred to as "examinations" with specific goals — for example, a limited monthly examination leading to interim balance sheets and interim income statements. You should not use the term "audit of the company" unless you are expressing the intent of the parties that the examination lead to an accountant's opinion (which, unfortunately for the accounting profession, is incorrectly referred to as a "certification").

Auditors do not certify, guarantee, or insure the financial statements on which the auditors express an opinion. They give only their opinion for what it is worth, and you should recognize this limitation when counseling your client and drafting an agreement. With this caveat in mind, the attorney can shed his blind faith in the alleged total reliability of the "audited" financial statements.

Audit clause

In partnership agreements, an attorney may draft a provision stating that:

the books of account shall be audited by an independent public accountant and a copy of the audit shall be mailed to each party. Said audit shall be conclusive upon the partners unless, within —— months, . . .

Such a provision may be a disservice. The requirement for an audit may be unnecessary under the circumstances, and the partners may not want to incur the cost of an audit.

Flexibility needed   A more appropriate clause, giving greater flexibility to the partners, would be:

After the end of each fiscal year of the partnership, the independent certified public accountant shall examine the accounting records and present the balance sheet and income statement pursuant to the scope of examination established by the partners.

Other language can be added as to whether the report shall be final, but you must realize that in no event will it be final if a protesting partner proves fraud or misrepresentation.

Financial statements

Boilerplate in buy-sell agreements, merger agreements, and partnership agreements frequently recite clauses containing the words "audited" and "audited financial statements." Generally, clients are unaware of the significance of their commitment in the word "audit."

Clients confuse "audit" with an examination not leading to an opinion. For example, a "monthly" audit is ordinarily a limited examination by the CPA to give the client some financial information in the form of a balance sheet and income statement.

By themselves, these "monthly" interim financial statements are often notoriously inaccurate. Be wary of relying upon them unless adequate auditing procedures have been used by the CPA to verify the assets and liabilities.

Comparison with income tax returns   A listing of some common differences between financial statements and income tax returns emphasizes the undesirability of referring in agreements to the income tax returns as the basis for net income.

A comparison of the reporting of various items in financial statements and income tax returns is set forth in Table 17-1.

Generally accepted accounting principles

These four words are used in agreements as though they had a definite and easily ascertainable meaning. Would that it were true! Unfortunately the business community at times makes a mockery of them.

Recognizing this, the accounting profession is concerned with developing definiteness in these principles. The public, including the SEC, unhappy investors, confused security analysts, and plaintiffs in liability suits are coming to the belief of some harsh critics of the accounting profession that there are no principles, and that what are used are not generally accepted.

[T]hese 'generally accepted' principles are so varied, and can be applied so flexibly, that investors can hardly be blamed for

---

TABLE 17-1: Differences between items as reported in financial statements and income tax returns

---

Financial statements   *Income tax returns*

Profits on installment sales

Financial statements	Income tax returns
Reported in financial statements when sale is made.	Reported in tax return as income when cash is collected.

Expense for pension costs

Reported in financial statements when accrued actuarially.	Reported in tax return as expense when contributed to the pension plan.

Estimated losses in inventory

Reported in financial statements when reasonably anticipated.	Reported in tax return as expense when in fact sustained.

Provision for major repairs and maintenance

Reported in financial statements when accrued in books systematically based upon estimates.	Reported in tax returns as expense when in fact incurred.

Depreciation expense in early years of asset life

Reported in financial statements on an accelerated method and with short lives of assets.	Reported in tax return on the straight line method and using longer lives.

Gains on sales of property leased back from buyer

Reported in income statements over the period of the lease.	Reported in tax return when sale is made.

Interest and taxes during construction

Reported in financial statements as addition to cost of construction.	Reported in tax return when in fact paid or accured.

Research and development

Reported in financial statements as asset and deferred and amortized over life of product or an arbitrary number of years.	Reported in tax return when paid or accrued.

---

sometimes throwing up their hands in confusion when trying to compare a company's current results with past performance. *Wall Street Journal*, May 12, 1966.

Sources of ambiguity

The attorney must therefore be wary when, without inquiry or investigation as to applicability, he inserts the wording, "generally accepted accounting principles," into an agreement.

First, these principles are manmade conventions developed within the accounting profession to cope with changing economic problems as the problems developed, or they were created by ingenious management seeking to circumvent prior principles. The attorney should view the principles not as fundamental or as natural laws but as guidelines and working rules developed by the accounting profession to assist management and members of the profession.

Second, because of the need to exercise judgment as to which principles management or the CPA should apply and because of the evolutionary nature of the principles, the attorney should accept their limitations.

Misuse of phrase   This paragraph from a merger agreement illustrates the misuse of the phrase, "generally accepted accounting principles":

The consolidated net pretax earnings of the XYZ Corporation for the years 1969 through 1973 will be computed by Blank & Co., or such firm of certified public accountants as may be designated by Purchaser, using generally accepted accounting principles.

This clause leaves the following questions unanswered:

• Which principles apply to the XYZ Corporation?

• Were the principles that apply to the XYZ Corporation used consistently each year, or were new ones developed?

• What was the effect in dollars of the change, if any, in accounting principles?

Sample clause

The following paragraph might better state the intent of the parties and lead to a more correct result as to the Purchaser.

The earnings from operations before nonrecurring items and before federal and state income taxes shall be computed for the years 1969 through 1973 by Blank & Co., or such firm of certified public accountants as may be designated by the Purchaser. Said earnings shall be prepared on a consolidated basis pursuant to section 2051 of the American Institute of CPA's Volume No. 1 of Accounting Principles. Said earnings shall be computed in accord with the accounting principles used by the XYZ Corp. in 1968 with the following modifications:

1. An allowance for uncollectible accounts shall be established at 50 per cent of face value on all accounts receivable balances on which no payments have been received for 90 days.

2. Inventory cost shall be computed (a) on an average cost for those items of the inventory that are purchased for sale to customers without modification in the factory of the XYZ Corp., and (b) on the first-in, first-out basis for raw materials plus direct labor cost and excluding overhead for those items manufactured within the factory of the XYZ Corp.

3. Research and development expenditures shall be deferred and amortized over a three-year period from the end of the fiscal year in which the amounts are charged in the accounting records, although for income tax purposes the research and development expense shall be charged against income.

To assist you in side-stepping the pitfall of uncertain accounting principles, you might refer to the newly established looseleaf service of the American Institute of CPA's on Accounting Principles, and to the excellent tretise by Paul Grady, *Inventory of Generally Accepted Accounting Principles for Business Enterprises* (Accounting Research Study No. 7, American Inst. of Certified Public Accountants, New York, N.Y., 1965).

Alternative accounting methods

The following list, adapted from Grady's monograph (cited above), illustrates some of the alternative methods of implementing "generally accepted accounting principles." Note that the principles are not different — Grady, a distinguished writer on accounting subjects, characterizes the variations as "alternative methods of implementation."

It might also be noted that some of these alternatives are similar to those compared in Table 1.

Inventory "Inventory cost is determined under:

- Fifo (first in, first out);
- Lifo (last in, first out);
- Average cost;
- Base stock; and

- Various combinations of these methods.

"In addition to the foregoing cost methods, standard costs are acceptable, if they approximate actual costs, and a zone of tolerance is permitted in undercapitalization of overhead costs; for example, some companies omit depreciation. Cost is reduced to market, where lower, and market means current replacement cost, except that (1) it should not exceed net realizable value, and (2) should not be less than net realizable value reduced by a normal profit margin. Market may be applied on an over-all basis or by individual items. Some companies in metal mining and meat packing carry inventories at market rather than cost.

Intangibles "Unlimited term intangibles, such as goodwill not necessarily expected to have value over the entire life of the enterprise, are:

- Not amortized, but charged off when there is clearly no remaining value; or
- Amortized over an arbitrary period.

Research and development "Research, development, and experimentation costs are

- Accumulated as deferred charges and then amortized over an arbitrary, but relatively short period; or
- Charged to expense as incurred.

Spare parts "Spare parts of machinery are

- Carried in fixed assets; or
- Included, by some companies, in inventories.

Tools "Patterns, jigs, and small tools are:

- Capitalized and depreciated over estimated lives;

- Carried at estimated depreciated values as determined by inspection from time to time; or

- Charged to expense as purchased."

Conclusion

The requirements for reasonable care in drafting agreements extend further than the items discussed in this article, because the variations between industries — and between companies in the same industry — demand that an attorney confer with the certified public accountant of his client before the attorney drafts or accepts a draft of an agreement containing financial terminology.

Failure to comply with this caution almost inevitably will result in renegotiation or litigation, because the vagueness or ambiguity of general nonspecific terminology gives a dissatisfied party to the agreement leverage to extract benefits not intended by the other party to the agreement. Such a result diminishes the worth of the attorney who was not sufficiently vigilant to prevent the controversy.

GOVERNMENTAL PROGRAMS FOR AIDING SMALL BUSINESS

18

Perhaps few topics would arouse more emotional outbursts among small business people than that of the government's attempts to aid them. There are those who stoutly maintain a policy of not having anything to do with the government. However, the Small Business Administration and the programs with which it is connected are a reality and should be studied whether or not they are used.

This reading describes the Small Business Administration.

A new day at the SBA

Dun's Review†

†*Dun's Review*, **June 1971, pp. 42-44.**

Reprinted by special permission frum DUN'S June, 1971. Copyright, 1971, Dun & Bradstreet Publications Corporation.

"This agency has been a sleeping giant for eighteen years," says boyish-looking Anthony Chase, the Small Business Administration's 33-year-old Deputy Administrator, "but it's finally beginning to stir. And it's about time, because the SBA has the potential to solve every problem a small business might have."

Chase is surely right on both counts. Despite the fact that the SBA guarantees loans (up to $350,000) to fledgling entrepreneurs, helps them to land government contracts, provides technical expertise if needed, and acts as a catalyst for venture capital, it has never quite lived up to its potential. "How could it?" asks Chase. "The top jobs here have simply been way stations for people on their way to something else. The average tenure of the Administrators has been fourteen months, and even lower if you take out the guy who stayed five years back in the Fifties."

But 51-year-old Thomas Kleppe, who was tapped by President Nixon early this year for the SBA's top job, is determined to stop the revolving door and breathe new life into the agency. A government," he notes, "are going to cut down on many a small businessman's profits, and he is going to need a loan to get him over the hump."

What kinds of business are kept afloat by these SBA loans? The lion's share of the loans, which have numbered some 145,000, totaling $2.5 billion, since the agency's inception, go to typical Mom and Pop enterprises like barbershops, butchers and boutiques. In recent years, in fact, an increasing proportion of these loans have gone to budding entrepreneurs who want to purchase franchises of one kind or another. "Franchising," says Eachon, "is an excellent way for an inexperienced guy to get into business. The franchisers generally have a prescribed formula for a novice to follow. Sure," he admits, "there have been some fly-by-night operators in franchising. But we have had excellent experience with such outfits as McDonald's, Burger King and Western Auto."

The SBA, however, is not only involved in staking Mom and Pop. It is constantly lending money to more sophisticated companies. Among its recent loans are $330,000 to Photo Magnetic Systems, Inc. of Greenbelt, Maryland, which makes a device for programming a computer over the telephone, and a loan of $350,000 to Continental Conveyor Co., which is building a highly automated materials handling plant in Jasper, Alabama.

In fact, under recently passed legislation, the SBA can go over the $350,000 loan ceiling to assist companies damaged by foreign competition. Under this law, the agency has loaned $2 million to Chicago's Emil J. Paidar Co., whose sole business of manufacturing barber chairs has been severely damaged by Japanese imports, and it has loaned $1.4 million to Mas-

sachusetts' Benson Shoe Co., which is in a similar bind.

All of these loans are, of course, risks that the banks were unwilling to assume without a government guarantee. But given the fact that the loans are generally "unbankable," the loss of the taxpayer's money has been relatively small. The SBA's loan loss record since its inception has been 3.8%. The typical commercial bank's loss record runs somewhere between 1.5% and 2%. "But our losses are bound to go up in the future," warns Tom Kleppe. "Both the President and Congress want us to make an all-out effort to increase business ownership among the nation's black and Spanish-speaking minorities. I believe deeply in this program. But since so many of these people have had little business experience, the risks are naturally much greater. Right now, 37% of our loans and 21% of the dollars involved are going into minority business," adds Kleppe.

The man carrying the ball in the SBA's drive to increase the number of minority businesses is, on the face of it, a very unlikely candidate for such a task. Marshall J. Parker is a well-tailored businessman-farmer and former state senator from the country town of Seneca, South Carolina. And he is quite sensitive to the skepticism among some blacks that a man from the South, who happens to be a close associate of Senator Strom Thurmond (R.-S.C.), could be dedicated to creating more black businesses. But the highly articulate Parker is determined to dispel any existing skepticism. "If 17% of the population [the black and Spanish-speaking minority] continues to own less than 2.5% of the businesses and 0.5% of the nation's manufacturing assets," says Parker, "the whole former North Dakota Congressman, self-made-millionaire Kleppe brings to the job a missionary zeal that was never exhibited by his multitude of predecessors. A small businessman himself, Kleppe became president of the Gold Seal Co., a North Dakota bleach and wax manufacturer, at the age of 38. By the time he left to go to Congress, he had, in his own words, "made an awful lot of money."

The restless, energetic Kleppe is determined that the nation's 5 million small businessmen, who account for some 37% of the GNP, shall have the same opportunity to strike it rich that he had. The key, as Kleppe sees it, often is access to sufficient working capital. "Small businesses," says Kleppe, "are generally not prime candidates for bank loans. That's where we come in. We don't make the loan, but we guarantee 90% of it. It's all handled through the local bank," he explains.

If these loans are 90% guaranteed by Uncle Sam, why have so many banks heretofore been reluctant to make them? "The red tape has been simply horrendous," says Tony Chase. "It often took as long as six months to get a loan approved, and no less than 42 forms had to be processed to do the job. And if there was a default," he adds, "the SBA first conducted an investigation to find out why before it made good."

With that kind of legendary bureaucracy, it is not surprising that many banks were gun-shy about getting involved in these "guaranteed" loans. "But we have changed the whole system," says Chase proudly. "Now if a bank submits a loan application, we have just three days to say no. If they don't hear from us in that time, it's approved. The 42 forms are now two forms, and we pay off the defaults first and investigate later. Now our

problem," adds Chase, "is that many banks do not realize things have changed."

The job of convincing the nation's 14,000 banks that "things have changed" belongs to Jack Eachon, SBA's Associate Administrator for Financial Assistance. A former president of the First National Bank of Englewood, Colorado, the personable Eachon spent twenty years in the banking business before joining the SBA last year. "I traveled 200,000 miles last year telling bankers how they can benefit themselves and their communities by making SBA loans," says Eachon. "After all, when a community grows, nobody stands to benefit more than the local banker."

More money is needed

A good indicator that Eachon's efforts are bearing fruit is the fact that his till is practically empty. "We'll only have about $60 million left by June 1," he says. "And since our loans have been running at about that rate each month, the cupboard is going to be pretty bare by July."

But Eachon is fully confident that Congress will raise SBA's loan ceiling from the present $2.2 billion to $3.1 billion for the fiscal year beginning July 1. And having former Congressman Kleppe at the helm will not exactly hurt the agency on Capitol Hill. "With the economy turning up," says Eachon, "our loan demand next year should be at an all-time high." And there are still other reasons, he adds, why small businessmen will require additional working capital. "The rash of environmental and plant safety laws coming from every level of free-enterprise system will be in jeopardy."

Garnering government contracts

One of Parker's key vehicles for increasing minority enterprises is the SBA's set-aside program. Under it, the government not only sets aside a number of direct federal contracts for small business, but puts pressure on big contractors to subcontract to smaller enterprises. Only recently, in fact, SBA landed a $5-million Defense Department contract for Garland Foods, a minority-owned Dallas, Texas processor of canned hams. "But we don't want to make them dependent on Uncle Sam," says Parker. "This year, they have $5 million in government business and $6 million in commercial business. Next year, the government contract will be $3 million and the year after it will go down to $1 million. This should give them time to find other business to take up the slack."

This year, Parker's people have managed to garner some $11 billion in government contracts — $7 billion in prime and the rest in subcontracts — for small business. "Those subcontracts can be an awful tough nut," says Parker. "The big contractor always resists giving the subcontract work to small companies because it's naturally easier to give the job out to one big concern. What we try to do is to get him to break it down so the little companies can handle it. One of the toughest companies to move on this is Pratt & Whitney; they simply won't budge."

Parker particularly resents any allegation that small companies do not perform as well for the taxpayers as big ones. "Small companies often bid lower than big companies because they need the work. Therefore they are willing to take less profit. And smaller enterprises are often more efficient than larger ones," he adds.

An integral part of the SBA's program to aid small business are the Small Business Investment Companies — more familiarly known as SBICs — which were created amid great fanfare some thirteen years ago. An SBIC is a government-licensed private corporation that provides equity capital and long-term loans for small business. The minimum requirement of the SBIC is $150,000 in private money, which the government will match with $300,000.

Not surprisingly, the lure of government money matching private funds on a two-for-one basis stimulated a boom in SBICs in the early years of the program. Inevitably, there was a big shakeout because, as Arthur Singer, SBA's Associate Administrator for Investment put it, "a lot of people got into the SBIC business who had no business being in it."

But Singer, formerly president of El Paso, Texas' Alemite Co., believes that the shakeout was a good thing for the entire program. Although there are now only about half the SBICs there were five years ago, they are, in the main, much stronger enterprises. Says Singer, "While 645 SBICs invested $220 million in small business in 1965, last year 331 SBICs invested $187 million. I think that this puts the entire program on a much more solid footing."

Of the 331 SBICs now in existence, 37 are publicly owned. Among the most successful are Narragansett Capitol of Rhode Island, headed by retired Textron Chairman Royal Little; the First Connecticut SBIC, which specializes in real-estate development companies; and Midland Capital, whose largest stockholder is New York's Marine Midland Bank.

The lure of the SBIC has proven so attractive, in fact, that some of the nation's top corporations — including General Motors — have gotten into the act. And applications are currently being processed for ITT and Union Camp.

Without a doubt, however, the SBIC is an ideal vehicle for the banks, which are already in the business of evaluating the prospects of small companies through their loan departments. Thus it is not surprising that some of the nation's largest and most successful SBICs are owned by such major banks as First National City, The Bank of America, Continental Illinois and Chase Manhattan. Says President Louis L. Allen of Chase Manhattan Capital Corp., whom Anthony Chase calls "the greatest venture capitalist of them all": "We are now in sixty different investments, from the $5,500 we have in a dry-cleaning store in Brooklyn to the $2 million we have in a computer firm in Boston. We had 1,000 small companies come to us last year," continues Allen, "and after extensive investigation, we decided to invest in eleven of them."

In an effort to pump more money into the SBICs — and thus into small business — the SBA has come up with a plan to market some $30 million in the debt obligations of various SBICs. The entire issue, much like a federally insured mortgage, will be backed by Uncle Sam. The issue is being floated this month by a blue-ribbon underwriting syndicate headed by Solomon Brothers and Goldman, Sachs. To head off criticism that they are giving this business to the giants of the investment world, SBA has shrewdly insisted that the syndicate include four small regional underwriters. "It will be kind of a baby Fanny Mae offering," says Arthur Singer.

But even if the offering is successful and SBA also gets the money it hopes for from Congress, the agency can never hope to have the $14 billion the Federal Reserve estimates as the capital requirements of small business. This huge need, which often means life or death to a small enterprise, can only come from using the SBA's funds to tap private resources, or "leverage," as Tom Kleppe puts it. "We must get maximum leverage for every dollar that we have by tapping private capital both through the banks and the SBICs," says Kleppe, puffing on a cigar.

But as the once sleeping giant on Washington's L Street begins to stir under Tom Kleppe's firm leadership, both bankers and venture capitalists should soon be convinced that small business is where the action is. — GERALD R. ROSEN

This reading is a criticism of the SBA. There is no shortage of that! Note that it appeared one year after the previous article.

Urgently required: A reordering of SBA priorities to save small business

Harold K. Charlesworth†

†Harold K. Charlesworth, pp. 45-58, *MSU Business Topics,* Summer 1972.

Reprinted by permission of the publisher, Division of Research, Graduate School of Business Administration, Michigan State University.

The most persistently troubled sector of the U.S. economy is that of small business. Joseph Martin, Jr., general counsel for the Federal Trade Commission, predicted that inexorable economic forces may eliminate small and moderate-sized businesses in the near future. Unfortunately, the programs proposed and enunciated to resolve small business problems are largely ineffective and unimaginative.

In testimony before the Senate Committee on Small Business, Edward H. Pendergast, Jr., vice president for Legislation of Small Business Associations of the Northeast, outlined the dilemma that faces small business and the federal government. He contended that the Small Business Administration (SBA) is "woefully inadequate to perform its mission" of furthering the growth of small business and encouraging a healthy, competitive business environment. SBA's efforts have been diminished by having heaped upon it "additional responsibilities without additional manpower to carry out new programs." As a consequence, this lack of personnel and the necessary supportive funding has limited the SBA's activities almost exclusively to those of servicing borrowers, while neglecting such vital programs as procurement and management assistance.

What is particularly troubling about the neglect of small business is the significance of this sector to the U.S. economy's future growth and economic viability. As shown in Table 18-1, the small business share of gross national product amounted to 37 percent in 1967; for 1970 "the small business share of Gross Business Product (Gross National Product less Government output, agricultural product, and miscellaneous adjustments) has about drawn even with the share of its big business competitors." Moreover, "this

trend toward a progressively higher small business share of gross business product is expected to continue through the 1970s."

The share of GNP generated by small business is divided up among thousands of firms having widely different characteristics as to the size of business receipts, number of employees, number of firms per industry group, and legal form of organization.

According to Internal Revenue Service (IRS) data for 1966, 32 percent of all business firms had receipts under $5,000; 12 percent had receipts between $8,000 and under $10,000; and 56 percent, $10,000 or over. In terms of the number of employees, 26 percent of these firms had no employees; 55 percent had 1-9 employees; 13 percent had 10-49 employees; 3 percent had 50-99 employees; and 3 percent had 100 or more employees.

Increases in human population and in personal and per capita income are the basic ingredients which induce a favorable rate of growth in the business population. As shown in Table 18-2, between 1963 and 1971 the total number of businesses increased roughly 16 percent, from 4,797,000 to 5,560,000.

Of critical importance is the small business share of the total business population, currently estimated to be about 95 percent. [See discussion of the definition of small business below.] In 1970, 5,200,000 of the 5,480,000 firms in the United States were considered small concerns, and the SBA estimated that, for 1971, small business firms would account for 97 percent or 5,280,000 of the total business population. Assuming that 95 percent of all business firms may be classified as small business, and recognizing that Table 18-2 is based on fiscal rather than calendar years, the number of small

TABLE 18-1: Distribution of Gross National Product, by sector, 1967

	Billions of 1958 dollars	Percent-age of total
Total GNP	673.1	100.0
Business	580.5	86.0
Small[1]	248.5	37.0
Other[1]	332.0	49.0
Agricultural, forestry, and fisheries	25.4	4.0
Government and government enterprises	66.9	10.0
Rest of the world[2]	4.5	1.0
Residual[3]	−4.2	−1.0

SOURCE: Office of Business Economics, U.S. Department of Commerce and Office of Planning, Research and Analysis, Small Business Administration.

[1]Estimates of the Small Business Administration.

[2]Difference between income of foreign concerns in the United States and U.S. concerns abroad representing compensation of employees, corporate profits, and net interest.

[3]Difference between GNP measured as sum of final products and GNP measured as the sum of gross product originating by industries.

businesses at the end of calendar year 1977 would be about 5.9 million.

The small business share of individual industry receipts or sales reflects its importance to a particular sector. In 1970, for example, only in manufacturing, where small business receipts accounted for but 30 percent of the industry's total, did big business dominate the industry. However, small business accounted for 85 percent of sales or receipts in the contract construction industry, 82 percent in the service industry, 72 percent in retail trade, and 70 percent in wholesale trade.

The record of business failures, starts, and discontinuances

The growth in the numbers of small business hides the true state of the patient's health because the figures cover up an increasing number of business failures and a rising number of business discontinuances.

Dun & Bradstreet reported that the failure rate per 10,000 firms of all sizes was forty-four in 1970 as compared with thirty-seven in 1969, an increase of 17 percent (see Table 18-3). More favorable economic conditions for small business are reflected in the 1968 and

**TABLE 18-2:   Estimated number of business firms:
1963, 1969, 1970, 1971, and 1977[1]**

FISCAL YEARS
(thousands)

Industry	1963 Amount	%	1969 Amount	%	1970 Amount	%
All industry	4,797	100.0	5,420	100.0	5,480	100.0
Construction	470	9.8	540	10.0	541	9.9
Manufacturing	313	6.5	340	6.3	340	6.2
Wholesale	332	6.9	380	7.0	384	7.0
Retail	2,032	42.4	2,240	41.3	2,255	41.2
Services	942	19.6	1,090	20.1	1,115	20.3
Other	708	14.8	830	15.3	845	15.4

[1]The IRS estimates the total number of business firms in the United States in 1966 to be 8,251,200. The fundamental difference between IRS and SBA business population statistics is that the SBA concept "excludes firms with no employees, and no established place of business as well as agriculture and professional services."

1969 low failure rates than are reflected for 1970. If the current 6 percent level of unemployment cannot be reduced in 1972, and if inflation remains unchecked, a rise in failure rates, possibly to the level shown in the early sixties, might be expected.

On the average over the past decade, new business starts have accounted for about 9 percent and old business discontinuances for approximately 8 percent of the business population. While business discontinuances must not be identified with business failures, evidence presented by different studies indicates that, "of all new business entrants, about one-third are discontinued within one year; about 50 percent are discontinued within 2 years; and about two-thirds are discontinued within five years." The studies also indicate that "about half of the discontinued businesses were discontinued for

the purpose of avoiding or minimizing losses."

If the above estimates of starts and discontinuances are applied to the business population forecast figures in Table 18-2, in 1977 there will be about 561,000 new starts and 498,000 discontinuances. Assuming one-half of the discontinuances are to avoid or minimize loss, about 249,000 businesses in 1977 will close their doors for this reason, and almost all of these discontinuances will be small businesses.

This violent cycle of births and deaths which accompanies expansion of the business population has been described as healthy and normal because it is the expected outcome of a market-oriented society where the owner-entrepreneur assumes the risk of doing business. But this cavalier attitude hardly is justified when it is recognized that both the probability of the business failure rate

TABLE 18-2 (Continued)

1971 Amount (estimated)	%	1977 Amount (forecast)	%	Annual percentage Increase 1971-1977
5,560	100.0	6,230	100.0	2.0
555	10.0	670	10.8	3.5
342	6.2	355	5.7	0.6
390	7.0	445	7.1	2.3
2,270	40.8	2,430	39.0	1.1
1,140	20.5	1,280	20.5	2.1
863	15.5	1,050	16.9	3.6

SOURCES: 1963 and 1969: *Recent Trends in Industry*, Office of Planning, Research and Analysis, Small Business Administration, 2 October 1969, Table 1; 1970, 1971, and 1977: *Small Business Administration Economic Review*, annual issue, 1971, pp. 21, 65.

and the number of discontinuances have a heavy impact on sustained and rapid national growth.

TABLE 18-3: Business failure trends since 1960

Year	Failures per 10,000 firms
1960	57
1961	64
1962	61
1963	56
1964	53
1965	53
1966	52
1967	49
1968	39
1969	37
1970	44

SOURCE: *The Failure Record Through 1970*, Dun & Bradstreet, 1971, p. 1.

Major problems facing small business

President Nixon, in his Message to Congress on 20 March 1970, reported that his Task Force on Improving the Prospects of Small Business had identified three major problem areas: (1) the need for sound management counseling; (2) the need for capital and for recognition of the special financial problems small firms may face in their early years; and (3) the need for people, and especially for trained people. While the President's Message to Congress correctly identified the three major problems facing small business, the SBA has been slow in undertaking positive and corrective steps to remove these problems. Certainly the question must be asked, "Why?"

In passing the Small Business Act, Congress gave to the agency the mandate of counseling, assisting, and protecting the interests of small business concerns, thereby strengthening and maintaining free competitive enterprise and contributing to the strength of the national economy. In carrying out its mandate, the SBA chose the funding of small business as its first, and by far most important, assistance activity. While it recognized the legitimacy and the need for management assistance, it never assigned to such assistance equal priority with its loaning or funding activities. For example, out of more than 4,000 SBA personnel, only seventy-three currently are assigned to offer management assistance to small business.

Moreover, the SBA has adopted a passive role by dispersing its assistance on a first come, first served basis. In so doing, it has failed to promote the importance of small business in the restructuring of the U.S. economy, with the ultimate aim of a redistribution of prosperity. That is, many geographic locations and linguistic and ethnic minorities are not included in the growing U.S. abundance because employment and growth patterns are unevenly distributed. Minority groups do not have the same level of per capita income or employment opportunity as the predominantly white population. The SBA estimates that only 3.7 percent of all U.S. businesses were owned by minorities in 1968, and that "it would require an investment of at least $40 billion at 1968 prices from all sources to raise the status of minority persons in the small business community to a point where their disadvantaged status would be no greater than that of small business in general."

Furthermore, while the growth of small business (which has increased over 75 percent between 1945 and 1969) has paralleled the nation's economic affluence, geographically this growth pattern has been extremely uneven. Income expansion has been more rapid in the Southeast, Southwest, and Far West than in the midwestern regions of the country.

What the SBA must do if it is to expand the importance of small business is to change its policy and become actively concerned with the role small business can play in restructuring the economy. Moreover, to achieve maximum effectiveness, the SBA must reorder its priorities.

Reordering SBA priorities

Thus far, the very magnitude and diversity of small business has hindered development of a sound small business assistance policy. It is this author's contention that the SBA must reorder its priorities by first identifying and defining the major elements of the small business community through a determination of common characteristics and needs. Following this, there is a need for a major shift in program emphasis and policy away from financial and toward management assistance. Further, the SBA can promote small business growth and development, particularly among disadvantaged groups and areas, by establishing a capital bank to provide discount facilities for long-term paper. The initial step, however, must be that of defining the basic elements and needs.

The definitional problem

In analyzing the problems inherent in defining small business, C. N. Hooper concluded that "a definition of small business is not, in fact, independent of the policy problem being considered and that any argument about definition is essentially an argument about policy."

The very concept of *smallness* itself is a relative term. The Small Business Act of 1953 defined a small business as

one which is independently owned and operated and which is not dominant in its field of operation. In addition to the foregoing criteria the Administrator, in making detailed definition, may use these criteria, among others: Number of employees and dollar volume of business. Where the number of employees is used as one of the criteria in making such a definition for any of the purposes of this Act, the maximum number of employees which a small business concern may have under the definition shall vary from industry to industry.

An obvious issue in the definitional problem is the unit of measurement to be selected, for example, the number of employees, asset value, net income, or the annual volume of business receipts. For use in its business loan program, the SBA currently defines a manufacturing firm as *small* if its employment in the preceding four calendar quarters did not exceed 250, and as *large* if average employment exceeds 1,500. In contrast, for construction, wholesaling, retailing, and service industries, a yearly dollar volume of business is used to determine whether a firm is large or small. For example, a wholesaling firm is classified as small if yearly sales do not exceed $5 to $15 million, and in retailing, annual receipts cannot exceed $1 to $5 million.

Yet definitions useful for loan programs are not appropriate if the emphasis of the SBA policy and programs is to shift from financial to management assistance. What is needed is a *behavioral approach* which focuses its attention on differing kinds of business behavior. The following

section examines one attempt to identify different types of small business organizations using this approach.

Suggested behavioral definition

A study of the trip reports of program officers (small business management consultants) of the University of Kentucky's Office of Business Development and Government Services to five hundred small business clients visited between July 1968 and January 1972 yields the matrix of small businesses by behavioral patterns shown in Table 18-4.

As indicated by the columnar headings, the identification or unit of measurement of each business client was behavioral rather than deterministic, that is, small business was not identified as to the number of employees, value of assets, or volume of sales receipts. Rather, the behavioral definition recognizes that the small businessman is a product of his sociocultural environment and seeks to group his activities around some central tendency which is either social or cultural in character. About 50 percent of the small business clients studied were self-employed, that is, a one person (male or female) or a family (ma and pa) type operation. At best they may employ a few people, but never more than five. Obviously, they are found predominantly in wholesale and/or retail establishments and in the service industry (dry cleaning, fast foods).

About one-third of the clients were identified as craftsmen. A craftsman clearly evidences a strong talent in some economic activity; he may have a particular talent as a mechanic or

TABLE 18-4:   **Clients by types of business operations (based on sample of 500 small business clients)**

	Self-Employed[1]		Craftsman[2] (one talent)		Organization pattern[3]		Total	
	Amount	%	Amount	%	Amount	%	Amount	%
Manufacturing	50	10.0	83	16.6	34	6.8	167	33.4
Wholesale/retail	123	24.6	48	9.6	33	6.6	204	40.8
Service	73	14.6	31	6.2	25	5.0	129	25.8
Total	246	49.2	162	32.4	92	18.4	500	100.0

[1] Ma and pa type of operation, entrepreneur key figure.

[2] Attention concentrated on machinery or production. Business developed because of the owner's mechanical techniques, buying, selling.

[3] Large operation with department heads or specialized functions, sophisticated organizational pattern.

engineer, or he may have built up his business because of his skill in repairing cars, trucks, and other machinery. While the one talent need not be mechanical, it often is. However, it may be a buying or bargaining ability or a selling capability which makes him outstanding, or perhaps he is innovative and produces an item which has found a market and is selling well. The significant factor is that this talent is so outstanding it has permitted him to operate successfully a small business typically employing between five to twenty people. Yet his success hangs exclusively on this one remarkable talent and everything is subordinated to it. As a result, the other necessary decisions required to efficiently operate a small business are often ignored until their demands severely hamper or perhaps even destroy the craftsman's business. The most commonly ignored demand is for good accounting records to meet payments, pay for taxes, record accounts receivable and payable, and so

forth. In a sense, the craftsman is top-heavy in one talent and inadequate in another, and his management practices may be characterized as being strongly imbalanced among the different management functions.

Less than 20 percent of the clients fall within the final category of organization pattern. Organization pattern represents that sophisticated group of small businesses which undertake business operations in a well-balanced manner. Each function, such as personnel, sales, administration, accounting, or planning, is recognized and assigned its proper order of importance or priority. The number of employees ranges from about twenty to 250, which, by SBA definition, is the limit for a small manufacturing firm. The term *organization* also indicates that the small business group tends not to be dominated by a single personality or function. Rather, the business is organized around all the necessary functions required to produce an

TABLE 18-5: Small business problems ranked by frequency of appearance

Problem	Frequency	Percentage
Financial planning	79	16.8
Accounting	76	16.2
Marketing	70	14.9
Plant layout	39	8.4
Inventory control	32	6.8
Collections	32	6.8
Credit	29	6.1
Personnel	29	6.1
Technical process	27	5.8
Tax problems	23	4.9
Production planning	17	3.6
Production control	11	2.3
Quality control	6	1.3
Total	470	100.0

efficient economic unit, and each function, as indicated, is given its proper voice in management.

Corresponding to the column totals, the row totals identify the clients by type of business, with one-third categorized as manufacturing, two-fifths as wholesale/retail and slightly more than one-fourth as service oriented. This kind of behavioral definition establishes not one single statistical universe, but, rather, several different universes, each with its significant behavioral and business characteristics. To lump them all into one massive universe is to deny the diversity which exists among small businesses with regard to abilities, need for assistance, and attitudes toward such assistance. To rely on a single universe is to assure that the bulk of small business assistance programs will go to the more sophisticated and knowledgeable, who value such

assistance. The rest will remain without aid.

Identification of basic needs

An additional group of 200 business clients (randomly selectly from among the 500 businesses discussed previously) identified their business problems, needs, and attitudes toward assistance programs. As with the 500 businesses, the 200 clients were classified by type of organization (self-employed, craftsman, or organization pattern) and by type of business (manufacturing, wholesale/retail, or service). Thirteen different business problems were identified. The frequency with which each problem occurred varied from a low of only six for quality control to seventy-nine for financial planning. Table 18-5 ranks the different problems in terms of their relative frequency of appearance. Most clients had more than one identifiable problem, and the mean number of problems was 2.4 per client. As might be expected, the most frequent combination consisted of financial planning, accounting, and marketing, ranking first, second, and third among problems encountered.

When the thirteen problems were allocated among the clients by type of organization, the bulk of the financial planning, accounting, and marketing problems were found among the self-employed, as is to be expected. As the sophistication of the organization grew, the problems increased in complexity. The clients classified as organizational pattern expressed considerable concern over problems in technical process, production planning, and control.

Similarly, clusters of problems were found when allocated among the clients by type of business. The whole-sale/retail clients accounted for a large share of the financial planning, accounting, marketing, credit, and collection problems. Most problems found among service clients were similar to those facing the wholesaler/retailer. Manufacturers encountered problems of plant layout and quality control.

All clients were found to be short of money, and undercapitalization of fixed assets was a common characteristic. However, only 16.8 percent of the problems clearly could be identified as being caused by acute money stringency. And even here, more money was not the answer to the problem; the need was for better management of funds. For the majority of clients, financial assistance or funding would not fulfill their needs. The clients indicated that, of the thirteen problems, lack of good management was the most likely reason for small business failures.

It must be recognized that answering small business management needs with more financial assistance acts as a palliative, preventing corrective action from being taken. Second, until a behavioral definition is made, differences and similarities among small business cannot be identified. Moreover, each type of small business operation must be given a management assistance program oriented toward solving its particular problems. Using a general and impersonal assistance program for all types of small business is of little value because each owner or manager views his problems in a personal light and resents the impersonal approach. The obvious need is for management assistance, and means must be found to deliver it.

Search for an effective delivery system

If poor management is the basic problem confronting small business, why hasn't the SBA devised effective programs to correct this deficiency? In part, it is because the SBA never has been given the funding to support an effective nationwide management assistance program. A second, more basic, reason is that achievement of an effective delivery system of management assistance requires an understanding of small business attitudes and behavior, and the recognition that such knowledge must form the basis for any assistance program. Past programs offered by the SBA, universities, and state and federal agencies have failed to recognize that behavioral patterns and attitudes are an integral part of small business problems. One possible explanation of this oversight is that such behavior patterns have become so routinized as to pass almost unnoticed. Whatever the reason, the fact remains that past programs have not been notably successful. The question then is: What criteria can be used to determine whether a delivery system is effective? It can be measured in part by the attitudes of small business toward an assistance program. In particular, was the program well received and did it help induce corrective management practices?

As an illustration, a total of 585 visits were made to the 200 randomly selected clients, identified by type of organization and type of business in Table 18-6. Seventy-eight percent of all clients were receptive to visits, 19 percent were indifferent, and only a negligible number were hostile or refused assistance. The average number of visits was nearly three per client.

There was little difference among the clients as to the average number of visits when classified by type of organization. However, when classified by type of business there was a noticeable variation; the average number of visits to manufacturing clients were 23 percent greater than to service clients.

Table 18-7, which shows the analysis and distribution of visits by type of organization, reveals important characteristics about the visit pattern. Among the self-employed, 339 visits were made, 70 percent of which were favorably received; the largest percentage of total visits (52 percent) were made to wholesale/retail clients who, while not as receptive as manufacturing or service clients, still were relatively receptive (65 percent).

There was greater total receptivity among craftsmen (87 percent) than among the self-employed (70 percent). Within the 135 visits paid to craftsmen, manufacturing received the greatest number, with receptivity at 78 percent. Wholesale/retail clients and service clients had fewer visits but were more highly receptive, with 93 percent and 94 percent respectively.

Among the organizational pattern clients, manufacturing again received the greatest number of visits (46 percent) with receptivity of 82 percent.

TABLE 18-6: Classification of clients and visits by type of organization

	Self-employed	Craftsmen	Organizational pattern	Total
Number of clients	115	44	41	200
Number of visits	339	135	111	585
Average number of vists	2.9	3.1	2.8	2.9

By type of business

	Manufacturing	Wholesale/Retail	Service	Total
Number of clients	51	86	63	200
Number of visits	166	253	166	585
Average number of visits	3.2	3.0	2.6	2.9

TABLE 18-7: Analysis of visits by type of organization

SELF-EMPLOYED

	Manufacturing		Wholesale/ Retail		Service		Total	
	Amount	%	Amount	%	Amount	%	Amount	%
Receptive	44	73	114	65	78	76	236	70
Indifferent	16	27	58	33	19	18	93	27
Hostile	0	0	4	2	6	6	10	3
Total	60	100	176	100	103	100	339	100
Percentage of total visits to self-employed		18		52		30		100

CRAFTSMAN

	Manufacturing		Wholesale/ Retail		Service		Total	
	Amount	%	Amount	%	Amount	%	Amount	%
Receptive	42	78	37	93	39	94	118	87
Indifferent	8	15	3	7	2	6	13	10
Hostile	0	0	0	0	0	0	0	0
Total	54	100	40	100	41	100	135	100
Percentage of total visits to craftsman		40		30		30		100

ORGANIZATIONAL PATTERN

	Manufacturing		Wholesale/ Retail		Service		Total	
	Amount	%	Amount	%	Amount	%	Amount	%
Receptive	43	82	33	89	22	100	98	88
Indifferent	7	14	4	11	0	0	11	10
Hostile	2	4	0	0	0	0	2	2
Total	52	100	37	100	22	100	111	100
Percentage of total visits to organizational pattern		46		33		20		100
Total visits	166		253		166		585	
Percentage receptive		78		73		84		

NOTE: Total visits to the craftsman group include four visits to manufacturing firms which were refused.

Again, wholesale/retail and service clients had fewer visits but higher receptivity; 89 percent of the former were receptive and all of the latter. One would expect to find a greater number of manufacturing businesses in the organizational pattern sector because more sophisticated business concepts are associated with manufacturing.

Table 18-7 reveals that, for the manufacturing industry, visit receptivity increases from the self-employed through the craftsmen to the organizational pattern. This same pattern exists for the service visits; all twenty-two visits made to service clients in the organizational pattern were favorably received. Yet the same pattern does not exist for the wholesale/retail clients.

As for the distribution of total visits, an equal number were made to the manufacturing and service clients (166), yet the service clients proved to have greater total receptivity (84 percent as compared to 78 percent). The wholesale/retail clients had the lowest total receptivity (73 percent) and the highest indifference (26 percent). The distribution of visits within the manufacturing industry were approximately equal. This is to be expected since the smaller number of self-employed businesses probably reflect the higher fixed investment requirements of the manufacturing industry. In all, a total of 452 receptive visits were made, or 77 percent of all visits. Of these 452 visits, about twice as many were made to the self-employed as to the craftsmen or to the organizational pattern. When classified by type of organization, small business clients who follow a craftsman or a wholesale/retail business pattern are relatively more receptive to business counseling than the self-employed who, as a group, are the least receptive.

However, even here the percentage showing favorable response to offers of assistance was 70 percent (Table 18-7). When classified by type of business there is less variation in the distribution of receptive visits than exists when classified by type of organization. But the pattern of visits strongly identifies the wholesale/retail industry as the least receptive. Overall, the most receptive clients by type of organization were in the grouping organizational pattern, and, by type of business, among the service clients. In both groupings, over 80 percent of the clients responded favorably to assistance visits (Table 18-7).

A second measure of the effectiveness of a delivery system is the number of new jobs created or old jobs protected through management assistance. An estimate of the value of the program to the economy of the state for the fiscal year 1970-1971 shows 1,088 jobs created by expansion of the firm or protected from business failure. In the preceding year, the estimated jobs created or protected were less than half as large, reflecting a growing awareness of the program in the business community as well as a change in client attitude from indifference and even hostility to greater receptivity.

Finally, the question needs to be asked: Should the SBA itself mount a management assistance program? One answer was presented during the hearings before the U.S. Senate Select Committee on Small Business. Replying to the question whether scientific and technological research assistance could be delivered economically by the SBA, Wilfred Garvin, assistant administrator for Planning, Research and Analysis on SBA observed: "Within the framework of our organization today, we very candidly have not the expertise in this area from the standpoint of management assistance. And I think it would be too costly to provide it through the vehicle of the people of SBA directly, but rather to use the facilities of our educational institutions when it can be better done."

For the SBA to undertake the provisions of an effective delivery system would require enormous funding, create a whole new bureaucracy centralized in Washington, and require a staff needlessly duplicating many already existing staffs in universities and colleges. A more reasonable approach is that the SBA's role in management counseling should be as an expediter and catalyst by helping to fund staffs of management consultants at educational institutions where experience in behavioral attitudes and knowledge of business problems already exist.

While management assistance provided by the change agent concept is a necessary condition of small business growth and development, it alone is not sufficient. A necessary ingredient for the future development of small business is "risk capital." This aspect of the problem often is referred to as the "small business capital gap."

Overcoming the small business capital gap

Attempts to measure the existence of a small business capital gap have been impeded severely by the variety and haziness of definitions.

The concept of a capital gap is suggested in Section 207 (a) of the Small Business Act: "(1) No financial assistance shall be extended pursuant to this subsection unless the financial assistance applied for is not otherwise available on reasonable terms. (2) All loans made under this subsection shall be of such sound value or so secured as reasonably to assure repayment."

Thus, according to the act, a gap existed if a small business failed to secure "on reasonable terms" capital which it needed and could "reasonably" be expected to repay. No standards of "reasonableness" were set forth in the statute.

A small business capital gap can be said to exist "if the marginal return on funds invested in small business exceed the marginal cost of capital; in other words, if opportunities to improve the allocation of scarce financial resources are being lost due to inadequate financing of small concerns. Second, a gap exists if the cost of money to small concerns (the riskless rate of interest plus allowances for differentials in risk and loan administration costs) exceeds the cost of money to large concerns."

In 1958 the Federal Reserve System made a comprehensive study of the financial needs and problems of small business. In its report to the House and Senate Banking and Currency and Small Business Committees it found "some evidence in the background studies . . . that there is an unfilled margin, perhaps a rather thin one, between the volume of funds available to small concerns in general, and to new firms in particular, and the volume that could be put to use without prohibitive risk."

Subsequent studies by the SBA based on the financial reports of some 22,000 borrowers indicate that for many small businesses a capital gap does exist, particularly with regard to intermediate and long-term credit. By contrast, short-term funds (generally under one year) are available for small business from a variety of sources such as credit lines extended by commercial banks, 30- to 90-day paper, and trade credits.

Unable to secure capital from the organized capital markets because "his needs for equity and loan capital are too small to interest the investment banker or to be marketed in the national capital and credit markets," the small businessman has turned to the commercial banking system. Yet his capital needs have remained largely unsatisfied, in part because of the liquidity problems associated with long- and intermediate-term paper of small business.

"The largest disadvantage of small size in business is the inability to absorb error." This remark by Louis Allen, president of Chase Manhattan Capital Corporation, mirrors the problem of liquidity. A commercial bank investing in small business must be prepared to suffer through several business "errors," all of which will require additional capital. Commercial banks are not organized to continue advancing capital in the face of repeated errors because they are not set up as venture capital institutions. Based on cash flow projections, the commercial banker inevitably will expect repayments of the loan to begin in the third month of operation. Repayment will commence, but more often than not with the businessman's personal savings.

However, the long-term capital needs of small business will not be overcome by resolving only the liquidity problem, important as that is. The 1958 Federal Reserve study of the capital requirements of small business was primarily concerned with the demand side of the problem. But the demand side reflects the borrower's search for capital; it does not reflect the lender's views or actions, and it must be remembered that discrimination against small business or the lack of

discrimination "is essentially, though not completely, a lender rather than a borrower's characteristic."

A study by William L. Silber and Murray E. Polakoff, using the same data as that on which the Federal Reserve study was based, found that "the banking system desired to discriminate against relatively small business borrowers during the 1947 period of tight money," and that "banks wished to favor large business by raising the portion of funds available for large-business loans while, at the same time, desiring to discriminate against small business by reducing the portion of funds available for small-business loans.

Viewed from a lender's perspective, the capital gap problem is as much the result of banker attitudes as it is a question of the credit worthiness of the borrower. Either ignored or unrecognized is that the indifferent and even hostile attitude of commercial banks toward small business creates an effective barrier to business growth and to an area's development. In the ghettos, commercial banks have discriminated against a minority group, albeit many times unwittingly, simply because the bank's attitude does not include understanding of a life style different from its own. Often the minority applicant loses a loan because "loan officers and loan forms measure things he lacks"; emphasis is placed by the bank on "previous bank association, age, years on the job, years at residence, home and property ownership. All these are things that most minorities . . . run short on." If commercial banks are to become an effective force for ghetto development, they must understand the minority culture which is quite different from the culture of middle class white America with whom they have most of their business dealings.

Similarly, the attitude of the commercial banker inhibits small business growth in rural areas. Many commercial bankers in rural America have a fear of any new and different business venture. They hesitate to make even the smallest loans outside well-known economic activity. This is well-exemplified by many Kentucky communities which owe their economic existence to coal mining or tobacco, and where banking communities have never seen or realized solid income derived from anything except coal and coal-based activities, or tobacco and tobacco-based industries.

In comparison with other rural communities, which have as much as 60 percent of their deposit money out on loan to small businesses to sustain the community's economic growth, 73 out of the 120 counties in Kentucky have lower loan-to-deposit ratios than the state average of .63. In many Kentucky towns, money that is not involved in coal or tobacco is placed in U.S. government securities; 38 banks in Kentucky have more funds in U.S. Treasury bonds than in loans, and many hold substantial amounts of federal agency securities and cash excess reserves. These banking preferences, so harmful to small business development, are built on the fear of accepting any risks in underwriting a business venture. This fear has been described by anthropologists as a kind of social paralysis where acceptability is generated by strict adherence to the status quo, and leadership is gained by "rote recitation of the epic past."

Unfortunately, the SBA's current guaranty loan program may support restrictive banking practices toward small business. At the end of fiscal 1971, the SBA's guaranty loan program accounted for 88.8 percent ($1,262.9 million) of total SBA-approved loans of $1,422.6 million. Of this, one-half ($696.1 million) represented guaranty loans. It is the nature of the loan guaranty program that the local banker determine which small business is an acceptable loan risk. In practice, this may result in banks favoring those clients whose business organization places them among the organizational pattern group because the banker has less to fear from faulty records, poor management decisions, and untried and new business ventures. Assuming that the 500 clients studied represent a fair cross section of all types of small business, then the SBA's loan guaranty program may be servicing less than 20 percent of the total small business population, leaving 80 percent and more unfunded. The SBA's direct loan program, which does not work through the local banking structure, but goes directly to the small business, accounts for less than 1 percent ($13.8 million) of total loans approved.

To be sure, the difference between the two programs is a large one. Under direct loans the SBA lends its own money; under guaranty loans it generates the local bank's loan. And since the SBA's funding for direct loans is very limited, it usually has chosen to expand its financial assistance through the guaranty loan program. Also, the SBA has pushed its economic opportunity loans to help disadvantaged minority groups as well as its Displaced Business and Local Development Company loans. But the SBA's share of the total of these three programs came to $186.2 million in fiscal 1971, or 26.7 percent of its guaranty loan program. Clearly, the guaranty loan program is by far the most important for small business, and clearly, it is this program which is most likely to be subjected to the fears and even hostilities of the local banker, to the detriment of small business.

One possible solution to the dilemma is that the Federal Reserve Board give immediate attention to its rediscount policies and practices governing small business intermediate and long-term paper. In particular, the federal government should adopt a long-range legislative program covering small business capital needs which would lay the foundation for the development of small business in the 1970s to the turn of the century. Recognition by the federal government of the special capital needs of agriculture was a significant reason for the rapid increase in agriculture production during the first half of the century, and surely the needs of small business are no less significant or important.

Such a program should include: (1) the establishment of a capital bank as a discount facility for term paper; (2) a policy of permitting commercial banks to take an equity position (for example, conversion privilege) in small firms which are nonpublicly held; (3) a recognition that management assistance must be given after a loan is made as well as before; and (4) active encouragement of small-town bankers in rural areas and big bankers in urban ghettos to adopt a positive attitude toward small business loans.

Conclusions

What steps can be taken to reorder SBA priorities and thereby promote the role small business can play in restructuring the economy? In the area of management assistance, the SBA can inaugurate a major policy shift away from financial to management assistance and thereby give material encouragement to "maintain and preserve free competitive enterprise."

Such recommendations have been made to the agency before. In fact, one common thread running through three separate evaluations of the SBA's minority enterprise program was "an emphasis on the importance of management training and counseling and a finding of insignificant deficiencies in both the quantity and quality of training and counseling actually furnished to borrowers." Similar needs have been expressed for small business in the rural areas, where it is recognized that the small businessman who refuses to either seek or accept professional assistance faces growing business risks and dim prospects for business success.

It is the hypothesis of this article that the role small business can play in the promotion of national or regional economic development can and must be one of great significance. However, that role will never be achieved until the importance of behavior patterns in the decision-making process of small business owners and managers has been recognized and incorporated into a management assistance program.

Furthermore, acceptance of management assistance as the principal SBA goal toward promoting the development of small business can be a meaningless gesture unless an effective delivery system is adopted. The use of a change agent as a management assistance technique can be the basis of an effective delivery system to reduce business failures and discontinuances. As suggested by SBA administrators and the analysis of this article, universities and colleges are in a better position than federal agencies to identify small business problems and to develop appropriate solutions, given the sociocultural environment facing small business. The SBA's role should be that of a catalyst and expediter of management assistance programs, rather than a participant.

The sociocultural environment, both of the businessman and the banker, often has been the inhibiting influence preventing rural areas and ghettos from being offered or accepting social and economic change. Coupled with the establishment of a capital bank for small business, a significant step can be taken by the SBA, the Federal Reserve System, and other interested federal and state agencies to promote confidence and acceptance by the banking community of small business loans.

✳✳✳✳✳

Congress recognized the need for more venture capital and passed legislation to make such investments more attractive. Here is an evaluation of the SBIC and MESBIC programs.

A perspective on the MESBIC program

Richard H. Klein†

Considerable attention has been given by government, business, and academic communities to the Minority Enterprise Small Business Investment Company (MESBIC) concept over the past three years. Essentially, the MESBIC is a Small Business Investment Company (SBIC) devoted solely to the extension of loans and/or equity investments in enterprises owned and operated by socially and/or economically disadvantaged entrepreneurs. Primarily designed as a conduit whereby the skills

†**Richard H. Klein**, pp. 45-51, *MSU Business Topics*, **Autumn 1972.**

Reprinted by permission of the publisher, Division of Research, Graduate School of Business Administration, Michigan State University.

and finances of large- and medium-sized national corporations could be utilized to assist disadvantaged entrepreneurs, the MESBIC concept has been enlarged, and several community-based groups have initiated their own MESBICs.

While this approach does have considerable merit, it is the thesis of this article that only with some substantial modifications will the MESBIC program be able to provide significant venture capital and other financing for minority-owned businesses.

The MESBIC program benefits the disadvantaged entrepreneur, the community, the federal government, and the MESBIC-sponsoring organization. Because MESBICs are willing to extend credit, some of which may be subordinated to other creditors, or perhaps to even invest "front money," disadvantaged entrepreneurs can obtain needed capital. Even more important, MESBICs provide requisite managerial and technical assistance. Therefore, because of the MESBIC program, the disadvantaged entrepreneur may obtain such advantages as management assistance, seed capital, long-term loans, and the possibility of loans for periods as short as thirty months.

Numerous benefits accrue to the disadvantaged community through MESBIC activities. These include psychological uplift and self-pride, the infusion of capital leading to the establishment of an expanded economic and tax base, the creation of new and stable jobs in areas within reasonable commuting distance for disadvantaged workers, and the furnishing of managerial and financial skills to a community generally inexperienced in business. Perhaps the most important benefit that can be attributed to the MESBIC concept is that it contributes to the establishment of an entrepreneurial class.

Quite interesting are the advantages secured by the federal government from the MESBIC program. Because the MESBIC is a privately owned financial intermediary, and is only regulated by the Small Business Administration (SBA), the substantial paperwork, time, and costs that normally would be required in making a direct government loan are significantly reduced. Thus the MESBIC concept enables the government to fulfill the social objective of attracting venture capital for small disadvantaged entrepreneurs from the private sector. If the newly financed firms are successful, federal tax revenues will be increased. In addition, because the MESBIC can borrow funds at a given interest rate from SBA, the federal government can show a net "income" from the program while encouraging the financing of small disadvantaged businesses.

A variety of benefits are available to the sponsoring firm or organization which establishes its own MESBIC. These include good public relations; tax advantages such as the tax deductibility of 100 percent, rather than 85 percent, on dividends received from portfolio (client) companies; and the opportunity to learn about the specific needs of disadvantaged groups.

The MESBIC record

As of mid-July 1972, a total of fifty MESBICs have been licensed with a total paid in capital and surplus of $16,483,910. Total SBA funds loaned to these concerns amounted to $5,430,000. The availability of government funds on a two-for-one or, in some cases, on a three-for-one basis relative to private capital, has not been taken advantage of because of the limited length of time that these MESBICs have been in existence and because of the present relatively high cost of borrowing as required by statute.

MESBICs can receive revenues from items as interest on short-term securities (for example, certificates of deposit), interest on portfolio loans, dividends from equity investments, gains from the sale of securities, and consulting service fees. Costs of maintaining a MESBIC include operations costs, losses from defaulted loans, and the cost of capital. The U.S. Department of Commerce anticipates that the "sponsor" of a MESBIC will have to spend, on the average, about $60,000 on annual operating expenses alone, much of which will not be recovered, and they encourage firms to consider this possibly recurring expenditure as a "social investment."

That this pessimistic prediction has evolved can be seen by the fact that the twenty-one MESBICs reporting for the fiscal year ending 31 March 1971 revealed a negative 19.6 percent net return on invested capital for the year. However, the $816,962 loss reported is not representative of the MESBIC program's future capabilities because much of the amount can be attributed to the difficulties sustained by one MESBIC and to start-up costs of new MESBICs. Given a possible incubation

TABLE 18-8: Number and size distribution of licensed SBICs and MESBICs (private capital size groups)

	Size 1: $300,000 or less	Size 2: $300,001-$1,000,000
SBICs*	94	126
MESBICs**	33	14

SOURCES: *Small Business Administration, Office of Reports, Washington, D.C., 31 December 1971. The main offices of licensed SBICs only are included in this category. **Small Business Administration, Office of Reports, Washington, D.C., 15 March 1972.

period of about six years before MESBICs become profitable and given the cyclical nature of the industry, losses such as the one for the 1971 fiscal year should be anticipated. However, because of the present objectives and structure, the MESBIC program still might engender substantial losses.

Even though the program itself is presently unprofitable, MESBICs have furnished needed funds to disadvantaged entrepreneurs. According to the Department of Commerce, as of 1 April 1972, thirty-six MESBICs had financed 422 businesses in the total amount of $7,600,000, and these businesses employed more than 4,400 persons. An additional $23,000,000 in government guaranteed loans were made to these businesses largely because of previous MESBIC financing. The MESBIC program can already claim some success in that these financings generally would not have been made if not for the program.

In order to encourage the further extension of funds to disadvantaged entrepreneurs by MESBICs and in order to make the MESBIC program itself more viable, the Small Business Administration has modified the MESBIC program and has made it

somewhat different than its original foundation, the SBIC program. For instance, MESBICs are exempted from diversification limits which apply to SBICs. The percentage of MESBIC funds available to a portfolio concern for purchases of goods and services from MESBIC sponsors or associates has been increased from less than 50 percent of the funds to less than 75 percent. The latter change should encourage franchisers to establish MESBICs.

SBICs compared to MESBICs

Inasmuch as the MESBIC program is based primarily on the SBIC program it is necessary to examine some aspects of the older SBIC industry in order to forecast possible MESBIC trends. From its inception in 1958 until 31 March 1971, 817 SBICs were given licenses. At that latter point in time only 288 companies were reporting out of 442 licensed, and they had total assets of only $611.9 million. This information clearly indicates a "shakeout" and readjustment of present MESBICs.

Table 18-8 provides further credence to this thesis, and it shows the number

TABLE 18-8 (Continued)

Size 3: $1,000,001-$5,000,000	Size 4: $5,000,000 or more	Total number
52	14	286
0	0	47

and size distribution of SBICs and MESBICs. The differences in category proportions are significant and indicate that there will be a growth of MESBIC asset size.

Because the SBIC industry is more than ten years old, the data presented in Table 18-8 attest that economies of scale do exist in the industry. Table 18-9 is more explicit in illustrating the prevalence of these economies, and it provides annual SBIC data for the past four fiscal years. Of additional interest is the fact that only 97 out of 210 SBICs in the size 1 category reported data as of 31 March 1971, while for the size 3 category, 49 out of 52 reported. According to SBA, the ratio of reporting SBICs to licensed SBICs is a general indicator of the quality condition of the industry. Thus the economies of scale concept is again substantiated. Table 18-9 also demonstrates that the SBIC industry is highly cyclical by nature.

In promoting the MESBIC program, the Office of Minority Business Enterprise, U.S. Department of Commerce, has claimed that because of the uniqueness of the concept, MESBIC client concerns may be able to obtain $15 of financing for every $1 supplied by the MESBIC. It is highly doubtful that such a leverage ratio can be generally achieved, and this fact may cause

economic difficulties for MESBICs and the clients, especially if subsequent financing is required. A 1969 study showed that SBICs have enabled their clients to borrow only an additional $1.35 from commercial banks and other sources for each dollar invested or loaned by a SIBC. On the other hand, SBICs never were promoted on the leverage concept basis, while such is the case with MESBICs.

Obtaining funds through the sale of debentures to SBA by SBICs has been, at times, exceedingly difficult because of a lack of funds, and this situation would have portended poorly for the SBIC offshoot, the MESBIC. In some periods redemptions of SBIC debentures exceeded new credit extended by SBA thereby placing great financial strain on SBICs. However, a new law (Public Law 92-213) has changed the outlook for SBICs and MESBICs significantly. Now the 100 percent guarantee of the full faith and credit of the U.S. government can be placed on paper sold by SBA to finance SBICs and MESBICs if specific and adequate funds are not appropriated by Congress. Similar to the Federal National Mortgage Administration (FNMA) arrangement, the law purports to aid SBICs in those periods when they are unable to secure adequate funding. This possible

TABLE 18-9:   **Number of SBICs reporting and return on investment received: 1968-1971**

End of fiscal year	Private capital size group	Number of SBICs reporting	Percentage return on investment
31 March 1971	Size 1[a]	97	(0.2)
	2[b]	129	(1.7)
	3[c]	49	1.8
	4[d]	13	(9.1)
31 March 1970	Size 1[a]	125	1.4
	2[b]	144	3.1
	3[c]	48	5.0
	4[d]	14	2.0
31 March 1969	Size 1[a]	159	0.4
	2[b]	156	6.0
	3[c]	45	11.1
	4[d]	13	12.4
31 March 1968	Size 1[a]	221	1.1
	2[b]	175	4.2
	3[c]	31	7.6
	4[d]	14	7.5

NOTE: Private capital: a: $300,000 or less; b: $300,001-$1,000,001; c: $1,000,001-$5,000,000; d: $5,000,000 or more.

SOURCE: Small Business Administration, *SBIC Industry Review*, Washington, D.C.

repackaging and resale of SBIC debentures to institutional investors is guaranteed by SBA and is a significant advance because it creates a permanent source of funds for SBICs and MESBICs.

MESBICs encounter both economic and social problems, with the lack of present profitability being the most serious difficulty. Each loan has to be tailored separately and includes provisions for time period, repayment schedule, equity involvement, restrictions, and collateral. Thus the interest earned on the loan and the opportunity for additional gains through equity options must more than cover the cost of making the loan if the MESBIC is to be a viable financial institution rather than just an appealing concept.

Economic issues

The idea of establishing a small ($150,000) MESBIC was first offered to large private corporations, but that approach had its drawbacks. In the short run the sponsoring firm may be satisfied to be "reimbursed" through favorable public relations, but it is doubtful that such an outlook would continue to exist. If profits are not forthcoming and annual subsidies are required, the goodwill of the firm and the "fashionability" of the MESBIC program rapidly decline. It is quite revealing that most of the later MESBICs were established by nonprofit civic corporations or by a consortium of commercial banks. The banks' objective is probably to establish a financial intermediary to which a given bank in the consortium can refer a disadvantaged loan applicant in lieu of a final rejection.

The promotion of a number of smaller MESBICs was done under the mistaken premise of some government officials who argued that the objective should be to inject money into the disadvantaged community, and that once the concern is funded and the MESBIC provides managerial assistance, economic growth will be facilitated. Such an attitude neglects the profitability requirements of the MESBIC itself, ignores the concept of economies of scale, and is probably injurious to the long-term growth of the MESBIC industry.

Another economic issue facing MESBICs is the total amount of loans and/or equity investments extended to disadvantaged entrepreneurs. Of the $156 million disbursed by SBICs and MESBICs for the twelve-month period ending 31 March 1971, 3.5 percent or $5.4 million went to firms owned or controlled by socially or economically disadvantaged persons. Significantly, this figure is a substantial increase over previous years. Some explanation for this low percentage can be found in the fact that the total capital stock and surplus for the 288 SBICs reporting as of that date was $320.5 million, while the comparable figure for the 21 MESBICs was $3.3 million. These figures clearly indicate the need for additional investments in MESBICs.

Social issues

The social issues facing MESBICs are interrelated with the profitability issue. First, MESBICs make loans and/or equity investments to small businesses which, by their very nature, have a high probability of failure. Second, the objective of the entire MESBIC program is to aid the disadvantaged entrepreneur. MESBICs may be more apt to incur losses than SBICs because their particular clientele generally lacks a business tradition. While the individual disadvantaged entrepreneur may be knowledgeable about the operations of the business, he is usually unsophisticated in financial and managerial skills. Venture capital intermediaries such as MESBICs depend more on the skills and motivations of the individual entrepreneur than on any other factor. Thus, because the disadvantaged entrepreneur may not have had any opportunity to see how a business is managed nor been trained in the requisite technical skills, he is handicapped at the start.

Adding to the training deficiency is the fact that most of the disadvantaged entrepreneurs establish businesses in inner city neighborhoods. There they face the overlapping problems of poverty, a destructive environment, inadequate public transportation and parking facilities, lack of self-confidence, inability to obtain insurance, high crime rates, inadequate housing, and high taxes. Clearly, the difficulties enumerated here provide MESBICs with a monumental challenge if they are to be successful in aiding the disadvantaged entrepreneur and simultaneously in making a profit.

A social or a moral issue generated by some MESBICs is the fact that they desire to avoid equity involvement in the disadvantaged enterprises they finance. However, SBIC experience has shown that some type of equity financing such as convertible debentures or loans with stock warrants are the most profitable financing vehicles. The interest on the loan would cover the operating costs while the possibility for capital gains through stock warrants is what makes the financing attractive. Limiting the financing to the extension of loans only, even under the aegis of social consciousness, is untenable if the MESBIC industry is to prosper and be able to supply adequate financing to client firms.

Changes already proposed

In order to alleviate some of the problems facing MESBICs and to make them profitable, SBA already has made some changes to the MESBIC program and has proposed legislation (H.R. 13805) before Congress. Recognizing the existence of economies of scale, SBA is encouraging smaller MESBICs to merge. Such is the case of the merger between Opportunity Capital Corporation and Provident in California. In addition, both SBA and the American Association of MESBICs are encouraging the formation of consortiums of MESBICs in order to make larger loans or equity investments (more than $50,000) to a single client. In this manner the cost of the loan or equity investment per dollar is reduced, the restriction on the loan size that an individual MESBIC can make is overcome, the risk is spread over a number of participants, and MESBIC portfolio concerns can obtain adequate financing.

In order to help overcome the unprofitability problem and other

objections to the MESBIC program, SBA submitted innovative proposals for modification to Congress. Included in the recommended legislation is a request for authority for SBA to offer limited equity leverage to MESBICs. MESBICs would be allowed to sell nonvoting cumulative preferred stock to SBA, and this stock would carry a dividend rate of 3 percent. MESBICs capitalized at $500,000 or more would be able to sell to SBA an amount equal to its private capitalization. With this preferred stock concept, a federal regulatory agency for the first time would have as its policy the purchase of equity securities from a private concern.

The suggested bill also would grant an interest subsidy for the first five years on MESBIC debentures purchased by the administration. The interest rate paid by the MESBIC would be pegged at the greater of 3 percent or 3 percentage points below the borrowing cost of the government for comparable U.S. government securities. If the bill is passed, the cost of debt would be reduced during the MESBIC's formative years.

Also included in the legislation is the idea that MESBICs with only $500,000 in paid in capital and surplus would be permitted to borrow funds from SBA on a three-for-one rather than a two-for-one basis. Thus, the bill not only recognizes the existence of economies of scale but also encourages it with the provision for additional leverage, both primary (through debentures) and secondary (through preferred stock).

The proposed legislation also facilitates the favorable tax treatment of gifts by individuals or organizations to nonprofit MESBICs. Admittedly, tax benefits are tangible, but a tax shield provides for only a portion of the contribution. In other words, while all the proposed modifications to the MESBIC program are substantial, reasonable profitability in the long run still may be illusory.

Recommended changes

While some modifications to the MESBIC program have been made and others are being considered, additional changes will have to take place. Included in these proposed modifications are: direct government subsidies for reasonable operating costs; recognition of the MESBIC by the sponsor as a profit center rather than a charitable contribution; the encouragement of larger size loans and equity investments; stress on the size and efficiency of the individual MESBIC rather than the number of MESBICs; use of the Office of Minority Business Enterprise consultation centers for MESBIC clients in order to reduce MESBIC advising costs and to provide the client with free technical assistance; and realization that the MESBIC program should be part of a coordinated "product mix" of programs designed to alleviate economic disparities facing disadvantaged groups.

In order to establish a viable venture capital industry utilizing the MESBIC concept, a company contemplating the formation of its own MESBIC must be able to anticipate profitability in the foreseeable future. Conceivably a method of fulfilling this goal may be through direct government subsidization such as that received by the defense industry. At least in the first five years of existence, MESBICs should receive reasonable subsidies for operating costs because (1) they help fulfill the social objective of furnishing funds to disad-

vantaged businessmen; (2) they assist in the creation of a skilled entrepreneurial class; (3) they help train disadvantaged group members in venture capital financing; and (4) their costs of operations are apt to be higher than the typical SBIC due to the additional problems they confront.

The recognition of the MESBIC as a profit center would encourage the growth of the industry because profitability, rather than the short-term public relations advantage, is primary. Especially in recessionary periods, social responsibility will not generate the substantial funds that are needed to provide realistic economic assistance to disadvantaged entrepreneurs.

In order to be profitable, MESBICs normally should concentrate on making larger-size loans and equity investments and should permit the Economic Opportunity Loan (EOL) program, also administered by SBA, to make the smaller-size loans. Under the EOL program, an economically or socially disadvantaged entrepreneur can borrow directly up to $50,000 at 6 percent interest. As previously mentioned, as of April 1972 there were 422 MESBIC financings and $7,600,000 in current investments. This averages out to $18,000, although the median figure might be $15,000. Clearly, the cost per $1,000 of loans outstanding is considerably higher if the loan portfolio consists of small loans.

Furthermore, the MESBIC can couple its loan or equity investment with an EOL loan and/or a regular SBA loan under the 7(a) program so that the portfolio concern can obtain a substantial amount of money at a reasonable cost. Under the 7(a) program, SBA can guarantee a bank loan up to 90 percent, and the amount of the guarantee can be as high as

$350,000. Thus, the EOL loan on a direct basis should be used for amounts of $50,000 or under, and MESBICs should be used to engender loans and/or equity investments for larger sums. By concentrating on the larger size loan or equity investment and by limiting the number of portfolio concerns, the MESBIC will be able to keep its overhead costs to a minimum and still be able to provide adequate advisory services to client firms.

Because MESBICs generally should be used to make the larger size (more than $50,000) loan or equity investment, because of the existence of economies of scale, and because of the present lack of trained manpower to operate client concerns, the number of MESBICs actually needed may be limited. Therefore, the emphasis should not be placed on establishing 100 or more MESBICs, but on the quality and efficiency of each MESBIC. Only then will the MESBIC industry be truly viable and have favorable long-term prospects.

Conclusion

Finally, because of its limited capabilities and objectives, the MESBIC concept should be regarded only as an element of a synchronized "product mix" of programs dedicated to alleviate economic and social disparities encountered by disadvantaged groups.

While the MESBIC concept is worthwhile, it is our thesis that only with significant changes will the program attain the capability of being able to supply substantial venture capital and debt financing for the disadvantaged businessman. Some of these changes, such as those proposed in H.R. 13805, already have been recognized, and this bill should be passed. Other changes, such as the direct government subsidization of operating costs during the MESBICs "incubation period," have yet to be promoted.

Nevertheless, the MESBIC industry will grow only if the individual MESBICs are profitable and healthy.

III

CREATING THE VALUE

This section is most frustrating to both the reader and the authors for it cannot really come to grips with the production problems that an entrepreneur faces. The problems of the furniture maker and those of the chemical compounder are so varied that they can only be covered in a general way. The actual production problems of an industry cannot be covered. While it is possible go into plant layout, work flows, and the like, such information would be useful to only a small number of readers. Retailers and non-production manufacturers would have no use for the information. The new businessman will have to look to his industry for information concerning the details of production in his industry.

It is difficult to be specific in this section, for the spectrum of business opportunities is so wide that the process of creating the value is infinite. Suffice it to say that the guts of business operations revolve around creating a value and then taking it to market and exchanging it for money, making something and selling it. The following two chapters make a few observations about the production side of the business.

ACQUIRING
PRODUCTIVE CAPABILITIES

19

A great deal of money can be saved by astute buying practices. Indeed, in some businesses profit is to be made on the buying side rather than on the sales side. One example is the defense electronics industry. Profits on defense electronics contracts are usually less than one percent of sales. Yet many times the contracts are bid under the assumption that the purchasing department, in buying the parts, will realize at least ten percent savings on the bill of materials as projected by the cost estimators. Thus the company's profit comes from buying acumen. If the purchasing agent fails to do his job, large losses will follow. To put it concisely, it is difficult to make money if a person doesn't buy right.

A rather wealthy businessman of varied interests related a misadventure he almost had with a promoter who has now been dethroned and is in hiding, if not from the law, at least from his former investors. At the peak of this promoter's power he was wheeling and dealing, buying every business that was for sale, using his worthless paper for money. It seems that one day the promoter and the businessman went to a nearby large city to buy a savings and loan company together. It developed that there was a difference of about a quarter of a million dollars between what they wanted to pay and what was being asked for the firm. This quarter of a million was in real money, not paper, a difference that is not to be taken lightly. After haggling for about fifteen minutes over the price, the promoter suddenly got up, stretched out his arms, and at the top of his voice shouted, "Gentlemen, gentlemen! What are we doing sitting here quibbling like fish mongers when we could be out making millions?"

The businessman said, "I knew right then and there that I didn't want to be in business with any man who wouldn't sit there and talk about a quarter of a million dollars, so I bailed out right then and there and had nothing more to do with the man."

It so happened that one big factor underlying this promoter's downfall was his obsession with the sales side of his enterprises and his distinct disdain for the buying side. He paid far too much for everything he bought and this helped collapse his empire. Indeed, he had paid so much for his company headquarters that when the mortgagee took it over no one would buy it for any significant portion of the mortgage. He had paid too much for the building. One must pay careful attention to buying, lest his cost structure render him uncompetitive.

Another example is provided by a company that was introducing a new product into supermarkets. It had to buy some racks for its merchandise. A wire rack manufacturer quoted a price of $11.25. The company needed about 1,000 racks which was going to cost about $11,000. The entrepreneur, pondering other ways of solving the problem, began thinking about wood; he devised a wooden rack which could be made for $5 as needed. He didn't have to place an order for 1000 units. Thus he saved $6000 and that's a lot of money. Such are the tactics of the successful entrepreneur. He operates viciously on the buying side.

As a further illustration: one successful mail order seller of mountaineering and camping equipment would take a tour each evening behind the stores of every merchant in the downtown section, picking up corrugated boxes that had been put out for the trash man. Why? Because corrugated boxes are expensive, 50¢ to $1 for any sizable box, and he needed about 100 a day. That trip in his little truck made him anywhere from $50 to $100 a day.

The entrepreneur can't stand to waste money. If he can find a cheaper way to do something, he will do it even though it may be inconvenient and cause him some work. Time he has; dollars he may not have.

LEARN ABOUT USED EQUIPMENT

Many times the price of new equipment is shockingly high in comparison to what the same goods can be purchased for in the used market. The used equipment may be perfectly functional. One restaurant owner wanted to buy a food mixer for a baking operation he was going to start. A new food mixer cost $800; he located a used mixer for $50 in a restaurant that had failed. A mobile food concessionaire at fairs needed some booths. The cost of manufacturing a booth of the size he had in mind was quoted at $12,000 each. He discovered some small steel sheds that an oil company wanted to get rid of for $700 each.

This process, of course, requires time to find what is needed and negotiate for it, but it is time well spent. It is far more convenient to put in everything new, pay the price, and let other people worry about all the problems, but it is expensive. Without a lot of money, one must learn the used equipment market.

In putting in a men's apparel store with 4800 square feet of space, the total costs for fixtures and everything needed to finish off the concrete shell was $35,000. Another men's apparel merchant located across the mall finished off similar quarters for $90,000. The difference? The latter merchant purchased his fixtures from supply houses, paying full price for everything. The first merchant purchased nothing from existing fixture suppliers, but rather he had learned how to have them made inexpensively by local craftsmen. Where one merchant paid $300 for a commercial tie rack the other made an original one from some lumber for $75. Original, creative thinking can save much money in buying. Don't automatically assume that you must follow in the trodden paths on which tradition thrusts you.

The availability of "incubator space," low rent quarters in which new enterprises can grow and prosper before they are forced to pay a market price for their building, is an important factor in locating the venture. Many old, obsolete factories in the East have been converted into a number of smaller units to house new ventures. In some areas there is a shortage of low cost space for the enterpriser. The differences in space costs can be astounding. In surveying Los Angeles, one might wonder why all industry isn't located near the coast. Well, the answer is costs. To get into any commercial or industrial property in the Irvine Industrial Complex, it costs 50¢ a square foot for space. The same space in Anaheim costs 15¢ a square foot per month. In South El Monte it is even less.

A businessman who had just started a screen printing operation in South El Monte but who lived in Anaheim was asked why he did not locate closer to home. He replied, "Couldn't pass up this deal. We moved in practically free. It was built by a screen printer who didn't make it. All the modern equipment was in place and everything. It was for rent by the bank that took it over. They put us in with two month's free rent and a line of credit."

In such a circumstance, the buyer is often in a position to extract extremely favorable terms, for there isn't much of a market for used screen printing plants. When an established screen printer comes along and says he is willing to take over the facilities, not only can he get favorable rent, but he also is in a position to ask for a rent moratorium until operations commence. One must remember that the owner of an empty plant is under pressure to get somebody into it.

Incidentally, another reason the screen printer went to South El Monte, again on the buying side, was that the school district had a program in which high school students would work in the plant for 85¢ an hour with the school district picking up the difference between that and the minimum wage. Moreover, the kids were more productive than the other workers.

In many businesses astute buying can give the enterprise a competitive advantage which allows it to successfully compete in the marketplace. Without such a cost advantage, many times the firm would perish. A cost advantage allows lower prices to be quoted which guarantee sales, for in many industries the firm that quotes the lower price gets the order. The problem is not sales, but one of costs in such instances. Get the low costs and the sales will follow.

OVERHEAD

Overhead takes more than its proportionate share of casualties. Some businessmen call it "the monster" because it must be fed regularly and eats so much. The truly perfect enterprise has no overhead, only variable costs. If nothing is sold, nothing is spent. The larger the overhead, the riskier the enterprise. If feasible, overhead should be converted into a variable cost. Rent a store on a percentage-of-sales basis rather than a flat amount. Pay salesmen a commission rather than a monthly salary. The management of overhead is one key to success in small business. In fact, it is the very reason that small businesses can frequently compete against bigger enterprises.

In the field of publishing, the price of the books most companies sell includes a 30 percent charge to pay the overhead of their large organizations. Those organizations have hundreds of secretaries, editors, and so on. Those costs go on every month regardless of sales. The beginning publisher who does not have this overhead and who is publishing just a few books has a 30 percent cost advantage immediately on which to operate. Either he can sell at a lower price or he can put that much money into profit or into his product. In any case, it is a definite advantage. Indeed, one could theorize that one of our national problems is that the overhead of our large organizations has grown too large.

A young man had successfully established a small plant for manufacturing very small diameter stainless steel tubing that was sold to hospital supply houses for disposable hypodermic needles. He had been told by his friends that he should expand into other fields, that he should hire a metallurgist, and that he should do this and do that. He hired a consultant for guidance who looked over the operation. When he walked into the outer office no one was there; everyone was in the plant working. There were no staff people, no accountants, no secretaries, no personnel people, only production workers who were turning out the product. The company was making handsome profits. It was selling everything it could produce because its prices were significantly lower than its only other competitor in the industry who had a staff of 22 people performing the usual work done by staffs. The consultant thought for about ten minutes on the situation and made two recommendations. First, the man should quit listening to his friends; second, he should fire the consultant.

He had one of the most ideal situations one could ever get into and he ought to just relax and enjoy it. He was positioned in a highly lucrative market that was growing; he had a cost advantage over his competition; he had no marketing problems in that he sold his product to two firms that stood in line for it; there was nothing his competitor could do to meet this situation; and his production expertise was such that it couldn't be copied. Thus, the last thing in the world he needed was to hire a staff, no personnel men, no metallurgist, nothing! He had been doing everything right and was making a ton of money.

Which brings up another lesson in business. Most of the people you meet think they know more about your business than you do and they are not at all hesitant about telling you so. If you listen to everybody, you will lose your shirt. The beginning entrepreneur is usually so unsure of himself that he is tempted to listen to everything everybody tells him. The only protection that can be suggested is that he needs to obtain the advice of one man whom he trusts and in whom he has confidence. Listen to a few select advisors and tune out all other people, for they have other axes to grind.

SUBCONTRACTING

Initially there are advantages to subcontracting as much work as possible. Financial requirements for productive equipment are lessened and a firm price is usually received which can be relied on in cost calculations. If one attempts to do the production work himself, mistakes and inexperience make costs uncertain. Moreover, do not be tempted to believe that subcontracting is automatically more expensive than making it yourself, for such may not be the case. Under many circumstances a subcontractor may be able to make an item cheaper than you can make it yourself if he wants to be competitive. After all, he is operating his plant at a large percentage of capacity and may have the power to buy raw materials more advantageously than you. Also, subcontractors may help finance your operations by extending credit.

Admittedly, there are instances in which a subcontractor's price would render an entrepreneur uncompetitive. The lowest costs come when the entrepreneur makes an item in his own business. Do not assume that the prices of all subcontractors will be close. When buying one small coaxial cable unit, a small electronics manufacturer was quoted prices from $1.15 to $17.00 for the same item from a group of 14 bidders. Subcontractors vary tremendously in their technology and their cost structure. More importantly, they vary in how badly they want your business. This matter of how hungry they are is of critical importance. Let's explain what goes on in a subcontractor's mind.

Suppose you walk into a shop that is loaded with business. Since they have a six month backlog of orders, they are not really eager to do business with you. You ask them for a quote. They throw you a "high ball," a high price. The subcontractor has no way of knowing how competitive he must be to get the job. If he is lucky he will get the order at the high profit figure. Then he will take it, even if it means dislodging some of his low profit work in process. After all, the name of the game is profit. The subcontractor who will quote a low competitive price is the one who is hungry. He may be new in business and need the volume badly or business may

be slow for him at that time for some reason or another. So an entrepreneur must obtain bids from several subcontractors before committing himself. Some time can be saved by asking people with whom one does business for information about good subcontractors.

Observation indicates that the lowest prices do *not* come from large, nationally recognized concerns. The large company has a large overhead and general administrative expense burden that it must include in all prices; this frequently renders them uncompetitive with some smaller concerns. Look for the smaller contractor who not only may have a lower cost structure, particularly for small runs, but who is eager for the business. Moreover, in dealing with such small concerns frequently one is dealing directly with the owner, who will be flexible in the arrangement he makes, whereas the hired help of a large corporation must stay strictly within company policy. Also, large concerns frequently have minimum order requirements so large that the small buyer cannot do business with them.

One of the problems in dealing with subcontractors is the matter of specifications. It is impossible to be too explicit in what is needed. Always submit a purchase order which explains in detail precisely what you want them to do. Many new businessmen have been severely damaged by their failure to fully communicate to the subcontractor what was wanted. Get all specifications and terms of the sale down in writing.

Another matter is the ownership of dies and art work. Usually in subcontracting the buyer must pay for the cost of dies, art work, or other such items that are used. You should state in your purchase order, if you are paying for such things (and you usually are), that you retain ownership and possession of them. You may not always want to do business with this concern and may have trouble getting possession of costly dies and/or art work if you want to change suppliers.

Do not be surprised at the seemingly high cost of some of these dies, molds, or artistic endeavors. One manufacturer of a baby walker made from aluminum tubing realized that he could save a great deal of money yet have a product far more appealing to the market if he could make it out of plastic by an injection molding process. His unit costs would drop from the present $4 to 75¢ which would allow a retail price that would vastly expand sales volume. The research people at Phillips Petroleum in Bartlesville had precisely the plastic and the process which he needed. The only problem was that the molds and set-up costs would be $250,000! There was no way the company could justify investing that much money in tooling, even if it had the money. Admittedly, $250,000 is rather extreme, but it is not at all unusual to incur tooling costs of $5,000 to $10,000 for a product. Simple art work can run hundreds of dollars, even thousands.

Truly, this matter of finding a way of producing the product with a minimum investment is a most difficult step in founding a new business. Many times the start-up costs are so large that it is simply not prudent to go ahead with the enterprise. The potential risks exceed the potential profits.

*****

Three approaches to inventory control

E.O.Q. — Is there a better way?

Harris Zeitzew
Peter Wulff†

Chances are you're making a mistake if you're using E.O.Q. to determine how much to buy.

The Economic Order Quantity concept was originally developed to determine batch-production quantities, where a trade-off was possible between machine set-up costs and inventory carrying costs. It was defined as that quantity which would minimize the total of set-up and carrying costs.

This production-scheduling concept was borrowed for use by purchasing. It has been widely applied to procurement decisions, by naively substituting "ordering cost" in place of "set-up cost" in the formula. However, reordering costs are often trivial, so they are not analogous to production set-up costs. In addition, most companies don't really know what their ordering or carrying costs really are, so they have to use estimates.

More importantly, it is simple-minded to assume that *only* the ordering costs and the carrying costs are relevant to the determination of order quantities.

For example, we should also be concerned with one or more of the following factors:

†Harris Zeitzew and Peter Wulff, *Purchasing*, September 2, 1971, pp. 29-37.

- Storage space limitations.
- Price speculation.
- Quantity discounts and freight costs.
- Perishability or obsolescence risk, and salvage value.
- Inventory turnover policy, and inventory investment.
- Stock-out costs.

Instead of E.O.Q., it would be better to use an order quantity system flexible enough to account for all variables. This can be accomplished by modernizing an old technique: the MIN/MAX system.

Under this system, order quantities can easily be varied in response to demand forecasts. This is particularly true in computerized installations, where the machine does all the clerical computations. The computer can also adjust the formula for price breaks, minimum order quantities, and the like.

The old MIN/MAX system fell into disfavor because it was inflexible. But it was simple and easy to use. The new "variable" version is highly responsive.

In the "variable" MIN/MAX system, the minimum acts as a floating order point. It is based on the amount of safety stock, the replenishment lead time, and the forecasted usage.

The maximum functions as the floating replenishment level. It is based primarily on the inventory turnover rate desired. Inventory turnover relates the average size of the inventory to the current usage rate.

The average size of the inventory is the result of two related but separate factors: the amount of safety stock and the order quantity.

Once the average inventory is determined, you divide the annual usage by the average inventory. This gives the annual inventory turnover rate.

The MAX in the system is based on the turnover objective. But before the MAX can be established, it is necessary to determine the desired average time between reorders. This is a function of both the turnover rate and the safety stock.

FINDING THE MINIMUM

MIN = Forecasted leadtime Usage + Safety Stock
Example: Forecasted usage = 10 units per week
Reorder leadtime = 3 weeks
Safety Stock = 2 weeks supply
MIN = (3 x 10) + (2 x 10) = 50 units

AVERAGE INVENTORY

Average inventory = (½ x Order quantity) + (Safety stock)
Example: Order quantity = 90 units
Safety stock = 20 units
Average inventory = (½ x 90) + (20)
= 65 units

FINDING THE ANNUAL INVENTORY TURNOVER RATE

$$\text{Annual inventory turnover rate} = \frac{\text{Annual usage}}{\text{Average inventory}}$$

Example: Annual usage   = 520 units
            Average Inventory   = 65 units

            Annual turnover rate = $\frac{520}{65}$ = 8 turns per year

After the desired average time between reorders ("Q") has been determined, the MAX is found by taking the sum of the MIN and the forecasted usage during "Q".

Using the above steps, the buyer has a simple basis for determining the variable reorder quantity:

Whenever the available inventory drops below the Minimum, it is time to reorder. The reorder quantity is simply the *difference* between the Maximum and the available inventory.

The reorder quantity can then be easily adjusted to allow for packaging, price breaks, or storage considerations.

Since both the MIN and the MAX are recalculated every time the forecast of usage is revised, the system is much more flexible than the old "fixed" MIN/MAX one. Changes in inventory turnover policy, safety stock, or replenishment lead time also call for new calculations.

For example, if the desired annual turnover rate in our example is increased from 8 to 10, "Q" then becomes 6.4 weeks. The MAX decreases to 114 units, and the reorder quantity drops to 74 units.

Under this system, the buyer is not locked into a fixed order quantity. Thus he is in a better position to adjust his inventory to both declining and expanding requirements.

FINDING THE DESIRED AVERAGE TIME BETWEEN REORDERS

$$Q = \frac{104}{T} - 2(S)$$

Where:
   Q = Desired average time between reorders, in number of weeks.
   T = Desired annual turnover rate.
   S = Safety stock, in number of weeks.

Example:
   T = 8 turns per year.
   S = 2 weeks supply.

   $Q = \frac{104}{8} - 2(2) = 13 - 4 = 9$ weeks.

FINDING THE MAXIMUM

MAX = MIN + Usage during Q

Example:

Min	= 50 units
Forecasted usage	= 10 units per week.
Q	= 9 weeks

MAX = (50) + (9 x 10) = 140 units

FINDING THE REORDER QUANTITY

Inventory (units)

140	MAX	
50	MIN	Reorder quantity
40	Inventory level	
20	Safety stock	
0		

Variable reorder quantity = MAX − Inventory

Example:

Inventory	= 40 units
MAX	= 140 units
Reorder quantity	= (140 − 40) = 100 units

Leadtimes:
Key to MRO
inventory

Accurate leadtime information is vital when 90% of your time is devoted to the purchase of maintenance, repair and operating supplies. That's the job of Plant Buyer George Klein at Allied Chemical's industrial chemicals division in Baltimore. He buys everything from one-at-a-time V-belts to gears and castings costing thousands of dollars.

"We establish accurate reorder points for each of the 7,800 items in our stores," says Klein. "These points are based not only on use but also on leadtimes. If leadtime on a bearing suddenly jumps from four weeks to eight, it's going to critically affect our reorder needs. If we fail to keep that information up-to-date, we may well have part of our plant shut down."

Maintenance supplies make up the bulk of Allied's inventory, some quarter million dollars' worth. While that figure is substantial, it's the very minimum Klein considers necessary to keep the plant running.

Each item of capital equipment carries a different utility value at Allied. Some items are essential to the entire operation. Other equipment can, in an emergency, be shut down for a few weeks. The only people who can decide the relative importance of an equipment item, according to Klein, are production experts. "Their decision determines what inventory of spares we should carry."

Once the decision on spares inventory has been made, the maintenance department breaks down all the individual items needed to keep capital equipment running. Maintenance forecasts parts' wear, estimates replacement dates, and lists each part on a stock instruction sheet. It also adds a suitable figure for min/max stocking, based on production's estimate of the item's usefulness.

Equipment leadtime is all-important

The completed forms — one for each piece of capital equipment — are sent to purchasing. Klein finds a source for each part and obtains a price, which he periodically updates. Most important, he asks his supplier for an accurate lead-time estimate.

"Unless it's an exceptionally expensive component, which we might risk not stocking in order not to tie up needless inventory money, the question of cost hardly enters our inventory decisions," says Klein. "What does count is the relative need for a part, plus its leadtime."

If usage of a replacement part is four per week, and leadtime is four weeks, purchasing and maintenance may decide on a reorder point of 16, plus a few extras as a safety margin. If leadtime increases to six weeks, the reorder point must be worked out anew.

Based on the reorder point, storekeeper Frank Loewer makes out two cards for each component. One is a traveling requisition; the other a perpetual inventory card. On the former, Loewer writes in the reorder point. The minute the stock falls below this point, he pulls the TR and sends it to purchasing for reordering.

While some pieces of capital equipment have unique components, others contain parts in common with dissimilar equipment. "A stores catalog allots each component a code number," explains Klein. "A certain bearing will have the same code number, and be stocked in only one location, even though it may be common to several machines.

"Of course, we add this multiple use consideration into our calculations of reorder points. But, again, it's leadtimes that ultimately determine how much we carry in inventory."

EDP assures on-time orders

Standard production items are easy to schedule. But specials are another story. And, in a small company, a computer is a big help in keeping accurate track of every order in the plant.

Materials Manager Richard Brooks is the first to admit his debt to the computer, a relatively unusual possession for a company the size of Formsprag — less than 250 employees. The Warren, Mich. based company manufactures a variety of power-transmission products, including sprag-type clutches. Its chief customer is the machine tool industry. About half of its sales are of standard equipment; the other half are specials. So

Brooks — in charge of production control, purchasing, shipping, and receiving — uses a computerized scheduling system which keeps track of all the elements needed to complete an order on time.

On orders for specials, engineering first receives a copy of the sales order. All specially designed parts are drawn up. Then engineering sends a breakdown of the bill of materials to production control. This shows the origin of each part: whether it's made in-plant, purchased as a raw material, or comes in as a finished component.

The production controller consults one of two computer printouts. The first shows all items currently in inventory — about 15,000 different parts. The other lists only the inventory items on which there has been activity during the past 12 months.

Computer shows up-to-date inventory

If the inventory reports show a part is available, production control merely withdraws it from stock and issues a work order for the shop. If sufficient quantities aren't on hand, the controller issues a requisition for purchasing to buy. The leadtimes on such purchased items determine the final delivery date to the customer. But, since there's close rapport between purchasing and production control, it's simple to keep abreast of any problems.

The production controller then prepares a route sheet showing each operation needed on the part, and how long it will take. Attached to the bill of materials, this goes to EDP together with the date when all components must be ready for assembly.

Information for each part is assembled in the computer to give a complete picture of the finished product. The computer works backward — like a PERT system — to schedule each operation for a work center on a particular day. The aim: to have every component arrive at assembly on the same date.

Big problem: Finding good small-order suppliers

Every week, the computer issues a schedule based on the route sheets for all jobs in the plant. A copy goes to each shop foreman, showing priorities. The foreman then has the discretion to schedule jobs to make optimum use of set-up times to reduce costs. This also gives him the opportunity to squeeze in rush jobs.

Copies of all the schedules also go to Brooks, who is responsible to sales as far as meeting promised delivery dates is concerned. Since he's in charge of production control, Brooks can re-schedule any job he feels is falling behind.

"Purchasing fits into the picture in a very special way," says Brooks. "Creative buying here consists of developing suppliers who are willing to produce our specialty items in small quantities and at reasonable cost.

"It's one of the problems of a small company that its orders rarely represent sizable business for any one supplier. We often feel lucky if we can find even a single good supplier who's willing to give us continuing high quality at a reasonable price. But, once we've found him, it's purchasing's first order of business to find a reserve supplier, in case something goes wrong.

That's why developing new sources is so important to us."

QUESTIONS

1. Which of the three inventory control methods would be most appropriate for your business?

PRODUCT PLANNING

20

Countless hours go into carefully thinking through all aspects of the product, for there are hundreds of decisions that must be made on every attribute and many times there is scant basis upon which to make them. What colors should be used? What sizes should be made? How many models are needed? Should we put this jim-crack on it or not? Should aluminum or steel be used?

Errors at this stage frequently prove fatal when the product fails to find market acceptance. Thus it is difficult to overly stress the importance of carefully thinking through and working out all details of the product before beginning production.

Unfortunately, the realities of production must affect product decisions. Ideally one might like to do thus-and-so with the product, but it proves to be too costly. The production man says do this-and-that for realistic costs. You accept this-and-that. Production realities frequently veto market preferences. Be prepared to make many compromises. However, it is important to realize when one should not compromise, when it would harm

the enterprise. Certain things may be so important to the consumer that they must be provided. To compromise in such critical spots also jeopardizes the enterprise.

An interesting dilemma arises as to when the product is ready to go to market. One of two mistakes can be made. Some engineering-oriented people tend to keep the product in the laboratory, perfecting it, pouring more and more money into it, far beyond a reasonable period of time. There is no such thing as a perfect product. Any thought that the initial product will be flawless is unreasonable. All products are compromises and inherently contain some flaws or disadvantages. Somewhere along the line the boss must draw the line and say, "This is the product we will take to market."

On the other hand, the entrepreneur in his haste to get to market is under pressure to release a product so faulty that his long run chance for success is jeopardized. If the company, in its haste, sells the distributive middlemen a product that causes them grief, it will be difficult to come back later to those same middlemen and say, in essence,

"We found what was wrong, so now let's try again." Middlemen are not famous for their forgiveness. They dislike doing business with amateurs. So by all means, make certain that the product is satisfactory, not perfect, necessarily, but at least sufficiently good that no serious problems will be encountered by either the middlemen or the users.

No matter how well a product may work in the laboratory or experimental stages, bugs usually show up in actual usage. No matter how much thought is given to things, something comes up in actual testing that was not previously considered. Consider limiting the scope of marketing until the bugs have been worked out of the system. There is no sense in contaminating one's entire potential market initially. Limit the scope of possible damages by proceeding slowly to introduce the product market by market.

A floral supply wholesaler in Denver, Colorado, developed a chemical compound for preserving the life of carnations. It worked marvelously well and the company began selling the compound nationwide. Later in the fall, complaints came from wholesalers in the southern states. The compound had turned brown and was ruining flowers. Investigation disclosed that the product had been developed in Denver where the climate is very dry and generally tends to be cool. There was a chemical in the product which, when exposed to high humidity and heat, turned to sulphuric acid. The product had to be recalled and that troublesome compound replaced with another chemical that would do the same job without decomposing. A great deal of testing is usually necessary before going to market and the temptation to cut it short and start bringing in the money is exceedingly strong.

BRANDING

Pay special attention to naming the enterprise and its products. The entrepreneur should avoid using his own name unless he knows it will help sell goods. Rather, try to develop a brand name which, in itself, communicates exactly what the product is. Some examples of this type of brand name are Frigidaire, Snap-On Tools, Kool-Aid, Dairy Queen, Der Weinerschnitzel, Rototiller, Roto-Rooter, etc. Take care to get all the legal protection possible by copywriting advertising material, trade-marking brand names. Those processes are inexpensive and can provide excellent protection. Copyright forms are available from the Library of Congress, Washington, D.C. Trademark information is contained in a booklet available from the U.S. Department of Commerce, Washington, D.C. The matter of patents is something else, a far more complex matter.

PATENTS

Part of entrepreneurial mythology is that if the inventor can only get a patent on his widget, he has protected himself from the pirates who are bent on stealing his brainchild. Remember, we said it was mythology. The facts of patent life are rather grim. Let's approach this matter by making some flat statements about the patent situation without delving into all of the supporting arguments behind them. The supporting data is available, but it would constitute a book. Just be advised that the entire patent process as it now stands in the United States is a mess, one that Congress has been trying to clean up for years but really doesn't know what to do about it.

First, patents are expensive. One almost always needs a patent lawyer to handle it. It is unlikely that you will be able to get a patent for less than $3000 and the chances of spending more are large. It depends upon the complexities of the idea and the difficulties encountered.

Second, there is a good chance that the patent search will discover that your invention is not new and cannot claim patent protection. Thus, you have spent money and have nothing to show for it except that perhaps a violation of someone else's patent, which is another problem.

Third, assuming one is granted a patent by the U.S. Patent Office two or three years after it was filed, the patent may not really mean much after all; it may be challenged in court. In a very real sense, no patent is valid until the U.S. Supreme Court says so and they don't say it often. The bulk of patent cases taken before the U.S. Supreme Court are declared to be void because they do not truly represent new inventions. The courts have rather severe tests of invention. One cannot simply nail two boards together in a different way and patent it, as the Great Atlantic & Pacific Tea Company found out when it tried to enforce a patent on its way of bringing up groceries at the check-out counter.

Fourth, bear in mind the great costs that will be incurred in trying to defend your patent in court. If you are not financially prepared to defend your patent, then you might be better advised to follow other procedures.

Fifth, consider the advantages of not patenting the product but rather keeping it as a trade secret. A product used in commercial flower arranging sold to the floral trade was patented. A competitor wanted to copy it, for it was an extremely lucrative item. A copy of the patent papers was obtained (they are for sale from the Patent Office) which related in detail exactly how the item was made. The competitor copied the procedures and was in business. The patent owner could do little about it for he was small and there was doubt that the patent would have held up in court. In short, all the patent owner had done was tell everybody how to make his product. He would have been much wiser to have kept it as a trade secret such as Coca Cola has done with the formula for its syrup. Bear in mind that a patent only lasts for 17 years. A trade secret lasts for as long as it can be kept.

There are ways of keeping secrets in certain instances. One chemical compounder took pains to put into his product certain inert chemicals, solely for the purpose of confusing chemical analysis of them. An electronics manufacturer protected the circuitry for some of its proprietary items by encasing them in a solid block of epoxy in which the circuitry would be destroyed if the epoxy were shattered. So examine whether or not something would be better kept as a trade secret and the extent to which a patent could be protected if there were one.

Here are some reasons to apply for a patent for an idea. First, it may scare off the naive venturer. Second, it becomes an asset that can be sold. Many firms will not buy an unprotected idea but will talk sale if the idea is backed by a patent. Third, it does provide certain tactical advantages in the event of legal difficulties. Finally, there are some products which can be protected by patents.

KEEP IT SIMPLE

The old "kiss" principle (Keep It Simple, Stupid) is particularly valid for product planning. Too many new enterprisers feel that they must offer a complete line of products or a multitude of models right from the start. They are urged to do this by self-serving middlemen who insist that they won't do business with "short line producers." It is true that many middlemen disdain dealing with the firm that has but a few items in its line. Manufacturers' representatives, wholesalers, and even retailers like to buy from a firm selling a large number of items. It simplifies their ordering problems. Moreover, if something goes sour with one or two of the items they can get credit on their accounts against future purchases. The one-product manufacturer poses a big risk to these middlemen.

While all of this is true, it is nevertheless beside the point at times for the beginning enterpriser. Trying to put out several products at one time not only is financially back breaking but also results in many mistakes. Market experience is needed before one can be sure of what needs to be added to the line. A manufacturer of aluminum baby walkers originally produced the product in three colors, blue, pink, and yellow. On one of his first calls to a large department store he was told that it only wanted to buy one color; it didn't want to be bothered stocking three colors, for it complicated inventory. Experience proved only one color was needed.

Production and financial considerations, plus the practical aspects of managing a business, may have to take precedence over the preferences of some middlemen, contrary to everything devout marketing men proclaim. There is little point giving the middlemen everything they want if it means going broke. Moreover, middlemen can be ridiculous in some of the "suggestions" they make. In their bent to either play the role of

the expert or to rationalize not buying the product, they feel compelled to come up with some improvement that is needed. One buyer for a large supermarket chain, when asked to buy a 12-inch diameter plastic wheel that gave the nutrient content of most foods, said, "It is too big. Make it 4 inches in diameter." And how was anyone to read it? The print was a bit small as it was. Bear in mind that the middlemen care not one whit for your problems or your costs nor have they agonized long hours over the problems which they so glibly solve with a few offhand remarks.

A primer on patent, trademark, and know-how licensing

Bernard J. McNamee†

Even though their balance sheet value fails to present a reliable index to their true economic worth — patents, trademarks, and know-how represent some of the most valuable assets of many companies. These assets, unlike inventories, plant, and equipment, are intangible property rights. One way of making them work for the firm is the

†Bernard J. McNamee, *MSU Business Topics*, pp. 11-20, Summer 1970.

Reprinted by permission of the publisher, Division of Research, Graduate School of Business Administration, Michigan State University.

licensing of property rights to others; in these days of increasingly complex technological methods, seldom does one company possess all the technology it needs to operate efficiently.

A common pitfall in discussing the negotiating licenses is a failure to understand the nature of patent, trademark, and know-how rights as well as the legal constraints involved in their licensing. The information in this article is intended to orient the business executive to some of the more salient legal ramifications of patent, trademark, and know-how licensing so that he is in a better position to conduct his negotiations. It is not intended as a substitute for the technical, legal, and financial advice that the business executive should seek.

A *patent* is a public document issued by a government describing an invention which the government considers worthy of protection in view of its novelty and utility.

There are two principal types of patents: product and process patents. A product patent provides that the product itself is patented; a process patent only covers a phase of the manufacturing procedure in making a product which itself is unpatented. Some patents contain both types of claims.

A patent represents a right created and granted by the government to a person; it cannot be created by agreement of private parties. In granting the patent there is no transfer of property to the inventor. The patent grant from the government confers on the owner only the right to exclude others from making, using, and selling the patented invention. In the case of a process patent only, this means the right to prevent others from using the patented process; in the case of a product patent, it is the right to prevent others from manufacturing, using, or selling the patented product.

In granting a license the patent owner merely agrees not to sue his licensee for infringing on his patent rights. Since exclusion of others is the only feature of a patent right, the patent owner cannot legally impose restrictions on the licensee which go beyond this right. On the other hand, reasonable restrictions that do not amount to a misuse of the patent right are accepted.

A *trademark* is a word or symbol identifying the owner, maker, or source of the product on which it appears, or the service with which it is used. The trademark is also a symbol of quality identified with the owner. As such, trademark rights under U.S. law arise only from actual use of the mark, and not from registration of the trademark in the U.S. Patent Office, although such registration provides greater procedural protection to the owner in enforcing his trademark rights.

The theory underlying the trademark right is that the trademark identifies the source of the goods. If a third party, not the trademark owner, were to employ the same trademark on his goods, the public would be misled into believing these goods were the trademark owner's goods and of the same quality as those sold by the trademark owner. As a protection not only to himself but also to prevent deception of the public, the trademark owner can exclude others from use of the same or deceptively similar trademarks in connection with similar products. To this extent the trademark owner has a monopoly which is recognized and protected by the government. But such recognition and protection is limited geographically by each nation so that a trademark owner must, like a patent owner, develop his rights separately in each country.

Licensing of a trademark is more than a covenant not to sue. Since the trademark has become a symbol of quality in the minds of the public, a trademark owner stands in jeopardy of losing his trademark unless he retains effective control over the licensee to see that the products manufactured by the licensee and bearing the trademark meet the standards of quality that the trademark owner has established.

Trademarks should not be confused with trade names. Trademarks are symbols placed on a product to indicate source of the goods; a trade name is a stylized name under which a company may be doing business. A license of a trademark does not of itself grant a license to use the trade name of the licensor, nor does the assignment of a trade name carry with it a right to use a trademark, although both are similar. However, a trade name may infringe a trademark, and vice versa.

While *know-how* is not easily defined, it is a term used to embrace all sorts of secret proprietary information, whether it relates to manufacturing procedures, research developments, marketing intelligence, trade secrets, or even specialized machinery and raw materials.

Unlike patents and trademarks which are public knowledge and the use of which by outsiders is prohibited by law, the owner of unpatented confidential know-how has a property right in such know-how only to the extent it does not become public knowledge, and once it becomes public knowledge anyone can use it freely. Unlike a patent, know-how has no statutory life span and so long as it remains secret, the owner can prevent others from using it. Unlike patents and trademarks, know-how is not given any specific monopoly

protection. Possession of know-how does not create any right to prevent others from independently developing and using the same know-how.

In licensing others to use its know-how, the owner is not merely giving a covenant not to sue; a license of know-how involves the disclosure and transfer of previously unknown information to the licensee. Except for unauthorized expropriation of such know-how from the owners, for example, by a former employee in breach of his employment obligation, or a third party in breach of his obligation to keep such know-how confidential, the rights of any recipient of such know-how to use that information is governed solely by the contract under which it was disclosed to and received by the recipient. For this reason it is important that the owner not disclose the information freely, but only on a confidential basis which will require the recipient not to disclose or allow the disclosure of such know-how to other than designated employees of the recipient who agree to keep such information secret.

Technical assistance

Along with the patent and know-how license, a licensee generally wants technical assistance: to lay out a plant, to procure and assemble equipment, to train workers, to start up production, and to provide assistance in solving manufacturing problems. In agreeing to provide technical assistance, the licensor should specify what type of assistance he will give, where it will be given, which party will bear the costs involved, and whether there will be any separate fee.

The range of technical assistance should be spelled out as to whether it will be limited to consultation or actual construction work, the number and qualification of technical personnel to be made available, and the duration of their availability. Sometimes the technical assistance will be required on the spot; other types of training can be given at the licensor's plant. Provision should also be made for allocation of expenses. Generally the licensee bears the expenses incurred by his own employees while at the licensor's plant as well as the travel and living expenses of the licensor's employees while at the licensee's plant.

The licensing relationship

Identification of topics for negotiation is an important preliminary step. Such identification highlights the alternatives available and the probable parameters for negotiation. These are some of the topics to be dealt with in considering a license:

1. License, assignment or dealership. The fact that a product is patented or bears a trademark does not mean that a company purchasing and reselling the product must obtain a license to do so. In selling the product the patent or trademark owner has exhausted his monopoly of excluding others from making, using, or selling the patented invention or selling the trademarked product. This principle is not simply an implied license to use or resell the product whenever and however the purchaser chooses — although it is often referred to as such. Consequently, a distribution agreement should not be cast in the form of a patent or trademark license, nor should it impose on the distributor redistribution restrictions which can be imposed only on a licensee.

A patent "license" involves use of the patent; a trademark "license" involves manufacture of the trademarked product. These licenses legally amount to consent of the owner not to sue others for infringement of his patent or trademark.

The consent of the owner can be achieved in two principal ways. He can assign his patent or trademark or he can merely license it. An assignment is a transfer of all rights of ownership. It is a sale. Under a license, the licensor (or grantor) remains the owner of legal title to the patent or trademark, and the licensee (or recipient of the grant) receives the consent of the licensor to use his patent or trademark. While a patent owner can assign title to his patent, an assignment of a trademark may not be made under U.S. law unless the assignor also transfers the business and goodwill associated with the trademark to the recipient. In a license, however, an owner can license merely the patent or trademark without regard to transfer of the business or its goodwill. Since the owner retains greater control over his patent and trademark by merely licensing their use, licenses tend to be more common than assignments.

2. Country to which license applies. Patents and trademarks are territorial rights, that is, they are rights which are conferred or recognized by a government and extend only as far as the territorial boundaries of a country. Since patent and trademark rights in a country are conferred by the law of a particular country, rights to a particular trademark in the United States or a U.S. patent will not thereby confer any rights or protection to the trademark or patent in a foreign country, unless the appropriate local patent and trademark filings and procedures are pursued. If licenses to use the trademark or patent in several countries are desired, each of such countries should be identified and the status of the respective patents and trademarks in those countries verified. Notwithstanding the fact that a license agreement provides for a governing law, the validity of the patent and trademark will be judged by the law of the country for which a license is given. Any provisions relating to governing law will apply only to the contractual rights between the parties. When dealing with licenses under foreign patents and trademarks, it should not be assumed that the foreign law is identical to U.S. patent, trademark, or contract law; nor should it be forgotten that some U.S. laws will be applicable. Knowledge of the various rights and obligations conferred by laws of the countries where the license is given is helpful in determining what responsibilities are being assumed. When a license involves rights under patent or trademark rights of several countries, which may not have uniform laws, it is of even greater importance to specify what obligations will be assumed by the licensor and licensee.

3. Exclusive and non-exclusive licenses. In an exclusive license, the licensor agrees not to appoint any other licensee in the same territory or field. Generally, an exclusive license also is interpreted to mean that the patent or trademark owner himself cannot use the patent or trademark in that territory or field. Consequently, if the owner desires to retain the right to use his patent or trademark, he should specifically so provide in his license agreement.

An exclusive license, without more, does not imply a prohibition against the licensee in selling the product outside the exclusive territory or field.

Exclusive licenses as such generally are regarded as lawful, although other restrictions in the license may make the exclusive nature of the license unlawful. For example, direct restrictions against resale of a licensed product outside the exclusive territory have come to be regarded as an invalid use of the patent or trademark right. If the licensor has established a pattern of exclusive territories with several licensees, with prohibitions against each licensee selling outside the licensed territory, such a pattern is considered an illegal combination among the licensor and the several licensees to prevent competition among them, notwithstanding that each licensee was granted territorial rights co-extensive with the national patent and/or trademark rights.

As the term implies, non-exclusive licenses give no guarantee to the licensee that others will not receive a similar license.

4. Royalties. Determination of royalties generally has the most direct economic impact of all provisions in an agreement. Consideration must be given not only to the rate of royalties, but also the base on which they are calculated.

Base for calculation

The simplest base on which to calculate royalties is sales. However, care should be taken to define sales precisely. Often the preferable base is "net proceeds from sales," rather than gross sales or even net sales. Discounts, commissions, returns, allowances, and credits are the usual offsets. In addition, the net sales price may include other charges which do not accrue to the benefit of the licensee-seller. These would include transportation charges and sales and excise taxes collected by the seller. A reduction in the base should also be made for such items, either by reference to actual costs or by an allocated figure.

One or many royalties

Sometimes a product or its manufacture is covered by several patents which are licensed by the same patent owner. To avoid paying of multiple royalties on the sale of a single product, it is well to provide that only one royalty will be payable to the licensor regardless of the number of licensor's patents covering the product or its manufacture. This is especially desirable for a licensee who may want or need licenses under future improvement patents. A licensee would want to reduce royalties payable to the licensor in the event and to the extent the licensee may subsequently be held to infringe a patent held by a third party and required to pay royalties to such third party on the same product.

Patented component or whole product

Designation of the base for calculating royalties becomes especially important where the final product is a complex one, and the specific patent in question covers only one component of the final product. There is no uniform rule of thumb because each situation will present its own peculiarities in determining whether to use the total final product or the patented component as the base.

Royalties based on sales of all products

Where the licensor is in the position of licensing a pool of patents, convenience sometimes dictates using as a base the sales of all products, whether or not all such products were covered by any of the patents. Care must be exercised to avoid antitrust problems if this alternative is selected, and its use should be supported by data showing the impracticability of identifying sales of the patented products. Moreover, such a package rate proposal should not be made a condition by the licensor in granting the license and the licensee should always have the option of paying royalties only on sales of products covered by the licensed patents. It is certainly the safer alternative to provide for royalties only on sales of products covered by the licensed invention.

"Most favored nation" clause

A non-exclusive licensee will generally want to incorporate into the license agreement a clause which will give him the benefit of more favorable terms which might be granted by the licensor to other licensees of the same patent.

Minimum royalties

The requirement of reasonable minimum royalties as a condition of maintaining the license is a common provision in a license agreement, especially in exclusive licenses. Such a clause provides incentive that the patent be used and that the patent owner be assured of some minimum economic benefit from ownership of the patent.

Duration

If many patents are involved in the license royalties, as well as the license, they can be extended until the last of the patents expire. However, no royalties may be required after all the subject patents have expired. Since trademarks and know-how have no predetermined life, royalty requirements can presumably continue as long as the trademark and know-how license continues. In most instances, the know-how licensee will want to put a limit upon the period during which it will pay royalties. The licensee will want to include a similar royalty termination provision if the patent never issues. In such event this should be clearly provided for.

Where the agreement grants a license under several corresponding patents in several countries, expiration of a patent in a particular country before expiration of corresponding patents in other countries presents problems of accounting, taxation, and sometimes of payment. For example, if the product was made in a country where an unexpired patent was in existence, final sale of the product in a country where there is no patent or where the local patent has expired is of no consequence and the royalty would still be payable. Only if the product were manufactured and sold in countries where the patent was no longer in force can the licensee avoid payment of royalties.

Types

Royalties can be a single lump sum, or as is more common, they can consist of periodic payments calculated as a percentage of sales, costs, use, or other appropriate variable which has relation to the quantitative use of the invention or trademark by the licensee. Royalties can be in cash, in securities, or in other types of properties agreed upon by the parties.

5. Warranty of ownership. The grant of a trademark or patent license carries with it the implied warranty of ownership of the patent and trademark rights, but no implied warranty of validity. While the licensor should be certain of his ownership rights in the countries where the license applies, the prospective licensee should satisfy himself that the patent and/or trademark is valid in the countries where he is to be licensed, and that his use of the patent and trademark will not infringe on third parties' rights. Too often the assumption is made that if a patent or trademark is owned or developed in one country it is valid elsewhere as a matter of course. The contrary is the rule, and the licensor should take steps to establish his ownership rights to the licensed patent or trademark in each country before he attempts to license those rights.

6. Infringement. Important to the prospective licensee is knowledge that the license he is paying for is worthwhile. Not only does the licensee want assurance that the licensor owns the patent or trademark, but also that his use of the licensed patent or trademark will not infringe upon the rights of third parties. To get this assurance the licensee must ask for it, since a licensor does not impliedly warrant that use of the patent and/or trademark is noninfringing upon the rights of third parties. The licensor for his part may want to have the licensee, especially if he is an exclusive licensee, prosecute infringers of the patent or trademark.

Where there may be a question of infringement by a third party of the patent or trademark licensed to the licensee, the agreement should provide which party is to take action against the alleged infringer, who is to bear the costs of prosecution of the infringement suit and share in the rewards of a successful litigation. Provisions should be made for the other party to take over such litigation if the first fails or declines to do so, and for cooperation between the parties in prosecuting the litigation. Where the primary responsibility of prosecution is on the licensor, the licensee may wish to provide for withholding of further royalty payments pending successful action against the infringer by the licensor. Since infringement suits generally must be brought in the name of the patent or trademark owner, the agreement should provide that the licensor will join in such litigation and lend its name as a party.

7. Improvements.   Both the licensor and the licensee may want improvements developed by the other. While the licensee wants the option to have a license under the improvements without payment of additional royalties, the licensor generally wants use of the improvements made by the licensee to the basic process or product licensed. Both can probably be achieved to the mutual benefit of both parties. Where the licensee obtains a license to an improvement patent owned by the licensor, the licensor presumably collects royalties for a longer period since the newer patent will most likely expire later than the original patents which have been licensed. On the other hand if the licensor receives a non-terminable royalty free license under the improvements made by the licensee he at least reaps a costless benefit of use. Caution must be used in attempting to require the licensee to assign all his improvements back to the licensor. Such "grant backs" are now being challenged by the Department of Justice.

8. Patent and trademark markings. Requirements vary from country to country concerning patent and trademark markings to be put on the product or its labeling. Failure to put the correct marking on the product can result in the loss of the right to damages for past infringement by third parties. Since the requirements vary from country to country, the licensor should check the local laws on marking.

9. Duration of license.   A license should state not only its intended duration but also the occasions for earlier terminations. While a patent license may not exceed the life of the last of the licensed patents to expire, a trademark or know-how license can be extended indefinitely. The license agreement should provide for an initial term of years, even if there is provision for the parties to extend the license for additional periods at the end of such term. Consideration should also be given to reasons why the agreement may be earlier terminated and which party may terminate.

A licensee generally will want the option to cancel the license at any time for any reason or for no reason, but will not want to give the same option to the licensor. One of the principal reasons for such a provision is that the licensee doesn't want to build up a market only to find the license cancelled and the licensor entering the market himself. On the other hand, if the licensee doesn't or can't establish a market, he may wish to cancel the license — especially if it contains a minimum royalty requirement.

The licensor generally wants the option to cancel the license if the royalties to him and sales of the licensed products are too meager. Thus, the licensor may establish minimum royalties and provide that if such minimum royalties are not paid, the licensor shall have the option to terminate the license; or if it is an exclusive license, the additional option to make it non-exclusive. While some license arrangements allow the licensee to keep the license alive by making up deficiencies in royalties, such an arrangement is not always satisfactory to a licensor who may feel the market potential for the licensed product is greater than actually developed by the licensee and the mere payment of the minimum royalty is unsatisfactory. Whatever approach is adopted, the agreement should clearly state the options available.

The licensor may also wish to terminate the license earlier than its stated term for other reasons including bankruptcy or insolvency of the licensee, acquisition of the licensee by a competitor of the licensor, failure of the licensee to pay royalties on time, and other breaches of the license agreement.

10. Post-termination restrictions. Once a patent expires it can no longer be the subject of a valid license, and any attempt to require royalties on the basis of an expired patent is unlawful and unenforceable. If a patent license is terminated prior to expiration of the patent, the former licensee has no right to continue practicing the patent and can be sued for infringement. On the termination of a trademark license the former licensee has no right to continued use of the trademark, and may be prevented from such use by the owner of the trademark. While such restrictions are implicit, it is wise to state in the licensing agreement that upon termination of the license all rights of the licensee to use the patent or trademark revert back to the licensor.

When a know-how license is terminated, special care must be taken to provide that all the know-how is to be returned to the licensor and that the licensee shall not thereafter disclose or itself use such know-how — at least until such time as it becomes public knowledge. While such a restriction of unlimited duration is considered by some as unenforceable, allowing the terminated licensee to again use the know-how at some later date destroys the value of the know-how to both the licensor and presumably to other licensees. Nevertheless, the alternative of a time period might be adopted, for example, ten years. Presumably in that period non-use of the know-how, change in personnel, and improvements in the know-how will depreciate the value of the original know-how to the former licensee.

To be contrasted with such restrictions is a license that provides for payments of royalties for only a specified number of years after which the licensee is free to use the patent, trademark, or know-how. Where this is the case, as is common in know-how licenses, provision should still be made that the licensee is obliged not to disclose the know-how to others until such time as it becomes public knowledge, and to meet the quality standards of the trademark owner, all on the penalty of loss of license if the licensee breaches the license. The point is that a license does not necessarily come to an end once royalties cease.

Antitrust limitations

Patents and trademarks are a form of monopoly; and even though they are monoplies protected by the government, misuse of that monopoly can result in loss of patent or trademark benefits as well as antitrust fines, penalties, injunctions, and treble damage suits. The Department of

Justice and the federal courts have taken a very narrow view of the scope of the patent monopoly. Recently the Department of Justice announced formation of a special antitrust patent litigation section; it is a favorite defense in an infringement suit to allege misuse of the patent in violation of the antitrust laws. It is likewise an accepted rule that agreements and practices that go beyond the patent or trademark monopoly are to be judged like every other agreement in restraint of trade and judged under the Sherman and Clayton Act standards.

The Sherman Act prohibits agreements in restraint of trade and attempts to monopolize. Since licenses are agreements, they come within the purview of this Act. A violation will be found where the patent or trademark rights are misused to restrain trade. While one patent as a monopoly standing alone is permissible, attempts to accumulate a group of related patents in a field by acquisition, assignment, or license will be subject to challenge as an attempt to monopolize a part of commerce. The Clayton Act prohibits, among other restraints of trade, tying arrangements and exclusive dealing.

The following discussion touches upon some common restraints of trade which have been commonly found in license agreements. A word of caution, however: many foreign countries, as well as the European Economic Community (Common Market), do not consider many of the following restrictions as abuses or misuses of the patent or trademark monopoly. Nonetheless, the effect of such provisions in a license covering foreign trademarks or patents, may affect U. S. foreign commerce and thus be subject to U. S. antitrust standards.

For some years it was common to include a clause in patent licenses prohibiting licensees from challenging the validity of the patent being licensed. In 1969 the Supreme Court of the United States struck down such a clause on the ground that anyone should be able to challenge the validity of a patent for the use of which he is paying royalties. In effect the Court laid down the rule that such clauses may no longer be used.

Since the Department of Justice is attempting to extend this rule to trademark licenses as well, and may well succeed, continued use of this type of clause in trademark licenses must be carefully weighed. While novelty is not a criterion in determining the registration of a trademark, and since third parties have the opportunity to challenge the issuance of a trademark registration, the reasons expressed by the Supreme Court against such a clause in patent licenses do not apply to trademarks. On the other hand, the status of a mark as a trademark can be lost or abandoned; the licensee should have the same opportunity to challenge the mark as third parties, if such rights have not been dissipated by acts of the licensee.

Approval of sublicenses

The grant of a license does not give the licensee any right to sublicense others. To secure this right, the licensee must obtain the express consent of the licensor. It has been the practice in many license arrangements for the licensor to require the licensee to get the licensor's approval before the licensee may grant sublicenses.

At the present time the U. S. Department of Justice is alleging that requiring the licensor's approval before a sublicense is granted constitutes an unlawful agreement in restraint of trade, on the ground that a licensee

Buskirk & Vaughn—Man. New Ent.—16

should be able to make his unilateral judgment in appointing a sublicensee. To the extent that it is challenging this practice where the licensee has not been given any right to sublicense, the government is unlikely to win unless it overturns the basic theory of patent rights, that is, the right to exclude others. Where the licensee has received the right to sublicense third parties, the licensor still has much at stake in terms of royalties and proper maintenance of the patent. Nonetheless, such approval of the licensor constitutes, in the eyes of the Department of Justice, an agreement in unreasonable restraint of trade. Having initially transferred the right to sublicense, the licensor, according to the government, cannot hold back some controls. Whatever the logical merit of the government's theory, it is likely to find support by the courts. Therefore, if the right to sublicense is granted, the licensor should specify reasonable criteria under which the licensee may or may not grant sublicenses. These might include conditions similar to those in the principal license between the licensor and the licensee. Sharing of royalties from sublicenses should be provided for in such proportions as the licensor and licensee initially agree upon. After this point the licensor should not attempt to exercise any control over the selection of a sublicensee.

The practice of obligating the licensor to secure the approval of his licensee(s) before granting licenses to others is clearly illegal, since such a restriction redounds to the benefit of the licensee and not the licensor. To the extent that the restriction is not for the benefit of the patent owner, no reliance can be placed on patent rights; they are intended to benefit solely the patent owner.

Field of use restrictions

Patents: Sometimes the patent owner desires to parcel out the rights given him to different licensees, whether this be to achieve a greater amount of royalties or to prevent competition with itself or other licensees in certain areas. Where the patent covers the product and not merely the process of manufacturing it, such division of fields of use have been accepted as lawful use of the patent monopoly. Where a process patent *only* is involved, a direct attempt at restricting the use of the product made from the process is generally less supportable as within the patent monopoly; the patent does not extend to the product itself, but merely to employment of the process. To the extent that reasonable standards of quality imposed on the licensee in using the patented process result indirectly in restrictions on the product's utility to certain fields of use, they are generally acceptable. Under foreign patents, field of use restrictions are generally accepted as lawful exercise of patent monopoly rights, whether the patent covers the product or only the process for making it. Field of use restrictions in know-how licenses generally can be no more restrictive than those for process patents.

Trademarks: Attempts to divide fields of use through trademark licenses where each trademark (valid only in connection with the specific types of goods) must be used on goods manufactured by the licensee are also under attack by the Department of Justice. While use of a trademark in connection with types of products in areas for which there is no trademark registration can result in infringement of other trademarks and possible misuse and loss of the trademark, a deliberate pattern of using different trademarks to divide fields of use and competition in the same product goes beyond legitimate use of the trademark rights.

Absent a "pattern" of market division, restrictions on the licensee to put a licensed trademark on a product only in certain fields of use for which there is trademark protection are reasonable; they avoid unwarranted expansion of use of the trademark into areas where the trademark is unregistered, where the trademark use is more likely to result in infringement, and for which use the trademark owner has made no warranty of ownership.

Restrictions on sale and resale of licensed products

Patents: The patent monopoly extends only to excluding others from making, using, and selling the product covered by the product patent or the use of the patented process in making a product covered solely by a process patent. Attempts to control channels of distribution and sale prices present pitfalls. Where the product itself is unpatented, even though made under a patented process, the patent owner cannot lawfully and directly restrict the channels of distribution, field of use, or prices at which the unpatented product is sold. In the case of a patented product, the rule of law still allows the patent owner to state the price at which the licensee may sell the patented product and the initial channel of distribution and fields of use.

Once the initial sale of the patented product takes place by the licensee (or the patent owner), the general rule is that no further restrictions may be placed on the purchasers of the patented product. The reason is that by the initial sale of the product, the patent monopoly has been exhausted; the product, by such sale, comes into the public domain like any other product. Stated otherwise: the licensee, once having sold the product, has also given the buyer a covenant not to sue for infringement. Any attempt in a license agreement to directly impose any resale price or field of use restrictions thus becomes illegal. Other methods of controlling the distribution of patented products (such as use of a lease-only system) have also been stricken down as an anti-competitive misuse of the patent monopoly. A licensor of know-how cannot impose restrictions of minimum price, fields of use, and channels of distribution to be followed in sale of products made with the know-how.

Trademarks: The owner of a trademark can prevent others from using the same mark without his approval or license. However, once a licensee has received a license to use the trademark and puts the mark on the product in accordance with the terms of the license, the trademark owner cannot dictate the channels of distribution in which the trademarked product may be sold or resold. To the extent " fair trade" states allow resale price maintenance by the trademark owner or licensee not in competition with his customers, the licensee-manufacturer may dictate the price at which the trademarked product is to be sold by the licensee or resold by its customers.

Tying arrangements

A tying arrangement is an agreement by a party to sell one product only on the condition that the buyer also purchases a different product. The Supreme Court has said that "tying agreements serve hardly any purpose beyond the suppression of competition." Conditioning the grant of a license upon the licensee purchasing raw materials or other products from the licensor would fall within this proscription. Even where a licensor honestly feels that his reputation, sales of the licensed product, or the trademark would be jeopardized unless the licensee used the licensor's quality raw materials, such a tying requirement will almost always be considered illegal. However, the licensor can certainly impose reasonable standards of quality for the licensed product to insure that sales and royalties will be maintained and the quality of the product, especially if it bears a licensed trademark, is maintained. Under such standards, the licensee should be left free to deal with vendors other than the licensor who can meet the designated quality standards.

Grant-backs

While a number of patent license agreements have provided that the licensee shall assign back to the licensor any improvements, inventions, and patents developed by the licensee and relating to use of the licensed patent, such provisions have also currently come under attack by the Department of Justice. In view of the risk attendant with this practice, a less objectionable and safer method of assuring the licensor the ability to use the improvements developed by the licensee is to provide that the licensee grant the licensor a worldwide non-terminable non-exclusive royalty free license under the patent or improvement. While this does not assure control over the improvement by the licensor, it will assure him the freedom to use it.

Patterns in several licensing agreements

While certain provisions may be reasonable restrictions when considered in isolation in a single agreement, a pattern of such restrictions throughout the licensor's agreements with several licensees may make the practice unreasonable. For example, grant-back provisions in all license agreements or prohibitions against sale of licensed products in other territories have been considered unreasonable restraints.

Pooling of patents

Patent pooling and cross-licensing are considered opprobrious anti-competitive practices, especially when significant or basic patents in a field are shared exclusively among a few companies. Provisions requiring future patents to be pooled on the same basis are likewise deemed anti-competitive.

Tax considerations

The tax effects of licensing play a significant part in determining the economic benefit to be derived from the transactions. As a general rule, the royalties paid under a license constitute taxable income to the licensor and a deductible business expense to the licensee.

Some further tax considerations are the following:

License vs. assignment. Patents, trademarks, and know-how can be "capital assets" within the meaning of the United states Internal Revenue Code and the sale or assignment of "all substantial rights" in such property will qualify for capital gains treatment. Although an exclusive license which amounts to an assignment will be considered as a sale for capital gains treatment, royalties from non-exclusive licenses are taxed at ordinary income rates. Exclusive licenses which fall short of an assignment of all substantial rights will subject the payments to the licensor to taxation at ordinary income rates. The term "all substantial rights" is not met, for example, where the licensor reserves the right to terminate the license, to grant other licenses, to use the patent itself, or to approve or disapprove sublicenses. The licensee on his part must consider the tax benefit of currently deducting from income royalties under a license versus capitalizing the payments for purchase of the property right under an assignment.

Depreciation. Only capitalized assets which have an ascertainable life span are subject to depreciation. Patents meet this standard since the patent grant is for a fixed term, for example, in the United States it is for seventeen years; the purchase price or cost of obtaining a patent may be amortized over the remaining life of the patent. On the other hand, trademarks and know-how have an indefinite life span and their cost cannot be amortized until lost or abandoned. In such instances the licensee would prefer a true license rather than an assignment so that it can deduct the royalty payments against income and reduce taxes.

Conclusion

Licensing is not a simple transaction, but presents traps for the unwary. Perhaps the first of a number of general rules to remember is that successful licensing depends on careful planning, sound financial, tax and legal advice, artful negotiation and a basic understanding of patent, trademark, and know-how rights.

QUESTIONS

1. What are some of the difficulties encountered in licensing agreements?
2. How good is the protection offered by a patent?

*

IV

MANAGEMENT

Much has been written about the critical role played by management in the success or failure of any enterprise so there is little point to repeating it here. Rather these chapters dwell on a few aspects of small enterprise in which management theory might lead the unsuspecting entrepreneur astray.

All is not as it is written in management books. One cannot manage a small concern the same way as a large one. The focus here is on a few of the more important differences.

PEOPLE AND ORGANIZATION

21

Businesses are people, people who do things to make money. Early in economic endeavors it was clear people did more things to make money if they were organized in certain patterns. Thus the concept of management was born for managers are people who organize and direct people in their work. Therein lies one of the great problems inherent in small business. Many, if not most, small businessmen are not managers. They do not direct the work of other people but rather do the work themselves. Even those who do hire other people to do work for them may not truly manage them but instead work beside them, with them. Not many people are managers, even fewer are good managers. But this is not the place to try to instill managerial skills, that is far too complex. Instead, be advised that the ownership of a business does not make one a manager. You will have to work diligently to acquire that skill. Now for some general observations.

THERE IS NO MAGIC ORGANIZATIONAL STRUCTURE

One of the myths harbored by some alleged executives is that if they could only discover the "right" organizational structure most of their managerial troubles would be solved. Such people continually tinker with their organizations, drawing chart after chart, rearranging the people in their employ until nobody is certain who reports to whom or who is supposed to do what for whom. It is largely nonsense. *There is no one "right" organization.* You are free to form whatever structure seems to make sense to you for your situation. The key is: Does it work? If the work gets done at an acceptable cost, then it is a good organizational structure.

There is great virtue in organizational stability. Letting people alone long enough that they learn how to work with one another. In a healthy organization, they will get the work done within almost any structure provided. It is not wise to tinker with relationships within an organization. Change can begat unforeseen consequences. People can become upset by changes far beyond what any rational analysis would predict.

DO NOT BE OVERLY CONCERNED WITH ORGANIZATION

Closely related to the previous admonition, it is not good to worry too much about organizational structure. What seems natural, right, and sound is probably the best organization. Whatever organizational means are developed will be workable; the key factor is the people who fill the organization. Concentrate on the people, not on the form.

DO NOT BE A COPY CAT

Just because some other businessman has been successful using a certain form of organization does not mean that you should employ it. One merchant observed another merchant's organization with great admiration; he had been able to free himself from the day-to-day harassments of operations by developing a store manager who reported directly to him who was responsible for supervising all floor operations leaving the merchant free to buy merchandise. The first merchant tried to copy that structure. He hired a store manager. Unfortunately the situation was such that it just did not work out. Neither the store manager nor the merchant were of such a nature that they could function successfully in such a structure. This merchant had to run operations. He could not stay off the floor. He could not keep from issuing direct orders to the sales clerks, orders

that frequently countered those given by the manager. An entrepreneur must develop a structure in which he can be successful. Contrary to management theory which holds that an organization should not be built around personalities, in small businesses it must be that way because the boss is one factor in the situation who cannot be ignored. In big business, one might be fired for not fitting into a particular organizational slot. In one's own business, that bit of nonsense goes out the window. The organization must fit the person.

DIVISION OF LABOR

Organizational structure is a means for dividing up the work to be done in some meaningful way and fixing the responsibility for doing it upon one person. These are possibly two of the most important basic principles of management.

Western industrial prosperity has largely been based on the discovery that if the work that must be done by an organization is divided up between the people in that organization in certain ways the total output, or productivity, of the organization is vastly increased. Thus a great deal of time is devoted to determining how best to divide up the work. Who does what? One way is to isolate everything that must be done and assign each task to someone. Everyone must understand what it is that they are supposed to do. Moreover, they must recognize that they will be held accountable — responsible — for doing it.

UNDERSTAFF

There are successful businessmen who maintain that an organization should be deliberately understaffed. One should hire fewer workers than may really be needed. In such a manner, productivity will be increased. They maintain that a healthy organization will find a way to get the work out. If they fall behind a bit, they will work a little harder and get the job done. If too many workers are hired, the same work is done, but for a higher cost. Most entrepreneurs are most careful not to over hire. Hiring a person is a serious responsibility. Once hired, it is difficult, if not costly, to get rid of the person if it is later discovered that he or she is not really needed.

In particular, most successful small businessmen are most reluctant to hire staff personnel — accountants, personnel managers, market researchers, credit managers, purchasing agents, or whatever. These people are overhead and overhead can strangle a company. Instead, they try to farm such work out to independent contractors. They use outside accounting firms, consultants, employment agencies, or other such firms to avoid putting staff people on the payroll.

STRENGTHS

A small businessman has certain significant organizational strengths that make big business envious. They provide a definite competitive advantage.

PERSONAL RAPPORT WITH WORKERS

One classic tale told over and over relates the fate of the entrepreneur who was successful because of his relationships with his people. He worked closely with them and they loved him. They really put out for him. Then in success, he removed himself from that relationship only to lose the basis of his success. A small businessman has an opportunity to develop a productive team that the large corporation cannot have. It is a real advantage to develop it.

FLEXIBILITY

Classic management theory extols the virtue of flexibility, the ability to quickly take advantage of opportunities. Large corporations cannot move fast. Indeed, usually they move with exceptional slowness. Things can be done quickly if one wishes to do so.

COMMUNICATIONS

Management theory lauds the excellent communications within a small organization. Everyone should be better able to know what is going on in a small organization than in a large one. Particularly the boss should know what is occurring. One of the complaints of the president of a large company is that he seldom gets the word about developments until late in the matter. Indeed, unfavorable events are screened from him by subordinates whose fates may be jeopardized should the boss find out what is going on. A small businessman can find out what is going on if he tends to his business. Granted that the annals of business are filled with small businessmen who have failed because they did not tend to their affairs and did not know what was happening to their enterprise, that is but a reflection of managerial ineptness.

MOTIVATION

It is much easier to motivate people in a small organization than in a large one. Granted that this is a result of the previous factors, it seems sufficiently important that separate mention should be made of motivation.

The small businessman has a much better opportunity to get to know each of his employees because of face-to-face interaction with them. This type of interaction makes it possible to recognize the fact that people differ, not only in their ability to do their jobs, but also in their desire to perform. With this knowledge, the entrepreneur should utilize those motivating factors that are effective with various employees. These factors, to mention a few, may be: appreciation for their performance, sympathetic understanding of their personal problems, job security, consideration of employee ideas in attempting to solve organizational problems, good working conditions, promotion and growth opportunity with the company. Employees are often motivated through recognition and affiliation.

PROBLEMS

Small business is not an unblemished organizational virtue. There are some problems.

GETTING GOOD PEOPLE

The small businessman has a difficult time hiring talented people in most instances. People are worried about their future, their security, their welfare. A small businessman can seldom offer them much along those lines. They know that he may fail, sell out, or simply quit business at anytime. Where will they be? There seems to be more security with the larger corporation, at least that is the way most people see it.

Usually, there is little opportunity for advancement in small business. There is the boss and there are the workers with no place to go. There may be little the boss can do about it. After all, he went into the business to be boss and hired them to be workers, not management or partners. Thus the labor pool open for the small businessman may be quite limited and those people in it may not be what he would like them to be. It all depends upon your business.

TRAINING

Most large concerns spend considerable sums of money training their new people. IBM hires reasonably bright young men who have no experience and train them to do things the IBM way. They are good at this tactic. The small businessman has neither the money nor the skills to do such training, not to mention the time and inclination to do so. Not many small businessmen do much that can be classified as training. Yet they need to do it as badly as the large concern.

Over a period of years one woman built up a rather profitable business selling equipment to outdoorsmen both by mail order and through two retail outlets. She tired of the business as her health failed; she perceived that what was needed was someone to manage the enterprise full time for her. After hiring and firing five different men for the job she finally had to dispose of the company. She had been unable to hire a manager. Each story was about the same. She would hire a man; he would make some mistakes; she would fire him. "I just can't find anyone who knows how to run the business," she would complain. Of course not! She had to train such a person. Unfortunately she had neither the talent nor the temperament to train a manager.

In contrast, one men's apparel merchant built a chain of stores upon the managerial philosophy that each sales person hired was a potential store manager who required training. Each man was provided careful and thorough training in how to run an apparel store.

SMA

SMALL BUSINESS ADMINISTRATION
SMALL MARKETERS AIDS No. 136

FIRST PRINTED JAN. 1969   **WASHINGTON D.C.**   REPRINTED MARCH 1972

HIRING THE RIGHT MAN

SEE OTHER SIDE ▶

When he was ready for the responsibility, a store was built for him. Training takes time and patience. But it is a must!

ONE MAN BANDS

Possibly the most frequent weakness in the management of small businesses is that the owner tends to become a "one-man band." He does everything, delegates nothing. Not only does such an individual find himself bogged down in a mass of detail, but the people who work for him fail to develop. The boss who insists on doing everything will discover that other people will be perfectly happy to let him do it. He'll hear no protest; he will just be overworked.

A "one-man band" faces severe limitations on his growth and happiness. His business cannot grow unless he develops people to do the work. He will not be able to get free from his business unless he develops other people to do the work. A manager who is a one-man band is really a worker.

1. KNOW WHAT YOU WANT NEW EMPLOYEE TO DO.

2. DECIDE WHAT SKILLS NEW EMPLOYEE WILL NEED TO DO THE JOBS YOU WANT HIM TO DO.

3. DON'T HIRE UNTIL YOU FIND AN EMPLOYEE WHO HAS THESE SKILLS.

FOR MORE INFORMATION
Get a Free Copy of SMA 106
"Finding and Hiring the Right Employee"
FROM THE NEAREST SBA OFFICE

DO THIS

FILING CLASSIFICATION: PERSONNEL MANAGEMENT—Copies of this Aid are available free from field offices and Washington headquarters of the Small Business Administration. Aids may be condensed or reproduced. They may not be altered to imply approval by SBA of any private organization, product, or service. If material is reused, credit to SBA will be appreciated. Use of official mailing indicia to avoid postage is prohibited by law. Use of funds for printing this publication approved by Bureau of the Budget, June 29, 1970.

HOW TO PICK PEOPLE

Possibly the single most important thing a manager does is select the people he hires. If he hires the right people, he will be successful and his life will be relatively uneventful. The people will get the work done. Hire the wrong people and little but problems will result. It is difficult to over emphasize the importance of hiring the right people. It takes time to do it but it is time well spent. So a few observations that may not be found in the many books written on the topic will follow.

DO NOT COMPETE
WITH BIG BUSINESS

You need a different type of person from the classic college graduate sought so vigorously by big business. A small business has little to offer him that he wants.

DEPENDABILITY-LOYALTY

Hire people you can count on, people who show up for work and do so on time.

You need people who will do their jobs as directed. You can forgive many faults to get dependability.

HONESTY

Never hire a crook. Sounds silly to say it for few people would do so knowingly. Let us put it another way. Seek people whose character indicates that they can be trusted. There is no way you can protect yourself from someone who is of a mind to steal from you, particularly when they are working for you. No control system is foolproof. They all can be beat in some way. Character is your only defense. Look for people who tell the truth and whose attitude is such that they feel no compulsion to cheat. There are ways to detect such people from their conversations and attitudes in life. The man who cheats one place will cheat another. Look at the record.

No comments had best be made on the following bit of nonsense. Read it for fun.

How to know a comptroller from a personnel manager (A concise guide to basic executive characteristics)

Position	He wears	He eats	He believes
Chairman of the Board	Double-breasted blue suits	Yogurt	He's an industrial statesman
President	$150 suits	Banquet chicken and peas	He makes all the decisions
Executive vice-president	$300 suits	Steak	He's running the company
Comptroller	Vests	Pot roast	People don't know the value of money
Sales manager	Sports coats	On his expense account	He can sell everything they can produce
Production Manager	Shirtsleeves	Salami sandwiches	He can produce everything they can sell
Advertising manager	Brooks Brothers suits	On the Agency's expense account	Advertising sells the company's products
R&D director	Sweaters	When he thinks of it	He's another Einstein
Purchasing director	Robert Hall suits	On the suppliers' expense accounts	Purchasing is a profession
Public relations director	Bell bottoms	With financial reporters	He should report to the president
Personnel manager	Horn-rimmed glasses	In the company cafeteria	He likes people

He hopes	He knows	He wants	He'll settle for
Other people believe it too	Everything	A cabinet position	Writing a book
He's indispensable	He isn't	To be an industrial statesman	Making a speech at the Rotary Club
The president will retire	He won't	Power and prestige	Power
He can teach them	He can't	To cut costs 20 percent	Cutting costs 2 percent
They'll build up inventory	The production department is dragging its feet	More salesmen	A bonus
He can reduce inventory	The sales forecast is ridiculous	New machinery	A bonus
He's right	The Nielsen ratings	A bigger ad budget	A bigger office
He can prove it	$E=mc^2$	Professional recognition	Patent rights
Other people think so, too	They don't	Top value for low prices	Low prices
The president knows he's alive	He doesn't	To place an article in Fortune	A paragraph in the local paper
People like him	They don't	The best man for every job	Anyone the agency sends him

CONTRACTOR OR EMPLOYEE?

22

A small manufacturer of an elastic rope tie down device designed for the sailboat market subcontracted the sewing together of the loops to a woman to do in her home for two cents a rope. It was a marvelous arrangement for both parties. Was the woman a contractor or an employee? Well, read on!

Some small businessmen avoid paying payroll taxes and other costs that are related to hiring people by carefully arranging to have work done by independent contractors rather than employees. Care must be taken, for the governments take a most strict look at such arrangements. They want their taxes. *WARNING:* The cooperative "employee" who eagerly seeks to be an independent contractor, for he has visions of being able to beat the income taxes by doing so, may be the one who makes a report to the IRS. His motive? He wants coverage under social security and sees an opportunity to have his boss pay all of his coverage.

Here is an authoritative treatment of this subject.

Current factors that distinguish between "employee" and "independent contractor"

Aaron Levine †

The federal employment taxes impose on an employer significant excise and withholding tax obligations with respect to wages paid to their "employees." As a result, it is extremely important that a taxpayer be able to determine accurately who,

†**Aaron Levine,** *The Journal of Taxation,* **September 1972, pp. 188-193.**

Aaron Levine, of the District of Columbia and Illinois Bars, is with the Chicago law firm of Lapin, Panichi, & Levine, Ltd. He is a member of the Tax Section of the American Bar Association.

among those individuals involved in his business, are his "employees" and who are "independent contractors." In addition, it is necessary for a taxpayer to know who his "employees" are for purposes of several other important provisions of the Code.

Even though there are a significant number of Code sections whose operative provisions are related to a class of individuals designated as "employees," there is extremely little guidance to be found in the Code or the Regulations as to what constitutes an "employee."

To mention only a few of the potential problem areas, failure of the taxpayer to make an accurate determination of who his "employees" are may result in the disqualification of a pension or profit-sharing plan or have other undesirable consequences in the area of qualified stock option plans. However, for purposes of the Federal Employment taxes, a taxpayer faces the largest potential exposure if his "employee" determinations are inaccurate. If a taxpayer has not withheld employment taxes with respect to individuals who are a part of his business and it is later determined upon an IRS audit that those individuals are "employees," the taxpayer faces the prospect of a large assessment for the taxes which were not withheld, along with accrued interest. However, it is possible to abate part or all of the assessment relating to the actual taxes themselves if the taxpayer can prove that those individuals, with respect to whose remuneration he did not withhold and pay the applicable Federal employment taxes, paid the taxes themselves. However, *Rev. Rul.* 58-577, 1958-2 CB 744 provides that a taxpayer who filed a supplemental return reporting the tax which should have been withheld from an employee originally thought to be an independent contractor, must pay interest even though the additional tax shown on the supplemental return was abated when it was determined that the employee had filed a return and paid the tax that was shown to be due on the return in full.

Putting the interest question aside, the taxpayer's main concern will be proving to the Service that the employee paid the employment taxes himself. This will be especially difficult for those taxpayers who engage large numbers of individuals in their operations and who suffer a high turnover rate. In addition, the author's recent experience leads him to understand that the Service will not make its computer records available to a taxpayer who is seeking to abate an employment tax deficiency assessment.

Finally, an examination of the question of which individuals a business engages in its operations are its "employees" is becoming increasingly more important since the author has learned that the Service is now encouraging its Agents to examine more closely a corporation's compliance with the Federal employment taxes. This increased activity is the result of a determination by the Service that their Agents have tended to ignore this area in the past and as a result, compliance has slackened to some extent in many cases. The taxpayers who are likely to be confronted with assessments for Federal employment taxes are those companies who engage, as part of their marketing system, large numbers of individuals in their businesses as manufacturer's representatives, distributors, field salesmen, local plant operators and similar types of individuals. These individuals typically operate on their own, in the field and away from the direct control of company headquarters.

Statutory guidance

As indicated earlier, the Code and its Regulations give extremely little guidance as to what criteria are to be used in ascertaining who is an "employee." This stems, in large part, from the fact that the original legislation establishing the 1935 Social Security Act set forth no definition of the term "employee" but merely specified in Section 1106(a)(6) (48 Stat. 620, 647) that the term employee "includes an officer of a corporation." The situation has improved somewhat from the original 1939 Code provisions and now Section 3121(d)(2) (relating to the Federal Insurance Contributions Act) provides that an employee is "any individual who, under the usual common law rules applicable in determining the employer-employee relationship, has the status of an employee." Section 3306(i) (relating to the Federal Unemployment Compensation Tax Act) adopts a somewhat similar approach to the definition of the term employee. That Section provides that there is excluded from the term "employee" (1) any individual who, under the usual common law rules applicable in determining the employer-employee relationship, has the status of an independent contractor, or (2) any individual (except an officer of a corporation) who is not an employee under such common law rules." Section 3402(c) (relating to the withholding of income tax) provides virtually no guidance as to how to ascertain which individuals will be designated as "employees" for Federal income tax withholding purposes.

As a result of this virtual dearth of statutory guidance as to what standards and criteria are to be used in defining the term "employee," the practitioner must resort to the extensive case law and Treasury pronouncements for assistance in determining who are "employees."

Case law considerations

The case law has developed a number of factors which are useful in analyzing whether a particular relationship is one of employer-employee. In *Illinois Tri-Seal Products, Inc.*, 353 F.2d 216 (Ct. Cls., 1965), the court set forth those factors as follows:

" . . . degrees or extent of control which the principal may exercise over the details of the work; whether or not the principal has the right to discharge the individual; opportunity of the individual for profit and loss; investment by the individual in tools and facilities for work; whether the individual or the principal supplies the tools and places to work; the degree of skill required in the particular occupation; the permanency and length of time the individual is engaged; the method of payment (whether by time or job); whether the work is part of the employer's regular business; and whether the parties believe they are creating an employer-employee relationship or a principal-independent contractor relationship."

Even when applying the above factors in analyzing a particular relationship one must keep in mind that no "one factor is controlling nor are these factors exclusive. The relationship is to be ascertained by an overall view of the entire situation, not by any rule of thumb, or by the presence or absence of a single factor. The result in each case must be governed by the special facts and circumstances of the case itself."

Although many of the factors noted in the *Tri-Seal* case would appear to be obvious when viewed in the normal business office context, the presence or absence of certain of these factors is not always immediately discernible when the situation involves a manufacturers' representative, a moving van operator, storm window installer, or other individual who is engaged by a business to carry out a portion of its activities outside of the plant without immediate close field supervision. Therefore, it would be useful, especially to those practitioners who have had little or no contact with the "common law" of the employment tax field, to briefly analyze the substance of each of the above-cited factors and how they are applied to particular relationships.

Degrees or extent of control which the principal may exercise over the details of the work. What the courts, and the employment tax Regulations look to here is whether the principal has the right to instruct the agent as to the precise details and methods which he will use in accomplishing a given task rather than the end result of the agent's labors. It is here that many controversies between the Service and the taxpayer begin; the taxpayer contending that he only specified what was to be accomplished by the agent and not how the agent was to achieve the result. To determine whether the principal has enough control to constitute him an "employer," one must examine the ground rules governing the relationship between principal and agent. In a case currently in our office, the following are the characteristics of the relationship between a manufacturer and his distributors. The distributors were not required to do any of the following:

1. Devote their full time to their distributorships;

2. Attend sales meetings;

3. Make reports;

4. Work any set number of hours a day or number of days a week;

5. Call on any particular customers at any given time;

6. Adhere to any instructions, rules, or procedures as to how to make sales presentations;

7. Submit contracts of sale for home office approval;

8. Maintain any specific inventory level; and

9. Produce any minimum amount of orders for any given period.

Clearly, the lack of restrictions to which the distributors were subject in their relationship with the home office should leave no doubt that the manufacturer did not have the right "to control and direct" the distributors as "to the details and means by which" they conducted their distributorships. Regardless of this seemingly clear-cut example of a principal not retaining enough control over the details of how the distributors sold his products, the Examining Agent is taking the position that the "control factor" existed, and that the distributors were actually employees. In *Illinois Tri-Seal Products*, the Court of Claims found no employment relationship to exist where these similar facts were involved:

" . . . The installers determined for themselves when they would work and their hours of work. They prepared their own work schedule. . . . The installers were free to work alone or with partners or associates of their own choosing and the compensation paid them was decided among themselves without interference by plaintiffs . . . All work was done away from plaintiff's premises and plaintiffs never attempted to control or direct the manner in which the installers did the work. Plaintiffs had no foremen or supervisors to direct the installers in the manner of doing the work and other than instructions contained in the worksheets — which the installers were expected to follow so that the work would be accomplished in accordance with the specifications contained therein — plaintiffs gave no directions or instructions to the installers concerning the manner or method of accomplishing the work."

Whether or not the principal has the right to discharge the individual. In applying this factor, the practitioner must scrutinize the basis upon which the principal can exercise his right to terminate an individual. If the principal terminates an agent because he failed to adhere to company rules and regulations such termination will tend to support a finding that the discharged individual was an employee and he was fired because he refused to take instructions as to how his work was to be accomplished. On the other hand, if the agent's discharge is for failure to meet a prescribed sales quota or produce a finished product satisfactory to the principal's specifications, the discharge of the agent is on the basis that he failed to achieve the result desired by the principal. The fact that an individual is fired for failure to achieve the intended result of his assignment does not establish that he was an "employee" merely by virtue of the fact of his discharge.

Opportunity of the individual for profit or loss. In the normal employment relationship, the employee's opportunity for profit or loss does not exist, or at best, is only a nominal one. Therefore, if the facts and circumstances of the situation indicate that the individual does, in fact, have the opportunity for significant profit or loss from his endeavors, this will weigh in favor of a finding that the individual is an independent contractor. For example, in *Nevin, Inc. v. Rothensies,* 58 F. Supp. 460 (DC Pa., 1945); *aff'd.* 151 F.2d 189 (CA-3, 1945), the court, in determining that an independent contractor relationship existed between the parties made the following observation about a licensee who was in a separate (though not a fully independent) business in which he had a personal interest. "He could make or lose money in the business. The possibility of profits could be enhanced by efficiency, economy and skill. He took the risk of considerable personal loss in case the business was not successful — a risk which involved a good deal more than the mere possibility of loss of position. He obtained complete freedom in connection with his own time, working hours, etc., and an opportunity to increase his income not only by sales records (as in the case of a commission salesman), but by business judgment in most of the matters which are in the province of any independent retailer."

Investment by the individual in the tools and facilities for work. What this factor attempts to look at is whether the extent of the individual's personal investment in the equipment which he uses in carrying out his assignments is so significant that such an investment would not be found in the customary employer-employee relationship. For example, the installers in the *Tri-Seal* case supplied their own trucks; furnished their own tools and equipment for performance of the work; paid all expenses for upkeep and maintenance of their trucks and equipment; and stored doors and windows for assigned jobs at their own expense.

Similar investments were made by the distributors involved in the case currently being handled in our office. Even if a substantial investment in tools and facilities is made by the individual, he may still be classified as an "employee" if he is subject to extensive detailed instructions by the principal as to how he will use his equipment.

The degree of skill required in the particular occupation. Where the particular occupation involves the services of a highly skilled individual (except in circumstances of attorneys, accountants, doctors, dentists and other professionals working in firms or clinics), it is likely that the particular individual is not an "employee" due to the lack of control which the principal would normally exercise over the work performed by such an individual. In a case involving so-called "gypsy chasers" (individuals who assist a moving-van operator in loading and unloading) the factor of the degree of skill required by the occupation was discussed and the court in *Lanigan Storage & Van Co., Inc.*, 389 F.2d 337 (CA-6, 1968), stated as follows:

"These 'gypsy chasers' are skilled in furniture handling, a skill which requires perhaps several months of concentrated effort to obtain. *They are in a real sense 'specialists' in their work and do not require nor would they welcome detailed supervision.* They jealously consider themselves 'independent.' That the driver does not, in fact, exercise such control is not

dispositive, but does tend to indicate that he does not possess the right to control." (Emphasis added.)

The importance of this skill factor is that if such skill is possessed by the individual in the particular situation, it will assist the practitioner in proving that the over-all control factor is not present in the relationship.

The permanency and length of time the individual is engaged. A benchmark of a basic employment relationship is the fact that it is of a permanent nature, usually involving a specified initial term of service, and provides for specified notice periods before either party can terminate the relationship. In commenting on this factor, a district court in *Silver*, 131 F. Supp. 209 (DC N.Y.), made the following observation:

"Permanency of relationship can hardly be said to exist or be a weighty element where each obligation was of comparatively short duration and the worker was free to accept or reject the offer of a new or similar obligation."

If the given situation involves facts such as those of *Silver*, this factor will be favorable in arriving at the conclusion that no employment relationship exists. However, if a manufacturer's representative maintains a long-standing relationship with his manufacturer, the permanency factor may militate against the case. On the other hand, this factor alone, while it is not generally determinative of the issue, should not be ignored. Even if the relationship between manufacturer and representative is of long-standing, this only demonstrates that each party has consistently achieved the *result* he expected to derive from the relationship and does not go to the question of control by one party over another.

The method of payment (whether by time or job). This particular factor has not been given a great deal of scrutiny by the courts and its relation to the determination of the existence of an employment relationship is not entirely clear. It would appear that if an individual were paid on an hourly basis, an argument could be made that he was an employee (if certain other factors existed), because it would be expected that the principal would give his agents more detailed instructions so that they could accomplish their jobs in the least amount of time.

On the other hand, if the payment is on a job basis, it is more likely that the agent involved is not an employee because the principal would not be interested in how quickly the job was completed, but only with the final result. Therefore, he would not be likely to require the agent to follow detailed instructions in completing the job. On the contrary, it would be up to the agent to devise the most expeditious methods for his own accomplishment of the jobs assigned to him, as the more jobs he completes, the higher will be his compensation. This analysis, obviously, would not apply to a factor situation where workers are paid on a piece-work basis.

However, this question of the manner of payment arises indirectly when the Service contends that the drawing account of a salesman is, in fact, a salary paid to him as an employee. In general, the courts have tended not to consider the normal drawing account arrangement between the manufacturer and salesman to constitute a salary. If a drawing account is involved in a particular case it can be expected that the Service may characterize the account as a salary.

Whether the parties believe they are creating an employer-employee relationship. As in many other instances of the tax law, the intent of the parties (while often expressed in self-serving statements) is very important in deciding the question involved in this article. Factors which are substantial in ascertaining the true intent of the parties were set forth in *Illinois Tri-Seal, Inc.*, where the court stated:

"A further factor here is that the parties believed that they were creating a principal-independent contractor relationship and not an employer-employee relationship. The installers considered that they had their own business and that they were self-employed; they paid self-employment taxes; some had their own business cards; they carried personal and property liability insurance and were required to deposit with plaintiffs a certificate showing they had such coverage before being given any installation work. Plaintiffs did not carry any workmen's compensation policy covering installers; did not pay State unemployment insurance on the earnings of the installers; and did not withhold income taxes or assume liability for unemployment taxes on installers' earnings."

While the intent argument is essentially a self-serving one, it is one which should be utilized in support of the factual aspects of a case.

In addition to the factors which the courts have developed for analyzing a particular relationship for employment tax purposes, the Service also provides somewhat similar guidelines which can be gleaned from an analysis of its Regulations and Rulings.

Guides for determining whether an employer-employee relationship exists are found in three substantially similar sections of the employment tax Regulations. Reg. 31.3121(d)-1(c) provides, in part, that generally, the relationship of employer and employee exists when the person for whom the services are performed has the right to control and direct the individual who performs the services, not only as to the result to be accomplished by the work, but also as to the details and means by which that result is accomplished. Thus, an employee is subject to the will and control of the employer not only as to what shall be done, but as to how it shall be done. In this connection, it is not necessary that the employer actually direct or control the manner in which the services are performed; it is sufficient if he has the right to do so. The right to discharge is also an important factor indicating that the person possessing that right is the employer.

Thus, the employment tax Regulations look only to control of the details of performance and the right to discharge the person performing the services. It is because of this lack of more detailed regulatory guidance that so many cases have been litigated in the courts concerning the determination of whether a particular individual performing the services for another is the employee of the latter. The only additional instruction, outside of the case law itself, are the Rulings published by the Service.

Current IRS attitude

Comparison with employee's responsibility. Rev. Ruls. 70-442 and 70-602, 1970-2 CB 218, 226, deal with two situations containing fairly divergent fact patterns. What makes them interesting to compare is that they appear to have been decided on the finding of one particular element. *Rev.*

Rul. 70-442 dealt with rural telephone exchange operators who operated company-owned equipment, followed prescribed operating procedures, made regular reports to the central office, and whose services could be terminated if not satisfactory to the central office. In addition to other obvious control factors which this relationship contained, the Ruling states: "The nature of the work of the operator is the same as that of the regular employees on the payroll of the companies."

Rev. Rul. 70-602 involved individuals who owned their own trucks, entered into oral contracts with a retail company, paid all the expenses of operating their trucks (including the hiring of helpers), and were paid on a truck load basis. The truck owners were required to report for duty at a specified time each day, to report when leaving with a delivery, to wait for loads, to give notice when they were unable to perform services on any particular day, and to purchase gasoline from the company. In addition, the drivers could be transferred by the company from one retail outlet to another. Although it would appear obvious that there were enough control factors present in the relationship to constitute the truck owners (despite their own heavy investment in their equipment) employees of the company, the Ruling indicated it was necessary, as in the case of the rural exchange operators, to make this statement:

"The names of the drivers are carried on the Company's payroll records and the conditions and circumstances under which they perform their services are substantially similar to those under which the drivers of company-owned trucks perform services."

The comparison of the above two Rulings demonstrates that when a particular arrangement involves the performance of services, which are also performed by regular employees of a company, that those individuals who perform the same services, on a temporary basis, or outside the central office will, in all likelihood, be classified as "employees," regardless of the fact that the temporary employees may have a heavy personal investment in their equipment or are not under the close supervision of the company's central office.

Operators of bulk oil plants. In *Rev. Rul.* 70-444 1970-2 CB 214, the Service concluded that the operator of a bulk oil plant leased from an oil company was an "employee" for Employment tax purposes because he: (a) was required to sell at fixed prices; (b) could not extend credit; (c) was required to make periodic reports; (d) could not sell competitor's products; (e) could not alter the premises; (f) could not assign his lease; and (g) was required to devote his full time to the plant.

In contrast to *Rev. Rul.* 70-444 is the bulk oil plant operator described in *Rev. Rul.* 70-446, 1970-2 CB 215. In that Ruling, the bulk oil plant agent was found not to be an "employee" for employment tax purposes because: (a) he bore all expenses, including freight and taxes; (b) he provided his own equipment (including construction of the plant itself); (c) he conducted his own local advertising; (d) he was not required to follow oil company instructions or use its operators' manual; (e) he could fix his hours and days of operation; (f) he was not required to devote full time to operating the plant; (g) he could extend credit to customers at his own risk; and (h) he could sell products below company established prices.

From a comparison of the two bulk oil plant operator Rulings it is possible to obtain a fairly clear understanding of the factors which resulted in the agent being classified as an "employee" in *Rev. Rul.* 70-444 and as an independent contractor in *Rev. Rul.* 70-446. Although the conclusions of those Rulings would appear to be obvious, the predecessor of that Ruling (I. R. Mim. 5925, 1945 CB 371) was not issued until the taxpayers were successful in *American Oil Co. v. Eugene Fly*, 135 F.2d 491 (CA-5, 1943) and *The Texas Co. v. Joseph T. Higgins*, 118 F.2d 636 (CA-2, 1941).

Manufacturer's agent. In *Rev. Rul.* 70-586, 1970-2 CB 223, a manufacturer's sales agent was found to be an "employee" for employment tax purposes because: (a) products could only be sold at fixed prices; (b) the contracts specified that all agents would follow manufacturer's rules and regulations governing their activities; (c) all sales were subject to manufacturer's approval; (d) any office set up by an agent had to carry the manufacturer's name on the door, in the telephone book and on the building directory; (e) warehouse space was required to be obtained in accordance with manufacturer's specifications; (f) regular inventory and other reports were mandatory; and (g) no deliveries could be made by the agent without the manufacturer's approval.

Rev. Rul 70-587, 1970-2 CB 224 concluded that such agents were not "employees" for employment tax purposes because: (a) manufacturer had no contact or knowledge of agent's customers; (b) no reports were required; (c) agent could set his own hours; (d) agent was given no instructions as to how to canvass his territory; (e) cash sales did not require manufacturer's approval; (f) attendance at sales meetings was not required; and

(g) agent was not required to follow manufacturer's instructions or rules regarding his activities.

These two Rulings, involving fairly clearcut contrasting situations, provide good criteria to be used by the practitioner in determining whether, in a given situation, a manufacturer's sales agent should be classified as an "employee" or independent contractor.

Operators of gasoline service station. Rev. Rul. 69-305, 1969-1 CB 259 involves an individual who operated a gasoline service station under the following circumstances: (a) a fixed monthly rent was paid for the station; (b) company products could be sold at any price set by the operator; (c) competitors products could be sold; (d) credit could be extended at operator's own risk; and (e) he operated under his own name.

As would appear obvious by this point, the Service concluded in that Ruling that the service station operator was not an "employee" of the lessor oil company.

Rev. Rul. 70-443, 1970-2 CB 213, provides a contrasting set of circumstances where the Service concluded that the service station operator was an "employee" of the oil company involved. The operator was classified as an "employee" because of the following conditions to which he was subject: (a) maintainance of the service station in a manner satisfactory to the company; (b) periodic reporting; (c) displaying of advertising matter in company approved manner; (d) accounting for all funds, products and property of every kind belonging to the company coming into his possession; (e) sale of products at fixed prices; (f) extension of credit only as directed by the Company; and (g) sale of competitors' products prohibited.

As was the case in the other previously cited contrasting situations, where seemingly similar occupational categories were involved, the two service station operator Rulings disclose the factors which distinguish an independent contractor from an employee.

Merchants police. Rev. Rul. 70-529, 1970 2 CB 220, held that individuals referred to as "merchants police" were "employees" of those merchants who used their services because: (a) each merchant gave the policeman specific work instructions; (b) policeman was required to turn off lights in display windows at a certain hour, check to see that all windows and doors were locked; (c) instructions were subject to change at any time; and (d) the policeman was paid directly by the merchant.

In *Rev. Rul.* 70-530, 1970-2 CB 221, an individual and his assistants performing patrol services (identical to those in the above Ruling) for various merchants were not deemed to be the "employees" of the merchants for the following reasons: (a) the patrol service operator contracted with each merchant individually; (b) specific services were contracted for; (c) no merchant could contract for services which would be incompatible with rendering services to all other merchants; (d) all equipment and uniforms were supplied by the operator; and (e) no merchant had any control over any of the patrolmen used by the operator.

This Ruling distinguishes itself from *Rev. Rul.* 70-529 on the basis that, in the situation covered in that Ruling, each patrolman was subject to specific instructions as to what duties would be performed, whereas in this situation, the merchants contracted for specific services with the patrol force operator.

The details as to rendering those services were apparently spelled out as specific services in the contracts. It would seem that the instructions given to the merchant patrolmen as to how they would render services to the merchants in *Rev. Rul.* 70-529 constituted control "as to the details and means by which" the duties were to be carried out by the individual patrolman. The difference between not finding requisite the control in *Rev. Rul.* 70-530 can probably be traced to the fact that the detailed instructions given in the first Ruling were translated into specific services (results) to be rendered in the contracts contained in the second Ruling. Therefore, the merchants who contracted with the patrol force operator specified only the results to be accomplished and not the means for doing so. They, therefore, had no "control" over the operator or his men even though the services contracted for were very nearly the same as those described in the instructions which the individual patrolmen received from the merchants in the first ruling.

Construction subcontractor. Rev. Rul. 70-618, 1970-2 CB 227, dealt with a fact pattern where an individual entered into a written contract with a construction company whereby he would, in return for a specified percentage of the construction cost, furnish the labor, tools and equipment for the construction of houses. The construction company would reimburse him for the cost of the labor and building materials required and other construction costs. The Ruling concluded that the individual, and those assisting him, were "employees" of the construction company because: (a) the company had the right to select, approve or discharge any persons which the individual engaged to assist him; (b) the individual was not responsible for faults, construction defects or wasteful operations; (c) a company representative frequently visited the construction site and kept current on the progress of the construction; and, (d) the individual submitted a weekly statement to the company for all amounts expended by him including labor costs for which the individual was not liable.

It seems reasonably clear that the key aspects which the Service focused on in holding that the individual and his assistants were "employees" were that the construction company had complete control over the assistants, no expenses were paid by the individual, the individual was not responsible for quality or cost control, and the construction site was visited frequently by a company representative.

Auto salesman. Rev. Rul. 72-74, IRB 1972-8, 9, involved a salesman engaged in the wholesale purchase and sale of used automobiles between dealers. The Service concluded that, even though state law prohibited the salesman from working for more than one dealer at a time, that he was not an "employee" because: (a) the salesman developed his own leads; (b) the salesman could sell the cars for whatever prices he could obtain; (c) the salesman was not required to observe prescribed working hours or follow a prescribed routine; (d) the salesman was not guaranteed a minimum amount of profit or permitted a drawing account against future profits; (e) the salesman paid all expenses incurred in transporting, reconditioning, and selling the used cars sold; and (f) the salesman was liable to the dealer if the car was sold for a price below its acquisition cost.

There should be little surprise that the Ruling reached the conclusion it did, based on the facts as set forth above, since practically all the elements evidencing an employment relationship were clearly absent in the situation.

Summary of IRS ruling position

From the preceding analysis of the current Service ruling policy, it can be determined that there are certain "primary control" factors which if present in a given situation, will result in a finding by the Service that an employment relationship exists. This list of "primary factors" consists of the following:

1. Full-time commitment;

2. Prescribed hours and routine;

3. Mandatory rules and regulations;

4. Requirement of reports;

5. Required attendance at sales meetings;

6. Control over assistants;

7. Provision of customer lists and sales leads; and

8. No opportunity for profit or loss.

In addition, if not all of the "primary control" factors exist in a given relationship and the "secondary control factors," set forth below, are found to exist it is probable that the combination of the primary and secondary control factors would result in the Service finding an employment relationship. The secondary control factors consist of:

1. Sale of competitor products not allowed;

2. Provision for drawing account;

3. Reimbursement of expenses;

4. Lack of substantial individual investment in tools and equipment; and

5. Requirement of a sales quota.

Planning possibilities

In order to prevent the imposition of a large deficiency for failure to withhold and pay Federal employment taxes, there are a number of precautions which can be taken by a business.

1. Ruling Request; Form SS-8. By filing a Form SS-8, a business concern can determine in advance whether or not the Service will consider certain of those individuals associated with it as its "employees" for Federal employment tax purposes. Although this form requires fairly substantial information, an advance ruling obtained from the Service will serve as an invaluable insurance policy against any future employment tax deficiency.

2. Adequate instruction to independent contractors. If it has been determined by a business concern, either by a ruling or on advice of counsel, that a certain class of individuals should be deemed independent contractors, such individuals should be adequately informed of their legal responsibility to pay estimated Federal Income and self-employment taxes. If called upon by the Service, the company should be able to produce official company memoranda which contain instructions to independent contractors as to their Federal tax responsibilities. In addition, it would be advisable, where practical, to have each independent contractor sign a form acknowledging receipt of the Federal tax information memorandum.

3. Do not use detailed instruction guides. Unless it is deemed absolutely vital, a company seeking to have a certain class of individuals be accepted by the Service as independent contractors, should not provide detailed operating manuals. If a company feels

that it is necessary to use manuals of any kind, such manuals should contain a printed statement that the independent contractor is not required to use the manual, and that it is available to him only for his reference and need not be adhered to.

4. Do not require unnecessary reports. If reports of salesmens' progress are not essential to the company's marketing program, it is inadvisable to require any form of mandatory reporting by salesman or distributors. The requirement of periodic reports, as noted earlier, is one of the primary factors the Service looks to in attempting to establish an employment relationship in a given situation.

QUESTIONS

1. Why do small business people so strongly want to make people who do things for them into independent contractors?

MANAGEMENT IN A CLOSELY HELD COMPANY

23

Special problems arise in the management of companies which are owned by a few people most of whom are active in its operations. One of the more frustrating problems is that of getting out of the organizations with one's money intact. Business folklore is redundant with terrible tales of how minority stockholders in a closely held company are squeezed out, frozen out, and plain cheated out of their equity.

Here is an oft-told tale, just the names change as the plot unfolds again and again everywhere.

Caught in a closely held company

Harold Smith†

†Harold Smith, *Dun's Review*, **December 1971, pp. 57-58.**

One day last winter they carried me out of my office on a stretcher. I was in the hospital for nearly three weeks. The doctors diagnosed it as collapse brought about by mental and physical exhaustion. How right they were. I was completely strung out from trying to manage my end of a closely held company.

I was with a $125-million-sales specialized manufacturing and services company, serving as vice president and general manager of a division that accounted for some 60% of total business. Unhappily, most of the company's shares were held by the aging chairman, who had acquired it just before World War I, and his family.

There was something of the reluctant dragon about the firm. Here was a company that had built an international reputation in its particular field of specialization. Yet throughout its history, sales and profits went up and down like a roller coaster, and even in boom times it hesitated to expand and modernize.

I joined the company five years ago, just before the old chairman finally retired and turned the job over to his son. I was an experienced executive with a background in operations and marketing. I suppose you could call me a bottom-line guy who was also sold on long-range planning, EDP, modernization, research and development and just about everything else that growth companies boasted of doing.

I was, of course, elated when the new regime took over. With the old man in retirement, the company could at last institute some innovative management, perhaps take a few risks and bring the entire organization up to snuff internally. Surely, I believed, our young chairman and our new president, who had been elevated from the ranks, were bright and daring enough to bring some new thinking and efficiency into the company.

Nothing of the kind. Even in retirement, the old chairman's influence hung over the place like a pall. He kept coming into the office regularly, and some of the old-timers swore they could feel him breathing down their necks. It soon became obvious that the new management's only commitment was to preserve the status quo. They stood in such awe of the old man's presence that they feared to rock his boat.

Oh sure, the new management tossed us operations chiefs a few token crumbs of authority. We were allowed some latitude in hiring, in promoting and some in reorganization. But in a company crawling with family and favorite sons, the authority was meaningless. To my dismay, I discovered that many of the old-time employees thought nothing of going straight to the top with problems they should have solved themselves or taken to their immediate superiors.

The nepotism and paternalism obviously made it impossible to maintain lines of authority. And try getting rid of one of these favorite sons!

Those of us who did try ended up pleading the point far beyond any reasonable show-cause requirement. And we always lost.

Nor, in a family-controlled company like this, was the board of directors any help. Most of the directors were in their middle or late sixties; a couple were even older. The board was strictly cosmetic — it certainly was not inclined to buck the old chairman who had put them there.

If the new chairman and president had any game plan at all for the company, it was not visible to the rest of us. When they assumed ostensible control, infiltration into our markets by European and Japanese companies had already begun. But our boys sat resolutely tight.

They made a few feeble gestures toward plant modernization and R&D, but barely enough to protect our present markets and offset product obsolescence. Yet we were in a field ripe for growth. Other companies our size were committing $20 million-$30 million to expansion and modernization; our commitment was less than a quarter of that.

And when it came to internal improvements, not even Arthur Murray could outperform our president at the hesitation waltz. At one point, he agreed that industrial relations, engineering and all the other functional disciplines necessary to proper division operation should report directly to the general manager of the several divisions. Considering how reporting lines had previously crisscrossed like a cobweb, some going right up to corporate headquarters, I viewed this attempt to decentralize as a good — albeit not daring — decision.

But when our treasurer, a holdover from the old regime who exercised considerable power, learned that the rookie president had approved of accounting heads reporting directly to division heads, he let out a squawk that could be heard clear out to shipping and receiving. Sure enough, our president — stout fellow — backed off. "Let's wait and see what happens" were his inspiring words on the subject. Of course, the plan was never heard of again.

To the modernists in the company like myself, the treasurer was a far tougher adversary than the chairman or president. He was the torchbearer for the old ways, and we had to fight him every step of the way. Often we conspired to bypass him, at no small risk to our jobs.

You never spoke of debentures, long-term debt or stock issues to the treasurer, because he hated like the devil to borrow money. Perhaps it was due to his Puritan ethic, but I prefer to think it was a throwback to the old regime's house rule of "keeping the books clean." I also think he was miffed at not getting the presidency.

He was especially tough on acquisitions. Even if you could marshal conclusive data supporting a proposed acquisition right down to the last bolt in the plant, you could be sure that the treasurer would argue against it.

The new management talked a lot about market diversification, but got cold feet when it actually came to spending money to modernize facilities and develop new products and processes. Why commit so much capital to just one new product for one or two markets, they would argue. As a result of their hedging, European and Japanese companies got an even bigger foot in the door.

For a long time, I vented most of my anger and frustration on the treasurer. But I soon came to see that the villain of the piece was really the new chairman, who had the power to bring about change but shrank from using it. He was still running the company like a family fiefdom. He was so involved in civic and charitable work completely unrelated to our business that he never seemed to be around when you needed him. Worse, he had a knack for taking off on long vacations right in the middle of a corporate crisis.

The president, for whom the rest of us had such high hopes, was an up-from-operations man who was thoroughly knowledgeable about the business and proved to be an excellent politician. But a leader of men he was not. He never backed his managers or took a determined position on any company problem. He also deliberated uncommonly long before making decisions. Some saw this as deep thinking. I saw it was procrastination.

Looking back, I see a company that had two ways to go at the time I joined it. The new management could have swept away the old cobwebs and made it a far more important company in its industry. Or it could preserve the status quo, content itself with halfway measures and continue to be vulnerable to economic downturns. It chose to go the old way because the company's "grand old man" refused to let go and the new management was too weak or too afraid to buck him.

I am at another company now, second in command. Decisions are made firmly and implemented swiftly. Lines of authority and accountability are spelled out. There is corporate politicking, yes. But life as an executive is no longer a living agony. While the work is demanding, I no longer dissipate my energies definding lost causes or bucking my head against stone walls.

But just to stay on the safe side, I am keeping up my major medical insurance.

QUESTIONS

1. How can you try to protect yourself
   in a closely held company?

THE ADVANTAGES OF MANAGING A SMALL ENTERPRISE

24

Much has been written about the advantages of large scale enterprise — financial power, political power, specialization of management, and the ability to attract capable people. As a consequence, some people come to believe that the small business person is doomed to be crunched under the large corporation's steamroller. Such is not always the case. There are situations in which the small enterprise has definite economic advantages. Moreover, there are managerial advantages which have been documented many times over — flexibility, quick decision making, and low overhead.

Here is the real reason why small business can compete with big. It is in overhead costs. The small man must save enough in overhead that it offsets his productive disadvantages.

*****

Peter Drucker attacks: Our top-heavy corporations

Dun's Review†

Despite the profit-crunching, belt-tightening impact of a

†*Dun's Review*, **April 1971, pp. 38-41.**

near-recession the past year, management scientists and savants have continued to predict great new changes in the corporation during the 1970s — bold new organizational forms, a new breed of fast-moving, streamlined young executives armed with superior knowledge and decision-making ability and a host of sophisticated new techniques designed to provide almost instant management.

But some nagging questions arise. Is there really anything new under the corporate sun? Have the upper corporate echelons truly learned anything from the many mistakes of the

1960s? And are management's horizons really changing and taking hold of the promises of the recent past?

To one of the most respected and honored thinkers in the management field, it does not seem so. Peter F. Drucker has been a close observer of management trends and practices for the past thirty years — as a consultant to many of the biggest companies in the U.S. and abroad, including General Motors and General Electric, as a teacher and as author of nearly a dozen books, among them such business bibles as *Managing for Results, The Practice of Management* and *The Effective Executive*.

Below, the 61-year-old, Vienna-born Drucker takes a down-to-earth, no-nonsense look at the realities of business today, offering pungent criticisms and observations about a subject that is too often treated as a mystique. His warnings on the mistakes companies are making and where they are heading should give every chief executive a great deal to think about.

Q: Mr. Drucker, aren't corporations headed in the direction of more participation in management, more diffusion of responsibility and authority to lower levels of the organization?

A: Hell, no. Nothing is simpler than to use a decentralized organization as a tool of autocracy. It is much easier than using it as a tool of genuine participation. From where I stand, I do not see organizations moving toward greater flexibility, or less hierarchical structures, or even the ability to use different organizing principles according to the logic of the situation.

Q: Yet many management observers, as well as executives themselves, believe that the hierarchical organization is headed for an overhaul

or even total banishment. You don't agree with this, then?

A: No, I see no signs of change here. Indeed, most companies are just building, building, building on the old — adding layers of vice presidents, overstructuring and getting horribly topheavy. I personally think there is no excuse for having an executive vice president, a group vice president or any of this type of executive. We are title-happy.

Q: What's the reason for this tendency to overbuild?

A: Structures are always dominated by a prototype. But in our society the prototype is not found in business. It is the government. Consciously or unconsciously, we are adopting typical bureaucratic structures. And in any bureaucracy, according to an old truism, status always conquers function.

Q: What do you mean by that?

A: Business is becoming Byzantine, because, like civil government, it has failed to learn one thing that the military understood a long time ago: that title and job are two separate things, not one. Business, like the civil government, believes that title and function must correspond. As a result, it reacts to the problem of how to get things done when a man is incompetent by working around him and creating another layer of titles.

Q: Is this true throughout industry?

A: The big companies have already been through it; they already look like Victorian gingerbread. Now the medium-sized companies have caught the same disease. In fact, they are worse — naming managers of assorted, fancy staff.

Q: It's hard to believe that after the recent economic crunch and all the belt-tightening programs we've been hearing about that this could still be so widespread.

A: There is not one company I know of where a sharp cut in the number of executives wouldn't be a real improvement. They are all grotesquely overstructured. Far too much time is spent maintaining hierarchical systems.

Q: Isn't one of the reasons for these executive structures to relieve the chief executive?

A: A friend of mine, one of the best-known management consultants in the country, asked me if I had ever met a chief executive who really was a chief executive. He said he hadn't. Most of them spend their time on things they shouldn't be doing. Mind you, he wasn't being critical, just making an observation about the gap between theory and practice and between the optimum and normal. And one of the main reasons for the chief executive's frittering away his energies is that all these levels of executives below him clamor for his attention.

Q: You do not go along, then, with the idea that the corporation has to cater to the life-style of the young people who are entering business?

A: I'm not a great believer in that juvenile talk about converting an institution into a love-in. Love-ins that extend for more than one night become a deadly bore, even at age 17. I think 28 minutes is roughly all the time you need for a love-in. Whether people are happy is really a secondary consideration. The first question is, do they perform and achieve? What the young people are demanding — and they are right — is more responsibility, more challenge, more self-discipline and a more demanding job.

Q: Then these young people are not breaking down the hierarchy, as we so often hear.

A: On the contrary; they want more of it. The kid who has nothing more than a big title at age 24 wants more rungs on the ladder, because the more rungs there are, the more you can climb the first two years. As a result, the steps are getting shorter and the ladder is getting longer.

Q: Yet we hear a lot these days about how companies are changing their structure to extend responsibility down the line.

A: All that talk about democratic organizations — which really means joyful chaos — is purely rhetorical flourish to cover up the reality of dangerous overstructuring. Take a man with eighteen people reporting to him. Maybe that is too many, so he should make his subordinates more responsible, give them more authority. Instead, he is made a group executive with only two men reporting to him, which looks nice on the organization chart. But all this has done is create more insulation. There is nothing worse than a job in which the executive does not actually do something. Having nothing to do except make sure that other people work is not managing — it is busyness.

Q: And the young managers aren't really being given more authority, more complex jobs?

A: Don't believe anybody who tells you that jobs have become more complex. It just ain't true. Sure, the salaries have changed, and the titles, and the diploma one has to have. But the jobs have not been restructured. The trouble is that these young people — and many of my students among them — are hired with great expectations of challenging jobs, then dropped into training programs. They are given fancy titles and salaries and then given a file clerk's work. It serves no earthly purpose. It's work that doesn't have to be done.

Q: This hardly jibes with the claims made by many companies for their management-development programs. What went wrong?

A: Look, we have a very big age-distribution problem in the United States today. We have a very old senior executive group, a lean group of managers in their forties [the Depression babies] and then all the highly trained young people who were born in the Forties [when the birth rate shot up 45% within five years]. Because there was a shortage of educated young people in the 1960s, we all got panicked into thinking there was going to be a shortage in the Seventies (although anyone who read page 8 of the *Statistical Abstract* would have known that the 1970s were going to bring a glut of educated young people). Mind you, I made the same mistake. I'm not saying I was brighter. I'm saying we should have been brighter. Now we are grossly overstaffed in young, educated people.

Q: Then the massive recruiting programs of the 1960s were really a big mistake.

A: The recruiting craze of the past ten years was insane. Nobody was asking, "How many do we need?" They were saying, "How many can we get?" Companies felt, rightly or wrongly, that they had to hire a good many of these well-trained young people, and raised their expectations with fairy tales about how every clerk is given a division to run. Now there are no jobs for them.

Q: It's as bad as that?

A: These kids go to college and then to business school. By the time they go to work after all that schooling, they are 25. In work experience they are the equivalent of the fifteen-year-old of a generation ago. But in theoretical knowledge they excel any one of their elders. So they go up fast — only to find themselves senior vice presidents at age 29, but working for the same old bookkeeper I worked for years ago.

Q: So all the new management techniques they are learning are not doing them any good?

A: There's a lot of highfalutin jargon around about management science, when all that really means is running the petty-cash ledger. I'm only half kidding. It once took me half an hour to catch on to a learned fellow who was talking about an "organized logic information system"; he meant the telephone book.

The young people today expect to see business run by theory, knowledge, concepts and planning. But then they find it is run like the rest of the world — by experience and expediency, by whom you know and by the hydrostatic pressure in your bladder.

Q: Yet with all this greater knowledge they are bringing into companies, surely they have a large contribution to make despite their lack of experience?

A: Not unless we change the structure to fit them in. We have an indiscrimate input of people who have been trained to use knowledge, but we haven't learned how to put them to work.

Twenty-five years ago, I made a study of General Motors as a consultant. I always asked for a biographical background on the men I was to deal with. But while I always got more than I needed about everyone else, I could get no information about the vice chairman, Albert Bradley, the third most powerful man in the company. You know why? They didn't want to admit that they had at the top of the company a man who didn't go to work at age 14 — who, in fact, had a Ph.D. It was a disgrace to admit such a thing in those times.

Q: That's hardly the case today.

A: No. In fact, I see a real danger that we will fall into the deadly sin of intellectual arrogance. We may end up saying that unless a man has gone to college, he's hardly a human being. We can hire such a man only to clean the latrines. We may write off the 50% of the population that didn't sit on its behind forever getting a college degree, and deny them access to opportunity.

Q: How can we avoid this "intellectual arrogance"?

A: If I were in business today, I would make sure that it was our practice to find the able, ambitious, striving people whether they have degrees or not. I would want to know what a man can do, not how much money has been invested in his education. The worst thing that can happen is to develop an elitest group. I am almost at the point where I think someone should shock the rest of us by saying that a degree is an automatic disqualification.

Q: What about the business schools? What kind of job are they doing?

A: I'm not terribly impressed with many. They may have an excellent curriculum and a good staff. But then they expend both on students who can't learn much about business because they don't have enough experience. I personally don't believe a 22-year-old belongs in a business school. He belongs in a job. Five years later, when he has had some experience, he belongs there. The experience will make the learning more meaningful. Case histories and business games are not enough.

Q: So business is really penalizing its young managers?

A: Nothing creates disaffection faster than a big title, a lot of money and only donkey work to do. It destroys your hope, because where else is there to go. Sure, you can make more money and get a bigger title, but what does it really mean? The absence of demand, responsibility and the chance to fail and achieve is very discouraging. Especially when you are surrounded by a sea of contemporaries in the same situation. Business still requires experience, and they don't have it.

Q: But many of them will soon be running the companies themselves. Won't they be inadequately prepared to do it effectively?

A: They are very vulnerable because so many of them have ridden too far, too fast. They haven't had a chance to learn enough about their jobs. Also, a lot of them haven't enough compassion.

Q: Compassion?

A: Yes. They haven't learned that character is more important than abilities. That, of course, isn't learned at an early age. For this, one has to be betrayed by one's brilliance a few times.

Q: Considering the predicament the younger people are in, do you see a clash coming between them and top management?

A: A clash is definitely coming, but not between the old and the young.

Q: Where will it be?

A: Among the young people themselves.

Q: Why is that?

A: The age-distribution factor is the cause. Ten years hence, most of them will have risen so fast, they will be in their terminal jobs. There will be no place else to go because there will be so many of them. If you are thirty, you are willing to accept a 55-year-old executive vice president; you know he will retire soon enough, and then you will have your chance. But when you are forty, and your boss is also forty and just one graduating class ahead of you, and his boss is just one class ahead of that, what then?

Like any unbalanced age structure, this is going to create an enormous problem within ten years. There will be a great many good people who are frustrated not because they have been unsuccessful, but because they have reached the end of the line too soon. There is going to be a problem of finding second careers for people who have been successful very early but who by sheer arithmetic can go no further where they are.

Q: Do you think this will be especially severe in any particular industry?

A: Banks have one of the largest groups of young executives, so they are going to have a particular problem. If you are a bank vice president at 28, where do you go later?

Q: What should companies be doing to avoid this?

A: There should be someone strong enough to honestly tell these young people to go work somewhere else. To tell them, "Look, what you want to do, we don't want to do; what you can do, we don't really need; and what we need, you cannot and do not want to do."

Q: What about the chances of some modification of the hierarchical system?

A: In any organization there is a contingency of common peril, which is a fancy way of saying it can get into trouble. When that happens, there is a fantastic premium on clear authority. So the question really isn't whether the hierarchical organization is ever going to go away; it is whether we are going to move away from a mechanistic model to a biological one.

Q: What do you mean by biological?

A: The main difference is that a biological system has a number of systems, or authorities, or commands or communication centers within it — rather like the human body, although it doesn't have to be as complicated.

Q: Are there any corporations today modeled on such a system?

A: Most companies have several systems going. It's more complex than the books tell. Years ago, for example, the human relations people were surprised to discover that there was nothing more rigid than the informal organization within a formal organization. You can change the organization chart, but you cannot change the perks of a good secretary. Just try it. The formal organization is really a fluid one. But the informal one, like all custom, is hard to deal with.

Q: Why do you think this is so?

A: If you look at an effective executive, the question is what makes him effective. Is it because he's bright and imaginative, or is it because he has a boss who kicked him and said, "Wake up."

But it's really more complex than that. He has this plant manager out there who is really his customer; 99% of the time he works laterally with that man, organizes his own work on the logic of information and knowledge. So he's not depending on the formal chain of organization; he only needs it when he gets into trouble. But that doesn't mean he doesn't have a boss. And it doesn't mean that if he's in the boss' "black book," the support of the plant manager will help him much. On the other hand, he may be the boss' white-haired boy, but if the plant manager can't stand him, he isn't going to get very far.

*

V

MARKETING

Now the entrepreneur must get his product to market and sell it. Most entrepreneurs claim that marketing is the key to success. If there is a good market for a product, he should be able to figure out a way to sell to it. But be not deluded. Marketing takes a great deal of effort and time. Sometimes investments must be made to build distributive channels. Rarely is an item an overnight success. It will pay you great dividends to apply yourself diligently to the study of marketing for there is much to learn.

BUILDING DISTRIBUTION

25

The difficulties involved in building distribution have been forcefully demonstrated to the authors time and again through the consulting efforts they have been requested to undertake. Almost invariably the businessman has but one question for which he wants an answer: "How do I get distribution?" He does not know how to get his widget to market!

In most cases, building distribution is many times more difficult, more costly, and more time consuming than any of the steps we have heretofore discussed. It is not at all unreasonable to be able to establish the enterprise and have a product ready to market within three to six months of sustained effort, whereas it may take three years to get adequate distribution. One can buy a machine or a plant but channels of distribution have to be developed, and that takes time and effort. True, there are cases, not always exceptions, in which a new enterpriser has taken his product to a big mass merchandiser such as Sears, J. C. Penney, K-Mart or whatever, and obtained nation-wide distribution rather rapidly. Even in those cases,

however, several months elapse before the chain has completed its paperwork and made arrangements to handle the item. One does not put a new product into more than 1000 stores overnight. Selling to mass merchandisers is attractive to the new enterpriser since they do represent the easiest course of action for him to follow.

THE MASS MERCHANDISERS

The advantages of distributing through such firms as Sears or J. C. Penney are rather obvious: immediate large volume, no credit risk, and a minimum of selling expense. Such firms are readily available to the entrepreneur. Sears and J. C. Penney can serve as illustrations, although there are hundreds of firms that could be classified as large buyers.

These firms do everything in their power to make it easy for the supplier to do business with them. Call one of their regional offices for information about where your type of product is bought. Usually such negotiations take place in the home office, Sears Tower in Chicago or 1301 Avenue of the Americas in New York City for J. C. Penney.

At times the manager of one of their retail stores can help you. If the department in which it should be sold is known, such as sporting goods, one asks for the name of the sporting goods buyer in the home office. It usually takes several visits there to arrange a sale if they are interested. If the buyer is not interested, he will make it clear. Buyers want to see new products because that is their business; they make their money by finding unusual merchandise at attractive prices. They cannot risk not looking at a product because it may be a big winner. They have no way of telling without seeing it. Keep in mind that these people are experts; they have considered thousands of new products. They have had their failures and more than their share of winners. They have a good feel for what their customers will buy and the prices they will pay, not that they are always right, but usually their advice is good. In fact, it is wise to talk with one of these buyers early in the planning stages of the enterprise, for the person can provide a great deal of guidance in such matters as pricing, packaging, and much product information.

The buyer forms a judgment quickly on whether or not an item is something her customers will buy and whether or not it is something that her firm can handle. It must be made quite clear at this point that most items submitted to such large buyers are rejected. There are several reasons for rejections. First, most frequently the buyer thinks her customers will not buy the article. She does not see sufficient demand to warrant carrying it. Remember, these buyers are mass merchandisers. They are not interested in something that will sell a few units a month. They want to move substantial volume of goods. Thus, if something is not likely to sell in sufficient quantity, they are not apt to handle it. So a large number of products are rejected outright for this reason.

Interestingly, these buyers are almost like umpires. They may make decisions rather quickly. If they see something they like and they get a feeling they can rapidly make the decision to buy. In their minds it is almost as if they decide after looking at the pitch whether it is a ball or a strike. If the buyer likes it she will ask, "What are the prices?"

A large number of good products fail at this point, for the buyer has already formed an idea of what she is willing to pay for it. When she looked at the item she decided, "That will retail for $5." If her department operates on a 40 percent margin, she knows that all she can pay for it is $3, so if the supplier quotes anything above $3 he will be told of the buyer's evaluation of the product's value. If the price is not right, a sale will not be made. Mass merchandisers make their money on the buying side. They buy advantageously, trying to squeeze every dime they can out of the suppliers. That is how they offer low prices in the stores. It is not that they operate on lower margins, for they usually do not.

Do not be discouraged if the buyer turns down a product, she may change her mind. There have been numerous instances of new products that were rejected at first but later accepted after some experience proved the item's marketability. Buyers like proof of a product's salability.

Once the buyer has decided that the product and its price are right, she then investigates two other critical areas which can disqualify the deal rather quickly. Look at it from the point of view of the mass merchandiser who has seen hundreds of of excellent products brought in by people and has issued a purchase order for a sizable quantity, only to discover one or both of two things: either the enterprise was unable to supply the quantities demanded on time or, if it did so, the quality was not as specified. Large retail organizations have problems obtaining timely deliveries of the quantities they need. Also, the new enterprise many times is simply unable to control the quality of its output satisfactorily. Bear in mind the tremendous physical task of shipping sizable quantities of goods to over 1000 stores. The physical work alone is tremendous and the goods must all be sent out at about the same time. If they are not on the store shelves by a certain date, the market may be missed. It does little good for toys to be received in stock in late December; they should have been on the shelves in October.

The buyer has reservations about the entrepreneur's ability to deliver the goods as specified. This is not an easy objection to meet unless the nature of the product is such that production and quality control should be no problem. In selling a book, the buyer knows several hundred thousand copies can be run off quickly and that quality is no problem. However, try to sell him a new bicycle and he would worry.

One should question whether or not mass merchandisers should be used. Bear in mind that when selling to mass merchandisers, it is not usually possible to sell also through traditional channels. When Sears took on the Arnold Palmer line of golf clubs, most golf pro shops threw them out. Traditional merchants seldom feel that it is to their best interests to carry the same brands that are available in chain operations, although in certain cases, if the item has extremely strong demand, they might

be forced to do so. Mass merchandisers are famous for taking on some item, pushing it as hard as they can, and then, when demand falls off, getting rid of it. Businessmen who firmly believe that their products have a good steady demand if sold through traditional channels, feel it wiser to take their time and slowly build conventional channels, thus protecting the image of their products.

If a product has large market potential, another problem may be posed: it may be taken over by the middleman. Sears has been known to buy the manufacturing facilities of its suppliers of staple goods. There is some likelihood that a firm supplying such staple products may find itself a captive of the mass merchandiser. In other situations, the mass merchandiser may take the product and have another firm copy it for them. So be warned that dealing with mass merchandisers is not an altogether unblemished virtue. However, these risks have been exaggerated. With reasonable wisdom, they can be avoided or at least minimized.

The biggest drawback to using the mass merchandizer is the continual pressure placed upon the supplier for lower prices. If he has relied almost exclusively on the mass merchandiser as his channel of distribution, rest assured that the buyer is aware of it and knows that she has tremendous leverage in forcing price reductions and other concessions. Suppose a plant is built up on the basis of large orders from Sears and has a few other steady customers. If Sears cancels the contract the business may well be out of business, or at least in serious difficulty. Managers with only a few customers do not sleep very well. For this reason, many entrepreneurs, from a policy standpoint, refuse to allow any one customer to account for a substantial portion of their volume. A businessman is always in a much stronger bargaining position if he can let a customer walk out the door without jeopardizing the enterprise.

The matter of manufacturing a slightly different product or a private brand for the mass merchandiser will frequently arise, but that is getting a bit too involved for this discussion. Suffice it to say that the mass merchandisers strongly prefer to push only their own brands of goods. They do not want to promote someone else's brand name. They like to own the rights to the things they sell and promote. One should prepared to put the middleman's brand on a product in such a case.

Selling to the mass merchandisers requires special marketing techniques. To do business with them, one must learn to meet their requirements. They will not waste time with suppliers who will not fit into their routine systems.

How to sell the mass merchandiser (Interviews with two experts on *selling*)†

An interview with
Carl Maurantonio

Let me begin by reviewing the four major points that must be discussed: 1) The selection of a proper listing for the account you're working with. 2) An

†*The Discount Merchandiser*, **August 1971**, pp. 84-93.

advertising format. 3) The display technique to be employed. 4) Reordering technique, (which many manufacturers do not concern themselves with).

First, let me discuss the selection of a listing, and basically what happens now. An appointment is made, the day comes, and you are ushered into the buyer's office. In many cases, it's so small it's difficult to find a place to sit. You start your prepared 15 minute presentation, and you try to capture the buyer's imagination with your line. An hour later, we look in on you, and you're still trying to finish. You ask, "What's taken so long?" Well, there were 6 or 8 telephone calls, naturally, all of an emergency nature; there were 5 other emergency interruptions, all of which were necessary. The buyer's mind has started to wander. You now finish your presentation, and naturally, you ask the question, "What do you think? Isn't this the greatest program you have ever seen? When can I have you order?"

How can this buyer make an intelligent decision? Buyers are overburdened with tremendous number of projects which many manufacturers fail to realize. Most manufacturers, if asked to define a buyer's functions would reply, that they are:

1) Selectors of merchandise. 2) Negotiators of terms. 3) Communicators of product information to the field.

To be perfectly truthful with you, this only consumes between 10 to 15% of his time. The rest is consumed by various other duties, namely:

1) Assistant advertising director. 2) Markdown specialist. 3) Accountant. 4) A statistician. 5) Freight expert. 6) Space allocation expert. 7) Re-order clerk. 8) Tracer of missing shipments. The list goes on and on.

Let's get down to how lines are really selected:

A) Personal relationships between reps. and buyers (don't kid yourself — this accounts for a tremendous amount of business and also accounts for a great deal of problems).

B) Profitability and turnover.

C) Pre-sold merchandise to consumers. (Such as G. E. lightbulbs, Prestone antifreeze, Black and Decker tools etc.).

D) A very convincing selling job by the salesman.

What are buyers *Really* Interested In?

1) Price. 2) Your ability to deliver. 3) Freight costs. 4) Profitability and turnover. 5) Advertising information. 6) Percentage fill of orders. 7) Preticketing. 8) Plan-O-Grams. 9) Display techniques.

A particular gripe: While I am on the subject of selecting a listing, I would like to bring out something that really gripes me. This is when a salesman has come in, has gone through his presentation, and now it comes time to get down to serious discussions. All of a sudden, I find out he's not authorized to do this, and he must get back to me on that. This is something I just can't understand. If selling is the lifeblood of your company, and this gentleman is charged with that responsibility, then why isn't he given the authority to act?

So much for that. Let's discuss what you can do to help correct these situations.

1) If possible, when calling on an account, get the buyer out of his office, take him to your factory, take him to your motel room, take him to the rep's office, take him somewhere so he can give you his undivided attention. It's fair to you, it's fair to us, and it's fair to him. Know what you're talking about.

Check your freight costs from your factory to major cities across the country. This problem of increased freight costs is eating us all up alive. We are all fighting to keep our margins up. Chains that operate as we do, that is drop-shipping everything to the stores without the availability of a warehouse, are facing an increasing dilemma as each day passes. Should we widen our inventory cycles and order more goods each time? This would enable us to make a minimum shipment but it does cut down our turnover. Should we switch more and more of our lines to feeders? Naturally, our costs on these lines now increase, but so does our turn, or should we look to those manufacturers who are widening their assortments to cover more and more of our everyday needs? I think the latter will become the most important agent in the future: the super manufacturer, a vendor who can supply a majority of the merchandise in a given category. I think the smaller manufacturers, those who specialize in an individual commodity, are going to be hardpressed.

Pre-ticketing has to come: Another area in which you can be of tremendous service is preticketing. It has to come. Most of your prime feeders are doing it now.

If you're looking to improve your business, it's an area you must explore. I realize it isn't an uncomplicated problem. Every potential customer of yours uses a different ticket and a different coding system. But if you can concentrate on how to preticket the goods for your customers, or at least have them inserted in an envelope, in the carton, you will find that your shipments become privileged. We have certain vendors who do this now. When a shipment from one of these vendors hits the back door, it's the first shipment brought to the sales floor. The order is checked in, and on display normally within an hour. Other shipments may sit there for days to weeks, before they are sorted out, priced, and put on display. It's definitely an area you must look into.

I would like now to move into the area of advertising. Let me review what happens now. Everyone's the specialist. The buyer, the advertising director, the merchandise manager, and in the case of National Hardgoods, the operator, who owns the total store. Everyone feels he knows what's best. The people we hear the least from are the manufacturers. You are affiliated with many different chains. If anyone should know what's successful, it's you. Let's hear from you. Again, present us with a program that we can advertise throughout the year, not just one promotion. We also have a serious problem trying to obtain ad mats, glossies etc. I don't have a solution, but it's a problem. Many times we pass up advertising an item because we don't have the proper materials in our file.

Headaches with display: Display. Talk about a problem and this is it: National Hardgoods is a leased department operation in sixty discount department stores. These departments range in size from 3,000 to 15,000 sq. ft. We have departments in the north, south, east, midwest, and southwest. Each department with its own particular needs, and each a different size. This presents mammoth problems. And, I can tell you most of the manufacturers we deal with haven't been much help. Some have no idea at all how their merchandise should be displayed at store level. Relative to this, I'd like to share with you an experience I went through at one of the factories I recently visited. My buyer

and I had finished touring the factory, and we were now in the showroom reworking our listing. This particular showroom is outfitted with glass shelving and plenty of illumination, all in the right places. One of the salesmen picked up a particular item, put it directly under a brilliant light, and said: "This is a new item. Isn't it gorgeous? It has to be a winner at this price."

That's when I got up, took the item, put it onto a bottom shelf of a gondola out of the light, and then asked the question: "How does it look now?" The answer was obvious — not as good. It no longer looked like a "steal." In fact, it didn't even look like a value. You know you have to visualize what happens in the store. Get some fixturing into your plant — the type we use. Now display your program. Does it look like a value? If it does you may have a winner.

Do not sell individual items. Sell a program. It produces more dollars. There is another important point which you must always remember: selection by the buyer is only the first phase. This doesn't insure the success of your program. Your program becomes a success when the consumer buys your product, takes it into her home, and is completely satisfied with it. This insures re-orders. Then you have a success. Most manufacturers put forth a tremendous amount of effort and money in trying to sell buyers on their products. But they simply forget the people who actually sell the merchandise; the store-level personnel. If these people aren't sold as well, your program may be doomed to failure. I'd like to see more effort put forth in the area of training store-level personnel in the proper display technique of your products. I realize, this is an area which has always been very difficult. Top management of every discount organization has always wanted it.

Many have tried, but few of us have achieved success. Why?

Train at supervisory level: In many discount organizations, this training is aimed primarily at the department manager level. This area has one of the highest turnover rates in any company. When a man does stay with you for any length of time and becomes a good department manager, he is quickly moved into some higher position. A few years ago someone happened to have the bright idea of having the manufacturers train the people in our departments. After all, wasn't the manufacturer the expert in his own field? The idea was excellent, many vendors cooperated, but again, they ran into the same problem we've been facing for quite some time; high turnover rates at the department-manager level. Many vendors became disheartened, and I think, took a negative approach afterwards.

Others went a step further, using their own factory people to take inventories and place re-orders. Still, others have hired service organizations to basically do this same type of service.

Some of these programs have been very successful, and I certainly won't knock them, but I have always felt a company is as good as the people in its employ. I further believe we must teach these people as much as we can, so they will become more qualified. We don't want other people running our business. We want our people to become merchants — not just robots doing our every whim.

Let's aim more of this training at our supervisory level. This is where we have a much lower turnover rate. These men are constantly in the stores and they are the authority. Once they believe in your program, the job will get done. You, the manufacturer, can't do it

by yourself. We must work with you, even if it costs us both something initially. The key word here is "motivation." You must be able to motivate the buyer and also the field-level personnel.

Every major chain has some way of replenishing stocks on depleted lines. Most of us use some type of an inventory preprint, send it to the stores, ask for an inventory and have it sent back to the home office for order writing or we authorize the store to release the order directly to the vendor.

Study inventory cycle at each store: Do you know how often each of your accounts inventory your line? Is it every four weeks, every eight weeks, or every ten weeks? If a chain were inventorying every four weeks, you then could rightly expect 13 re-orders for the year. Have you checked recently? Do you know what's going on? Let me give you a hypothetical case. Let's say we have a chain of twenty stores inventorying your line every four weeks. If everything went perfect, you should expect 13 re-orders for each store. Let's say we now sit down and it's one year later. We now analyze this particular situation. This is what you could expect to find: Five stores placing about eight re-orders, eight stores placing between four and eight re-orders, and seven stores placing between one and three re-orders. Do you know how much business you have lost? The question now is, why and how can we correct this situation? Some stores send in an inventory, the counts are bad, and the order is passed. In other cases, we never receive an inventory from the store, again, no order. The final and most important reason is that the vendor's minimum shipping requirements were larger than the amount needed on this particular order, and again, we passed, even though, we needed some merchandise.

Just a few months ago, I discussed this same situation with some of the major people with three large companies. They never realized this was happening. When we pass ordering on a particular cycle, we don't take another inventory for at least four more weeks. If an order is placed, it takes another three weeks to get the merchandise — that's seven weeks without needed merchandise. Again, we've both lost. That's why many of the feeders are getting more and more of the business. They have such a wide range of merchandise; there is never any problem making a minimum shipment.

Freight allowances for low-volume stores: It may be to your advantage to analyse your present accounts. We all have A,B,C,D, and E stores. Maybe some type of a freight allowance could be worked out for only the low-volume stores, where minimum shipments are very difficult to make. If you were to walk into a given store right now, and take a physical inventory on every item they should be carrying, you would find approximately between a 15 and 30 per cent "out" situation, unfortunately, on the best selling items. The primary reason is this minimum problem. If you shipped in this manner, you couldn't stay in business. Do you know if you could help correct this problem with some of your top accounts, you could have as much as a 15 per cent increase in sales without soliciting a new customer?

Another concern of mine is the follow up of orders, whether they be ad orders, new store opening orders, or season distribution orders. In calling some of your factories, it is like dealing with the Russians. Everything is top secret. The conversation goes something like this:

"Good afternoon, Bell Wire, may I help you?"

"Yes, this is Mr. Maurantonio, I'm the merchandise manager for National Hardgoods, and I would like to check on an order that should have been shipped on March 1st."

"Just a moment, sir. I'll connect you with Mr. Sanders. He handles these particular problems."

At Mr. Sanders office, I go through the same procedure: "I'm sorry, Sir. Mr. Sanders, is out of town. Let me connect you with Mr. Smith. Maybe he can be of some help."

Again I go through the same thing. I now find that Mr. Smith can't help but he's willing to take a message for Mr. Sanders. I wonder if a man as important as Mr. Sanders, should ever be allowed to leave the factory. Surely, there is someone who can handle these types of problems when Mr. Sanders is out.

Let us know problems: If you are having a problem, let us know. Maybe we can be of some help. Don't let us call and hear every reason why it wasn't shipped. We're not interested at that point.

Just recently, I called a vendor on such a problem, and he said: "Carl, we shipped all of your stores with the exception of three. What are you raising such a fuss about?"

I replied, "I didn't think it necessary to call you. All of the stores are of equal importance. My job is to satisfy all of the customers that shop each and every one of my stores. It's better to ship each store a little than to skip three. Call us. We'll let you know what to do. Don't take it on your own."

In closing, I would like to pass on a story I was once told. It seems, there was a captain who ran a very tight ship and he had his men constantly busy scrubbing the decks, painting the bulkheads, and shining the brass. One day, while at sea, they developed a leak in one of the lower decks and this shiny, clean, well-painted boat went to the bottom. All was lost, because no one had the responsibility of checking for leaks. Everyone was too busy doing other things.

Now what does this all mean to you? Well, while your new products department is coming up with new and better items, and your sales force is selling more and more merchandise, and your factory foreman came up with another way to save you money, your shipping departments are starting to develop leaks. Where it used to take three days to get an order out, it's now taking two weeks. Your percentage of fill has dropped from 97% to 80%. Gentlemen, it's time to start looking for leaks.

An interview with
J. Michael Loughlin

First you have to know the mass merchandiser, know the industry, and individually the companies that are a part of it. The simple facts are that the so called mass merchandisers have: a) Grown from $2 billion in sales in 1960 to $24 billion in sales in 1970. b) The annual growth rate is about 14 per cent a year. c) Currently, we are the number-one outlet for general merchandise in America. Yet, we're still in our infancy — 20 years old. Growth like this in such a short span of time creates big problems.

Top executives of manufacturing firms may know all of this

information . . . Do your Field Representatives know it? Do they know us? Can they relate to us in their sales presentations?

Is a representative who's called on the department stores for the majority of his career capable of swinging over to a mass merchandiser without some education? If you manufacture a product that is common to department, grocery, variety, and specialty outlets such as drug or hardware, is your same salesman capable of adjusting to the needs of each of these outlets in addition to the mass merchandiser? Is our volume potential worth a specialist? . . . Only you can answer that!

We want to be sold. A poor salesman is a tragedy for both of us. He might have the right item in every respect, but, unfortunately, never be able to sell to us. The result is that we both lose.

Assume your representative is an effective salesman with a thorough knowledge of our industry and the particular account he is calling on. What should he be armed with? Or what do we want? What are we looking for?

The name of game is "value": If I were allowed only one word it would be "VALUE". Value means a lot of things and requires explanation. We don't control it. You as the manufacturer do. We can only offer your products to our customers at a price that will enable us to make an acceptable markup. This is particularly true of branded merchandise. On unbranded merchandise the company with the best *complete* value gets our business.

How do we arrive at purchasing decisions? Basically, there are only two categories of items and/or lines to evaluate: New items, and items currently on the market that we don't stock. In arriving at a purchasing decision on a new item we consider the following points:

a) Is it being advertised? How many dollars have been *firmly* committed? Over how long a period? What media is being used?

b) Does the item measure up to its advertising claim? Can you prove it?

c) Is there a consumer need or demand for it? This applies particularly to additional sizes of the same item, whether it be fifth size of a brand of toothpaste or the sixth size of a frying pan!

d) By purchasing the item do we trade dollars and profit or do we increase it?

e) If it's a novelty item . . . will the appeal last?

f) Is it a seasonal item? Does it have seasonal ups and downs? When is the season? When does it peak?

g) Is there an initial stocking incentive? Extra Dating? Co-operative advertising?

h) Is it consumer-tested? How? In the market place? Panel Test? What were the results?

For new and old items: There are certain points that are common to the purchase evaluation of both new items and items currently on the market. Once again the importance attached to each point varies by item:

a) How much volume can we expect from the item or category?

b) Is it priced competitively? Does it offer better markup opportunity? Or at least the same as *our* best item in the category?

Several months ago a major manufacturer introduced a new line with items in several categories currently stocked. As part of their introductory package they offered an initial markup based on list that was less than the top two items in the category, and had an opening offer that was far less than the normal periodic deal offered by the leaders. They presented an impressive advertising program, yet we turned them down cold. To us their program was simply unrealistic.

c) Case packing: Is the quantity per case in proportion to the volume we can anticipate? This is extremely important when we're drop-shipping merchandise. If we are taking it into a warehouse what is the inner wrap?

d) What is the minimum drop shipment? Is there a quantity discount or warehouse allowance *if* we wish to take advantage of it?

e) What merchandising material is available? Floor Displays? Posters? Back Cards? Shelf Talkers? Or signs of any nature?

f) Do you have a complete program? This could apply to instore service, pre-ticketing, and frequency of promotion, both to us and to our customers.

g) Can we eliminate a similar item? Does it mean increasing our overall inventory?

h) Can we expect deliveries in a reasonable period of time? Will you be in stock at all times?

i) Will the packaging sell itself? How much space does it take versus the dollar volume we can anticipate? (A 24" diameter beachball with a retail of .19¢ obviously presents a problem.) Can it be easily merchandised on the shelf? On an end-cap? Feature table? Check-out?

j) How do you handle damaged merchandise?

k) What are your terms? Dating, or anticipation?

The following points pertain to evaluating items currently:

a) Is it better value than a comparable item we stock?

b) Who carries it?

c) What volume are they doing with it?

d) What is it retailing for?

e) When replacing an item or a line, what confusion will be created at store level? What will you do to help us consolidate inventories on the current line? After a period of time will you relieve us of odds and ends?

Once we buy we expect the lines of communication between us will remain active. They are essential to our normal turnover business and to possible promotional consideration.

How we select ad items: How do we select items for both in-store, newspaper, and circular featuring? In selecting these items we consider some or all of the following points:

a) How many customers will it attract? At what price?

b) Will it attract the customer for value? A young mother? The head of a household?

c) Does it have broad appeal?

d) What past experience have we had with it or a related item?

e) Can we get the quantities needed? Can we be assured of delivery at the specified time?

f) Will it generate related sales? Such as: a label-maker, with potential for additional tape sales; a toy, that can be added to.

g) If it is not successful as a feature item, how long will it take to liquidate our inventory at regular price? Will you accept returns?

h) What is the handling cost? Price marking is expensive, particularly with a low-ticket item with tremendous volume potential. How many styles, colors, shades, must we include in the assortment? Hair coloring is a perfect example. Ordering, packing, and shipping 15 shades is expensive. And in what proportion do you ship it?

i) How bulky is the item? Storage presents a problem.

j) Is it a high-ticket item that we can anticipate selling in limited quantities or a low-ticket item that will move in vast quantities?

k) Is a deal available to contribute to a reduced price? A deal in the form of cooperative advertising, quantity discounts, merchandising allowances. If there is, how much *lead time* is available?

Lead time is a topic in itself. We need almost 4 months advance notice on the availability of a deal in order to consider it for our rotogravure circulars; 8 to 10 weeks advance notice for a newspaper ad!

If you are armed with a thorough knowledge of our industry, a thorough knowledge of the particular account and the right item presented with all of the surrounding facts, the door is wide open to sell the mass merchandiser in 1971. We're looking for items for regular stock and promotions. We can't find enough of the right items to promote. I've seen ads killed, circulars cut down in size just because the right items were not available. When I say not available, we didn't see them. I'm sure they are out there. Bring them in!

QUESTIONS

1. Why are mass merchandisers so demanding in their requirements upon their suppliers?

SELLING TO SMALLER CUSTOMERS

26

Many new enterprises that plan to distribute through smaller merchants try to set up a system of manufacturers' agents or representatives to act as the firm's salesmen. Many times the new venture cannot afford or even procure a good sales force of its own. Moreover, there are advantages to using agents with established market contacts, for it facilitates market penetration. More will be said of them later.

To locate good agents, ask a few good merchants for information about the best agents who call on them. Once a good agent has been located and brought into the structure, he can provide leads to other good agents in other parts of the country. The biggest advantage of such agents is that their cost is variable, a percent of sales, usually five to ten percent. If they do not sell anything, they do not cost anything.

Sometimes distribution through wholesalers is required. If so, the task is a tough one because they will not buy until there is a proven demand for an item from their customers. Demand for the item has to be built before wholesalers will be receptive.

INDUSTRIAL CHANNELS

Industrial products are apt to require direct selling to the user. The amount of money likely to be involved in an industrial sale makes such direct selling economically possible.

If the item is such that it should be distributed through an industrial wholesaler or distributor, then the enterpriser faces a task similar to that of selling through any wholesalers — they want to see a demand before they will buy. Much depends upon whether the product is to be sold to a horizontal or vertical industrial market. A typewriter has a horizontal market, all industries use it. Textbooks are sold to a vertical market, educational institutions and students. Sometimes a product is sold to a single market. Oil well drilling bits have one customer, drilling contractors. Obviously, the more focused the market is for a product, the easier it will be to market it.

Indeed, today many leading concerns are organizing their sales forces along industry lines; each salesman calls on one type of customer. Experience indicates that such an arrangement greatly increases the salesman's effectiveness.

USE OF TRADE SHOWS

Display at trade shows facilitates building distribution. Vernell's Butter Mints built distribution in supermarkets for its candy rather quickly by taking a booth at the National Food Brokers Trade Show. Every industry and every type of trade has its trade shows and conventions. They can play an important role in building distribution.

BUY EXPERIENCE

A small new enterprise developed a product that had to be distributed through floral supply wholesalers to retail florists. Its fortunes floundered for a year until it hired a sales manager who had thirty years' experience in selling to that industry. Within a week the product was carried by 300 floral supply wholesalers. He did it over the telephone. Such is the power of contacts. Knowing the people who must be contacted is of tremendous assistance. The new enterprise that has such a man in its organization has a definite advantage.

ESTABLISHING TRADITIONAL CHANNELS

The new enterprise is frequently faced with the task of placing its wares in the distribution system supplying some trade. It is important to realize that each industry has its own distribution system that has evolved for good and substantial reasons; it does not exist by accident. An industry's distributive system is a network of institutions that do the work of moving the product to its users. The distributive practices of these institutions can be discovered by simply talking to people in the industry. They know how things work. The furniture dealer will describe how he goes about buying from the manufacturers and their representatives by going to the furniture shows held in the various regional marts. The gift store owner will disclose the manufacturers' representatives who call on her, the gift shows she attends, and the trade marts in which the manufacturers' representatives and the direct selling manufacturers locate their sales offices.

A great deal can be learned by visiting these trade marts and talking with manufacturers' representatives or other such middlemen. They can relate rather quickly what it takes to do business in that industry.

MANUFACTURERS' REPRESENTATIVES

The managers of new enterprises are attracted to using manufacturers' representatives, at least in the initial stages of development, because the costs of their services are variable. A manufacturers' representative is a salesman who has put together a line of products from various manufacturers so that when he calls on a customer he has enough merchandise to sell that his commissions will cover his costs.

Salesmen are expensive. It takes a minimum of about $25,000 a year in earnings and expenses to keep a salesman in the field, perhaps more. If a firm can only afford to spend five percent of sales on the selling function, one of its salesmen would have to sell

$500,000 a year to support his costs economically. If an item is relatively low priced and does not sell in large quantities, the likelihood of a salesman being able to sell such a volume is remote. Such products simply cannot support a sales force of their own. This is where the manufacturers' representative steps into the picture. For five or ten percent of sales, depending upon the industry, the agent will represent one. Most representatives only cover a limited territory, thus it takes several representatives for nationwide coverage.

Attendance at trade shows is a good way of meeting various representatives. Also, the recommendations of the intended customers can be quite helpful, for they know who the good representatives are. Make no mistake, there are good representatives and bad ones, just as there are good salesmen and bad salesmen. It is not too difficult to determine a representative's skills from looking at the lines he carries and his reputation with those to whom he sells.

MAIL ORDER AND DIRECT MAIL

New enterprisers are able to get into business relatively rapidly by using the mails and/or mail-order advertising. Direct mail refers to mailing out sales promotional literature to likely prospects and receiving orders in return. It is a nice business in that it can be operated with few people and one can contact an entire trade rather quickly.

One new enterpriser selling an item called "Vita-Wheel" to health food stores tested his product by making a direct-mail promotion with a sample enclosed to 1000 health food stores whose names had been picked from the Yellow Pages. He got more than a 20 percent return; over 200 merchants sent him orders with checks. True, this is an exceptionally high rate of return, but remember it did include a sample and sampling is the best possible promotional device one can use.

Be warned that the Postal System does little to facilitate this business. In fact, it is a tremendous headache. Postage costs are high, so consider third class mail.

In the Vita-Wheel mailing, a first-class envelope cost 24¢ to mail and a third-class cost 12¢ — a 12¢ per unit difference. On 1000 units, that is $120, which is a lot of money. So why not mail everything third class? Because the Postal Service is slow, despite their protests to the contrary. One mailing that went out in May was delivered in the middle of August. If time is at all important, third-class mail poses problems.

For the right type of situation, direct mail is an attractive channel of distribution. Some firms rely on it exclusively. It is easily managed but it is an industry unto itself, for it gets the enterpriser into all of the various problems of efficiently conducting direct-mail campaigns, a field requiring considerable specialized knowledge.

Mail order advertising is slightly different. The orders are solicited by advertisements in various advertising media and the goods sent either by mail or by United Parcel Service. Whenever possible, it is strongly advised that you use the UPS, for it is not only cheaper, but offers much superior service to the Postal System.

A young man wrote and published a book on how to get a better job. He took an advertisement in *The Wall Street Journal* costing $2200. He sold 400 copies of the book priced at $10 a copy. Granted, the promotional costs were rather high, but he still made a profit on the deal.

Certain types of items can be sold very well through mail order advertising, but it largely depends upon the product. The product and price must both be right for mail order to be successful. As a general rule, two factors stifle mail order sales. First, the customer cannot accurately perceive exactly what is being offered. Second, the price is too high. Perceived risks in such transactions are lowered by the seller who offers a money-back guarantee. This is mandatory in such marketing programs.

It is not uncommon for a manufacturer to use direct mail in promoting sales to dealerships if he cannot afford a sales force. Retail buyers will buy something through the mail, particularly if a sample is provided. Sometimes such direct efforts can be complemented by telephone calls. Bear in mind that the telephone and the mail are relatively inexpensive when compared to the high cost of a salesman's visit. Moreover, they can cover territory faster than the salesman.

ABOUT WHOLESALERS

Wholesalers tend to be very nasty people (according to many manufacturers, at least) with whom to do business. The new enterpriser will usually find a cold welcome in the wholesale buyer's office. Wholesalers are interested in carrying items that are demanded by their retail customers. They are not particularly eager to

pioneer new items and generally refuse to do so. Typically, the manufacturer must establish the demand for his product at the retail level before the wholesaler becomes interested in it. If he is able to do this, wholesalers will come to him. In the Vita-Wheel case mentioned previously, the direct mail program to dealers managed to establish a sufficient distribution base that salesmen of various wholesalers saw the product in the stores and learned that it was selling well. Subsequently the company received an unsolicited order for 1000 wheels from a wholesaler in Tulsa. Another wholesaler in Los Angeles wrote a letter asking to be contacted about the wheels, saying that its salesmen were requesting them.

From a bargaining standpoint, one should endeavor to get the wholesalers to come to him rather than he going to them. Even so, in the case of the Vita-Wheel, the wholesalers were not used as a primary channel of distribution because they were just too expensive. They wanted a 25 percent margin; the company was spending less than that on its direct mail campaign to dealers. Moreover, the wholesalers were not carrying sufficient quantities and one of them wanted the goods on consignment, he would not pay for the goods until after they were sold. Well, that was a lot of nonsense, so the wholesaler was not used.

So it goes in business. There are some people whose price is simply more than they are worth. In this matter of distribution systems, everything comes down to dollars and cents. What can be economically afforded usually *dictates* what is done.

LOGISTICS

27

Logistics is the science of physically moving goods from one point to another. It entails not only transportation but physical handling and storage. These seemingly mundane activities are given far too little attention in most books about business yet a bit of experience will soon drive home to the entrepreneur not only the importance of logistical decisions but their cost as well. A great deal of time can be spent trying to solve logistical problems. Sometimes transportation proves to be so costly that it seriously limits the market for goods. The field is so complex that all that can be said here is a warning about it and a few hints about transportation that may be of some help.

For all of its tremendous importance to both business and living standards, transportation is given scant attention in eduction. Yet its problems pose serious obstacles to most businessmen. It is wise to learn about the field because a lot of money can be saved by doing so.

Transportation report

Peter Wulff
Tom Finnegan†

What's the best way to ship?

"Ship best way." "Ship cheapest way." There probably isn't a purchasing man in the business who hasn't written these words on a purchase order at some time.

Yet what do they actually mean? Is there one best or one cheapest way to move freight? When the purchasing manager writes up the shipping instructions on the p.o., should he

†Peter Wulff and Tom Finnegan, *Purchasing Magazine*, September 30, 1971, pp. 25-41.

288

simply indicate whether to ship air, rail or truck, or should he go further and name names?

Naming names is in the interest of both parties, say the carriers themselves. "It's a poor purchasing manager," notes one transportation executive, "who would go to a distributor and order electrical equipment without specifying the manufacturer. By the same token, the purchasing manager should pick his freight supplier just as carefully. If he did, the best carriers, like the best manufacturers, would prosper, and the purchasing manager would end up getting better service."

A traffic buyer notes: "If you let your supplier determine shipping methods, you may be losing out on one very important area of potential savings. In our case, we always specify freight methods by the simple expedient of buying everything f.o.b. supplier's plant. That way savings — or mistakes — are ours to make."

How good — or how bad — is the service available from carriers in 1971? Opinions range all over the spectrum. There's a printing company executive in upstate New York who says succinctly: "Trucking service stinks." Others use even more descriptive language about rail and air freight services. Still others are content with what they're getting, aware that no supplier can be perfect 100% of the time.

Pay more
get better service

And one purchasing manager recently filed suit, as a private citizen, to have the truck rates he pays raised. His reasoning: a higher rate boost than the one already proposed will do more than compensate truckers for recent wage increases, and assure him of continued quality service.

No matter how purchasing managers feel about the service they get for their freight dollar, it will pay them to take another look at how they buy transportation services. Could the blame for poor service lie at purchasing's door? Is the purchasing department making any of the mistakes carriers single out as hampering their operations? And is purchasing getting all the service it is entitled to?

Talk to the people who sell freight services — as *Purchasing* Magazine did — and you'll hear the same comments over and over again. Here's a selection:

Purchasing uses competitive methods to buy raw materials. But it forgets all about competition when it comes to freight. The purchasing manager shouldn't lock himself into one mode of transportation forever. He should remember that circumstances change from year to year. For example, computerization on the railroads and the advent of the 747 have changed quite a few established "facts" about rail and air freight.

It's the overall cost
that counts

The smart purchasing man doesn't stop with the cost of materials, or even with the cost of point-to-point transportation. He considers the overall cost of everything from raw materials through freight, inventory, and production delays to getting his product into the customer's hands. That's materials management — and an argument for not necessarily buying what appears to be the cheapest transportation mode.

Don't assume that air freight, because of its higher cost, is for emergency shipments only. Instead, think of the total concept of physical distribution, from receiving dock through production and final shipment. Often, the greatest savings can be accomplished in this area. Efficient use of air freight — even though it costs more per pound — may cut a company's operating expense.

Consider consolidation of small shipments bound for one destination, either into trailers via piggybacking, or into air shipment containers, for later local distribution via freight forwarders.

Don't route truck shipments via two or three carriers where single-line service is available. It's a matter of knowing your carriers and their capabilities. Single-line carriers mean fewer split claims and better tracing service.

Don't route truck shipments in a roundabout way by picking a carrier with terminals that do not suit your needs. It can add hundreds of miles, and many hours, to delivery schedules. As a general rule, a straight line route is the best way.

Consider the costs of keeping inventory. Can an efficient freight system become your traveling warehouse instead? Any one of the three modes, with proper planning, can deliver supplies to your plant a day or two ahead of production needs.

To obtain expert advice on how to ship the best way, *Purchasing* Magazine went to the men who know — the carriers themselves. Then to ascertain where the problems are, we asked representative purchasing managers to comment on each mode. Here are the results — for air freight, truck, and rail.

Air freight — Fast, competitive[1]

Q: Mr. Cooke, what steps can the purchasing manager take to obtain better freight service from the airlines?

A: The first thing a purchasing manager should do is try and evaluate what the inbound product is, and what its use is going to be to his company. I am talking about inbound raw materials and semi-finished components, which will be collected at one or more assembly plants.

He must evaluate the cost of moving that raw material to a manufacturing plant in terms of its relative cost to surface transportation. The cost of air freight is higher because it's a premium service — faster delivery, less damage and pilferage, less insurance claims, and all the inherent advantages of air freight. But the purchasing manager must look into the offsetting factors.

More than anyone else, the purchasing manager knows that, when it comes to stockpiling raw materials, inventory costs money. Stockpiling exposes a company to oversupply of an item that may not be needed over the original projected period. Quite often, these supplies become obsolete, and cannot be returned to the vendor.

Through regular air freight service, purchasing can order materials on a shorter delivery cycle, getting exactly what is needed by production — and no more — at the precise time. Inventory

[1] As Director of Air Freight Sales for Trans World Airlines, Clifton N. Cooke heads a worldwide staff supervising direct cargo sales. He has wide experience in overseas and transcontinental air freight operations.

can be reduced to near zero and obsolescence can be eliminated. These are important factors. And many cost reductions can be achieved by ordering in quantities that insure a smooth flow of materials to the production line.

Q: What new services are you offering to encourage purchasing managers to use air freight?

A: We have introduced new 747 daylight container rates, where the user, in effect, buys a container. He pays a flat rate and can put as much into the container as it can carry, up to its structural limit.

Previously, users paid a flat rate up to a so-called pivot weight, and paid so many cents per pound for each 100 pounds over that. Now there is no pivot weight. And no penalty for density. A purchasing manager who orders a shipment of ball bearings can be way ahead. The more use we can make of the increased weight capacity of an aircraft, the lower the rates we can offer.

Q: How can the purchasing manager get a comparative view of freight costs?

A: Purchasing people should ask their suppliers the delivered cost. Most goods are sold f.o.b. Now, some companies are selling c.i.f., with the freight cost added. By establishing the freight costs, purchasing managers can get a better fix on the total cost of the product.

Freight and delivery charges are sometimes almost hidden because the cost of transportation is off in another area and is not directly related to the specific item being shipped. It's very difficult for purchasing to go back at the end of the quarter and find out just what costs should be assigned to each piece of material that flowed into the plant.

Q: How can a purchasing manager assure himself of getting your best rates?

A: There are several sources. Individual airlines can quote rates immediately over the phone. Or the buyer can have a sales rep sit down with him and discuss the product to be shipped. The rep will quote exact rates based on the commodity itself, the commodity description, and the density.

Many companies use air freight forwarders. The forwarders have separate rates that differ from those of the airlines because they are based on consolidation. Ofttimes consolidations can bring substantial savings on a regular basis.

Q: How about theft?

A: We have concentrated very heavily on this problem in the past 18 months. Our claims now represent less than one and one-half percent of our revenue, which means we are not losing a lot of freight, and we are not damaging it. Containerization or unitization helps tremendously. We now have a large igloo that carries up to 12,000 pounds. It's completely sealable and is padlocked. It cannot be cut through. It's really a flying safe.

Q: Mr. Becker,[2] how can a purchasing manager get the most out of your services?

A: He can contact our air freight service in his city and ascertain the best

[2]American Airlines has established freight marketing on the highest level, appointing Otto A. Becker as senior vice president to head the division. Becker has 30 years of wide-ranging airline experience, and heavy service in freight sales and services.

rate, the best arrangement of services, and the best type of movement. He should familiarize himself with tariffs. Or, better yet, he can call our sales department and present his requirements in terms of original points, general destination, and type of cargo, both in pounds and volume.

The salesman and our specialists will analyze the complete situation and present a solution that will be to purchasing's best advantage. However, if we establish that we cannot meet his requirements, we will recommend against air transportation.

Q: What do you see as the main advantages of your mode of transportation?

A: Naturally, the principal one is speed. Other advantages for the user are high sales expansion, a better marketing thrust, lower packaging costs, lower insurance rates, and a lower rate of damage claims.

The overall advantage from a physical distribution view is that total service of air freight can be purchased for a cheaper dollar cost than surface transportation.

Purchasing executives will be greatly interested in our recently launched E container program. The E container has 18 ft. of cubic space, carries 500 lbs., and offers maximum flexibility. It has been designed to fit the bellies of all our passenger planes, from the smallest two-engine job to the 747. This means that for the first time every city in the country is now accessible for air freight.

The new container lets a shipper place a lot of small shipments in the one container. There's less damage, less material handling. It's an efficient way to send a product mix to a distributor or a primary customer.

If shipments have different destinations, a freight forwarder or a break bulk man can route each individual shipment when the container is opened at the air terminal. Shippers thus can obtain an advantage in rates through consolidation.

Q: What are the disadvantages of your mode?

A: The high rate on a point-to-point basis, as compared to the rates of other means of transportation. But as I have said, the rate must be measured against lower insurance, less claims, and the fact that efficient use of containers makes air freight competitive with other modes.

Q: There has been widespread publicity on airport cargo thefts. Is the picture worse than before? What's being done to improve matters?

A: There has been wide publicity on airport thefts. The problem looks greater than it is. If one looks at the true statistics, such as the total volume of shipments and total value of the percentage of cargo affected, the ratio of theft is much lower than generally presented. By eliminating statistics that relate to outside of the gate thefts and truck hijackings, the rate of airport theft comes into better focus.

Still, we are not satisfied. However, for the first time we are attacking the problem on an entire industry level. Instead of individual airlines instituting their own protection measures, all companies are coordinating their efforts in conjunction with the newly-established Airport Security Council. There has been a marked improvement, shown by the lower theft rate. We are beginning to see our way clear to maximum protection against thefts.

The buyer's view:
small towns are a problem

Q: Mr. Watters,[3] do you see any improvement in the air freight service you've been getting recently?

A: I see no improvement. Advertising and sales calls promoting door-to-door expediting service just aren't working out. The job is too big for the few operating people in the air terminal office.

Q: What's your chief problem with air freight? Have you considered switching to another mode?

A: Problems arise in small towns where some of our suppliers are located. In many of them, a pick-up truck travels a route once, or maybe twice, a day. Miss the truck by minutes and you can lose 24 hours.

Another gripe: Freight handlers at the terminals don't use their imagination in re-routing parcels to effect fastest possible delivery. The result? We're using United Parcel Service more and more. At least we're not disappointed, since we don't expect overnight service from them.

Q: You say you're not too happy with some of the service you've been getting. Have your carriers suggested any ways by which you could help yourself get better service?

A: Not that I'm aware of.

Q: Whom do you rely on for accurate rate information?

A: Our traffic manager. While purchasing is responsible for incoming freight, we work very closely with him and rely on his experience and knowledge. And we get direct reports from our receiving manager as well. Though he reports to the traffic manager, he lets us know if the carrier isn't doing his job.

Q: Have you ever used outside traffic consultants? Or does your own traffic department meet all your transportation needs?

A: As far as I'm aware, we've never used traffic consultants here. The reason is simple. Our own traffic manager has over 35 years of experience and can handle almost any problem.

Q: Is the theft picture better or worse?

A: We don't seem to have a theft problem — probably due to the nature of our product.

Trucking — The real
door-to-door system

Q: Mr. Davis,[4] what steps can the purchasing manager take to help himself get better freight service from a carrier?

A: A purchasing man knows that if he guarantees a supplier a certain volume of business annually, purchasing is most likely to get a quality product at the right price and on-time delivery. The same principle applies to carriers.

[3] A major user of air freight is Ralph Watters, Director of Purchases for Sybron Corporation's Taylor Instrument Process Control Division in Rochester, N.Y. Watters discussed the use of air freight with PURCHASING Magazine.

[4] "Purchasing managers should treat motor freight carriers the same way they treat ordinary suppliers," says David H. Davis, vice-president/sales, Wilson Freight, Cincinnati, who rose to his present position from a trainee in Wilson's freight training program. Sitting in on PURCHASING Magazine's interview was Wilson Freight's Paul A. Selzer, executive vice-president, and a pioneer in motor freight.

By consolidating his purchasing power with a few selected carriers, a purchasing executive can use their services to the best advantage. He will find that many of his shipping problems can be solved by careful selection of the carriers who handle his inbound business.

At Wilson Freight, we have prepared a brochure aimed at purchasing men. It tells them how they can have less congestion, less dock costs, and fast, on-time deliveries on a daily basis if they make enough shipments.

Q: What additional tips can you offer purchasing managers so they can obtain the best advantages from a carrier?

A: Check your receiving conditions to see if you are getting a lot of late shipments. You may have only one door. At times there may be three carriers waiting to unload. It costs 12 cents per minute for a truck's operating time. So, if a carrier has to wait 20 minutes every time he makes a delivery, he will see to it that the delivery is made on the last stop. If a purchasing man finds his material is all tied up and he's not getting deliveries, it may be due to inadequate loading facilities.

Q: What about the relationship of purchasing to physical distribution problems?

A: The purchasing man must stick his neck out and learn routing, traffic concepts, various modes, and how to consolidate shipments. Whether he has a traffic department or not, he's the one who has the say on inbound shipments. He's always looking to increase purchasing's contribution to company profits. He can do a better job if he knows traffic. Whether he's in a small or a large company, this is knowledge that will pay off.

Q: Mr. Selzer, what are the principal advantages of truck transportation?

A: Trucks are the optimum. They are cheaper and faster, especially for less than trailer lots (LTL). Purchasing managers don't realize that inbound truck shipments, depending on the day they are shipped, frequently arrive ahead of air.

As an example, if a supplier in Cincinnati routes a shipment by air on Thursday in response to purchasing's request, that shipment will not be delivered until Monday in New York. We can also deliver that shipment by truck at the same time and the rate will be drastically lower.

Of course air is faster on a coast-to-coast setup, often a vital factor with perishables. But on lesser distances, trucks often offer greater benefits.

The one disadvantage to trucking is the price of small shipments. Here I recommend batch deliveries, especially under 500 pounds.

The purchasing manager must figure out how much it's costing him to save a day on early shipments by air. If he can wait another day, he may find that his savings will be greater if he ships by truck.

Q: Mr. Mellen,[5] what are the chief advantages that trucking has over other modes of transportation?

[5]McLean Trucking Company, headquartered in Winston-Salem, N.C., is the country's fourth largest Class 1 Common Carrier. It specializes in LTL freight, serving 31 states and the District of Columbia. McLean operates more than 7,500 tractors, trailers and city delivery trucks from over 90 terminals ranging from Maine to Texas. Telling the large trucking company's point of view to PURCHASING Magazine is the company's newly-elected president, Amory Mellen, Jr.

A: Two: speed and flexibility. We're the only mode that can offer door-to-door delivery without a premium price. Sure, airlines can get a shipment across the country much faster than we can, if you're prepared to pay for their service. But remember, their service is only from airport to airport. It's still trucks which actually pick up and deliver the shipment.

For lesser distances, a direct shipment is often as fast as a truck-plane-truck shipment. A large company such as ours can reach three-quarters of the nation's population within its own route system and, of course, we work with all other truckers to get shipments to points we don't reach.

As for flexibility, consider that only two railroads in the country are still in the LCL business, while fully 60% of our volume is in LTL. This means that, no matter what the size of your shipment, trucks can handle it. And, because there are more roads than rail lines or airports, we can go anywhere. Try to get from Philadelphia to a small town in South Carolina, and rail might take a week. A truck can deliver on the first or second day. It's a question of having a pipeline versus an inventory.

Q: How about disadvantages? Are there any shipments which air or rail handle better than trucks?

A: Yes, and they relate chiefly to pricing structures. For some bulk commodities, rail has an overwhelming economic advantage. And, for the urgent 50-pound package going across the country, there's no question that the extra premium for air freight is worthwhile.

However, we don't consider either rail or air as our competition. Our true competitors are other motor carriers.

Q: What can the purchasing manager do to get better service from truckers?

A: The first step should be to analyze where his shipments are coming from and with what frequency. Does he really need that frequency? Could he consolidate shipments and ship greater quantities less often? That way he could obtain a tidy cost reduction.

The single best method of improving truck service, however, is to get to know the truckers who serve your locality. Each has a different route and terminal system. By taking advantage of the differences, purchasing and traffic can easily determine the one best way.

As for rates, use the rate clerks on the trucking company's staff to help you find the cheapest way. Rates are tremendously complicated and they're experts in getting you the best price. The only "secret" in getting the best rate is to describe your shipment accurately.

Q: Theft remains a major problem. What are truckers doing to improve the picture?

A: Beefing up security in individual companies. Forming such industry-wide associations as TICOTH (Trucking Industry Committee On Trailer Hijacks). Working in conjunction with the FBI on preventive measures and an alert system in case of hijacking.

The greater internal security measures which companies are taking reflects the fact that it's easier to prevent theft from the outside. If the thief is a member of your own organization, you have a real problem.

Truck user:
classification's the secret

Q: Mr. Giese,[6] has your trucking service improved or worsened recently?

A: There's been a steady improvement as trucking companies realize that service is the watchword. Most rates are fixed beyond a company's control, and when a carrier asks "What can we do to attract more business?" it soon realizes that service is the answer.

Service, of course, goes beyond reliability of deliveries. It also includes better tracing ability and faster claim handling. And better tracing has to be the result of increasing reliance on the computer. The computer also helps truckers in another way. It allows a trailer to be loaded more scientifically so that shipments can be routed to the most suitable terminals.

Q: Is there any aspect of your trucking service you're not satisfied with? Could you switch to another mode, such as rail?

A: The biggest problem we have is when a carrier either gets overloaded or else doesn't have enough material for a full trailerload. In both cases, he's likely to "gypsy" the material he can't handle

to another carrier. This creates a problem of tracing.

Neither of our solutions to this problem is entirely satisfactory. If we insist that the carrier handle it himself, rather than farming the shipment out, we're likely to have a delay. And if we switch to rail, we either have problems with LCL, or, with CL, we have to consider the availability of sidings.

Q: Mr. Gentsch,[7] what special advantages can rail freight offer the purchasing manager?

A: There are several, apart from the obvious one of being able to handle tremendous volume at low cost. The most surprising may be that railroads are offering ever-increasing reliability and scheduling. Thanks to computerization coming into almost universal use, a railroad can pinpoint every car in its system to make sure it gets to its destination on time. More than that, a shipper can dial a number for instant information from the computer on where his shipment is at that moment.

Another major advantage is that cars can be virtually custom-designed for a particular shipment, insuring added safety. For regular customers, railroads can reserve or set aside a fixed number of cars so that they're always ready when a shipper needs them.

The people who say that railroads are stick-in-the-mud are mainly those who

[6]Henry Giese, with a lifetime of traffic activity under his belt, is Vice President — Purchasing & Traffic with General Battery & Ceramics, Reading, Pa. In addition to using common carriers, General Battery owns its own fleet of over 100 pieces of trucking equipment. Giese is pretty well satisfied with the trucking services he buys.

[7]The Norfolk & Western Railway Company, on the basis of its freight operations, has the distinction of being one of the two or three most profitable railroads in the country. At Roanoke, Va., headquarters, Edward Gentsch, vice president of materials management, gives his views on what rail freight has to offer.

haven't had a chance to see what's going on today. Given the opportunity to be a member of the purchasing-transportation partnership, we can really do things for you.

Q: And the disadvantages of rail?

A: We're not equipped to handle less than carload shipments, nor short-haul traffic economically. But don't forget the possibilities of piggybacking. It's probably the closest thing we have to a truly intermodal means of transportation.

Q: How can the purchasing man be sure he's getting the best rates on rail freight?

A: Consult the traffic expert who can be part of your staff without costing you a penny: the local railroad representative. Let him come up with the best means of moving your material. If that means isn't rail, he'll tell you so. Getting the cheapest rate is usually a matter of classifying the material correctly. That's what the railroad rep is expert in.

And keep this in mind. Today the materials management concept is taking over from the purely purchasing function. This means that you must consider the overall costs of materials flow from suppliers of raw materials right to the customers of the finished product. "Ship cheapest way" is inadequate for purchase orders these days.

Q: What about traffic consultants? Should the purchasing manager use them?

A: The fact that they exist and prosper shows they must fill a need. But I hate to pay for anything I don't have to pay for. The local freight representative can probably do a similar job for the purchasing man — and he's free!

Q: How can purchasing get the best service from today's railroads?

A: Keep up with what the railroads are doing to modernize, then avail yourself of what modern technology can offer. Take computer pinpointing of individual cars, as an example. With this tool, the purchasing manager needn't wait until a shipment is overdue before trying to find out where it is. With a simple phone call, he can track his shipment across the country and schedule such matters as unloading times, dock space and production planning almost to the minute. Even if a shipment should be delayed — like other transportation systems, railroads are sometimes at the mercy of very bad weather — this tracing system allows the manager to make alternate plans to keep production on schedule. In a very short time he may be able to re-route another shipment already in transit. This makes a modern rail system his warehouse on wheels and helps reduce inventory.

Q: How do you get the best possible service?

A: Usually by buying f.o.b. supplier's plant. That way we're responsible for freight. If we get bad service, we have no one to blame but ourselves.

Q: You say you like to handle freight yourselves. How do you make sure you get the best rates?

A: If there's one secret to favorable rates it's making sure you classify your material correctly. A mistake in stating the gauge of steel you're shipping, for instance, can cost thousands, and after a certain time period you have no recourse. Conversely, familiarity with classifications can turn a traffic department into a real profit center.

Q: What's your opinion of traffic consultants?

A: They have their good and bad points. They can often save you money by checking freight invoices. But remember, if you classify a material incorrectly, there's nothing they can do without checking thoroughly into the commodity you ship — which costs money.

However, if you have a well-organized traffic department, a consultant may be something of a luxury. There's nothing he can do that a good man in traffic can't.

One of the places where I'd recommend a traffic consultant is for a small company that can't afford a high-priced qualified traffic manager. Purchasing may be able to handle the day-to-day chores, but, for real savings, look to the consultant's expertise.

Rails — Customized service makes the difference

Q: Mr. Austin,[8] how can you help the purchasing manager?

A: With 16 separate services to our customers, we can truly say we're in business to serve our customers' needs — all of them. We have a management that is willing to do little better than break even in some areas of our operations, because it feels that the long

range future of MoPac is being made secure by our ability to attract the heavy freight through our performance of various auxiliary services as well. With these services, MoPac is truly able to offer a total distribution system, or, as its slogan says: "A carton or a carload."

Among the most important of these services we count our ability to handle both LTL and LCL; five all-piggyback trains plus the six standard piggyback plans; several container-pack plans; split deliveries; intrastate trucking through our own subsidiaries; interchange with more than 400 motor carriers. Plus, of course, standard rail car service with more than 97% of our fleet in full operating condition at any time. With any of these services, or a combination, we can customize a distribution system for any customer.

If the MoPac system has any disadvantages, I'd say the fault lies with a customer's not taking advantage of the total distribution concept for cost savings and reliability. If he doesn't have the knowledge, for example, to use the proper mix of services, he could lose out.

What it comes down to is this. The purchasing or traffic manager can get better service from the railroads if he'll consult with the experts: the sales staff on the railroads' own payrolls. Free services to the customer go further than showing him how to buy the best package available. They show him how to reduce his total transportation cost and minimize damage.

Q: How does a purchasing manager find the best rates?

A: Once again, it's a matter of going to the experts — the transportation companies. All our charges are published in tariffs' on file with the

[8]The St. Louis-headquartered Missouri Pacific System is almost unique in the transportation picture today. It's one of the last of the railroads to offer LCL small shipments service. In addition, it owns two trucking subsidiaries that operate nearly 4,000 pieces of equipment in 12 states. MoPac's Vice President — Traffic is old-time railroader Joseph Austin. Here he talks to PURCHASING Magazine.

Federal Communications Commission. Our trucking subsidiaries also have their rates on public display.

Rail user:
Service needs improvement

Q: Mr. Fendrick,[9] from the user's point of view, how do you find rail service? Is the railroads' stress on the computer helping you?

A: Based on our use, rail service has worsened, though I'd never call it good, even in the past. We get shipments both by tank car and carload, and we've had innumerable problems with both types.

We're just 11 miles from Philadelphia, and many of our suppliers are on the same railroad as we are. Yet we've had shipments that have taken six days to cover those miles because of switching and delays. Something like this is fatal to us, since we pride ourselves on giving better than three-day service to our customers. It completely destroys our flexibility.

And one more horror story. Last week I got a call from our production manager: "Where's that tank car of oil coming from Charleston, S.C.?" I'd thought it was long in and gone. We'd been billed for it, and the shipper had sent us the papers and even the car number. We did some checking and found that the car had been sitting, fully loaded, on the supplier's siding for 31 days. Now we were at fault, admittedly, for not expediting sooner.

[9]Ronald Fendrick has a wealth of traffic experience. Prior to becoming Director of Purchasing at Quaker Chemical Corp., Conshohocken, Pa., he worked for one of the largest chemical companies in the country. And, at Quaker, Fendrick leases 30 to 40 rail cars on a permanent basis. He has some decided opinions on rail service.

But it's incredible to think that the railroads could allow a foul-up like this to occur.

Computerization
isn't helping us

Is the computer helping? We see no evidence here. But, in its defense, I feel that the basic logistics of railroading are so complex that it's impossible for service to improve.

Now we have no ax to grind. In fact, railroads are some of our best customers. And on a local level, we get good service from switchmen, etc. It's just that the enormity of the paperwork and the logistics of getting cars to their proper location defeat all efforts at reliability.

Q: Are there some good points about railroads?

A: Yes. In one area, their service beats trucking. Far too frequently, one of our suppliers can't load a truck with the pure material we buy because the truck hasn't been steam cleaned. Then the truck has to go back for cleaning and we lose a day. We hardly ever have cleanliness problems with rail.

Q: Why don't you switch to all truck freight for incoming material?

A: It's a question of cost. On some items, if we chose to receive them by truck, we'd be priced right out of the competitive picture.

Q: Have the railroads suggested any steps to improve their service to you?

A: That's part of the trouble. We have almost no contact with railroad representatives. The air freight people are especially good at this. They come in regularly and ask us how they can improve their service to us. So do truckers. If we see a railroad man more than once a year, we're amazed.

Q: What about rates? Are railroads helpful in giving you rate information?

A: No, they're not. It often takes a week to get the answer to one question. We rely on our traffic department to get the best rates and to classify our freight properly. They can make big savings by means of the manufacturing in transit provisions.

Q: Do you have any experience with traffic consultants?

A: Not directly. And I'm not sure that the use of such people to audit freight bills on a continuing basis would pay off.

On a one-time basis, to straighten out or increase the efficiency of a company's traffic department, I can see the merits of outside consultants.

QUESTIONS

1. There are many businessmen who would take strong exception to the statement that one should buy FOB seller's plant. Why?

GOVERNMENTS
AS CUSTOMERS

28

In reading about the huge government expenditures in the billions of dollars it is easy to lose sight of where a lot of that money goes. The government is a big customer for just about everything made. Indeed, for many concerns the government is the only customer. There are firms that have been established just to supply some need of the government.

The casual new businessman seldom knows much about selling to the government. What does the government buy? Where does one go to make contact with the potential buyer? How does one go about making the sale? How do you get paid? These and many more such questions are not easily answered for the government is so large and its needs so diverse. It buys in many places and in many different ways. There is a lot of bidding, but not always.

For one interested in investigating the government as a customer, the Small Business Administration has a number of publications that will give some idea of how to go about it.

But first, a few warnings about doing business with the government. When one sells to the government it is

necessary to obey or comply with a large number of laws and rulings most of which most people know nothing. One maker of clothing was placed on a blacklist — no government agency could do business with that company — because it would not open its books and records to government investigators from the Department of Health, Welfare, and Education who were checking to see if the company's hiring policies met with government rulings. In doing business with the government, the firm becomes an open book because in most contracts the government has the right to inspect records and premises. This latter aspect is true even if one does not do business with the government.

Then there is the matter of re-negotiated prices. Normally a customer pays the price asked. It is not so in many government contracts. The government reserves the right to renegotiate the price if profits are excessive. There have been many instances in which several years later the government has walked in for a large claim against some company on the grounds that too much money was made on some deal with the government. Bear in mind, that as far as the government is concerned, profits from it are evil. The government contracting officer considers himself successful if he is able to get the seller to work for wages. So be careful about what is in a contract with the government.

Some of the most successful firms dealing with the government will not grant it any special contractual considerations. Their policy is one of selling the government goods from its shelves just as if it were any other customer. No negotiations!

Then there is the matter of fraud. The government not only dislikes it but has the legal machinery available to it free of marginal cost to do something to the seller about it. One trucker in Los Angeles now resides in jail reflecting upon his "sins." He had a contract to haul beer to the Long Beach Naval docks for shipment to who knows where. His tale is rather discouraging. He would be given the run around at the dock as to where he should unload it. He was forced to wait for most unreasonable lengths of time to make deliveries. Many times he had to take his load back and return again at some other time. All of this ran up his costs significantly. He covered himself by making claims for trips and beer not delivered. Several years later after the man had sold his trucking business, the government somehow discovered his fraud and prosecuted him. His sad tale garnered no tears nor sympathy from the Federal judge who sent him to jail.

The moral of this tale is quite clear. The government is a tough customer. While the private concern would handle the matter of overcharges in a civil suit, the government can throw one in jail and does so. As a government

contractor, one is in the public eye, a target for every muckraker who is looking for a cause. Many business people say, "Who needs it?" They stay away from government business.

One person experienced with selling to the government advised:

1. Do not believe for one minute that it is cheaper to do business with the government than with other customers. Although the government refuses to recognize marketing costs in its contracts, the fact is that it is far more costly to sell to the government than to sell to other types of customers. Allow for it in the price.

2. Read the fine print in the contract. Know that the contract because the government certainly does and will hold a person to all its provisions.

3. Try to develop proprietary products which the government must buy off the shelf just as any other customer buys them. It is difficult to do this for the government hates such a situation and tries to avoid it whenever possible.

4. One should try to protect his rights. The government usually tries to take ownership of whatever ideas or developments one comes up with while working on their contracts. If you come up with some innovation that they accept, they will probably try to gain ownership of it so that they can put it out for bid the next time around. They do not want any one company to have a monopoly on something they buy. You can fight this sort of thing but you will have to be tough to do so.

5. Remember the name of the game is documentation. Bureaucrats have an everlasting passion for paperwork. There must be a piece of paper to back up everything. You must keep detailed records of everything.

6. One needs help from people who know how to deal with the government. It is an art; there are certain ways of doing things. You must gain access to this type of know how. For this reason, many firms hire former government officials to handle their government relationships. Supposedly, they know

where to go and who to see to get what is wanted.

7. Never forget that the government is not very forgiving nor bound by the restrictions of economy in prosecuting what it believes to be fraud. It will come after one years afterward with forces not calculated to win favor.

*****

There are some businessmen who would strongly advise the entrepreneur to shun government contracts or subcontracts from them because such volume is not the stuff on which solid businesses are usually based. This article provides some insight into the area.

The risks inherent for a small business taking a contract as a prime — or as a sub-contractor

Stanley D. Zemansky†

A good part of this country's economic well-being depends upon a competitive economy and the concomitant preservation of a strong small business community. We all are well aware of the competitive edge available from small business, as compared to large business, in those activities where small business is capable. Small business is

†**Stanley D. Zemansky,** *Journal of Purchasing*, **May 1971, pp. 43-55.**

Reprinted from Journal of Purchasing, Vol. 7 (May, 1971). Copyright by National Association of Purchasing Management, Inc., and reprinted with their permission.

needed if we are to maintain this broad base of economic support. We need the independent man in our economy; he is important to our national character. We need enterprising, imaginative small firms to give us new ideas and new competition. Some of the best ideas of merchandising, manufacturing, and efficiency have come from small firms. This may be because of the necessity of their making savings and improving productive efficiency in order to survive. Most of the great corporations of today started as small, independent firms. They were aggressive, they offered something, and today they are great national assets; we must make certain that the door remains open for others to follow.

There are other cogent reasons underlying the concern about small business and its share of government spending. It is good politics. The interest of political leaders in the over five million small U.S. businesses and their voting strength is natural. For over a century, Congress and other officials have sponsored plans to help small private enterprises. Such help has included homesteading, land sales, farm aid, subsidies, tax benefits, and loans.

Underlying the political interest, however, is a sincere and widespread public appreciation of the vital role that America's millions of businessmen and farmers play in our economy. One of the great advantages of our free society is the endless range of products and services available. All compete for the varying tastes and dollars of customers.

While big companies with their research laboratories are developing new products and uses, records of the United States Patent Office confirm that individuals and smaller firms still account for approximately seventy-five percent of all new inventions. Such ingenuity warrants support.

In the national economy there is a coalition of large and small business standing together as necessary complements of our national purpose. They are adjoining links in the chain of production and distribution of goods and services. Promoting small business requires the cooperation of large business as well as the government. To be effective, this cooperation must be a two-way street based on mutual understanding.

"Assists" to small business

A small business is an independently owned and operated organization having fewer than 500 employees and not dominant in its field of operation. The "500 employees" includes all divisions and subsidiaries. There are, of course, exceptions to this rule, but the exceptions pertain to specific industry or product interests and are not of sufficient general interest to warrant discussion here.

Small business has many things "going for it," if its management is willing to capitalize on this position. Some of the advantages are:

1. Public Law #85-536 (1958) states the national policy of using government procurements to enhance and preserve competition and placing a fair proportion of such procurement with small business concerns. Public Law #87-305 (1961) requires that government and prime contractors, and with flowdown to major subcontractors, with contracts in excess of $500,000 establish a firm program which gives small business a fair opportunity to bid on government contracts and subcontracts.

2. Most large companies feel that dealing with small business is nothing more than sound economics. Small business is a most-important part of our free enterprise system.

3. Small business generally can operate with lower overhead and has flexibility of operation and fast reaction time.

The Small Business Administration (SBA) was established by Congress in 1953. The original Small Business Act primarily empowered the SBA to aid small business by business loans and disaster relief. Succeeding legislation added the facet of support through government procurements. Figure 28-1 presents an overall view of the Small Business Administration and its programs. The SBA was created to help ensure that small firms continue to be an active and important part of the nation's economy. Strong legislative follow-up is maintained to ensure that the objectives of this law are met.

This follow-up includes hearings by both House and Senate Committees at least once a year to evaluate the small business programs of SBA, government purchasing agencies, and prime contractors. These hearings often result in new and more-effective programs.

Some products are beyond the normal capability of small business, due to the investment required. This is particularly true for the prime contractors which are called upon to

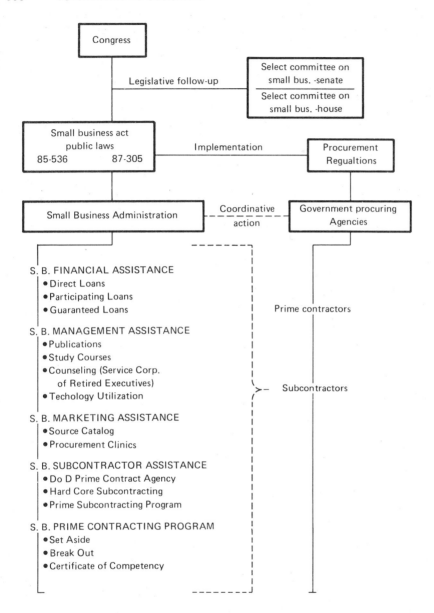

FIGURE 28-1: Government small business program

supply the large, complex weapon systems. But, in turn, they must subcontract a large portion of such systems at the major subsystem level.

Small business and ASPR

The Armed Services Procurement Regulations and sound business require that competitive pricing be established by a system of bidding on each procurement. Only "qualified" sources, suppliers which through survey demonstrate the ability to meet the prescribed procurement and quality control standards, are solicited. Each company bidding is in competition with equals or at least companies which have the capability of performing on a specific requirement. If a company in Philadelphia consistently underbids a company in Los Angeles, and does, in fact, meet quality (technical) and delivery requirements, then it will get the business. Why the company in Philadelphia consistently is the low bidder is the question that the higher bidders must answer if they are to be competitively successful.

Possibly the low bidder has a management that recognizes the merits of value analysis, zero defects, and overall cost reduction. As a result, its costs are less. If this is true, the other bidders must find a smarter way to secure business. It is in this area that one of the biggest risks of small business becomes apparent. In its anxiety to get orders, a small business may risk a bid at less than cost, hoping to make it up in the volume of additional business performed at profitable rates, or hoping to keep the business afloat until profitable business is available. For those small businesses which wish to perform on prime or subcontracts in the government field, they must (1) have the capability to produce the required product, (2) qualify the product, and (3) sell the product.

Selling the product is important to all businesses, but it is particularly important for the small business. Even though a small business meets the first two requirements, it cannot merely sit back and wait for the buyer to beat a path to its door. It just won't happen.

To meet successfully these three requirements requires an anticipatory investment, which involves considerable risk for a small business. Especially in the selling cost area, this risk expense may go on for some time. This is particularly true in doing business with the Department of Defense and other large prime contractors which have literally thousands of small businesses calling on them each month with just one idea in mind — selling.

Only those firms which demonstrate an active interest and make their product thoroughly familiar to the buyer will be given the opportunity to bid. Competition today is keen and it will become even more so. Although the buyer has an interest in buying from small business, the burden is on the small firm. The buyer can only assist. Small business must be the one to qualify, to sell, to bid competitively, to meet schedule requirements, and to provide a quality product.

Problems faced by small business

It would appear that small business should be able to obtain good sound business opportunities within its capabilities. The considerable support of the government and prime contractors will do much to enhance these opportunities. However, there are risks inherent to a small business taking a contract as a prime or a sub. Unfortunately, some of the problems and risks are so severe that they may encourage many small businesses into commercial endeavors and away from military, aerospace, and government work. Here are some, if not all, of the more significant problems:

1. Getting loans: The small businessman often has a tough time getting loans, especially if his credit references are not gilt-edged. Also, he often must pay a higher rate of interest than his bigger rivals.

2. Competition for raw materials: Small outfits frequently find it hard to get the relatively exotic materials needed. These include items such as aluminum, alloy steels, titanium, copper and copper alloys, and beryllium. In addition, lack of volume reduces the potential for purchasing economies.

3. Cutbacks and changes in government buying: At the end of any wartime period or as occasioned by the fast rate of technological change or fluctuations in the government budget leading to program modification, stretchout, or elimination, the volume of business for all manufacturers, large and small, may be heavily trimmed. In such cases, prime contractors may hold back work that would be subcontracted to other companies so they can avoid excessive layoffs.

4. Rapid technological changes: With the accelerated shift in emphasis from traditional weapons to missiles, atomic power, and space applications, there has been a change of materials and construction methods. One aerospace supplier, for example, reports that over half his business covers processes and methods unknown just three years ago. Many small companies have not had the facilities or money for research and new product development to keep up.

5. Mergers: Corporate mergers in the United States have had practically an exponential rise since the mid-1950's. Thousands of small firms have been merged into larger or stronger companies, and this has increased the competition for the remaining small concerns. Mergers have been especially numerous in the aircraft accessories, electronics, metals, and plastics fields.

6. Growth: Grow and compete — or die — is the alternative for many small businesses. Companies owned or controlled by one man, a family, or a small group often are unable to finance expansion.

7. Taxes: High corporate tax rates that take 52 percent of profits over $25,000 make it hard for many small companies to accumulate money for expansion.

8. People: Often it is a real problem for a smaller organization to recruit and keep high level management and technical talent. The smaller the number of people, the more important it becomes to choose with care. Loss or failure of a key man can threaten the company's survival. Few small companies can afford to have or set up programs to train or promote young talent. But these same firms must compete against the large companies that can mount a much broader effort to recruit and train people, have more fringe benefits, and offer the security of wider opportunities for transfer and promotion.

9. Low volume: To compensate for low volume production, small companies must have higher skills and efficiency.

10. Renegotiation loss and delays: Most companies, both large and small, are hesitant to reinvest their earnings because they do not know how much to set aside to meet the government renegotiation which may not be decided for three years or more. It is not unusual for the firm to experience a cut in profits earned three years earlier, in effect penalizing the firm for its ingenuity and efficiency.

Success of small business in obtaining contracts

Despite all these problems, small businesses have acquired many contracts. A recent analysis reveals the true capture rate of contracts by small business. This analysis consisted of reviewing the total procurement expenditures of a representative group of the nation's leading government prime contractors to isolate and identify the true small business market potential covered by these expenditures. This was accomplished by removing from the total procurement base those major subcontracts which clearly were beyond the capabilities of small business. For the years 1966 and 1967, the small business capture rate of the potential business within their capability approximated 70 percent.

There are several reasons why the share of small business does not reach its maximum potential. The most significant seem to be:

1. During periods of prime contract downward load fluctuation, large firms are forced to compete for contracts usually within the province of small business in order to maximize plant utilization.

2. The concentration of DoD on the procurement of weapon systems from a single prime contractor, accompanied by increased technological complexity of such weapons, tends to eliminate small businesses whose resources are inadequate for such work.

3. Small business was not responsive or not competitive.

Common problems shared by all government contractors

The problems and risks are basic to both large and small business. However, the impact on small business is greater and the effects may be catastrophic. For those small businesses dedicated to working in the government contracting environment, and whose product is due to the entrepreneurial or inventive character of the business, there are other elements of risk which merit discussion. The following common problems are shared by many who contract or subcontract on government procurements:

1. *Warranties:* Circumstances vary substantially in this area of exposure, depending on the product area, degree of design responsibility, and state-of-the-art. However, limitation of liability as to time period of warranty and inspection, latent vs. patent defects, consequential damages, and responsibility for satisfying the purpose intended must be considered. Most important is the proper method of disclaiming implied warranties which, unless disclaimed, are imposed by the uniform commercial code. Tight guarantees on mean-time-before-failure, time between overhaul, unscheduled removal rate, and cost per flight hour applied to items for which often there is no prior history available are current types of requirements.

2. *Data requirements:* Although great strides have been made in developing a reasonable approach in the demands for proprietary data, there

still persists in some areas the threat that unless data are furnished or sold as a separate item, the bidder may not be considered. It would appear that the buyer hopes a fearful bidder will supply the data for a nominal sum, and thus, assist the buyer in his next procurement. In some procurements, the buyer claims that the purchase order cannot be placed unless the seller furnishes all his data.

3. Defective pricing clauses and certificate: Defense Department interpretation of Public Law #87-653 is a constant source of trouble. Despite the law's clear wording, procuring agencies, contracting officers and prime contractors' buyers frequently call for cost breakdowns and price certifications even in situations where such requirements apparently are exempted. Several procurements have requested certification for orders under $100,000, when it apparently is not required. Documentation to support a determination that adequate competition does not exist is not regularly made available by the concerned buying activity, and audits (particularly those made during negotiation where a certificate will be required) are not always made available even though equity requires that both parties must be in an equal position at the bargaining table. Also, it is not unusual for a certificate to be requested even though it patently is not required by the statute. Some concerns even require a multiplicity of certificates reflecting a series of cost proposals made during negotiations.

4. Demands for financial consideration: There has been an increasing demand for financial consideration under prime contracts where the contractor is in default of

deliveries for reasons outside his control.

5. Termination clause – subcontracts: In prime contracts, terminations are permitted for a convenience of the government. A subcontractor normally would be governed by the same termination clause and suffers certain disallowables of termination, such as no profit on subcontracted items. This would include changes or other modifications caused by the government as well as termination under the prime contract. An example of a specific risk currently applied by some customers is that of absorbing recurring costs in the event the buyer does not sell his planned production.

Recent action by the ASPR Committee has further added to the risk of all suppliers by clarifying that the term "subcontractors and suppliers" includes firms at all tiers, and not merely first tier subcontractors. In effect, this modifies the default clause to make the contractor liable for delays of his subcontractors through all subsequent tiers.

6. Privity of contract: There are a number of problems at the subcontract level brought about by the subcontractor's inability to exert a claim against the government for those actions, or lack thereof, under rights the government acquires in the subcontract by virtue of flowdown provisions of the prime contract.

7. Flowdown: One of the defense contractor's more serious problems is flowdown of contractual requirements from the prime contract. While the prime contractor can negotiate contractual terms other than statutory requirements with the government, the subcontractor has no such opportunity to negotiate. It must agree to provisions accepted by the prime contractor. This creates severe problems for the small businessman who is neither organizationally nor financially equipped to cope with these complex requirements. Exhibit 1 gives a sample listing of such flowdown provisions as may be utilized by a typical prime contractor.

8. Paper profusion: Severe documentation requirements, imposed indiscriminately on the most-complex and simplest equipment alike, cause costs to increase out of proportion to value received. This can result in the government paying over $7,000 in non-recurring costs for a simple hand tool which costs $10 to manufacture.

9. Patent infringement: Many small businesses are private innovators. Therefore, the Patent Laws are of vital interest to such concerns. The government's current policy of purposeful infringement strips the inventive contractor of his most valuable asset, which is the exclusive right to the product of his own inventiveness.

10. Quality impositions: In many cases, government source inspection is imposed on the subcontractor. Many disputes occur when differences in interpretation of specifications arise. When such cases arise between a subcontractor and a prime, without the presence of government source inspection, negotiation and final arbitration are the usual course of settlement, with price adjustment if warranted. However, if the government source inspector takes a contrary position, usually the subcontractor will be forced to accept that interpretation, often with no direct contractual remedy available. Further,

the multiplicity of surveys is a heavy burden.

11. Forward pricing: This is the requirement of extending prices over a lengthy period (possibly 10 years), during a time of unknown inflation, and being contractually bound by these prices.

12. Extreme changes clauses: This approach is one which puts all the options for changes in the hands of the buyer, without recourse from the supplier.

13. Complete audit facilitation: This includes make-up of burden centers and imposition of disallowables.

14. Payment delays: Often the subcontractor will not receive payment until after the equipment has been accepted by the prime's customer.

15. Controlled spares pricing: Establishment of a catalog of spares for the original equipment, at a pegged price list.

16. Incremental funding: The use of incremental funding restrictions is a means of program control without contractual recognition of the effects of such action. This type of funding management increases contract costs and necessitates schedule extensions.

17. Insurance: A cost risk based on the ASPR provisions requiring insurance coverage as directed by the contracting officer, at no cost to the government.

18. Cost principles: The use of ASPR, Section XV — Cost Principles results in disallowing many of the true costs of normal business. There are a number of fluid elements currently

---

FIGURE 28-2   Fixed price general contract flowdown provisions

---

1. Definitions	13. Assignment
2. Invoices	14. Bankruptcy
3. Shipment and storage	15. Responsibility for articles
4. Changes	16. Notice of labor disputes
5. Warranty	17. Precedence
6. Inspection	18. Waivers, etc.
7. Default	19. Release of information
8. Termination	20. Buyer or government property
9. Patent indemnity	21. Utilization of small business
10. Reproduction of technical data	concerns & labor surplus
11. Stop work order	area concerns
12. Applicable laws	22. Terms and conditions

General ASPR fixed price flowdown provisions

ASPR	Provision
—	Equal opportunity — Executive Order 11246.
—	Government inspection — Under inspection clause rights.
1-315(e)	Required source for jewel bearings (Apr. 1967).
1-372.2	Required source for aluminum ingot (Mar. 1966).
1-1208(a)	New material (Jan. 1965).
1-1208(d)	Government surplus (Jan. 1965).
6-104.5	Buy American Act (May 1964).
6-403	Communist areas (Oct. 1966).
6-605.2	Duty-free entry — Canadian supplies (June 1967).
7-103.13(a)	Renegotiation (Oct. 1959).
7-104.12	Military security requirements (Apr. 1966).
7-104.15	Examination of records (Feb. 1962).
7-104.18	Priorities, allocations, & allotments (Jan. 1961).
7-104.21	Limitation on withholding of Payments (Sept. 1958).
7-104.40	Competition in subcontracting (Apr. 1962).
7-104.41	Price adjustment and audit
7-104.42	Cost and pricing data
9-104	Notice and assistance regarding patent and Copyright infringement (Jan. 1965).
9-106	Filing of patent applications (Oct. 1966.)
9-107.5(b)	Patent rights (License) (Oct. 1966).
9-203	Rights in technical data (Feb. 1965)
9-207.2(a)	Technical data — Withholding of payment (Oct. 1966)
12-303	Contract Work Hours Standards Act — Overtime compensation (June 1964).
12-605	Walsh-Healey Public Contracts Act (Jan. 1958).
13-704	Special tooling (Oct. 1967)
13-705	Special test equipment (June 1965).
E-620	Interest (May 1963)

If the contract is for an amount in excess of $500,000 —

1-707.3(b)	Small Business subcontracting Program (June 1965).
1-805.3(b)	Labor Surplus Area Subcontracting Program (Nov. 1967).

under discussion, including cost attributable to socioeconomic requirements and related bid and proposal costs.

19. Restraint of competition: This is use of a clause by the government in prime contracts binding the prime contractor against including in his subcontracts any provision on the subcontractor to bid or supply directly to the government or others items which the prime contractor would procure from such subcontractors. This clause would be a flowdown provision for subcontractor application in turn. This provision would eliminate prime and/or subcontractor proprietary interest in the technical data, the applicable patent, or any tooling or facilities owned by the prime or subcontractor.

20. Over-reaching by some price contractors: This is a generic problem and can cover a multitude of actions. Much of what has been said to this point concerns the pervasive influence of the financial element. Particularly pertinent in this context are those items which come under the general heading of the claims of the subcontractor upon the prime. These may be brought about by changes, constructive or otherwise; terminations; warranties; and audit negotiations, and all their attendant administrative and court costs. The dollar magnitude of the differences existing between the subcontractor and his customer can make it financially impossible for the subcontractor to survive or even complete performance of his on-going subcontracts if he must await the outcome of litigation before receiving funds justly due him. In such cases the subcontractor may be totally dependent upon his customer's appreciation and support of such problems.

Prospects for small business

Much has been said about small business and the country's need for its entrepreneurial performance. Much support has been given to small business in the name of this objective. Small business is, by nature, intensely and ruggedly individualistic. It takes a definite Horatio Alger spirit to start a small business and considerable tenacity and skill to make it survive. Unfortunately, the weak and least successful are likely to cry the loudest; it is they who most often run to Congress for handouts and special treatment. Of course, certain complaints may be legitimate, but Congress may make the logical mistake of assuming that the weak ones typify the lot. And so the weak request tends to become law. Such laws can be considered "bad" when they are out of kilter with the free enterprise principles. As a matter of fact, small business itself actually is threatened by many of the cures proposed in its behalf.

Oddly enough, at least in the government contracting area, a review of the small business community reveals some curious things. A strategic industries association survey of 1,000 small business defense firms found that nearly all viewpoints were allied closely to the views of their counterparts in larger industry. Seventy percent said "no" to the idea of giving small firms a price advantage in competing for government work; 67 percent felt renegotiation had a negative influence on subcontracting; only one firm in four preferred advertised bidding; 70

percent said they would rather compete for a negotiated contract, which is concomitant with the belief that such competition can be relied upon to keep prices fair; small business abhors close government regulation, with 80 percent saying the less the better; and two out of three thought small companies were holding their own against large firms.

To a great extent, the fortunes of the small defense business must follow that of large business. As the contracts won by large business go up, so does the volume of outside procurements. When large business suffers a drop in volume, or a contract is terminated, the business of its subcontractors and suppliers declines. Just as large business has no guaranteed workload and must compete on both quality and price, so likewise small suppliers cannot expect guaranteed business.

Suggested additional aids to small business

In addition to the current support given small business through both government and large business efforts, what else might be done to aid small business? The following should be considered:

1. Simplifying and reducing government reports.

2. Strengthening the government's hand in preventing mergers when they trend toward monopolies.

3. Furthering means by which the advances in technology and management can be made available to small firms.

4. Providing appropriate legislation to protect both the public and contractors against catastrophic occurrences in connection with government programs, including the limiting of the extent of consequential damages.

5. Recognizing the regular modes of conducting business so that the actual costs of business presently arbitrarily disallowed may be recognized as proper costs of doing business with the government.

6. Giving proper protection to patent and proprietary interests when earned by the company.

7. Supporting the work of the Commission on Government Procurement as currently operating under P.L. 91-129.

8. Fostering establishment of an Ombudsman, who would be concerned with the many problems germane to this general field.

Conclusions

It is easy but inaccurate to think of national defense, space, and government procurement in terms of a relatively few big companies. We must depend on thousands of companies of smaller size but not lesser in importance or skill. Many have been birthplaces of brilliant new ideas, materials, and methods that vastly have improved the products procured by the government. There is a true need in the United States for the small firm — independent, imaginative, resourceful, willing to experiment, and not easily discouraged. They are a very real part of the American industrial system and a bulwark of our free economy. In view of the vital support required for the sophisticated products needed by the government, it is essential to divide the mission up among as many capable organizations as can make an economic contribution, whether they be large or small firms.

QUESTIONS

1. Since such contracts pose large risks, why bother? Why not adopt a policy of refusing to deal with the government?

PRICING

29

Pricing problems depend entirely upon the nature of the business. In many instances prices and policies are determined by a market. If there is a market price for what is sold, and industry trade practices dictate policies, then one has to find out what they are and act accordingly. The first step is to make a study of the industry and its competitive practices. Typically in an industry the middlemen demand a certain markup and there are certain traditional cash discounts and other practices that are observed. The new enterprise is usually well advised to go along with industry practices, to counter them creates one more hurdle to be cleared in making a sale. Find out how the industry prices its goods and act accordingly. However, pricing a unique product which has no direct competition poses some difficulties.

THE COST RULE OF THUMB

Granted that rules of thumb can be misleading, still there is one that is fairly useful in pricing goods. It has been found by experience that unless a consumer product can be sold at retail for *at least* five times its direct production cost, the chances for making a profit on it are rather slim. Notice the rule is *at least* five times; preferably it should be higher. One giftware manufacturer's representative stated that for many products he feels more comfortable if retail is six times cost. The drug industry frequently operates on a ten-times-cost formula. If these ratios seem high, bear in mind some economic facts of life. While there are some exceptions, more than half of the retail price goes to pay middlemen. Retailers want 40 to 50 percent of the retail price and the wholesalers want anywhere from 10 to 33 percent of the price to the retailer.

Here are the discount schedules for several industries. Products sold to the health food industry carry a 40-25 percent discount, 40 percent going to the health food dealer and 25 percent of the remaining 60 percent going to the wholesaler. Note how chain discounts work. You do not add them. An item retailing for $1 sold on a 40-25 percent discount nets the manufacturer 45¢ ($1 x .6 x .75 = $.45).

	$1.00	Retail Price
− .40 ($1.00)	.40	Retailer's Margin
	.60	Retailer's Cost & Wholesaler's Price
− .25 (.60)	.15	Wholesaler's Margin
	$.45	Wholesaler's Cost & Manufacturer's Price

In setting up distribution to supermarkets through a manufacturers' representative, a manufacturer of housewares quoted discounts of 50-10-10. The fifty percent went to the supermarket chain, the first ten percent went to cover the chain's wholesaling activity, and the second ten percent paid for the manufacturers' representative. A discount of 50-10-10 nets the manufacturer only 41 percent at the mill. Subtract from that a two percent cash discount and the mill net of a $1 item is 40¢. In most manufacturing operations, if the cost of goods sold is much over 50 percent of the manufacturer's sales there is not much left to pay for marketing and overhead and still leave any profit. So the product should not cost more than 20 percent of retail if the cost of goods sold is to be held within reason — retail is five times costs.

Very early in examining a new product idea, apply the price rule of thumb. If it will not bring at least five times actual production costs, the chances for its success are slim. There are exceptions. Sometimes in selling big ticket items where there are many dollars involved and perhaps channels of distribution are direct or do not require a large margin, then one can modify this rule of thumb. But be warned that one of the biggest reasons new enterprises fail is that they are unable to get a sufficiently high price for the product to meet costs. Moreover,

bear in mind that buying distribution is expensive. Many times to get started in a business one has to offer middlemen higher margins than otherwise to motivate them to take on the item or line.

For industrial products, situations differ so widely that no such guidelines can be put forth. How one prices depends upon the situation. How much marketing and overhead is needed in the deal? In some industrial selling situations marketing costs may be low while in others they may exceed the costs of distributing a consumer item.

PRICE STRATEGIES

There are two basic, opposing strategies in pricing a product, penetration and skim-the-cream.

A penetration price is one in which the seller places a relatively low price on the product in the hope that by doing so he will achieve the fastest possible penetration of the market. Such a policy is adopted for one of several reasons. First, the seller feels that if he can get into the market fast and solidify his position he will have a nice, long run market. Once a new product is in the stores it is difficult for competitors to dislodge it if it remains competitive. The seller does not want to charge a high price, thus slowing down his rate of market saturation. If competition is imminent a high price will attract competitors, thus placing great downward pressure on price while dividing the market among more producers. Unquestionably, a penetration price discourages the entry of competitors into a business. In establishing a penetration price the businessman must be confident of his costs; if he is in error, losses may bankrupt him before he perceives the problem and can rectify it.

A skim-the-cream price is set as high as the market will bear. The reasons are several. First, in the early stages of operations it may be wise to limit the demand for an item because production capabilities may be unable to handle the volume that would be sold at lower prices. Second, at the beginning the seller may not want to sell much product for he is not prepared to handle the business physically or financially. He may need to go slow. Third, a high price can help establish a certain value in the customer's mind; thus, when the price is lowered later, demand may prove far more elastic than if the price had originally been set at a lower figure. Moreover, the initial costs of starting up a business and the desire to make relatively large profits to finance expansion make the skim-the-cream price policy attractive. Additionally, if an error has been made in costs, the skin-the-cream price can cover the mistake without incurring losses, thus saving the business the embarrassment of suddenly having to increase price simply because they made some errors in their cost estimates.

The general principle is that one should first consider a skim-the-cream price unless there are definite reasons why the product itself can prove to have a long run demand and, if the higher price is charged, competitors will be attracted into the industry.

THE PRICE LIST

A price list is one of those necessary details that is too often neglected. It is a most important document, for it communicates critical information to potential customers. The key factor to remember in developing a price list is that it must be a completely self-explanatory document. The price list goes into the customer's files. When he wants to order a product he pulls it out. It should tell the whole story. The ideal price list contains the following information.

1. The name and address of the seller.

2. Product information. Preferably pictures or drawings of the product are included so that the buyer can know precisely what he is ordering, rather than merely "Model 604A."

3. Prices clearly stated. The buyer needs to know exactly how much it will cost him to buy the item. Do not ask the customer to do mathematical calculations by giving him a list price and quoting a long chain of discounts. He will likely make a mistake in his favor and you will have to write him to correct it. Tell the buyer how much it is going to cost him and, if applicable, how much profit he will make from the goods.

4. A discount schedule, if applicable. Think about quantity discounts carefully, for they are a valuable tool for stimulating sales. A well thought out quantity discount schedule should motivate the customer to buy more goods than he otherwise would. Few quantity discount schedules will make the customer buy more than he should; at least no good buyer will. But the seller wants to encourage the customer to buy as much

as possible, as much as he should, and not underbuy. There is a natural tendency for a customer to buy "hand-to-mouth" since it minimizes his investment in inventory and, to his way of thinking, his risks. A quantity discount should overcome these fears; make him pay for underbuying. However, there are many instances in which a quantity discount will have no effect on sales. A lawyer needs a typewriter; a lower price for a second one will not induce him to buy the unneeded machine.

The actual setting of the quantities at which the price breaks and how much the price break should be are most difficult decisions for which there are few rules upon which to rely. Some guidelines are given below which may help.

By law (the Robinson-Patman Act) the amount of discount offered for buying a larger quantity cannot exceed the savings realized by the firm from selling in that quantity. Not many new enterprisers worry about, or even know of, this limitation. It is not at all easy to determine such savings.

Minimize the number of price breaks. A large number of price categories usually confuses the customer and results in little motivation to buy more because little price advantage can be given for each one of many categories, a violation of the next principle.

Make each price reduction large enough that it is meaningful to the customer. Small differences will likely be ineffective.

Study the natural buying preferences of potential customers, then set breaking points a bit higher than the buyer's natural inclinations. If the breaking point is too much larger than what the buyer wants, he is not likely to take the bait.

Do not include a low price for an unrealistically large quantity because it discloses to aggressive buyers to what extent the price might be lowered, encouraging them to push for that price for whatever buying arrangements they want to make. Bear in mind that a quantity discount schedule may convey information about costs.

Discounts do not have to be in the form of money. They can be merchandise or other values. The idea is always to try to move merchandise. Try to avoid giving discounts in dollars. To cut price, offer free goods such as one item free with an order of ten rather than a 10 percent discount. Free goods cost less than dollar discounts.

There are many instances in which an initial stocking deal should be made to encourage a new customer, usually a retail dealer, to being in a complete stock of the product. Usually a stocking deal will include a display rack of some sort if that is appropriate for the item. Make it easy for the dealer. Offer him a package and make it worth his while to buy it.

Bear in mind that a price list is sales promotional material, so do not be bashful about putting sales information on it. One other thing about price lists, use the "kiss" principle again. Some businessmen make their price lists so complicated that only they can figure out what the price of an item is.

NEED FOR A PRICING SYSTEM

In certain types of businesses in which the seller does not offer a standard, on-the-shelf, product which has been previously priced, he must quote a price to the potential customer. Many times the quote is legally binding.

Several problems arise in such instances.

First, if the price proves to be in error, either too high or too low, unfortunate consequences result. If the price is too low, the firm loses money on the deal. If the price is too high, it is not likely to get the business.

Second, the time it takes to develop quotes can be excessive thus making the process too expensive if a large percentage of the quotes do not turn into firm orders. Yet the company must make quotes if it is to make sales. Thus some inexpensive way must be developed to quote prices.

Third, working up quotes is not the favorite activity of able men, yet if a talented person does not do the work great risks are created. An inept price quoter can lose the firm a great deal of money rather quickly. Many entrepreneurs feel so strongly about the importance of quoting prices that they will not delegate the task to others. It is just too important.

Thus some quick, accurate system should be developed by which quotes can be given. One swimming pool contractor developed a set of tables which could be used to quote a price. The salesman just looked up the type of pool, its square footage, added on the various nonstandard equipment wanted, and, presto, a price was developed within a matter of minutes.

A wire rack manufacturer developed a standard price per foot of wire used in the rack. He would figure up the wire in a rack then multiply by the standard price per foot to arrive at a final price quote.

A screen printer used a figure developed for the square inches of surface to be inked.

Notice that such pricing systems are far more prevalent in industrial selling in which the buyers have unique requirements which must be met.

QUOTING STRATEGY

Some businessmen quote a flat price for the item requested complete — a package price. However, this poses problems. Experience shows that buyers many times are uncertain of exactly what it is that they really want. They may not know a business or be aware of all the aspects of a product or service. They are uninformed buyers. Thus when they ask for *such and so*, they may not really want *such and so*; they may end up wanting *this and that*. One man quotes a price on *such and so* and his competitor quotes on *this and that*; the competitor gets the business because *this and that* is cheaper than *such and so*.

To avoid such non-equal comparisons, many firms break down price quotes into basic units showing the cost of each thing the customer is buying.

A customer asks a color printer for a price on a certain catalog sheet and is quoted $495 for 6,000 sheets. The printer gets the business and delivers the goods; the final bill — $695. It seemed that there were some charges for paste ups, art work, etc. That was the last time the buyer used that printer. That is not a recommended way to build up patronage. People do not like surprises in their bills. They feel tricked, cheated, and foolish when something like that is pulled on them. It is best to make all such costs clear right from the beginning so that there will be no surprises at the end.

In fact, one clever young businessman would deliberately over quote slightly so that he could render a final bill less than the one quoted.

Needless to say, his customers were pleasantly surprised and quite pleased when they received the bill. And to top it off, he was an auto mechanic. He built up a large, loyal clientele quickly.

Put a time limit on a price quote for several reasons. Costs increase so a quote cannot be left out indefinitely. Moreover, putting a time limit on it also puts some pressure on the buyer to act quickly.

There are legal aspects to a price quote. If the quote is not intended to be a firm offer to which one can be held legally responsible, take steps to make that clear. All terms should be clearly spelled out. Thus the price quote is nothing to be taken casually.

BIDDING

Bidding is a critical managerial skill in many industries particularly those selling to the construction markets, the governments, and to large industrial firms. Large buyers have a strong preference for letting contracts to the low bidders for they believe that it results in their getting the lowest prices. Perhaps so, perhaps not; it all depends upon the situation. However, bidding does create problems. The matter of quality can be a serious problem. The buyer must go to great lengths to specify the exact product he wants and specify the exact qualities it must have. This poses problems to the seller whose products do not match those specifications exactly. Indeed, one of the strategies of industrial salesmen in such fields is to get the buyer to write the specifications in such a way that either the salesman's product is the only one that meets the specifications or at least has an advantage over other bidders in some

way. There are also the sellers who quote low prices knowing full well that their products are inferior.

A major state university operated under rules that required all purchases to be made on an open bidding system. This included the development of films of the school's football games. One year a small concern underbid all other processors and was awarded the contract. It was an unhappy season for the coach. The firm ruined the films of the first four games before the coach could get through all the bureaucratic red tape to get rid of the processor. Of course, all bids say that the contract goes to the lowest *responsible* bidder, but how does the buyer discern whether or not the lowest bidder is responsible. It is not easy. Thus bidding attracts the attention of many fly-by-night concerns that hope to get into business, or keep their faltering business going, by getting a big contract with a low price hoping against hope that somehow the Lord will provide.

Smart businessmen do not like to compete in such a competitive setting. It is largely a waste of time and money. After all, it does cost money to prepare a bid; sometimes a great deal of money. The bidding costs for some government contracts run into the millions. A bid is a gamble, a wager of bid costs against potential profits from the contract.

One small electronics manufacturer would not bid on a contract unless he felt that there was a one-in-three chance of getting it. If the bidding for some government IFB (Invitation for Bid) was to be intense, he would refrain from the fray.

The really skillful entrepreneur tries to avoid all bidding. Some develop such skills and reputation that they are able to sell directly to the buyer without bidding, usually on a cost plus or negotiated basis.

Bidding is a risky business. *"Low bidders go broke"* is not idle saying. One middle aged man had been an estimator for construction jobs for 20 years for various concerns. He was a skillful engineer and had a great deal of experience. He decided to go into business for himself. To get his first contract, he was low bidder on a small job laying water pipe to a school in the mountains. It was not a big contract but one that would get him into business. Unfortunately, things did not go as he had planned them when making the bid. The weather proved to be unreasonably severe so his costs soared; he lost his shirt. The loss was far more than a matter of a few dollars; it was eating money for his family. Real hardships followed. The family broke up when it could not weather the storms. Low bidders have reason to worry. Did they overlook some costs? Will things go as planned?

One defense contractor had an interesting strategy. He would deliberately not be low bidder: "I know that at least three idiots will underbid me. One will do it from sheer stupidity, one from carelessness, and one from desperation. So I bid my price, then after the Department of Defense announces the award, I go to work contesting the action. I get the others disqualified as being not responsible. I win enough times that I stay in business. And I get the contracts at my price. The whole key to success is to get the business at your price. If you can't get your price, you don't want the business."

Good advice! There is no point to working for nothing. Walk away from unprofitable contracts.

COLLUSION

When competitors get together to agree on things, it is called collusion. It is usually illegal. Nevertheless, it happens. Bidding encourages collusion.

One large state university required bids for all its food buying. The trading area had two egg wholesalers from whom the university solicited bids each month. The bids were quoted as so many cents over or under the daily price on the Chicago Board of Trade. The two egg wholesalers saw no reason to get into an unprofitable fight over the university's business, so they agreed to submit the same bids each month. The business was then split between them. Both firms made good money.

Then there came the day when a new purchasing agent smelled collusion and demanded that they submit different bids or else he would ask for an investigation by the state's attorney general's office. So they agreed to do things a bit differently. One firm would submit the low bid one month and the other firm would be low bidder the next; they split the business again but in a way that would be more difficult to prosecute. The one thing they would not do is get into cutthroat competition over the university's egg business.

There is far more collusion among small businessmen than one would ever believe. Of course, there is no way of proving this statement officially. The basis for making it is from personal experience.

The merchants in a shopping mall agree in their leases not to conduct discount operations on the premises. (This is being challenged by the government at the present time.)

Various merchant associations get together to agree on a wide number of things, among which price is not an infrequent topic.

The ready mix concrete suppliers in one town were in collusion on their prices.

The reason for such collusions is easy to understand. In most instances, the small businessman views his market as inelastic; there is only so much volume that can be done in the territory and lowering price does not increase it sufficiently to offset the loss of margin. So the businessman feels very strongly that he must protect the price structure for the goods he sells. He knows price cutting quickly leads to losses. Thus the price cutter becomes a hated foe. One must understand the strong emotions underlying this matter for they are not to be taken lightly. The businessman's entire life and the welfare of his family are tied up in his business. If it goes under, he is ruined. His life is a shambles. The corporate bureaucrat can go on to another job with only some inconvenience if his firm fails, but not so with the small businessman. Indeed, some commit suicide when their business fails. It is a matter of great tragedy. Small wonder that small businessmen are so protective of their prices?

Thus the basic strategy of the adept small businessman is to gain control over the pricing of his wares. He does not want to quote prices or bid for contracts. He prefers to set his price, then get it. Whether or not he is able to do so depends upon his managerial acumen.

*****

What is the best selling price?

Victor A. Lennon†

Summary

In setting prices, the goal should be to maximize profit. Although some owner-managers feel that an increased sales volume is needed for increased profits, volume alone does not mean more profit. The ingredients of profit are costs, selling price, and the unit

†**Victor A. Lennon,** *Management Aids No. 193 for small manufacturers,* **Small Business Administration, 1968.**

sales volume. As in baking a cake, they must be in the proper proportions if the desired profit is to be obtained.

No one pricing formula will produce the greatest profit under all conditions. To price for maximum profit, the owner-manager must understand the different types of costs and how they behave. He also needs up-to-date knowledge of market conditions because the "right" selling price for a product under one set of market conditions may be the wrong price at another time.

The "best" price for a product is not necessarily the price that will sell the most units. Nor is it always the price that will bring in the greatest number of sales dollars. Rather the "best" price is one that will *maximize the profits* of the company.

The "best" selling price should be cost oriented and market oriented. It should be high enough to cover your costs and help you make a profit. It should also be low enough to attract customers and build sales volume.

A four layer cake

In determining the best selling price, think of price as being like a four layer cake. The four elements in your price are: (1) direct costs, (2) manufacturing overhead, (3) nonmanufacturing overhead, and (4) profit.

Direct costs are fairly easy to keep in mind. They are the cost of the material and the direct labor required to make a new product. You have these costs for the new product only when you make it.

On the other hand, even if you don't make the new product, you have manufacturing overhead such as janitor service, depreciation of machinery, and building repairs, which must be charged to old products. Similarly, nonmanufacturing overhead such as selling and administrative expenses (including your salary) must be charged to your old products.

Direct costing

The direct costing approach to pricing enables you to start with known figures when you determine the price for a new product. For example, suppose that you are considering a price for a new product whose direct costs — material and direct labor — are $3. Suppose further that you set the price at $5. The

difference ($5 minus $3 = $2) is "contribution." For each unit sold, $2 will be available to help absorb your manufacturing overhead and your non-manufacturing overhead and to contribute toward profit.

Price-volume relationship

Any price above $3 will make some contribution toward your overhead costs which *are already there* whether or not you bring the new product to market. The amount of contribution will depend on the *selling price* which you select and on the *number of units* that you sell at that price. Look for a few moments at the figures in the table on this page which illustrate this price-volume-contribution relationship.

In this example, the $4 selling price, assuming that you can sell 30,000 units, would be the "best price" for your product. However, if you could sell only 15,000 units at $4, the best price would be $5. The $5 selling price would bring in a $20,000 contribution against the $15,000 contribution from 15,000 units at $4.

With these facts in mind, you can use a market-oriented approach to set your selling price. Your aim is to determine the combination of selling price and unit volume which will provide the greatest contribution toward your manufacturing overhead, nonmanufacturing overhead, and *profit*.

Selling price	$5	$4	$4
Projected sales in units	10,000	30,000	15,000
Projected dollar sales	$50,000	$120,000	$60,000
Direct costs ($3 per unit)	$30,000	$90,000	$45,000
Contribution	$20,000	$30,000	$15,000

Complications

If you ran a nonmanufacturing company and could get as much of a product as you could sell, using the direct costing technique to determine your selling price would be fairly easy. Your success would depend on how well you could project unit sales volume at varying selling prices.

However, in a manufacturing company, various factors complicate the setting of a price. Usually, the quantity of a product that you can manufacture in a given time is limited. Also whether you ship directly to customers or manufacture for inventory has a bearing on your production and financial operation. Sometimes your production may be limited by manpower. Sometimes by equipment. Sometimes by the availability of raw materials. And sometimes by practices of your competition. You have to recognize such factors in order to maximize your profits.

The direct costing concept enables you to key your pricing formula to that particular resource — manpower, equipment, or material — which is in the shortest supply. The Gail Manufacturing Company[1] provides an example of doing it.

Establish contribution percentage

In order to use the direct costing approach, Mr. Gail had to establish a contribution percentage. He set it at 40 percent. From his past records, he determined that, over a 12-month period, a 40-percent contribution from each price would take care of his manufacturing overhead, his

[1] All names in this reading are disguised.

nonmanufacturing overhead, and profit. In arriving at this figure, he considered sales volume as well as his overhead costs.

Determining the contribution percentage is a *vital* step in using the direct costing approach to pricing. You should review your contribution percentage periodically to be sure that it covers *all* your overhead (including interest on money you may have borrowed for new machines or for building an inventory of finished products) and to be sure it provides for profit.

Mr. Gail's 40-percent contribution meant that his direct costs — material and indirect labor — would be 60 percent of the selling price (100 − 40 = 60). Here is an example of how he computed his minimum selling price:

Material	27¢
Direct labor	+10¢
	37¢

The 37 cents was 60 percent of the selling price which worked out to 62 cents (37 cents divided by 60 percent). The contribution was 25 cents (40 percent of selling price):

Selling price	62¢
Direct costs	−37¢
	25¢

In this approach, raw material is given the same importance as direct labor in determining the selling price.

Value of material

The value of the material used in manufacturing the product has a bearing on the contribution dollars that will accrue from each unit sold.

Suppose, in the example above, that the material costs are only 15 cents instead of 27 cents while the direct labor costs remain the same — 10 cents. Total direct costs would be 25 cents.

In order to get a maximum contribution of 40 percent — as Mr. Gail did — the direct costs must not exceed 60 percent of the selling price. To arrive at the selling price, divide the total direct cost by 60 percent (25 cents divided by .60). The selling price is 42 cents. With this new selling price, the contribution is 17 cents (42 cents minus 25 cents for direct costs).

The point to remember is that when the material costs are less, the contribution will be less. This is true even though the *same* amount of direct labor and the same amount of machine use is required to convert the raw material into the finished product.

Contribution-per-labor-hour

What happens if Mr. Gail is unable to man his equipment fully at all times? In order to *maximize* profits, he must realize the same dollar contribution per direct labor dollar, *regardless* of the cost of materials. To do this, Mr. Gail could use the "Contribution per Labor Hour" Formula for setting his selling prices.

In this formula, you determine a mark-on percentage to use on your direct labor costs. This mark-on will provide the required contribution as a percentage of selling price. For example, if direct labor is 10 cents and contribution is 25 cents, then contribution as a percentage of direct labor will be:

$$\frac{.25}{.10} = 250\%$$

The mark-on factor to use on direct labor costs is 250 percent of direct labor costs.

Now suppose that material cost is 15 cents and direct labor cost is 10 cents. The selling price would be 50 cents, figured as follows:

Material costs	15¢
Direct labor	+10¢
	25¢
Contribution	+25¢
Selling Price	=50¢

The "Contribution per Labor Hour" approach assures Mr. Gail a 25-cent contribution for each 10 cents of labor (250 percent) used to make a product regardless of the value of the raw material used.

Contribution-per-pound

If, and when, *raw materials* are in short supply and are the limiting factor, then the base to use is the dollar contribution-per-pound of material. This formula is similar to the one for contribution per labor hour. The difference is that you establish the contribution as a percentage of material cost rather than as a percentage of direct labor cost.

Contribution-per-machine-hour

Determining the contribution-per-machine-hour can be a more involved task than figuring the contribution-per-pound. If different products are made on the same machine, each may use a *different* amount of machine time. This fact means that the total output of a certain machine in a given time period may vary. As a consequence, the dollar contribution-per-machine-hour, which a company realizes, may vary from product to product. For example, products A, B, and C are made on the same machine and their contribution-per-machine-hour is:

$28.80 for product A
$26.00 for product B
$20.00 for product C

When machine capacity is the *limiting factor*, you can maximize profit by using dollar contribution-per-machine-hour when setting prices. When selling to customers, you should give priority to products which give the greatest dollar contribution-per-machine-hour. In the above example, your salesmen would push product A over products B and C.

To use this pricing approach means that you have to establish a base dollar contribution-per-machine-hour for each machine group. You do it by determining the total number of machine hours available in a given time period. You then relate these machine hours to the manufacturing and nonmanufacturing overhead to be absorbed in that period. For example:

Total machine hours
  available in 12 months = 5,000
Total manufacturing
  and nonmanufacturing
  overhead = $100,000
Contribution required
  per machine hour to
  cover manufacturing
  and nonmanufacturing
  overhead = $20^2

In this example, during periods when the company can sell the output of all of

^{2}$100,000 divided by 5,000 hours

its available machine hours, it must realize a return of $20 per machine hour in order to cover its manufacturing and nonmanufacturing overhead. When the full 5,000 hours are used, the $20 per-hour return will bring the company to its break-even point. When all of the company's available machine hours cannot be sold, its return-per-machine-hour must be more than $20.

Notice that in the above example, only the breakeven point is considered. There is no provision for profit. How do you build profit into this pricing formula?

Return-on-investment is a good approach. If the Gail Manufacturing Company, for example, has $300,000 invested and wants a 10-percent return, its profit before taxes would have to be $30,000. Mr. Gail can relate this profit goal to the machine-hour approach by dividing the $30,000 by 5,000 (the available machine hours). This means that he needs $6 per machine hour as a mark-up for profit.

Selling price for product C

Now suppose that Mr. Gail wants to use the contribution-per-machine-hour and profit-per-machine-hour approach to set a price for product C. For product C, the direct labor cost per unit is $1.80. Machine output (or units per hour) is 1.25, required contribution per machine hour is $20, and desired profit per machine hour is $6. The formula to set the unit selling price is shown at the top of the following page.

If Mr. Gail is to get a 10-percent return on his investment before taxes, the selling price must be $43.97.

But suppose competitive factors mean that Mr. Gail cannot sell product C at $43.97. In such case, he might:

Material cost	$21.37
Direct labor	1.80
Contribution per unit	16.00[3]
Price before profit	$39.17
Desired profit	4.80 ($6 × .80[3])
Desired selling price	$43.97

1. Not make product C if he can use the machine time to manufacture another product which will give his company its profit of 10 percent — provided, of course, that he has orders for the second product.

2. Reduce the selling price, if refusing orders for product C means that the machines will be idle. Any price greater than $39.17 will generate some profit which is better than no profit.

But suppose that $39.17 is also too high. Should Mr. Gail turn down all orders for product C at less than $39.17? Not necessarily. If he has no orders to run on the machines, he should accept orders for product C at less than $39.17 because $16 of that price are a contribution to his manufacturing and nonmanufacturing overhead. He has to pay these costs even when the machines are idle.

Keep in mind that the direct costing method of setting a price gives you flexibility. For example, Mr. Gail has to get $43.97 for product C in order to make his desired profit. But his price for that product can range from $23.17 to $43.97 (or higher, depending on market conditions).

Any price above $39.17 brings in some contribution toward profit. Mr. Gail can break even at $39.17. Any price between $39.17 and $23.17 brings in some contribution toward his overhead. And in a pinch, he can sell as low as $23.17 and recover his direct costs — material and direct labor.

However, Mr. Gail must use his flexibility with care. It takes only a few transactions at $23.17 (recovering only his direct costs) to keep him from maximizing his profits over a 12-months period.

QUESTIONS

1. In the first paragraph, Mr. Lennon states that the goal of pricing is to maximize profits. Is this always so? What might be some other goals the price maker seeks? What are some of the practical difficulties encountered in trying to set a price that will maximize profits?

Pricing and profits in small stores

Edward L. Anthony[†]

---

[3]Calculated as follows: With a machine output of 1.25 units per hour, .80 of a machine hour is needed to produce 1 unit; the required contribution per-machine-hour is $20; therefore, $20 × .80 = $16.

[†]**Edward L. Anthony,** *Chief, Management Methods Division, Small Business Administration, Washington, D.C.,* **1960.**

Summary

In small retailing operations, profits ordinarily depend on the proper price-volume combination. There is no single success-producing formula. Rather, price-setting decisions should be based on a combination of competition and experimentation — especially when you're dealing with distinctive merchandise of the specialty or shopping types. Three important aspects of price setting are: (1) whether or not to follow a one-price policy; (2) how to offset the lack of markup on promotional or leader merchandise with wider markups on other items; and (3) what policy to follow in regard to price lining. Once you have decided these overall considerations, you can concentrate on meeting price competition by doing better than the next fellow in such areas as service, specialization, and timing.

According to one popular theory, the key to success in a small retailing business is *volume*. "Yes," say some, "when you get your volume up, everything works out all right." Another common idea, however, holds that the vital factor is *margin*. "Remember," say supporters of this view, "price to hold up your margins on each item and the whole line will be in good shape."

Price-volume-profit relationships

Actually, there is no single success-producing factor. It is a combination of price and volume which tells the profit story. A few typical situations with illustrative figures will support that statement.

Three cases in point. Suppose, first, that you buy an item at $2.62½ net. You price it at $4.50 and sell 300 in the course of a given period of time. This gives you an income of $1,350 with cost of goods of $787.50 and a gross profit of $562.50 for the period.

Next, suppose you think that the item might move better with a lower ticket. Accordingly, you cut the price to $3.95. Volume over an equal period expands to 600 units and income rises to $2,370. Cost of goods still at $2.62½ net per unit, jumps to $1,575 and you earn a gross profit of $795 for the period. This is better than before, just as you had hoped.

Then finally, suppose you decide to push for the still greater volume and, therefore, cut your price to $3.79. Sales during a like period rise, but only to 675 units. Income goes up to $2,558.25 and cost of goods increases to $1,771.88. In this situation you end the period with a gross profit of $786.37. You did get an increase in volume, but you're worse off. In the second case your gross profit was the largest in terms of total dollars.

The conclusion to be drawn from these cases is that the best price was in the $3.95 range. The price-volume-profit relationship at that point yielded the most dollars at the end of the period. It isn't a question of price alone or volume alone; you have to consider both at once.

A word about expenses. "That's a good line of reasoning," some businessmen will say, "but what about expenses?" The answer to that question is that, here, they were left out of the calculations. In relation to any individual item in a store, most big retailing expenses are "fixed" in the short run. "Variable" expenses, like wrapping paper and string, are usually insignificant. But major expenses like rent, wages, and advertising would, in most cases, hardly be changed if a single item were added or dropped from stock. The exceptions are the situations where rent is based on a percentage of revenue, where salespeople get a percentage commission, or where both techniques are used together.

Unless you operate with such percentage arrangements, it is a highly complex job to estimate what expenses per item really add up to as volume changes. Therefore, when expenses are largely fixed in relation to a single item, it is usually good sense, in determining its price, to consider the effects of a price change on dollar gross margin. That's what was done above.

Watch the overall effects. Along this line, in making price decisions try to size up the broad implications and long-range effects. For instance, some retailers plan to enlarge their clientele by pricing one of their items so low that they only cover their costs. Other merchants plan to build prestige by pricing certain lines so high that they appeal only to a very special class of customer. While such policies may not yield the biggest profits at the moment, they are designed to do so over the long pull by the effect they have on the store's total trade.

There is wisdom also in watching the profits for your business *as a whole.* This means that some items you carry may not necessarily make a given profit percentage — or even a profit at all. But they will tend to build business. The principle of leaders rests on the fact that one of the best ways of attracting customers is to offer certain articles at exceptionally low prices. Shoppers coming in for the leaders are encouraged to purchase other merchandise in sufficient quantity to more than make up for the leaders' lack of margin. Salespeople, of course, must

concentrate on moving other goods besides just the leaders.

Unquestionably it is not always easy to apply the reasoning outlined by the price-volume-profit examples. In practice, it is hard to look ahead, as it were, to try to determine how many units of a given item would be sold at various prices. To find out, you have to experiment. But most small retailers, having hit on a price which produces a reasonable volume and profit, are hesitant to risk any further experimenting. Moreover, in many cases, the typical merchant is pretty much forced to keep his prices in line with those of competitors.

By and large, the nature of the item you are trying to price is the most important consideration. For example, a housewife normally will buy only as much salt as she needs whether the price is high or low. But as the price of electrical appliances drops off, more and more housewives tend to buy them. However, with standard, nationally advertised, widely used items, reductions by one seller will usually be met with similar price cuts by others.

In those cases, the important question becomes, "Which way would we all be better off — as things stand, or at a lower price level?" Many retailers will remember the answer when that question was posed some years ago in regard to phonograph records: when a general price reduction was tried it brought dramatically increased sales and profits to all. Obviously, of course, every situation can't be expected to follow that pattern.

"That's all very interesting," you may say, "but what does it mean to me as a small retailer?"

The answer is this: Your best bet for experimentation with price-volume-profit relationships is usually in the field of distinctive, or specialty and shopping goods, where you are the only seller of an item, or at least one of a very few.

The one-price policy

If you follow a one-price policy, you offer each item at a single fixed price to everybody who buys in the same quantity. You give no special prices to special people. To many merchants, single fixed prices are customary and logical. They are evidence of fair and equal treatment for all. Besides, haggling is time-consuming both for the salesperson and for the customer. However, conditions today make it necessary to consider carefully just where you stand on the one-price policy. Most small retailers believe in one price to all comers for a given article. But sometimes it is hard to stick to your guns when a customer says:

Your prices are out of line. I can go over the the "PDQ Sales Company" right now and for $12.95 get the very same item you're trying to sell me for $15. I'm ready to give you $12.95, cash on the barrelhead. I want the article and I'd like to do business with *you*. How about it?

Many small retailers under this kind of pressure would find it hard to refuse to shade their prices. Hence, it is essential to make up your mind in advance what kind of store you want to have. You can't have both a fixed and a flexible policy. You have to decide before you get into a bargaining situation whether or not you will mark down a line just on the basis of what a customer says. Some stores do. Others refuse to consider price changes until they have checked up on what competition is really doing. Many feel that over the years they would be better off if they were to compete on a broader

basis than just price. They believe that continuous price cutting would not yield an adequate return on the capital invested in the business. They claim that merchants who shade prices, even on only a few items, soon find that customers regard *all* prices merely as starting points for haggling.

The markup problem

The markup problem is an old story to small retailers. It is always important to pricing and to profits, but it can be handled in different ways.

Most small merchants find it preferable to handle markup and pricing largely on an individual basis. The reason is the many factors which influence the decision — factors which vary according to the goods involved. For example, some of these influences are what your competition is doing, how the item fits into your price-lining setup, the promotional or leader value of the item, the season of the year, and whether resale-price maintenance is exercised by the manufacturer.

However, even though most items are marked up individually, it *is* useful to obtain some average markup as the result of your overall operations. This means that you should try to balance slim margins on some items with wider margins on others so that the combined volume produced will maximize your total profit. You may need to carry some unprofitable items just because they regularly bring into your store customers who buy other things, too. With goods for which you are the exclusive dealer, or where you don't have much direct price competition, you may find that you can take a longer markup, still maintain volume, and thus add to profits.

Price lining

The term "price lining" has come up earlier in connection with markup. Essentially, it means setting prices on given classes or lines of merchandise and marking all items at one of these established prices — with nothing priced at points in between. It works because most customers have narrow ranges of prices which are acceptable to them. It offers both opportunities and problems.

Price lining opportunities. For example, there is a large group of men (and women buying gifts for men) who are willing to pay from $1.50 to $5 for a necktie. Within these limits, of course, the demands of this group vary. But if you set prices for an assortment of ties at $1.50, $2.50, $3.50, and $5 only, most members of the group would accept these four price lines as satisfactory. Other groups, of course might look for higher or lower lines.

Price lining is best suited to shopping goods; that is, to merchandise of which customers want to look at style, color, size, weight, material, and the like before they buy. It can work well with inexpensive gift items, clothing, and home furnishings in the popular price ranges.

There are various advantages to recommend price lining. For one thing it helps avoid confusion both on the part of the salesperson and on the part of the customer. Prices are simplified. There are seldom more than two or three prices to choose from. Often only a single price is feasible. For another thing, increased sales can result because of (1) bigger assortment in each price line, and (2) greater ease in getting customers to make decisions and buy.

In addition, inventory planning can be made easier by the demand groupings which develop at the relatively few selling prices. Similarly, price lining can lead to reduced expenses because of smaller stock requirements, greater turnover rates, fewer markdowns, quicker sales, and simplified buying and marking procedures.

Price lining problems. One drawback is the unsuitability of setting price lines on prestige items and high-style goods where price is a minor consideration. Thus, in the "real" jewelry market — as distinguished from novelty and "costume" jewelry — most customers are not looking for assortments in certain price brackets. Typically, they want one-of-a-kind items with particular characteristics. Likewise, with costly antiques, price lines seldom fit the usual buying psychology. Customers don't generally think in terms of: "What can I get for $50?" They start instead from an inquiry like: "Do you have any English sterling silver of the Queen Anne period?"

Another question is the difficulty of trading up because of the relatively big jumps between lines. For instance, you might set $9.95, $13.50, and $16.85 as prices. There may be some customers who would pay more than $9.95 but not so much as $13.50, or more than $13.50 but not up to $16.85. With only the three lines, you might lose chances to make, say, a $15-sale.

Another problem is inflexibility in a rising or falling market. For example, you might set one price line at $9.95 and a higher one at $13.50. Goods retailed in the first line might cost around $5.89 and those in the second around $8. A 10-percent rise in wholesale prices would bring the cost of your first line up to $6.48. To price it at $13.50 would be too high, competitively. But if the goods are marked at your lower price line ($9.95), your margin is only $3.47 compared with $4.06 previously obtained.

Meeting price competition

The question which numerous small retailers are asking today is, "How am I going to meet competition from the price cutters when I can't go down to their levels without losing money?"

One answer is: Do things better than the other fellow. What things? Here are 10 plus-values which help in reducing the effect of price competition:

Specialization. In some cases, distinctive merchandise and private brands will help to offset price competition. To many shoppers, the most significant feature of any price is the way it compares with other prices quoted for the same article. But if the article you sell has different features — and is, in fact, *not* identical with what your competitors sell — the significance of price comparisons can be reduced.

Personal salesmanship. The human element is important, too. This means doing a more effective job than your competition on personnel selection, training, and motivation.

Timing. Doing the right thing at the right time often isn't easy, but it is nevertheless important in meeting price competition. For instance, you can gain an advantage by following weather conditions and coordinating your advertising with them. Likewise, skillful timing of special sales can be a big asset. Good timing helps you avoid overstocking goods which were once popular but which are now meeting

increasing sales resistance. It also helps you capitalize on new merchandise coming into the market for which strong price competition has not yet developed.

Sensitivity to trends. Recent trends have had great influences on retailing; for example, interest in do-it-yourself activities, hi-fi radio and phonograph equipment, gardening, and amateur photography. Watching these trends and adapting operations to them has paid off in many small stores.

Prestige. Here again your objective is to do something the other fellow can't do. Partly, it is a matter of always seeking to improve the quality and appearance of the merchandise you stock; partly, it is a matter of working steadily to improve the impression your store makes on customers. Attractive display, topnotch maintenance, good lighting, and quiet selling conditions are also involved. And don't overlook the effect of your storefront and the "personality" of your advertising.

Services. Among the most effective means of combating price competition are such services as delivery, installment and repair work, and permitting returns and allowances.

Convenience. People are often willing to pay a little more when it is easy for them to shop. Nowadays, this often means parking facilities more than anything else. A handy place to leave the car is extremely important to most customers. In addition, you should not ignore the possible value of night openings.

Selling conditions. Worthwhile improvements can often be made in this area. Consider, for instance, extra emphasis on impulse selling, better point-of-sale displays, face lifting and streamlining of stores and shopping districts, and appropriate simplified selling techniques such as self-service and automatic merchandising.

Expense control. You may be able to find ways of managing your costs and expenses more skillfully so as to provide larger margins. Among the techniques to investigate are machine operations for record-keeping, better control of inventories, and new techniques for reducing losses from pilferage and damage.

Consumer and community relations. This is a combination of goodwill and customer loyalty, effective public relations, and the acceptance by the business of its proper responsibilities to the community in which it operates. The concept of rendering a useful service rather than simply making a profit is fundamental to improving consumer and community relations.

*****

Pricing arithmetic for small business managers

Jules E. Anderson
Earl C. Gassenheimer†

Summary

A recent study revealed that only 4 out of 155 leading industrial companies had written price policies. The survey also brought out that an understanding of pricing arithmetic is comparatively rare even among the best managed companies. Yet, pricing has a direct bearing on any company's success. Several important factors are involved in pricing arithmetic: (a) The profit-margin formula (P.M.); (b) standard costs; (c) replacement value in costing; (d) pricing for maximum profits; (e) effect of capacity on pricing decisions; and (f) pricing flexibility. This *Aid* discusses each of those factors.

The costs of operating a business may be considered in two major categories. In the first are costs related to your plant capacity, more commonly called "fixed" costs. Among them are rent, depreciation, salaries, research costs, and many others throughout all departments of the business.

Their characteristics are—

1. They vary with capacity changes (production, selling, and the like) but do not vary directly with day-to-day shifts in how many units you make or sell.

2. They are set mostly by management decisions as to how many dollars you will spend per period of time, and can be altered by your decision (property can be bought or sold, personnel hired or laid off, and so on).

3. They have only an indirect influence on product cost.

4. You can record and check them best in terms of total dollars spent in a given length of time.

In the second category are product costs, more commonly called "variable"

†Jules E. **Anderson** and Earl C. **Gassenheimer,** *Management Consultants, New York, N.Y. Small Business Administration,* **1961.**

costs. Production items such as raw materials, packaging, direct labor, and sales variables such as outgoing freight, commissions, and cash discounts are typical examples. They have the following characteristics:

1. They vary directly with the number of units you sell.

2. They apply directly to each individual product.

3. Market conditions influence them more than independent management decisions.

4. You can record and check them best in terms of dollars per unit of production, per dollar of sales, or per similar volume measurement.

Some costs, by management decision, can be either fixed or variable: Advertising costs may be appropriated as fixed dollars in a period, or as variable dollars figured as a percentage of sales volume. Some expenses require careful study to determine their specific category. However, simplicity may lead you to treat unimportant doubtfuls as fixed costs.

of profit-margin dollars which can be applied to overall fixed costs.

The profit-margin formula is a highly practical measuring tool because it gives you a basis for sound management decisions. It helps, for example, in deciding whether to make or to buy a part, to purchase additional machinery or to replace old equipment, to expand or contract capacity, to increase or decrease advertising outlays.

Here is a simple example. A businessman considers putting on new salesmen at a total monthly cost of $2,000. He also plans an increase in advertising of $5,000 per month. Based on recent experience, he estimates that these moves will increase his sales by at least 10 percent and, possibly, by as much as 50 percent. Currently, 5,000 units are being sold at a per-unit margin of $11.06. Thus he anticipates a dollar gain ranging between $5,530 (with a 500-unit increase), and $27,650 (with a 2,500-unit increase). All he needs to cover his gamble of $7,000 monthly is a sales increase of 12.66 percent (633 units x $11.06 = $7,000).

Profit-margin formula

The profit-margin formula (P.M.) of pricing takes into account cost, volume, and profit relationships. This formula distinguishes between variable and fixed costs. It uses only the variable element as the starting point in setting prices. The fixed element is accounted for separately as a part of general plant overhead. The profit margin is the difference between net sales revenue and the total variable costs of the products sold. The first pricing objective is to cover all the variable costs charged directly to the item. The second pricing objective is to produce, in addition, the largest possible number

Standard costs

It is not the purpose of this *Aid* to discuss standard costs in detail; there are textbooks and articles on this subject. Suffice it to say here, that soundly established standards are the gages for checking costs and expenses. Variances above or below a standard are the profits or losses of internal operations.

For example, suppose you use a certain liquid in your process. Over the last few years, you've paid an average of 52 cents per gallon. So you take that as the "standard" cost. Then you get a chance to pick up 1,000 gallons at 49 cents per gallon.

When you come to work out the effects of that purchase, you make a distinction. You still figure each gallon of liquid going into your product at the standard 52 cents. But you chalk up a profit of $30 ($0.03 per gallon saving on 1,000 gallons) for your purchasing operation. You'd keep right on using 52 cents as the basic cost per gallon of liquid when you put a price on the finished item.

Later, you might have to pay 55 cents for another 1,000 gallons of liquid. You would then account for the variation from standard by showing a $30 loss due to purchasing inefficiency. You would figure that for pricing purposes each item you made still cost the standard amount.

Having variances isolated in this way makes it easier to see where a good or poor job is being done. A "bad break" in buying should not be charged off as an added manufacturing cost.

Replacement value in costing

Replacement costs are often the most helpful ones to use in selling-price determination. In some industries, steadiness of raw material prices may reduce the day-to-day importance of this principle.

In rising market conditions, the cost of replacing inventories should have a strong influence on the pricing of finished products currently being sold. Even in a declining market, the replacement approach is important because companies may delude themselves by refusing sales which are below their "actual" cost. Unfortunately, the loss has already been incurred on the inventory itself and it may be urgently important to take some sales profit on the lowered inventory value before further declines occur.

In defining replacement cost, you should not necessarily tie it down to the basis of narrow market trading. Frequently, the most recent transactions are too small or too scattered to be a fair gage of replacement value. In such cases, replacement value may be *your* own considered judgment. In other words, it is a prediction, rather than an actuality. Thus, if the present price of a raw material is $9 per unit — but you think that competition will force the price down to $8.50 by the time of your next purchase — the replacement cost you should use in pricing is $8.50.

Pricing for maximum profits

The optimum selling price is one that will net the most dollars (after allowing for applicable selling costs) during the time the product is on the market. It depends in part on whether you have a short- or a long-run item. Also, it represents the profit-margin concept on the basis of standard replacement cost. For a case in point, see Table 29-1.

The effect of capacity on pricing

In the preceding situation, it was assumed that production capacity is 1,000 units, based on the fixed cost rate of $3,000. Consider now some additional arithmetic involved in arriving at a final conclusion.

First, you note that based on the assumption of a 1,000-unit capacity and of 800-unit sales at the optimum price of $15, you have idle capacity of 200 units. This represents an additional profit potential of 200 units at $6.60 per unit, or $1,320. It may be that you can earn part of this $1,320 by offering 200 units

TABLE 29-1

	Operating profit forecast at various selling prices			
Unit selling prices under consideration	$18.00	$16.00	$15.00	$14.00
Direct variable selling costs[1]	$1.08	$.96	$.90	$.84
Freight and delivery costs	$.50	$.50	$.50	$.50
Direct product variable replacement costs at standard	$7.00	$7.00	$7.00	$7.00
Total direct variable costs ...	$8.58	$8.46	$8.40	$8.34
Profit margin per unit	$9.42	$7.54	$6.60	$5.66
Estimate sales volume (units)	400	600	800	900
Total P.M. dollars	$3,768.00	$4,524.00	$5,280.00	$5,094.00
Fixed costs and expenses @ 100-percent capacity (1,000 units)	$3,000.00	$3,000.00	$3,000.00	$3,000.00
Operating profit	$768.00	$1,524.00	$2,280.00	$2,094.00

[1]Computed as a percentage of unit selling price as follows: sales commission, 3.5 percent; cash discount, 2 percent; provision for bad debts, 0.5 percent; total direct variable selling costs, 6 percent.

These estimates lead to the conclusion that $15 is the optimum selling price. Other considerations, such as a need for particular price lines, might call for a decision to set a price which would yield less profit. However, correct pricing arithmetic is essential in reaching a sound conclusion.

at a special price, or by giving special inducements to the sales force, or through additional advertising and sales promotion.

Second, you see if you can cut total fixed costs by economy in all operations. Remember, with that $15 price, only 80 percent of capacity is used; facilities for turning out 200 units will lie idle. Thus, if you can reduce any costs relating to this idle capacity, you should do so.

Third, you find out whether the firm could improve its total profit picture by reducing fixed costs to a capacity of only 600 units and selling at the $16 price.

For example, suppose you got rid of enough productive facilities to cut down to a 600-unit capacity. And suppose that by doing so you also eliminated at least $756 worth of fixed costs (heat, rent, maintenance, and the like). In that case, you could earn more profit by selling fewer units at a bigger price. Here is the arithmetic:

Total P.M. dollars:
  800 units at $15.00 equals----$5,280
  600 units at $16.00 equals---- 4,524

  Difference --------------------- 756

To go a step further, a reduction of, say, $1,000 in fixed costs would yield a profit advantage of $244. (Bear in mind, of course, that these are not the only considerations which enter into a decision to reduce capacity and sales.)

Flexibility for salesmen

Manufacturers who set prices and stick to them rigidly often miss worthwhile profit opportunities. Hence, the need for pricing flexibility under the profit-margin formula gives rise to "soft" and "firm" pricing policies. Pricing uniformity admittedly has many advantages. But pricing flexibility, properly and moderately employed, can create daily profit opportunities. While all pricing decisions must be carefully weighed against customers' and competitors' reactions and possible long-term effect, no such opportunity should be discarded without positive reasons.

When a company's sales order backlog is below what is required to operate at full capacity, soft pricing is needed. Conversely, the higher the sales order backlog, the firmer the policy. Soft pricing means: price concessions, special discounts and allowances, liberalized credit policy and terms, special drives and contests, and increased advertising and sales promotion.

In an actual example, the profit plan of a food-products company forecast a profit margin on sales to a certain large customer which made up 20 percent of its total forecast P.M. for the quarter. The offering price of the particular product was $2.20 per pound. The replacement cost was $2 with selling commission at 2 percent of sales price. A total of 50,000 pounds was offered at $2.20. The customer stated he would buy at $2.18. At $2.18, a P.M. of $6,800

would be earned after brokerage of $2,200. But in this instance — at the suggestion of the sales manager — the customer was offered a $2.16 price, if he would buy 100,000 pounds. The broker agreed to a 1½ percent commission. Result: a P.M. of $12,760 after paying the broker $3,240.

Increasing profits — a case history

The "Cassette Co." (name disguised), a small manufacturer of bedding products, had a production capacity of 15,000 units per month. During 4 months of the year, Cassette was able to sell its entire output. And for the remaining 8 months, its sales averaged 10,000 units monthly. Capacity months were profitable, but slack periods showed losses which made total early results unsatisfactory. As a result, management consultants were called in. They reviewed the company's operating forecast for the month of July which was set up as shown in Table 29-2.

The consultants worked out a standard-cost system, and recast the operating forecast using the margin-of-profit formula, based on 100 percent of capacity and on predicted sales. The results of this approach are shown in Table 29-3.

Market studies revealed greater volume potential at higher retail prices. Cassette's volume actually suffered because its low prices denoted an inferior product to the buying public. Analysis also showed that competitors with higher prices were spending considerably more in cooperative advertising and in retail sales incentives. Cassette, because of inadequate knowledge of costing and pricing principles, believed it could not offer greater advertising cooperation

TABLE 29-2

	Dollars	Percent
Sales revenue	400,000	100
Less discounts and allowances	8,000	2
Net sales	392,000	98
Cost of goods sold:		
Material 160,000	....	40
Direct labor 60,000	....	15
Manufacturing expenses 80,000	....	20
Total	300,000	75
Gross profit	92,000	23
Selling and advertising costs 60,000	....	15
General and administrative costs 40,000	....	10
Total	100,000	25
Operating loss	8,000	2

without losses. However, when the P.M. formula in pricing was introduced, the following actions based upon it were taken by management: The average sales price was increased from $40 to $48; the provision for advertising was increased from 3.5 percent of gross revenue to 5.0 percent; a more liberal credit policy was adopted (from past experience, no increase in bad-debt provision was felt necessary); and a special promotional fund of $25,000 was appropriated to be spent at the discretion of the sales manager.

A revised forecast for the month of July wasthen prepared. It is shown in Table 29-4 together with the actual operating results.

The Robinson-Patman Act

In addition to marketing factors, the legal aspects of pricing must be considered. No attempt will be made in this *Aid* to discuss the Robinson-Patman Act or other laws affecting pricing. However, controllers, marketing and other executives should not reject economically sound pricing policies because of legal uncertainty. This should be left to a legal expert. His advice should be sought on the attainment of pricing objectives which do not violate any laws or regulations.

TABLE 29-3:   Revised forecast (based on 100 percent capacity and on predicted sales)

	Profit potential at 100-percent capacity		Original sales forecast	
	Percent	Dollars	Percent	Dollars
Sales:				
Percent capacity	100.0	....	66.7	......
Units	.....	15,000	.....	10,000
Average selling price	.....	40	.....	40
Dollar revenue	100.0	600,000	100.0	400,000
Deductions:				
Discounts and allowances	2.0	......	.....	8,000
Sales commissions	4.0	......	.....	16,000
Provision for advertising	3.5	......	.....	14,000
Provision for bad debts	.5	......	.....	2,000
Total	10.0	60,000	10.0	40,000
Net realization	90.0	540,000	90.0	360,000

Direct costs of goods sold at standard:	Per unit				
Material	$16.00	40.0	240,000	40.0	160,000
Production labor	5.00	12.5	75,000	12.5	50,000
Variable expense	.75	1.9	11,250	1.9	7,500
Total		54.4	326,250	54.4	217,500
Profit margin		35.6	213,750	35.6	142,500
Fixed manufacturing expense		.....	82,500	.....	82,500
Expenses:					
Selling expenses		.....	30,000	.....	30,000
General and administrative expenses		.....	38,000	.....	38,000
Total		25.1	150,500	37.6	150,500
Operating profit or loss		10.5	63,250	−2.0	−8,000

TABLE 29-4   Operating statement and Comparson to Forecast

	Amounts	
	Forecast revised	Actual
Sales:		
Capacity (percent)	100	97.9
Units	15,000	14,680
Average selling price	$48	$45.64
Sales revenue	$720,000	$670,000
Deductions:		
Discounts and allowances	$14,400	$14,740
Sales commissions	28,800	31,490
Provision for advertising	36,000	28,810
Provision for bad debts	3,600	3,350
Total	$82,800	$78,390
Net realization	$637,200	$591,610
Cost of goods sold: (At standard):		$234,880
Material at $16 per unit	$240,000	75,102
Direct labor at $5 per unit	75,000	
Variable expenses at $0.75 per unit	11,250	12,918
Total	$326,250	$322,960
Profit margin	$310,950	$268,650
Unit P.M.	20.73	18.30
Fixed expenses:		
Manufacturing	$82,500	$81,800
Selling	30,000	30,000
Special promotion	25,000	23,000
General, administrative	38,000	38,600
Total	$175,500	$173,400
Operating profit	$135,450	$95,250
Breakeven sales:		
Units.............................	8,466	9,475
Sales revenue	$406,368	$432,439

[1] Analysis of net realization nonvolume variance:

Unfavorable variance due to price decline $34,640

Less: Sales Deductions: 11.5 percent 3,984

  Variance: Net 30.656

Unfavorable varience due to increase in sale deductions of 0.2 percent 1,340

Total unfavorable variance in net realization as above 31.996

Table 29-4 (Continued)

Percent to sales revenue		Variances	
Forecast	Actual	Favorable volume (F)	Unfavorable nonvolume (U)
.....	.....	......	....
.....	.....	320 U	....
.....	.....	......	2.36 U
100.0	100.0	$15,360 U	$34,640 U
2.0	2.2	$307 F	$647 U
4.0	4.7	614 F	3,304 U
5.0	4.3	768 F	6,422 F
0.5	0.5	77 F	173 F
11.5	11.7	$1,766 F	$2,644 F
80.5	18.3	$13,594 U	$31,966[1] U
33.3	35.0	$5,120 F	0
10.4	11.3	1,600 F	$1,702 U
1.6	1.9	240 F	1,908 U
45.3	48.2	$6,960 F	$3,670 U
43.2	40.1	$6,634 U	$35,666 U
.....	.....	....	2.43 U
11.4	12.2	....	$700 F
4.2	4.5	....	....
3.2	3.4	....	2,000 F
5.3	5.8	....	600 F
24.4	25.9	....	$2,100 F
18.8	14.2	$6,634 U	$33,566 U
.....	.....	1,009 U	....
.....	.....	$26,071 U	....

PROMOTION

30

To hear some people tell it, all one has to do is spend a lot of money on advertising and the demand will come rushing in. Nonsense! Probably in no other area of business is the entrepreneur so inadequately prepared as in the field of promotion. Advertising is a complicated field and a most expensive one. It would be impossible to cover the techniques of promotion here; it is a separate field of study. Rather, let us itemize some of the classic promotional mistakes that are made by the new enterpriser.

PREMATURE ADVERTISING

In their haste to get to market, many new enterprisers advertise their goods before they have enough distribution to satisfy the demand; thus the money is almost totally wasted. It is pointless to spend money to create demand, to get people to go to the store to ask for something, if the goods are not there. True, one can build a case for distribution-building promotion aimed at getting retailers to stock goods, but this can be expensive. While it is granted that some dealers are made susceptible to carrying a line if it has been nationally advertised, still a great deal of money is wasted on nationally advertising some product that is not available for sale. The coordination of promotional efforts with distribution is critical.

THE PARLAY THEORY

Parlay players die broke. In a parlay, the bettor wagers on an event, then takes all of his winnings and wagers them on the next event, then takes all of the winnings from that occurrence and wagers them again. Sooner or later he must lose if he does not stop the series. And it is usually sooner than later. Firms have been known to employ the same strategy. A small concern was established in Oklahoma City to market a line of chemical products designed to treat glass surfaces to make them more resistant to dirt. The firm had $80,000 to spend on advertising. It spent the entire amount on TV spots in Oklahoma City with the idea in mind that from the profits of the goods sold from that promotion the firm could advertise in other areas; they would parlay their profits. The only firm of which the author is aware that has used this strategy successfully was Hadacol in the early fifties in which Dudley Le Blanc parlayed all of his profits by plowing them back into more advertising, but he bailed out at the top for $8-million and left someone else holding the bag when the scheme collapsed.

In the Oklahoma City case, the concern lost all of its money. It had also made the mistake of advertising without having good distribution. But do not jump to the conclusion that was the reason for its failure. Even if it had distribution, the firm would have failed, for the ads were technically quite poor. It was amateur night.

AMATEUR NIGHT

The difference between a professionally developed advertising campaign and one prepared by amateurs or incompetents is the difference between night and day. Unfortunately, there are too many people who feel they are advertising experts. They shoot some film of the company president telling about the features of his product, the results of which are exceedingly painful to watch, and expect to sell millions. If the entrepreneur intends to spend much money on promotion, he should find someone who is proficient in the art to help him. Hire a professional. Amateurs lose a business' money. Then why don't new businessmen hire professionals? Money! They are expensive! Then what does the small businessman who cannot afford professional advertising services do for help? He must make an effort, and many times it takes much effort, to locate some individual with a flair for

advertising who will handle his promotional affairs on the side (moonlight) or perhaps a small agency may exist that is reasonable.

THE AGENCY STRUCTURE OF THE ADVERTISING INDUSTRY

The economic facts of life almost prohibit the new enterpriser from availing himself of professional talent in the advertising field. First, advertising agencies make their profits mainly from large scale advertising on television in which they can create one good spot advertisement and have it run nationwide for thousands of times, each time collecting a 15 percent commission on the time charges. In particular, there is no profit in such mundane advertising as direct mail, trade advertising, brochures, etc. Thus a great many agencies simply refuse to do business with any firm that does not spend more than a quarter of a million dollars on advertising a year. Even the new enterprise utilizing the services of a small one- or two-man agency can be expensive. It is easy to spend thousands of dollars in advertising and have little to show for it. The new enterpriser should be most careful about how he spends his advertising money.

Make no mistake about it, advertising, if done right, can be effective. New enterprises have been built on a particularly effective advertising campaign. An interesting twist which illustrates this point is the establishment and success of the 4 DAY TIRE STORES in Los Angeles. The chain was started and owned by an advertising agency that developed a unique advertising format. It is not uncommon for advertising experts to start businesses using their skills to promote them. A man in Seal Beach, California, made a great deal of money running the ad shown in Figure 30-1 which promoted his book on mail order advertising and direct mail selling.

There is no easy solution to the advertising problem. The entrepreneur will have to muddle through it on his own, depending upon his own knowledge of the field and what he can learn about it.

IGNORING THE IMPORTANT LITTLE THINGS

Too many businessmen ignore the promotional value of such things as letterheads, product tags, information booklets, sales literature, and signs in front of the establishment. In the total scheme of things, sales literature is the single most effective promotional material used. A good sales brochure can be very effective, but it is not easy to create one. Do not be surprised at the costs of preparing such brochures. If four-color printing is necessary, a brochure can run anywhere from 10¢ to 50¢, depending upon its size and the number needed. A good sales brochure can take the place of a salesman, giving a sales pitch and asking for the order.

PUBLICITY

A great deal of good exposure can be obtained for low cost by a good publicity program. The press, both public and trade, is hungry for news. Trade journals carry new product columns that feature a picture of the item along with a description of it. There are public relations concerns that are able to execute such programs if there is money to pay them.

Only rarely will one encounter an entrepreneur who is not an adequate salesman. Many are even great salesmen. They must be, for they are continually persuading people to do what they want them to do, customers to buy goods, employees to work hard and diligently, bankers to loan them

---

FIGURE 30-1: Ad run to promote book on mail order advertising

---

Advertisement

The Lazy Man's Way to Riches

'Most People Are Too Busy Earning a Living to Make Any Money'

© 1973 Joe Karbo 17105 South Pacific, Sunset Beach, Ca. 90742

Do we bring you back every 5,000 miles so we can sell you something more?

When you buy tires at 4day, we ask you to return to us every 4,000 to 6,000 miles for inspection, and free rotation if needed.

Some customers object to that.

It's a nuisance. Too hard to remember. They live too far away.

Or maybe they're suspicious that we want them to keep coming back so we can sell them additional things or services.

Other dealers don't require them to keep returning.

Well, we don't force anyone to come back either, for a free inspection or anything else. It's up to you.

We do, however, offer (except at cash & carry prices) a free minimum mileage guarantee on every tire we sell. We don't know of anybody else who does that.

You have to come back for inspection *only if you want to keep that minimum mileage guarantee in effect.*

The free inspection enables us to make sure your tires aren't underinflated or overinflated, or out of alignment, or wearing too fast because of some other mechanical problem.

Also it enables us to rotate the front and rear tires if needed.

Since we're the ones who have to make good if your tires are wearing too fast, obviously these inspections are for our protection.

But they're for your protection also.

When we guarantee a tire for a certain number of miles, we expect 99% of our customers to get several thousand more miles than our minimum. If the tire wears prematurely we lose, but you lose too, because you didn't get those additional miles, above and beyond the guarantee, that were coming to you.

What if you come in when we're very busy? Do you have to wait your turn for an inspection?

Usually not. We place a numbered cone on every car that enters.

If you're in for an inspection, say so immediately. On your cone we'll place a little tab saying, "Inspection Only."

The minute one of our men has a free moment, he'll bring his portable inflation equipment right to your car. He'll check the pressure in each tire and inspect the tread and sidewalls. If everything's ok you'll be on your way promptly.

Only if your tires require rotation must you wait your turn in numbered cone sequence. And then the extra wait is worth money to you.

Meanwhile, lower your guard. We won't try to sell you something else.

We do offer simple alignment in some of our stores. If you need alignment you can get it from us, or bring us a receipt from any qualified mechanic on your next inspection visit to keep your guarantee in force.

Other things and services we do not sell at 4day. No batteries, gasoline, brake relining, front end over-hauls, lube jobs, ball joints, mufflers, windshield wipers, sewing kits or chewing gum.

Keep your money in your pocket when you return for those inspections every 4,000 to 6,000 miles. These 4day service costs you nothing.

4day services

NXC means No Extra Charge, if retail invoice is presented, because included in original price.

5,000 mile inspection, & rotation if needed. (Up to $4 a car elsewhere.) If bought at 4day.....NXC If bought elsewhere or cash & carry, per tire............75c

Mounting. If bought here.....NXC If bought elsewhere or cash & carry at 4day
—on standard rims........$1.50
—on mag wheels, or commercial or hand mounted rims........$3
Flat repairs............$3 If tire bought at 4day.....NXC

Adjustment. If tire was bought at 4day........... no service charge If elsewhere or cash & carry....$2.50

Valve stem, rubber. (85c to $1.35 elsewhere.) Ours, EPDM ozone resistant.............75c

Valve stem, steel. ($1.50 to $2.25 elsewhere.)...........$1.50

Bubble balance. Weights NXC. ($1.50 to $2.50 elsewhere.).....$1.50
Dynamic balance. 2 plane. Weights NXC. Tire balanced off car. Schildmeier, Hofmann, Schenck Trebel. ($2.75 to $4 elsewhere.) If tire bought from 4day........$2.75 (If unsatisfactory, return within 2 weeks for correction or refund, at your option.)
—if tire bought elsewhere........$3
Mag wheel & commercial or hand mounted rims..........$4
—if tire bought elsewhere.....$4.50 (If adjusted at 10,000 miles or over, we charge for rebalancing.)

Alignment. At Irving Store only. Guaranteed 5,000 miles. (Average $13.95 elsewhere)$12.50

How big is an 80.7% increase?

Some of the things you read can be rather misleading.

For instance, the other day there was a big headline saying that Goodyear's quarterly earnings had jumped 80.7% in 1974 over the same quarter of 1973.

Sounds alarming, doesn't it?

Before you get elated (if you're a stockholder) or angry (if you're a consumer), let's take a careful look at the rest of that figure.

Their earnings went up from a little over 2½% in 1973 to a little over 4% in 1974. That's still quite moderate for a company that needs to attract the enormous amounts of capital required by a major tire manufacturer.

Price Elsewhere is based on average of dealers offering the same or comparable tires. Prices are checked frequently for accuracy.

Mighty low % of bad checks here

If you think we're extra careful about personal check identification, it's for your benefit.

In 1974 our bad check losses on our Texas stores totalled only 42½ cents for every $1,000 in sales. In our California stores they totalled only 31½ cents per $1,000.

And they'll end up even lower than that, because we follow up vigorously and still expect to collect a good % of what we're holding.

Some retailers allow for as much as $8 to $10 bad check loss per $1,000.

As price cutters, dedicated to underselling other tire dealers, we base our pricing on a loss factor of less than 50 cents per $1,000.

Last year we did pretty good. This year we intend to do even better.

	Sun	Mon	Tue	Wed	Thu	Fri	Sat
	Gone fishing	Gone fishing	Gone fishing	Open 9 to 8	Open 9 to 8	Open 9 to 8	Open 9 to 6

52-185

4day Tire Stores

Open only during 42 most efficient selling hours. We can sell at cut prices by developing maximum sales with 1-shift overhead.

RICHARDSON 640 South Central Expwy (Exit 24 on Southbound access road). 234-2424. Joe Higdon

OAK LAWN 7046 Oak Lawn (6 blocks E of Stemmons Freeway). 526-4001 Joe Crawford, Ron Thurman

OAK CLIFF 410 W Elmore adjacent to Enter Elmore from Zang Blvd. 943-5100. John Beyless, Jim Kerr.

WHITE ROCK 7347 Gaston Avenue (at E Grand & Garland Road). 328-5434. Nathan Hunsucker.

IRVING 713 N Belt Line Rd (1/2 mile S of Hwy 183 & New Irving Mall). 255-0564. Jack Wallace.

Supervisor: Bill Ewton.

Also 16 stores in California. Los Angeles, Beverly Hills, Whittier, Santa Ana, San Bernardino, San Diego, Chula Vista and San Jose.

Help us improve our service. If you see any irregularity or inform our owners promptly, Floyd Ewton or Bill Weems, 713 N Belt Line Rd, Irving, Texas 75062. Or, in Dallas area, phone collect 252-7581.

*Credit means Bank Americard or Master Charge. We offer 4% off for cash. The 4% difference on a 30 day charge is a 48% annual percentage rate. The deferred payment price is our cash price plus federal excise tax plus finance charge

†Note: No mileage guarantee on tires sold at our wholesale or unmounted cash & carry prices.

©1975 Lansdale & Carr

money, whatever. It will pay large dividends to master the art of persuasion.

A helluva way to learn salesmanship

Jim Lavenson†

"Keep your eyes and ears open and your mouth shut. Got it?"

"Yeah!" All we sales trainees shouted in unison to the inspirational words of the sales manager of the Pioneer Suspender Company. "And whatever your senior salesman asks you to do, you do it. Got that?"

"Yeah," we again answered, a little less enthusiastically.

"O.K., men, I'll see you in six weeks after your swing through your territories. And remember one more thing. Your senior salesman is your teacher, your judge, and your jury. Make it with him, and you'll make it with the company. Any complaints? Discuss them with him alone. Go over his head to me, and I'll consider it your resignation. So long and good luck"

---

†**Jim Lavenson,** *Management Review,* **August 1972, pp. 41-43, as condensed from** *Sales Management, the Marketing Magazine.*

Reprinted by permission from Sales Management, the Marketing Magazine. Copyright 1972.

I thought the whole thing was a bad dream. Actually, I didn't even work for Pioneer Suspender directly. I was a junior account executive with the advertising agency, and my boss thought it was a nifty idea for me to see the selling process first hand. The client agreed and quickly suggested I follow their regular sales training.

Well, I told myself, it's only six weeks and then I'll be back in the office telling other people what to do.

My senior salesman was Dick Dashiell, a natty, wax-mustached, wiry man in his early 50s. He'd been with Pioneer for 20 years and was a top producer. When we met, I immediately liked him.

He smiled graciously as he gave my hand a really firm shake. "Meet me downstairs at the back entrance of my apartment house at six tomorrow morning."

"Where do you live, Dick?" I asked, hiding my horror at the hour of rendezvous. "Find out," he said and left. That was my first clue that maybe he wasn't going to become my love object.

Sure enough, there was only one Richard Dashiell in the phone book and I arrived at the back entrance of his building about 6:03. He was waiting.

"Good morning, Dick," I said cheerfully, thinking we'd get off to a good start.

"You're late," was his only acknowledgement. He pointed to four large sample cases and got into the driver's seat of his car.

I looked at the sample cases, then at Dick, then at the trunk of the car, and suddenly I had the crazy impression that he wanted *me* to put them in the car.

"Do you want me to put these in the trunk?" I asked.

"I don't think they'll fit in with the motor," he replied as he started the engine. I put the cases in and climbed in the front seat beside him. Almost as if he changed his mind, he got out of the car and came around to the passenger side.

"You drive," he said, and we switched places.

"Where are we going?"

"Hutzler's in Baltimore."

"Where's that?" I asked, getting more and more nervous.

"Find it."

I retrieved a map from the glove compartment showing the route from our point of origin in Philadelphia to downtown Baltimore, and drove off. Some hours later I pulled up in front of Hutzler's. Dick didn't budge and I soon got the feeling that we were outsitting each other. He just stared straight ahead and seemed to redden around the neck. Finally he said, "Let me out."

In disbelief I got out of the car, walked around to the passenger side, and opened the door. He stepped out, said, "Thank you," and told me to meet him in the buyer's office.

I was tempted to just abandon the car in the middle of the street and take a train back to Philly. But I parked the car and went into Hutzler's to find Dick blithely discussing baseball with the buyer.

"I'd like to show you our new line, Howard," Dick said to the buyer.

"O.K., Dick, where is it?"

Dick turned to me. "Where is it, Lavenson?"

"In the trunk of the car," I answered brightly.

"Well, now, Jim, should we all go out and get into the trunk of the car, or do you think Howard might prefer to see the new line right here in his office?"

"There are four big bags, Dick," I pleaded.

"I know, I counted them," he responded, and turned the conversation back to baseball with Howard, the buyer.

More than slightly angry, I returned with the four bags, dropped them on the floor of the buyer's office, and pouted.

"Howard," Dick said, still not looking at me, "you can probably guess what's inside the sample cases. I don't think it's necessary for Jim to open them up and actually show you the merchandise, do you?"

By this time the disgustingly lazy and uncommunicative Dick Dashiell was getting to me. So without further prompting I displayed the merchandise, wrote the order, repacked the line, carried the cases back to the car, and drove around to the front of Hutzler's. I even got out and opened the door for him to get into the car.

By dinner time at the hotel I worked up enough courage to tell Dashiell just what I thought of his behavior.

"You've got a royalty complex," I told him. "You expect me to wait on you hand and foot and act like I enjoy it. I came on this trip to learn how to *sell*. Remember?"

"You're learning," Dick said smiling at me.

"Learning *what*?" I demanded. "All I've learned is how to treat you as if you were some kind of king who also happens to be an invalid."

"You're learning," Dick said slowly, "how to treat customers."

QUESTIONS

1. Do you agree with the philosophy put forth in the article?

Unfortunately, there is a scarcity of good material on advertising that is helpful to the small businessman. There is no answer for this problem here except to admonish the entrepreneur that much attention must be given this problem. It is something that will require considerable study and effort. Here are some materials published by the Small Business Administration on the problem.

Sales promotion pointers for small retailers

Bernard W. Smith†

Summary

Sales promotion is any special effort a retailer makes to improve his business and to hold on to his existing customers. In the broadest sense, it is anything he does to move goods and services out of his store. All business activity that is intended to influence sales, such as a retailer's putting an "Open for Business" sign in his window, can be considered sales promotion.

However, this Aid deals with some of the basic specifics of sales promotion. It discusses objectives the retailer should strive for and lists ways to help him in planning to achieve those objectives in his sales promotion.

†**Bernard W. Smith,** *Associate Professor of Retailing, New York University, School of Retailing, New York, N.Y. Small Marketers Aids,* **No. 60, Small Business Administration.**

Point one: Determine policy

The first step a retailer must take is to determine what type of sales promotion policy is best for him. He should decide what clearcut "image" he wants his store to convey to the customer. The face the store presents must be clear, recognizable, and pleasing to the customer. Some of the categories in which these images may be classified are:

Location	"At the Crossroads" "Opposite the Bus Terminal"
Economy	"The Bargain Store" "The Thrift Center"
Fashion	"First in Fashion" "The Smart Shop"
Assortment	"From Triple A to Triple E" "We have it or we will get it"
Quality	"Every Item Guaranteed" "Laboratory Tested"
Service	"The Friendly Store" "Delivery" "Your credit is good" "Exchange" "Fast Service" "Adjustment"

Establishing an image is important because it will influence everything you do in sales promotion. If, for example, you want to develop an image for exclusive fashions, your store must convey the feeling of smart fashion through its windows, wrapping, supplies, salespeople, decor, and advertising.

Surveys show that 70 percent of all customers have a store of "first choice" even though they shop in many stores. To get on a customer's first-choice list, your store must stand for something concrete in her mind.

Point two:
Analyze the market

To find out what image will be most acceptable to your customers, you should analyze the market. The market analysis that you need is comparatively simple — but essential. There are five major things you must know:

1. What are the characteristics, economic and social, of the customers to whom you will cater? How much do they earn? Kind of industry they work in? Are they blue-collar or white-collar workers? Are they members of the country club? What are their social interests?

2. Where do they come from? How do they come (walk or ride)? In what areas do they live? How do they live (type of homes)? Are there any topographic or other geographic limitations that will hinder shopping in your store?

3. What is the size of the market: population, size of family, age of residents? Relation of transients to permanent inhabitants?

4. What points of superiority does your store have to offset direct competition in its community?

5. What are the counterattractions of other shopping centers and their effect on your store? Which stores do customers like? Why?

Much of this information can be obtained from buying power indices, the chamber of commerce, or your local newspapers, as well as Government publications such as those of the Small Business Administration and the Department of Commerce. Talking to salesclerks and people in the community is also helpful.

Point three:
Decide what to promote.
The common denominator

A good concept of a retailer is one that defines him as the purchasing agent of his customers. It is your function to give the customer what she wants (or what you think the customer will want in the case of new items). The common denominator for all items to be promoted, therefore, must be *wanted merchandise*. In other words you must promote:

• *The right merchandise* — merchandise that is in good taste and that conforms to the customs of the community.

• *At the right price* — a price that your customers are able and willing to pay.

• *At the right time* — the time when your customers are ready to buy.

• *Of the right quality* — merchandise of a quality that is suitable for the function it is to perform.

• *In the right fashion* — the style that is in current demand.

• *In the right quantity* — in amounts sufficient to satisfy your customers' demands. The question "How long does it take to reorder?" is important here.

Each item must also reflect and help further your store's image in the customer's mind.

Point four:
Decide where to promote

Many promotional media are available to you. These can be divided into two major groups:

1. External advertising media — newspapers, shopping publications, direct mail, handbills, outdoor signs, radio, and television.

2. Internal advertising media — tear sheets, proofs, blowups of advertisements, handbills, manufacturers' literature, gift novelties, merchandise attachments such as tags and labels, catalogs, signs, posters, public address systems, floor and window displays, and telephoning.

The choice of media is dependent on many interrelated factors, such as the nature of the merchandise, the amount of merchandise available, the amount of money available, and the efficiency of the medium.

No hard and fast rule can be made. Each situation must be weighed by you as an individual retailer. For instance, if your store is in a small community, the newspaper can be a potent medium when it is the only one your customers see. On the other hand, if your community has no newspaper you may have to do your sales promotion through the medium of a bulletin board in the village square or by word of mouth. However, the choice of items suitable for a specific medium can be stated in general terms for all retailers.

Newspapers. First, items to be advertised in newspapers must have all the elements described above under "common denominator."

Second, the items must conform to the nature of the medium. A newspaper is purchased for the *news.* The item therefore should have *news value.* It may be news in fashion, news in price, news in utility, news in timeliness — that is, seasonal or special-occasion news in availability.

The newspaper is popular as an advertising medium with retailers because it has a low cost per reader, wide market coverage, family readership, quick public response, flexibility, and public acceptance.

The newspaper, like all media, has limitations. It offers you a ready-made circulation, which you accept or reject. Sometimes its circulation extends to areas so remote that readers from those neighborhoods are unlikely to come to your store. In the newspaper, as in several other indirect media, your advertisements are competing with those of other stores.

Other indirect media. There are other indirect media; that is, media that may reach wider audiences than the groups who are customers or prospective customers of the retailer. Examples of such media are signs, car cards, radio, television. You must pay a rate for space or time based on the medium's entire circulation, rather than on just the part of the circulation which reaches your customers.

Moreover, you must adjust the form of your advertising messages to the physical limitations and mechanical regulations prescribed by the medium employed. To overcome some of these limitations, many retailers turn to direct mail in place of or to supplement the indirect media.

Direct mail. This type of advertising offers you the opportunity to select not only the item but also the audience to which your message is directed. Here are the criteria for selecting an item for direct mail advertising:

First, the item must have the elements described above under "common denominator."

Second, the message must be personal, in the sense that the item presented must correspond to the needs and wants of the person receiving the message.

The success of a direct-mail campaign is dependent, therefore, on good mailing lists. The compilation of such lists takes time and effort, but it is worth it. Direct mail going to general lists or wrong lists can be very expensive.

Windows. Store windows are often referred to as "show windows." They constitute the face your store shows the public. The nature of the merchandise put into windows, more than anything else, should reflect the store's image. It must be merchandise that, in addition to fulfilling the requirements of the "common denominator," has eye appeal and *attention-getting qualities*, as well as being something you are proud to show off to your customers. To tell the customer the complete story, put a price sign on your merchandise.

Internal displays. (Permanent and Semipermanent). The qualifications for items to be used for internal display are the same as for show windows. Such displays have the added advantage of being useful as outposts for different sections of your store, and they lend themselves to coordinated displays of related items.

Point-of-purchase display. These displays are used (1) to highlight selling points of a fast-selling item, (2) to keep customers interested while they are waiting for a salesclerk, and (3) to help increase sales of a desired item, as is done with mass displays of current, wanted or advertised items.

The merchandise selected must help accomplish these aims. The display, therefore, must be clear as to the message it wishes to convey, attention getting, eye appealing, and self-explanatory.

Radio and television. You should remember a few fundamentals of two of the fastest-growing media in sales promotion — radio and television. In many cases, radio is used most effectively for promoting the store image. When it is used for merchandise selling, the item must be of such a nature that the customer can recognize and identify it by a word description.

Many have found that presenting this picture in an entertaining way, such as with a jingle or comic or dramatic presentation, is more effective than straight reporting. Of course, the item must have all the elements listed above under "common denominator."

Merchandise that is to be presented on television must meet the requirements for windows and radio. In addition, it must make possible good use of the element of movement.

The nature of the programs and their positions (time and relation to other popular programs) are important factors in securing an audience for your presentation. The research division of the local radio or television station can help you greatly in making this determination.

Public relations. It is the effort on the part of the retailer to develop a gracious personality or favorable image for his store and then to publicize this personality to his present and potential customers. This takes time and persistence. If you have your own image (see above) clearly in mind and consistently promote it, you will have made an impression on your audience.

The most common avenues used by retailers to accomplish this purpose, in addition to the regular channels of advertising described above, are (1) participation in community events; (2) special events away from the store — for instance, fashion shows; (3) exhibitions, demonstrations, and so on at the store; and (4) special customer services.

Point five:
Decide how much to
promote (budgeting)

There are many variables to be considered in determining the amount of money a store needs and can afford to spend on promotion. The right answer for your store may be wrong for another. The factors are:

• *Age of store.* A new store needs more promotion than one that is well established.

• *Policies of the store.* A women's shoestore needs more advertising than a pastry shop in a shopping center.

• *Size of store in relation to the size of the community.* In a large community, a small store needs more advertising.

• *Location of the store.* A neighborhood bookstore needs more advertising than an airport bookstore.

• *Size of the trading area.* A farm equipment dealer may need to advertise in several surrounding counties.

• *Competition.* Your store can fade away in the din of your competitors' heavy advertising.

As a starting point in deciding how much to spend, you may consult the figures supplied by trade associations or advisory services which report the average experiences of other retailers. Averages, however, lump together the experience of highly successful stores and those of stores having mediocre operations. They should be used with good judgment.

As the next step, you should estimate how much promotion you need and can afford. You can compare your past sales against your past promotional efforts to try to determine what kind of promotion pulls customers into your store.

Finally, you must determine when and what to promote, and allocate your

promotional money to the various media.

Point six:
Decide when to promote

A study of consumer buying habits will indicate that they follow a fixed pattern, with only fractional variations from year to year. For example, a monthly breakdown of department store sales shown by Federal Reserve reports (1957), shows a pattern that runs somewhat as follows:

Percent of year's sales		Percent of year's sales	
January	6.7	July	6.5
February	6.2	August	7.7
March	[1]7.3	September	8.0
April	[1]7.9	October	8.7
May	8.2	November	10.1
June	7.5	December	15.2

[1] Subject to larger variation because of differing dates of the Easter season.

The reason for this fluctuation in consumer demand is that consumer buying habits are related to:

1. Climatic factors.

2. Calendar factors (holidays and special dates such as Mother's Day, Baby Week).

3. Traditional factors (retail customs and traditions).

The first two are pretty well fixed. The third factor is subject to variation within a limited range. As an example, some stores will run February furniture sale in January (calling it a midwinter sale) if budgeting, competition and other business conditions warrant a change. The schedule on page 33 shows some of the most important events in each month. You should consider that climatic scheduling will differ in various sections of the country and should be modified to meet conditions in your region.

Also, your promotional plan should include special events that are characteristic of your store, community events such as Dollar Days or Pioneer Days, and those resulting from opportune purchases.

You can chart each month's plan on a sheet such as this:

Week date	Sales	Dollars for advertising	Window (items)	News- paper (items)	Mail (items)	Other (radio, T.V., and so on)
	Last year_____ This year_____	Last year_____ This year_____				
	Last year_____ This year_____	Last year_____ This year_____				
	Last year_____ This year_____	Last year_____ This year_____				
	Last year_____ This year_____	Last year_____ This year_____				
	Last year_____ This year_____	Last year_____ This year_____				

✳✳✳✳✳

Advertising for profit and prestige

D. Peter Bowles†

†D. Peter Bowles, Consultant, Atlanta, Ga. Formerly Advertising Manager, Revlon, Incorporated; Group Supervisor, McCann-Erickson, Incorporated. *Small Marketers Aids*, No. 56, Small Business Administration.

Summary

Advertising can be a sales aid and a prestige builder. Ideally, it should be both. Good ads can help create immediate profits and long-term consumer good will. But an advertising campaign should be the result of careful planning; haphazard ads will cost you money without adding to your profits or prestige.

It makes good sense to pay as much attention to what you're getting from your advertising dollar as to what you're getting from, say, your inventory-and-innovation dollar. You

Schedule of retail promotion events

Month	Climatic	Calendar	Traditional
Jan.	Clearance of winter merchandise; resort wear.	Inventory clearance.	White goods sales, drug sales.
Feb.	Advance showing of spring merchandise.	Lincoln's Birthday, Washington's Birthday, Valentine's Day, Boy Scout Week, Lent.*	Furniture, piece goods, housewares.
Mar.	Spring clothes.	Girl Scout Week, Easter gifts,* St. Patrick's Day.	Home furnishings.*
Apr.	Spring cleaning, garden supplies and outdoor furniture, fur storage.	Baseball season opening, Do-It-Yourself Week, Baby Week.	Spring Anniversary Sales.*
May	Spring clearance, summer sportswear, air conditioning.	Mother's Day, camp wear.	Bridal promotions.
June	Summer wear.	Graduation gifts, Father's Day, vacation needs, barbecue needs.	Housewares, drug sales.
July	Summer clearance.	4th of July, inventory clearance.	
Aug.	Advance showing of fall merchandise.	Back-to-school needs.	Furniture,* piece goods, fur sale, housewares.*
Sept.	Fall clothes.	Christmas layaway promotion, back to school.	China and glass, draperies and curtains.
Oct.	Fall clothes and accessories.	Columbus Day, Hallowe'en	Fall Anniversary Sale,* woolen piece goods.
Nov.	Fall clothes and accessories.	Election Day, Thanksgiving, Christmas opening, toys.	Linens, china, and glass.
Dec.	Winter clothes, resort wear.	Christmas gifts, evening wear.	

*Subject to variations.

can make your advertising successful by creating or supervising the creation of your ads with care; by pinpointing your public; by using the one medium or the combination of media best suited to your firm's purpose; and, finally, by selecting one product or sales claim and presenting it with force, clarity, and originality.

Advertising is often treated as a stepchild by small businessmen. Their opinion on the subject is typified by one owner-manager who recently expressed his views in this fashion:

Yes, I advertise. I place ads in a newspaper; sometimes I send out flyers, and occasionally I buy a few "spots" on radio — now and then even on TV. My ads tell people what I've got to sell. That's all there is to it, isn't it? There is no mystery to advertising.

Advertising is an art.   True, there's no mystery to advertising, but there is an art to it. Yet this fact is all too frequently overlooked by small business advertisers. Many of them, in fact, appear to spend their advertising dollar without much reflection. Blithely unaware of the need to spend it with much care, they seem to feel that any slap-dash, hurriedly-conceived ad will bring in customers and profits. This is a dangerous and expensive delusion.

You might protest: But I have lots of customers. They come in, and they buy. So, nothing much can be wrong with *my* ads.

Think again. How do you know that the right kind of ads might not attract *more* people to your store? How do you know that the right kind of ads might not attract customers with larger spending ability? How do you know that the right kind of ads might not sell those higher-priced, slower-moving items at a more rapid pace? You don't.

But profit alone should not be your sole motivation in advertising. There is the matter of what might be called "image building." Briefly, it means creating among customers and non-customers alike a favorable impression of your business. But more about this important point later. Right now let's turn to certain decisions you as owner-manager must make. They are decisions facing both the newcomer to advertising, and the man who intends to place his advertising efforts on a more "scientific" basis.

Advertising decisions

Before you advertise, you should make certain definite and vital decisions. But before you can make them with any degree of intelligence, you might review in your own mind a basic question: Why Advertise At All?

Why do you advertise?   You advertise to (1) let people know you're in business; (2) let them know what you're selling; (3) keep the firm's name before customers — actual and potential, and (4) make special offers on special occasions. And (you might as well face it) you advertise because your competitor advertises. Finally, if you use advertising with the broadest possible long-term aim in view, you advertise because you want to create a favorable image for your firm.

These are sound, practical reasons for advertising. But their conversion into an actual campaign must be preceded by equally sound and practical decisions on your part. These decisions are:

Decision one: Determine your use of funds.   No one but you knows how much you can afford to spend. And there is no easy answer to the question,

"How much should I spend?" But several sources can help you make the best possible determination in *your case*. They are: (1) your trade association and trade publication; (2) your business acquaintances who have had experience in advertising; (3) a professor of advertising in a college or university near you, and, finally, (4) your own judgment.

Whatever figure you arrive at, it should be one that will allow you to make your campaign effective. There is little point wasting money whispering if your competitors are shouting.

Decision two: Pinpoint your public. In your trading area, there are probably several advertising media: Radio, TV, newspapers, shopping guides. Use one or all of them, depending on your financial resources. But first, be sure you know what audience you want to reach through them: Women? Men *and* women? Teenagers? Young people? Older people? The upper income level only? The lower income level? The middle income level? Householders? Apartment dwellers? Farmers or city people?

Of course, chances are that you might want to reach several of these groups plus some other groups not mentioned here. But it is unlikely you'll want to reach *everybody* in the trading area. Of course, you are the best judge of what public or publics you do want to appeal to.

You are also the best judge of your merchandise (or service) and who the potential purchasers are. You know full well, for instance, that the modern furniture you carry appeals mostly to the younger set in the community. Your ads, then, might stress the "modern look" lines, luxuriousness — rather than simple comfort and convenience,

attributes that might appeal more to the older group.

Decision three: Select your sales claims. What do you want to sell? When possible, stress one claim (two at most) in your ad. Be specific: A claim such as "You can't beat our prices" is fine if you can substantiate it. Your ads, remember, will create an image (an impression) of your store beyond the immediate item or items you offer. If you want your store known for its high quality items, your ads should reflect this desire. But if you want to sell to a broader market, don't intimate that you carry luxury goods, and then strengthen that impression by leaving out prices. This is a sure way of putting your message across — in the wrong way.

Decision four: Judge your advertising media. This decision calls for study. You have a choice of several media through which to convey your message: Radio, TV, newspapers, shoppers' guides, flyers, car cards, and direct mail. What can each do for you? For instance, how much of an audience does the radio or TV station reach — and what type of audience? How about the newspaper? And how much will it cost you to reach that audience? Can you afford one or more of these media? And what about those flyers and car cards and direct mail? Will they be effective, and is the expense involved low enough to justify their use?

Compare and contrast the costs involved, and the audiences reached by each of the available media. Then make up your mind how to spend that valuable advertising dollar.

One way to waste money is to select the wrong medium — wrong, that is, for a particular advertiser. Few small stores, for example, are in a position to advertise in national or regional magazines. Few are likely to get a return from such advertising which would compensate them for the money spent. Another good way to waste funds is to advertise in the wrong local radio or TV show — wrong for a particular advertiser. Advertise your teen age apparel on a local disk jockey show known to broadcast pop music; not (generally speaking) on a classical music program.

But the type of show is not always the sole criterion of suitability. Sometimes *approach* counts. You sell (say) perfume. Is that an item to advertise during a boxing match? It *can* be. Make the copy read (particularly around Christmas): "Why not give the woman in your life a touch of Perfume X? She'll love that delightful fragrance . . ."

If you have the money to use several advertising media at one time, fine. If not, you have to make a decision based on facts and figures you have gathered: Which is the *one* medium which will do the most for *my* store?

This, too, is important: Whatever medium you finally select, advertise in it *consistently*. An ad now and then won't do much for you, unless it is intended to advertise a special, one-day sale for instance. If you can advertise only once a week, advertise on the day when your message will have the greatest impact. If Friday is the big shopping day in your community, you might advertise that day or the day before . . . every week. People thus will expect to see your ad, will even look for it. That's one way of building trade.

Creating the good ad

Ads — good ads — can be profit-and-prestige producers. But too few owner-managers pay sufficient

attention to their advertising and its preparation to let ads become as helpful to business as they should be. What are the objectives of a good ad?

Immediate aims:

1. Attract attention and arouse interest

2. Establish a major claim

3. Prove that claim with specific facts and figures

4. Sum up the sales argument

5. Attract the customer and motivate him to visit the store

6. Identify the store clearly and memorably.

Long-term aim: Create a favorable "image."

Getting the picture. To be specific: Think for a moment of how you may have been dealing with a supplier, largely by phone, occasionally in person in your office. What do you *really* know of him? You know his merchandise, you know that he delivers it on time. Apart from that — nothing.

Suppose, at the beginning of the business association, you wished you knew more about him. How could you have managed it? By going through his building, by talking with him in his office several times and over extended periods, by even talking to his employees. *Then* an image of his organization would have formed in your mind. You would feel more at ease dealing with him. And that image would come to mind whenever you thought of that particular supplier, perhaps just when the term *supplier* was mentioned in your presence.

Image of a business. Such a mental picture — if it is favorable — can be a great asset to a small business. But all your *potential* customers can't know you and your store on a personal basis. Most of them know very little — if indeed anything at all — about you. Even those people who already are your customers, may drop in only occasionally to buy an item or just look around. In this situation, advertising can be used to fill the gap in personal acquaintance.

Advertising, properly used, can help you build up in a potential customer's mind the *right* image of your firm. He will get a good feeling. As a result of that good feeling, he will think about your store each time he is about to make a purchase of an item which you carry. That's the objective of image creation . . . one aim of advertising.

How advertisers go astray

Is there one single, simple way of creating sales and a positive image through an advertisement? Unhappily not. Many ingredients go into a good ad, the most important of which will be discussed later. First a look at some "trouble-makers."

The busy, busy ad. It "spills ink." This advertiser, anxious to get his money's worth, has filled up every available inch of white space. (Or, on the radio, he has jammed in too many words.) The result? Confusion — not communication.

The who-sells-it ad. It tells all about merchandise sold, prices charged, store hours, parking facilities. But where is all this available? This advertiser seems to believe that his name and address are non-essential.

The come-and-see-us ad. It is like an invitation to a masked ball. You can't tell what you're going to see if you go. Its message: "We are friendly, nice people. So why not drop in?" This advertiser seems to believe his ad is irresistible, that it will lure people in as if by magic.

Ingredients of a good ad

What are the ingredients of a good ad? This *Aid* can't be all-inclusive, but here are some of the musts of a selling, favorable-image-creating ad (more details on this subject can be found in "Individuality in Retail Advertising," in *Small Marketers Aids: Annual No. 2.* available from the Superintendent of Documents, Washington, D.C. 20402, for 40 cents).

Originality. Special type faces, unusual headlines, a catchy slogan, a unique approach to copy in print and on the air: Use them — but don't overdo them.

Simplicity. Stress *one* item, *one* sales claim, *one* point. Couple simplicity with clarity and meaning.

Strength. Make a definite claim. Be positive, be forceful, be direct. Hedging shows lack of conviction, can cause loss of customer confidence.

Believability. Sell your wares hard, but don't oversell them. Extravagant claims may work once, often boomerang later. Consumers have a good memory for a bad deal.

Quality. Let your ad create a good image. Your ad, after all, can tell a lot about you — and your business.

Restraint: Use as much space (or air time) as you need to tell your story — and no more. Give the reader-listener the information he needs to make an intelligent appraisal of your store, but don't drown him in a sea of words or pictures.

Building an ad

How do you go about fixing up an ad that will include those ingredients? To tell others about yourself, you have to know something about yourself. So it is with a business advertisement.

Composing the text. Before putting anything on paper, you should:

1. Take a fresh look at your firm

2. Find the one or two key points you want to communicate

3. Present these points in a concise, dramatic, clear-cut way

4. Be certain that the message does three things:

> States quickly in the headline, opening line or paragraph of body copy what you're about to say;
> Then gives the basic details, and
> Ends by summarizing what's been said. This method is particularly vital for radio or TV, where the listener cannot refer back to the ad

5. Look for non-essentials and, if you find any, cut them out.

Illustrating the ad. Use any device that will drive home your message. If a picture will help, use it. Good, appropriate illustrations can strengthen an ad's appeal; and they can convey information, too. Funds permitting, don't use a static picture of, say, a toaster if, instead, you can show a girl using one. It won't be any news to you, but the latter picture will "flag" more readers than the former.

Judging results

When an expensive item is bought in your organization, you size up the value of that item before you reorder. Do the same with your advertising.

Some people love to criticize any advertisement they see. So, discount casual remarks which disparage your advertising program and don't be discouraged by them. Don't, furthermore, as a result of such criticism hastily decide that there is something wrong with your advertising methods.

Guides for judgment. Instead, be guided by actual customer behavior. Ask "first-time" customers what made them come to you. You may find, of course, that many came in because they liked a certain item they saw in the window. But some, without doubt, will have been attracted by your ad. By asking them, you will not only gather some interesting and valuable information, you will also (provided you phrase your questions well) make a friend; customers like to feel they aren't just faceless people to the store owner and personnel.

Ask your steady trade, too, if they have seen your latest ad; and did it lead them to come in to buy a certain item you offered in it. If practical, you might also put special offer coupons in your ads. But don't hope for too much if you do: a 5-to-10 percent response spells success.

But whatever you do, refrain from quick revisions of your advertising campaign just because a few negative voices are heard from. Wait for long-term results.

The *trend* in advertising results is the important point. Therefore, it usually pays to keep on experimenting with ways of improving an advertising program.

Sources of help. You may get some useful ideas for your ads from suppliers, trade associations, and trade publications. Your newspaper and radio station can also give you aid and counsel. You may want to hire the services of a local advertising agency. This may not always be easy: A good many such agencies are not set up to handle relatively small accounts. But it may be worthwhile nonetheless for you to talk to agencies in your area. Should you find one that will take you on (and one which you can afford to hire), its personnel can take much of the detail work and most of the ad execution off your hands. But be sure that you and your agency agree from the beginning on the purpose of your campaign. (In this connection, you may want to refer to "How Advertising Agencies Help Small Business" in *Management Aids for Small Business: Annual No. 2*, available from the Superintendent of Documents, Washington, D.C. 20402, for 55 cents.

Summing it up. The *right* type of advertising, pursued with taste, vigor, and imagination, can bind more closely the ties with your customers, attract new trade, establish your business firmly in the minds of the public. It can build a positive image of your business for the future while building current profits. This double-barrelled effect is hard to beat — and your competition will find it so.

For further information

Readers who wish to explore further the subject of advertising may be interested in the references indicated below. This list is brief and selective. However, no slight is intended toward authors whose works are not included.

"Promotion Policies and Techniques" *Stores*. May 1959. National Retail Merchants Association, 100 W. 31st Street, New York 1, New York. $6 per year; 65 cents per copy.

Successful Store Advertising, by Kenneth Collins. Fairchild Publications, Inc., 7 East 12th Street, New York 3, N.Y. 1959 $1.75

"Effective Advertising for Small Retailers" in *Small Marketers Aids, Annual No. 1*. 1959. 45 cents. Small Business Administration. Available from the Superintendent of Documents, Washington, D.C. 20402.

Newspaper Advertising for the Small Retailer, by Isabelle M. Zimmerly. Business Management Service Bulletin No. 851. 1954. 85 cents. University of Illinois, College of Commerce and Business Administration, Urbana, Ill.

VI

CONTROL

Control is perhaps the most difficult aspect of business for the entrepreneur to master, yet it is one of the earmarks of a well-run enterprise. Without adequate controls, the venture will most assuredly encounter difficulty. The wise entrepreneur takes care to institute adequate controls over his operations.

CONTROLLING
THE ENTERPRISE

31

It seems to be inherent in the basic personality of entrepreneurs that they not only detest the philosophy of control and accounting systems, but sometimes go out of their way to avoid learning much about them. They can be quite contemptuous of such important matters. While one might understand this feeling, still in our system such an attitude is not only foolhardy but also hazardous to one's continued personal freedom of movement. Many enterprises have floundered because the manager failed to institute a good control system that disclosed the things he must know, such as: How much does it cost to make the product? How much money will we need to bring in this month to meet our obligations? Are we making any money? Should we make or buy a product? What do we owe? Who owes us what? A good accounting system is needed and the entrepreneur had best grit his teeth and get with it, or he most assuredly is headed for a great deal of trouble.

The graduate students at Southern Methodist University's Business Clinic accept many assignments from the Small Business Administration to go to

the aid of some small enterprise that is floundering in the hope that some way can be found to save the venture. By far, the most common problem encountered is the entrepreneur who says, "I need some help with my books." Then the student has thrust into his hands a brown paper sack crammed with receipts, cancelled checks, and a half-eaten sandwich or two. In one such case, a plumbing contractor in Dallas, Texas not only did not have anything even closely resembling a set of books, but he also had not even filed an income tax return for the past three years. His personal expenses were mixed with the business expenditures in such a way that separation of them was a hopeless task. And to top it off this plumber was asking a bank to lend him more money. It would be comforting to say that this was an exception. It is not! Such entrepreneurs are in continual trouble and cannot grow and prosper for they keep getting deeper and deeper into trouble as they pay a frightful price for their financial mismanagement.

Initially, small enterprises are usually best advised to hire the services of a public accounting firm to set up the system, take care of their books, and handle all the paperwork that must be done for the governments. Notice it was said a "public" accounting firm. That does not preclude the use of a CPA if one can be found who is interested in your business and who also is reasonable. Unfortunately, there is a big difference between CPAs and public accountants, both in their prices and their skills. CPAs are not cheap. It is difficult to find one who will work for less than $25 an hour and sometimes the costs are more than $50 an hour. For some reason, the hours it takes to do the work are usually far more than one expects. Thus, the fixed monthly fee services many public accountants offer are attractive. One average-sized restaurant had all of its accounting and tax work done for $70 a month by a public accounting firm whose system was computerized. Each month the manager would get a computer print-out of the restaurant's performance. It would be impossible to hire a full-time accountant for less than $1,000 a month, so it is sensible to farm out the work until the size of the business is sufficiently large to justify hiring a full-time, in-house accountant.

GOOD RECORD KEEPING BEGINS WHEN YOU START THE BUSINESS

Rather interestingly on the other side, when one studies the history of highly successful enterprises, he will usually find someone in the organization who installed an excellent information system (records) early in the firm's existence. The history of the J. C. Penney Company is a case in point. J. C. Penney in his autobiography, *The Man with a Thousand Partners*, attributes much of his success to Mr. George H.

Bushnell who was responsible for developing a detailed inventory control system. Right from the start it was apparent that Mr. Penney was most concerned about accurate and timely records.

When I moved my headquarters from Kemmerer to Salt Lake City I had in mind not only centralized buying, but also centralized bookkeeping, accounting, and finance, for the stores in which I had a financial interest to begin with, but ultimately for all the stores. None of us who had developed the business up to that time had any experience in modern accounting. I knew how to strike a trial balance, to make a statement, and to keep track of my bank accounts, but my bookkeeping knowledge was limited to the elements of single entry. I always knew where I was at, by and large, but I had no means of keeping tab on the transactions of all my stores. There was no one point where I could put my hand on everything that I found it convenient to know. I wanted a system of accounting that would give me a consolidated picture of the business as a whole, as well as a current analysis that would show the strength and weaknesses of individual store management.[1]

One cannot help but be impressed with the importance of an excellent system of records if he will study the operating systems of leading successful firms in our economy.

PURPOSE OF RECORDS

The accounting system serves five main masters: management, Internal Revenue Service, the financial community, the owners, and other governmental agencies.

[1]J. C. Penney as told to Robert W. Bruere, *The Man with a Thousand Partners*, (New York: Harper, 1931) p. 89.

MANAGEMENT

Management needs information in order to guide operations intelligently. What sections of the business are making money? Which operations are losing propositions? What does it cost to do certain things? What does each product cost to make? What does it cost to sell the output? There is no end to such questions that an alert management continually asks itself. Without a good flow of information it must resort to guesses in order to answer them. It is difficult to manage a business properly without good records, records that provide accurate information about what is under study at the time it is being studied.

INTERNAL REVENUE SERVICE

The law of the land dictates that every business must maintain an adequate set of records with which its tax liability can be accurately assessed. The entrepreneur who neglects or who fails to keep an adequate set of records flirts with jail. Most assuredly, few things aggravate a tax man more or quicker than to encounter the person who treats lightly this aspect of business operations. Those who somehow see humor in handing a shoe box full of receipts and cancelled checks to the inquiring tax agent will not likely appreciate their audience's reception. Bear in mind that the tax people can arbitrarily assess a high tax and then let you try to prove in court that it is incorrect. Without records, you are not likely to enjoy your day in court.

OR TO PUT IT MORE BLUNTLY, WITHOUT AN EXCELLENT SET OF RECORDS THE TAX PEOPLE WILL CRUCIFY YOU.

Become knowledgeable about income taxes. Do not rely solely on other people for advice on income tax matters, for that will be of little protection to you in the event of trouble with the IRS. Ignorance of the law is no excuse! Moreover, it pays big dividends to understand in explicit detail what is deductible and what is not, and how to arrange your business affairs to minimize your tax burden. In the matter of tax administration, substance appears to be of little consequence and form a great deal. You may spend money on some perfectly legitimate business expense, yet if you call it one thing you may lose the deduction while if you call it something else it is deductible. It is important to master the jargon of the tax man so he can be best accommodated. The time you spend studying income taxes will pay you big dividends, for in business today income tax considerations are critical factors in most decisions.

Bear in mind at all times that sooner or later (and it is usually sooner) you will be audited by the IRS. The time to worry about such audits is during the tax year and when preparing the tax return. It is too late to do much about your plight when the tax man knocks at your door. Conduct your business and keep your records in such a way that audits are routine affairs.

THE FINANCIAL COMMUNITY

If the business requires funds from outside sources, banks, venture capitalists, or investors, rest assured that excellent financial records must be made available for their study. Few things will chase a potential investor away from a deal quicker than to see that the operation's manager has a disdain for accounting and control mechanisms. They know this signals trouble. It is the mark of an inept businessman.

OWNERS

While in most small enterprises management and ownership are identical, still they are separate functions. While management wants information in order to make better managerial decisions, owners want information to know how well management is doing with their money. Without good accurate records owners have a difficult time determining how well the enterprise is faring.

OTHER GOVERNMENTAL AGENCIES

If the firm has sold stock to the public, various state and federal regulatory agencies demand that detailed and timely financial reports be filed lest the wrath of the law come down on the offending company. This aspect of financial records is growing increasingly important each year and cannot be ignored or minimized. These people are not kidding!

DO IT NOW

An accounting system relies on original documents. If one has the original documents, he can reconstruct and do his accounting at a later time. The entrepreneur is sorely tempted to become a paper collector. He allows invoices, receipts, checks, and other papers containing details of his transactions to accumulate with the idea that he will sit down "when he has the time" to catch up on his bookkeeping.

Don't do it! Typically, the mess one encounters when he "finds time" is so frightening that he is likely to postpone it further. Finally the time comes when he cannot remember the transactions and the papers are not self-explanatory or they get lost or whatever. Accounting is something that must be kept up to date. The businessman who writes checks without keeping an accurate running balance of his bank account will inevitably jeopardize his relationships at the bank, as he will be habitually overdrawn. The wise businessman makes certain that he keeps up with his paperwork daily — repeat: *daily*. If he does not, he will forget too many things, largely to his detriment. Such matters as spending some money on this or that and failing to record it are costly.

KEEPING A DIARY

One of the most valuable and money-saving documents the businessman can create is a daily diary recording his cash expenditures and providing a careful list of the business dealings and meetings of the day. The human memory is such that it simply cannot recall the details of who was seen where or when, and what was talked about even a few days afterward. Yet that is information the IRS demands to know when examining the tax status of a transaction two or three years later. Get in the habit of keeping all the details daily. Granted, it goes against the grain of the entrepreneur, for he detests such nonsense, but he must realize that he is being governed by bureaucrats and bureaucrats have a passionate affair with paperwork.

PAY BY CHECK

Try to pay everything by check, supported by an invoice clearly stating for what the money was spent. The check alone is not sufficient to satisfy the IRS, for the tax men may suspect it to be in payment of a personal expense. The name of the tax game is documentation; you must have the documents to prove what you are claiming. Moreover, the IRS gets extremely suspicious when one deals in cash; the possibilities of tax evasion loom large in cash businesses. The IRS, knowing this full well, carefully scrutinizes cash transactions whenever possible.

INVENTORY CONTROL

Control of inventory assortments is a ciritical aspect of retail management. Here is a look at it.

Using the computer for distribution of fashion goods

The Discount Merchandiser†

As retail chain stores expand, the distribution of merchandise becomes more complex and costly. It is becoming increasingly more difficult to maintain

---

†*The Discount Merchandiser*, **December 1971, pp. 28-30.**

an uninterrupted flow of merchandise and information through the distribution center.

The cost of distribution varies dramatically depending upon the number of stores in the chain, the number of receipts and the number of distributions to be made for the average receipt. Our studies have revealed a wide range of from $1 to $10 per receipt.

As the number of stores, receipts and distributions increase, several problems become evident.

• the experienced distributor has less time to spend on each distribution resulting in unbalanced color and size mix by store

• new, less experienced, distributors are added to the staff resulting in increased distribution cost and, because of their inexperience, unbalanced color and size mix by store

• to avoid the excess cost of distributing, many chains do not distribute down to the color/size level. This means the picker must scale the selection store by store resulting in unbalanced color and size mix by store.

Fashion distribution – old style: The key point is that many distributions of styles to the stores do not reflect the way in which the buyer bought merchandise. A buyer has the right to assume that a style he purchases for the chain will closely approximate his order in regard to color and size mix at the store level. Unfortunately, this is too often not the case and the unbalanced distribution at the store level can result in unnecessary markdowns.

Before we explore a possible solution to our problem, let us take a quick look at the environment of a typical fashion distribution center.

Upon receipt of the merchandise and its movement to the proper area in the center, the merchandise is opened and listed on a copy of the purchase order or on a separate listing sheet. A copy of the purchase order/receipt is then sent to order checking. For those that fail the rules of order checking, the order checker would hold the receipt for approval by the buyer.

If it passes the order checking process, a notification is sent to marking and to the distributor. While it is being marked, the distributor utilizes the open-to-ship report, which contains a Unit Plan by class and price point for each store, to determine how each style should be shipped. Some chains will record the quantity by style only, others by style and color for each store, and others by style, color and size. Those chains who do not record the units for each store to the size/color level must rely on the pickers to choose the best merchandise selection.

The distribution process is a time consuming one involving repetitive addition and readjustment. Completed distributions are then usually sent to the key punch department. Store charge cards and/or picking slips are prepared. The next step is the physical picking of the merchandise. After merchandise is picked, it is moved to the staging area by store where it is consolidated for packing and moving to the stores. In the shipping area, the stubs of the picking tickets are removed for entry into the retail stock ledger and into the Unit Control System.

Almost without exception, this system is representative of the data processing effort in the chain environment for a distribution center. It has not materially changed since the early 1950's. Only innovations have been added, for example, optical scanning is often used instead of key punching. But, basically, the system has remained the same and only until recently are significant breakthroughs being made. Let us now discuss the solution to the problem.

Fashion distribution – new style: After completion of the order checking process, the quantity received by size and color is entered into the system. The quantity to ship by store to the style level will be determined by the distributor using the open-to-ship report which contains a unit plan by class and price point for each store. The distributor will not have to keep track of goods by color and size. The decision to be made is: Within the quantity of a style to be sent to each store, how should the style received be allocated to these stores by size and color to give each store the best assortment of that style.

Style no. 123x – Junior dresses

Color	Size						
	3	5	7	9	11	13	S/T
Green	12	12	26	38	38	24	150
Purple	24	24	52	76	76	48	300
Grey	34	34	66	100	100	66	400
Burgundy	12	12	26	38	38	24	150
S/T	82	82	170	252	252	162	1000

Let's assume that one of the styles received is the one depicted here. It shows the quantities received for each color/size combination within the style. This is just one of the many styles that apply to junior dresses. The sizes range from 3 to 13 and there are four colors. The subtotals are summarized by color and size. They reflect the color distribution and the size distribution for this particular shipment of merchandise. This merchandise is to be distributed to a number of stores in the chain.

The objective of this selection process is to distribute to the stores a "good" selection and this is the key to the problem.

Let us define what we mean by a "good" selection. First of all, you will notice there is a certain size distribution within the available merchandise shown here. This size distribution reflects the sizes in the population and the way dresses and other wearing apparel is bought. Normally, it is known as a bell-shaped curve or size curve by buyers and merchandising people. A "good" selection has to satisfy the size distribution. Also note that there is a certain color variety.

Need for color variety: In a "good" selection, the color variety has to be as wide as possible. The third characteristic in a "good" selection is that it has to satisfy the quantity requirements of the store.

Store group	"Open-To-ship"	No. of stores	Store Group sub total
1	8	20	160
2	10	24	240
3	12	50	600

This shows a tabulation where open-to-ship quantities are listed with the number of stores to receive these quantities. In this case, there are 20 stores that are to receive 8 pieces each, 24 will receive 10 pieces, and 50 stores will receive 12 pieces.

The shipping quantities are totaled by store group. The grand total is 1,000 units. Notice this is the same amount as shown previously as being available. Merchandise has to be taken from the available to ship and distributed to the stores in fixed open-to-ship quantities. (The number used in this example comes from an actual distribution in a large chain.)

			Size				
Color	3	5	7	9	11	13	
Green		1			1		2
Purple	1		1		1	1	4
Grey				2	1	1	4
Burgundy			1	1			2
	1	1	2	3	3	2	12

Let's take a look at some of the patterns that will be shipped to various stores. The color and size distribution is very close to the one originally furnished. The store shown here received at least one of every size.

			Size				
Color	3	5	7	9	11	13	
Green			1		1		2
Purple		1	1	1	1	1	5
Grey			1	1	1	1	4
Burgundy				1			1
	0	1	3	3	3	2	12

This store did not receive any size 3. An examination of the merchandise available to ship will show a total of 82 pieces for size 3. The requirements indicate that we are distributing this style to a total of 94 stores. Thus, there are necessarily at least 12 stores that cannot receive any size 3. There will be some cases where some stores will receive duplicates of a particular color/size item.

An examination of the merchandise available indicates 100 pieces in grey in size 9. Once again, as we are distributing to only 94 stores, some stores will receive two copies of this color/size. The algorithm used will tend to cause this duplication to occur in the large store groups.

Look-ahead features: The algorithm is dynamic in that it examines the state of the system at every assignment step as a prerequisite for the following assignment. Moreover, it has look-ahead features in the sense that the array of colors and sizes available for distribution is examined at the very beginning to uncover those characteristics that will affect the distribution.

The system analyzes the total number of items available to be shipped and normalizes this with the number open to ship for the first store. After allocating the sizes and colors for this store, it will deduct these quantities from the sizes and colors available to be shipped and renormalize this reduced quantity with the quantities open to ship at the next store. The procedure is repeated for each store in the distribution.

Color	Size						
	3	5	7	9	11	13	
Green	1					1	2
Purple			1	1		1	3
Grey			1	1	1		3
Burgundy		1			1		2
	1	1	2	2	2	2	10

If we examine the allocation of sizes and colors for stores receiving 10 units, we can see that regardless of the number of items open to ship for a store:

Color	Size						
	3	5	7	9	11	13	
Green		1				1	2
Purple		1		1	1		3
Grey				1	1	1	3
Burgundy	1	1					2
	1	1	2	2	2	2	10

The size and color distribution has remained good and closely follow the original size/color distribution as purchased by the buyer.

The patterns you have seen are "good" if taken within the overall framework of multiple stores and many pieces. Any specific pattern can possible be improved when taken individually as we have already indicated. You can look at one of these patterns and say, "How come this store isn't getting any green"? or, "This other store isn't getting any size 3." But, if we look at the problem from the point of view of overall assignment of colors and sizes, this collection of patterns provides good color/size distribution for practically all the stores in question.

When there are exceptions: What about exception conditions?

Computer distribution can handle exception conditions including:

• Limiting the number of colors and/or sizes per store

• Restricting a color and/or size for designated stores

• Partial distributions, distribute 600 and leave 400 in stock. The 400 would contain a balanced color/size mix.

• Contiguous sizes such as 3, 5, 7, not 3, 7, 9 skipping size 5

• Direct store shipments — run the distribution at the time of order (rather than at the time of receipt) and use it as a basis for vendor shipping instructions by store

• Specific distributions such as promotions, tests and store openings can override the system

The entire computer distribution process can overlap the time available while marking and thus not slow down the flow of merchandise.

Computer post distribution pays off when you have either:

- Many stores
- Many orders
- A long lag between order and receipt or a combination of these three.

The benefits: The advantages we receive with computer distribution are:

- It is based upon need at the time of receipt
- There is an uninterrupted flow of merchandise and information
- Rapid distribution by size and color without bias
- We can get stock by store in units and dollars
- Reduced cost and increased speed of distribution
- Readable picking and shipping instructions are machine printed

The results we have achieved so far are based on 100's of arrays run in the last few months. The size range of these arrays varies from one size in four colors to ten sizes in six colors. The open-to-ship range that was used varied from three to 72, that is, we had stores that were to receive three units of a style and other stores that were to receive anywhere from four to 72. These runs were made on actual test data. Styles were distributed to up to 200 stores in a single run. The last store in the distribution received as balanced a color/size mix as the first store. Merchandising and distribution center executives considered the distributions good.

Computer distribution is being implemented today in several chains. There are definite cost savings. However, the most significant benefit is that the stock in the stores reflects the proportions in which it was purchased by the buyer.

QUESTIONS

1. Do you really need a computer for such systems?

COST CONTROL

When the enterprise in in jeopardy a cost reduction program is an immediate solution to stemming the flow of needed cash. It is quick and sure. Sales stimulation programs take time to institute, cost money, and are uncertain of success. Those executives whose fame is based on saving sick businesses are adept cost cutters. Here is some material on that skill.

Cost reduction: "Panic from the word Go"

George J. Berkwitt†

In the corner office of a medium-sized Pittsburgh steel distributor, the president is poring over operations costs. Suddenly, he realizes that his labor costs for moving materials from the storage yard into the plant have skyrocketed. In a kind of reflex action, he grabs the telephone and puts through a call to Frank H. Chester, national accounts executive of the

†George J. Berkwitt, *Dun's Review*, **June 1970, pp. 43-45.**

industrial truck division of Clark Equipment Co.

Although Chester always likes to get an order, particularly in a year like 1970, this one made him wonder. "Right then and there," he recalls, "this man ordered a $25,000 piece of mobile yard machinery he had been considering. But he didn't even bother to look at the specifications he had on file, and — you might guess it — the truck he ordered was two feet too wide for the aisles in the plant."

So, far from cutting costs, the panicked distributor added some useless freight and cancellation charges to his ledger and lost valuable time. "He just got scared," Chester concludes. While it may be little consolation to the harried steel executive, the fact is that he has plenty of company — in corporations spanning the entire spectrum of U.S. industry.

In the year of the shrinking budget, cost-cutting announcements are a daily phenomenon. Collins Radio trims its work-force by 20%. Tight money forces utilities to trim marketing plans. Pan Am concedes it is undergoing a massive executive shakedown. Hanes Corp. realigns its knitwear unit, releasing 500 to 600 workers from one plant.

Officially, such moves are usually described as "readjustments." But at best, the cost-cutting news is evidence of a failure of a good many long-range plans. And at worst, it is indicative of "panic management," a virus that many corporations in 1970 have fallen prey to. "Panic programs do irreparable damage to attitudes, systems and personal relations," states Joseph H. Humberstone, group vice president of Air Reduction and a long-time advocate of planned cost reduction. "They are a sure sign of mismanagement. They show that the organization has failed. It has allowed costs to get out of hand. It

has, in fact, failed to apply the simple truth that the best producer is also the lowest-cost producer."

Today's cost cuts are characterized by the fact that they are usually sudden, one-shot affairs. They can hit any segment of the company. They can eliminate people, substitute a cheaper material for a more expensive one or consolidate or lop off production operations. While layoffs and cutbacks in spending are making monotonous news day after day, consider just two other ways in which, according to charges by lower-ranking executives, management is hurting itself with cost-cutting moves:

• Operation changes. Top management is demanding reduced reject rates, reductions in inventory, but also the use of cheaper fabrication materials — a move certain to fan the flames of consumerism still higher. In the office, secretarial labor is being replaced by costsavers such as stenographic pools that receive dictation by telephone, which fosters resentment (and a slowdown) by employees still on the job.

• Moratoriums on sales and promotional campaigns. Advertising, public relations, direct mail and other promotional programs are feeling the traditional pinch of lean profit years. Several companies have completely eliminated their advertising, thus robbing 1971 sales.

The trouble, of course, is that all too many of these programs represent last-ditch maneuvers to salvage a respectable profit year — or to keep it from dipping into red ink. Yet, as middle managers are charging, the cost-cutting is simply the midpoint of a three-part debacle that starts with top management miscalculations and ends with a long-term weakening of the business affected.

A classic example

Litton Industries' new publishing enterprise is a classic example. Four years ago, Litton decided to build a "cradle-to-grave" educational capability and acquired five companies. Insiders joked that the company had formed "Litton's instant McGraw Hill."

In the fall of 1965, Charles Hutchinson Jr. joined what had become Litton's Van Nostrand-Reinhold Co. and became editor-in-chief of the professional and reference-book division. Early last April, Hutchinson was released with others. Litton headquarters described the firings as a company-wide cost-cutting effort, but the way the move was handled had all the earmarks of corporate panic.

Hutchinson says he was called in on a Friday morning and told flatly that, as of the end of the day, he and a half dozen others were out. He does not question management's right to fire as much as its habit of painting everything with same brush. "You don't run a book company like a factory," says Hutchinson. "But management's solution to the profit problem is traditional in manufacturing — knock guys off the production line. Since when is a book company equal to an aerospace operation?"

Only in a conglomerate, perhaps. "We were told at first that the book company was funded for growth and that it was to be a new and viable force in the industry," says Hutchinson. "Of course, this stimulated us into thinking that we could assume some long-range planning and some knowledge of book publishing. We assumed wrong."

Financial management, sent down from headquarters, did not know the field, says Hutchinson. "And it caused no end of trouble. For one thing, earlier staff cutbacks upset the organization and the continuity of personal relations that is essential to a publishing house. Some of those fired were operating managers from the original staff, managers who know the technicalities of our business better than anyone else. I see this as the real beginning of our troubles."

Admittedly, not all the woes heaped on the troubled book division were the handiwork of top management. An over-rated backlist that failed to generate the sales expected of the books on hand and the inexplicable loss of critical marketing records are both contributing to a poor showing in the division's second half (its fiscal year ends July 31). But management's cost-cut reaction has, in Hutchinson's mind, exacerbated the situation. "In planning acquisitions," he asserts, "management cleverly thought that it could consolidate operations to trim overhead and operating costs. Again, the traditional nuts-and-bolts approach was wrong for the business. You just can't consolidate some operations," says Hutchinson. "Schoolbooks may be shipped in carloads, other types of books are shipped one at a time. The costing operations can be entirely different."

The economies of Litton's big-cost roundup are doubtful. In its attempt to put the book operation back on its feet, asserts one insider still with the division, "headquarters is spending enough money to start another company."

In other companies, cost-cutting effectiveness is dissipated through mishandling. A little more than a year ago, for instance, a directive was sent out at W. R. Grace & Co. "to eliminate all unnecessary frills." As one ex-Grace manager recalls, "Most of our divisions were asked in a nice way to cut down on spending and reduce overhead.

Naturally, each department head felt that his department was spending as little as possible already, and the attitude was, 'The other fellow will do it.' "

Of course, no one did. In fact, staff overhead actually increased. So management simply ordered a percentage cut across the board, department by department. Typically, underraction was followed by overreaction. In the department of the ex-manager, a cut of 50% of the personnel was ordered, and the department chief chose a Christmas party to break the news to layoff victims.

Worse, news of Grace management attending $1,000 political fund-raising dinners, executives living high on the company tab and the wholesale redecoration of top managerial offices further provoked the resentment of the remaining middle managers and other employees. Says one Grace executive: "Seniority meant nothing. One man was let go after 22 years with the company. There was no evaluation of performance or contribution, no guidance from the top on whom to fire."

A layoff was bungled differently at National Environment Corp. A California diversified construction outfit, National Environment spent heavily on a year-long morale-building campaign. Among other things, it handed out tie clips with the number "80" emblazoned on them, meaning that management was exhorted to reach an 80-cents-per-share year. Then, suddenly, 65 headquarter men were thrown onto the unemployment rolls. The reason was soon evident. Earnings for the year, at 60 cents, were 25% off target.

When cost-cutting involves layoffs and most crash programs do, it often results in long-term damage to the company's relationship to its community. Nowhere is this more evident than in the crippled aerospace industry.

A good many California towns are now under a dark recessionary gloom because of aerospace cutbacks. But defense-oriented layoffs are occurring throughout the country as well — invariably accompanied by a flood of negative public opinion sparked by the victims. Take the case of James O. Lee, until April 1 a research specialist in defense oceanography for General Dynamics' Electric Boat division. Lee, who survived a first cut of 500 men at the division but was nailed by the second, is bitter. "It was panic from the word go," he says.

"Electric Boat," he believes "is a captive company that hasn't assumed the responsibility for its own fate. It adjusts itself to the whims of the Navy. Caught up in the massive work on the Hyman Rick over-inspired atomic submarine, some of the men got to calling the Admiral 'the chairman of the board.' Had Electric Boat truly believed in research and development, it might have used its outstanding staff of engineers and scientists to come up with more commercial products and retained more of its most valuable and creative assets instead of just lopping them off. But they don't seem to have a notion on how to pitch civilian work. This company," Lee concludes, "is a twentieth-century enterprise lost somewhere in the eighteenth century."

The consequences of a cost-cutting layoff can, of course, hit closer to home than the adverse effects on the community. Management at a Philadelphia warehouse, for example, struck 55 workers from the payroll and replaced them with a fleet of lift trucks that clamped onto materials rather than lifting them on pallets. With labor grievance already in the air at the facility, says an insider, "The men were in a nasty mood as it was." This mood was heightened by their sympathy for their associates who got the axe. Result: "They beat hell out of the trucks, and maintenance on the normally tough units zoomed," the insider reports. "It cost the company about $70,000 to go back to the old system."

In other cost-cutting maneuvers, the debits may not show up for some time, but they are an implicit consequence. A typical move among utilities these days is to slash marketing budgets. At Northeast Utilities, which serves part of Massachusetts and Connecticut, ad spending has been almost eliminated. "There ought to be some adverse effects," admits Boardman G. Getsinger Jr., advertising manager, "but not for at least a year."

Can cost reduction be properly planned? Some companies try. At Union Carbide, it can take as long as a year to phase out a key group. During that period, its men are put through a battery of seminars and interviews to help them define their ambitions and redeploy their skills. A solid effort is made to retain them — but elsewhere in the company. When this fails, they are groomed and their resumés refined for a well-focused job search outside Union Carbide.

While a $2.7-billion (annual sales) monolith like Carbide obviously can afford such a program better than less well-heeled concerns, even in the smallest companies most employees are aware of the need for a company to operate in the black and to reduce costs when profitability is jeopardized. But when management begins to fire blindly, to cut costs mindlessly and, as in so many cases, to make cost-cutting attempts that end up raising costs, then it is time to ask just how well the top-management dollar is being earned.

QUESTIONS

1. While the article deals with some large businesses, do the same principles apply to a small one that is in difficulty?

2. Where does the small businessman first look to reduce costs?

SOME BASIC ELEMENTS OF ACCOUNTING

The following article was prepared to help the reader who knows little or nothing about accounting to understand the terminology and basic elements of the field. *If you have had a course in accounting, you will find the following material to be quite elementary and probably of little use to you. Moreover, if you know nothing about accounting, this material will not teach you all about how to keep a set of books.*

But it will:

1. Provide you with some of the terminology used by accountants so that you can better understand them and talk with them.

2. Give you some idea of the basic ideas underlying accounting systems.

3. Give you some idea of how to go about setting up a control system, what is needed, and some of the problems encountered.

Designing a bookkeeping system for a new small enterprise

Richard H. Buskirk

You have just incorporated your promising new venture — MONEY TREES, INC. —and now need to start some sort of bookkeeping system.

Do it correctly right from the start!!!!

Time and again the beginning businessman starts out with some overly simplified bookkeeping "system" only to discover quickly he needs a more comprehensive one. *It matters not whether you plan to do the books yourself or hire an outside accountant to do the job for you!! A system is still needed and you should be the one to develop it, or at least help design it so you will understand it better and thus make it more useful to you!*

First, diagram the flow of information in and out of your firm such as is shown in Figure 31-1. Here are the things your bookkeeping system needs to know.

- Information relating to Sales:
  Goods Sold
  Dollar Volume
  Cash or Credit Sales
  Returns
- Information relating to Credit Sales:

Name and Address of Customer
Amount of Purchase
Payments Received
Amounts Owed

- Information relating to things you Buy (Purchases):
  Goods Ordered and from Whom
  Goods Received
  Goods Returned
  Amounts Owed
  Amounts Paid
- Information relating to Internal Flow of Values and Funds:
  Inventories
  Cash on Hand
  Cash in Bank
  Payroll
  Expenses
  Assets
  Debts

List in detail other things you want to know! Now put it together visually!!

Now begin thinking about the documents you need to make your accounting system work. Paper is the stuff from which books are kept. You need documents, records, written or visual symbols which communicate to people the information they need to do their jobs properly. The shipping clerk won't know where or what to ship unless so informed. Long ago wise management learned to put things in writing. Oral orders repeatedly result in mistakes. Actions are usually based upon written documents.

First, begin with sales information. Some sort of document is needed as a sales order form. A multipurpose document can be created to serve several masters. Let's plod through a transaction. The hot shot Money Trees sales woman, Lotta Cash, sells a bundle of goods to a new customer, Fly-by-Night Airlines. She writes up the order in her order book even though

FIGURE 31-1:   Information flow system

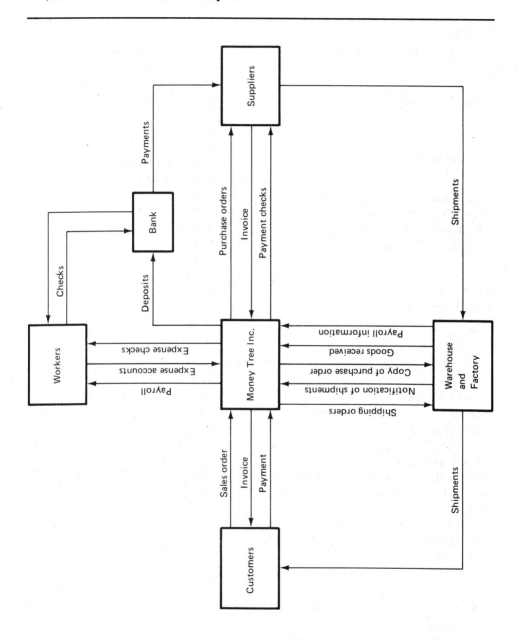

the buyer also issues a purchase order. Most professional buyers will write a purchase order as do the buyers working for Money Trees, Inc. Each firm needs to know exactly what has been bought, what it is committed to buy, and what it will receive and must pay for in the future.

So the company needs a sales order form!

Do not jump to the conclusion that designing one is a minor matter; the designing of all forms can be tricky. Remember, make an error and you're stuck with the erroneous forms. And they do cost money. One standard sales form is shown in Figure 31-2.

Several printing firms sell standard forms through office supply stores. The new enterprise is advised to use standard forms at first for several reasons: (1) less money is tied up in forms, (2) with some experience the management can better design the form that it needs, and (3) it is the quickest source of forms. Tailor-made forms can be obtained from the many firms specializing in them.

FIGURE 31-2:   A Standard sales order form for retailers

No. 1661   Dept._____ Date_____ 19___

Name_____

Address_____

| SOLD BY | CASH | C. O. D. | CHARGE | ON ACCT. | MDSE. RETD. | PAID OUT |

QUAN.	DESCRIPTION	PRICE	AMOUNT

Customer's Order No._____   Rec'd By_____

Redifform 5H 32

KEEP THIS SLIP FOR REFERENCE

The order form shown in Figure 31-2 is more applicable for a retail store than for a manufacturer.

How many copies of the sales order are needed? That is an important consideration.

Perhaps three might be needed: One for the home office, one to be given to the buyer for his records, and one retained by the sales person for her records.

Lotta puts the sales order in an envelope and mails it to the home office. When the person responsible for opening the mail sees Lotta's sales order, it is forwarded to the sales department where it is checked for accuracy and completeness. Sales people do make mistakes — wrong prices, wrong stock numbers, wrong addresses, or missing information. Buyers who receive the wrong goods are apt to buy elsewhere next time. Thus, right from the beginning make certain that the order form has been completed correctly. Usually at this point an INVOICE is prepared with as many as eight copies which are distributed as follows:

Copy 1   Sales Office Records

2   To Accounts Receivable

3   To Customer for His Records

4   To Customer for Return with Payment

5   To Shipping Department for Its Information

6   To Shipping Department for Use as Packing Slip

7   To Bank for Collateral on Loan

8   To Sales Person or to Regional Office

As you can see there are a number of people who need to know the information that is on the INVOICE. A standard INVOICE form is shown in Figure 31-3.

The main idea is to minimize the number of times someone has to place the sales information in writing. If all needed documents can be created with one writing, much time and money is saved. Moreover, each time something is copied there is a likelihood of error. If the original is correct, then all copies are correct. One of the advantages of a computer control system is that the computer print out can accurately provide all the documents that are needed with little effort. Many times the actual labels which will be used for shipping the goods to the customer can be created at the same time the invoice is typed — one of the copies going to the shipping room being made by them into shipping labels.

The invoice is the backbone of most accounting systems. It is the original document from which sales information is gained.

On the buying side of the business, the basic document is the PURCHASE ORDER. It tells exactly what is wanted; when it is wanted; where it is to be shipped; and the terms of sale to the seller, to the receiving department, to the requisitioner, and to accounts

---

FIGURE 31-3:   Standard invoice form

Rediform 7H724	INVOICE		OUR NUMBER 9568

payable. Thus perhaps five copies may be needed:

Copy 1   Stays in Purchasing Department Records

2   To Supplier

3   To Person in Organization Wanting Goods

4   To Accounts Payable

5   To Receiving Department

Many small enterprises would not find it necessary to have that many copies because they do not have separate purchasing and receiving departments. The owner, requisitioner, and purchasing agent are one and the same person. Such a business might need only two copies of the PURCHASE ORDER.

Some documentation must go with the shipment of goods because the receiver (customer) needs to know:

• Exactly what goods are in each box

• How many boxes are in the shipment

• The Purchase Order Number of the order

A standard packing slip is shown in Figure 31-4.

If the goods are shipped by common carrier, (a public trucking firm or railroad) a BILL OF LADING must be prepared. A standard form for Motor Carriers is shown in Figure 31-5. The trucking company with which you do business will furnish such forms if you ask.

You will need checks for paying bills but that is a simple matter that need not be gone into here.

There are internal forms that may or may not be needed. Perhaps you will need some payroll records — a way of knowing how much each worker has earned for the pay period. The law requires that careful records be kept of such matters.

FIGURE 31-4:   Standard packing slip

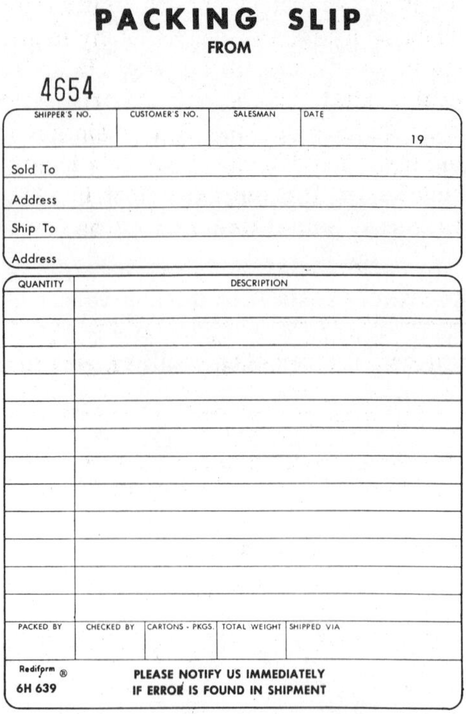

Perhaps you will need some credit forms if that is important in your enterprise. And what happens when a payment is received from a customer? How is it recorded in the books? Perhaps a log is needed. Or perhaps some receipt is made to record such payments. Whatever, some record must be made of every transaction — everything that happens to change the location of values.

Logs can be useful

And we are not referring to trees! A log is some kind of notebook in which a record of every event of a particular category is kept. Some professional people keep logs of all telephone calls, both outgoing and incoming. Others just log long distance calls. Some firms log in all correspondence in addition to all sales orders and checks. Many firms log in all visitors to the plant. Bear in mind that each log represents something to be done. Only maintain a log if you need it, but it can be a handy time saver. It is quicker to look in a log to see if something has or has not happened than it is to search through a stack of documents.

You have your documents, now what?

The information from the documents must be transferred to the firm's books—the journals and ledgers. In the early days of bookkeeping, all transactions

FIGURE 31-5: Standard bill of lading for motor carriers

This Memorandum is an acknowledgment that a Bill of Lading has been issued and is not the Original Bill of Lading, nor a copy or duplicate, covering the property named herein, and is intended solely for filing or record.

Shipper's No.

Carrier Agent's No.

RECEIVED, subject to the classifications and tariffs in effect on the date of the receipt by the carrier of the property described in the Original Bill of Lading,

From ______ Date ______ 19____

at ______

The property described below, in apparent good order, except as noted (contents and condition of contents of packages unknown), marked, consigned and destined as shown below, which said company (the word company being understood throughout this contract as meaning any person or corporation in possession of the property under this contract) agrees to carry to its usual place of delivery at said destination, if on its own railroad, water line, highway route or routes, or within the territory of its highway operations, otherwise to deliver to another carrier on the route to said destination. It is mutually agreed, as to each carrier of all or any of said property over all or any portion of said route to destination, and as to each party at any time interested in all or any of said property, that every service to be performed hereunder shall be subject to all the conditions not prohibited by law, whether printed or written, herein contained, including the conditions on back hereof, which are hereby agreed to by the shipper and accepted for himself and his assigns.

Consigned to ______

Destination ______ Street ______ City ______ County ______ State

Routing ______

Delivering Carrier ______ Vehicle or Car Initial ______ No.

Collect On Delivery
$ ______ and remit to: ______
Street ______ City ______ State

C. O. D. charge to be paid by { Shipper ☐ Consignee ☐

No. Packages	Description of Articles, Special Marks, and Exceptions	* Weight (Sub. to Cor.)	Class or Rate	Check Column

Subject to Section 7 of conditions, if this shipment is to be delivered to the consignee without recourse on the consignor, the consignor shall sign the following statement.

The carrier shall not make delivery of this shipment without payment of freight and all other lawful charges.

(Signature of Consignor.)

If charges are to be prepaid, write or stamp here, "To be Prepaid."

Received $ ______ to apply to prepayment of the charges on the property described hereon.

Agent or Cashir

Per ______
(The signature here acknowledges only the amount prepaid.)

Charges Advanced:

$

*If the shipment moves between two ports by a carrier by water, the law requires that the bill of lading shall state whether it is "carrier's or shipper's weight."

NOTE — Where the rate is dependent on value shippers are required to state specifically in writing the agreed or declared value of the property. The agreed or declared value of the property is hereby specifically stated by the shipper to be not exceeding ______ per ______

______ Shipper, Per ______ 3 ______ Agent, Per ______

Permanent post-office address of shipper.

6A 683 Rediform

were logged into a daily journal, but that is burdensome. Too much writing. So simplier methods were developed. Several firms sell specially designed bookkeeping systems for different types of businesses. Two of the more popular systems are the Ideal and the Simplified bookkeeping systems. Some pages from the Ideal system are shown in Figure 31-6, along with the directions for using the system. These systems are available in most office supply stores.

What is all this about "double entry" systems????

For sake of completeness, not to try to teach you all about accounting here, let us delve into some basics so that you can better understand what is going on in the accounting process. *Let us start with the basic unit of all business . . .*

The transaction!!!!

When you buy something or when you sell something, you are involved in a transaction. In a transaction there is a buyer and a seller — two sides to the deal, each of whom keeps books.

Suppose you are the seller.

Two things happen to you. You gain something and you lose something.

Plus
and
minus
or (as the accountants
prefer to put it)
debit
and
credit

You've got to know your debits from your credits, your pluses from your minuses.

When you have a debit you have a plus, you have gained something.

When you have a credit on your books, you have lost something.

Back to the sale. You sold a truckload of money trees for $12,000. *You gained* $12,000, so that is debited to your cash account. *You lost* a truckload of money trees so that is credited to sales.

Now suppose you are the buyer. You bought some office supplies for $100. You gained some office supplies, so that account would be debited, and you gave up $100, so cash would be credited.

Two things happen in each transaction and all a double entry bookkeeping system does is record each of those things in its proper account?

What is an account?

In order to know where one's money has gone and to better understand the exact nature of one's assets and liabilities, all happenings are classified by their nature. It would be possible to have but three accounts — assets, liabilities, and net worth, but that would hide the exact nature of expenditures, information that is most helpful to management. Moreover, the IRS would be most displeased with such an arrangement. It demands details.

Many expenditures are defined by the Internal Revenue Code. The difference between an automobile expense and a traveling expense is carefully spelled out in the law. Allowable entertainment expenses are similarly spelled out.

You will have to decide upon the accounts that will be needed. These are fairly well recognized by accountants but you should feel free to add or delete accounts as suits your business.

An account is simply a resting place or a pigeon hole into which all debits and credits of the same type are recorded. For example, all cash receipts are debited to the cash account and all cash payments are credited to the cash account.

Thus, an account is the place, usually a sheet of accounting paper, where debits and credits of a certain type are recorded. These sheets of paper are usually kept bound together in a ledger.

If you want to know how much money you owe other people, you look at the accounts payable account. If you want to know how much you are spending on telephone calls, you look at the telephone expense account.

Recording the debits and credits of a transaction as they appear in the journal into their proper accounts in the ledger is called posting. If books are not kept posted up to date, then management is not likely to have an accurate picture of what is going on. The accounts will be inaccurate if not current. This is a large problem in all businesses; big businesses frequently are several months behind in their books and this does cause serious problems in times of difficulty.

Common accounts used

The following accounts will most likely meet your needs. You add whatever accounts you feel are needed for your information on your enterprise. If your concern does a lot of direct mail promotion, perhaps you will want several accounts detailing the expenses on that activity. If salesmen's expenses are significant to your firm, then perhaps you will have a separate account for them.

- Asset accounts:
  Cash
  Accounts Receivable
  Notes Receivable
  Inventory
  Plant
  Equipment
  Automobiles
  Patents and Goodwill
- Liability accounts:
  Accounts Payable
  Notes Payable
  Taxes Payable
  Interest Payable
  Wages Payable
  Mortgages Payable
- Equity Accounts:
  Capital Stock
  Surplus or Retained Earnings
- Profit and loss accounts:
  Sales
  Returns and Allowances
  Wages
  Payroll Taxes
  Taxes
  Interest
  Contract Labor
  Postage
  Advertising
  Telephone
  Auto Expenses
  Travel Expenses
  Entertainment
  Employee Benefits
  Office Supplies
  Legal and Accounting
  Insurance
  Depreciation

THE FINANCIAL STATEMENTS

You've probably heard much about the two basic financial statements: *the balance sheet and the profit and loss statement.* Sometimes the profit and

FIGURE 31-6: Ideal System

BALANCE SHEET

ASSETS AND LIABILITIES
AT BEGINNING OF YEAR
ASSETS

CURRENT ASSETS:

Cash on Hand.............................._____

Cash in Bank............................._____

Notes Receivable ...._____

Accounts Receivable ...._____

Inventory Stock on Hand.............._____

     TOTAL ...._____

FIXED ASSETS:

Land ...._____

Buildings ...._____

Equipment ...._____

Furniture and Furnishings............_____

_____......._____

     TOTAL ...._____

OTHER ASSETS:

_____......._____

_____......._____

_____......._____

TOTAL ...._____

  TOTAL ASSETS ...._____

LIABILITIES

CURRENT LIABILITIES:

Notes Payable ...._____

Accounts Payable ...._____

_____......._____

_____......._____

    TOTAL ...._____

FIXED LIABILITIES:

Mortgages ...._____

_____......._____

TOTAL ...._____

    TOTAL LIABILITIES ...._____

NET WORTH (Deduct Total Liabilities from Total Assets
and enter the difference here)......................._____

    TOTAL LIABILITIES AND NET WORTH........_____

YEAR 19____

ASSETS AND LIABILITIES
AT END OF YEAR
ASSETS

CURRENT ASSETS:

Cash on Hand........................_____

Cash in Bank........................_____

Notes Receivable ...._____

Accounts Receivable ...._____

Inventory Stock on Hand.............._____

    TOTAL ...._____

FIXED ASSETS:

Land ...._____

Buildings ...._____

Equipment ...._____

Furniture and Furnishings.............._____

_____ ...._____

    TOTAL ...._____

OTHER ASSETS:

_____ ...._____

_____ ...._____

_____ ...._____

TOTAL ...._____

  TOTAL ASSETS ...._____

LIABILITIES

CURRENT LIABILITIES:

Notes Payable ...._____

Accounts Payable ...._____

_____ ...._____

_____ ...._____

    TOTAL ...._____

FIXED LIABILITIES:

Mortgages ...._____

_____ ...._____

TOTAL ...._____

  TOTAL LIABILITIES ...._____

NET WORTH (Deduct Total Liabilities from Total Assets
and enter the difference here)......................_____

    TOTAL LIABILITIES AND NET WORTH......._____

INSTRUCTIONS
(V-9, 3221)

EXPENSES AND PAYMENTS

In this section use as many lines daily and as many pages monthly as may be necessary to list all payments made from your business, including payments for merchandise, expenses, equipment, etc., and owner's drawings, but not including bank deposits. Enter each payment on a separate line across the page as follows:

DATE, CHECK NUMBER, TO WHOM PAID, and MEMORANDA. Enter date and, if paid by check, the check number, then the name of the individual or firm. The "Memoranda" column is for any special notation as the date or number of the invoice or bill the payment is for, or the month or period the payment of rent, wages, etc., covers. (This will help prevent errors of paying the same account twice.)

BANK DEPOSITS—Column 1 may be used as a memorandum record of bank deposits as they are made.

BANK BALANCE—Column 2 may be used as a daily record of your bank balance. To maintain this balance, add the entries in column 1 to the balance in column 2 and subtract from this amount the entries in column 3.

PAID OUT BY CHECK—Column 3. Enter the total amount of the check, if paid by check, and then enter the amount under the proper heading in columns 4A to 20 inclusive to show what the payment was for.

PAID OUT BY CASH—Column 4. Enter the total amount of the payment, if paid by cash. Then enter the amount paid under the proper heading in columns 5 to 20 inclusive to show what the payment was for.

DEDUCTIONS FROM EMPLOYEE'S EARNINGS—Columns 4-A to 4-C inclusive. Enter the amount deducted from the employee's total earnings, including social security taxes, withholding taxes, etc.

PAYROLL—EMPLOYEES TOTAL EARNINGS—Column 5. Enter the total earnings of the employee for the day, week or other period which the payment covers. Include in this column 5 amounts deducted for the same period for social security taxes, withholding taxes and the cost of meals, etc.

FOOD, GROCERIES AND OTHER PURCHASES—Columns 6 to 9 inclusive. In these columns enter the net amount paid for food, groceries, beverages, tobacco, cigars and cigarettes, confections, etc., and other similar purchases for resale under the proper heading.

DISTRIBUTION OF EXPENSES PAID—Columns 10 to 18 inclusive. In these columns distribute expenses paid. When paying the Government social security taxes and income taxes that you have deducted from employees' earnings, enter in Column 20. Enter employer payroll taxes in Column 13. Include supplies used in your business that are not included in the Purchase columns or other Expenses columns of this Section such as brooms, office supplies, etc., under "Operating Supplies"—Column 12.

Columns 17 and 18 are to be used for miscellaneous or other expenses. Write the name of the account in Column 17, such as sales expenses or entertainment expense, and the amount paid in Column 18. This enables you to identify each miscellaneous expense which can be totaled separately and summarized at the end of the month.

OTHER PAYMENTS—Columns 19 and 20. Enter in these columns all other payments including owner's drawings from the business, payments for equipment or other business property, payments on notes, etc., loans made to others, contributions, and any other payments made that do not come under columns 5 to 18 inclusive. In column 19 show the name of the account and in column 20 the amount of the payment. Then transfer the amount paid to the proper account in another section. For example: The owner draws $50.00 from the business by check. Enter on the left hand page the date, check number, owner's name, and in column 3 $50.00, then on the opposite page write "Proprietor's Account" in column 19 and $50.00 in column 20, and then turn to the "Proprietor's Account" section and make the necessary entry in his account on Form 70. This posting is done only with "Other Payments" columns 19 and 20.

By entering all payments in the "Payments" section and distributing each payment on the same line across the double page from column 3 to 20 inclusive, you have a complete record of all your disbursements, and of your expense distribution and of other payments, that will enable you to see at a glance what your money is being paid out for, to look up any item quickly, and to prepare the "Summary of Business and Statement of Income" and any other necessary reports easily.

Carry the total of each column forward to the next page until the end of the month. At the end of the month transfer the totals for the month to the "Summary of Payments, Distribution of Expenses and Other Payments," in the back of this section (the last page under Expenses tab) and to the "Summary of Business and Statement of Income" in the Summary section.

To balance the pages in this section the total of columns 3, 4, 4A, 4B, and 4C should be the same as the total of columns 5 to 20 inclusive.

Start a new page in this section the beginning of each month and do not bring any totals forward from the previous month as monthly totals are transferred to Summary pages only.

PAYMENTS — ALL CASH AND CHECKS PAID OUT

THE IDEAL SYSTEM, REG. U. S. PAT. OFFICE. MADE IN U. S. A.

	1	2			
	BANK DEPOSITS	BANK BALANCE (2+1—3)	DATE 19___	CHECK NUMBER	TO WHOM PAID
1					
2					
3					
4					
5					
6					
7					
8					
9					
10					
11					
12					
13					
14					
15					
16					
17					
18					
19					
20					
21					
22					
23					
24					
25					
26					
27					
28					
29					
30					
31					
32					
33					

RESTAURANT & CAFE RECORD

IDEAL SYSTEM · FORM 223

MEMORANDA	PAID OUT BY CHECK (3)	PAID OUT BY CASH (4)	DEDUCTIONS FROM EMPLOYEE'S EARNINGS			PAYROLL, EMPLOYEES TOTAL EARNINGS (5)	FOOD AND GROCERIES (6)	
			F.O.A.B. & UNEMP. INS. (4A)	WITHHOLD-ING TAX (4B)	OTHER DEDUCTIONS (4C)			
								1
								2
								3
								4
								5
								6
								7
								8
								9
								10
								11
								12
								13
								14
								15
								16
								17
								18
								19
								20
								21
								22
								23
								24
								25
								26
								27
								28
								29
								30
								31
								32
TOTALS								33

DISTRIBUTION OF EXPENSES

THE IDEAL SYSTEM, REG. U. S. PAT. OFFICE. MADE IN U. S. A.

	7	8	9	10	11	12	13	14
	BEVERAGES	TOBACCO CONFECTIONS, MISC. PURCHASES	OTHER PURCHASES FOR RESALE	LAUNDRY & LINEN SERVICE	REPAIRS AND REPLACE-MENTS	OPERATING SUPPLIES	TAXES AND LICENSES	INTEREST AND RENT
1								
2								
3								
4								
5								
6								
7								
8								
9								
10								
11								
12								
13								
14								
15								
16								
17								
18								
19								
20								
21								
22								
23								
24								
25								
26								
27								
28								
29								
30								
31								
32								
33								

RESTAURANT & CAFE RECORD

IDEAL SYSTEM - FORM 223

15	16	17		18	19		20	
TELEPHONE, LIGHT, POWER, HEAT, WATER	ADVERTISING AND PRINTING	OTHER EXPENSE			OTHER PAYMENTS			
		NAME OF ACCOUNT		AMOUNT PAID	NAME OF ACCOUNT		AMOUNT PAID	
								1
								2
								3
								4
								5
								6
								7
								8
								9
								10
								11
								12
								13
								14
								15
								16
								17
								18
								19
								20
								21
								22
								23
								24
								25
								26
								27
								28
								29
								30
								31
								32
								33

THE IDEAL SYSTEM

REG. U. S. PAT. OFFICE
PUBLISHED BY
THE IDEAL SYSTEM CO., LOS ANGELES

AND STATEMENT OF INCOME

RESTAURANT & CAFE RECORD

IDEAL SYSTEM - FORM 224-A

JANUARY	FEBRUARY	MARCH	APRIL	MAY	JUNE	
						1
						2
						3
						4
						5
						6
						7
						8
						9
						10
						11
						12
						13
						14
						15
						16
						17
						18
						19
						20
						21
						22
						23
						24
						25
						26
						27
						28
						29
						30
						31
						32
						33
						34
						35
						36

THE IDEAL SYSTEM

REG. U. S. PAT. OFFICE
PUBLISHED BY
THE IDEAL SYSTEM CO., LOS ANGELES

MONTHLY SUMMARY OF BUSINESS

THE IDEAL SYSTEM, REG. U. S. PAT. OFFICE. MADE IN U. S. A.

	JULY	AUGUST	SEPTEMBER	OCTOBER	NOVEMBER	DECEMBER
1						
2						
3						
4						
5						
6						
7						
8						
9						
10						
11						
12						
13						
14						
15						
16						
17						
18						
19						
20						
21						
22						
23						
24						
25						
26						
27						
28						
29						
30						
31						
32						
33						
34						
35						
36						

MONTHLY SUMMARY OF BUSINESS

THE IDEAL SYSTEM, REG. U. S. PAT. OFFICE. MADE IN U. S. A.

MONTHLY SUMMARY - YEAR 19_____

1	**INCOME—CASH RECEIPTS:** **Meals and Lunches** (From Income Section Column 1)
2	**Beverages** (From Income Section Column 2)
3	**Tobacco, Confections & Misc. Sales** (From Income Section Column 3)
4	**Other Sales** (From Income Section Column 4)
5	**Other Income** (From Income Section Column 5)
6	**Other Cash Received** (From Income Section Column 6)
7	**Meals to Employees, Included in Payroll** (From Income Section Column 7)
8	**TOTAL INCOME** (Total Lines 1 to 7 inclusive)
9	**Sales Tax Included Above** (Subtract from Line 8)
10	**TOTAL NET RECEIPTS FROM SALES** (Line 8 Minus Line 9)
11	**PURCHASES PAID:** **Food and Groceries** (From Expense Section Column 6)
12	**Beverages** (From Expense Section Column 7)
13	**Tobacco, Confections, Misc. Purchases** (From Expense Section Column 8)
14	**Other Purchases for Resale** (From Expense Section Column 9)
15	**TOTAL PURCHASES** (Total Lines 11 to 14 inclusive)
16	**PAYROLL:** **Payroll—Employees Total Earnings** (From Expense Section Column 5)
17	**EXPENSES PAID:**
18	**Laundry and Linen Service** (From Expense Section Column 10)
19	**Repairs and Replacements** (From Expense Section Column 11)
20	**Operating Supplies** (From Expense Section Column 12)
21	**Taxes and Licenses** (From Expense Section Column 13)
22	**Rent and Interest** (From Expense Section Column 14)
23	**Telephone, Light, Power, Heat and Water** (From Expense Section Column 15)
24	**Advertising and Printing** (From Expense Section Column 16)
25	**Other Expenses** (From Expense Section Column 18)
26	(From Expense Section Column 18)
27	(From Expense Section Column 18)
28	**TOTAL EXPENSES PAID** (Total Lines 17 to 27 inclusive)
29	**Depreciation** (From Form 5)
30	**Contributions and Other Deductions** (From Form 60)
31	**TOTAL EXPENSES, DEPRECIATION AND DEDUCTIONS** (Total Lines 28, 29 and 30)
32	**MONTHLY STATEMENT OF INCOME** **TOTAL NET RECEIPTS** (From Line 10, above)
33	**TOTAL PURCHASES & PAYROLL or TOTAL NET COST OF SALES** (See Instructions)
34	**GROSS PROFIT FROM BUSINESS** (Line 32 Minus Line 33)
35	**TOTAL EXPENSES, DEPRECIATION AND DEDUCTIONS** (From Line 31, above)
36	**NET PROFIT FROM BUSINESS** (Line 34 Minus Line 35)

AND STATEMENT OF INCOME

RESTAURANT & CAFE RECORD

IDEAL SYSTEM - FORM 224-B

TOTAL FOR YEAR	STATEMENT OF INCOME - YEAR 19_____
	TOTAL NET RECEIPTS FROM SALES...................
	PURCHASES:
	TOTAL PURCHASES or Cost of Sales._____
	PAYROLL:
	Payroll—Employees Total Earnings...._____
	TOTAL PURCHASES AND PAYROLL...................
	(or Total Net Cost of Sales)
	GROSS PROFIT FROM BUSINESS......................
	(Sales Minus Purchases and Payroll)
	EXPENSES:
	Taxes on Business Property.
	Licenses ...._____
	Rent and Interest........._____
	Repairs and Replacements_____
	Telephone, Light, Power,
	Heat and Water........_____
	Laundry & Linen Service_____
	Operating Supplies ...._____
	Advertising and Printing.._____
	Other Expenses_____ _____
	TOTAL EXPENSES: ....
	DEDUCTIONS:
	Depreciation ......_____
	Contributions ....._____
	Other Deductions.._____
	TOTAL DEDUCTIONS ....
	TOTAL EXPENSES AND DEDUCTIONS (Subtract from Gross Profit from Business)...................
	NET PROFIT FROM BUSINESS ....
	Plus All Other Income Not Included Above.........
	Total......................................
	Less All Other Deductions Not Included Above.....
	TOTAL NET INCOME FOR YEAR...................

THE IDEAL SYSTEM

REG. U. S. PAT. OFFICE
PUBLISHED BY
THE IDEAL SYSTEM CO., LOS ANGELES

loss statement is called the income statement or operating statement.

The balance sheet reflects the financial state of the enterprise at one point in time. It is a statement of the firm's assets, liabilities, and owner's equity or interest in the firm. The basic balance sheet equation is:

$$ASSETS = LIABILITIES + NET\ WORTH$$

Or to look at it another way, a business owns a number of assets and someone has claim to each of them, either the owner or some creditor. If a business owes no money, then all assets will be owned by the owner. As it progressively owes more money, those creditors have increasing claims on the assets. Thus the balance sheets show what the enterprise owns and the claims against those assets.

The profit and loss statement is a completely different matter. It reflects the moneys that flow in and out of the enterprise over a period of time because of operations. Thus the basis for the other name for the statement — The Operating Statement.

Note that while the balance sheet is a snapshot in time, the profit and loss statement reflects a period of time. The profit and loss statement simply reflects all revenues received by the firm and all expenses incurred in operations for some time period. The basic formula is:

$$SALES - EXPENSES = PROFIT$$

How do the balance sheet and profit and loss statement tie into each other? The profit from operations shows up in two places in the balance sheet: First, those profits take the form of some assets, perhaps cash, or accounts receivable, or inventory, or plant, but they are in the assets somewhere. On the other side, the profit belongs to the owners so it is in net worth.

Figure 31-7 shows samples of a balance sheet and a profit and loss statement for a hypothetical company, with explanations of each account.

A final word . . .

Yes, it will take a lot of time and effort to keep a good set of books. Good control over your operations won't happen by itself. You will have to do it. And if you don't, brace yourself for trouble because it will not be far away.

FIGURE 31-7:   Sample financial statements of X company

Income Statement for the Period of December 31, 1970 to December 31, 1975

Gross Sales		$75,000
Less Returns and Allowances		5,000
Net Sales		70,000
Less Cost of Goods Sold:		
Beginning Inventory	$9,500	
Purchases	25,500	
Goods Available for Sale	$35,000	
Ending Inventory	12,000	
Cost of Goods Sold		23,000
Gross Margin		$47,000
Less Expenses:		
Administrative Expenses	20,000	
Marketing Expenses	20,000	
Financial Expenses	1,000	
Total Expenses		41,000
Net Profit before Taxes		$6,000
Federal Income Taxes		1,320
Net Profit after Taxes		$4,680

Gross Sales. This is what we thought we had sold — it moved out the door.

Returns and Allowances. But some goods came back through that door — they didn't stay sold.

Net Sales. Now here's where things really begin. We sold this much.

Less Cost of Goods Sold First, let's find out what the goods actually cost that stayed sold.

Beginning Inventory. This is what we had on hand at the beginning of the period.

Purchases. We bought this much goods during the period.

Goods Available for Sale. So we had available in our place of business at various times during the period this much that could have been sold.

Ending Inventory. But this much didn't sell; we still have it.

Cost of Goods Sold. So we sold this much — simple logic.

Gross Margin. Subtracting the cost of goods sold from Net Sales gives us our gross margin. Some people call it gross profit, but that is misleading for it is in no way profit.

Expenses. Now let's subtract all our expenses. We have grouped them into three simple categories. In actual practice they are detailed out; e.g., postage, travel.

Administrative Expenses. Under this heading come a great many overhead items such as rent, postage, salaries of administrative personnel, administrative travel and entertainment, supplies, depreciation on office equipment, property taxes, etc.

Marketing Expenses. Such expenses as sales men's earnings, travel costs, entertainment of customers, advertising, etc. would be included here.

Finance Expenses. Interest, accounting costs, and bank charges would be included here.

Net Profit before Taxes. Depending upon your theory of profits, here is your profit on operations.

Income Taxes. The federal government takes 22 percent of the first $25,000 profit, 48 percent of all over that amount — unless this corporation has filed the proper papers to be considered a Sub Chapter S corporation, in which case there would be no corporate tax. We assume that this company is located in a state that has no corporate income taxes.

Net Profit after Taxes. For people who consider taxes a cost of doing business, this is the true profit from operations.

Balance Sheet as of December 31, 1975

Assets — Any item of value owned by the business.

Current Assets — Cash and all assets that will be converted into cash within a year.

Cash — Money in the till and all bank accounts.

Accounts Receivable — Goods that have been sold, but for which the money is uncollected.

Bad Debts — Some of the people who owe money will be deadbeats — won't or can't pay — so we guess how much we are going to lose and take the loss now.

Inventory — Goods we have in stock for sale.

Prepaid Expenses — We have already paid out money for expenses, but have not used what we bought — rather like carrying expenses in inventory for future use.

Fixed Assets — Property that will not be converted into cash in the near future — buildings, land, equipment.

Depreciation — Fixed assets usually lose their value with time. Depreciation is an attempt to show the property's value more accurately.

Investments — Firms make investments to employ idle cash or to acquire interests in other companies for strategic purposes. Investments of cash in marketable securities are usually placed in current assets.

Intangible Assets — The estimated value or the amount of money the firm has spent developing such things as patents, goodwill, trademarks, and research knowledge.

ASSETS

Current Assets:			
Cash		$7,000	
Accounts Receivable	$10,000		
Less Allowance for Doubtful Accts.	−500	9,500	
Merchandise Inventory		12,000	
Prepaid Expenses		1,500	
			$30,000
Fixed Assets:			
Building		30,000	
Less Accumulated Depreciation		−10,000	
			20,000
Store Fixtures		5,000	
Less Accumulated Depreciation		1,000	
			4,000
Investments:			
Investment in XYZ Corp.			11,000
Intangible Assets:			
Patent Rights	1,000		
Goodwill	1,000		
			2,000
			$67,000

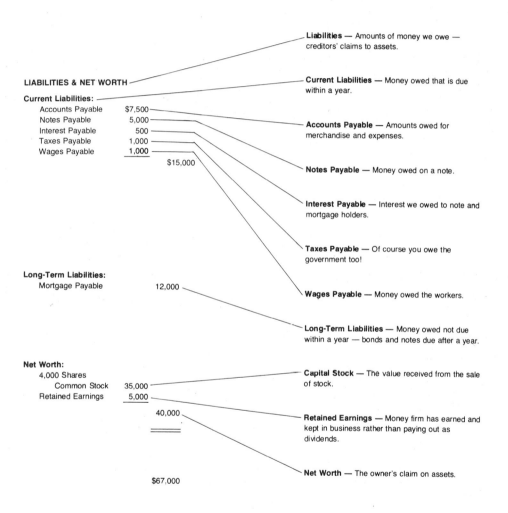

LIABILITIES & NET WORTH

Current Liabilities:

Accounts Payable	$7,500
Notes Payable	5,000
Interest Payable	500
Taxes Payable	1,000
Wages Payable	1,000
	$15,000

Long-Term Liabilities:

Mortgage Payable	12,000

Net Worth:

4,000 Shares Common Stock	35,000
Retained Earnings	5,000
	40,000
	$67,000

Liabilities — Amounts of money we owe — creditors' claims to assets.

Current Liabilities — Money owed that is due within a year.

Accounts Payable — Amounts owed for merchandise and expenses.

Notes Payable — Money owed on a note.

Interest Payable — Interest we owed to note and mortgage holders.

Taxes Payable — Of course you owe the government too!

Wages Payable — Money owed the workers.

Long-Term Liabilities — Money owed not due within a year — bonds and notes due after a year.

Capital Stock — The value received from the sale of stock.

Retained Earnings — Money firm has earned and kept in business rather than paying out as dividends.

Net Worth — The owner's claim on assets.

INCOME TAX

32

One of the authors was having lunch recently with a highly successful entrepreneur who now headed his own $30 million operation. While the main topic was to have been his up coming sales promotional program, at six different points in the meeting he digressed into some income tax problem he was facing. Such is the importance of taxes. Everything done in a business has tax implications. If you do not handle your tax affairs intelligently, you'll not likely keep whatever profits you make. Uncle will take them.

Taxes are far too important and too complex to undertake any real presentation of them here. However, the following article delves into matters that are not commonly included in most academic discussions of the income tax law.

Income taxes are so important and tax troubles so painful that great benefits accrue to those people who study the topic in detail. Detail is necessary, for the taxman levies his charges based on details, minute ones.

A practitioner's guide to avoidance v. evasion: Basic concepts change

Harry Graham Balter†

Much has already been written on the subject of the difference between tax "avoidance," tax "gimmicks" and tax "evasion." Yet, the problem remains sufficiently troublesome to warrant a fresh look at the basic concepts and applications.

There are only three practical ways in which increasingly harassed taxpayers may try to lift the impact of high taxes: (1) by seeking legislation beneficial to

†**Harry Graham Balter,** *The Journal of Taxation,* **July 1972, pp. 12-16.**

their particular situation; (2) by "avoidance" or "minimization" plans or schemes (including "gimmicks") or (3) by evasion.

The legislative route, of course, is the most direct and effective, creating "loopholes," sometimes of scandalous nature and proportions; but only the wealthy, the politically powerful, or well-organized group interests can successfully pursue this means of eliminating or reducing a particular tax impact.

The next level of opportunity is taking advantage, by lawful means, of all the opportunities which the present laws provide for reducing or minimizing taxes. This is labeled "avoidance" or "gimmickry," and can be referred to as the "high-bracket" game, generally affordable only to the wealthy who are able to pay for astute tax counsel.

At the bottom of this ladder of tax-reducing opportunism is tax evasion, available to those who are unable to obtain relief either by legislation or "avoidance" planning. Basically, tax evasion is the willful or intentional failure to pay part or all of the tax, which is known to be due, by fraudulent, dishonest, deceitful, or misrepresentative means. Euphemistically, it has been repeatedly stated that "avoidance" is the elimination or minimization of tax by "lawful" means, while "evasion" seeks the same result by "unlawful" means.

This may sound simplistic enough, but beneath the surface nagging problems lurk.

Helping to obfuscate the theoretical distinction between the "legal" and "acceptable" *avoidance*, and the supposedly mutually exclusive "illegal" and "unacceptable" *evasion*, is the unfortunate fact that the two terms have been used interchangeable in court decisions, statutes, Regulations, and by public "figures."

Denominators of "fraud" situations

Administratively, enforcement activities cannot reach all conduct which, while fraudulent, is more or less in the area of *de minimus*. This is so because the administrators of our revenue laws recognize, as we all do, that to a greater or lesser extent, nearly everyone is guilty of practicing some form of tax evasion. Failure to report small amounts of interest on bank deposits, padding of business entertainment expenses, or exaggerating contributions to charity are simple examples of tax evasion practiced on a wide scale by rich and poor alike.

The means of "evasion" in the usually accepted term of willfully paying less taxes than that known to be legally due are as ingenious and limitless as the imagination of the particular wrongdoer permits. There are, of course, the usual patterns: keeping double sets of books, fictitious bank accounts, counterfeit invoices, false entries, fictitious transactions in the names of dummies or figureheads, non-recordation of sales, personal expenses deducted as business expenses, conducting business transactions in cash so as to avoid bookkeeping and bank records, etc.

Then there are more devious and complicated schemes, such as distribution of corporate income in the guise of unjust and unreasonable "commissions" to the principal shareholders, depositing to his personal bank account by the principal shareholder of checks made out to the corporation for corporate sales and not accounting for the receipt in either his own return or that of the corporation, fraudulently claiming as a deduction alleged losses from sham sales of shares of stock which the taxpayer later bought back in cash from the accommodating purchasers, failure to report monies received as bribes, kickbacks, gambling profits, etc. As indicated, the common denominator of all fraud situations to which civil or criminal sanctions may attach is basically the same, namely, willfully paying less tax than that which the taxpayer knows is legally due, and would include, of course, willfully paying no tax when the taxpayer knows that a tax in some amount is legally due.

In the typical fraud or evasion case, where misrepresentation of fact, concealment, artifice, trick or device are the dominant characteristics, there is no problem. The bad faith, or the willfulness, or the intent to evade tax is clear from the act or transaction or evasion device itself; as, for example, changing entries in books, false sets or double sets of books, secret bank accounts or bank accounts under assumed names, a repetitive pattern of substantial understatement of income, a repetitive pattern of substantial overstatement of deductions, etc.

Sometimes, however, the transaction or device itself, which at first blush would seem to be clearly fraudulent, may, when examined more closely in the light of all factors relevant on the issue of intent or "state of mind," disclose that the error which is the falsity, was honest rather than dishonest, or perhaps due to honest reliance on the misguided advice of others, or to the incompetence of bookkeepers and accountants, or perhaps even to an honest or mistaken interpretation of the applicable law.

Permissible plans, honest mistakes

If at one end of the spectrum of tax-saving efforts we find fraud or evasion which is based on the intent to evade the tax known to be due by means which are illegal, in that they involve deception, deceit, misrepresentation, or other devices usually labeled "badges of fraud," then at the other end of the spectrum is the taxpayer's effort to reduce his tax to the minimum by means which are lawfully available to him, although discernable perhaps only to the astute and the knowledgeable.

The tax laws literally abound with tax-saving opportunities, usually based on alternatives, choices, or elections. To name only the simplest and the most common: permissible investment in tax-exempt securities, splitting of income available on marriage, cash-basis taxpayer delaying collection of debts until past the close of the calendar year, reporting the sale of property on the installment basis, election of accounting method, use of *inter vivos* gifts to reduce both income and estate taxes, setting up one's sales of capital assets so as to take advantage of long-term capital gains treatment rather than short-term treatment, expensing rather than capitalizing intangible oil well drilling costs, use of accelerated depreciation method, etc., etc.

There are hundreds of other tax-reducing specific opportunities provided in the Code itself. Is the taxpayer even "avoiding" his taxes by taking advantage of these provisions? While probably not, nevertheless, for the purpose of our discussion, the "avoidance" label will be accepted. Regardless and obviously, we have no penalty problems here, either civil or criminal, because of the very nature of the lawfulness, *per se*, of the tax reduction alternatives.

Apart from avoidance clearly allowed by law, there remains a vast area of avoidance situations where the legality or success of the device or maneuver remains in doubt until tested by adversary proceedings with the Internal Revenue Service.

For our purposes, we may divide the residue of avoidance situations into a workable dichotomy: (1) an avoidance plan clearly carried out in an honest belief that it is allowed by law, but which fails because, on test, it is held to be invalid, and (2) an avoidance plan which also fails on test as being invalid, but where the dominant intent in the planning therefor or in the method of execution is not clothed with that degree of *bona fides* to prevent the "fraud" label from being pinned on it by the Service.

Taking up our first category of "avoidance" plans, we have the typical and common situation where the taxpayer honestly believes, either on the basis of his own interpretation or on the advice of competent counsel, that a reasonable construction of the applicable tax laws permits him lawfully to pursue a route which leads to tax reduction, minimization, alleviation, or avoidance, and he proceeds to do so. He may or may not find it necessary to change his legal status as, for example, the form in which he conducts his business, or to set up devices in order to qualify for travel on this tax avoidance route.

Let us assume, however, that he decides that he cannot qualify for avoidance unless certain changes are made, or certain devices, arrangements, or plans are carried out, for example, in the manner of conducting his business, that is, whether as a sole proprietorship, as a partnership, or as a corporation, or in the postponement of the enjoyment of income, or in the assignment of income, or in the transfer of property by way of gift or in trust, or by setting up a hoped-for tax-free corporate reorganization, etc.

Now let us assume, as usually is the situation, that the taxpayer honestly believes that under the applicable law he has the right to do what he sets out to do, tax-wise. If he goes about his tax-avoidance plan by completely honest means and if in fact the law is not so clearly opposed to his plan that it may be said that he embarks on his tax-avoidance program in reckless disregard of the law, then, even if his plan fails and even if his plan or device is labeled a "sham," lacking in *bona fides*, or in "business purpose," the result would still be the imposition of only a simple deficiency plus interest and, only occasionally where the facts justified, the imposition of a negligence penalty; but rarely would a civil fraud penalty be asserted by the Commissioner, or, if asserted, upheld by the courts, absent as supposed, actual deceit or misrepresentation.

Some "avoidance" may be "evasion"

Now suppose that in his zeal to achieve a tax-saving status by device, arrangement, plan, or scheme, the taxpayer begins to cut corners and creates an obviously sham and unreal device, which under no realistic analysis could have served any other purpose than that of saving taxes. Suppose further that the taxpayer's professed belief that the applicable law permits his tax-avoiding device patently is not in good faith because there could be no room for reasonable doubt as to what the law permits; and supposing that in his return our taxpayer conceals or beclouds the true nature of his tax-saving device. The taxpayer now is dangerously close to the area of fraud and evasion, because now a serious issue is presented as to whether he did not pay a lesser tax than was legally due, knowing that a larger tax was due under the applicable laws. His professed claim that in setting up a tax-avoidance device he did not know a larger tax was due, when taken in the light of all the relevant facts, may now lose its force.

Here we are in the unsettled area where the transaction may be determined to be either a penalty-free avoidance, or a penalty-imposed evasion. Both civil fraud penalties and criminal charges may be involved.

Civil fraud penalties. Since the imposition of the civil fraud penalty essentially is the result of the exercise of administrative discretion, whether a given arrangement, device, or transaction is treated as a fraud-free avoidance, or a fradulent evasion, may depend ultimately upon: (1) the decision made by the Commissioner in the first instance, or (2) by a court or jury in the last instance. It may be helpful to indicate a bare sampling of some decided cases where the Commissioner has asserted the fraud penalty in situations which tax men would be inclined to call "avoidance," and find out whether the fraud penalties were sustained or set aside on review:

1. Avoidance by dealings with closely-owned or controlled corporations, or with family intimates. Innumerable avoidance cases involve dealings between the taxpayer and his wholly-owned and dominated corpora-

tion, or by a taxpayer and members of his intimate family group. But if, for example, sales, or gifts to the controlled corporation or to members of the family group are genuine, so that the taxpayer has in fact divested himself of dominion or control, the transaction may be upheld. Usually, however, the validity is attacked and the Commissioner sometimes asserts civil fraud in addition to assessing a deficiency. On review, as far as the fraud issue is concerned, the determining factors, of course, would relate to the "avoidance" versus "evasion" aspects of the transactions.

For example, in *John T. Smith*, 40 BTA 387 (1939), the fraud penalty was asserted by the Commissioner, but a majority of the Board of Tax appeals held that there was no fraud in the case of a sale by a taxpayer of stock to his wholly-owned corporation, although losses on such sales were later held nondeductible. However, five Board members vigorously dissented on the ground that in their judgment, the taxpayer was guilty of fraud.

In a landmark case, *Mitchell*, 32 BTA 1093 (1935), the facts were that for many years prior to 1929, the taxpayer had been president of the National City Bank of New York and the National City Company. The Commissioner charged fraud for the year 1929 as the result of a purported sale by the taxpayer to his wife of 18,300 shares of stock of the National City Bank of New York. The sale was evidenced by an exchange of letters between the taxpayer and his wife. The sale price was approximately $4,000,000. The wife's total fortune at the time was less than $1,000,000. The taxpayer, by "gifts," provided his wife with sufficient funds to pay taxpayer the agreed "interest" on a loan which the taxpayer had made and in connection with which he had pledged the stock as collateral.

No notice of a sale was given to the bank with which the stock was pledged to secure taxpayer's loan. No revenue stamps were affixed to the stock, no bill of sale was executed, no entry of the indebtedness was made on the wife's books of accounting, and, although taxpayer's wife claimed to have bought the stock in order to resell at a profit, no sale was in fact made, notwithstanding that there was an improvement in the market and that the stock could have been sold at a profit to her of three-quarters of a million dollars. Subsequently, when the market price was $45 per share, taxpayer went through the form of a re-purchase from his wife at a price of $212 per share. The entire transaction was handled on advice of counsel, but not in the exact manner suggested by counsel. The Board of Tax Appeals held that the transaction was not a bona fide sale, and that the alleged loss did not constitute an allowable deduction from income; the fraud penalty asserted by the Commissioner was sustained.

In *Pleason*, 22 TC 361 (1954), the taxpayer was the sole owner of a wholesale whiskey business known as Royal Distillers Products. Being unable to obtain renewal of a license to carry on the business, he caused it to be transferred to his daughter's name, and it was thereafter known as Anne Davis, d/b/a Royal Distillers Products. However, taxpayer himself continued to manage the business as theretofore. The Tax Court not only held that the transfer was a sham and that the taxpayer is accountable for the income from the business, but sustained the fraud penalty on several grounds, one of which was the fraudulent nature of the transaction itself.

In *Jacksonville Paper Co.*, TCM 1954-116, the record showed that over a period of nearly 15 years, the corporation had paid no dividends, but that large salaries for the three principal officer-stockholders had been taken as deductions. However, only a portion of the deducted salaries were actually withdrawn. The largest part remained in a "pool," presumably subject to withdrawal at a later time. The fraud penalty was sustained by the Tax Court on the basis that the corporation should not have taken as a deduction all of the salary when only a portion was withdrawn.

In *Flato*, TCM 1955-216, the Commissioner, by amended answer at the close of the hearing in the Tax Court, asserted fraud penalties against the taxpayer, a subdivider, on the basis that he reported a profit from the sale of lots at capital gain rates, when he knew that he should have reported the same at ordinary rates. The Tax Court held that he had properly reported on the capital gain basis; therefore, the fraud penalty was automatically set aside.

And finally, in *Court Holding Co.*, 2 TC 531 (1943), involving a situation under the 1939 Code, which was drastically changed by the 1954 Code, there is an excellent illustration of how the fraud issue may enter into a seemingly clear "avoidance" transaction. The facts were that the taxpayer was a corporation with two stockholders, husband and wife. The husband, who largely looked after the business, acting for the corporation, orally agreed to sell the corporate property upon specified terms; and $1,000 was received on the purchase price. At a meeting between the parties for execution of a formal contract of sale, the stockholders were informed that a sale by the corporation would cause imposition of heavy income taxes. They refused to sell, but immediately caused the corporation to distribute the property in kind to them as a liquidation dividend, and they then passed title to the purchaser for the same purchase price. The Commissioner held, that for tax purposes, the sale was made by the corporation, and assessed deficiencies, delinquency penalties, and fraud penalties. The Tax Court affirmed the Commissioner on the issue of the sale being one by the corporation, but disapproved the fraud penalties. The Fifth Circuit (143 F.2d 823 (1944)) reversed the Tax Court, holding that since the contract of sale made by the corporation was legally unenforceable under state law because it was oral; the sale was actually made to the shareholders in liquidation. The court set aside the deficiency as well as the fraud penalties; finally, the Supreme Court reversed the Fifth Circuit and sustained the Tax Court.

Criminal cases.   The case of *Carleton*, 138 F. Supp. 516 (DC Okla., 1956), appears to be a startling misuse of the criminal statutes for what the record seems to indicate was no more than an avoidance situation. Taxpayer assigned commissions totaling $3,828, which he had earned, to his parents, who included these earnings in their own tax returns and paid the tax. For this, he was indicted for criminal tax evasion. The district court found him not guilty and indicated that the matter should have been handled by the Service as a civil and not a criminal case.

In *Pechenik*, 236 F.2d 844 (CA-3, 1956), the defendant was indicted and convicted for having caused the Colonial Products Company, a corporation of which he was president, to have filed a fraudulent tax return, in that through the device of treating capital expenditures as operating expenditures, the full amount of which were deducted by the corporation, its expenses were incorrectly increased and its net income

correspondingly decreased by charging off in a single year expenditures which should have been charged off during a period of years through depreciation. However, the conviction was reversed on appeal, but on grounds other than the propriety of bringing criminal charges on this particular concept of fraudulent tax evasion.

And finally, in *Hall, Sr.*, 32 TC 390 (1959), *aff'd.* 294 F.2d 82 (CA-5, 1961), the Commissioner reallocated income between the taxpayer, an individual, and a Venezuelan corporation which he organized and dominated, and also asserted a fraud penalty. The Tax Court affirmed the reallocation as proposed, but set aside the fraud penalty on the ground that the intent was to avoid, rather than to evade.

2. Partnership arrangements. In *Harmon*, TCM 1955-204, the Tax Court held that a partnership between a taxpayer and his stepson was a sham, but refused to sustain the fraud penalty which was asserted by the Commissioner.

In *Biles*, 149 F. Supp. 642 (DC Okla., 1957), the U. S. defended a refund suit on the ground that the taxpayer's claim, that a valid partnership existed between him and members of his family, was a sham and fraudulent, and counter-claimed for deficiencies based on civil fraud penalties; however, the jury found for the taxpayer on both issues.

In still another case, notwithstanding a written partnership agreement between the principal owner of a business and his key employees, the Tax Court held the relationship to be merely that of an employer and not that of a partnership; the fraud penalty was asserted by the Commissioner, but the Tax Court set it aside.

3. Sham transfer to others of income-producing assets and of evidence of ownership; assignments of future income. Affirming the determination of the Tax Court that fraud penalties were supported by the evidence, the Second Circuit in *Heyman*, 176 F.2d 389 (1949), *cert. den.*, held that a purported transfer of capital assets by a corporation to taxpayer's son and husband was merely an assignment of the right to receive future interests and did not relieve the stockholders of any tax liability. The facts in the case disclosed that the taxpayer (Mrs. Heyman) was a substantial stockholder in a corporation which was declared dissolved in 1933, existing thereafter only for the purpose of winding up its affairs. At this time the corporation owed its stockholders approximately $29,000 as a debt, and its primary asset consisted of a claim against the City of New York for over $700,000. In 1935, the corporation transferred to its stockholders and/or their assignees, in their alleged capacity as creditors holding a $29,000 debt of the corporation, the claim against the city in consideration of their waiver of interest and payment of expenses of the litigation against the city, which was to be continued in the name of the corporation. Taxpayer's son and husband were listed as owners of the designated share in this claim by the instrument affecting the assignment.

This case seems to present an attempt to short-circuit the well-established principle in tax law that an assignment of income will not operate to divest the assignor of his tax liability for the entire income. The fraud penalty could well have been the sanction imposed for persisting in using or attempting to disguise a tax-avoidance device long held to be invalid.

4. Miscellaneous avoidance plans. In *Brock*, 22 TC 284 (1954), the taxpayer arranged to open stock and commodity trading accounts with a broker in the names of each of eight relatives. He was granted a limited power of attorney to give, buy and sell orders to the broker. Taxpayer made the initial deposits as well as subsequent deposits in each of the accounts. These deposits were neither gifts nor loans to the relatives. No relative contributed any funds to these accounts. The understanding between the taxpayer and each relative was that profits thereby derived from the account standing in each relative's name were to belong equally to each of them; but that each relative would not bear any part of the loss of the amount advanced to the account by the taxpayer; and that before any division of profits, withdrawals from the account should be applied first to reimburse taxpayer for the amounts advanced by him. The various accounts were in fact managed by the taxpayer, utilizing his judgment, skill and acumen. The Tax Court held that taxpayer is accountable in full for the profits derived from the capital furnished by him. However, the court refused to sustain the fraud penalty which the Commissioner asserted.

In *Schwartz*, 213 F. Supp. 306 (DC Pa., 1964), the taxpayer was a Philadelphia attorney whose practice was primarily devoted to financial matters, many of them on an international scope. Taxpayer's practice required that he give counsel at various times on tax matters. During 1953, taxpayer suffered a capital loss of $174,000 which could be carried forward under the law then in effect, for five years. This loss carryforward, however, would be of no practical advantage to the lawyer unless there were capital gains against which it could be applied.

During 1954, 1955 and 1956, the taxpayer reported capital gains against which he applied the capital loss carry forward. The Government contended that in each instance in which a capital gain was reported, the taxpayer should have reported such income as ordinary income from legal services. Some of the assertions of capital gains by the taxpayer were not completely untenable; however, the clearest transaction adverse to him involved instances in which he took fees and invested them in real estate and similar investment outlets. He was found guilty by a jury and the trial court denied motions for acquittal and for a new trial. In stressing the evasion rather than the avoidance aspect of the case, the court referred to the taxpayer's evasive tactics during the course of the investigation, as well as the repetitive pattern of the reporting of what seems to be ordinary income as capital gains.

And in still another case, *Wenger*, CA-2, 1/26/72, the defendant, an accountant for a Union pension fund, was indicted, convicted, and conviction sustained, for tax evasion, where he attempted to avoid tax on ordinary income (a $15,000 finder's fee for persuading the Union fund which he represented to make a loan of $150,000 to another entity). He arranged to purchase antiques for $5,000, and then within a month resold the same antiques to the same dealer for $20,000, thus netting the $15,000 which he treated as short-term capital gain, offset by long-term capital losses.

And finally, in *Unger*, 159 F. Supp. 850 (DC N.J., 1958), the defendant, an attorney, was indicted on tax evasion charges for advising his client to prepare an income tax return for 1949 which did not disclose a capital gain resulting from the sale of stock by the client, which the Commissioner contended had been received by the defendant as agent for the client in that year. The deal for the sale of the stock was consummated on December 30, 1949, the last banking day of the year; on that date the defendant received a certified check for a substantial amount which he deposited in a trustee account in his own bank. On the following day, December 31, 1949, the defendant prepared two checks in favor of his client in discharge of his liability to her, which were deposited in her name in accounts maintained by her in her own bank on January 3, 1950. The district court, disregarding the strict rules of agency, sustained a motion made by the defendant to dismiss the indictment on the ground that under these circumstances the amount represented by the certified check was not reduced to the possession of the defendant's client in 1949 in the sense that the client could not have drawn upon it. Therefore he was not accountable for the amount as income constructively received that year.

Safeguards in avoidance situations

This sampling of cases demonstrates that the Commissioner on occasion does assert civil fraud penalties in what would appear to be avoidance situations, and that there is certainly no guarantee that the taxpayer, either at the lower or at the higher level of review, would prevail.

It is therefore highly practical to lay down a few safeguards for the benefit of the taxpayer and his tax adviser, which, if followed, may obviate the risk of the

Commissioner initially asserting the fraud penalty in a situation which the taxpayer and his adviser believe is a permissible avoidance plan, but where a difference of opinion as to whether any element of fraud is present, is probable:

1. Making a full and honest disclosure of what the transaction really is. By his return the taxpayer must place the Commissioner on notice as to the manner in which he is seeking a tax avoidance. A full disclosure should be made in all of the taxpayer's dealings with the Treasury Agents. Let the legal chips fall where they may; but let there be no doubt that the taxpayer has concealed anything as to what the facts are, either in his records, in his return or in his dealings with the Treasury.

In *Jarvis*, 5 TCM 459 (1946), the fraud penalty imposed by the Commissioner was set aside by the Tax Court even though the deficiency asserted by the Commissioner in a family partnership situation was sustained. One of the motivating factors for setting aside the fraud penalty was a disclosure of all the facts in the taxpayer's return.

Similarly, in *Jemison*, 45 F.2d 4 (CA-5, 1930), a fraud penalty which had been asserted by the Commissioner and sustained by the Board of Tax Appeals was set aside by the Fifth Circuit on the ground, among others, that all relevant matters affecting the transaction were shown on the return.

In *Dilks*, 15 BTA 1294 (1929), the petitioner stated in his return that he had received $74,604 which he was not reporting as income because he claimed it to be a gift. The Board of Tax Appeals held that the transaction was not a gift, but was income; nevertheless, it refused to impose the fraud penalty because the disclosure had been made in the return. Although this is not a true avoidance case, the analogy is strong.

And in yet another case, the fraud penalty asserted by the Commissioner was set aside by the Tax Court in a sham partnership situation, principally because a full disclosure had been made by the taxpayer.

Finally, in *Harmon*, although the partnership involved was held to be a sham so that all income was taxable to the taxpayer, the Tax Court set aside the fraud penalty principally on the ground that the return itself, which had been prepared by the taxpayer's accountant, stated that it was "incomplete" and that an amended return would later be filed, even though in fact no later amended return was ever filed.

2. From the start of evolving the tax avoidance plan, the taxpayer should keep a complete data file. The taxpayer should be prepared to prove his good faith at every step. If legal advice has been sought, the correspondence and legal memoranda should be made available for future inspection. Where corporate transactions are involved, the minutes of meetings of Board of Directors and shareholders should be up-to-date and properly executed. If a specific date of a transaction is important, supporting data should be available for verification purposes.

3. The taxpayer should fortify his position by the independent advice of competent and qualified tax counsel to whom a full disclosure of all the pertinent facts surrounding the purported avoidance plan has been made.

If these three rules are faithfully followed, we can be reasonably certain that if a fraud penalty is asserted by the Commissioner, it would not be sustained by the courts.

A word of caution

It should be clear by now that reliance on a tax avoidance device is not free from the risk of a fraud penalty being asserted by the Commissioner, or even on rare occasions, the risk of criminal prosecution. While it is true that the burden of proof would be upon the Commissioner as to the issue of fraud, if his assertion of fraud is contested, as a practical matter, the fact remains that a great deal of time, expense, mental anguish, and possibly the imposition of the fraud penalty itself may be the ultimate price which must be paid by the taxpayer by attempting a questionable avoidance device.

The tax adviser who suggests such a program bears a heavy responsibility, both to the Government and to his client, and he is not only entering what has been referred to as a "mystic field which only the initiated may enter," but, additionally, he is assuming the calculated risk that, should the avoidance plan fail, mere restoration of the taxpayer to the *status quo ante* will not heal the breach in the relationship between the tax adviser and the client, which the sudden call upon the taxpayer to pay up his tax deficiencies, together with interest, may create.

VII
GROWTH

Those who are successful grow and, thus, the seeds are sown for yet another round of managerial problems. Wise growth policies are needed if the enterprise is to weather this phase of its existence.

THE MANAGEMENT
OF GROWTH

33

Ironically, when the new venture has weathered the first storms of business (the concept has been proven and management tested) it is subjected to a second severe test, management's handling of its growth. Growth creates many problems, some of which can ruin the enterprise.

A small automobile battery manufacturer prospered in a regional area. He made a good product and his price was right. As his reputation grew he was approached by a large merchandising chain and given a large, lucrative contract to make its private brand for the year. The battery manufacturer accepted the contract and, on the basis of it, greatly expanded facilities, borrowing money to do so. The contract was renewed the next year but at a lower price; profitability was severely affected. The following year the price offered was below cost. He had to sell out, for he was committed to overhead costs and loan payments that he could not meet. It was simply a case of a man expanding too fast on the basis of business which could not be relied upon with funds which were too

expensive and had to be repaid, a most hazardous position for any enterprise. The man failed to manage the growth of his firm in a sound manner.

A small women's wear merchant was very successful with his small collegiate shop which catered to well-to-do coeds and town women who wanted to pass as coeds. As is wont with most successful entrepreneurs, the thoughts of expansion came forth from where they had been lurking in the recesses of his mind. He opened a larger store in another college town, only to have it quickly go broke for lack of his personal attention, among other things. While the merchant was a good manager of his one store, he did not know how to grow.

A small manufacturer of ski boots whose unique product was readily accepted by skiers rapidly expanded operations, adding buildings and most of the symbols of big business. He quickly encountered trouble. Sales dropped as the market became saturated and competition entered to counter his innovation. Costs rose rapidly because of the overhead that had been added to operations.

Managerial problems mushroomed, for the growth had been too rapid to allow a careful selection of personnel.

These three examples are given to illustrate some of the classic pitfalls into which the entrepreneur can fall in trying to grow. Now let's analyze them.

THE ENTERPRISE HAS NO GROWTH POSSIBILITIES

There are some businesses that cannot and should not grow. Sometimes an enterprise can prosper in one location serving one small market segment, but the market and the management is such that any attempt to grow will meet with disaster. Many small merchants feel that if they can just obtain a larger store they will automatically sell more goods and make more money. It may not happen that way. Frequently all they discover is that their overhead has increased. The acid questions which the entrepreneur must answer are:

• Is the market for my proposition sufficiently large that I can grow?

• Do I have the managerial depth and skills to operate a larger organization?

• Do I have the resources on which to expand?

Some entrepreneurs have no business at all trying to build a large organization, for their talents are inadequate to do so. It is one thing for a man to personally operate a small shop or plant; it is quite another for him to manage other people. Running a larger organization is an entirely different matter, for one is dealing with different problems than he was when he was small.

Two brothers started a small drive-in restaurant on a good corner location in a small western town. They prospered. As business grew bigger they hired more waitresses and expanded facilities. Then, to quote the owner, "One day I woke up and found I was doing five times the business I had been doing but making less money. I took a careful look at things and found out that I was working my tail off to support all these other people. So I fired 'em all, cut operations back to where my brother and I could run the whole show, and you know . . . we're doing less work and making more money!"

Growth is not synonymous with profit. There is an optimum size for every operation and many times it is at a lower level than one might think. By expanding such operations, all one encounters is increasing costs. Why then are entrepreneurs so eager to grow? Several hypotheses can be put forth. First, there is the definite myth that growth automatically means more profits. Second, and perhaps a more forceful impeller, growth can be an ego trip. Some entrepreneurs feel inferior simply because their businesses are small. They think that by building a larger company more prestige from their community will be forthcoming. There is some basis for this thinking, but only if the larger enterprise prospers. Third, the attractions of economic power are many. The small businessman has difficulty obtaining many of the things he wants because he is small. Certain popular brands of merchandise that the small merchant might like to carry may be unavailable to him because the manufacturers prefer not to deal with such small dealers. A package manufacturer may have a minimum order that precludes the small businessman from dealing with him. The small buyer pays a higher price for the things he buys, many times a prohibitively higher one. He must get bigger to buy competitively. Thus, the businessman sees that with a larger operation he will have more power in his resource markets. The desire to grow is strong; it takes a strong manager to control it.

INADEQUATE MANAGEMENT DEPTH

Many enterprises fail in their growth attempts because they lack the management depth to execute their plans. Too often the entrepreneur gets to feeling that he is omnipotent, that he can do no wrong, that he can manage a bigger plant as well as he can manage his small one, that he can manage two stores as well as he can one. He thinks, "I'll spend a half-day at each store." Famous last words! All he has is two half-managed businesses.

It is axiomatic that an enterprise cannot expand any faster than it has the personnel with which to do it. One successful men's apparel chain expanded only when it had a trained manager ready to take over the operation of a new store. Until a manager was available, no new store was established. The average small merchant does not have the management depth nor the ability to train it, thus his growth possibilities are limited until he somehow manages to develop such talent. The manager who is tempted to spread himself too thin frequently jeopardizes his entire operation.

INADEQUATE RESOURCES

It takes money on which to expand, preferably equity, for the use of debt poses severe risks. Debt increases overhead, interest costs. Debt must be repaid, usually rather quickly. These two factors place a great burden upon the growth to pay off rapidly. If calculations are wrong and the new growth's profitability is inadequate to meet its increased costs, then existing operations are burdened with its support. If those additional burdens are large enough, they jeopardize the solvency of the whole enterprise. Conservative financiers usually insist that there be considerable equity involved in expansion plans.

LACK OF PROFITABILITY

Amazingly, one would think that growth only occurs when an enterprise is profitable, but frequently such is not the case. Many enterprisers have plunged into ambitious expansion programs while their original enterprise was still unprofitable. One principle of finance is that one should not grow faster than his profitability. But the thinking of some entrepreneurs is that the reason they are not profitable is that they are too small; therefore, it follows in their thinking that if they grow bigger they will become profitable. Perhaps, but not likely. Usually all that occurs is that the man becomes more unprofitable. Until the enterprise has a solid profit base it has little upon which to expand and it is folly to do so.

WRONG INTERPRETATION OF SALES FIGURES

A new enterprise starts and its sales are immediately heartening. The business seems to be making money and sales are good, so why not expand? Well, a sales figure alone does not tell much. Sales can be high for a number of reasons, some of which mislead the unwitting entrepreneur.

Some unsophisticated entrepreneurs are not able to perceive the difference between ultimate sales and pipeline sales. Initially a lot of the sales may be going to fill the pipelines and once those pipelines are filled, repeat buying may be slow. The true key to future sales in many enterprises is the amount of repeat business, i. e., how sales hold up once the distribution pipelines are filled. In other instances, a business may have a large number of one-time sales but little repeat business; people try the product but do not like it. New food items are particularly subject to this risk; first sales may be meaningless.

Many times sales are good simply because the industry is riding the crest of a boom and when that boom slackens, sales will fall. It is important for the entrepreneur to judge where his enterprise is positioned in the business cycle. Expansion at the height of a boom just prior to a recession is a risky undertaking. The expansion is best undertaken at the bottom of the business cycle as it moves into an upswing. Resources are cheaper and a better perspective of the market is available at that time.

CONGLOMERATE GROWTH

The successful entrepreneur's general feeling of omnipotence leads him onto dangerous trails. On the national scene, large business organizations have already shown the fallacy of this thinking in their policies for growing by going into non-related businesses — the conglomerate movement. The economic history of conglomerates is rather dismal. They have not been particularly successful. Business theorists predicted this, for there are certain economic facts of life that make conglomerate ventures hazardous. The theory, of course, is that the enterprise diversifies into many different businesses and thus is no longer a prisoner of the forces of any one market which, of course, has some merit.

The conglomerates chanted a term called "synergism," the idea that one part of the conglomerate could help another part, thus make the whole greater than the sum of the parts. This sounded good in theory, but it just did not happen. In practice, there was very little communication between the various divisions of a conglomerate. Moreover, in practice a negative synergism developed in which a division that was in trouble would pull down the other divisions. For example, one profitable division of Litton Industries had its budgets cut and its resources curtailed to finance the losses in other Litton operations, much to the consternation of the manager of the profitable operation. However, the real Achilles' heel of conglomerate growth is inadequate managerial knowledge of the various industries. Frequently financial people who know little about an industry would take over management of some enterprise and proceed to make unwise decisions based on their preconceived general business principles that were at odds with industry realities.

One must remember that no matter what business he is in, there is a great deal of expertise required to be successful in it, expertise that cannot be gleaned quickly from books or talking with people. Only experience in the industry will provide such knowledge. Many businessmen have learned bitter lessons when the wisdom of the old adage, "Shoemaker, stick to your last," was painfully brought home.

Great care should be taken by the businessman who contemplates entering a different line of business. One successful men's wear merchant was being constantly harrangued by various people, including many of his own staff, to open a women's wear department since there were many stores that had put in women's departments with some success. He adamantly refused, saying, "I don't know anything about the women's wear business so I don't think it is likely that I'll make much money being the dumbest man in town in that business. I know men's wear, so that's where I'll stay." It was a sound business decision, for it is difficult to be particularly impressed by the success of operations that try to keep a foot in both markets. If you insist on venturing into another business, be prepared to pay for the lessons that must be learned in it. If you insist upon such ventures, try to obtain help from people who are experienced in that business. Go out and hire some expertise.

PLANNING FOR GROWTH

One excellently managed business is the Adolph Coors Company in Golden, Colorado. In particular, their policies toward growth command respect. The market for their product is phenomenal. Many people are unable to understand why Coors has not expanded rapidly to take advantage of the market situation in which they find themselves. Many unserved markets are crying for Coors beer. It is in short supply in many other areas, yet it does not have national distribution. But Coors management

adheres to its policy of planned growth. It has a policy that it will make its product in Golden, Colorado, from the resources located there. It will not build plants elsewhere. Moreover, it is expanding the capacity of the Golden brewery at a fixed rate each year on schedule. Its growth is so programmed that it maintains a permanent staff of construction workers to build the new capacity. Management controls its growth, making certain that it is profitable and sound while not jeopardizing the image of its product.

In contrast, there have been concerns that in haste to take advantage of market opportunities, have expanded so rapidly that product quality deteriorated, thus permanently damaging their reputation.

Try to isolate the policies of this company that have facilitated its rapid, profitable growth.

Jet propulsion in drug discounting

The Discount Merchandiser†

Does drug discounting win friends and influence repeat buying? It does in the case of Rite Aid, Harrisburg, Pennsylvania which has run its store count from 15 in 1965 to 170 by the end of 1970, and is opening units at almost

---

†*The Discount Merchandiser,* **August 1971, pp. 40-46.**

the rate of one a week. Lewis E. Lehrman, president, discusses the Rite Aid program for competing at a profit with all comers in drug merchandising.

What sort of volume do you do as an average per store today?

We are going at the rate of $600,000 per unit in our chain of 180 self-service drug stores.

What are your objectives?

We expect to operate about 1,000 stores by 1980. The annual compound rate of growth of our retail stores division has been the highest in the industry. We operate 180 stores today, after having started from zero in 1962. Of these, 110 were developed internally, the remainder by acquisition. Since January first of this year, we have been opening one store a week, and we are continuing our search for desirable acquisitions.

What explanations do you have for being able to achieve so much so fast with very little previous background in drug retailing?

One of the unique advantages our management team had was simply that we were not hung up on any of the prejudices that handicapped all the old-line retail drug chains. We didn't know whether a pharmacist was necessary to a store or not. We opened discount health-and-beauty aid stores along the lines of what we knew from our own rack jobber operations. If we had decided to incorporate pharmacies at the beginning, we would never have been able to open so many units. What we have done since, however, is to go back and review specific locations and install prescription departments in many of our older successful stores. Incidentally, during the past 5 years we have opened and acquired 86 full line pharmacies. A pharmacy is expensive.

Properly cost-accounted it runs to at least $8 an hour. If you are open 80 hours, it means $640 a week as a standing cost. That would require about $2,000 a week in prescriptions just to underwrite.

Do you cost-account all your departments the same way?

Yes. Unlike many conventional drug stores we demand that every department stand on its own. We have five major departments in our operations; health and beauty aids, housewares, grocery-related items (these are the household products such as waxes and cleaners sold in super markets), prescriptions and seasonal goods. We have added a sixth recently: franchised cosmetics. Each group is cost-accounted for the amount of service it takes to handle both at warehouse and store. For instance, we are completely self-service with respect to franchised cosmetics, because our figures show us that we ought not to do it any other way.

Could you give us a breakdown of sales by these various divisions?

About 75 per cent is in health and beauty aids, cosmetics, toiletries and prescriptions. Then there is 15 per cent in tobacco and cigarettes, and 10 per cent in sundries and seasonals. Sundry goods would include stationery, housewares, and the grocery-related items I mentioned before.

How different are your methods from discount stores when it comes to handling the same classification?

We think we are more discriminating as to selection of items, methods of merchandising, and tools for maintaining inventory control. Our store order-store delivery turn-around time is between 24 and 48 hours. We distribute out of our warehouse within a radius of 350 miles. One of the reasons why we are able to complete this cycle so fast is that we don't use the U.S. mails. Our telephone lines transmit merchandise orders in digital form during the day and night — via MSI system.

What is your turnover rate?

We are running about 9 turns in stores that are in business at least one year. This is comparable to super market drug turns, and as I understand it, higher than in discount stores. It is also twice the average annual turnover in a conventional drug chain.

When you talk of cost-accounting do you mean that this is also on an individual-item basis? Have you reached the point where you can determine costs of handling every unit?

We have the capability for doing it now, but since we are determined to sell all the name brands, we must carry them regardless of our handling costs. About 90-95 per cent of our sales are in these items. The rest is in our own private label. By the way, our *Rite Aid* private brand line now consists of over 400 items. We think our whole distribution program from warehouse to stores is one of the strengths that make it possible for us to maintain a highly competitive price structure.

Could you elaborate on these procedures?

We have around 250,000 square feet of drug warehouse space in Harrisburg, Pennsylvania. In addition, we have a warehouse of 160,000 square feet across the road which is our food distribution center. But 60 per cent, in dollar value, of the merchandise in the food distribution center goes to our Rite Aid stores. That applies to such goods as paper, housewares, household chemicals, tobacco goods, candy, and all the other merchandise which tends to overlap between super markets and drug stores. We also have a plant where we build our own fixtures, saving upwards of a half million dollars a year in capital and construction costs.

The warehouse is highly automated, relying on conveyor systems to move goods to consolidation points for shipment to the stores. All the merchandise leaves the warehouse already priced and store and date-coded for rotation purposes.

The merchandise arrives at the receiving dock and is moved by forklift past an IBM automatic data entry system. This communicates with our computer and logs in all received goods. It receives a communication back as to where to place the shipment in the warehouse — whether on the line or in the "floating" reserve. The forklift truck then follows the instructions. If delivery is made to the floating reserve, the merchandise is later moved onto the line as the line is depleted by the picking crew. The conveyor system is utilized to organize each store's order in the marshalling area for loading onto the 40-foot trucks which go to the stores. The marshalling area is elevated near the ceiling so that goods can roll down by gravity into the loading area.

Is it necessary to count the merchandise after it reaches the stores?

No. Here is the reason why. The computer system ties into the warehouse system; it invoices and prices each store directly. Suppose we start with the store order since that seems more logical for our discussion purposes. Every week the store manager and his assistants have to write the order. There is no automatic reordering — no forced distribution, nor orders generated by computer systems. We have watched attempts to develop automatic reordering and our conclusion is that good management right now is much better and no more expensive than so-called automatic replenishment systems.

The manager is assigned a specific day to compile his order based on what is in his four IBM order books. These contain twelve thousand line items, which are available to every store. The size of store will determine how many of those ten thousand line items it carries. That is established when the new store is set up. We use computerized shelf molding tags to determine the merchandise framework at the store level. Each item in the store, in other words, has been assigned a position along with a shelf molding tag that contains all the computerized information in our data bank referring to that specific item.

The orders are typed onto a tape by a clerk at store level and fed through the MSI system to the computer at the distribution center. All the store clerk does is transmit the order by telephone. As many as 12,000 line items might be handled on a single order. We have stores that order as many as 3000 lines per week — which is more than many super markets will order in a week in groceries. It takes only a few minutes to get the order to Harrisburg. The computer than invoices the complete order and sends it on to the drug distribution warehouse and the food distribution warehouse. To facilitate handling of goods at store level, we have set the warehouse up as a mirror image of the store. In that way all the items are organized by family groupings.

As the people working on the selection line pull merchandise, they affix price tags which have been printed out also as a mirror image of the invoices. If there are six pieces of Listerine ordered and our price is 99 cents, six tags looking exactly like tags made at store level are printed out on a separate sheet of paper to correspond with that order of six pieces. The selector puts those six tags on six packages of listerine and this goes on the conveyor along with all the other merchandise ordered by that particular store.

As you can see from this, we have a control built right into the system and therefore do not have to check receipts of the merchandise at the store. Should a person on the selection line be short of an item, she will have an extra tag on hand for that item. That forces her or him to pull another item. It is therefore very difficult for a person to make a mistake. If she were selecting two dozen can openers, for instance, she knows that she has to use up every price tag before she is through. All of the price tags are in the same sequence as the items on the invoice. The merchandise is placed into the tote box and sealed, then it goes on the conveyor and into the truck. The truck itself is sealed. At the store our security system requires that the truck be opened in the presence of the manager.

How often do you take store inventories?

About 3-4 times a year. As a result, we don't get to the end of the year and write off millions of dollars in inventory as a surprise to stockholders.

How much emphasis do you give to so-called merchandising in the stores?

Merchandising is important, but probably more important are our systems, our operating procedures. These systems were emphasized because of our limited financial resources, and because we had no trained manpower pool to draw on. The only way we could keep everything together was by instituting strong controls. We can tell you at any day in the week exactly how much merchandise is in any particular store throughout the chain. And we can give it to you in retail value. Our security department goes in and does inventories as part of its regular routine. If it finds the shrinkage in any store to exceed a certain tolerance, then we move in to correct the situation.

What do you consider intolerable?

We would not be happy with anything over 1-2 per cent, depending on the neighborhood. It would be unreasonable to look for less than one per cent in some places but quite reasonable in other areas.

Our assumption is that all these hard controls are designed to make you as competitive as possible. Are your shelf prices consistently lower than in discount department stores?

Positively. That doesn't mean we are always under everybody's individual prices. But overall, 365 days a year, we don't take a back seat to anybody on pricing structure.

Are you doing comparison shopping?

We have two people who work on pricing. Our computer has the capacity to deliver 4 pricing structures to our stores. We shop every area prior to a store opening to see what the competition is doing. We call these two people "inventory supervisors." They are not only involved with pricing, but also with inventory conditions.

What are the lines of organization like? Can you sketch out the chart?

It starts with the three senior operating officers: Alex Grass, chairman of the board, myself, as president, and David Sommer, senior vice president. Reporting to us are the many other officers and department heads, among whom are the director of

personnel, director of store security, controller, director of data processing, vice president of distribution, vice president of real estate, director of retail accounting and house counsel.

To continue: We have four division managers who take care of approximately fifty stores each through five supervisors each; a director of advertising and a director of outside vendors. This last person does nothing but monitor, control and correct errors in payment for merchandise and services sold to us by vendors. Only three per cent of our store goods come from outside vendors — but that is substantial when you are going at the rate of $130 million. He negotiates with every window washer, every pharmaceutical house that supplies us with "outs." He makes sure that we get 100 per cent on the dollar. It doesn't matter what kind of vendor is involved — a floor polisher, a book wholesaler, and so forth. If they don't serve us correctly, don't maintain our stocks, it is his responsibility to cut them out.

We try to focus each department head's functions in such a way that there is little overlap except at the top. We have a total of around 22 store supervisors who serve the four division managers. They continually train and retrain the store staff. Each has about eight stores to supervise. They also have to make sure that the orders are being written every week, that the merchandise is in good condition.

What is the size of store that you are building now?

We are putting in 6,000 square foot units on the average. But we are opening units as big as 12,000 square feet — one in Philadelphia and another in New York, for example. But that is as big as they are going to get. The 12,000 square foot store, however, is not merchandised with additional classifications. All we do is beef up the inventories in the lines we already are carrying. When we open a store that size, we expect to utilize the shelf-carrying capacity to the fullest to serve the heavy traffic we anticipate. With self-service we can use shelf space as a substitute for the labor involved in running into the backroom for stocking again and again. In a 12,000 square-foot store we consider a number of variables such as: What is the rent? In fact, the size of our store is almost always a mathematical function of the amount of rent.

How is that?

Well, if someone in a big regional mall is asking us for $6 a square foot, we are surely not going to build a store more than 5,000 square feet in size. Our rents vary substantially on a per square foot basis. In short, we have to determine the size by the rental cost as well as the volume anticipated. We usually tie our buildings up for fifteen to twenty years but we are generally obligated only for five to ten years.

Question: With approximately 40 stores in the bank, so to speak, what kind of locations are they going into?

Answer: They will go into 35 shopping centers and five downtown locations. Originally, we were only able to get downtown locations, because shopping center developers turned us down. We didn't have the net worth they required. Now that we have a better balance sheet than some of the bigger drug chains, the developers come knocking at our door.

Are you in shopping centers with discount stores?

Sure. We are the only drug store in that circumstance. We go in with a

super market and discount store and a few other satellite stores. But no other drug store, naturally.

How do you shape up against other drug chains?

We're rarely out of stock. Our prices are better. Our stores are neater. Our prescription prices are cheaper. We're more efficient and we make more money.

Where are you going to put all those 700-odd stores you plan to build?

We are expanding through contiguous geography. We will go in all directions, but in an orderly and planned fashion. Certainly, we will and are locking horns with other progressive chains like ourselves. But we think the market for our type of store is huge. There is a replacement factor involved also — the independent drug stores are on the wane, for instance. In 1970 about 1200 drug stores dropped out of business. A number of conventional drug chain stores also are facing difficult times. That is not to say that there is no more room for the independent. There is if he wants to do a good job. We have some very successful competitors among them now. The best managements will win.

What is the administrative function of the pharmacist if any?

He is always the co-manager of the store. He works in tandem with the front end manager.

In a 12,000 square-foot store, how many items are available to a manager?

He'd have about 12,000 line items available to him. We have 6,000 line items in health and beauty aids. We believe in carrying most sizes of items, not cutting them down as other firms do in discounting. The shoppers have different size medicine cabinets, and they are not going to buy larger sizes just because we want them to. We are out to satisfy the different inclinations of the consumers.

Do you handle some of the vendor-serviced displays such as appear in cosmetics lines?

No. Almost everything goes through the warehouse. All cosmetic items go through the warehouse.

Have you considered leasing departments in discount stores?

We have been approached by many requests of that kind, and our answer is always the same: We are not interested.

As you grow bigger, do you see yourself spreading out into wider assortments?

Not really. We see it more as an intensive cultivation of already existing lines. We are developing the lines we already have, because those lines are the best consumer non-durable lines that have national prominence. We don't have to worry about expanding them. We leave that to the manufacturers who are constantly doing that. Our job is to deliver brand name goods at a low price under the most convenient and comfortable circumstances.

Do you favor guaranteed sales from manufacturers?

We like that, yes. Most manufacturers are reasonable with us in that regard. After all, you have to see our situation as it exists: — Imagine in Central Pennsylvania, a small town with one drug distribution system doing $130 million worth of business. How many other points in the country are there like that? And isn't it efficient for a manufacturer to run a good part of his

production line through Rite Aid corporation? And when it comes to relations with salesmen, we have helped turn many of them from "rural" sales representatives to men who can produce as much and more than many salesmen responsible for giant metropolitan territories.

Since you have knowledge that combines food and drug strength have you considered the idea of going into family centers as well?

Yes, we have given thought to the idea but we are not interested in it. You know we have a rack jobbing business that does about $4 million and food wholesaling which accounts for $18 million, and we feel that we will be able to do well in excess of $100 million in the Rite Aid stores this year. Therefore, we are investing most of our money and manpower in the Rite Aid stores, because they contribute 90 per cent of our profits. We have a momentum that will probably carry us into the position of being among the top five drug chains in America in the not-too-distant future. In number of units we are in the top fifteen at the moment, but if you classify by volume, we are in the top twenty.

We see no reason to change from our very successful formula.

QUESTIONS

1. To what extent does the company's logistics system facilitate its growth?

2. What classic growth mistakes has the firm avoided?

TABLE 33-1   Five year financial review

YEAR ENDED FEBRUARY 28 OR 29

	1967	1968	1969
NET SALES			
Retail drug	$32,643,633	$40,831,820	$54,230,350
Wholesale drug	4,336,309	4,572,192	4,381,578
Grocery	11,777,813	13,161,005	15,266,271
Other	322,469	393,990	1,047,271
	49,080,224	58,959,007	74,925,470
COSTS AND EXPENSES			
Cost of goods sold, including occupancy costs	38,785,642	46,006,303	58,211,070
Selling, general and administrative expense	8,161,138	10,274,426	12,493,119
Interest expense	102,687	170,614	220,676
	47,049,467	56,451,343	70,924,865
INCOME BEFORE INCOME TAXES	2,030,757	2,507,664	4,000,605
Federal income taxes	805,067	1,018,103	1,722,295
State income taxes	116,052	134,376	270,674
	921,119	1,152,479	1,992,969
INCOME BEFORE EXTRAORDINARY ITEM	1,109,638	1,355,185	2,007,636
Gain on sale of real estate, less related income taxes			
NET INCOME	$ 1,109,638	$ 1,355,185	$ 2,007,636
AVERAGE NUMBER OF SHARES OUTSTANDING DURING PERIOD (a) PER SHARE	2,444,456	2,528,266	2,698,096
Income before extraordinary item	$ .45	$ .54	$ .74
Extraordinary item			
Net income	$ .45	$ .54	$ .74
NUMBER OF RETAIL DRUG STORES	83	105	117

(a) Shares outstanding for all periods have been computed on the basis of the average number of shares outstanding during such year after giving retroactive effect to a 2 for 1 stock split and companies acquired on a pooling of interests basis during fiscal 1970.

Adept management can create growth in the most unlikely situations.

1970	1971
$63,811,398	$79,498,953
3,980,445	4,160,125
15,871,904	18,563,655
1,489,869	2,102,527
85,153,616	104,325,260
65,035,734	79,686,748
14,703,759	16,873,646
385,014	797,515
80,124,507	97,357,909
5,029,109	6,967,351
1,884,039	2,617,244
398,766	542,762
2,282,805	3,160,006
2,746,304	3,807,345
	131,903
$ 2,746,304	$ 3,939,248
2,816,617	2,974,178
$ .98	$ 1.28
	.04
.98	$ 1.32
132	170

Homey hustlers — down-East look helps Maine outdoors store build national business†

FREEPORT, Maine — An old customer heard a disturbing rumor about L. L. Bean Inc. not long ago and went straight to the company with it. "Not going to put in a computer, are you?" he asked. "I remember '69 when you put the rug on the stairs. Place hasn't been the same since."

Customers like this make Leon Gorman, Bean's 38-year-old president, chuckle. "I'm surprised by the amount of detail they can remember," he says. And, though Bean does plan to get its own computer, Mr. Gorman doesn't intend to let it change the place any more than the rug did. Insistence on doing things in the tried and true way has been a big factor in the success of this hunting, fishing and camping emporium founded 60 years ago by Mr. Gorman's late grandfather, Leon Leonwood Bean.

In a retailing world of plastic, neon and the get-with-it sell, Bean's rambling wooden store remains a reassuring haven of durable wool,

†**Thomas Ehrich,** *The Wall Street Journal,* **December 5, 1973, p. 1.**
Reprinted with the permission of The Wall Street Journal, © Dow Jones & Company, Inc. 1973.

hand-stitched leather and no-nonsense styling. Bean sells outdoors gear to more than a million loyal customers each year. They include kings, presidents, housewives, insurance salesmen, students and factory workers. Four-fifths of them shop by mail, browsing Bean's homey, cluttered catalog. Bean's switchboard is lit up most of the time with calls from customers around the country who want to place orders, discuss merchandise, get a fall foliage report or just listen to the twangy accent of someone in a state most of them never even will see.

Open 24 hours a day

Many, however, do make at least one pilgrimage to this isolated town in southeastern Maine. Customers drive up in vehicles ranging from Jeeps to Rolls-Royces. They walk up two creaking flights of stairs to a merchandise-packed salesroom decorated with snowshoes and mounted trout. The salesroom is open 24 hours a day, 365 days a year, and often it is jammed. "In the summer it's wall to wall until three or four in the morning," says Buckey Arris, who runs the four-to-midnight shift. "Every year it gets more amazing."

Most customers spend several hours wandering through Bean's narrow aisles, inspecting shirts and sweaters piled on plain wood tables and trying on jackets wedged tight on pipe racks. "I've been coming here for 40 years," says one browser, Thomas Brown, of Madison, N.J. "Their goods wear like iron, and they're the nicest people. They gave me a new hat once when the stitching on the old one went bad. I probably wouldn't even have tried to return it to a New York store."

"It looks fabulous, doesn't it?" says A. M. Jones, a farmer from Iowa on his first trip to Freeport after years of shopping from the catalog. "I was afraid it would be fancy with a lot of trimmings."

Leon Leonwood Bean, known universally as L. L., launched his curious empire in 1913 with $400 of borrowed money and a hunting shoe of his own design, calling it the Maine Hunting Shoe. It had a rubber bottom and a waterproof leather upper. Fishermen and hunters discovered the homely but practical shoe — still Bean's best-selling product — and spread the word to other customers. And L. L. expanded his lines to include outdoor stockings, jackets and trousers. He also added factory and warehouse space to his building.

Night owls and ladies

L. L. didn't get around to opening a salesroom until 1940 or so. Until then, says Mel Collins, a longtime employe, "people wandered through the factory. We'd fit 'em right in the factory. They'd look around, see if anyone was lookin', and try on pants right there in the aisle."

Tired of getting up late at night and early in the morning to serve outdoorsmen and newly arrived vacationers who awakened him at home, L. L. started keeping the store open all night in 1954. Under pressure from his daughter-in-law, Hazel Bean, he also added a small ladies' department. It accounted for only 2% of sales last year, but Hazel Bean points out that wives formerly "stayed down in the car" while their husbands shopped because "there was nothing up here to interest them."

Bean began attracting a world-wide clientele of sportsmen and celebrities in the 1940s. The merchandise drew many. But others came to swap hunting and fishing yarns with L. L. "He was slightly deaf, so his voice boomed, and you could hear him 100 yards away," Mr. Gorman recalls. When sales of hunting products were banned during World War II, Mr. Collins says, "L. L. changed the name of the Maine Hunting Shoe to Leather-Top Rubbers and kept selling 'em." Then L. L. was called to Washington to advise on military procurement. His grandson says that "L. L. spent half his time in Washington at the ballpark. He was quite a baseball fan."

L. L. built customer loyalty by sticking with a no-questions-asked guarantee and refund policy. Not long ago, Bean refunded the $1.75 purchase price of a shirt purchased at least 32 years ago but never worn.

Tall tales and plain talk

When L. L. died in 1967, the store was selling some 400 items, and Harvard Business School was using it as a case study. Even so, Bean was more of a curiosity than a successful business. Sales had leveled off at $3 million a year, and earnings were only 2% of sales.

Then Mr. Gorman took over, modernized the marketing, latched on to the outdoors boon and turned Bean into a fast-growing, highly profitable enterprise. Sales now are climbing by 25% a year and should reach $20 million for 1973. Profits are a hefty 6% of sales. Employment has doubled since 1967 to 400 people.

To keep up with the expansion, Mr. Gorman has automated most paperwork, including mailing-list maintenance; the list used to be kept on three-by-five cards. Mr. Gorman also has instituted centralized buying and stricter inventory control, and he has tripled the advertising budget to $150,000 a year. But he is careful to preserve Bean's down-east image. He hires retired game wardens as salesmen just to have some yarn-spinners on the floor. "This is my first trip here in 10 years," says John Clancy, a salesman from Lake Harmony, Pa., "But it still has the same homey style."

Bean's principal selling tool is its 128-page catalog. Four times a year it mails a million catalogs to 50 states and 70 foreign countries. It gets 250,000 new requests a year for catalogs. The requests cost Bean less than 50 cents each, an astoundingly low figure compared with the several dollars that many advertisers expect to spend to fetch one inquiry. And 25% of new catalog recipients buy something within a year. The rest are dropped from the mailing list.

The catalog has changed little over the years. Product descriptions are straightforward. One flotation jacket, the catalog notes, is "not a substitute for Coast Guard approved life saving devices required aboard boats." Adjectives are low-keyed; flannel pajamas are "good," walking shoes are "comfortable," boat shoes are "practical," and a cardigan sweater is "rugged."

Prices seem reasonable. The Maine Hunting Shoe, for example, starts at $18.50 a pair. The Trap and Skeet Shoe made by Bass fetches $25. Abercrombie & Fitch calls the same shoe a Safari Boot and sells it for $32. Bean lists Stanley vacuum bottles at $14.80 to $21.60. Abercrombie prices the same bottles at $19.25 to $28. Scattered through the catalog are items like the popular $8.85 chamois-cloth shirt, wool shirts, unusual caps, trout flies, axes, animal traps, duck calls, tents and many others. Few cost more than $50 each. The most expensive, a canoe, is $375.

Bean leaves the market for gear used on highly technical expeditions like rock climbing to such outfitters as Eddie Bauer of Seattle and Eastern Mountain Sports of Boston. Bean also leaves the fashion market to others, such as Abercrombie. None of Bean's men's trousers, for example, is bell-bottomed or even flared. "We cater to the average guy who likes to enjoy the outdoors," Mr. Gorman says. "Most of us are average sportsmen ourselves. We know what works and what doesn't."

An occasional blunder

Bean takes pride in its antiquated factory, where it manufactures about 20% of its merchandise. (Its outside suppliers include Pendleton, the woolen weavers; Lee, the denim producers, and Bass, the shoemakers.) In Bean's 80-man workforce are 10 hand sewers who shape, track, trim and sew shoes and boots at old cobblers' benches at the rate of one an hour. Morris Hilton, production manager, says a machinery salesman once tried to talk him into gluing rather than stitching the soles of Bean's Ranger Oxford shoe. But Mr. Hilton balked. "It doesn't cost that much to stitch," he says, "maybe 85 cents a case (of 12 pairs). I like to see the stitches, and the customer likes to see them, so it's money well spent."

Bean tests merchandise offered by outside suppliers but only buys a few new items a year. "There aren't enough good new products around," Mr. Gorman says. Occasionally Bean blunders. Consumer Reports, for example, recently knocked a Bean sleeping bag with a combustible cotton cover. Bean promptly changed it.

Bean boasts next-day shipment of mail orders (except at Christmas) despite its staggering volume of 650,000 packages and one million pieces of first-class mail a year. The store is so well-known to the U.S. Postal Service that letters simply addressed "Maine Hunting Shoe" or "L. L. Bean" get delivered promptly.

VIII

TERMINATING
THE ENTERPRISE

Ironically, little has been written about one important managerial skill: how to go out of business — profitably. So far this book has shown how to start a business and operate it, but it is also necessary to know how to go *out* of business in the best way possible. In desperation some uninformed owners have been known to just walk away from an enterprise empty handed. They throw their cards in the middle of the table, get up, and walk out the door. While this may be advisable in some rare circumstances, there are other approaches that are usually more profitable.

It has not been unknown for people to declare bankruptcy and come out well off. This book will not dwell on that possibility because it usually involves skullduggery (the illegal hiding of assets) which cannot be condoned here. But suffice it to say that bankruptcy is one of the ways a business is terminated and there are people who use it skillfully.

This discussion is divided into two sections: selling a successful enterprise and getting out of a loser. They are two different games.

SELLING A
GOING ENTERPRISE

34

The classic method which most entrepreneurs dream of in selling their enterprise is to "go public," that is, having a public sale of the stock with the corporation becoming a publicly-owned concern. This method is most attractive because it usually results in the entrepreneur getting the highest price for his stock. Many times he not only sells his enterprise by going public but also maintains control of it if that is his desire. If the enterprise has a good record of profits, is of a nature that is tangible and substantial, and the amount to be sold is sufficiently large that the stock market institutions are interested in handling the action, by all means the entrepreneur should first examine this way out. Meetings with underwriters will guide his actions.

At this time in 1975 exceedingly few public offerings are being made because of the terrible condition of the securities market. People are just not too interested in buying stock. Going public is most feasible in the later stages of a bull market. Timing is everything.

SELLING TO
ANOTHER ENTREPRENEUR

Many small businesses are not able to go public because they are either too small to be of interest to the securities market or there is some characteristic of the business that makes it an unsuitable investment medium. Thus the business must be sold intact as a going enterprise to someone who wants to own such a business and has sufficient money to buy it. Such buyers are not easy to find. The price asked for a successful, going enterprise may be so high that few people have the money to buy it. Moreover, many would-be entrepreneurs are sufficiently egotistical that they prefer to start their own businesses from scratch in the belief that they can do so better, cheaper. However, there is merit in buying a proven, going enterprise in preference to starting one. A going enterprise is an operating system of proven capability. Its buyer is stepping into a reality, not a dream. He escapes the trials and tribulations that are always encountered in starting up an enterprise. He is off and running at full gallop. He does not have to crawl before he walks and this is worth a great deal of money, make no mistake about it. Thus, there are shrewd businessmen who prefer to buy a proven, going concern than take the time and trouble to build their own operations.

The focal point of negotiations is usually over price. What is the value of the going concern? There are a few rules of thumb, but they are only that, to guide you.

An enterprise has two values. First, there is the net value of its assets, what those assets could bring if sold independently in various markets. What are the values of its plant and equipment, inventories, accounts receivable, patents and other assets? These may or may not be accurately reflected by the company's book value. The minimum a business is worth is the cold, hard market value of its assets minus whatever liabilities are against them. The businessman who sells for less is a fool, but it has been done and not infrequently. This approach to the valuation of a business comes down to a matter of appraising the market value of the assets, which is not too difficult, although there is room for some disagreement in most instances.

The other approach to the valuation of an enterprise is by capitalizing the profits of the enterprise. A businessman does not particularly want to buy assets, for he can purchase them without too much difficulty. What he really wants is a profit machine. He wants a machine that will grind out a profit every year and he is willing to pay a certain amount of money for every dollar of that profit, depending upon the rate at which he wishes to capitalize those profits. Suppose a buyer wants a

minimum of 20 percent return on his investment; the rate of capitalization is then 20 percent. He should be willing to pay $500,000 to buy $100,000 of profit. Thus, if an enterprise apparently would generate a million dollars of solid profit, its value as a going concern at a 20 percent capitalization rate would be $5-million.

Now two problems arise: determining the true profit potential of the enterprise and fixing the rate of capitalization. Unfortunately, profit and loss statements seldom reflect true economic profits. Sometimes the reported income is much lower than the true profit. The businessman has taken excessive compensation or has written off many personal expenses against the business, thus lowering the apparent economic profits of the enterprise. This brings up a matter that many entrepreneurs overlook in trying to minimize the income reported from operations. If they wish to sell their enterprise, they may be wise to pay some income taxes. The records one keeps are one proof of the profit making potential of a business. However, existing records at best only show past experience. Only the naive focus on the past. What the buyer is interested in is the future profitability of the business. Thus, in a very real sense, the businessman can sell future profits if he can prove them. The basic trends in the industry, the economic soundness of the business, and its particular strengths and weaknesses all affect the buyer's profit expectations.

The appraiser examines the firm's operating statement, revising it to better reflect its true economic profit. Then the matter of capitalizing that profit arises, which depends upon the risks involved in the case. The higher the risks, the higher the rate of capitalization. If a businessman were buying into an operation that was risky, he might want to capitalize it at 50 percent or two times earnings. An operation that looked fairly secure might command a capitalization rate as low as 20 percent (five times earnings) but that would be most unusual. As a rule of thumb in selling a small business, it is very difficult to get more than three or four times earnings for the enterprise. Many sales are made for less.

In selling an enterprise, not only is the price negotiated but the terms of sale also are subject to negotiation. Many times the buyer has no cash with which to swing the deal or in his desire to protect himself, he wants the seller to carry a sizable note.

A word about this strategy. In buying a business it is unwise for the buyer to give the seller all cash and let him walk away from the deal, for he may have sold the business under false pretenses. He may have grossly misled the buyer in some respect so that the buyer would have recourse against him in court. If the seller has all of his money, not only may it prove difficult to find him, but the burden of getting him into court and collecting can be horrendous. On the other hand, if the buyer still owes the seller a great deal of money, he can stop payment and force the seller to go to court to collect, thereby settling disputes much easier. As a matter of insurance, smart buyers do not want to put up all of their money right away. They may put money into escrow to be delivered at a certain time in the future when everything has proven to be as represented and the seller has fulfilled his obligations. The income tax laws even encourage such contract sales. If less than 30 percent of the selling price is paid down, the seller can spread his taxable gain over the years of the contract.

In other cases, sellers are so desirous of getting rid of their businesses that they are willing to give attractive terms to the buyer, allowing him to literally pay for the business from the earnings of the enterprise. In such matters, the seller had better make certain that the buyer at least puts up a sufficient down payment to protect him from losses if the buyer runs the enterprise into the ground and ruins it. Keep in mind that if you sell your business on terms to someone who proves incompetent, he may ruin the total value of your assets. It happens!

From the buyer's point of view, buying on such terms is extremely attractive. It not only measures the seller's confidence in the ability of the business to make a profit, but it also enables him to get in on a minimum investment. When everything is boiled down, it really is a matter of how bad the seller wants to sell in comparison with how bad the buyer wants to buy, taking into consideration the financial resources of each party and his motivations.

It is impossible to generalize, for no two business deals are alike. The more one is involved in the buying and selling of businesses, the more he is impressed that there are few guideposts. Two parties can work out any sort of strange deal they want. Sometimes the seller takes his money out in the form of a royalty, he gets paid so much per unit. Sometimes he holds a mortgage on all the property. As a general principle, the seller is advised to gain all the security he can get for his investment in the enterprise; if things go sour he wants to make certain that he can get control of the hard assets before the general creditors seize them.

Along this line, some owners will sell the business but retain ownership of all the hard assets such as buildings and equipment, which are then rented to the business. In that way, if anything goes wrong the seller still owns the property. In the meantime, he has a good rental income. Moreover, it lowers the price of the business.

The seller's tax position should also be taken into consideration, for there may be definite tax advantages for him in stretching out payments over a period of time. It all depends upon his situation. Most sellers are wise to grab the money and run. Taxes should not lure one into a bad business deal. Time inserts huge risks into any transaction. The longer one is in a deal, the larger the chance that it will go sour, so take the money, pay taxes on it, and go play golf!

METHODS OF SELLING A GOING ENTERPRISE

There are business brokers who list and sell going concerns. Experience with them has not been good. Not only are they expensive (10 percent of the sales price), but also they are not on the side of the seller in negotiations. They know that it is to their advantage to cater to the man with the money, the buyer, and they do everything in their power to please him. One should be most careful about using a business broker. If one signs an agreement giving one the right for six months or so to sell a business and then if the business is sold during that period of time by anyone else, a commission of ten percent of the sales price is still due the broker, whether or not he did one lick of work. There are brokers who list every business possible, then do nothing; they collect commissions on those businesses that happen to sell by some other means.

In selling your business sometimes it is best not to let others know how eager you are to sell it. The minute other people think you must sell or are eager to dispose of your enterprise, your bargaining power is lessened. If you are running a successful operation, people will regularly drop hints to find out about your interest in selling it. How these are answered is important. The inquiries should not be cut off abruptly, but on the other hand, one should not appear eager to sell. Rather, you want to let them know that under the right circumstances you might consider talking.

One businessman liked to answer such feelers with, "Well, there's an old saying that everything is for sale. Under the right circumstances I could be interested, but I can't really give you much encouragement, for I have a good thing here."

But be warned that there are many people posing as potential buyers who are just plain nosey. They pretend to be buyers, but really just want to look at your books and find out about your affairs. The man who is really interested will ask you to put a price on your business. If it is ridiculously high he will walk on, but if it is within reason then negotiations may start.

A good faith potential buyer will insist not only on full access to the company's records but also will want to closely observe operations for a period of time. Moreover, he will want to talk with the people who do business with the firm, suppliers, bankers, customers, employees. He is looking for booby traps. Are big, important customers about to go elsewhere? Is a key employee about to leave? Is keen competition about to make itself felt? Is an important supplier about to cause problems? The buyer is fearful that the real reason for the owner's desire to sell is that something bad is about to happen to the company's fortunes. It is difficult for the buyer to understand why someone would want to sell a good business since he wants to buy one; thus, the buyer is continually trying to ascertain the seller's motives.

SELLING A FAILING BUSINESS

Few things are more difficult to unload than a business that is not doing well. The buyer must be a man of great perception, able to see values that others do not. He sees what is wrong with the enterprise and thinks he can correct it. Thus, he is in a position to buy a bargain. The trouble with buying a truly successful operation is that one pays a large premium for success. There are few bargains in successful ventures. The bargains are to be had in failures that can be turned successful, but there is a shortage of people with such foresight or talent. Perhaps a business has a location or a product or some obvious asset that a buyer may want to acquire. If so, fine; the business may be salable. All too frequently, however, it doesn't have any such assets. The owner is faced with the unenviable task of unloading a dead elephant.

Even though the business may be failing, the important thing is to not let other people know it. Keep your mouth shut. Everything should appear to be going fine. Businessmen are bigger gossips than their wives. The minute they see a vulture flying overhead it's all over town. So it is most important that the businessman maintain, insofar as he can, the facade that he has a good business.

Which brings up another point. It is important that an entrepreneur recognize when to abandon ship, for if he waits too long he will go down with it. The sooner the entrepreneur recognizes he has a loser on his hands and he can't do anything about it, the better; many times he can unload it before the overt signs of failure are observable. Bear in mind that the man who is operating a business, if he has any gumption at all, should know far in advance when his company is getting into trouble. Many times he will know a year or two in advance; thus he is able to make his move before there is much evidence of the plight of the enterprise. Do not wait till the sheriff knocks on the door, for he will not be there to buy the company. He will be there to seize it.

In old days an owner of a played-out gold mine would distribute some ore samples around to entice naive buyers to believe there was still gold in the hole. "Mines" are still salted today, but by more devious means. Let's recount a few.

Doctoring the books is not unknown, even in the highest of circles. Some businessmen report sales not made. Just because a merchant says he took in so many dollars in a month does not really mean that such sales were made. He could have floated some of his own money through the cash drawer and into the bank account, drawing it out again. Don't worry about income taxes; he knows there is no income about which to worry. He may not report some of the purchases made, thus inflating his gross margin. He may not record some of his costs of doing business. Thus, a profit and loss sheet can be totally fictitious.

Do not for one minute jump to the conclusion that this course of action is recommended for sellers, for it is not. It is fraud and the buyer has legal recourse against the seller when he finds out about it. It is only mentioned here because it is done and buyers should be aware of it. The other fellow's books cannot always be believed. It is better to reconstruct a profit and loss statement of one's own.

One merchant desiring to sell his store would sandbag potential buyers by creating a false scene of activity. Suppose a buyer made an appointment to see the business at 3:00 p.m. The merchant would have all of his family, relatives, and friends continually troop in and out of the store to create a false sense of activity. Nothing scares a potential buyer off faster than an empty store or inactivity. Smart buyers will sit outside a business and observe its operations, counting the people going in and out and what they buy. Take a look at the amount of mail coming in and out of a business. A prosperous business receives and sends a lot of mail. Any buyer of experience can walk into an enterprise and immediately tell whether or not it is prospering just by what is going on. One can tell whether goods are moving out or sitting on the shelves, whether a shipping room is busy or not. Inventory levels tell a great deal.

Try selling the business to a competitor; he may be harboring a desire to grow and taking over the operation may represent the cheapest and quickest growth opportunity for him. It may be the highest price one will get for the business.

Can a business be transformed into other enterprises of more value? The owner of a small downtown department store was unable to rent the premises after the business in it had failed. It did not seem likely that an enterprise could survive in that location. He saved the day by converting the building into

offices and he bailed out over time by leasing them.

A manufacturer was failing and was unable to save his business, but it was in a large plant. He converted it into a storage warehouse and was able to come out of the situation in fine fashion.

The questions the entrepreneur must ask are, "What is it I really have to sell and who might be interested in paying me the best price for it?"

GIVE IT AWAY OR RENT IT

If the business cannot be sold, perhaps it can be given away advantageously. A franchisee for a fast food chain ran into financial difficulty when the concept failed. He wanted out but couldn't find a buyer. He did find a couple who was willing to take over the operation but who had no money. He put them into the business without any money down with the understanding that they would pay him so much a month rent if it was earned. In essence, he rented his enterprise. It is better than letting it sit there and go to pot, for one of the salient principles in most instances is that no matter what, it is very important that the entrepreneur do everything possible to keep his enterprise operating. Once he closes the doors the value of his enterprise drops precipitously. Creditors immediately begin taking actions that the businessman is not apt to enjoy. Creditors will usually hold off as long as the business is still operating and there is some hope of being repaid. Remove that hope for repayment and court actions are apt to follow quickly. Once one creditor runs for the courthouse, the stampede is on.

Lest the seller become discouraged about his prospects of selling his business, let him read the words of one observer of the scene.

On this subject of selling the business, one of the most amazing things is the number of investors who stand ready with cash in hand to buy the businesses of the imaginative entrepreneurs, seemingly lured by the romance of some of these wild endeavors. Perhaps these potential buyers have no imagination of their own and simply admire the fortitude it takes to start a business. Many of them seem to have no business sense at all and are simply playing with Daddy's dollars. Suckers is what I call them.

There are other explanations for the supply of buyers. Business holds a fascination for many people. They feel compelled to get into something, but lack the skills to begin a business. Then there is the call of freedom, "Oh, if I could just be my own boss!" Thousands of people work and save for years to buy their own businesses. A man in his fifties told the consultant whom he had retained, "I am an accountant with a large company. I have saved $60,000 and want to buy a business. I need help in evaluating them."

The two men looked at several enterprises, but each was rejected for one reason or another. After six months of searching, they found a liquor store in an excellent location that looked good. A sale was negotiated; $30,000 front money was put up against a sales price of $50,000. The $20,000 remainder was placed in escrow to be paid in one year if the seller's representations proved truthful.

STOCK FOR STOCK EXCHANGES

If you have been moderately successful and have built an enterprise that has some merit, you may be approached by some larger concern with an offer to buy you out. Perhaps the buyer is a corporation whose stock is listed on some exchange. Usually such offers are not for cash. Rather they offer to exchange stock. The ratio is set by fixing the valuation of your firm and giving you that much stock value in theirs for it.

The bait that makes you tempted to go for such a deal is twofold. First, stock-for-stock exchanges are tax free; no tax is paid on the transaction and that is a big temptation because there will probably be a big tax bill on a cash sale. Chances are that your initial investment was quite small and that you have built up an organization that is very valuable. Practically all of the sales price is gain.

Second, the buyer usually gives you the full asking price, which is highly inflated. You are so delighted to get your price that you park your brains at home. The reason that the buyer is giving that price is that you are giving him his on how you value his stock. And he knows he is a bigger liar than you; his stock's price is more inflated than yours is. True, you are tempted to believe the price of his stock because it is listed or is traded over the counter and it seems to have a market value, but wait until you try to sell it.

First, many times the buyer stipulates that you can not sell the stock for a certain period of time. Thus, there is no way of knowing how much the stock is really worth until it is sold. Experience clearly has been most bitter with these deals. When you go to bail out, you get little.

Second, even if you are allowed to sell the stock, you will find the market will be so thin that you will depress the price quickly and will run out of buyers for it.

The only situation in which to go for a stock transfer deal is when the buyer is a large firm whose stock is sold on a big exchange and one can unload it at his own discretion. And that discretion should not be too delayed.

If the buyer does not give the right to sell his securities, then you should try another tactic; get some cumulative preferred stock on which the seller must pay money each year if it is earned. When a person is left holding just common stock, there is a good likelihood that in the end he may get absolutely nothing for his business. It has happened. Many times!

The best advice is usually to take cash and pay the taxes.

The bulk sales laws must be observed. When a person or company is selling a business in total (bulk) he must notify all creditors of the impending sale so that they may press their claims for payment. If they have not been so notified, their claims against the assets will follow the assets into the hands of the buyer.

While it is true the buyer would have claim against the seller in such circumstances, he might find it difficult to find the seller or collect from him if the matter arose. The key is to set up a deal in which the chances for such legal actions are minimized.

Again, now is the time a lawyer is needed. However, care should be taken so that he does not spoil the deal. It happens! A buyer and seller have a meeting of the minds about selling a business and take the deal to their respective attorneys who start earning their keep by telling what each must do to protect himself to get a good solid deal. Now be clear about this, the interests of the buyer and seller conflict at many points; there is plenty of room for disagreement. Each lawyer points out all of these problems and demands a contract to protect his client, as he feels he should. Each party reacts adversely to other's demands and the deal is blown out of the water.

Actually, if the seller is totally cooperative and agrees to everything the buyer's lawyer wants, the buyer has reason to worry. One tale about this aspect. Two men were buying a small jewelry manufacturing concern that was in terrible shape; it was a worthless enterprise but it looked like it had a good product line. The seller told a good story and had the documents to support it. The buyers brought their lawyer into the act, the seller had none (he did not need one in this instance!), who made an astounding number of outrageous demands — strict covenants not to compete, all sorts of representations, an agreement to buy the business back if it was not as represented, an agreement to pay for all repairs to equipment for the next six months, and so on. The lawyer had not been out of school more than two months and they hadn't told him about these matters in law school. The facts were that the seller could not have cared less. He was going to take the money and leave town. The buyers could no more have collected on any of the representations than they could make a profit on the business. Papers are no better than one's ability to make the signers do what they say they will do.

If a deal is not sound for both parties, it is not a good deal and will likely fall apart.

From the seller's point of view, he should realize that just selling the business does not necessarily free him from all concerns. The buyer may be back with some claims if he feels some misrepresentations have been made. Normally, the buyer's lawyer tries to make as part of the contract all the documents and statements the seller has made in selling the business to the buyer as proof of what the buyer was told by the seller. Care must be taken with what is said and given to the buyer. Even the truth may prove to be false and used against one later. A person's attorney may try to block such moves against him by placing in the contract statements as to exactly what he does represent and then say that he represents nothing more than that. But then the buyer begins to get suspicious, so . . . the deal may blow up.

SOME CAUTIONS

With a valuable business, do not assume that you can take a note from the buyer using the business for security with the thought in mind that if the buyer fails to perform you can always walk back into the business and salvage your investment. First, the buyer may have ruined the business; it can happen quickly without the seller's knowing it. Second, he may have run up a great deal of debt which is against the business so all you will be taking over are his debts.

Bear in mind the thinking of the person who has bought the business and has run into trouble. He wants to salvage what he can for himself. So he will grab the cash and other valuables that are available, run up debts, and not maintain the property. He can do this for some time before you will sense what is going on. Then he may, or may not, run for cover. In any case it would be difficult to recover losses.

Deals in which the buyer pays the seller out of the profits of the firm should only be considered out of sheer desperation. You would not be selling a business, you'd be renting it. And in the end you would not even own it. Get substantial front money or you'll likely rue the day you made the deal.

If you must sell on some pay-out-of earnings deal, make certain you keep title to the property until you have been paid. It greatly facilitates your legal repossession of the enterprise.

SOME LEGAL ADMONITIONS

Both the buyer and seller should have legal advice in making a sale for there are many serious legal problems that must be resolved.

Sellers may have tax problems to consider for the wording and substance to the sales contract may greatly affect how the IRS will treat the sale. If the business is being sold for a profit, the seller wants to make certain that they are treated as capital gains. However, if the contract contains clauses in which the seller agrees not to compete or agrees to do some managerial work or advisory services for the buyer, separate values may be placed on those aspects and they would be treated as ordinary personal income. The matter of value of the various things sold is of critical importance; only the sale of capital assets are treated as capital gains. Other assets can be treated as ordinary income.

Goodwill is a capital asset and the seller would be interested in having that part of the purchase price which is in excess of the value of the assets designated as goodwill. However, the buyer would want no part of that for goodwill can not be depreciated. Thus the valuing of the firm's assets is a critical step in the sale of a business.

If the enterprise is a corporation, the basic decision must be made as to whether the buyer is to buy the corporation's assets from the corporation or buy the owner's stock in the corporation from the owner. If the sale concerns the stock, then the sale is clearly a capital gain or loss.

However, usually the buyer's lawyer prefers that his client buy the corporation's assets for fear that the corporation may have debts or liabilities that are unknown. It is rather shocking to buy a company and then discover that what one really has acquired are some large debts that were previously hidden. There is really little the buyer can do to discover some of these liabilities so the risk is quite real.

But buying a company's assets is no sure way of avoiding such difficulties. In certain instances, liabilities will follow the assets right through a sale to the hands of the new owner. If the seller has not paid property taxes on the assets, the county tax collector will place a lien on the assets no matter who owns them. Make certain all taxes are paid on what you buy.

Here is a short article warning the seller about his problems in seeking advice. It also points up a big problem area — the mental barriers to selling one's offspring.

*****

How to play "You Bet Your Company"

Arthur Cuse†

Selling a company can be a lot tougher than buying one. The reason is simple. The businessman who wants to sell his company likely has never sold a company before. But the businessman who is buying a company may have extensive experience.

In regards to the experience of the two parties making the deal, selling your company is similar to buying a car. You may buy a car only every few years, but the man you are dealing with sells a couple of cars a week, maybe one every day. Obviously, the odds are against you that you will outsmart the car salesman.

When you sell your company, the disparity between your experience in selling and the buyer's experience in buying can be even greater. What's more, the stakes are a lot higher.

Most often, buyer and seller fail to agree on price vs. value. The buyer makes an offer, but the seller values his company at a higher figure. Perhaps 85 per cent of deals people would like to make don't go through ostensibly because of failure to agree on price.

But in many instances, price is not the real issue to the seller. The real issue is that the seller is not psychologically ready to sell, regardless of the price. The seller is playing "You Bet Your Company" for the first time, and he is worried, maybe even scared.

To begin with, the seller worries that if the buyer has agreed to a deal, then he must know something that the seller doesn't. Is there going to be a boom in his industry next year? Will shortages

---

†**Arthur Cuse,** *California Business*, **July 11, 1974.**

Mr. Cuse is a Los Angeles based independent business consultant who specializes in long-range planning and acquisitions. This material initially appeared in *California Business*.

suddenly appear and force up prices and profits? Is the government going to fund some massive program that will mean extra business?

In thinking over the deal, the seller becomes disturbed. Obviously, he thinks, his company is worth more than he asked, more than he agreed to. He is giving his company away. His friends will laugh at him. His wife will remind him of his bad judgment for the rest of his life. His children, deprived of their rightful inheritance, will scorn him. His dog will snarl at him.

Besides all that, the seller believes the buyer to be a heartless, soulless, mechanical man. All he talks about is money. He doesn't understand that the seller is selling his child, his baby, his life. The very smoothness and casualness of the professional buyer strikes fear in the heart of the seller.

These feelings, groundless though they may be, are the classic symptoms of seller's remorse. In a reverse situation, they would reflect buyer's remorse. But the net effect is the same: I never should have made the deal.

Such reactions are the reason that a good many deals get to the closing day and suddenly fall through. It happens all the time with automobiles, houses, boats and weddings — corporate or personal.

The basic problem is that the seller, who may be very good at building a business and running a business, has no experience in selling a business. Naturally, he will seek advice.

Most often he turns first to his old friend, the corporate attorney. This is the guy who incorporated the business 20 years ago, wrote the seller's one-page will, got his kid off on a marijuana rap, and handled the buying and selling of several houses or lots.

Seeking his advice appears to be a logical move, but it really isn't for three reasons.

First, even in major law firms in big cities, the number of attorneys who are experts in mergers and acquisitions are few. Chances are that your corporate attorney, however competent he may be, simply doesn't have the experience to make a sound judgment in this area.

You wouldn't go to a general practitioner for open heart surgery, but the equivalent happens all the time in the legal field — and with not better results, usually.

After all, when you are playing "You Bet Your Company," you don't want anyone learning at your expense, especially if the people across the table are professionals. That's like a grade schooler playing poker against Amarillo Slim.

Second, your attorney has a vested interest in your not selling out. If you do sell, he is sure to lose your company as a client.

Third, recommending against a deal is a lot safer than recommending in favor of it. If an attorney advises "no" but you go ahead and make the deal, he is in the clear if anything goes wrong. If he says "yes" and something does go wrong, even though he's blameless you might sue him. It's no surprise, then, that your attorney is likely to decline to take the risk of advising yes, especially in rough economic times, when more things can go wrong with a deal.

For these same reasons, seeking the advice of your accountant is rarely helpful. He likely isn't an expert in mergers and acquisitions, and he doesn't want to lose your business or be sued either.

Nor are finders or brokers of much help. Most aren't willing to take a deal through to its completion. They run an introduction service and think that's enough. But if you aren't experienced in this kind of negotiations, then it's not enough.

What to do?

You have to be willing to work as hard and as shrewdly in selling your business as you did in building it. And that means that you must seek out, through arduous research, specialists who can help you make a sound decision.

Although it's a comfort to have old friends like your attorney and accountant around in a time of stress, which selling your company is, remember this: If you are not careful and do not have expert advice, a deal to sell your company can be like the joke about insurance policies — what you get in the large print is taken away in the small print.

Statistics suggest that a lot of sellers are victims of the small print. They do not realize what has happened until months, maybe years after the deal is made. Most often, it's then too late to make corrections.

So when you are ready to play "You Bet Your Company," bring in the specialists rather than the general practitioners. Otherwise, like that grade schooler playing against Amarillo Slim, you are not going to get even odds.

QUESTIONS

1. Why do sellers so frequently make bad deals in selling their businesses?

✻✻✻✻✻

The expert's role in a company valuation

Gerald A. Sears†

When the value of a company must be determined for legal purposes, courts and counsel are often confronted with a complex and confusing area of judgment

†**Gerald A. Sears,** *The Practical Lawyer,* **January 1971, Volume 17, No. 1, pp. 11-34.**

Reprinted with the permission of *The Practical Lawyer,* 4025 Chestnut Street, Philadephia, Pa. 19104. Subscription rates: $12 a year; $2 a single issue.

that can only be traversed with the aid of a qualified financial expert.

The question of value can arise in many contexts; it is a critical factor in determining a distribution of the company's assets and can be a major element in litigation arising from tax, estate, and corporate matters. Given the importance of both the money involved and the significant number of times when a corporate valuation is a key element in a trial, it is felt that a thorough treatment of this area could be helpful to the practicing lawyer.

This article will focus on what an expert — such as an investment banker — does in company valuations. It will explore those areas where an expert can reasonably be expected to make a contribution, while also indicating the limitations in the use of any valuation expert.

Unfamiliarity with the different methods used to arrive at value often gives rise to apparently conflicting values, which tend to confuse both the court and the trial lawyers. A clearer understanding of the various types of valuation can materially reduce these conflicts.

The expert's approach to value

When the financial expert approaches the valuation of a company within the framework of a legal problem, he not only must determine what the company is worth, but also must set forth his ideas of value in as straightforward and simple a way as possible. Furthermore, he must realize that the court's duty to set a value between two conflicting viewpoints can be very different from the business approach of negotiation to arrive at value.

Definition of value

There are classic definitions of value. A common one is as follows:

"The fair market value is the price which the property will bring if exposed for sale in the open market by a seller, who is willing but not obligated to sell, allowing a reasonable time to find a buyer, who is willing but not obligated to buy, and who buys knowing all of the uses to which it is adapted and for which it is capable of being used."

This definition has been used so universally that experts, lawyers, and judges do not give it too much thought anymore. It is important, however, to understand what constitutes a "willing buyer or seller" and what a "reasonable time period" means in the context of a given situation.

The value of a company depends not only on its inherent worth, but also on the time frame in which it is offered, the number of potential buyers, the "popularity" of that company or industry at the moment, and a myriad of other factors.

Combination of assets

Any company consists of a collection of some or all of the following: some bricks and mortar, machinery, people who show up every morning for work, and customers who tend to do business with the company in preference to others. The last item, customers, gives the company that attribute known as good will. Bringing all these functions together in one place gives more value to the sum of the parts than to each part individually.

Clearly, the laborer skilled in working in the vineyard is not quite as valuable if there is no vineyard, nor does an unfinished subassembly necessarily have its pro rata share of the value of the completed product. The job of the expert is to quantify how much value is added merely by having all of these factors together in one place at one time. Therefore, the expert is not only responsible for establishing, for example, how much more a boat is worth in navigable water than it is sitting in a desert, but also for explaining the difference in value in as simple and convincing terms as possible.

Types of valuation

Economic and asset valuation

Two major types of "accepted" valuation should be distinguished:

• The "going concern," or *economic* valuation; and

• The engineering, or *asset* valuation.

They are not incompatible — quite the contrary. The asset valuation can be an important aspect of the economic valuation. The asset valuation cannot tell the whole story because it simply lists the tangible assets that the company owns without addition (or subtraction) for the value of the company as a going concern.

Concepts of value

Some counsel and the courts may tend to view the company valuation expert with a jaundiced eye because about eight different concepts of value can be used. These are:

• Passive values

Book value

Reproduction value

Net depreciated value

Substitution value

• Active values

Investment value

Market value

Going concern value

Capitalized earning power value

Active values are those that give effect to the "going concern" nature of the company and should be used whenever a company is in operation. Passive values assume that a company has ceased operations or is in liquidation, or that liquidation is contemplated. Because some of these valuation terms are used so interchangeably, they can be rather confusing.

Primary and secondary factors

The value issue is often further clouded by factors that are relevant outside the court but with which the court may not be entirely familiar. These can be illustrated by showing considerations of primary versus secondary relevance in most company valuations:

• Primary relevance

Financial considerations about the company

Management

Economic conditions

The company's products and position in its industry

• Secondary relevance

Nature of a proposed transaction

Nature of the consideration that might be paid

The way in which the stock of the company is distributed

Financial requirements of large stockholders

As can be seen, those factors under primary relevance all point toward the value of this company without outside influences — including the type of present ownership and hypotheses as to the owners' willingness to accept a certain type of transaction. Simply stated, if the company is owned by a little old lady from Chillicothe who will only sell to a white-haired, brown-eyed Presbyterian minister from Springfield, the result is that she has significantly decreased the market for the company and therefore the price she can receive. But in most cases this should have no effect on the real value of the company.

Public offering
or acquisition
as basis of value

Usually there are two types of actual transactions that establish the highest value of a company — a public offering or an acquisition. Value may have an assumed transaction as a basis. No attempt will be made here to divorce possible types of transactions as a basis of establishing value. Rather, it is suggested that every type of transaction be considered in a valuation.

In acquisitions, the difficulty in adjusting value by making assumptions about an assumed purchaser of the company is that it can open the door to unlimited conjecture. In order to determine the quality of the securities received, if this is the form of payment, one would have to do a complete analysis of the acquiring company.

A responsible expert will assume that the acquiror is reasonably well managed and has a good financial position, a conservative capital structure for its industry, reasonable earnings stability during adverse periods, and an earnings growth trend better than that of the seller's company, or at least equal to it. He will further assume that, if the seller receives securities, they have a reasonable basis of return or yield, a record of some price stability during market declines, and a reasonably liquid market.

There is, in addition, the overall assumption that the securities received were not overpriced in relation to the acquiring company's earnings trend when compared to a list of high-grade comparable stocks.

In a public offering, the expert will assume that the public offering has occurred in neither a rampantly "bull" market nor in a demoralized "bear" market. Whichever assumption he uses, he will — if both the acquisition and public offering options are viable — usually take the higher of the two values. This reflects the price a willing buyer and seller would arrive at.

Timing Each of these two alternative ways of arriving at a value varies with the economic climate at the moment. There are situations where, had the expert rendered his opinion a year prior, the value of the company could be substantially different. This arises simply because timing in an acquisition or in going public is a critical consideration.

Not only is timing important by itself, but the right time may vary for different companies. A company with cyclical earnings can generally make a better deal at the top of the market. Conversely, a company with stable but slowly growing earnings might not make as good a sale at the top of the market as at the bottom. The stable company might bring a higher price at the top of a market, but probably not as much higher as the stock to be received or the market in general. The net position could be a standoff or loss.

This is illustrated in Figures 34-1 and 34-2, which show how values in two industries — aerospace and chemicals — have changed with time.

There are times when, regardless of the merits of the company, it simply could not go public. The market is unreceptive to new stock issues. At these times the company still could complete a good acquisition.

When considering the public market as an index of value, the expert should be concerned with the price at which the stock will stabilize in the immediate after-market rather than with the price

FIGURE 34-1: **Historical price-earnings ratios of chemical industry**

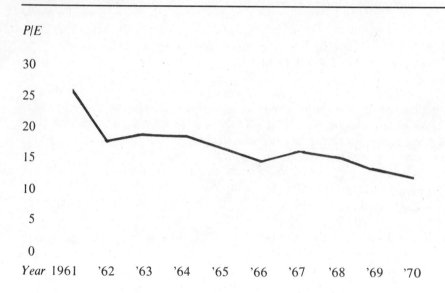

at which the stock would be offered to the public.

The initial offering price is not always a criterion of value. This can be seen by reviewing the price action of hundreds of stocks that have declined (or increased) dramatically shortly after their offering.

Value is in the eyes of the perceiver, and therefore the expert must know what the economic and emotional climate of both the acquisitions and public stock market is at the moment. He should know it in the sense of having lived it, not observing it as a bystander.

The valuation process

Asset values can be misleading

A company valuation analysis is different from a compilation of assets such as might be prepared by an

appraisal company. It may use an appraiser's compilation of assets as one input to reinforce value arrived at in a number of ways.

If current cost or replacement value of machinery, equipment, and other fixed assets was all that comprised the value of an operating company, very few companies would increase in value significantly. The value of an operating company is usually well in excess of the price at which it could sell its used machinery and equipment.

In considering the way a valuation is conducted, it is important to identify the major elements that distinguish the eight common methods of valuation listed above. The easiest way to do this is to consider first the four passive values — book, substitution, reproduction, and depreciated value.

Reproduction and substitution In our present economy, the reproduction and substitution values of tangible assets

FIGURE 34-2:   Historical price-earnings ratio of aerospace industry

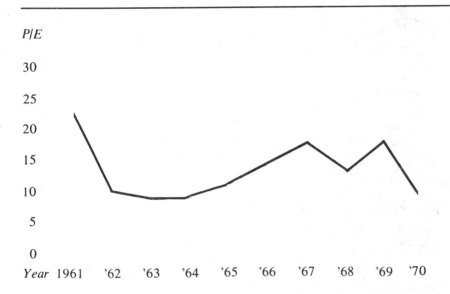

generally exceed their gross or net book value by several times. Both gross and net book value of tangible assets are interesting historic accounting figures showing an accumulation of costs used to acquire the hard assets necessary to operate the business. They also show the allowable depreciation practices applied to those assets. Beyond this, they really do not prove very much.

The value of companies may someday return to something approximating gross or net book value of hard assets, but since the end of the Depression there has been little relationship between the book value of assets and actual transaction values when companies have sold out or gone public. Occasionally there have been exceptions to this — usually when the nature of the company's operations are such that they require a very substantial plant relative to sales, cash flow, or earnings, such as the steel industry or railroads.

The technical difference between reproduction value and substitution value is that reproduction value assumes the duplication of the properties at prices prevailing as of date of the valuation, whereas substitution is the value based on the cost of building properties that would have the same capability and capacity as those being valued.

Both of these values can be helpful when one is thinking of building a new plant. However, it would be unusual when valuing a company to do it on the basis of reproducing or substituting the assets elsewhere. They are primarily engineering analyses used for such things as a make-or-buy decision, an auxiliary method of determining plant location, or fixing the amount of possible damage to a facility in a fire insurance award.

Book value   Book value of assets has the same type of drawback when an attempt is made to use it as a base price or platform below which the company's value cannot go regardless of its operating performance. It is important to bear in mind when considering gross and net plant as carried on the financial statement that accountants make no representations that these accumulated historic costs bear any relationship to the current market for this plant and equipment.

When a company has significant operating problems, it may become worth more dead than alive, such as when it has accumulated substantial losses, the outlook for its industry is bleak, it is poorly managed, its ability to compete in the foreseeable future is nil, and its cash flow is negative. It may have become, at that point, a corporate corpse that simply has not acknowledged the fact that it is dead.

In this situation, using accumulated historic asset costs can be very misleading. It could be equivalent to totaling a man's estate on the basis of his remaining productive years, after he is dead.

Liquidation of assets The approach to value in this situation is to try and determine which product lines, if any,

have sufficient attractiveness or profitability such that they can be sold as a line to others who may be in a position to make better use of them. In addition, a determination has to be made of other possible uses for the company's plants and productive equipment to identify a basis on which they could be sold.

The composite, or total, of this analysis results in value. If, in order to sell the plant and equipment, it would be necessary to dismember the physical facilities, the value may well be under that shown in the balance sheet as gross and net plant.

Relationship to market value Table 34-1 illustrates the relationship between gross and net plant and value of the company for a number of companies selected at random. The only criteria for the companies selected is that they be reasonably profitable.

As can be seen, even in a depressed stock market, the market value of these companies is significantly above their gross and net plant and equipment.

Questions about asset account To try and put some perspective on this

---

TABLE 34-1: Examples of the relationship between gross assets, net depreciated assets, and market value (figures in millions)

Company	Market value	Gross assets	Net depreciated assets
General Motors	$17,700	$14,800	$5,600
Corning Glass	1,090	463	220
Caterpillar Tractor	2,000	1,700	700
G. D. Searle	507	141	35
New York Times	134	102	41
Mattel	414	97	15

relationship of cost of assets to corporate valuation, the following series of questions about the asset account can be helpful:

• What are the company's policies for deciding whether to capitalize or expense?

• What controls exist for the recording of additions to fixed assets?

• How would a different depreciation method affect the book value of the assets?

• Does the company have sufficient retained earnings or cash flow to replace its plant and equipment?

This list of questions could be extended to much greater depth. However, the purpose is merely to illustrate that even a not too detailed look at the asset accounts will show their limited use in most valuations.

Economic valuation

It is not possible in an economic valuation to have the misleading degree of precision that asset values alone appear to give.

What is the basis of valuation that reflects the realities of the marketplace? It is that value which takes into account all of the factors concerning the company, its management, and industry.

Growth rate For example, the company's growth rate will generally have much more effect on value than the company's assets. This is because, in both acquisitions and public offerings, what is being purchased is a future stream of earnings or cash flow and a given trend or growth in them.

This area of prediction of the company's future earnings capability illustrates the difference between a passive asset valuation and an active operating valuation. It is the basis on which the businessman sets value when he is a buyer. Because projection of future growth rates is so highly judgmental, this aspect of value also illustrates the difference between the difficulties in arriving at real value by considering all the factors affecting the company and the mere toting up of a list of the company's assets.

Short- and medium-term prospects There are certain accepted practices within which these judgmental areas are confined. For example, in capitalizing the earnings on the basis of the company's past growth and its growth prospects, the expert should take the same position as that taken by the marketplace. He is not concerned about the 25- to 50-year growth of the company, and rightly so. His concern is about the short and medium term.

The marketplace has a simpler way of expressing its lack of concern about the long term, as characterized by the saying, "The short term is for traders, the medium term is for investors, and in the long term we're all dead." Usually the focus is on a five- to 10-year time horizon.

Price-earnings multiple In stock market, there is a very general correlation between average annual compound growth rate and the price-earnings multiple at which earnings will be capitalized. If a company is growing at a 10 per cent average annual compound rate, its earnings can be capitalized roughly 10 times to arrive at value. If that growth rate doubles to 20 per cent, the capitalization doubles along with it to 20 times.

Therefore, on this basis alone, a company's value could double merely because of this difference in its earnings growth rate. This of course, is very general — it varies in different industries and other factors do not remain stable — but it does give some indication of the wide differences in value that arise from the company's operating results.

Business valuation

The valuation of a company involves four major areas:

- The company, its products, and its competitive position;
- Its financial situation;
- Its management; and,
- Its relationship to other comparable companies as an index of value.

The company

In order to value a company, it is necessary first to understand it and how it relates to its industry. This helps the expert to form an opinion as to what the future stream of earnings is likely to be.

This aspect of a valuation is concerned with what the company is doing to generate its sales and earnings. It involves an understanding of the company's products or services, how they relate to other allied companies, and therefore what the subject company's competitive position is.

A financial analysis of the income statements and balance sheets alone would be sterile for valuation purposes. It is necessary to understand how those income statements and balance sheets were generated and what effect the company's position in its market may have on future results.

The fundamental position This area of valuation is frequently called the fundamental position of the company. It usually includes the following:

- Identification and analysis of the company's major products and services;
- The markets for the company and their trends, including the growth or decline of these markets for each of the company's products and alternate markets as they relate to value;
- The amount, degree, and type of competition, including the uniqueness of each company's products or sales efforts and the geography of the market;
- The nature of the corporate goals, including attitudes toward expansion versus stability, and the success the company has achieved in reaching these goals.

These are the broad areas and are more or less applicable in different situations.

Marketing The company's products or services, as elements of value, can be addressed from a number of standpoints. These vary according to the specific situation. The start is a review of the sales and profits trends over the past five years. This can be further broken down into important product, customer, or geographic groups. Another way of looking at product is to determine the company's share of the market.

If the company's sales and earnings are increasing at an annual compound rate of 10 per cent while their share of the market is declining each year, this could mean that they are picking off the more profitable market segment. On the other hand, if sales and earnings are declining while market share is increasing, they could be either buying their way into the market or there could be a decline in the industry to which they are selling.

It is possible, of course, to have one of these elements (for example, market share) remaining stable, while the sales and earnings trends are going in two different directions. The important point is that, as each of these trends changes, it can have important effects on value.

Distribution   Another area of value affected by marketing is the way in which the product or service is distributed. For example, if the company has "gone direct" versus agents and distributors, this can be either an indication of significant strength or weakness, depending on other factors about the company.

If the company is selling directly at a significantly lower cost than competition, but its market share is declining, this may indicate the development of an unfavorable trend with regard to the company's technical or sales ability.

When a company's competitors are going direct and it is still using agents and distributors, and the sales trend is downward, the company might be able to correct the trend by going direct itself. The important question is, How much value has been affected by the resultant loss in market position? This may be difficult to recoup in the short- to intermediate-term period.

Proprietary nature of products   A critically important attribute of value can be the proprietary nature of the company's products. For example, even though the names "Coca-Cola" and "Frigidaire" are not carried on their respective companies' balance sheets at any value, there is significant value attaching to the established market position and proprietary nature of the consumer's identity with those names. This type of proprietary market position can exist in a number of ways other than for trade names and consumer products.

In the industrial field, proprietary position exists with generic descriptions of the function of the equipment or service. For example, in high-speed mailing, the mailing pieces are "Cheshired" rather than addressed. The Cheshire Company is the leading manufacturer of such equipment, which is used by substantially all of the large high-volume mailers.

In a transaction where Cheshire was acquired by Xerox, there was significant value attached to the proprietary nature of the company's equipment. This proprietary nature, which was evidenced by the use of the company's name in describing the function, resulted from Cheshire's early lead in developing such equipment and ability to stay on top of the technology.

Technology   Technology is part of the fundamental position. It can be isolated and identified by observing values that attach to technologically oriented companies in both the public and acquisitions marketplaces.

In favorable public markets, technologically oriented stocks tend to sell at a higher multiple of earnings than the same earnings growth rate would command in a non-technology-oriented company. Sometimes it is possible, if other factors are present, to merge a technology-oriented company at a favorable price, even when that company is at or near bankruptcy.

All of this presupposes that there is some protection for the company's proprietary technological position. This can be in the form of patents or state-of-the-art development that places the company ahead of others by an identifiable and maintainable margin.

The attributes of value from technology are not in the technology itself. If that were the case, not-for-profit basic research organizations would have a very high value. Value derives from technology or proprietary position because it can result in a protected stream of earnings. There is greater value as well, because of the earnings growth that can occur given a technological breakthrough.

Latent values An interesting aspect of company valuations often occurs in the case of valuing older companies. In this situation, the company may well have established a proprietary market position through earlier efforts. However, in recent history the company's advertising and promotion may not have kept pace with changes in the marketplace.

It is not uncommon in these situations to see a company that has both a good product and market position but that has only stable or only slightly growing sales. This occurs when the company has not redesigned its product, service, or advertising to keep pace with the market. This kind of operation could be called a corporate "sleeper."

One method of determining this is to plot product design and advertising costs as a percentage of sales versus other comparable companies. This tends to quantify what the expert might see superficially in terms of outmoded product and development.

Financial

Analysis of financial statements The results of all of the other areas of the company's products, its industry, and management are summarized and quantified in the financial statements. For purposes of valuation, the expert has two major concerns about the financial statements.

First, on what basis were they prepared? He tries to bring into focus the goal in preparing historical financials. Were they structured to minimize taxes or maximize earnings? Were they structured to show significant tangible assets or to show as lean a balance sheet as possible?

Secondly, he is concerned with both the quality and nature of the accounting and the accounting firm (or firms) that did the work. How independent was the accountant? What is the quality of his statements both as to presentation and as to the amount of work he did in preparing them?

These questions about the financial statements can be summarized into five important areas, including:

• The amount, trend, and quality of the current and historical earnings and cash flow, as reported.

• The determination of the adjustments that may be necessary to reflect true earning power on both a cash and accrual basis, if necessary.

• The classification of assets and liabilities that were made to reflect the corporate accounting goals and any adjustments that may be necessary to reflect a cumulative, materially misleading result.

• Comparative significant liquidity and margin ratios, before and after reclassification and adjustment for a more accurate reflection of value.

• The type, terms, revocability, maturity, and interrelationship of liabilities, both current and long term.

Profit-and-loss statements Since earnings are, in many cases, one of the most important criteria in determining value, it is necessary for the expert to take a critical look at the past and potential earning power of the company. This may require adjusting historic earnings to determine the true earning power.

These adjustments may involve a detailed look at depreciation policies, management salaries expensing versus capitalizing, research and development costs, general and administrative expenses, and any other significant item in the profit-and-loss statement. The purpose is to be able to apply reasonable capitalization yardsticks against a true measure of the company's earnings and cash-flow capabilities.

If the company is unprofitable, the expert may ask himself what would be necessary to put this company on a profitable basis. For example, there are situations where one or two items in a product line are so unprofitable that the overall company is operating at a loss. In this situation, it could be quite reasonable for the expert to make some valuation assumptions based on the elimination of the unprofitable lines.

Management salaries In some privately held companies, management salaries are equivalent to dividends and do not bear a necessary relationship between the management value and compensation. This may tend to be the case particularly where stockholders and key management are identical. This can depress earnings to a level where the company would appear to have significantly less value than is actually the case.

There are certain ancillary benefits that owner-managers of privately held companies may tend to have. Thus, if there are a significant number of automobiles, boats, airplanes, and so forth being carried by the company for the personal benefit of the owners, these should be adjusted for.

The reverse situation can be present as well. For internal reasons, management may not be paying itself adequate compensation and may be in effect subsidizing the company. This subsidy may take the form of use of personal automobiles and entertainment at personal expense for the company's benefit. Each situation must be evaluated separately.

It may be necessary in order to determine the company's true earning power to review the company's fundamental basis of casting an income statement. To illustrate, the method by which overhead burden or costs are absorbed could make a significant difference in earnings.

If there is a standard cost system, direct labor and material may vary significantly from a standard that was adopted in some earlier period. It is possible that management may be understating or overstating earnings significantly by "burying" them in inventory through the basis on which it both costs overhead into inventory and prices out inventory against sales.

Balance sheets A basic question in balance sheet analysis is the company's liquidity. There are a number of ways to approach this. One is the total of cash and securities relative to operating needs. The current items in the balance sheet (current assets and current liabilities) are short-term items. Therefore, this current ratio is a method of measuring liquidity.

The amount of cash necessary and the particular current ratio for a company depends on its industry and the nature of its operations. However, excess liquidity can be a significant addition to value, or lack of liquidity a significant subtraction from value. A more detailed analysis of the balance sheet can be made to determine whether both inventory and plant investment by major area or product are warranted.

Excess liquidity is illustrated in Table 34-2. This shows a balance sheet adjusted by using comparable companies. This adjustment resulted in a decline in total assets of 47 per cent and an increase in "excess liquidity" of over $2 million.

The long-term part of the balance sheet can be equally important. For example, if the company has debt, how do the terms compare with the present debt market and what would the possibility be of refinancing as a means of changing interest cost. The relationship between the course of long-term funds (equity and long-term debt) and the working capital necessary to carry on the company's operations can provide a significant clue.

If, for example, the company is heavily leveraged but is turning its inventory at a slower rate than other comparable companies, the question would arise as to whether the company needed that much inventory. If the inventory could be reduced, then there could be a reduction in the debt with a concurrent increase in earnings, and therefore possibly in value.

Quality of accounting Finally, the expert is concerned with the quality of the recording itself. Are the descriptions of the accounts clear and do they conform to the standards recommended by the American Institute of Certified Public Accountants and other accounting societies? Is the tax treatment adequately explained so that it is possible for an informed analyst to arrive at taxable treatment given a different basis of consolidation and reporting?

Have the auditors, and therefore the company, elected alternative tax treatments for items that are not immediately obvious but that can have an effect on earnings? These would include amortization of bond premiums, bad-debt deductions, treatment of installment sales, and non-cash charges.

Are the years ended for the reporting periods roughly comparable with the company's natural business year? Are each of the balance sheets drawn off at the low point of the company's activity so that on the balance sheet dates the company appears highly liquid, but as a practical matter uses that liquidity in high-volume periods?

Finally, are there notes to the financial statements, and what is their nature? Footnotes to financial statements can be as important as the statements themselves. Therefore, if there is not adequate disclosure in the footnotes, there may be problems in arriving at a valuation judgment until the financial statements are explained in detail.

Key ratios One method of summarizing some of the key elements that can be important in valuation analysis is to describe them in terms of ratios. In order to summarize this discussion, it may be helpful to set forth some of the key ratios that can be used to arrive at value judgments:

• Depreciation to gross value of depreciable assets.

• Long-term debt as a percentage of equity.

• Current ratios.

• Net income before and after taxes to sales.

• Net income before and after taxes to net plant.

• Receivables to sales.

• Inventory to sales.

TABLE 34-2: Balance sheet adjustments

	Balance sheet as reported	% of Total assets	Comparable average % of total assets*	Adjusted Balance sheet
Assets				
Cash	$ 400	8.6%	7.0%	$ 173
Marketable securities	2,000	43.0	1.7	42
Accounts rec. net	750	16.1	25.5	750
Inventory	900	19.3	25.9	900
Prepaid expenses	50	1.1	2.5	50
Fixed assets	550	11.9	37.4	550
Total assets	$4,650	100.0%	100.0%	$2,465
Liabilities				
Accounts payable	$ 850	18.3%	14.3%	$ 850
Wages	130	2.8	16.8	130
Income taxes	280	2.8	16.8	130
Long-term debt	0	—	12.2	0
Total liabilities	$1,260	27.9%	46.8%	$1,260
Net worth	$3,390	72.9%	53.2%	$1,205
Total liabilities and net worth	$4,650	100.0%	100.0%	$2,465

Note to balance sheet adjustments: Over the years this company has retained more earnings than could be profitably invested in the business and has accumulated an excessive amount of marketable securities. These securities are not necessary to operate the business, as indicated by the fact that comparable companies do not maintain large securities portfolios.

Thus, the company should be valued in two segments — its value as an operating company plus the value of the securities that could be withdrawn. In the example shown, an estimated $2,185 could be withdrawn ($227 from Cash and $1,958 from Marketable Securities) without impairing the earning power of the company.

● Net plant (or gross plant) to sales.

This list is not intended to be all-inclusive but merely to illustrate some of these key factors.

Management

The quality of management can be one of the most important factors to be considered in valuing a company. This is equally true when valuing a small, privately held company as it is in evaluating a multibillion dollar company.

The overall quality of management in the past operation of the business can be reflected in earnings levels, historical earnings growth rate, and the profit picture as a percentage of sales compared to other companies in the same industry. However, a valuation of a company at the present must be based on judgments of the company's ability to continue and to increase its earning power, and this requires a subjective appraisal of the overall capabilities of the management team.

Appraisal methods When valuations are being made for use in court, they can be made from one or both of two viewpoints — on a "shorn of management" basis or on the basis that the existing management team will continue to run the company for the foreseeable future. "Shorn of management" appraisals are more common in valuations for estate purposes, but most other valuations are performed assuming that existing management remains intact.

Steps to insure valid basis To summarize comparability analysis, there are a number of specific steps that should be taken in order to insure that there is a valid basis for valuation using comparables. The steps are as follows:

• Identification of the subject company's position in its industry, including the positioning of the company versus other related and affecting industries.

• The use of comparable companies and transactions as indexes of value, including: identification, selection, analysis, and application of other comparable operations; and weighing the type and degree of comparability as it affects the value of the subject company.

• Developing the basis for using comparables as support for the current value judgment.

Return on investment for valuation Historic operations are mainly important as indications of future earnings and cash-flow potential. In any transaction, value is determined by the benefit to the purchaser — and the purchaser is only willing to pay for the value of the company's future earnings. Therefore, it is important to project or predict the probable range of these earnings.

This can be done for a number of areas — including sales, profits, and cash flow, as well as for major balance-sheet trends. Because of the complexities involved, a ready-made computer program can be most helpful. This can generate a five-year forecast of financial statements and balance sheets.

Again, the validity of this kind of forecast depends fundamentally on the assumptions or judgments that go into it. Nevertheless, in certain situations these forecasts can be critically important in arriving at a reasonable valuation judgment.

Relationships with the expert

Company and counsel

The relationship between the client, counsel, and the valuation expert should be viewed as that of a team in which counsel is the leader.

A valuation is a living document, since any operating business is constantly undergoing change that can significantly affect its value. The expert hopes that the pretrial and trial delays will not be so significant as to require him to re-do his work. Therefore, he should be constantly appraised of the status of hearing and trial dates, particularly when there is a written report involved.

Representing management The expert's position can vary significantly, depending on whether he is working for the same interests as management or for the opposing side. In either case, he is responsible for exercising an independent judgment as to value.

However, the expert working for management will occasionally find subtle influences being exercised. Although he is not asked outright to change his valuation, he may be given information in a way that has the effect of changing the indications of value.

It is quite proper, of course, for management to give the expert all the reasons why it believes a certain value should exist. It is then up to the expert to decide which reasons are valid. However, he must guard against being presented with material that is incomplete or arranged in an order designed to lead to a certain conclusion.

The expert requires candor from his client, and the element of surprise is no less an anathema to him than it is to the lawyer.

The well-trained investment banker is skeptical by inclination. He has heard so many proposals and projections presented to him for financing that he is in a constant position of appraising the individuals and their numbers on the basis of his past experience to determine the likelihood of their success. He knows where to get information, having generally done work in that industry or a closely related one on prior occasions.

Therefore, he can have an intuitive feel as to where the bodies may be buried.

Opposing management The situation is more complex when the expert is working for the opponents of management. First, he cannot value a company without obtaining at least a minimum amount of information from management, and second, he should be allowed a personal inspection to form his opinions about management and the company's plants.

Many managements do not realize that the good, experienced expert can obtain answers to a lot of his questions from sources other than the company. This is particularly true of market, industry position, competition, government regulation, and similar types of information.

The appraisal of management capabilities is done in three ways:

• By personal interview;

• By examination and analysis of records; and

• By observation of operations.

Important factors The factors weighed most heavily in such an appraisal include:

• The "results orientation" that the management team displays, both presently and through its past record.

• The capacity to continue to perform effectively as measured by age, health, willingness, interest, and so forth.

• Management depth, as it affects the company's ability to maintain earnings trends and earnings growth if one or more key managers depart.

• The degree of attention to improvement in the company operations, staffing, business strategy, and the other elements of management's fundamental responsibilities.

Using these kinds of measures and the experience that results only from repeated valuations, an appropriate bracketing of the worth of any given company's management can usually be made.

Valuation by comparables

Comparables valuation relies heavily on a capitalization of the company's earnings or cash flow. It compares this with other comparable companies to arrive at a proper basis for capitalization of the subject company. The use of the comparables capitalization method of valuation brings two immediate questions into focus:

• First, how does one handle the fact that no two companies are exactly comparable?

• Secondly, if this type of valuation depends on positive earnings or cash flow, how can it be applied to a company that may have both negative earnings and cash-flow?

Uniqueness It is true that no two companies, just as no two people, are ever exactly alike. However, when public companies are used for comparison, the marketplace does not generally make this fine a distinction. Management may subjectively believe that its company has values substantially different from its competitors. The marketplace, however — given two substantially competitive companies in the same industry with roughly the same size, growth rate, and method of operation — tends to value them on about the same basis.

Because there are always some differences between even companies that appear superficially to be identical, this becomes a highly judgmental area.

Loss ratios When a company has negative cash flow and losses, comparables can be used to determine various ratios of market value to book, net assets, and operating plant. This can be done for companies that have similar losses, similar ratios of losses, a similar amount of losses, or a negative cash flow.

It is axiomatic in the stock market that stocks tend to sell at certain price-earnings ratios based on their industry. For example, lead producers tend to sell in a range of from 12 to 17 times earnings. This will vary as the fortunes of the lead market change. These price-earnings multiples are not arbitrary but rather reflect the valuation judgments of millions of buyers and sellers who collectively have put the stocks in their particular price ranges.

The judgmental area is to take this "consensus" and, first, to determine which companies, if any, are comparables. Then a decision must be made as to the degree of comparability to the subject company based on operations. After this is done, a further refinement must be made to adjust for differences, if any, in financial structure between the subject and comparable companies.

Two methods of pricing In some ways, a valuation is the same kind of pricing decision that an underwriter makes when he is pricing a stock for its initial public offering. The underwriter is concerned whether the offering price can be sustained in the intermediate- or long-term market. But since the long-term market is very difficult to forecast, the responsible underwriter is usually most concerned with pricing for the foreseeable future.

The underwriter is strongly influenced by the price-earnings ratios at which comparable companies are selling in the public market. For valuation purposes, there can be anywhere from one to 12 comparable companies. This comparative "spread" is one of the major tools any underwriter uses for pricing. Since in an underwriting, unlike a valuation, the decision will meet the immediate test of the market, underwriters have found that comparability valuation is most likely to indicate a price that is realistic for that company in a given market climate.

The other major market where companies are valued by the acid test method of an actual transaction is in completed mergers and acquisitions. The major difference between this and the general stock market as a comparative basis for valuation is that, in an acquisition, the entire company is sold and the purchaser is another company buying for operating rather than investment purposes.

The few surveys that have been done on this subject indicate that price-earnings ratios in acquisitions tend to correspond closely with the stock market industry averages and that there are identifiable differences in price-earnings ratios paid in corporate acquisitions, but that these differences vary from industry to industry.

Nevertheless, this data can rarely be obtained outside the company as rapidly as it can be obtained from management. Usually it takes a great deal longer and requires more analytical work. It can, in fact, take as much as 10 times as long; and since time is the direct determinant of cost, the end result can be the same valuation costing as much as 10 times more.

Management's lack of candor may have a double-barreled effect if it has also failed to tell its own expert the truth. If he has based his report on misleading information and is caught by surprise when the opposition independently uncovers the facts, his testimony will obviously have much less credibility in court.

The expert in court

The expert may find himself in somewhat of a dilemma when he tries to present his testimony on the witness stand.

On the one hand, it is unreasonable to expect that most counsel and courts will understand the depth of the basis of his position as well as he does. Therefore, it is up to the expert to put his testimony in terms that can be understood by the court. This is not only for good communication, but it also improves the possibility of the court rendering a favorable decision.

On the other hand, unlike the usual give-and-take of negotiation for value, he is faced with an adversary situation in which any opening he has left will be used by the other side to weaken his position or show a lack of ability.

Impression on court The expert should realize that it is those impressions that he leaves with the court in testimony that may be most influential. They may determine the case as much as the merits and documentation of his report as it might be viewed by another expert. This aspect of trial and cross-examination requires the expert to be prepared in a range of subject matter beyond that which would normally be questioned in arriving at a value by negotiation.

In a specific situation, the question of intercorporate preferred dividend credits came up in cross-examination, and the expert could not remember the specific provisions. Although the intercorporate preferred dividend credit could have made little difference in the value of the company, counsel hammered on this for at least 10 minutes and then brought it up again to refresh the court's memory as to the expert's inability to recollect the specific numbers. It is this kind of courtroom theatrics that causes many high quality professionals to decline to serve in the expert's role.

The valuation expert who realizes that the result of all his preparation can be decided in a brief period before the court is also aware that this type of cross-examination provides equal opportunity for him as a witness to reinforce his position before the court in a very convincing way. Cross-examination can be used by the good expert to set a trial tenor whereby the cross-examination period is reduced to a minimum by his adversary counsel.

Written reports   The dilemma that the expert faces in preparing a written report is to write it so that it is comprehensive enough to lay the basis for his value judgment but does not overwhelm with marginal or superfluous material.

The expert may write two reports. One would be a short and simple presentation of his judgments and computations arriving at value. It should not require a graduate, or even an undergraduate degree in finance to understand it. The other would be a detailed and documented backup for his conclusions.

Counsel using an expert should, in most cases, assure himself that no written report will be prepared on the general method to be used in determining value. The principal reason is that if the expert's papers were to be subpoenaed, such a report might mitigate against the expert's position if it showed different values resulting from other approaches, however innocent.

Conclusion

In the final analysis, the value of a company can generally be determined within a reasonable range. Most of the significant valuation problems occur when the attempt is made to narrow this range and fix on a specific value.

Establishing a fixed value brings into focus the wide area of intangible judgments. In spite of these intangibles, there are a number of specific methods and accepted bases for arriving at value. This article has attempted to distinguish between these accepted methods and the intangible areas that are most difficult to quantify.

Representing the seller of a closely-held business

Harold A. Segall†

†Harold A. Segall, *The Practical Lawyer*, January 1973, Volume 19, No. 1, pp. 59-72.

Reprinted with the permission of *The Practical Lawyer* 4025 Chestnut Street, Philadephia, Pa. 19104. Subscription rates: $12 a year; $2 a single issue.

A lawyer's pride in his acumen in commercial matters should be tempered by the reflection that, if he had a true bent for business, he would be enterprising enough to leave the practice of law for commercial pursuits instead of remaining in the profession.

On the other hand, a capable lawyer is not merely a technician. No matter how capable the client may be in his own métier, the resourceful lawyer can almost always make a significant business contribution in a contemplated transaction by asking pertinent questions about value, by suggesting options and safeguards, and by devising and negotiating solutions to apparent deadlocks. The lawyer — who by interest and habit focuses not on legal problems *per se* but on the legal aspects of business problems — can find no better opportunity to exercise these talents than in representing the seller of a closely held, sizeable enterprise.

The reasons are obvious enough. The typical buyer of a prosperous business is a large corporation with a thoroughly trained staff to screen, investigate, and evaluate opportunities. On the other hand, no matter how competent the typical seller may be in marketing, production, and management, more often than not he is a neophyte in the sale of a business. Since the businessman has devoted a good part of his life to building up a going concern that represents his personal fortune, it is imperative to dispose of this asset as advantageously as possible.

How can a lawyer, in addition to handling the legal and tax aspects, help to improve the financial return to the client? Should not a businessman who may wish to sell his company be thinking in terms of assistance from business brokers, commercial bankers, investment bankers, and experienced friends? It is submitted that whatever help a potential seller may secure from these sources, a lawyer can be of invaluable assistance not only during the course of negotiations, but even before negotiations commence.

Finding a buyer

List of prospective buyers

Who should buy the company?

It is not unusual for the owner of a business, before he has made up his mind to sell, to find himself suddenly confronted with a serious and well-calculated offer by a prospective purchaser. Such an unsolicited offer may come directly from a buyer or through an intermediary, and one of these offers may be attractive enough to induce the owner to sell.

It should be obvious that the sale of a business resulting from such a sequence of events is rather haphazard and unscientific, and it would be a matter of luck if the price and other terms thus negotiated were as good as those available after a careful survey. If custom dictates (or used to dictate) that a single girl must wait for a suitor to appear, there is no reason for the potential seller of a business to be similarly inhibited!

Logical purchasers   No one may be in a better postion than the owner of a business himself to know who the logical purchasers may be. The experienced lawyer should suggest that his client devote some thought and time to drawing up an appropriate list. The lawyer, of course, may modify the list to eliminate certain buyers who cannot qualify because of the antitrust laws or the restrictions of regulatory agencies.

Although there are some topflight business brokers whose fee is well earned when a buyer is found and assistance is lent in the negotiations, the businessman would feel foolish if he were to incur a brokerage fee in selling his business to a company with whom he does business regularly! Furthermore, the screening of possible buyers is essential if the businessman is to avoid squandering time by executives, incurring unnecessary legal and accounting fees, upsetting morale in the organization, and giving the impression that the company is being "peddled."

Weeding out prospects   It is hard to put too much emphasis on threshold decisions. A particular business may be worth a lot more to Company *X* than to Company *Y*. One company that appears as an interested buyer may enjoy a reputation for making decisions efficiently and quickly (while being most careful in its investigation), whereas another company may have unfortunately earned the reputation of being a "shopper," not a buyer, for one reason or another, such as the vesting of authority in a committee that is habitually incapable of reaching a decision.

A prospective and experienced buyer will be impressed by the statement that the company will not be offered to any other party if interest is indicated by a certain date and if the negotiations are diligently pursued to conclusion. This is a constructive approach that will facilitate reaching an agreement. On the other hand, an attempt to juggle two negotiations or to play off one prospective buyer against another usually ends unhappily.

Brokers

In employing a broker — even the most ethical and skilled — care must be exercised. Technically, a broker has earned his fee when he has produced a buyer ready, willing, and able to meet the specified price. *Siegel v. Liese*, 261 N.Y.S. 2d 400 (App.Div.1965).

Since negotiations for the sale of a business, however, are extremely complicated and since the deal may founder on any one of a number of comparatively subsidiary points, it is important to have a tight brokerage agreement that obligates the seller only in the event of the actual consummation of the transaction.

It is also highly desirable to have an agreement that the broker will receive his compensation in the same proportion and at the same time that installments of the purchase price are received, as well as in the same "kind." In other words, if some of the consideration is to be paid in the form of notes or stock, it is advantageous to provide in the broker's agreement that payment may be made proportionately in kind.

Some brokers will not hesitate to canvass a large number of prospective buyers in the hope that they will establish the first relationship and will have a claim for a commission if the sale is made to one of the persons canvassed, even though an actual sale is made at a later date through the efforts of another broker. Apart from the possibility of multiple claims, it tarnishes a business, in terms of its desirability as an acquisition, when a prospective buyer receives offerings relating to the company from more than one source.

The suggested form of brokerage agreement outlined in the Appendix to this article limits the broker's authority to contact purchasers not specifically designated.

Determining the right price

Value of the business

How does a businessman know what his business is worth?

The owner who is thinking of selling his business is sure to be inundated and confused by tales of businesses sold at fantastic multiples of earnings. These bits of information frequently are exaggerated and, even when reasonably accurate, are so fragmentary as to be misleading.

A prospective buyer is interested not only in earnings, but also in the earnings trend and in the reasonable expectations for the future. Astute investigation includes the net worth of the company, the real value of underlying assets, and a host of other things.

Obviously, if a company that is practically identical to the client's is publicly traded or has recently been acquired in a transaction whose details have been revealed through proxy statements or otherwise, this may serve as a useful guide. As a practical matter, however, it is unusual to find such a guide, and information that will lead to valid conclusions must be painstakingly acquired.

There are many useful articles, such as Sears & Sucsy, *The Expert's Role in a Company Valuation*, [THE PRACTICAL LAWYER, Jan. 1971, p. 11]. No set formula, however, can furnish the answer, since price is necessarily a function of what will actually be bid and what will actually be accepted. Much will be learned in the process of negotiations, and, of course, it takes great resourcefulness to learn the game while playing it with a skilled person at the opposite end of the board.

Motives and circumstances

Realistically speaking, the client's motives in selling will have a significant bearing on the purchase price. If the client wishes to sell a good and growing business because he does not want all of his eggs in one basket, or because he is concerned about estate tax, obviously, he will not sell except at a reasonably good figure. On the other hand, the man who has a more pressing need to sell — because the business is growing more rapidly than his ability to raise capital or because competition is creating concern — cannot hope to hold out for the top dollar.

Obviously, one business may command a higher price than another with the same earnings and net worth. For example, a premium may be paid for a business that enjoys a natural monopoly by reason of unique location or for a business that is not likely to invite competition because of the inordinate amount of capital required for entry.

A seller's sights must be reasonable. It is hardly productive to attempt to secure 25 per cent more than the business is worth. Buyers are not likely to be foolishly accommodating. It is reasonable, however, to hope for and to earn, by astuteness and effort in analysis and in preparation, a small percentage improvement either in the sales price itself or in peripheral monetary areas. Obviously, if a seller can secure five per cent more than the "true" worth (whatever it may be) of his business, this is an achievement worth striving for in a multimillion-dollar transaction.

Alternatives

Certainly, before accepting any offer, the seller must give careful thought to alternatives, such as going public or having a private placement.

Character of the consideration

It is the lawyer's duty to demonstrate to his client that the price, the timing of the payments, and the character of the consideration are all integral components and must be evaluated as a package.

It is easy enough to point out that no price, no matter how high, is attractive if the seller is to be paid one dollar a year, with no interest on the balance!

Disadvantages of stock-for-stock deals It may be much more difficult, however, to convince a client that a stock-for-stock deal cannot be considered the equivalent of cash. Not infrequently, a conference between the seller and his lawyer will open with the client's statement that he wishes to sell for stock. The answer to the question "Why?" is, of course, for tax reasons. When a lawyer asks whether a client intends to hold the stock forever, more often than not the answer is "no." What, then, happens to the tax considerations?

If a client hopes to sell a business for $6 million dollars, he certainly should be asked whether if he had that sum of money uncommitted he would put all of it in the stock of the buying company. This question frequently brings a pause, as does the observation that in such a transaction the client is not really selling — he is buying! This point was obvious enough, even before the 1969-1970 nose dive taken by many high-flying conglomerates. It is the lawyer's duty, without making the decision for the client, to be sure that the client understands that the lure and

flattery of a high price should be disregarded if it is to be paid in a common stock whose price on the stock exchange appears to be unreasonably high.

Need for careful evaluation Obviously, the sale of a business for stock is frequently indicated, and this trend may be fostered by the Tax Reform Act of 1969. [Any long-term gain in excess of $50,000 may be subject to federal tax at an effective rate of up to 35 per cent. IINT. REV. CCODE OF 1954 (hereinafter cited, IRC) §§ 1 and 1202. Furthermore, one-half of a long-term capital gain is an item of tax preference. IRC § 57(a)(9)-(A).]

A sale for stock, however, requires the most careful evaluation, whereas, cold cash is very easy to size up! In this connection, the restrictions on the stock, the provisions for registration, and so forth, must be carefully analyzed financially as well as legally. It is important for the client to understand that lettered stock, even in a fine, publicly traded company, is worth considerably less than unrestricted stock in the same company.

Incidentally, it is difficult to understand why, if there is to be a stock-for-stock exchange, the acquiring company should not make meaningful warranties and representations with respect to its own business and financial condition.

Without in any way glossing over the importance of legal craftsmanship in every facet of the transaction, the seller's lawyer must, above all, be sure his client understands what he is getting. If the consideration is debt or stock, is the buyer a blue-chip company? Or is the buyer in less than a happy financial situation and trying to bolster its earnings picture with a good acquisition? Is a note or debenture offered as part of the consideration to be subordinated to other obligations of the acquiring company? If so, what are the layers of debt?

If a new company is being organized as a subsidiary of the acquiring company to act as the buyer as is frequently the case, the seller should insist that the parent company issue its unconditional guarantee of the contract and of the notes to be issued at the closing.

Subsidiary points affecting the arithmetic

Even when the lawyer has been called in after the price for the business has basically been set, there are many contributions of a commercial nature that can be made.

The seller's future role

To evaluate the financial package being offered by the buyer, the seller must consider, in addition to the price being offered for the business, his role and compensation as an executive in the management of the business under the new ownership in the future.

Obviously, an experienced buyer will insist that, for a reasonable period of time, the owner-manager, under whose aegis the business has prospered, remain with the company being acquired, unless, of course, it is a business in which the buyer already has expertise. Conversely, if the purchase price is to be partly contingent, or if there is to be additional compensation for the seller that depends on the future prosperity of the business, the seller must have confidence that the new owner will give the seller, as the continuing manager, a free hand (within defined areas of supervision), will

provide the needed working capital, and so forth.

With the present 50 per cent limit on earned income [IRC §1348], as well as the present pooling-of-interests rules [Accounting Principles Board Opinion No. 16, Nov. 1970], the future salary to be paid the seller as an executive of the continuing enterprise and a suitable profit participation may be more important ingredients than ever before in the negotiations for the sale of a business. (Conversely, the present pooling-of-interest rules, coupled with Opinion No. 17 issued in November 19 0 by the Accounting Principles Board governing treatment of good will arising from an acquisition, may lower the price a sophisticated buyer would have been willing to pay prior to the issuance of Opinions Nos. 16 and 17.)

Drafting the Employment Contract The employment contract is of the utmost importance to an entrepreneur who in the future will assume the role of an employee. In addition to the money aspects of the employment contract, the client will want to know to whom, as an employee in the future, he must report and to whom he need not report. As a successful businessman, he will not suffer fools gladly.

With patience and understanding on both sides, the employment agreement can be fashioned to reconcile the seller's desire as a future executive to manage the business with a relatively free hand, while giving the buyer needed controls. One solution may be to define the executive's duties in terms of his prior functions, recognizing that he will be responsible to a board of directors nominated by the buyer.

Incidentally, care must be taken even with such a seemingly routine provision as the place of employment. It has not been unknown for an employer, who wanted to get rid of an executive with a seemingly ironclad contract, to inform him of his transfer to a locale that he and his family would view with the same relish as Outer Mongolia!

Interest in appropriate cases

Let us assume that the purchase is predicated on December 31st figures, with a prohibition against dividends and other distributions after that date. In our example, however, the buyer wishes to close two or three months later in order not to show the installment obligations on its financials for a fiscal year ending on the last day of February or March.

Despite the acumen shown by the seller in situations with which he is familiar, he may not think of bargaining for interest to commence as of January 1st. If the lawyer is alert enough to make this suggestion when the closing date is first proposed in the discussions, it is hard to see how the request can be denied. Negotiating an item like this at a subsequent conference is, of course, far more difficult.

Sale-leaseback of part of the assets

A wise and experienced buyer may realize the futility of attempting to bargain with respect to the price that a seller in a strong position has in mind. Instead, the buyer may concede the requested price and attempt to improve the deal from his point of view in other ways.

The buyer may suggest that, simultaneously with the acquisition of the business, the seller purchase from the buyer the land and buildings with a long-term lease-back. While there may be good commercial reasons for the seller to so agree, this arrangement may present problems for the seller (apart from the complications that may slow up — and therefore jeopardize — the consummation of an agreement). Before this is agreed to, the lawyer should go through the arithmetic with his client.

To illustrate, let us assume that a business with a cost basis of $2,000,000 is sold for $10,000,000, the entire price to be paid in cash at the closing. The federal capital gain tax will be $2,795,000. This leaves $7,205,000 before deducting state income tax and the minimum tax for tax preferences. IRC § 56-58. If the land and building are fairly valued at $2,500,000, then, in effect, the seller will have working for him only $4,705,000 (further reduced by state income taxes and the minimum tax), or less than 50 per cent of the capital that he had working before.

The seller might well be better off selling only part of the business and retaining a stockholder's stake in its future appreciation.

Warranties

The typical contract, the first draft of which is traditionally prepared by the attorney for the buyer, includes a set of air-tight, omnibus warranties, together with concomitant indemnity provisions that survive the closing. The attorney for the seller, drawing on his experience in past situations in which he has represented a buyer, knows what qualifications and exceptions can be negotiated.

Disclosure of contingent liabilities
The key here is to build up confidence by making a full and complete disclosure.

At the same time, an effort should be made to exclude from the operation of the indemnity clause those contingent liabilities that have appeared on the horizon in the form of claims or otherwise.

Every business has problems of this nature; undoubtedly, some will be dropped or be defeated, others compromised, and the remainder paid in full. After all, since many intangible pluses exist in the going business to be acquired, it is not overreaching to attempt to persuade the buyer to take the chance that certain of the disclosed, contingent liabilities may have to be paid in the ordinary course of running the business.

The importance of candor cannot be overemphasized. The buyer's representative in a sizeable transaction must necessarily be concerned with the possibility of making a very costly blunder. As a reasonable person, he will not be as concerned about relatively minor matters. The first task confronting the seller and his lawyer is to instill confidence.

Since they are dealing with shrewd and experienced people representing the buyer, they will not gain confidence unless it is merited. When a presentation is made, it is foolish to omit or to attempt to gloss over weaknesses. Such weaknesses almost inevitably will be discovered, and it is only common sense to include them in the initial presentation, with whatever explanation or qualifications may be appropriate.

The careful lawyer for the seller will closely question his own client as to possible claims. A claim that a prospective buyer would regard as significant may not have been logged on the books and may have truly escaped the seller's memory. It is awkward

when items of this nature pop up at a later time.

Limitations of warranties   The seller's lawyer should be armed with a draft of clauses he will propose as reasonable limitations on the warranties. It is easier to negotiate changes that are presented in written form. The seller's lawyer need not delay until the buyer's lawyer prepares the initial draft, as is customary, since the seller's lawyer is acquainted with the forms usually employed and knows what to expect.

In negotiating for limitations on the warranties, it is completely appropriate — and it will make the seller feel much more secure — to agree upon a reasonable time limit for the assertion of claims for breach.

In fashioning the warranties, thought should be given to the fact that in almost every situation there are bound to be certain minor matters arising after the closing for which the buyer would be entitled to indemnity pursuant to the usual warranties. Especially where there is a continuing working relationship between the buyer and the seller, these minor matters are bound to cause some irritation and friction.

The seller may feel that he has given the buyer good value and that he ought not to be charged for minor claims that he was not able to identify in the contract and thus to exclude from the warranties. On the other hand, the buyer may take the position that the seller should not object to paying, out of the millions of dollars received by him for the business, a claim that was not contemplated at the time of the contract; furthermore, if the buyer is a publicly held company, its executives may feel a responsibility to enforce the contract as written.

A bit unorthodox, but quite reasonable, is a request by the seller's attorney that there be no requirement for indemnity, unless discrepancies or claims covered by the warranties exceed a stipulated aggregate amount.

In a situation in which there are two or more unrelated selling stockholders, the attorney for the sellers should not take for granted that his clients must agree to joint and several liability on any continuing indemnity.

Right to defend suits

It is recommended that if the seller has an obligation to indemnify, he should contract for the right to defend any claim as to which he must indemnify the company, as well as the right to receive prompt notice and cooperation on the part of the buyer. [Unless there is a specific provision in the contract of indemnity, an indemnitee is not required to give to the indemnitor notice of claims against him. See *Delaware & H.R.R. v. Adirondack Farmers Co-operative Exch.*, 306 N.Y.S.2d 1002, 1005 (App.Div.1970.)]

The buyer, in turn, would be well advised to ask for the right to be able to elect at any time to take over the exclusive defense of any particular lawsuit or claim, as well as the right to settle it, provided that, if such election is made, the buyer should be exonerated from the obligation to indemnify with respect to such item.

Buyer's assumption of undisclosed liabilities The seller's attorney will not be fulfilling his function unless he recognizes that an unorthodox situation may properly evoke a demand for highly unusual provisions. As an illustration, the following clause, requiring the buyer to assume the seller's undisclosed liabilities, was accepted by a sophisticated buyer because it was justified by the circumstances:

Buyer shall assume, and the purchase price of the Property shall also include, all liabilities of Seller, accrued as of the Closing (including, but not limited to, the full amount of all liabilities shown on the unaudited preclosing consolidated balance sheet dated _____, attached hereto as Exhibit _____, as affected by transactions occurring between _____ and the Closing), but whether or not then due, known or unknown, contingent or otherwise, and whether or not disclosed on the accompanying balance sheets annexed hereto, including all taxes (together with penalties and interest, if any) of Seller in all jurisdictions, federal, state, local, and foreign, of every kind and nature, including, without limitation, income taxes, franchise taxes, sales taxes, use taxes, property taxes, payroll taxes, unemployment taxes, and taxes of every kind and nature. The obligation to pay such taxes, penalties, and interest shall be only to the extent that each of the same is attributable to property held, gross receipts derived, income realized or accrued, personnel employed, or any business or transactions carried on prior to the Closing, whether or not then due and payable or whether or not arising as a result of audit, assessments, or deficiencies with respect to any prior returns or failure to file same, and Buyer shall be entitled to retain any refunds, credits, or over-assessments of or pertaining to such taxes.

Some exceptions were made, but these do not diminish the extraordinary concessions secured by the seller on the basis that the circumstances of the transaction justified a broad assumption of seller's liabilities.

Miscellaneous considerations

Transmittal of drafts

Deals have foundered on many points and in different stages of negotiation. When there is a disappointed buyer, there is always the possibility of a lawsuit for specific performance or damages, and prudence dictates that a lawyer's letter transmitting a draft contain language such as the following:

In order to save time, I have not cleared this draft with my client, and a copy is being mailed to him today. Needless to say, no party is bound unless and until a formal agreement is actually signed by both parties, and the transmittal of this or any subsequent draft by either of us is made with this understanding.

Negative covenant

The seller must realize that in a large acquisition the buyer will insist on a negative covenant. Naturally, the buyer will wish to have the contract provide for a negative covenant drawn as broadly as possible with reference to duration and territory as his attorneys advise will be legally enforceable.

In a sizeable transaction, the buyer cannot reasonably object to such a clause, but he can insist that the negative covenant extend only to the business being purchased. If the business being sold consists solely of the

manufacture and sale of venetian blinds, perhaps it is reasonable for the buyer to ask that the negative covenant extend to window shades, but it certainly should not extend to curtains and drapes.

If the contract is carefully drawn, no part of the purchase price will be taxed as ordinary income to the seller. CCH 1973 STAND. FED. TAX REP. ¶4717.0977.

Exoneration

In a closely held business, it is possible that the chief stockholder has signed a guarantee of loans or provided his own collateral as security. It may well be appropriate for the contract to include a provision that there will be a novation of such loans at the time of closing; alternatively, the possible liability can be covered by indemnity from a responsible buyer.

Letter of intent

A letter of intent may be necessary in a situation that requires stockholder action on the part of the acquiring company. Otherwise, it is difficult to see much useful purpose to be served by a letter of intent. If counsel for both parties are diligent, a final agreement can be hammered out with dispatch, and the time spent over an appropriate letter of intent will only delay the preparation of an operative contract.

Conclusion

The lawyer should not hesitate to do battle for his client. Hard negotiating does not jeopardize a deal. Conceding a point that should not be conceded will not necessarily salvage a deal that the buyer is not convinced he should make. On the other hand, delays have often killed a deal that should have been made.

The lawyer, therefore, owes his client the utmost diligence in proceeding just as fast as he can with care, but he should never hesitate to negotiate vigorously, with force and perseverance, for a concession that has a logical basis.

EPILOGUE: SOME BASIC BUSINESS PHILOSOPHY

Money is not where its at, if use of modern street jargon can be permitted. Sorry to spoil your illusions that the successful entrepreneur is a money grubbing, miserly skinflint. There is too much evidence to the contrary.

First, the most successful and happiest businessmen are those who consider themselves professionals at what they do. They have a pride in their work; they consider themselves the best at what they do.

This matter of *pride* is not to be taken lightly for it seems to be most basic to superior performance in any field of endeavor. Football coaches work hard to instill pride in their teams for teams without it seem to be losers. A man who takes no pride in what he does seldom does it very well.

Every successful person with whom the author has had association has stoutly maintained that the money will come automatically when one is good at whatever it is that he does. Moreover, there comes a time when money is really not important.

Five outstanding members of the Los Angeles Young Presidents Organization, on a panel at the University of Southern California, were pressed on this matter of money rather sharply by the class. They steadfastly maintained that money will come if you are good at what you do. So concentrate on what you are doing rather than on making money. Indeed, they were of the opinion that those people who go into endeavors with the sole purpose in mind of getting rich seldom do well.

J. Paul Getty wrote a little book several years ago titled: *How to Be Rich*.[1] In it he put forth some rules he feels are fundamental to success: Rules he claims he has lived by in his lifetime. His rules were:

1. Go into business for yourself! It is the only way you will make a great deal of money.

2. Never forget that the purpose of your business is to sell more and better goods to more people for lower prices.

3. Practice thrift! Make your money before you spend it.

4. Be careful of growth. Forced growth is dangerous. Only legitimate

[1]J. Paul Getty, *How to Be Rich* (Chicago: Playboy Press, 1965).

471

opportunities for growth should be pursued.

5. Run your own business! You can not expect your employee to do as well or to think as well as you do. If they could, they would not be working for you.

6. You must be constantly looking for ways to cuts costs or improve your products.

7. You must be willing to take risks with your own money and with other people's funds. However, borrowed money must be repaid. A poor credit rating can ruin your business career.

8. Stand behind your work. Develop a reputation for being reliable.

START WITH A CAPTIVE CUSTOMER

Many successful businesses were started on a subsidy so to speak; they had a good customer on the books before they opened the doors.

Vernell's Butter Mints were started on the basis of the business from Van De Kamps in Seattle. Van De Kamps had been buying a high quality butter mint from some maker and had developed a good market for it when the candy maker for some reason discontinued making it. A Van De Kamps employee learned of the situation and offered to make the butter mints in his home. His offer was accepted. With that order firmly in his pocket he went into business making the butter mints in his kitchen with the help of his family. Once the secrets of the business were learned and the process mastered, he began looking for other customers who were not too hard to find for his products were quite tasty.

With a good customer in your pocket to pay the initial overhead and get you started, you have a great advantage over those people who start out cold.

One entrepreneur approached going into business by surveying the buyers of several large chain organizations to see if there was some product they wanted but were having trouble buying. After some time, he discovered a buyer who was having difficulty obtaining a good fence gate closer. With that lead, the man studied the situation, designed a closer, took it to the buyer who immediately gave him a opening order that put him into business.

The Handlers, founders of Mattel, Inc., the large ($300 million) toy maker, tell of getting into business with an order for some plastic gift items from Douglas Aircraft.

Bob Teller, the ice cream-lemonade entrepreneur referred to previously, tells about his first venture. "I was working in the warehouse of this coat maker in Phoenix while I was in college. I noticed that twice a week a truck load of linings would arrive from some shipper in Tucson. The shipping costs would be about $300 a load. I got to *thinking*. $300 for a trip; I should be able to do it a lot cheaper than that. I looked around. Found out that I could rent a truck for less than $100 so I went to the boss and told him I could deliver the goods for $200 a shipment. Save him money! He said go to it, so for the rest of the year I made two hundred dollars a week making two trips from Phoenix to Tucson and back with a load of linings."

Good approach! Look around your employer's business and see what problems you can solve for him. Look for some supplier who is "Ripping him off" and see if you can make the same thing cheaper.

The person who goes into business with a solid order in his pocket has a big advantage over the individual who starts cold.

WHAT IS A GOOD BUSINESS?

Risk is the essential ingredient of what constitutes a good or bad business. A good business is *thought* of as one in which the risks are minimal; a bad business is one in which the risks are so high that success is bound to be questionable. How much risk does the enterprise entail? There are all sorts of risks. Let us factor the risk equation to see its components.

There is no such thing as a perfect business. The ideal which will be put forth could not exist. Nevertheless, there is virtue in setting certain ideals against which one can compare an enterprise and see where the risks lie in a venture.

The factors are:

- Capital Requirements
- Labor Requirements
- Demand Characteristics
- Product Complexities
- Cost Characteristics
- Distributive System Availability
- Customer Characteristics
- Promotional Requirements
- Governmental Requirements
- Supply Problems
- Motivations of Buyers
- Monopoly

CAPITAL REQUIREMENTS:

In the ideal business, a person does not have to invest money. Yes, it is possible. As was mentioned previously, there are many deals which require little, if any, investment. The larger the investment, the larger the financial risk. There are times that investments in a venture are so large that the risk-reward ratio makes the investment economic nonsense.

The big wheeler-dealer entrepreneurs who go around buying up this and that operation with their paper are able to do so because when the dust settles it is found out that they have managed to do so without investing any money. Read the article in Part I on Mr. Gustafson, *The Aquisitor*.

LABOR REQUIREMENTS

Labor is trouble, costs, and problems. It is a risk. Most entrepreneurs try to stay away from so-called labor-intensive businesses because labor is something over which they may not have very good control. Labor goes on strike. Labor costs constantly rise. Labor brings with it governmental control and interference. Labor requires management. Someone must hire, supervise, and fire it. Labor can be a contingent liability for pension plans, etc. The ideal business does not hire labor or pay labor taxes; it is not dependent upon the variable labor inserts into the situation. Many businessmen have refused to grow from their family business because they just did not want the problems entailed with hiring people.

DEMAND CHARACTERISTICS

The ideal business is selling a product or service for which there is a big inelastic demand. It is not a fad. It is something for which the demand is well established and is growing. Basing a business on a fad is risky. What will happen when the demand dries up?

When establishing a business, why not do it once and then live off of it.

Build an annuity not a one shot pay off. Pick a good solid demand base which can be relied on.

The leading fortunes of the world are made in basics, things people need: oil, steel, shipping, land, commodities, clothes, etc. True, there are people who do quite well selling jimcracks, but usually they do not amass true fortunes doing so.

PRODUCT CHARACTERISTICS

Many subordinate factors could be discussed, but here are a few of the more common problems. The matter of product complexity can not be ignored. True, there is some disagreement, but on balance it would seem as if simplicity has its virtues.

Complex products pose grave risks. Some makers never get the product perfected to the point where it is commercially feasible. Others flounder when servicing troubles arise from the complexities. Complexities normally cost a great deal of money. The management of a complex product must deal with many problems not faced by those who have simple products to sell. Visualize the position of the hairpin maker in contrast with the maker of a TV set or automobile. Life is easier for the hairpin producer.

Look at the opposite strategy. Sarkes Tarzian, when contemplating his new venture, asked himself, "What will be the most complex, the most difficult component in a television set to make?" His answer was the selinium rectifier. So that is the business he started, with great success. He reasoned that the competition would be fierce in all components that were easy to make. Trusting his technical skill, he entered the business which would be most difficult for others to enter. It was a good strategy for him for he possessed the necessary technical talents to do the job. Simple products do attract great competition.

COST CHARACTERISTICS

The ideal business has 100% variable costs, no fixed costs. Costs vary with sales. No sales, no costs. Fixed costs are overhead and overhead is what ruins most businesses. A business can last a long time on very little volume with low fixed costs.

Moreover, the shape of the cost curve should be examined. Variable costs can decline with volume in some industries. A business should have one in which costs come tumbling down with volume.

The product should cost nothing and there are some businesses in which this ideal is approached. Some enterprises use waste products which are available at little or no cost. A beachcomber based a business on the driftwood he picked up from a Northern California beach. A woodworker went into business using scrap lumber his employer would let him take home at night. Profits can come rather quickly when raw materials are free.

MARKETING SYSTEMS

Ideally, the business should have available to it a marketing system that is ready and willing to accept its products. The enterprise that must build its own distributive system is a risky proposition.

A young man developed a plastic disc on which he printed information concerning vitamins and the ailments to which they were related. The product was promoted by one direct mail brochure to health food stores which resulted in a 20 per cent return, all with cash. Thereafter, word of mouth brought in a continual flow of orders. Little was spent for promotion.

Other new products are so newsworthy that free publicity will take care of the job for the businessman, at least initially.

GOVERNMENT REGULATION

Ideally, the business should be free of government regulation and whim. Many defense contractors rue the day they started dealing with the government. Contrary to common thinking on the matter, few are the fortunes that have been made from dealing with the government.

One problem is that frequently contracts give the government the right to renegotiate prices. Make too much money and they want some of it back. Moreover, the hassles and red tape one must suffer when dealing with the government makes one wonder why anyone cares to do business with it.

On another vein, some businesses are highly regulated by the government and that is no picnic because some bureaucrat can, and usually does, come along and make a person fight for his existence. A person who runs a TV station has to periodically face the fear that its license will not be renewed if he has not programed as the FCC deems proper. Run a trucking company and it will be run like the government says or else. These are not ideal businesses. Perhaps the ideal business is one the government knows nothing about: no product safety regulations, no special taxes and no regulatory authority.

SUPPLY PROBLEMS

A new enterpriser opened up a gasoline station in 1973 right in the face of the gasoline crunch late in the year. He was out of business within two months. He could not get gasoline.

The inability to get needed supplies has put many businesses into bankruptcy. Ideally, there should be an ample number of suppliers all willing to sell on competitive terms.

It is for this reason that the large chain buyers such as Sears, Penney's Wards, K Mart, Woolworth, and Safeway are so attractive to the new enterpriser. The Sears distributive system is ready to go to work for the businessman who is able to create some value it wants. It is not easy to do, but the system is there waiting the right proposition. Moreover, the system is quite large and can sell a tremendous amount of goods. In fact, it may be too large for the typical small businessman; he'may not be able to supply enough products to satisfy it.

The propensity of small businessmen to seek a situation in which they can sell directly to their customers reflects this need for a distributive system that is ready to use. The business that is able to sell directly to its market with relative ease has its distributive system at hand. Industrial products are particularly attractive in this regard for they can frequently be sold directly to the customer because of the large dollar value involved.

One man, working in an oil field supply house, saw an opportunity to go into the making and selling of drilling mud. The availability of a distributive system already set up to the oil well drilling contractors made the venture much easier. He was quite successful, selling out later to a large competitor.

Incidentally, he did not finance the venture himself, rather a wealthy drilling contractor backed the action; he recognized the potentialities of the proposition.

A family with a nice stand of trees on their farm decided that they should start a sawmill in order to get more money for their timber. The investment was made and all went well for two years, then the timber began to play out. It developed that there was not enough timber in the area to support a sawmill.

CUSTOMER CHARACTERISTICS

Cash is beautiful. Usually, the ideal business receives its money in cash either before or at the time of sale. Credit is always a problem. Even more of a problem is an industry in which the middlemen are poor credit risks. There is little point to doing business if you don't get your money for your goods. Many enterprises fail because of unwise credit practices.

There have been instances in which a customer has financed its supplier, even put him into business. One hospital supply company had a problem buying disposable hypodermic needles; there was one supplier and his prices were out of line. American Hospital Supply Company encouraged a young man to go into the business and supported his enterprise in its early stages just to create a second source of supply.

Some businesses are blessed with customers who can only be called beautiful; they are loyal, do not constantly complain, do not continually try to squeeze your prices down, pay their bills on time, and are cooperative. Then there are the other customers who are the opposite. It is a lot more fun doing business with cooperative customers who appreciate what you are doing.

PROMOTIONAL REQUIREMENTS

In the toothpaste business one can expect to do a great deal of promotion or not sell much toothpaste. Promotion not only costs much money, but takes a great deal of skill. The need for large scale promotion should cause the new enterpriser much concern. Ideally, no promotion is needed. The product or service is such that the market is waiting for it, there are such things.

MOTIVATIONS OF BUYERS

Ideally, one's buyers should be buying for emotional reasons rather than rational ones, for such people are less price conscious. Profits are easier to come by if one is not constantly under strenuous price competition.

MONOPOLY

While our cultural roots have glorified competition as the proper way of business life, the fact is that every business person is constantly trying to obtain some degree of monopoly control over a segment of the market. We hate competition. And for good reason! Remember that under the theory of perfect competition, there are no profits in the long run. Perfect competition is a fairly miserable existence for everyone. If you are fortunate, you make wages.

Well, that is not why most people go into business; they want a profit. And that profit can only be achieved if some monopolistic power is developed.

Ideally, the business person wants an absolute monopoly over his intended market. Seldom is such obtained, but it is a goal.

SUMMARY

These last few factors were given as an overall view of business strategy in hope that they will give you a better feel for what underlies success in business enterprises. It has been said time and again that most businesses that sour do so because of fundamental weaknesses in managerial skills. One of those weaknesses is certainly a lack of understanding of what business is all about. That is what we have endeavored to provide.

*

SUBJECT INDEX

absentee ownership, 70
accounting, 375
accounting principles, 168
accounts receivable, 140
activist, 65
advertising, 353
air freight, 290
analysis, cash flow, 133
    economic, 5
antitrust law, 45
    limits, of patents, 228
articles of incorporation, 82
assessments, 112
assets, capital, 233
    intangible, 220
    tangible, 140
audit, 167

bad debt, 133
bank loan, 139, 174, 190
bargaining position, 118
base year, 113, 124
behavior, managerial, 27
behavioral approach, 183
bidding, 320
black capitalism, 66
bookkeeping system, 376
book value, 161
bottom line, 164
brand, 218
    private, 276
brokers, 462
building contract, 105
bulk sales laws, 438
business, elements of a good, 473
business, sale of, 34
business brokers, 462
business failure, 22, 179
buyer, mass merchandise, 274
buying practices, 205

capital, 173
    asset, 233
    crisis, 155
    equity, 66
    gains, 84
    gap, 190
    initial, 156
    outside, 7
    proposal, venture, 152
    sources of, 139
    stock, 89
    working, 136, 154
capitalism, black, 66
capitalist, venture, 145
capitive customers, 472
cash flow analysis, 133
casualty insurance, 108
change agent, 28
channels of distribution, 273
    industrial, 284
    traditional, 285
Clayton Act, 48, 229
closely held company, 259
collusion, 321
commercial loan company, 141
common area, 116, 120
    expense, 123
communications, 239
competition, 125
    foreign, 175
    product, 48
computer, 215, 299
computer, inventory control 367
concept, soundness of, 4
condemnation, 127
contract, building, 105
    government, 176
    terminology, 160
contractor, independent, 247
contribution, 325

control, 145, 148
copyright, 218
corporate shield, 84
corporation, 89
  closely-held, 259
Corporation Code, 80
cost advantage, 205
  data, 11
  estimating, 18
  overhead, 207
  patent, 219
  start-up, 210
  transportation, 288
cost control, 371
cost rule of thumb, 315
covenant, restrictive, 115

debt, bad, 133
  use of, 153
delegation of authority, 242
depreciation, patent, 233
direct costing, 323
direct mail, 286
direct selling, 284
directors, 84, 89
discounts, 318
display, 278
distribution, 273
  traditional, 285
dividends, 138
division of labor, 238
domestic corporation, 91
drop-ship, 277, 282
drug discounting, 417

earnings, 166
economic analysis, 5
  climate, 23
  order quantity (EOQ), 210
electronic data processing (EDP), 214
employee, definition of, 247
  expense, 80
  selection, 19
  training, 19
employer's identification number, 80
employment contracts, 465
employment taxes, 247
enterprise, stage of, 146

entity, legal, 84
entrepreneur, characteristics of, 55
equipment, used, 207
equity, 143, 190
  capital, 66, 84
escalation, rent, 112
exclusive license, 224
exclusivity, 45
expense, common area, 123
  of employees, 80

fads, 4
failure record, 179
Fair Access to Insurance (FAIR) Plan,
  19
feasibility study, 7, 11
fictitious name, 84
field of use, 230
financing, 19, 131
  sources of, 139
  supplier, 150
financial statements, 383
financial terminology, 160
fire, 127
  insurance, 108
flexibility, 239
foreign corporation, 91
foreign trade, 229
forward pricing, 310
franchise, 38, 70, 174
  agreement, 43
franchisee, 4, 38, 70
freight, 280

government contract, 176
government, selling to, 301
governmental aid programs, 173
governmental regulations, 78, 96
  of patents, 228
grant-back, 232
Gross Business Product (GBP), 178
Gross National Product (GNP), 174, 178
group interview, 11
growth, 411
guaranty loan program, 192

high-ball price, 209
honesty, 243

households, 14

immunity, 109
income, median, 16
income tax, 89, 91, 137, 168, 400
    royalty, 232
incorporation, 80
incubator space, 207
indemnity, 110
industrial channel, 284
infringement, patent, 226
insurance, 19, 80
    fire and casualty, 108
intangibles, 171
Internal Revenue Code, 91, 233
    Section 1244, 84
interview, group, 11
introductory package, 282
inventory, 171
    control, 210, 367
    cycle, 277
    turnover, 211
    valuation, 163
Invitation for Bid, 320
I.R.S., 365

labor, 80
    division of, 238
leadtime, 213, 283
lease, commencement of, 122
    shopping-center, 116, 118
leasing, 105
    company, 142
legal aspects, 78
legal entity, 84
lending institutions, 139
less-than-trailer lots (LTL), 294
leverage, 177, 197
    price, 275
liability, accrued, 137
    product, 51
    profit, 137
licenses, 79
licensing, 220
life-cycle, product, 6
limited liability, 84, 87
limited partnership, 92
Litton Industries, 373

loan, bank, 139, 174, 190
    SBA, 142, 173
location, incubator, 207
    retail, 7
logistics, 288
loss, net, 164
    operating, 86
low-income area, 8
loyalty, 243

mail order, 286
managment, 235, 263
manager, small business, 27
manufacturer's agent, 254, 284
market study, 7
marketing, 271
    to small customer, 284
markup, 282, 330
mass merchandiser, 273
median income, 16
merchants' association, 126
middleman, 275
MIN/MAX system, 211
minority business, 65, 175, 194
Minority Enterprise Small Business
    Investment Corporation (MES-
    BIC) 67, 194
minority stockholder, 143, 259
money market, 152
monopoly, 228
mortality, 22
mortgage lender, 128
most-favored-nation clause, 225
motivation, 240

negligence, 109
net profit, 164
new business starts, 179
new issue stock, 144
non-exclusive license, 224

Occupational Safety & Health Act
    (OSHA), 96
one price policy, 330
operating expense, building, 113
operating loss, 86
order system, 211

organization form, 87
  pattern of small business, 184
  structure, 237
overhead, 207, 263

packaging, 282
parking, 126
partnership, 84, 90
  limited, 92
patent, 218, 220
  infringement, 310
  pooling, 232
percentage lease, 106
performance of contract, 106
personnel, 237
PERT system, 215
pirating, 4
preferred stock, 143
pre-ticketing, 277
price leverage, 275
price lists, 317
price quotes, 319
price strategies, 316
Pricing, 315
  arithemetic, 333
  lining, 331
  small stores, 327
  systems, 318
product evaluation, 282
  imperfection, 217
  liability, 51
  life-cycle, 6
  planning, 217
production, 205
  set-up cost, 210
productivity, 238
profit, liabilities of, 137
  net, 164
profitability, estimating, 18
promotion, 342
promotion policy, small retailers, 348
publicity, 334
public stock flotation, 143
purchase price, 164
purchasing, 210

quality control, 275

radius clause, 125
rail freight, 289, 298
rate of return, 146
records, purpose of, 364
rent escalation, 112
repair clause, 110
restraint of trade, 229
restrictive covenants, 115
retail location, 7
  opportunity, 8
  trading area, 14
return on investment, MESBIC, 195
revenue data, 11
  potential, 14
risk, 3, 84, 139
Robinson-Patman Act, 318
royalty, 224

sale-leaseback of assets, 466
salesmanship, 346
sales, tie-in, 231
sales force, 284
sales tax, 79
satellite tenant, 119
security, loan, 139
selling a closely held business, 460
selling business, 34
selling price computation, 322
selling the enterprise, 431
shell-and-allowance, 121
Sherman Act, 48, 229
shipping, 288
shopping-center lease, 116
signs, 126
small business, 22
  aids, 173
  definition of, 183
  major problems, 181
  management advice, 263
Small Business Act, 181
Small Business Investment Corporation (SBIC), 142, 176, 194
small-order supplier, 215
social issues, MESBIC, 199
Social Security, 80
specifications, 209
stage of enterprise, 146

standard costs, 334
stock, MESBIC issue, 200
   new issue, 144
   sale of, 143
stockholder, 84, 89
   minority, 143, 259
   Subchapter S corporation, 92
store lease, 105
store owner, training, 19
Subchapter S corporation, 84, 91
subcontracting, 176, 209, 303
sublicense, 229
subordination, 118, 129
subrogation, 108
supplier, financing from, 150
   small-order, 215
swindle, 144

takeover, 259
tax advantages of MESBICs, 195
   base, 112
   escalation, 112, 124
tax avoidance, 400
tax evasion, 400
taxes, 89, 91, 137, 246
   licensing, 232
   partnership, 93
   sales, 79
technical assistance, 222
tenant clauses, 105
   major, 117, 118
   problems, 106
termination, franchise, 51
tie-in sale, 231
trade secret, 219
trade show, 285
trademark, 218, 220
trading area, 14
traffic, 289
training, personnel, 240
transportation, 288
truck freight, 289, 293
trusts, 94
turnkey, 121
turnover, inventory, 211

understaff, 238
unemployment compensation, 80

Uniform Commercial Code, 51
Uniform Partnership Act, 90
use clause, 125
used equipment, 206

valuation of company, 442
value, book, 161
   creating, 203
   of a business, 463
   product, 281
   sense of, 60
venture capital 173, 194
   proposal, 152
venture capitalist, 145, 156, 177
Vernell's Butter Mints, 472

waiver of rights, 110
warranties, selling a business, 466
wheeler-dealer, 60
wholesaler, 284, 287
windfall, 109
withholding tax, 247
work letter, 121
working capital, 136, 174
   crisis, 155
workmen's compensation, 80

zoning ordinance, 78

NAME INDEX

AFL-CIO, 97
Allen, Louis, 191
Allied Chemical, 213
American Arbitration Association, 76
Anderson, Jules E., 333
Andrews, Frederick Douglas, 66
Anthony, Edward L., 327
Arapahoe Chemical Company, 143
Armendaris, Alex M., 68
Austin, Joseph, 298

Balter, Harry Graham, 400
Barry, B. John, 61
Becker, Otto A., 291

Berkwitt, George J., 371
Black Enterprise, 67
Bowles, D. Peter, 353
Bradley, Albert, 267
Brimmer, Andrew F., 68
Bureau of Labor Statistics, 16
Bureau of the Census, 16
Burger King, 175
Burrell, Berkeley G., 66
Bushnell, George H., 364

Carousel, 60
Central Bank & Trust Company, 143
Charlesworth, Harold K., 22, 177
Chase, Anthony, 173
Chase Manhattan Capital Corporation, 177
CIT, 171
Coca Cola, 219
Coco's, 3
Committee for Economic Development, 22
Cooke, Clifton N., 290
Coors, Adolph, 417
Cuse, Arthur, 400

Daugherty, William K., 87
Davis, David H., 293
Drucker, Peter, 263
Dun & Bradstreet, 26, 179

Eachon, Jack, 174
Ehruch, Thomas, 425
Equitable Life Assurance Society, 115
European Common Market, 229

Federal Reserve Board, 68
Federal Reserve System, 190
Federal Trade Commission, 178
Fendrick, Ronald, 299
Finnegan, Tom, 288
First Connecticut SBIC, 176
Formsprag Company, 214
Friedman, Milton R., 105

Garfield Organization, 66
Garland Foods, 176
Gassenheimer, Earl C., 333
General Electric, 264

General Mills, 109
General Motors, 177, 264
Gentsch, Edward, 296
Getty, J. Paul, 471
Giese, Henry, 296
Gold Seal Company, 174
Gottlieb, Leon, 38
Grace, W. R., 373
Gustafson, Deil O., 60

Handler, Ruth, 472
Harvard Business Review, 23
Hoel, Robert F., 8

Illinois Tri-Seal Products, Inc., 248
Institute for New Enterprise Development, 157
Internal Revenue Service, 80, 84, 93, 178, 246
International Business Machines, 240
International Telephone & Telegraph, 177

Jackson, Rev. Jesse L., 66

Karbo, Joe, 57, 344
Kellogg, Irving, 160
Kemker, Harry, 43
Kerin, Roger A., 8
King, Rev. Martin Luther, Jr., 66
Klein, Frederick C., 60
Klein, George, 213
Klein, Richard H., 194
Kleppe, Thomas, 173
K-Mart, 273

Laughlin, Lawrence, 26
Lavenson, Jim, 346
Lennon, Victor A., 322
Library of Congress, 218
Lilly Digest, 18
Little, Royal, 176
Loughlin, J. Michael, 281
Lyda, Thomas B., 136

McDonald's, 54, 175
McNamee, Bernard J., 220
Martin, Joseph, Jr., 178
Maurantonio, Carol, 276

Mellen, Amory, Jr., 294
Midland Capital, 176
Mitchell, Steve, 57
Motown Industries, 67

Narragansett Capitol, 176
National Business League, 66
National Cash Register, 18
National Food Brokers Trade Show, 285
National Safety Council, 97
Nicholas, Jack R., Jr., 96

Office of Minority Business Enterprise (OMBE), 67
Operation PUSH, 66
Oarker, Marshall J., 175

Pendergast, Edward H., Jr., 178
J. C. Penney, 273, 364
Phillips Petroleum, 210
Polakoff, Murray E., 191
Pollack, Benjamin, 118
Postal System, 286
Purchasing Magazine, 289

Ralston Purina, 5
Robinson-Patman, 338
Robo Car Wash, 34
Rudelius, William, 8

Sears, 140, 273, 442
Securities & Exchange Commission, 144

Segall, Harold A., 460
7-Eleven, 70
Silber, William L., 191
Singer, Arthur, 176
Small Business Administration (SBA), 18, 67, 84, 98, 142, 173
Smith, Bernard W., 348
Southland Corporation, 71
Syntex, 144

Teller, Bob, 131, 472
Thomas, Howard E., 115
Time, 58
Tropicana, 60

Union Camp, 177
United Parcel Service (UPS), 286
U.S. Department of Commerce, 195, 218
U.S. Department of Labor, 97
U.S. Patent Office, 219

Vernell's Butter Mints, 285
Vita-Wheel, 286

Wall, Douglas J., 87
Ward, Francis, 65
Watters, Ralph, 293
Western Auto, 175
Wulff, Peter, 210, 288

Yellow Pages, 286

Zeitzew, Harris, 210
Zemansky, Stanley D., 303

†

DATE   DUE